Christianity in South Africa

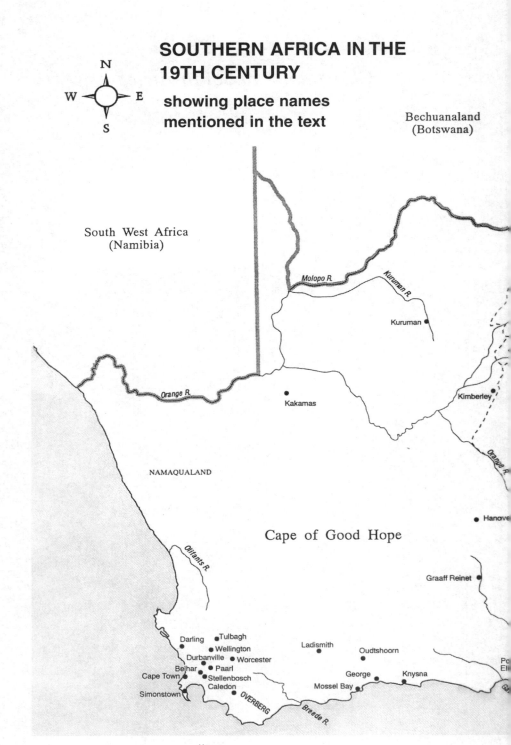

SOUTHERN AFRICA IN THE 19TH CENTURY

**showing place names
mentioned in the text**

N
W E
S

Bechuanaland
(Botswana)

South West Africa
(Namibia)

Molopo R.

Kuruman R.

Kuruman

Orange R.

Kakamas

Kimberley

Orange R.

NAMAQUALAND

Hanove

Cape of Good Hope

Olifants R.

Graaff Reinet

Darling   •Tulbagh
•Wellington   Ladismith   Oudtshoorn
Durbanville •Worcester
Belhar •Paarl   Po
Cape Town• Stellenbosch   George Knysna   Eli
Simonstown   Caledon   Mossel Bay
OVERBERG   Breede R.

Southern Rhodesia
(Zimbabwe)

Limpopo R.

SOUTPANSBERG

Letabe R.

Pietersburg

Portuguese
East Africa
(Mozambique)

South African Republic
(Transvaal)

Limpopo R.

MARICO

Zeerust   Rustenburg

Hammanskraal
Mamelodi
Pretoria   Cullinan
Krugersdorp   WITWATERSRAND
    Johannesburg
Randfontein   Germiston
    Soweto   Boksburg

Carolina

Potchefstroom
    Evaton
    Sharpeville

Klerksdorp

Vaal R.

Swaziland

Kroonstad

Welkom

Wakkerstroom

Charlestown   Vryheid

ZULULAND

Orange Free State

Caledon R.   Ladysmith

    Bloemfontein

MALUTI

Eshowe

DRAKENSBERG

Basutoland
(Lesotho)

Natal

Stanger

Wepener   Morija
    Orange R.

Pietermaritzburg   Verulam
    Pinetown
Richmond   Mt. Edgecombe
    Durban

Thukela R.

Zastron

Herschel

Umzinto

Kokstad

Aliwal North

Harding
Port Shepstone

Mzimkulu R.

TRANSKEI

Engcobo   Umtata

Queenstown

dock

Butterworth

AMATOLAS
Adelaide   Stutterheim
    Keiskammahoek
King Williamstown   Bisho
BRITISH KAFFRARIA
    (CISKEI)
mstown
VELD   Salem
Bathurst

Mzimvubu R.

Mtata R.

Mbashe R.

Kei R.

Fish R.

days R.

0   100   200 km

Lutheran

LR10	Amalienstein bz
LB54	Bethany cx
LH40	Bethany cw
LB30	Blaauwberg cv
LB43	Botshabelo cw
LR121	Carnarvon by
LS80	Ekutuleni dx
LM103	Elim az
LN79	Empangeni dx
LM63	Enon cz
LN17	Entumeni dx
LN18	Eshowe dx
LM9	Genadendal az
LB29	Georgenholz dv
LB45	Gerlachshoop dw
LH36	Harmshape cw
LH78	Hermannsburg dx
LH39	Kana cw
LR4	Komaggas ax
LH46	Linokana cw
LB25	Lobethal dw
LB31	Malokong cv
LM100	Mamre az
LN149	Mpande's Kraal dx
LB44	Mphome dv
LN77	Mphumulo dx
LB42	Neu Halle cw
LS83	Oskarsberg dx
LH38	Pella cw
LB127	Pniel az
LH19	Quelwasser dw
LR1	Richtersveld ax
LB24	Sekulane dw
LB28	Shewase dw
LB23	Shibovune dv
LM13	Shiloh inset
LR2	Steinkopf ax
LB158	Stutterheim inset
LR119	Upington bx
LB89	Wallmansthal cw
LR122	Williston az
LR8	Wupperthal ay

American Board Mission

AB74	Amanzimtoti dy
AB75	Lindley dx
AB76	Groutville dx
AB131	Mosega cw

Dutch Reformed

D98	Clanwilliam ay
D7	Ebenezer ay
D86	Kranskop dv
D168	Mabeskraal cw
D41	Moera cw
D35	Mochudi cv
D37	Saulspoort cw
D88	Seleha cv
D104	Swellendam az
D62	Zoar bz

Anglican

A61	Abbotsdale az
A166	Clydesdale cy
A163	Ekukanyene dx
A138	Hambanathi dx
A82	Kwamagwaza dx
A164	Modderpoort cx
A162	Springvale dy
A161	St Matthew's inset
A14	St Mark's inset
A65	St Luke's inset
A170	St John's cy
A60	ThabaNchu cx
A58	Thlotse cx

Roman Catholic

C169	Dunbrody cz
C141	Mariannhill dx
C56	Roma cx

Swiss Romande

S26	Elim dv
S87	Mhinga dv
S21	Matuarena dw
S22	Rikafia dw
S27	Vuldezin dv

London Missionary Society

L112	Bethelsdorp cz
L117	Bethesda bx
L120	BlijdeVooruitzicht ay
L137	Bushman Station inset
L105	Caledon Institution az
L151	Cradock inset
L125	Dithakong bw
L109	Dysselsdorp bz
L94	Fort Beaufort inset
L130	Graaff-Reinet by
L51	Griquatown bx
L11	Hankey bz
L129	Hephzibah bx
L6	Kamiesberg ay
L90	Kanye bw
L124	Kuruman bx
L123	Maruping bx
L34	Molepolole cv
L110	Pacaltsdorp bz
L108	Paarl az
L157	Peelton inset
L92	Pella ax
L93	Philippolis by
L113	Philipton inset
L128	Ramah bx
L32	Serowe cv
L33	Shoshong cv
L97	Silver Fountain ay
L114	Somerset East cz
L107	Stellenbosch az
L49	Taungs bx
L116	Theopolis inset
L47	Tiger Kloof bw
L132	Tooverberg by
L99	Tulbagh az
L111	Uitenhage bz
L101	Wellington az
L102	Worcester az

Scottish

SU71	Buchanan cy
SG152	Chumie inset
SU12	Emgwali inset
SG154	Iggibigha inset
SG69	Lovedale inset
SG156	Pirie inset

French (Paris Evangelical)

F143	Berea cx
F53	Bethesda cx
F52	Bethulie cy
F147	Cana cx
F133	Carmel cy
F134	Hebron cy
F50	Hermon cx
F85	Leribe cx
F59	Mekoatleng cx
F57	Morija cx
F48	Motito bw
F55	Thaba Bosiu cx

Wesleyan

W16	Buntingville cy
W67	Butterworth inset
W15	Clarkebury cy
W139	Edendale dx
W68	Healdtown inset
W95	Imvani inset
W140	Indaleni dx
W136	Kamastone cy
W145	Lesoane cx
W5	Lilyfountain
W126	Makwassie cw
W142	Merumetso cx
W150	Morley cy
W64	Mount Coke inset
W148	Mpharane cx
W146	Mpokane cx
W144	Platberg cx
W70	Shawbury cy
W60	ThabaNchu cx
W155	Wesleyville inset

KEY (Based on maps in J. du Plessis, *History of Christian Missions in South Africa* and B.A. le Cordeur and C.C. Saunders, *The Kitchingman Papers*, and other sources)

A	Anglican Church
AB	American Board
C	Roman Catholic
D	Dutch Reformed
F	French Mission
L	London Missionary Society
LB	Berlin MS
LH	Hermannsburg MS
LM	Moravian MS
LN	Norwegian MS
LR	Rhenish Mission
LS	Ch. of Sweden
S	Swiss Romande Mission
SG	Glasgow Mission
SU	United Free Church of Scotland
W	Wesleyan Methodist Missionary Society

(LB, LH, LM, LN, LR, LS bracketed as Lutheran)

Notes

1. The Roman Catholic Church established many more missions than th[ose] shown on this map, but the diocesan structure of R.C. missionary organiza[tion] is not easy to represent on a map of this scale.

2. No account is taken here of the separate establishment of the Nederd[uitse] Gereformeerde Sendingkerk, which set up branches in many centres in [the] Cape from the late 19th century.

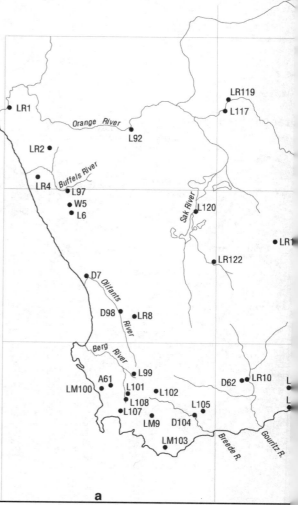

a

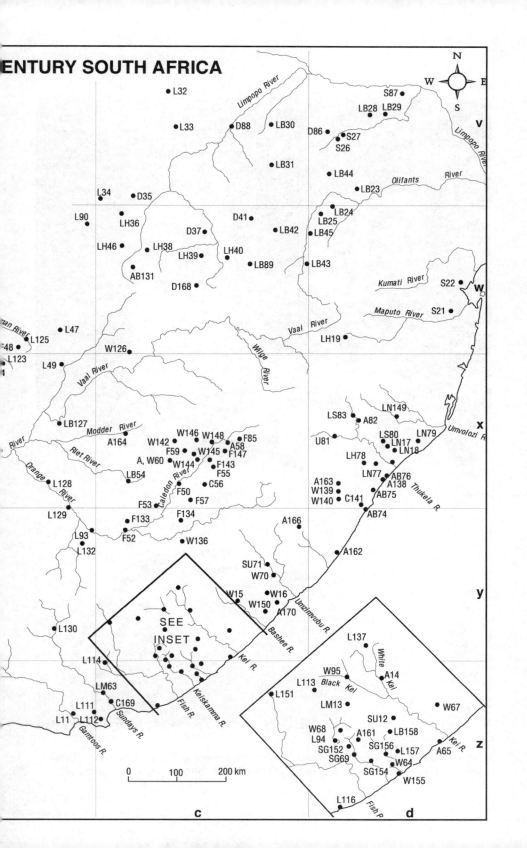

ENTURY SOUTH AFRICA

Temple of Zion Apostolic Foundation Church in a home at Khayelitsha, Cape Town. Child members with menorah, drums, trumpets, archbishop's gown, flag, and holy ropes.

Christianity in South Africa

A POLITICAL, SOCIAL, AND CULTURAL HISTORY

EDITED BY

RICHARD ELPHICK AND RODNEY DAVENPORT

UNIVERSITY OF CALIFORNIA PRESS
Berkeley   Los Angeles

Perspectives on Southern Africa

55. *Christianity in South Africa: A Political, Social, and Cultural History*
     edited by Richard Elphick and Rodney Davenport (1997)

First published in 1997 in Southern Africa by David Philip Publishers (Pty) Ltd,
208 Werdmuller Centre, Claremont 7700 South Africa;
in the United States of America and Canada by the University of California Press,
2120 Berkeley Way, California 94720;
and in the United Kingdom by James Currey Publishers, 73 Botley Road, Oxford,
England

ISBN 0 86486 306 3 (David Philip paper)

ISBN 0 520 20939 7 (University of California Press cloth)
ISBN 0 520 20940 0 (University of California Press paper)

ISBN 0 85255 751 5 (James Currey paper)

Printed in South Africa by Creda Press (Pty) Ltd, Eliot Avenue, Epping, Cape

Contents

CONTENTS

Contributors

Allan H. Anderson is Director of the Centre for the Study of New Religious Movements, Selly Oak Colleges, Birmingham, U.K.

Roger B. Beck is Professor of History at Eastern Illinois University, Charleston.

Joy Brain is Emerita Professor of History, University of Durban–Westville.

David Dargie is Professor of Music at the University of Fort Hare, Alice.

Rodney Davenport is Emeritus Professor of History, Rhodes University, Grahamstown.

John W. de Gruchy is Professor of Christian Studies at the University of Cape Town.

Elizabeth Elbourne is Assistant Professor of History at McGill University, Montreal.

Richard Elphick is Professor of History at Wesleyan University, Middletown, Connecticut.

Norman Etherington is Professor of History at the University of Western Australia, Perth.

Deborah Gaitskell is Lecturer in History at the School of Oriental and African Studies, London.

Jonathan N. Gerstner is Professor of Theology at Knox Theological Seminary, Fort Lauderdale, Florida.

Irving Hexham is Professor of Religion at the University of Calgary, Alberta.

Janet Hodgson is a Diocesan Advisor in Local Mission for the Church of England in Durham, U.K.

Lizo Jafta is Lecturer in Church History at the University of South Africa, Pretoria.

Johann Kinghorn is Professor of Religion at Stellenbosch University.

Eugene M. Klaaren is Associate Professor of Religion at Wesleyan University, Middletown, Connecticut.

Gunnar Lislerud is a Bishop of the Church of Norway in Oslo.

Tshidiso Maloka is a Lecturer in History at the University of Cape Town.

Wallace G. Mills is Professor of History at St. Mary's University, Halifax, Nova Scotia.

Jeff Opland teaches at Charterhouse School in Godalming, U.K.

Gerald J. Pillay was Professor of Church History at the University of South Africa, Pretoria, and is now Professor of Theology and Religious Studies at the University of Otago.

Karla Poewe is Professor of Anthropology at the University of Calgary, Alberta.

Hennie Pretorius is a liaison of the Dutch Reformed Church with African Initiated

Churches in Kuils River, Cape Town.

Dennis Radford is Professor of Architecture at the University of Natal, Durban.

Robert Ross is Coordinator of African Studies, Faculty of Letters, Leiden University, Netherlands.

Georg Scriba is Tutor at the Lutheran House of Studies and Lecturer in Reformation Theology at the University of Natal, Pietermaritzburg.

Milton Shain is Associate Professor in Hebrew and Jewish Studies, University of Cape Town.

Robert C.–H. Shell is Senior Lecturer in History, Rhodes University, East London.

Barry Smith is Associate Professor of Music, University of Cape Town, and Master of the Choristers, St. George's Cathedral, Cape Town.

Peter Walshe is Professor of Government and International Studies, University of Notre Dame, Indiana.

Editors' Preface

An underlying assumption of this book is that there has been an excessive tendency among modern historians to regard materialist motivation as the essential undercurrent of change. South Africans at least have the experience of noting the power of ideological shibboleths as a countervailing influence, above all during the last half-century. But we are still in danger of assuming that the South African story turns entirely on the twin pivots of obsessionist slogans and economic greed. If this book succeeds in effectively questioning such an assumption by drawing one of the world's great traditions of belief and morality into the mainstream of the story, the effort to produce it will have been worth while.

The extent to which the story of southern Africa is permeated by activities of the Christian churches gives the effort a special relevance. The present volume is a collective effort by scholars of differing disciplines, beliefs and commitments, from four continents. All have worked in South Africa. Together, they seek to provide accounts based on up-to-date research and in accessible form to general as well as specialist readers.

We have striven to cover the many ways Christianity has manifested itself in the political, social, and cultural history of South Africa. But we have not been able to eliminate all of the gaps in coverage. Important linguistic groups, like the Pedi and the Venda, get less than due attention, as do groups like the Quakers, the Eastern Orthodox, the Unitarians, and the influential African Methodist Episcopal Church (AME). There is no coverage of Christianity and the visual arts, inadequate attention to Christianity and education, and the story of Christian–Muslim relations is not told for the twentieth century. Yet, despite these and other gaps, we believe that this volume represents a significant step toward the creation of a comprehensive history of South African Christianity.

Initial planning of this project began in 1991, when Richard Elphick was a fellow at the Shelby Cullom Davis Center for Historical Studies at Princeton University. He is particularly grateful to Peter Brown, Natalie Zemon Davis, Kari Hoover, Grete Otis, Robert Shell, and Robert Tignor for warm hospitality, stimulating conversation, and sound advice. In August 1992, many of the authors gathered for a planning session at the University of the Western Cape, benefiting from the efficient hospitality of Henry Bredekamp and the Institute for Historical Research. The air fares of several participants were subsidized by an American family foundation, whose trustees wish to remain anonymous. This foundation also contributed toward phone, fax, photocopy, and courier costs. Without its generous help, the daunting logistics of coordinating twenty-nine authors in four continents would probably have been insurmountable.

In 1993 we began to edit first drafts, when Rodney Davenport, funded by the Pew Charitable Trusts, was a Pew Visiting Fellow at the Public Affairs Center at Wesleyan University. He is grateful to that university for its hospitality and support over a six months' period.

We are deeply indebted to Jeannette Hopkins for her encouragement, her counsel, and her rigorous developmental editing – a legend in North American publishing. Her relentless demands on editors and authors – and her even greater demands on herself – have resulted in a crisper, more accessible, and more unified volume than we could have created on our own.

Richard Elphick wishes to thank two Wesleyan students, Joshua Power Stevens for resourceful and diligent toil in standardizing the computer formats of the chapters, and Phil Stern for his computer wizardry, meticulous revisions, and above all for his willingness to work days, nights and weekends to prepare chapters for the authors and publishers. In South Africa, Susan Sturman, formerly of the South African Library, responded with great skill to the challenge of selecting illustrations. The mapwork was ably undertaken by Susan Sayers of the Department of Geography in the University of Cape Town, and the index by Leonie Twentyman Jones.

Having been most fortunate in finding supportive and competent publishers, we wish to record our gratitude to David Philip, Russell Martin, Monica McCormick, and William McClung, and to Dee Murch and Michelle Willmers at the Cape Town end for devoting further days, nights and weekends to the restandardization of North American computer formatting to conditions encountered in the southern seas.

Inevitably in a project of this magnitude, duration, and complexity we have incurred many debts, above all for hospitality and good advice. In particular, we wish to mention Surendra Bhana, Colin Bower, Lorenzo Duso, Richard Holway, Peter Randall, Wolfram Kistner, Richard Mendelsohn, Henning van Aswegen, the late Anna van Aswegen, Virginia van der Vliet, David Welsh. Many of the authors gave helpful advice to us and to other authors, but one – John de Gruchy – must be singled out for special thanks.

We wish to acknowledge our gratitude to Cluster Publications for granting us permission to use material that forms the basis of chapter 25.

Our special thanks are due to the Anglo American and De Beers Chairman's Fund for financial assistance towards the production of this book.

Richard Elphick
Rodney Davenport

1 Groote Kerk, Cape Town

2 Groote Kerk (interior)

3 Lutheran Church, Cape Town

4 M.C. Vos, NGK minister

5 H.R. van Lier, NGK minister

6 Lena, an early convert, meets returning Moravians

7 George Schmidt,
   Moravian missionary

8 Genadendal Moravian Mission Church

9 Genadendal church (interior)

10 J.T. van der Kemp,
LMS missionary

11 John Philip,
director of LMS missions

12 William Shaw, Methodist
minister and missionary

13 Bethelsdorp Mission (LMS)

14 Salem, Methodist settlement and mission

15 The "slave" church, Paarl

16 The workshop, Lovedale Scottish mission

17 Healdtown Methodist Mission

18 Tiyo Soga, Lovedale
graduate and minister

19 Janet, wife of Tiyo Soga

20 Tengo and Davidson
Jabavu, Lovedale

21 Eugene Casalis, Paris Evangelical missionary

22 Moshoeshoe, king of the Sotho

23 Allen Gardiner, missionary at Port Natal

24 John Colenso, Anglican missionary bishop of Natal

25 Robert Gray, Anglican bishop of Cape Town

26 Sophy, wife of Robert Gray

27 Ekukanyeni Mission, Natal

28 Robert Moffat, LMS
missionary

29 Mary, wife of Robert
Moffat

30 Daniel Lindley,
American missionary

31 Kuruman mission, LMS

32 David Livingstone, LMS
missionary

33 Sechele, Tswana chief

34 John Mackenzie, LMS
    missionary

35 Kgama III, Tswana chief

36 Mission house and church, Berlin Society's Botshabelo mission

37 Wagon shop, Botshabelo

38 "Notre Mère", Assumption
   Convent, Grahamstown

39 F.C. Kolbe, Catholic priest

40 Owen McCann
   (Cardinal)

41 Mackay's Nek R.C.
   mission, Transkei

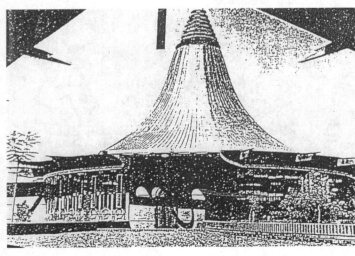

42 Hammanskraal R.C.
   mission, Transvaal

43 R. Stott,
Methodist
missionary
with Indians

44 Pastor J.F. Rowlands at Chatsworth

45 Dutch Reformed Indian evangelists

46 Catholic Indian Young Men's Society, Durban

47 Logo of Baptist Indian
mission

48 Enoch Mgijima,
   Israelite leader

49 Isaiah Shembe, Nazarite
   founder

50 L.M. Makhoba (bishop),
   African Congregational Church

51 James Dwane (centre) with American Methodist clergy

53 Edward Lekhanyane,
   Zionist leader

52 Ma Nku, Pentecostal evangelist

54 Andrew Murray, Calvinist
evangelical NGK minister

55 Erasmus Smit,
Voortrekker predikant

56 Dirk Postma, founder of
the Gereformeerde Kerk

57 Dirk van der Hoff,
founder of the
Nederduits
Hervormde Kerk

58 S.J. du Toit, Neo-Calvinist NGK
minister

59 T.F. Burgers,
liberal NGK minister,
later president of
Transvaal

60 St. John's Anglican church, Bathurst

61 St. Andrew's Presbyterian church, Cape Town

62 St. George's Anglican Cathedral, Cape Town

63 Nederduits Gereformeerde Kerk, Cradock

65 Nederduits Gereformeerde Kerk, Sunnyside, Pretoria (Byzantine style – Moerdyk)

64 Nederduits Gereformeerde Kerk, George

66 St. Mary's, Woodstock, Cape (Sophy Gray)

67 Nederduits Gereformeerde Kerk, Ladismith, Cape

68 Grahamstown Cathedral (Anglican)

69 Methodist Church, Cape Town

70 Architect's plan for St. George's, Cape Town

71 Anglican Church, Cullinan, Transvaal

72 Lutheran mission, Kimberley (now at De Beers Mining Museum)

73 St. Patrick's, Batho location, Bloemfontein: the design, its partial construction, and its nemesis

74 A garage church in a "white area" – targets of legislation in 1957

75 Holy Cross, Gaborone, Botswana

76 S.E.K. Mqhayi, Xhosa
    poet and praise-singer

77 "Totius" (J.D. du Toit),
    Afrikaans writer

78 The Xhosa praise-singer Mbutuma in
    traditional costume

79 J.H. Soga, author

80 Alan Paton, author

81 Johannes du Plessis, professor in NGK

82 B.B. Keet, professor in NGK

83 Beyers Naudé, NGK minister

85 Dutch Reformed and Anglican leaders meet at Cottesloe (Bishop Bill Burnett, Archbishop Joost de Blank, Ds. P.S.Z. Coetzee, Bishop Ambrose Reeves and Ds. C.B. Brink)

86 Michael Scott,
   Anglican priest

87 Geoffrey Clayton, Anglican
   archbishop of Cape Town

88 Trevor Huddleston, Anglican priest, later bishop

89 Smangaliso Mkhatshwa, R.C. priest (centre), with Albertina Sisulu and Dorothy Nyembe

90 Frank Chikane, secretary general of the South African Council of Churches

91 Denis Hurley, R.C. archbishop, in protest

92 Protest march to Parliament, 1988: Kheza Mgojo, (President of the Methodist Church), Archbishop Stephen Naidoo (R.C.), Archbishop Desmond Tutu (Anglican), Allan Boesak and Frank Chikane

INTRODUCTION
Christianity in South African History

RICHARD ELPHICK

"In my Father's house are many rooms." —John 14:2 *(NIV)*

About 72.6 per cent of South Africans now claim to be Christian, up from about 46 per cent in 1911. Over the twentieth century Christianity has grown most dramatically among Africans – the largest, fastest growing, and now politically dominant sector of the South African population – up from 26 per cent of Africans in 1911 to 76 per cent in 1990. In addition, by 1990, 92.1 per cent of South African whites, 86 per cent of Coloureds, and 13 per cent of Indians called themselves Christians.[1]

Long before Christians became an overwhelming majority, Christian ideas and institutions were prominent in the political history of the region. In the nineteenth century Christian missionaries fanned out into the southern African interior, injecting themselves into the power politics of the region; they were often opposed, occasionally supported, by whites as well as blacks. In the twentieth century South Africans have used Christian doctrine both to justify and oppose doctrines of racial segregation, most notably apartheid. Christian leadership provided much of the impetus for the founding, in 1912, of the African National Congress, the most influential black opposition to white rule, and now the dominant political party in South Africa. And in the accelerating struggle between white rule and black liberation in the 1970s and 1980s, Christian affirmations, symbols, and rituals were prominent among militants on both sides, and among the would-be conciliators in the middle.

Because Christians have been so numerous and so politically influential, Christian doctrine, language, and sentiment are also interwoven in the social and cultural history of South Africa. Starting with the missionary campaign to Christianize African societies, some of the most intimate matters of white and black culture in South Africa – initiation, marriage, divorce, sexuality, association with people of other races, and even dress and drinking patterns – have been debated at length and with passion, largely in Christian terms. Also, until the 1950s, churches and missions controlled almost all schools for Africans and, to this day, many private schools for the largely white elite. So, too, social work, medicine, and nursing all were, to varying degrees, sponsored by Christian missions and churches. And the literature of Afrikaners and Africans was, until the Second World War, largely shaped by churches, missions, and publishers with Christian agendas; both literatures, like that of English-speaking whites, were replete with Christian motifs and allusions. Rich Christian musical traditions have also flourished, some with

1

strongly African character. Many South African towns are visually dominated by the spires of a Dutch Reformed church or an Anglican cathedral, just as in African townships the numerous churches are among the most notable and most utilized public buildings.

The pervasive influence of Christianity in South African life is, however, poorly reflected in the historical literature. To be sure, there is an abundance of writings on churches and missions, one recent bibliography listing 6,491 books and articles.[2] But this literature, most of it highly specialized, fails to situate Christianity in the broad political, social, and economic context of South African history. It has had little influence on the "mainstream" historiography of South Africa, whose liberal and Marxist historians, long preoccupied with the struggle between black and white, have tended to assign in this dynamic only marginal roles to religion.[3] The literature on the Christian churches is isolated in a second sense – from itself. Until very recently, little effort has been expended in creating a coherent synthesis of the numerous existing biographies, theological writings, and histories of missions, Christian schools, charitable institutions, churches, hierarchies, and congregations.[4] The history of South African Christianity is found for the most part in local or "micro"-narratives, while the highly elaborated "macro"-narratives of colonialism, capitalism, and liberation – the backbone of the conventional histories of South Africa – give to Christianity, only a marginal role, or no role at all. Work on a macro-narrative of South African Christianity itself – combining the histories of congregations and missions into one coherent story – has barely begun.[5]

This volume seeks to insert the Christian micro-narratives into the macro-narratives of South African history; thus its subtitle, *A Political, Social, and Cultural History*. As for the second challenge – to develop a macro-narrative of South African Christianity – the contributions here, produced by 29 scholars, can only be suggestive. Each chapter reflects the present uneven state of research. Coverage is not complete. But in creating a macro-narrative, coherence, not comprehensive coverage, is most crucial. The authors have suggested comparative and speculative themes that transcend their own chapters; readers will no doubt find others.[6]

Part One of this volume covers the history of Christianity in South Africa from 1652, when whites first settled at the Cape of Good Hope, until 1910, when four colonies united to form the Union of South Africa. During the first phase of this early period, from 1652 to 1795, the public expression of Christianity was, with minor exceptions, monopolized by the Dutch Reformed Church, closely overseen by the ruling Dutch East India Company. Chapter 1 argues that Reformed piety and doctrine were far more influential in the shaping of white society, and by extension of white-black relations, than most social historians have allowed. White colonists, persuaded that their eternal salvation derived from God's promise to their ancestors, embraced Christianity as an exclusive and inherited religion which shored up their group boundaries, nurtured their sense of superiority, and laid the basis of a white-dominated racial order. But a minority of whites in the Dutch Reformed Church embraced another Christian tendency with very different social implications: the Continuing Reformation's belief that people's salvation depended, not on their ancestry, but on a personal conversion to Jesus Christ.

British conquest (in 1795 and again in 1806) exposed South Africa, not only to a dynamic global economy, but also to an explosive proliferation of Protestant movements. South Africa was soon awash in newly imported churches – Anglican, Congregational, Baptist, Presbyterian, Methodist – and new missions from Britain, Germany, France, Switzerland, and Scandinavia. Differences among the churches and missions should not be exaggerated. The British groups were predominantly Evangelical and the continental groups predominantly Pietist; they shared with one another, and with the Continuing Reformation in the Dutch Reformed Church, a concern for personal conversion; they emphasized Biblical authority, the cultivation of intense devotion, and the Christian imperative to preach the Gospel. The Roman Catholic church (chapter 11) was slow to get started in South Africa. Only the growing Anglo-Catholic current in the Anglican Church, and the liberal and Calvinist strands surviving in the increasingly evangelical Dutch Reformed Church, stood apart from the common culture of Evangelical and Pietistic Protestantism – a culture similar to that of nineteenth-century North America.[7]

The churches did, however, differ from one another in ecclesiology and in politics. Each brought to the Cape some practices, aspirations, or fears derived from European history, most notably from the Reformation and the French Revolution. Each strove to reproduce at the Cape its characteristic form of organization – episcopal, presbyterian, or congregational – and to establish the relationship with the state it had advocated in Europe. In retrospect it seems that it was inevitable that, since no church had a clear majority among the white settlers, the Cape would reject an established church and adopt instead a pluralist and voluntarist form of church organization, as did the United States and the Canadian and Australian colonies in the same period. The outcome was not so apparent to contemporary South Africans. The two churches – the Dutch Reformed and the Anglican – that had pretensions to established status learned the disadvantages of establishment only when the government curtailed their ability to discipline dissident clergy within their own ranks (chapter 3).

A dynamic in most churches at the Cape (including the Anglican and Dutch Reformed) was a zeal for Christian missions. By the early nineteenth century South Africa had become one of the most intensively "occupied" fields of Christian mission in the world. The story began among the Khoikhoi, then called "Hottentots," (chapter 2). Subsequently Christianity penetrated beyond the Cape Colony to the Xhosa (chapter 4), the Zulu and Swazi (chapter 5), the Sotho and Tswana (chapter 6), and to Africans and whites in Republics established by Dutch settlers beyond the Orange River in the 1830s (chapter 7). For the most part missions were directed at Africans, but, as on the American frontier, missionaries also sought to Christianize white settlers, some of whom were only nominally Christian.

Many common themes emerge in the seven chapters of Part One. In most cases, missionaries founded schools, studied African languages, and translated the Bible. Usually they made a few converts. Religious change was rarely rapid and never simple; it differed greatly from region to region. Among the Khoikhoi, many of whom had lost their political and economic independence to the Cape Colony, the gospel found eager adherents almost from the first; before long Christianity had

3

become a badge of identity of several Khoikhoi groups. Among some peoples, like the Xhosa and Zulu, still on the fringes of encroaching colonialism, the response to Christianity was cooler, with most rulers wary of missionaries, at least at first; the few converts in these societies came overwhelmingly from among outcast and marginal social groups. Among the Sotho and some Tswana, especially the Ngwato, a third pattern emerged, when some rulers took an interest in Christianity, or even, like Khama of the Ngwato, became fervent converts, encouraging an early surge of conversions, particularly among some factions of the aristocracy.

Wherever they went, missionaries were drawn into the internal politics of African societies and, often too, into their external relations with other African and colonial powers. Part of the fascination of this period is the variety of attitudes to society and the state, born in European conflicts, that missionaries imported, often uncritically, into the vast social laboratory of Africa. In general the British and American missionaries had a more activist (broadly speaking, Calvinist) attitude toward the state than did the Lutheran missionaries from Germany and Scandinavia, and hence were more inclined to come into open conflict with white settler societies or with Christian African rulers like Khama. But the Anglo-Saxons, too, were bitterly divided on the advisability of a missionary's engagement with politics – a difference epitomized by the debate between the London missionaries John Philip and Robert Moffat. In Natal and Zululand, missionaries brought a par-ticularly rich variety of social models they wished to implement in a Christianized Africa – from the communal solidarities of German medieval villages to the assertive liberties of the early American Republic (chapter 5).

These early chapters conclude, as do studies of Christianity elsewhere in Africa,[8] that the spread of Christianity owed more to the zeal of African converts than to the direct actions of missionaries, whose importance seems to have been more political and cultural than evangelistic. Most dramatic was the case of the Xhosa prophet Ntsikana, never part of a missionary community, who fashioned a form of African Christianity that profoundly influenced African music, literature, theology, and politics (pp. 72–73, 312, 322–23). Equally significant were the armies of African evangelists who, independently or under missionary supervision, carried the gospel to new regions and peoples, drawing on the assumptions, idioms, and even the spiritual resources of pre-Christian African culture. Many early African Christians, like most missionaries, regarded Christianity and African religious views as mutually exclusive and even hostile to one another; more recent analyses, including several chapters in Part One, tend, in contrast, to emphasize complex "negotiation" between the two worldviews and to argue that accommodation between them has been as common as conflict.

The advance of conservative theology and Evangelical piety, and the closely related zeal for missions among whites and blacks, had paradoxical effects on South African racial and ethnic identities. White Dutch-speaking settlers continued to rely on the Dutch Reformed Church as a bulwark of their identity and their exclusiveness, despite the Christian universalism entailed in that church's growing Evangelical and missionary commitments. Some Griqua also formed an ethnic identity around Christian affiliation, while Christianity provided the social back-bone of the new Khoisan community founded at the Kat River in 1829 (chapter 2).

Later in the century Khama of the Ngwato blended Christianity into the national ideology of his kingdom (chapter 6).

The missionaries' relations with colonial political powers varied greatly depending on the time, the place, and the missionary's nationality and social philosophy. Some comparatively radical missionaries clashed periodically with Cape officials in the early nineteenth century. But others, such as Joseph Williams, the founder, in 1816, of the first permanent mission to the Xhosa, were willing to serve as government agents. And, though many missionaries opposed the expansion of white colonies and Boer Republics into African controlled lands, most missionaries, particularly the English-speakers, backed the aggressive use of British imperial power (as opposed to local settler power) against the Zulu kingdom in 1877, and against the Boer Republics in the Anglo-Boer War (1899 to 1902). Throughout South Africa missionaries strove to inculcate in Africans an appreciation for European trade goods and values, and a confidence in the beneficence of at least some forms of European rule.

Yet Africans often made very different use of the missionary message. Christians of deep piety, such as the Kat River rebels in 1851, Dukwana of the Xhosa, and Johannes Dinkwanyane of the Pedi (chapters 4 and 7), took up arms against white colonialism. In subsequent decades, particularly in the Eastern Cape and Natal, a moderate but politically active response to colonialism emerged among members of the new African "middle-class," called *kholwa* in Natal, who had been educated in missionary schools and were for the most part committed Christians (chapters 4 and 5). Christian missions also sparked counter-reformations, as in Lesotho, where Christianity was overshadowed by resurgent African religion in the late nineteenth century. Similarly, among the Xhosa, an extraordinary chain of prophets arose, beginning in the second decade of the century with Nxele, whose anti-colonial and non-Christian message was salted nevertheless with borrowed Christian themes.

Over the course of the nineteenth century members of different, even hostile, groups found themselves members of the same Christian denomination. However, given the proliferation of mission societies in southern Africa, and the tendency of each society to concentrate on specific peoples, inter-ethnic conflicts among Africans in the churches were perhaps rarer in South Africa than in some other parts of the continent. Much more significant, both in the short- and the long-run, was the challenge to the Christian conscience presented by the membership of whites and blacks in the same church organization, at a time when the whites were increasingly dispossessing Africans of their land, their labour power, and their political freedom. South Africans, in consequence, debated issues of segregation and integration in their churches earlier than they did in their legislatures. As chapter 3 shows, different churches adopted different strategies for coping with this dilemma, the Anglicans, for example, maintaining black–white unity at the diocesan level, and the Dutch Reformed eventually creating separate churches, one for each of four races. All denominations adopted segregation to some extent, but it was the Dutch Reformed model that later inspired the doctrine of apartheid.

In this book the chronology of South African Christianity is divided at 1910, when four white-ruled colonies (the Cape Colony, Natal, the Orange Free State, and the

Transvaal) became the Union of South Africa. Around this time the political and economic histories of South African regions began to flow increasingly toward a single channel – as did the ecclesiastical history, though rather more slowly, with early moves to consolidate national denominations. In forming the new Union, white settlers were motivated partly by their desire to coordinate their "native policies." The new Union parliament promptly began to craft segregationist legislation that would come to shape the black–white struggle of the coming century, posing an acute challenge to believers in Christian universalism.

The early twentieth century was a time of profound change in South African as well as in global Christianity. In 1910 South African Protestant missionaries joined colleagues from around the world at the Edinburgh Missionary Conference, an event widely regarded as the climax of optimistic, progressively oriented Protestant missions. Only four years in the future lay the assassination at Sarajevo, the First World War, a profound shaking of confidence in Western civilization, and an accompanying crisis in Protestant theology. In South Africa itself religious change was rapid. The Roman Catholic Church, though still comparatively small, had more than 90,000 adherents by 1911, and was building up a head of steam that would later make it one of the largest churches in South Africa. Members of new mission societies – some with novel Holiness and Pentecostal doctrines – were trickling into South Africa. The formation of African Initiated Churches (AICs), underway for a generation, had already entered a second, or Zionist phase, as Africans began to fashion traditions markedly more Pentecostal, and more African, than those of the churches they left behind.

To reflect all these reorientations Part Two of this volume is organized, not on regional or ethnic, but on ecclesiastical, lines. Each chapter deals with a church or group of churches, ranging from the Roman Catholic church (chapter 11), through the clusters of Reformed, English-speaking, Lutheran, and Pentecostal churches (chapters 8, 9, 10, and 13), to the greatly fragmented AICs (chapter 12). The themes of these chapters reflect, in part, the varying agendas of the churches in twentieth-century South Africa. The Roman Catholics, for example, who began the century somewhat on the margins of South African social and political power, concentrated on building up parish and diocesan life, on training well-educated and tightly disciplined priests and bishops, and on creating the characteristic Catholic institutions of evangelism and social service – schools and hospitals. By the 1960s the Catholic Church, now much larger and influential, became increasingly outspoken in social and political affairs, especially through the Southern African Catholic Bishops' Conference. The Afrikaner Reformed churches, too, moved more aggressively into education and social service in the twentieth century. They were motivated largely by their tight identification with the social and political struggle of the Afrikaners, and assisted by their comparatively easy access to government policy-makers, both before and after the 1948 electoral victory of the (Afrikaner) National Party. For their part, leaders of the English-speaking churches (especially the Anglican, Presbyterian, Methodist, and Congregational) were much preoccupied with Christian unity and with issues of social justice; they took the lead in creating the South African Council of Churches and several non-denominational organizations, such as the Institute for Contextual Theology and the Christian Institute, both prominent in the struggle against apartheid. Lutherans, by contrast, felt largely marginalized in a society dominated by Afrikaans- and English-speaking whites. Concentrating on the preservation of German and Scandinavian cultures among white immigrants, and on building up a distinctive culture of quiet piety among African converts, they joined the anti-apartheid struggle relatively late. Even more remote from political and social power were the Pentecostal churches, both white and black, and the AICs, which generally steered clear of overt political involvement and concentrated instead on spreading their distinctive forms of Christianity, often with spectacular success.

All these groups, except the AICs, had large numbers of black and white members, with the black members becoming the majority in most denominations during the twentieth century. The leadership of all but the AICs, however, remained firmly in white hands until the apartheid era: the first black Catholic bishop was appointed in 1954, the first Anglican bishop in 1960, and the first black president of the Methodist church in 1964. Even Pentecostalism, despite its birth in inter-racial settings in America and South Africa, quickly adapted to South African social norms, with the whites retaining firm control of interracial churches.

Despite their subordinate position in ecclesiastical structures, Africans (and among Pentecostals, some Indians) continued to be the key agents of Christianization in the twentieth century, most obviously in the AICs, which grew from almost nothing in 1890 to embrace somewhere between a third and a half of the Africans of South Africa by the 1990s. The mission societies remained under white control, but by 1928 they were employing almost twenty times as many blacks as whites,[9] who increasingly served as supervisors and trainers, but not as pastors and evangelists. In the Roman Catholic Church, African believers carried Catholicism to new districts and maintained it without benefit of sacraments until the arrival of a priest. Male migrant labourers were particularly crucial in the spread of Christianity, carrying it first from missionized rural areas to the mines or city, and later from the mines or city back to the countryside (chapter 14).

The result of all this activity was a massive growth of Christian adherence among Africans in the twentieth century, a process still almost totally ignored by scholars, though it far overshadows the much slower – but more adequately studied – spread of the Christian faith in the nineteenth century. While it is still too early to understand this process as a whole, the chapters of this book give some clues. Chapter 7 says, for example, that fission and competition between churches accelerated Christianization in the nineteenth century; this might be even more true in the twentieth. By the 1990s few places in the world, apart from the United States, matched South Africa in the proliferation of Christian denominations and sects – evidence that Christianity has apparently adapted to a striking variety of cultures and social classes, a reason for its dramatic advance.

This explosion of Christian adherence coincided with massive social, economic, and intellectual transformations that some theorists call "modernization," while others, especially those influenced by Marxism, see as products of "industrial capitalism." Three aspects of these transformations were of particular importance to the churches: urbanization, secularization, and a closely related intellectual current, theological liberalism.

In the early twentieth century, Afrikaans-speaking whites and Africans flooded to the cities in the wake of the mining boom, the subsequent growth of secondary industries, and the deterioration of life in the countryside. Most middle-class members of English-speaking churches had little empathy for the white and black workers, who began to press the demands of organized labour on South African politicians, or for the black peasant populations left behind in the deteriorating rural reserves. By contrast, the Afrikaner Reformed churches, acutely aware of economic and spiritual dangers the cities posed to Afrikaans-speaking whites, undertook to alleviate the "poor-white problem" with work colonies, boarding houses for the poor, hostels in town for rural school children, industrial schools, orphanages, and hospitals. Similarly, many missionaries of all denominations thought that the urbanization of Africans would lead to crime, sexual immorality, and religious indifference, and from this concern arose an influential body of South African Christian social thought, often called "Social Christianity" (chapter 23).

The churches whose members had little political power often responded to urbanization by aggressively planting new churches in the cities. Thus, new forms of Zionist Christianity emerged that offered physical healing, a supportive community, and spiritual solace to newly urbanized Africans. As a consequence of such vigorous evangelization, the majority of urbanized whites and blacks became members of Christian churches. In this respect the history of South African Christianity more closely resembles the pattern of the United States than that of European countries; in Britain, for example, the church failed to implant itself in the working-class culture of nineteenth-century cities and went into decisive decline.[10]

The growth of cities coincided with the organization of "modern" institutions such as universities, professions, and sciences, and with the growth of a bureaucratic state willing to intervene in social matters. These processes, which echoed earlier European and North American developments, were bolstered by certain assumptions, imported from overseas, about the desirable and inevitable "secularization" of society. That was the belief that the state and various expert bodies should take over functions formerly fulfilled by the church, while the church withdrew from the public arena to confine itself to private devotion and the needs of local communities. The state, on this view, would increasingly intervene in the funding, management, and curriculum planning of formerly church-run schools; anthropologists would replace missionaries as "experts" on the culture and social problems of "the native"; and psychiatrists, social workers, nurses, and doctors would provide solutions to problems once approached chiefly through religion.

South African society has, in fact, been substantially secularized over the twentieth century, a secularization overlooked by historians, perhaps because it has provoked little anxiety among Christians, and hence little public controversy. In South Africa, unlike in western Europe, secularization has been accompanied, not by a decline of religious devotion, but by a dramatic rise. Moreover, it has proceeded slowly and unobtrusively. In South Africa, as in other societies influenced by Britain, ruling elites have promoted secularization less aggressively than in, say, France or the United States. Moreover, the comparatively weak South African state has had to rely on the churches to provide services, particularly to Africans, long provided in wealthier countries by secular agencies. Secularization in South Africa has sometimes been camouflaged. It is easy to forget that the massive system of apartheid, created by the state in cooperation with numerous expert elites, was in many respects a secularizing process, despite the government's theoretical allegiance to the anti-secularizing ideology of Christian Nationalism. The most dramatic step in the secularization of South African society – the taking over of the mission schools in the wake of the Bantu Education Act of 1953 – was imposed on the churches by a government that proclaimed its Christian commitment.

Urbanization and secularization affected all churches. However, only those with significant political power – the English-speaking, the Dutch Reformed, and later, the Roman Catholic – had the resources to attempt organized, nationwide responses. In this they were both inspired and troubled by theological impulses that reached them from overseas Christian churches. Early in the century two divisive forces from European and American Protestantism arrived in South Africa: "modernism," the critique of traditional doctrine in the light of science, Biblical criticism, and the presumed needs of modern society; and the Social Gospel, the belief that Christians were called to combat sins embedded in the structure of society. Except among Afrikaners, these imports caused far less rancour and division than they had in the United States, where several major denominations had split into "modernist" and "fundamentalist" camps. In South Africa, Social Gospel ideas were particularly popular among leaders of English-speaking churches and of the English-led South African Council of Churches, and among Christian activists in secular organizations such as the South African Institute of Race Relations (chapters 9 and 23). The notion of structural sin may well have paved the way in these circles for the more radical Black and liberation theologies of the era of apartheid, but their influence on ordinary churchgoers was probably slight, at least until the 1970s. Similar influences reached the South African Roman Catholic Church from the Vatican II Council (1962–65), whose various directives for updating the church's responses to the modern world were to enable greater cooperation with other South African churches, and a more vigorous Catholic opposition to apartheid.

In the Dutch Reformed Churches, which were deeply attached to the ethos of rural South Africa, the controversies over theological modernism coincided with the crisis of urbanization. These controversies caused painful divisions, particularly in the 1920s, when the popular theologian Johannes du Plessis threw himself against the conservative establishment of the NGK, the largest Afrikaner church, and was tried for heresy. In the ensuing turmoil the conservatives, who drew increasingly on neo-Calvinist ideologies from the Netherlands, emerged victorious. Afrikaner nationalist thought of the 1930s and 1940s, largely shaped by Reformed theologians and other Reformed thinkers, was comprehensive in its indictment of modernity and confident that it could provide a Christian antidote. One strand of this thought was later to shape the ideology of racial apartheid.

While Parts One and Two of this book deal broadly with Christianity in the history of white settlers and Africans, the five chapters of Part Three examine

9

INTRODUCTION

Christianity in specific settings bounded by gender or race. Two chapters explore Christian responses to the social and psychological disruptions of modernity, chapter 14 looking at the artificially all-male world of migrant labourers on the Witwatersrand gold mines, and chapter 15 at Christian African women's daunting new burdens of motherhood, particularly in the city. Under these conditions both men and women founded novel Christian organizations – choirs and groups of young volunteers among the men, *manyano* prayer and support groups among women – often under missionary oversight. In each case Africans engaged in pastoral ministries and undertook the conversion of other Africans. However, Christianity on the gold mine compounds was seriously undercut by the miners' needs for social consolations only feebly provided by the church. Miners were attracted to drinking and dancing, behaviours unacceptable to most missionaries, and drawn into the townships on weekends in search of the company of women. Christian fellowships in the all-male compounds were, in consequence, frequently tenuous. Women's groups, in contrast, provided strong support to African women while remaining loyal to the middle-class model of family life favoured by missionaries; the manyanos have flourished to this day, in rural areas as well as in towns and cities.

Although research on gender aspects of South African Christianity has barely begun, it is clear that, in most South African subcultures, Christianity appeals more to women than to men – this despite a nearly universal male domination of formal church structures. In the Roman Catholic Church, women have exercised considerable power in female religious orders, but always under the jurisdiction of a male bishop. Among Zionist and Pentecostal-type African churches, many women prophets arose, with at least one, Ma Nku, becoming a founder of a major church; women have participated energetically in the life and worship of such churches, where, by one estimate, they outnumber men by three to one. Yet this vigour has not dislodged male leadership; even Ma Nku's church has come under the control of men. In this respect spirit-oriented Christianity in South Africa seems to have followed the earlier patterns of revivalism and Pentecostalism in Europe and America, where an initial empowering of women preachers gave way to a reassertion of male leadership.[11]

The interaction between Christianity and African worldviews in South Africa has been fluid and led to many novel syntheses. This is less true of Christianity's interaction with the three other world religions – Islam, Judaism, and Hinduism – which, though small in numbers, have been influential in particular South African cities, regions, and social classes. Islam took root in South Africa as a result of both immigration and conversion of non-Muslims at the Cape, and of Indian immigration to Natal. Judaism was brought by immigrants from Europe, Hinduism by immigrants from India. Apart from a small growth of Islam among Africans, the three world religions have each remained confined chiefly to their base communities.

Christian missions have been directed at Jews, Muslims, and Hindus, but with much less effect than among Africans. Very few Jews have converted to Christianity (chapter 17). Among Coloureds of nineteenth-century Cape Town, as chapter 16 shows, complex patterns of social interaction – marriage and the manumission and emancipation of slaves – produced conversions from Christianity to Islam, and vice versa, with a net gain for Islam. Only among Hindus has Christianity made significant advances, largely propelled by dynamic Pentecostal witness since the 1920s (chapter 18): Christians now comprise about 13 per cent of South African Indians, a much higher percentage than in India.

Christians and adherents of the three great world religions in South Africa have tended to remain in parallel communities, meeting one another chiefly in the economic realm. Hindus, Jews, and Muslims have, like Africans, confronted Christianity as the religion of the country's rulers, with mixed consequences for the fortunes of Christianity. South African authorities have sometimes discriminated against non-Christians on grounds of religion (as well as on grounds of race). For example, the constitution of the nineteenth-century South African Republic denied Jews (and Catholics) the right to vote or hold high office; the 1913 judgment of the Cape division of the Supreme Court in effect invalidated Hindu and Muslim marriages;[12] and the Nationalist government imposed a Christian National curriculum on schools in the apartheid era. On the other hand, the policies of the Dutch East India Company in the eighteenth century, and the self-interest of Christian slaveholders, actually fostered the spread of Islam. In the nineteenth century liberal Cape governments responded favourably to requests from Jews and Muslims for support of their institutions and relief from discrimination (chapters 16 and 17).

By oppressing certain groups while proclaiming their devotion to Christian values, South African governments have doubtless tainted the image of Christianity in the eyes of their victims. Slaves in early nineteenth-century Cape Town preferred Islam to Christianity precisely because Christianity was the religion of their masters. In the apartheid era Hindu leaders countered Christian proselytization by pointing out the Christian ties of the apartheid government; some African anti-apartheid activists renounced Christianity altogether.

Because Christianity has become the religion of the vast majority of South Africans, including the rulers, it might well have contributed a common language, common aspirations, and common rituals to the integration of a highly divided society. Yet its integrative role has, so far, been slight, partly because it has so successfully adapted its message to many cultural traditions and to many social settings. Most South African Christians conduct their religious life within tightly bounded enclaves of race, of ethnicity, or of class – and sometimes of gender. One encounters, for example, highly distinctive Afrikaans, Sotho, Zulu, English, German, Coloured, and Indian Christianities, each with further male and female nuances. This capacity to be "translated" – first into another language, then into another culture – which the Gambian mission theorist Lamin Sanneh sees as the striking feature of Christianity worldwide, has, in South Africa, been in tension with the universalism of the Christian proclamation that "there is neither Jew nor Greek, slave nor free, male nor female, for you are all one in Christ Jesus."[13]

Part Four of this volume – with chapters on Christian literature, music, and architecture – provides evidence for the study of secularization and of translation (both linguistic and cultural) in the creative arts of South Africa. Chapter 19 explores Christian themes in South African literature, charting the pace of secularization in the different language groups. The English-speaking whites were the first to arrive at a point reached by highly secularized societies where literature is an autonomous sphere of activity distinct from religion; even though Christian and broader religious themes appeared in the writings of English-speakers, religion as such was no longer part of the their cultural identity nor of their professional identity as writers. Afrikaner and African authors arrived at this point much later – the former delayed by the close ties between religion and Afrikaner nationalism, the latter by white missionaries' control of the presses on which African authors relied – with the result that their published literatures remained more explicitly Christian than the literature of the English-speaking whites until, roughly, the 1960s. The belief that literature is an activity undertaken by inspired individuals free to incorporate or neglect religious themes is itself a facet of secularization.

In all the arts – and in intellectual life – African Christians faced the need to "translate" Christian doctrines, values, symbols, stories, and rituals into their own culture. Typically, two distinct modes of translation emerged, reminiscent of the Biblical distinction between putting new wine in old, or in new, wineskins. An old-wineskin choice in literature has been to praise the Christian God in classic African praise-poems; a new-wineskin choice to resort to formal, printed poems, plays, and novels. In music, Ntsikana, the founder of Xhosa Christianity, composed his Great Hymn in a thoroughly African musical mode, but before long many Africans in mission churches used Western hymn-tunes and cantatas, marked by Western melody and rhythms. Various compromises have also developed between Western and African styles, such as "Afro-diatonic" melody and the call-and-response musical performance common in AICs (chapter 20).

White Christians were at first inclined to resist the cultural translation of Christianity. Like immigrants to many other parts of the world, and like the Jewish, Muslim, and Hindu immigrants to South Africa, they tended to cultivate their European religious traditions tenaciously in their new land – Lutheranism as part of German identity, Anglicanism as part of English identity, and so on. They tended to remain highly conservative, until well into the twentieth century, in their tastes in church music and church architecture, as well as in their theology; they were willing to consider only those innovations imported from their mother country. Thus, centuries passed before South African hymnals and prayer books were compiled, and before the Dutch Bible was replaced by a version in Afrikaans, the language popularly spoken among the largest and oldest white community in South Africa. Long after white immigrants of diverse European origins had assimilated either to the English- or Afrikaans-speaking communities, they retained remnants of their original European traditions in their churches' liturgy, architecture, spiritual ethos, and even in the language of worship.

Ironically, the battle over segregation and apartheid shocked some white South Africans into the formation of new, distinctively South African cultural forms. This occurred most dramatically in intellectual life, as for example in the formation of Afrikaner nationalist theologies based on neo-Calvinist separate-sphere philosophies, and later in the more radical English-speaking and Black theologies designed to challenge the ideology of the apartheid state (chapter 24). While both theologies drew heavily on initiatives from overseas, their final form and application were distinctively South African. Similar aspirations toward engagement with South Africa, and more broadly with Africa, from the 1960s onward, led to innovations in Christian liturgy, literature, music, and architecture – a new phase in the story of translation.

Christians generally have found it hard to assert a universalist message in a society structured by systematic and often ruthless policies of social, political, and economic segregation. Many historians conclude, therefore, either that religion is irrelevant in political struggle, or that it serves as a mere reflection of the interests of dominant groups. Most chapters of this book deal at least implicitly with politics, presenting evidence useful in assessing these widespread assumptions; they show the ways religious impulses have coincided, or conflicted, with the political and economic agendas of various groups, both black and white. The four chapters of Part Five draw more explicit and systematic connections between Christianity and politics in twentieth-century South Africa. They discuss three periods when South African Christians, in the light of Christian universalism, have criticized the hierarchical and segregationist policies of South African governments: the demands of African middle-class "nationalists" for the rights of British subjects early in the century (chapter 22); the cautious call of social Christians, both white and black, for interracial accommodation in the 1920s and 1930s (chapter 23); and the more radical call for "liberation" among black and white activists and theologians in the anti-apartheid struggle (chapters 24 and 25).

All such views were, at most times, highly unpopular in ruling circles; Christians who advocated them – like liberals, radicals and nationalists of other religions and of no religion – faced the risk of ostracism and, in the apartheid era, of banning, imprisonment, banishment, and even death. To make matters more difficult, they sometimes received little support from church officials. They had to rely on an institutional or financial base that gave them some independence from the white ruling classes. The early African nationalists had accumulated some wealth in farming and commerce and were able to gain political leverage in some parts of the Cape by using their limited electoral rights. Social Christians of the interwar years relied heavily on their "Benevolent Empire" of schools, social welfare organizations, and publishing houses – in part funded from overseas – to give them a secure space for mounting cautious criticisms of government policies. The activists of the 1970s and 1980s, relying on a narrower institutional base and facing a more repressive government, depended even more on funds from overseas; by then, too, the leadership in some of the churches had moved towards a more boldly anti-government stance.

The voices of Christian universalism typically sought ideological support from narratives of world history that situated the history of South Africa in a broader context. Some early African nationalists, along with many more English-speaking white Christians, saw God's righteous purposes revealed in the successes of British Imperialism. The interwar mission-oriented Christians relied heavily on the spread of science, education, and Social Gospel notions to enlighten South African whites and induce them to change their policies. Activists of the later anti-apartheid movements sometimes drew on Marxist or other anti-colonial and anti-capitalist narratives of liberation. Such ideological alliances made the Christian universalists vulnerable to the charge of selling out to enemies of the faith. Thus, the early African nationalists were called dupes of the imperialists, the social Christians were denounced as "liberals" and "humanists," while the anti-apartheid activists were tarred with the brush of communism.

The Christian critics of the South African racial order also drew more directly on the Jewish and Christian religious traditions. Protestant activists, for example, were strongly inspired by "postmillennial" eschatology, the optimistic belief that improvement can take place in human history as a prelude to a second coming of Christ. Postmillennialism supported Christian engagement in the politics of this world, meshing neatly with the classic faith of missionaries, still strong in the twentieth century, that the living Christ could transform individuals in a personal encounter, and that through such encounters society itself could be transformed and the Kingdom of God ushered in. Many other South Africans interpreted the doctrine of Christ's second coming in a "premillennial" vein pessimistic about improvements in human history; this view, adopted by smaller Evangelical groups and by many AICs, has in general discouraged Christians from direct political action (chapter 22). So, too, the Judaeo-Christian doctrine of God's creation of the universe could support contrary political stances (chapter 24). On the one hand, Dutch Reformed theologians, arguing that humans should obey God's "creation ordinances", advocated an acceptance of existing authorities and hierarchies. On the other hand, practitioners of some Black and liberation theologies rejoiced that humans could extend God's creative acts by bringing about liberation in history. Another effective Christian resource in the anti-apartheid struggle, the tradition of Old Testament prophecy, was less amenable to alternative conservative interpretation. Confident that God calls the church to declare prophetic judgment upon social and political evil, many anti-apartheid Christians found courage to act in the face of extreme danger (chapter 25).

Christianity, then, has been far from irrelevant in South African political history; nor has it served merely to mask the interests of the ruling classes. While many Christians have used Christian language to support a segregationist and hierarchical social order, others have opposed this order in the name of Christian universalism. Christians have frequently found themselves on both sides of the political barricades, denouncing each another's political behaviour as heretical, idolatrous, or treasonous. Behind these divisions lie the interaction of two themes running through the long history of South African Christianity. On the one hand, Christianity has spread dramatically among South African people of varying cultures and social circumstances, diverging into numerous liturgical, theological and ecclesiastical forms. While the translation of Christianity did not cause segregationism, for a long time it accommodated it comfortably. On the other hand, before the rise of segregation and apartheid in the twentieth century, robust traditions of South African Christianity have opposed a variety of injustices, claiming that God's fatherly love, Jesus's sacrifice on the cross, the coming of the Holy Spirit, or some other Christian belief implies that all people are equal and thus must be equally treated. Christians themselves do not normally recognize a contradiction between the translation of Christianity and its universalism – between the "many rooms" and the one "house" that Jesus used to describe the Father's kingdom. Yet, in practice, translation and universalism have often been in tension, with powerful consequences for the course of South African history.

1

A Christian Monopoly: The Reformed Church and Colonial Society under Dutch Rule

JONATHAN N. GERSTNER

In 1652, a chartered trading corporation, the Dutch East India Company (VOC), set up a half-way station at the Cape for its ships sailing between Europe and the East Indies. This outpost was intended, at first, simply to provide a port of call for Dutch ships to pick up fresh supplies, but, as early as 1657, the Company allowed some of its former employees to settle and farm. In subsequent decades, immigration added to their ranks. Settlers received land grants for farms close to the Cape fort, and with rapid demographic growth the colony expanded, the settlers subjugating the indigenous Khoisan and seizing their land and livestock.

From the Cape Colony's beginnings as a garrison, the VOC provided for Dutch Reformed services, led by officially recognized religious workers. The first permanent minister arrived in 1665. The VOC, in collaboration with the Amsterdam Classis (regional assembly) of the Reformed Church in the Netherlands, maintained an almost continuous string of resident ministers from that time. As the established church, the Dutch Reformed Church exercised a virtual monopoly of Christian expression in the new colony.

Reformed church life and theology played a formative role in the development of South African culture and society. In particular, it contributed greatly to the formation of a distinctive identity among the white settlers and to their conviction of superiority to indigenous peoples and slaves.

The Dutch Reformed Tradition and Covenant Theology

Studies of South African history often refer to the doctrine of "Calvinism" quite loosely, without analysis of the historic doctrine of the Dutch Reformed Church. The Reformed faith, sometimes called "Calvinism," was one of the principal branches of the Protestant Reformation, a movement united on two basic points of doctrine: on salvation (how people could achieve forgiveness of sins and gain eternal life), and on the source of authority within the church. The leaders of the Reformation taught that human beings are justified (made right with God) only by faith in Christ as Saviour and Lord, that faith itself is a gift from God, and thus that salvation is solely a consequence of divine grace. The Bible alone, not the church hierarchy, was in their view the source of authority for faith and life. All religious teachings and all practices must be either directly scriptural or derived from scriptural principles. The individual believers, not the clergy, had the ultimate responsibility to decide for themselves what the scriptures said. The Protestant concept of "private interpretation" or "the priesthood of all believers" made it difficult for the Reformation churches to stay united amid divergent interpretations.

THE REFORMED CHURCH UNDER DUTCH RULE

The Reformation, after the Colloquy of Marburg in 1529, had permanently separated into three principal streams: the rather conservative Lutherans, who tended to retain from the medieval Catholic tradition all that was not strictly unscriptural; the radical Anabaptists, who granted baptism to adult believers only and also viewed civil authority as unspiritual; and the Reformed. John Calvin was the greatest theologian of the first century of the Reformed movement, but the term "Calvinism" was not used by the movement itself until centuries later. Lutheranism dominated the Protestant church of Germany and Scandinavia; the Reformed movement became the leading Protestant movement in France, Switzerland, Great Britain, the Netherlands, Hungary, and some regions of Germany.

The Reformed Church in the Netherlands was uniquely cosmopolitan, responsive to insights derived from throughout the Reformed world. It embraced distinct schools of thought represented best by its three confessions: the Belgic Confession of 1561, originally written in French, and influenced by John Calvin and his follower, Theodore Beza; the Heidelberg Catechism of 1563, emerging from the German and Swiss–German Reformed traditions, and influenced by the Lutheran Philip Melanchthon; and the Canons of Dort, a creed of Dutch origin, composed by an ecumenical gathering in 1618–19 of representatives from most of the Reformed Churches of Europe, including the Church of England.

The Reformed tradition maintains and is often associated with the doctrine of the sovereignty of God, or predestination. The sovereign God is seen as directing everything according to his eternal purpose, choosing or "electing" those who are to be saved. Salvation comes by grace alone, independent of an individual's own meritorious action. All people after the Fall are by nature spiritually dead and do not seek God or salvation. In order for persons to believe and be saved, God must give them a new heart to believe. God sovereignly chooses (or elects) those whom he will make into believers, and those he does not elect he allows to perish eternally as impenitent sinners. The majority of Reformed theologians viewed this decree of damnation as a passive or permissive decree.[1] God "will have mercy on whom He will have mercy; and whom He will He hardens"(Romans 9:18). A person gains evidence of election by faith in Christ, true sorrow for sin, sincerely striving to obey the Law of God. On the other hand, living an impenitent life does not prove that one is not elected or reprobate; only remaining unbelieving until death confirms that one was passed over by grace and left to choose the way of death that one had desired. Through repentance one becomes aware of being elect, but God's election is independent of one's actions. The doctrine of election was intended to mark an end to all human arrogance, for the elect and those rejected deserved the same fate of eternal condemnation. The only distinction between the two groups was the pure unmerited grace of God. On the cross Christ paid the penalty for the sins of all who will be saved, but he did not purchase potential redemption for everyone. Following the path of Calvin, the Synod of Dort of 1618–19 tidied up the Reformational understanding of justification by grace alone into a logically consistent system of which God's sovereignty was a central tenet.

The doctrine of the sovereignty of God that accompanied the Dutch colonists to South Africa imparted a strong confidence to them in encountering the uncertainties and dangers of life in a new land. A God who is in control of the infinitely essential matters of eternity is also in control of the smallest details of life. The Heidelberg Catechism summarizes this view: "herbs and grass, rain and drought, fruitful and barren years, meat and drink, health and sickness, riches and poverty, yea, all things, come not by chance, but by his fatherly hand."[2]

The tradition of covenant theology, that is, of God's sworn relationships with his creation, was the other chief aspect of the Reformed tradition. It sought to offer a biblical defence for baptising the children of believers. In response to Anabaptist challenges, covenant theology asserted a unity between Israel of the Old Testament and the Christian church of the New Testament, each being the people of God. In the Old Testament, children of believers received circumcision as the sign or seal of the need to receive righteousness by faith; in the New Testament, children of believers are to be baptized on the same ground. Covenant theology expanded beyond a defence of infant baptism into a doctrinal edifice explaining the fall of humanity into sin and the origins of all societal relationships. The continuity, through the covenant, of Christians with the Old Testament people of God provided a ground for group cohesion in the midst of the individualism inherent in Protestant doctrine.

One application of covenant theology in South Africa concerned the relationship between Christianity and slavery, an institution seemingly accepted in both Testaments and subject to Old Testament law. The Synod of Dort had addressed the question of the baptism of slave children held by Christian owners, concluding that slaves were part of the household of the slaveholder, following the practice of Abraham.[3] Generally theologians favoured delaying baptism until a slave was converted; however, a significant minority argued for baptism of slave children who were going to be brought up in a Christian household. All agreed that Christian slaves could not be sold out of the spiritual household in which they were born. The distinguished Genevan theologian, Giovanni Deodatus, even hinted at the most revolutionary understanding of all, that a Christian slave ought to be liberated, following the Old Testament covenant that no Israelite could hold another Israelite in perpetual bondage (Leviticus 25:39–40).

The seventeenth century, during which the Cape was first settled, was in many ways the golden age of the Dutch Reformed Church. It had weathered a controversy with Arminianism, whose core teaching was that human beings had the moral ability to reject or accept God's grace. After Dort, orthodox Reformed theology ruled in the Netherlands, although with remarkable diversity of practice and opinion. The followers of Gisbertus Voetius, a professor at the University of Utrecht, insisted on a unity between the Old and the New Testaments, while the followers of Johannes Cocceius, a professor at the University of Leiden, tended to de-emphasize the Old Testament, explicitly rejecting all Old Testament practices not explicitly reaffirmed in the New Testament. For the Cocceians Sunday was a day like any other, except for the practice of attending church on the first day of the week in memory of Jesus' resurrection. For Voetius and for his followers, non-essential work and recreation were forbidden on Sunday, the New Testament equivalent of the Jewish sabbath which was devoted instead to public, family, and private worship of God. Cocceius sharply divided the history of the world into separate covenantal systems or economies.[4] The controversy resulting from the profound differences on covenant theology between these two major theological figures engaged the entire Dutch Reformed communion.

The Voetians apparently exceeded their Cocceian counterparts in their own personal piety, and in producing committed parishioners. Even on some issues of reform, such as the rejection of Christian holidays, to which one would expect Cocceian theology to be more sympathetic than Voetian, leadership came from Voetians. The "serious Cocceians," a later branch, heavily emphasized personal piety but virtually accepted Voetian emphasis on law and the place of the Sabbath in the Christian life. In general, Voetian theology, in popularizing the identification of contemporary Christians with the Old Testament Israel, have had a more direct impact on the culture of the Dutch Reformed world.

Dutch Reformed believers in the seventeenth century also differed on how far reformation should go. Some believed that reformation had come to successful fulfilment with the establishment of a Reformed state church. By incorporating virtually all Dutch people in its membership, this church provided social cohesion and stability (through the assumption that all church members were true believers) which an emphasis on personal conversion and the search for evidences in the lives of church members could not do. Others believed equally vehemently that establishment of the Reformed church was only an initial step toward reformation of souls and revitalization of society through the Word of God. Known in the Netherlands as the "Nadere Reformatie," or "Continuing Reformation," this movement paralleled Puritanism in Great Britain and North America in its stress on personal conversion as a natural development of the Reformation's emphasis on individuals' justification by faith.[5] Families of the Continuing Reformation studied theological works as part of their after-meal devotions, putting biblical words to music, often the common secular tunes. For example, Willem Sluiter, the Voetian hymnist well loved in the Netherlands and colonial South Africa, set a psalm to the tune of "Prins Robbert was een Gentilman."[6]

Believers also differed on the timing of salvation. Some in the Dutch Reformed movement taught that children of believers were set apart for God, that is were "externally holy," but none the less in need of conversion to receive eternal life. Others held that most children of believers were already redeemed, that is "internally holy," at conception, a view embraced by the established church party. The three creeds of the Dutch Reformed movement seem to support the internal holiness view.[7] The baptismal form to be read at all baptisms ended with a prayer of thanksgiving to God for forgiving "us and our children all our sins."[8] Everyone presenting a child for baptism in South Africa would hear these words.

With the exception of the Khoikhoi converts of Georg Schmidt, no one was baptized in South Africa during the VOC period without the baptismal form. The practical differences flowing out of the distinction were immense, since Christians would view as unredeemed all indigenous peoples who had not yet heard of or who did not put their faith in Christ. Those who believed in the "internal holiness" of the children of believers counted the whole European community as having been redeemed, including the children, but regarded all the indigenous inhabitants – except for converts – as unredeemed. Those who believed in "external-holiness," on the other hand, considered all children – their own and those of the indigenous inhabitants – as requiring conversion to enter the kingdom of God. To external holiness thinkers, Christianity and ethnicity could never become synonymous. The identification of Christian and settler on the South African frontier, an identification with immense significance for the establishment of white supremacy in South Africa, clearly flows out of the internal-holiness version of covenant theology.

Governing in God's Name

The position of the Dutch Reformed Church in colonial South Africa was parallel to that of the church in the Netherlands at the time, except for some unique prerogatives claimed by the colonial administration. In South Africa, as in the Netherlands, the local governing board of each congregation, the consistory, was chaired by the pastor, and consisted of elders and deacons who were members of the congregation. In the Netherlands the next level of government was the classis, the regional church assembly, consisting of ministers and elders representative of local congregations. The classis in charge of South Africa, as of most of the Dutch colonial empire, was the Classis of Amsterdam, consisting of the churches in the capital region, but this distant classis could only exercise its jurisdiction by letter and could not effectively communicate its views to the colonial administration. An attempt in the mid-eighteenth century to form a classis in South Africa was suppressed by the VOC.

The colonial government had more direct influence on the Dutch Reformed Church in South Africa than the civil government in the Netherlands had over the mother church. Without a local classis as a counterbalance, the colonial administration could largely dictate to the church. In 1760, it even attempted to move a minister without his approval to a frontier congregation. The Council of Policy, the colonial executive body chaired by the governor, approved all candidates for church consistories, a role only rarely played by civil authorities in the Netherlands. When in 1708 the Rev. E. F. le Boucq attempted to remove members from the Cape Town consistory appointed by the Council of Policy, the Council deposed him from office and dispatched him to Indonesia to state his case to the Governor-General, rather than to the Classis of Amsterdam or to any of the other church assemblies to which he had appealed. The Council of Policy had dominant control of the authority structure of the church.

The VOC felt it had a responsibility to preserve and strengthen the Reformed church, which it regarded as the purest form of the Christian religion and a potential bulwark of societal unity, as it was in the Netherlands. The Company also claimed a God-given authority to direct the affairs of the church. Governor Simon van der Stel in a letter to the incoming governor, his son Willem Adriaan, invoked God's grace "for the directing of Church and politics to the benefit of the Company's profit and interest here which shall extend to the glorifying of the all holy name of God" and to the enhancement of the new governor's reputation.[9]

The desire for colonial unity was apparent in the VOC's treatment of the 126 French Reformed refugees whom it welcomed to the Cape after the revocation of the Edict of Nantes (1688) ended the toleration of Protestantism in France. The Council of Policy sought to merge the French into predominantly Dutch congregations, even though few of the refugees knew Dutch sufficiently well to understand the service. The French immigrant pastor, Pierre Simond, resisted the decision, appealing over the head of the governor to the Lords Seventeen, the VOC's governing board in the Netherlands. His appeal was granted, and a separate, predominantly French-speaking, congregation was established in Drakenstein (present-day Paarl). In retaliation Governor Van der Stel accused the French of being "rebels against their own king under pretext of religion," and encouraged the VOC, in future, to send German colonists instead, who, although predominantly Lutheran, would more easily merge with Dutch Reformed congregations. When Simond departed in 1702, the French colonists did merge into the mainstream of the Dutch population, by then having learnt the Dutch language. Nevertheless, a French Reformed piety survived, willing to question the Council of Policy on state–church relations, and in some ways similar to the emphases of the Dutch Continuing Reformation.

The Reformed church was more severe in its attitude to Roman Catholics than to other Protestants. As the Rev. Johannes Appeldorn, a seventeenth-century minister of Stellenbosch put it, Roman Catholics were "Antichristian, Papist, Babylon," since they rejected the doctrine of justification by faith alone.[10] During the seventeenth and eighteenth centuries the colonial administration engaged in largely successful efforts to suppress Roman Catholicism in the colony. Lutherans, on the other hand, were viewed as fellow Christians and followers of the gospel of justification by faith alone. Terms such as "Augsburger brethren" and "Lutheran brethren" are common in South African church documents of the time. Yet the VOC repeatedly turned down requests for the formation of a separate Lutheran church.[11] When the request was finally granted in 1780, only a trickle of colonists joined the Lutheran church, many Lutherans having already joined the Reformed church.

The Reformed also regarded Moravians as true Christians and could see no reason why they should have separate congregations. But Georg Schmidt, the first Moravian minister in South Africa, was admitted into the colony in 1737 only for the purpose of converting the Khoisan to Christianity. When Schmidt baptized his converts, the Dutch Reformed leaders concluded that he was founding a separate Moravian church and accordingly pressed successfully for his removal from the colony. To the Dutch Reformed Church and the VOC, South Africa was to be an example of the unity of the Christian church, whether Christians of different traditions approved or not.

The VOC was diligent in providing the South African settlement with ministers. Unordained comforters of the sick, who had been examined by the Classis of Amsterdam, were supplied to every ship and to any settlement without a pastor, and were also required to sign a statement of faithfulness to the creeds of the Dutch Reformed Church.[12] Many were deeply pious believers committed to the Continuing Reformation who had never had the opportunity to obtain a university education and were thus ineligible for ordination. One exception was the Rev. Johannes Backerus, the first minister to celebrate holy communion in South Africa, who had been ordained after exceptional service as a comforter of the sick in the West Indies.[13] Most of the comforters of the sick were held in high esteem in the colony, and several were popularly called "dominee," a title of respect officially reserved for ministers.[14]

Though the South African clergy were rarely involved in scandal,[15] some of them provoked settlers to explosive outbursts.[16] The church on the frontier was clearly identified with the colonial administration: this was evident in an unidentified parishioner's public outburst during a sermon which he viewed as too critical of the settler 1795 uprising in Graaff-Reinet: "Go ahead, little Manger [the Rev. J. H. von Manger], today is your turn, but tomorrow or the next day will be ours."[17]

There was a wide diversity in the philosophies of colonial pastors. Only three pastors are known to have been Cocceian. Most of the others, one surmises, were Voetian.[18] The first minister to serve a sustained period in South Africa (from 1655 to 1666) was the Rev. Johannes van Arckel, a student of the leading missionary theorist of his time, and a devoted Voetian. Most ministers, for a century after Van Arckel, showed little concern for the spiritual welfare of their parishioners as long as they attended services. The Rev. Petrus Kalden, minister from 1695 to 1707, did work diligently in an attempt to bring Khoikhoi and Chinese labourers to the Christian faith, but showed no such burning desire to lead the members of his own congregation to conversion. His critic, the Rev. E. F. le Boucq, while deeply concerned about external abuses in the church, did not speak publicly of the personal spiritual needs of his congregation.

The Rev. Frans le Sueur, minister at the Cape from 1729 to 1746, reported regularly to the Classis in Amsterdam that all was stability and peace in the church, although in one year one-quarter of the children he baptized were born out of wedlock. Sympathizers of the Continuing Reformation would have found such a peaceful state spiritually repugnant. Le Sueur deported two comforters of the sick, Louis van Dijk and William Raasel, who stressed the need for spiritual conversion, and was instrumental in the removal of the Moravian Georg Schmidt from the colony. He was more interested in the perceived threat Schmidt posed to the established Reformed church than in the Khoikhoi coming to faith in Christ.

Dutch Reformed clergy evidenced a clearer concern for Continuing Reformation in the later eighteenth century, and there is steady evidence of pastors who were dissatisfied with merely external peace in the church. In 1757, the Rev. H. Kronenberg observed that "the congregations still find themselves in a desired state from an external view, the desire and love of God and his blessed service are awakened in many. Our prayer is that God will follow this up with the heart-breaking grace of the Holy Spirit."[19] Around the turn of the nineteenth century the Rev. Helperus Ritzema van Lier, in Cape Town, and the Rev. Michiel Christiaan Vos, on the frontier, advocated a vibrant piety oriented to spiritual conversion and called on Christians to spread the gospel to ethnic groups outside the church.

One of the most practical means of conveying the Reformed faith to colonial South Africa was through the States Bible, commissioned by the Synod of Dort. This translation, which became a classic in the Dutch language, was accompanied by marginal commentaries summarizing Reformed theology. As in the Netherlands so in colonial South Africa many people read the Bible after every meal. A recent study found 281 copies of the States Bible in South Africa before the beginning of the nineteenth century, suggesting that it must have been widely used during that period.[20] The States Bible uses the term "heathen" (*heiden*) to translate the Hebrew *goi* and the Greek *ethnos* in reference to nations other than Israel, that is, "Gentiles." "Heathen" suggests uncivilized, not merely non-Jewish people. Its usage influenced colonial South Africa in ways its translators could not have intended. The Rev. M. C. Vos, a South African-born proponent of the Continuing Reformation, for example, had to correct a farmer who quoted Psalm 2:8 ("Ask of me and I will give you the heathen as an inheritance") to justify treating his slaves in any way he chose.[21] The commentary in the States Bible was apparently used by a farmer, Ignatius Ferreira, to justify his view that the Khoisan were cursed descendants of Ham.[22] In psalm-singing, which was the only vocal music in congregational worship, and commonly used in daily family worship, the Old Testament identification of people of God was emphasized, and the term "heathen" was regularly used.[23]

The other religious books known to be in South Africa during the Dutch colonial period were mostly works of the Continuing Reformation. Georg Schmidt spoke of settlers who felt they were saved "through pious living and book reading."[24] Shortly after the VOC period, James Campbell asked a frontier family how they spent their Sabbaths at such a distance from a church and was told that they spent their time "reading good books."[25] Heinrich Lichtenstein, who travelled extensively in the interior of the colony at the beginning of the nineteenth century, observed that daily family devotional times, in which books of sermons were read, were virtually universal.

> Evenings ... the whole family assembled again in the house ... A table is put in the middle, and all who are Christian sit down; slaves and Hottentots went again, just like in the morning to sit on their haunches on the ground next to the walls. The father read aloud a worshipful meditation out of one of the old books of sermons, followed again by the singing of a psalm and the evening blessing ... There were besides these books of sermons no other books except the Bible.[26]

Family worship on the frontier allowed the head of the household to become the pastor of his own family. John Barrow reported of many settler families: "They affect to be very religious ... Every morning before day-light one of William Sluiter's Gesangen is drawled out in full chorus by an assemblage of the whole family."[27] Documents of the period mention among others books of Johannes D'Outrein, Jodocus van Lodenstein, Bernardus Smijtegelt, Theodorus van der Groe, and Conrad Mel.[28] There were a multitude of avenues by which Reformed theology reached and influenced the colonial society.

The only public services almost every colonist attended were those for the administration of the sacraments. In the Reformed tradition, sacraments could only be administered as part of a public service.[29] To receive communion or to have a child baptized one needed to attend a service of worship. Since all children of colonists were to be baptized, all parents were exposed to the liturgical form for baptism, which implied the "internal holiness" view that their children were saved from the moment of conception. Many also attended the service of communion, called the holy supper, which was preceded by a service in the week before in which worshippers prepared for communion by examining their relationship with Christ. However, on the frontier, many came only for the communion service.

The first two commanders of the Cape garrison were influenced by Reformed piety. Jan van Riebeeck proclaimed a day of public confession for sin when he once detected the punitive hand of the sovereign God in an epidemic. His wife Maria taught the first Khoikhoi convert, Eva, to pray to God, and Eva, in turn, shared this teaching with other Khoikhoi.[30] Van Riebeeck's successor, Zacharias Wagenaer, who had arranged, against VOC directives, for secret services while serving in Japan, honoured the Voetian Sabbath, marking in his journal the rare cases when because of crises "to our regret, we were prevented from celebrating this day according to our custom, to the glory of God." Wagenaer left money in his will to the deacons of the Cape church to care for the poor.[31] There is also evidence of Reformed piety on the frontier at the turn of the nineteenth century. Lichtenstein spoke of "the universal religious turn of the colonists, bordering on bigotry." He also labelled the Rev. M. C. Vos, the leading Continuing Reformation minister on the frontier, a "bigot."[32]

Many observers perceived a general lack of Christian piety in the city of Cape Town throughout the Dutch period. One derives a picture of lax attendance at public worship, and a general pattern of sexual behaviour and exploitation inconsistent with Christian ethics, the slave lodge notoriously serving as a brothel, as also did some inns. A typical Continuing Reformation perspective on spiritual life at the Cape can be found in the comment that the colonist Jacobus Andries Bichert made in his copy of Jodocus van Lodenstein's work, *Observations of Zion*, "What would Lodenstein have said if he observed *present day* Zion? Oh dark days!"[33]

Religious Roots of White Dominance: Sacraments and Group Identity

The baptismal practice of the Netherlands, and, for that matter, of the rest of Reformed Europe, by the seventeenth century was rooted in a concept of the "thousand-generation covenant."[34] South Africa during the VOC period was a showcase for the thousand-generation practice. Any child who had an ancestor within the last thousand generations who was a believer in Jesus Christ was considered a member of the covenant and brought to the church for baptism. In practice this meant virtually all Europeans, even if their parents were excommunicated, living in unrepentant sin, or unbelievers. Even though the Reformed creed of the Belgic Confession considered the Roman Catholic Church a false church, a child of Roman Catholic parents might be baptized. The only exceptions to this thousand-generation covenant were Jews (the only sizable group in Europe seen as outside this covenant), Muslims, and "Heathen."[35]

At the Cape from its founding, it was considered imperative that all children known to have at least partial European parentage be baptized. For most of the period the VOC extended the policy further: slave children were baptized whose fathers were identified only as "unknown Christian."[36] Never was the validity of such baptisms doubted, for Christianity was seen as a birthright of Europeans. The first child recorded as baptized at the Cape was the son of Willem Barentsz Wylant, "the first born Christian who was born in this fortress."[37] Those without such parentage could enter the covenant only through personal conversion, but few

24

found their way through that narrow gate. There were only four converts to Christianity from the Khoikhoi in the seventeenth century, and all four eventually renounced the Christian life.[38] Christian status and European descent became increasingly identified in people's minds, as did "heathen" status and indigenous or slave descent.

A significant extension of baptismal practice beyond the European community concerned slaves owned by the VOC. Zacharias Wagenaer, the second commander, revealed his Voetian piety by opening baptism to all Company slave children regardless of their parentage, on the grounds that the Company itself would serve as "witness" (godparent) to ensure the children's training in Christianity. This minority view, evident at the Synod of Dort, was directly based in the external holiness view of baptism, a chief theme of the Continuing Reformation. Wagenaer was assisted in this practice by the first permanent minster at the Cape, Van Arckel, himself a follower of the school of Voetius. Van Arckel had also baptized a Khoikhoi infant rescued by the Dutch from being buried alive.[39]

This wider baptismal practice, which contradicted the majority of the opinions of the Synod of Dort, was challenged by a number of ministers at the Cape and repudiated by the Classis of Amsterdam in a letter received around 1697. During the period in which this policy was apparently suspended, some children of partial European background remained unbaptized, a troubling fact mentioned by Commissioner-General H. A. van Reede tot Drakenstein as a reason for his restoration in 1685 of the more open baptismal policy. It remained in effect until 1795.[40] Though the thousand-generation covenant idea remained in the background of even this decision to baptize some children without European descent, the VOC was relatively open in regarding upbringing in a Christian household as a sign of participation in the covenant.

Remembering the Old Testament promise of freedom for all Israelites, the company gave a conditional promise of freedom for any child of partial "Christian" descent. Males could be manumitted at 25 years of age, females at 22; they were required to reimburse the Company for their rearing and education, but not to pay a price for their own person. Children without a European parent, though baptized, had to work into their forties before possible manumission, repaying the Company the labour it considered it was owed. Very few survived to exercise this option. Notions of internal holiness apparently influenced the Company to favour children with a European parent.[41]

Other distinctions were made among baptized people. After 1695, the baptismal register had two distinct lists, "Names of Christian Children" and "Slave Children of the Honourable Company."[42] Being a Christian was still seen as related to ethnic descent. A child of European descent was baptized because it was regarded as already Christian or "internally holy"; a slave child was baptized not as a born Christian but as "externally holy" in virtue of its upbringing.

Unlike the Company, the private citizens who owned slaves did not regard children of the slaves as holy in any sense. With a few rare exceptions, such as the children of slaves held by some high-ranking Company employees (for example, Governor Simon van der Stel), no slave children of free citizens seem to have been baptized. Colonists, whether influenced by the covenant theology of Dort or from observing the practice of the VOC realized that if their slave children were baptized they should be set free or, at least, not sold, since the slave-owner would have to guarantee a Christian upbringing in the new setting. Also, fewer slave children of settlers than slave children of the Company had European fathers: private slaves, unlike many Company slaves, did not live in the Cape Town slave lodge, a brothel for sailors, where partly European children were often born. On the frontier only children of colonists themselves were baptized, and the contrary VOC practice strongly criticized. Apparently the Rev. F. le Boucq served as a spokesperson for many frontier farmers when he accused his Cape colleague of being willing "to baptize a sheep, if the Governor asked him."[43] The full implications of the thousand-generation covenant were apparent on the frontier, where all of European descent were considered to be in the covenant and all indigenous people outside, and where "Christian" became a synonym for settler.

The difference between the frontier and the Cape in respect of the observance of communion was equally significant. The Cape Town congregation, most directly influenced by the VOC, followed the pattern of the Netherlands, where many church members present at services failed to take the sacrament. Zacharias Wagenaer observed with dismay in 1665: "Though this place is occupied by a large garrison, many burghers and farmers, we were unable to count as many as twenty-four, which is a deplorable case."[44] Some have attributed this low response to the significant number of Lutherans present;[45] however, Lutherans were apparently permitted access to the communion table in the colonial church. Most likely the forbidding form of the service itself, and the preparation held the Sunday before, accounted for the low participation – both stressed that no one living in unrepentant sin was fit to come to the table.[46] In the Brothel of Two Seas, as Cape Town was then known, it may be that many persons were aware of the inappropriateness of their coming to the table. No such reticence was observed in rural areas. The settlers regarded themselves as quite fit for the Lord's table. Adam Tas, a colonial farmer whose journal shows few marks of Christian piety, writes that it was a responsibility of the minister to come and "invite" him to communion. The parishioners of Stellenbosch were offended when their minister sent a Khoikhoi servant to invite them.[47] The word "inviting," occurring often in colonial documents, marks a significant shift away from the Reformed tradition in which the minister and elder, or an elder alone, would visit a parishioner to ascertain if he or she was in a fit spiritual state to receive communion.

The celebration of communion helped link the settlers together as a people on the frontier. John M'Carter observed that farmers would travel for days for the quarterly celebration.[48] Such a universal partaking of communion on the frontier and not at the Cape suggests that the inability of most frontier settlers to attend the sombre preparatory service the week before communion made it psychologically easier to attend the communion service itself. The sacraments were also essential to settlers' identity: they would journey remarkable distances to partake of communion, and also to have their children baptized.[49] While their home worship provided the focus of their piety, their group identity centred on the sacraments. The settlers' understanding of religion was closely identified with being a Christian group, an identity that assumed that they all were redeemed. The mainstream of the Continuing Reformation, on the other hand, viewed all in the church as set apart for God, but only those truly converted by God as "redeemed." Much of the wording of the baptismal forms supported the settlers' impression.

The combination of baptismal and communion practice on the South African frontier is essential to an understanding of settler identity of the period. All the settlers were baptized as children and, as soon as they were adults, made a somewhat formal confession, and became partakers of the Lord's Supper. The indigenous inhabitants or imported slaves, for their part, were not baptized whether or not they had been reared in the settlers' own household and had received the same family Christian instruction; they never were permitted to receive the Lord's Supper. When successful Dutch Reformed missions at the turn of the nineteenth century baptized Khoisan converts, the consequence was a virtual revolt by some settlers, who refused to partake at the same table with those not of European descent, or, to use their term, not "born Christian." This led to the beginning of formal church apartheid.[50]

"Christian" became the mark of ethnic identity of the settlers on the frontier. Jacob van Reenen uses "Bastaard Christian" as a phrase for those of mixed Khoisan and settler descent. The traveller Carl Peter Thunberg encountered a farmer who explained that a lion would rather eat a Khoikhoi than a Christian. Khoikhoi, Griqua, and Xhosa all knew the settlers by their name of group identity, "Christian."[51] The assumption that all in the family were internally holy in the covenant, and thus Christian for all eternity, allowed "Christians" to appear to be literally an ethnic group. The conviction of spiritual superiority in the Christian religion was distorted into ethnic superiority.

Religious endorsement of white dominance can be found both at the Cape and on the frontier. At the Cape, while formal piety was less noticeable, the VOC and the church developed a sacramental policy that differentiated between the baptized. Slave children were baptized regardless of parentage, but black children were kept on a separate register and not regarded as spiritually equal to "Christian children," or internally holy children. On the frontier, only children with two colonists as parents were baptized. Christian became the unambiguous title for the group of frontier colonists in contrast with the baptized Europeans of the Cape. To equate the sign of baptism with the spiritual reality of redemption was to establish an infinite spiritual gap between the entire settler community and the indigenous inhabitants, regardless of the state of either from a perspective of personal conversion.

Under the Pear Tree: The First South African Missions

Christianity, in the view of all denominations at the Cape, was the only way to escape the judgement of eternal death and to receive the gift of eternal life. All other religions were seen as false, the religion of the Khoikhoi as virtually no religion at all. A comforter of the sick, Willem Barentsz Wylant declared, for example, that the Khoikhoi were "a very poor miserable people, both in body and soul, devoid of all knowledge of God, living like cattle."[52] The Moravian missionary Georg Schmidt, while attempting to learn about Khoikhoi religion, made clear that acceptance of Jesus Christ as Saviour required the rejection of this religion and its practices, which he declared to be superstitious.[53] On the frontier a comparable attitude developed towards the religions of the Bantu-speaking peoples.

Slaves and convicts from the Dutch colonial empire had brought other religions with them to South Africa. In 1703, the Rev. Petrus Kalden, instrumental in the conversion of two Khoikhoi, also baptized three Chinese converts, probably former followers of an Eastern religion.[54] The Rev. Henricus Beck baptized two converts from Islam during his ministry in Stellenbosch,[55] although Islam grew rapidly within the slave population, in part because slave owners considered Islam likely to produce "good" slaves without the implication of freedom that the settlers associated with Christianity.

Virtually no attempt was made by the Dutch in this period to allow prospective converts to maintain their own culture. The social barrier to conversion was immense. Nowhere was this more tragic than in the case of Eva, the Khoikhoi convert of Maria van Riebeeck, wife of the first commander. Eva responded so positively to Christianity that she attempted to share it with other Khoikhoi, and married a prominent European in a large church wedding. She was taught that Christianity meant adapting to the Dutch culture. Rumours had surfaced that she would run off from her new home, and revert to dressing in skins. When her husband died, her life collapsed, and eventually she died a drunken convict. In a tragic comment on the failure of Dutch Reformed missions, the official diary of the Cape noted that she was "made from a female Hottentot almost into a Netherland [sic] woman," only later to return "like a dog ... to her vomit."[56]

The breakthrough in South African missions came not from the Reformed Church but from the United Brethren, or Moravians, a pietist movement that developed within the Lutheran Church in Germany. The Moravians were settled at Herrnhut on the estates of Count Ludwig von Zinzendorf, who dreamed of converting not only Europeans but all nations to the gospel of Christ, and commissioned Georg Schmidt as a missionary to the Khoikhoi of South Africa. The pietism of the Moravians had much in common with the conversion emphasis of the Continuing Reformation, and Schmidt was accordingly welcomed warmly by Louis van Dijk, a sick-comforter with Continuing Reformation views. Still, the Moravians disagreed with much of the Reformed confessions as they understood them; in particular they emphasized the Arminian doctrine, condemned by the Synod of Dort, that in converting to Christ one accepted salvation that Christ had purchased for everyone. Schmidt often argued with settlers over the Moravian belief in universal atonement. In an explicit rejection of Reformed doctrine, the first question he posed to candidates for baptism was, "Do you believe that the Son of God died on the cross for the sins of *all men*?"[57]

Schmidt's diary illustrates why he was more effective than Dutch Reformed pastors in his ministry among the Khoikhoi. He tried to learn their language, falling back on Dutch, which was for him an acquired language too, only after he failed. Moreover, he was willing to ask the Khoikhoi about their own religion and learned the Khoikhoi names for God and the devil. He began his ministry along the Rivier Sondereind by helping Khoikhoi with their labours and later taught them to read the scriptures and to write. His decision to baptize his five converts, a final confirmation of the effectiveness of his labours, led to his deportation from the colony.

Schmidt's ministry continued under Khoikhoi leadership during the fifty-year period between his deportation and the arrival of the next Moravian missionaries. In 1792, the three missionaries found Lena, a Khoikhoi woman, holding religious services under the pear tree Schmidt had planted in his garden; she was the first indigenous Christian in South Africa to have indisputably found a home for her new faith in her own culture.[58]

The Beginning of the End of the Reformed Monopoly

At the end of the Dutch colonial period, two divergent developments were preparing the way for religious pluralism. One was the beginning of a drift from Reformed theological orthodoxy. The first South African-born ministers of the nineteenth century brought back a doctrinal liberalism from the universities in the Netherlands that cast doubt on the supernatural character of the scriptures and the miracles of Christianity. The argument that only one church can be tolerated holds only if its teachings are seen as absolutely true; the relativism of theological liberalism logically precludes any consistent claim to insist on one faith expression over another. A second trend, almost from the opposite pole theologically, was the furthering of Continuing Reformation emphases through the work of colonial minsters. This movement among ministers became personified by the ministries of Vos on the frontier and of Van Lier at Cape Town: both stressed personal conversion, and both challenged the view that all colonists were Christian by birth. Both paved the way for the revolutionary expansion of nineteenth-century missionary activity. Although their theology was diametrically opposed to theological liberalism, Vos and Van Lier worked for greater toleration of other Protestant churches, seeing a greater unity among all those who had experienced personal conversion to Jesus Christ than could be found in formal denominational structures. The growth of this "religion of the heart" through the great revival of the nineteenth century ruled out any possibility of return to domination by one church.

Christianity and Society under Dutch Rule

The Dutch Reformed Church supported the colonial administration of the VOC, the emphasis of covenant theology lending itself easily to a view that rulers are the Lord's anointed. Commissioner-General Van Reede tot Drakenstein made clear that the VOC and its agents were "not only owners of many treasures of wealth, but also patrons of Christ's church."[59]

The first minister born in South Africa, the Rev. Petrus van der Spuy, in a sermon at the centenary of the founding of the colony, quoted from the Psalms, "How blessed is the people whose God is the Lord,"[60] but by "people" he meant the Company and the settlers. The general covenantal confidence of being a people blessed of God was applied most exclusively on the frontier, where Khoikhoi, Xhosa, and settlers all used the term Christian as a synonym for settler.

Some indigenous inhabitants who converted to Christianity did so apparently in search of social standing, as in the case of Cornelius Goeiman, a man of partial Khoikhoi descent, who, when being discouraged from continuing to drink past the state of intoxication, "asked what right anyone had to restrain him as if he were a Hottentot: Was he not a Christian? and could he not have as much brandy as he pleased without being obliged to ask leave of any man?"[61] This identification of

Christianity with particular groups or social privileges clearly impeded the growth of a spiritual understanding of Christianity among the indigenous peoples. It also confined these peoples to the role of "heathen," while providing no clear way out, except by denigrating their own culture.

The history of Christianity in the VOC period reveals the remarkable success of the Continuing Reformation in conveying the basic concepts of Dutch Reformed theology to a population at the edge of the Dutch colonial empire. Yet it was also one of the Continuing Reformation's greatest failures, for it did not communicate its central tenet that every person needed to be converted in order to become a Christian and receive eternal life. The institutional monopoly of Christianity by the Dutch Reformed Church did help to unify Europeans of different backgrounds to a significant degree, but as Christianity became a source of social identification among the settlers, to most of the indigenous inhabitants it became all the more simply the foreign faith of a strange deity.

Nederduits Gereformeerde Kerk, Stellenbosch

2

Combating Spiritual and Social Bondage: Early Missions in the Cape Colony

ELIZABETH ELBOURNE & ROBERT ROSS

Protestant Revivalism and Mission Endeavour

"Go forth into all the world and preach the gospel to all nations," Jesus is said to have commanded his disciples. Christianity is clearly in theory a proselytizing religion, though the degree to which particular Christian communities have heeded this injunction has fluctuated greatly throughout history. In the late eighteenth century an international Protestant missionary movement arose in Europe and was exported to much of the world, including South Africa.

Scholars have until recently tended to assert either that the eighteenth-century rise of missionary enthusiasm was a consequence of the development of industrial capitalism or that it was the product of an internally generated evangelical drive to revitalize the church from within. Either explanation is simplistic in isolation; other factors were also influential. Notably, expansionist Protestantism was shaped by religious and political violence in Europe during and after the Protestant and Catholic Reformations.[1] For example, the Pietist movement, which sponsored the first modern Protestant missions to India in 1706, was closely tied to the religious and political ambitions of Protestant German princes, and it channelled local disaffection with Catholic Habsburg domination. The Renewed Unity of the Brethren, or Moravian Church, was founded by German-speaking Protestant refugees from Habsburg persecution who settled at Herrnhut, the Upper Saxony estates of a pious nobleman, Count Nikolaus Ludwig von Zinzendorf.[2] From the early eighteenth century, Herrnhut systematically dispatched missionaries, briefly to South Africa, and with more lasting effect to the New World, where they became exemplars for later British efforts.[3] Across Protestant Europe, out of religious conflict and in an atmosphere of millennial expectation, large-scale religious "revivals" emerged – broad movements of spiritual renewal, repentance, and conversion to evangelical Protestant Christianity. Britain, one of the principal countries that sent missionaries to South Africa, experienced two such waves of evangelical revival, one peaking in the 1730s and 1740s, with the wildfire spread of Methodism,[4] and a second, several decades later, re-invigorating the Calvinist dissenting denominations with roots in seventeenth-century Puritanism. Some common threads ran through these revival movements: beliefs about the actions of God in history working through human intermediaries, and expectations that individuals would be transformed at the crucial moment of conversion, or rebirth, which *every* person must experience in order to be saved.

The first British missionary societies arose from the second wave of revival: the Baptist Missionary Society, founded by the Particular (or Calvinist) Baptists in

1792, and the putatively interdenominational London Missionary Society (LMS) in 1795,[5] were both revivalist in emphasis. Other missionaries, from a different tradition or period, had other aims. In general, until the end of the Napoleonic wars in 1815, Anglican conservatives distrusted evangelical "enthusiasm" and ecclesiastical "irregularity" too much to sanction overseas mission work; despite the tentative early efforts of the fledgling Anglican evangelical Church Missionary Society, the earliest missionaries were thus dissenters, disbarred in England until 1828 from full political participation and attracted to militant and radical tendencies in Protestantism. As missionary activity became more widely accepted and admission standards tightened, missionaries tended to be of higher social class, better educated, and more likely to value social and ecclesiastical order.[6]

The first British missionaries were most often members of the upper working classes, especially in newly industrializing areas where the power of the Anglican Church was weak; but since missionaries needed a measure of literacy, they were never drawn from the ranks of the completely destitute. They tended to believe in aggressive self-improvement and the need to subjugate nature to human will. Often coming from recently rural areas made richer by a degree of industrialization and not yet devastated, they had a relatively benign view of industrialization. Indeed, in line with popularized precepts of the Scottish Enlightenment, many, like the Rev. Adam Ferguson, professor of philosophy in Edinburgh, tended to see the development of "commercial society" as integral to all progress.[7]

The missions of continental Europe had a different social, political and theological background. With key exceptions like H. Marsveld (a Dutchman) and H.P. Hallbeck (a Swede), most Moravians, who had preceded British missionaries to the Cape and re-established their mission in 1792, were born in the villages of Saxony, and remained members of the European Moravian communities. Most received their brides from there and sent their children to Europe for education, never building up kinship links in the Cape, either with whites or with Coloureds. Trained as artisans, they introduced craft production to Moravian mission stations, creating in South Africa central European villages, on a model probably never realized in the villages they had left.[8]

A few Dutch men (and women) had joined the LMS in its early years, but the mission work of the German and Huguenot churches did not begin until after the Napoleonic wars. While the French Protestant mission was primarily an imitation of British developments in minority churches,[9] German missionary societies emerged from a second wave of Pietism, a reaction to the secularizing modernism of the French Revolution, and were, as a result, politically acceptable to the establishment. The Prussian monarchy identified itself closely with the Berlin Missionary Society.[10] The principal backers of the Rhenish society, which was to work in the Cape and the future Namibia, did not come from the artisans and the "respectable" working class, as would have been the case in Britain, but rather from the local elite of factory owners and merchants in the Wupper valley north of Cologne,[11] although its missionaries came from a much wider area.[12]

The Religions of the Dispossessed: Khoisan and Slaves
The first work by European missionary societies in South Africa was among the

Khoikhoi, then known by whites as "Hottentots" – a formerly stock-herding people who inhabited most of the region later absorbed in the Cape Colony – and among the San, then called "Bushmen," a group closely related to the Khoikhoi but normally without cattle or sheep. The German-speaking butcher Georg Schmidt had begun work for the Moravians in 1737 among the Hessequa Khoikhoi of the Overberg region of the western Cape, then a centre of Khoikhoi settlement, now the village of Genadendal.[13] One of his earliest converts, Vehettge Tikkuie, recalled fifty years later that, in Schmidt's day, "the people had not been as poor as they were now." They had been numerous, and had had "plenty of cattle" and "more than enough meat and milk."[14] The VOC authorities forced Schmidt to abandon his work in 1743, as a result of pressure from the Dutch Reformed clergy (see pp. 28–29). By 1792, when the Moravians restored the mission, the Khoikhoi of the area had few cattle and were compelled to rely on farmwork for subsistence. Their last attempt at revolt occurred in the 1790s.[15] In the eastern Cape the mostly Gonaqua Khoikhoi tried in vain to resist dispossession. In a three-year rebellion from 1799 to 1802, they suffered large-scale loss of stock, land, and access to water, and were increasingly reduced to servitude to local white farmers.[16] The community structures of the Khoikhoi across the colony had been profoundly weakened before they came into contact with missionaries.

The fluid religiosity of Khoikhoi was able to absorb symbols from other cultures. Different groups used different but related terms for divinities. The nineteenth-century Nama worshipped a supreme being known as Tsuni-//goam, who could be approached through prayer and was possibly benevolent. Evil forces were concentrated in an evil deity, named Gaunab, whose centrality, however, may have grown after contact with Christian ideas of Satan. Mythic figures, such as the ancestral hero Heitsi-eibib, operated in the secular realm but reflected the nature of either Tsuni-//goam or Gaunab.[17] Sacred dancing was central to worship, the Khoikhoi dancing at night, especially before a full moon, to the accompaniment of sacred songs. Christian converts abandoned dancing at night, and refused to sing Khoikhoi songs, but often substituted all-night religious meetings and Christian hymns.

In Khoisan culture there were healing rituals, initiation rites for boys and girls, and a range of taboo beliefs and purification practices. Animals occupied an important place. An elderly man interviewed by Moravian missionaries in 1808 told them that all members of his community had a particular link with the spirit world in the shape of an unearthly animal that followed them throughout life and brought news in times of crisis.[18] Snakes were considered to cause illness and misfortune, and healers who had undergone special training were thought able to cure the bodies of sufferers. Storytelling bound together myth, heroic narrative, and the ordinary: the heroes of Khoisan folktales were not powerful figures, but often tricksters who escaped danger through cunning. Many Khoisan tales were about animals. Dreams were a crucial means of communication between human and sacred beings: they were considered prophetic, and their interpretation a matter of common conversation. Prophetic figures with particular powers to know things and to affect events could come to the fore, notably in the rebellions in both the eastern and western Cape just before the missionaries' arrival,[19] and adherence to war prophets continued at least until the Kat River rebellion of 1851.

The other main group of dispossessed were the slaves brought to the Cape from all the shores of the Indian Ocean – from Mozambique through Madagascar, Sri Lanka, South India, Bengal, to Indonesia. They came with a wide range of religious convictions. The vast majority of Cape slaves were not Muslims when they disembarked in Cape Town, and historians have been unable to discover any widely shared religious expressions among them before the spread of Islam (and Christianity), except for a general belief in various forms of magic.[20]

By 1770, Islamic services were held in Cape Town, and at least one man, Tuan Nuruman, was providing runaway slaves with Islamic talismans to protect them from recapture; however, until the foundation of the first mosques around 1800 only a tiny proportion of Cape Town's slaves was Muslim (see chapter 16). Christianity had a longer history among Cape slaves,[21] but had even fewer adherents than Islam. Most slaves, except those who belonged to the VOC (see pp. 34–35, 270–72), were not baptized as Christians unless they were manumitted. Most slave-owners resisted instructing their slaves in religion, because, at least after 1770, a converted slave could not be sold.[22] Some slaves were admitted to the household devotions, but the seats set aside for slaves in the Cape Town church were usually empty.[23]

"Going to Bethel": Settlers, Missionaries, and the Khoisan

In 1792 the Moravian brotherhood was able to resuscitate the mission which Georg Schmidt had been forced to abandon half a century earlier. After arriving in Cape Town, the first three missionaries, Hendrik Marsveld, Daniel Schwin and Christian Kuhnel, proceeded to Baviaans Kloof, later renamed Genadendal, "the valley of grace." There they met a few people, notably Vehettge Tikkuie, whom Schmidt had baptized as Magdalena, who had kept alive his message and who showed the missionaries the New Testament Schmidt had left behind. By 1792, when the Moravians restored the mission, the Khoikhoi of the area had few cattle and were compelled to rely on farm work for subsistence.[24] Initially there was considerable enmity against the mission on the part of the local farmers, but within a few years they recognized that many mission Khoikhoi had to continue to work on the farms, and that the mission formed no short-term threat to the established order. On the contrary, the discipline and artisanal labour which the missionaries imposed on the inhabitants of their station provided a model which the colonists believed should be emulated elsewhere, just as Genadendal was to form the model for the Christian communities that later missionaries wished to establish on their stations.[25]

The Moravians were soon followed by an LMS mission to the Cape. Johannes Theodorus van der Kemp – philosopher, theologian, doctor, soldier and courtier to the Prince of Orange – was its first head. He travelled in 1799 to the Ngqika Xhosa, accompanied by the reluctant John Edmond, an Englishman who had joined the LMS hoping to return to Bengal.[26] Johannes Kicherer and William Edwards headed north to the Sak River, in response to requests from three LMS Khoisan captains, Orlam, Vigiland and Slaparm.[27]

These first missionaries and those who followed them expected the lands of the heathen to be under the dominion of Satan, convulsed by moral and political chaos. They soon learned that the frontiers of the colony were bound up in colonial relationships in which the missionaries participated and from which they could not extricate themselves. They further decided that Satan was abroad in the colony itself. In the midst of the Third Frontier War (1799), the Xhosa ruler Ngqika, suspicious that Van der Kemp might be a colonial agent, considered having him killed, but instead granted him a tract of land and used him to communicate with the colony, to bring rain and also to heal the sick.[28] In contrast, the Sak River San initially welcomed the missionaries as potential white patrons, as well as diplomatic agents, of use in their continual warfare with European intruders.

Van der Kemp's first hard-won converts in Xhosaland were a handful of Khoikhoi clients of the Xhosa, most of them women and thus among the most powerless of their community. Kicherer's star converts and his most stable adherents were Khoikhoi and "Baster" (mixed-race) outsiders to San society (although in this case the Khoikhoi tended to be wealthier than the San).[29] The pattern was repeated elsewhere. The migrant Khoikhoi and Baster groups of Transorangia eagerly sought missionaries, as did the Nama, far from the colony.[30] The Moravian mission to the Hessequa was more successful than its founders had expected; the eastern Cape mission stations of Bethelsdorp and Theopolis developed a network of Khoikhoi preachers.[31] Despite its original expectations, the LMS (like the Moravians) soon came to focus most intensively on the Khoisan and their mixed-race descendants, establishing clusters of stations in the eastern Cape, in Transorangia, and in Little and Great Namaqualand. Missions to the Xhosa and later to the Tswana, in contrast, won few converts in their early days. Khoikhoi-descended groups thus tended to became spiritual and material brokers between Europeans and other Africans. Most missionaries worked formally through Khoikhoi intermediaries. At times, Khoikhoi, such as Cupido Kakkerlak and Jan Hendrik, ran their own missions. This later became a source of tension between Khoikhoi evangelists and certain white missionaries. Such links between Khoikhoi groups, and cross-cutting relationships across the wider community, help explain the relatively rapid acceptance of at least nominal Christianity by a surprising number of Khoikhoi groups. By the early 1830s, the Xhosa in the eastern Cape termed the Khoikhoi and their descendants "the people brought to life by the word of God."[32]

Those Khoisan who were already partially acculturated, and whose economic independence was largely eroded, responded more readily to the agenda of the missionaries than did members of more intact societies. On mission stations such Khoisan could regain a measure of authority over their lives. The appeal of Christianity was doubtless bolstered by the strong opposition of white settlers – who benefited from the equation between Christianity, a white skin, and economic and political dominance – to the Christianization of their Khoisan dependants. Khoisan, particularly those born of sexually exploitive mixed-race unions, knew the settlers' views, and for many of them an alliance with Christian missions was a defiant move, rather than a simple acceptance of the religion of their masters.[33] They had heard Van der Kemp and other missionaries castigate "Christian" Dutch settlers as the true enemies of Christ. Christianity furnished the means for a claim to equal status, and permitted some Khoisan converts to take over a familiar Protestant rhetoric of the pure remnant within the erring church, and to claim that they, not the local farmers, were the real Christians. Many of Khoikhoi descent, especially those in more desperate situations within the colony, came to believe that Christianity was in a sense for them, providing proof that their God had not forsaken them. In 1834, Hendrik Smit of the eastern Cape LMS station of Theopolis stated that he

> was surprised when the Bible came among us and asked the reason but no one could tell me; the reason was the oppression of the Hottentots which God saw. Previous to this we were like a man enclosed in a cask stuck full of nails, which cask was rolled down hill, and because it was down hill there was no cessation of suffering, it was always rolling.[34]

There were more concrete material advantages to Christianization. Beyond the colony, in Transorangia and Little Namaqualand, small groups living by trading, raiding, hunting and, where possible, pastoralism actively sought out missionaries. They had many reasons, among them the livestock the missionaries brought with them, their trading links to the colonial interior, their technological knowledge, their capacity to communicate in writing with the colony and with other groups, and the capacity of whites (though not necessarily the missionaries themselves) to help Khoisan obtain guns and gunpowder, those most coveted of goods in economies based on raiding and hunting. The mission station also offered the chance to acquire mechanical skills. In the colony it provided a place to leave stock and children, and served as a legal bastion against *de facto* enserfment.

The political implications of the eastern Cape "Hottentot" mission, on the other hand, were ambiguous. Consider the foundation of Bethelsdorp. Van der Kemp, recalled to the colony from Xhosaland, finding himself plunged into the midst of the Third Frontier War, was soon acting as a reluctant mediator between the British and rebellious Gona farm-workers who had recently lost their land, stock, and independence.[35] He persuaded a number of rebels to make peace in exchange for amnesty and a promise of land – promises which were to prove insubstantial. In the midst of struggles and negotiations, Read and Van der Kemp accepted the offer of Governor Dundas to allow them to establish a "Hottentot institution" at Algoa Bay. Of the 799 people worshipping with the missionaries at Graaff-Reinet, 301 decided to leave together to found the community which eventually became Bethelsdorp.[36] As the group departed, Van der Kemp read the language of collective purification in the text of Genesis 35:2-3, "then Jacob said unto his household, and to all that were with him: put away the strange Gods that are among you, and be clean and change your garments and let us arise, and go to Bethel, and I will make there an Altar unto God, who answered me in the day of my distress, and was with me in the ways which I went."[37]

The move was divisive for the Khoikhoi. Rebels living in the Zuurveld resented the withdrawal from conflict and attacked Bethelsdorp several times; Klaas Stuurman's kinsman Andries Stuurman was killed by a stray bullet in a dark night attack. Nevertheless, once the war had petered out and the incoming Batavian government that had replaced the British in Cape Town had imposed peace, a number of Khoikhoi rebels came in from the bush to Bethelsdorp, rather than return to white farms. Their presence intensified settler opposition to "a place of refuge for robbers and Murderers."[38] In one sense the Khoikhoi laid down their weapons when they moved to Bethelsdorp; in another, they took up new ones.

Van der Kemp and Read, as Calvinist pre-millenarians, believed, in common with several members of the LMS directorate, that the second coming of Christ was imminent. They held that God sends warnings to the guilty before punishing them, and believed, as did many European Protestants, that God acts through nations and other collectivities and passes judgement on erring communities.[39] Van der Kemp even saw the Third Frontier War itself as God's vengeance, anticipating in 1802 "that the desolation will go further" and that God would make the natives "the instruments of his wrath."[40] The political implications of this apocalyptic view were profound. In a comment encapsulating the inherent ambiguity of the missionary project, the Batavian governor Janssens complained that Khoikhoi soldiers from Bethelsdorp or the surrounding area were more likely to be good and trustworthy soldiers but also more likely to act as "ringleaders" in leading others to "disorder ... call[ing] out the name of Mr. Vanderkemp not in the way of lamentation, but in the tone of provocation."[41] After leaving the colony, Janssens wrote that, should the Cape ever be returned to the Netherlands, most of these "wretched missionaries" should be sent away with great haste.[42]

Throughout the first two decades of the century, settlers and missionaries competed to control the destiny of the Khoikhoi. The aristocratic Van der Kemp showed little interest in changing Khoikhoi culture fundamentally: "all civilization is from the Devil," he purportedly proclaimed.[43] Most other missionaries wanted the Khoikhoi to acquire the means to "settle" in an independent community, to become "respectable," and to acquire the rudiments of an individualistic capitalist culture. By contrast, labour-hungry local farmers and officials sought to remake the once-nomadic Khoikhoi into landless farm labourers, living permanently on white farms. They sought to intimidate mission stations into closing; they spread rumours that missionaries had nefarious designs against the Khoikhoi; and sought to bring mission Khoikhoi back under their control through a variety of legal and illegal techniques including, often, violence.[44] Andries Jager recalled many years later that this was "a time of sorrow" and "oppression under which I have often wished I was dead (God forgive me) to be eased of my burden."[45]

In the early 1800s, Van der Kemp, his close colleague James Read, and other LMS missionaries struggled, with some success, to obtain redress for crimes committed against the Khoikhoi. The investigation of criminal charges brought by Khoisan against Graaff-Reinet farmers and, more generally, the introduction of a circuit court were seen, probably correctly, as their doing. This campaign caused considerable dissension in LMS ranks, as dissident missionaries such as the Germans Messer and Sass protested against what they saw as their colleagues' focus on politics at the expense of good order and civilization, pointing to the Moravians' Genadendal as an example of a truly beneficial mission station. At issue was a fundamental disagreement about the sort of Christianity to be practised and propagated. The radical millenarianism of the first missionaries was being overtaken by a much more quiescent Christianity, both in Europe and in South Africa.

Quarrels between missionaries grew worse after the death in 1811 of the powerful Van der Kemp, and the arrival of George Thom and Robert Moffat, who held firm ideas about the appropriate relationship between "civilized" and "uncivilized" peoples. Matters came to a head in 1817, with the unveiling of a series of sex scandals, including the revelation that James Read, who was married to the Khoikhoi woman Elizabeth Valentyn, was the father of the illegitimate baby of a church deacon's daughter. In its wake, Read was dismissed from his post as director of LMS missions in southern Africa, and demoted to "resident artisan." These events were part of a general move to bring missions under tighter control, and to draw sharper lines between Europeans and Africans, as seen in 1820 when Robert Moffat took over and renamed as Kuruman the Tswana station "Lattakoo," now known as Dithakong, initially run largely by Khoikhoi agents.[46] Read's goal of rapidly ordaining an African clergy was quietly dropped, and, as elsewhere in the world, the LMS practice then prevalent of marrying into local congregations virtually ceased.

The Scottish Independent minister John Philip was sent to South Africa in 1820 to clean up the faltering LMS mission, especially in the turbulent eastern Cape.[47] Philip was a true son of the Scottish Enlightenment. He offered the Khoisan an identity somewhat different from that proferred by Van der Kemp's millenarian promises but one that offered converts the expectation of increased temporal power. He proposed that the Khoisan acculturate further and rapidly show what nineteenth-century Scots deemed the outward signs of "civilization," such as property accumulation, cleanliness, and Western-style clothing and housing, as a political tool to confound those critics who would deny them individual rights. This contract between Philip and the Khoisan coincided with the drive of the British government to liberalize the economy of the Cape Colony, so as to encourage trade, property accumulation, greater monetization, class distinctions, and the virtues of thrift and hard work among the populace. This moralized "modern" economy was a development Philip sought to encourage, on a much smaller scale, among Christian converts.[48]

Philip conducted his campaign on two fronts. First, he hoped to persuade the British government's Commissioners of Eastern Enquiry, sent to report on the governance of the Cape in 1822, to recommend improvements in the legal status of the Khoikhoi. To this end he organized visits to mission stations, recently redeveloped to look as "rational" and European as possible, with straight streets and square houses.[49] He then made a dramatic trip to London in 1826 to plead for equal civil rights for all free people in the colony, irrespective of colour, linking this cause to the general struggle for the abolition of slavery. He won an order giving the Khoisan "freedom and protection." Almost simultaneously, the Whig Acting Governor of the Cape, Richard Bourke, issued Ordinance 50, granting substantially the same privileges.[50]

Whether or not Philip was as instrumental as he believed in obtaining Ordinance 50, the ordinance was a major victory for the LMS.[51] It seemed to offer hope for the Society's promise that converts would be able to participate in the white economy on equal terms in exchange for undergoing fundamental cultural change. The link that the LMS under Philip's tenure made between economic and spiritual concerns depended on a particular idea of freedom. The economic arena could only function as a venue for salvation if individuals were free economic actors: the free choice to perform economic acts lent moral dignity, in contrast to forced labour, which degraded both employers and employees. In a parallel fashion, the moral arena both demanded and created freedom. Sin was slavery; true freedom was only to be gained through the knowledge of God and the self that conversion gave. Philip's famous statement that all he wanted for the "Hottentots" was the right to bring their labour to a free market and the rest would follow had many more implications than is immediately apparent.[52]

Ordinance 50 has been extensively criticized by historians, for its supposed lack of efficacy[53] and for its framers' liberal capitalist premises. It was, however, supported fervently by a wide range of Khoisan within the colony who benefited from it, as is suggested by the rush of protests against the projected re-institution of vagrancy legislation in the mid-1830s.[54] The ordinance allowed Khoikhoi to own land and abolished pass-law legislation and *de facto* forced labour. These were profoundly important changes, although crippling economic discrimination replaced the old legal restrictions, and Khoikhoi demands for the return of land in the wake of Ordinance 50 were never met.[55] "Every nation has its screen," said the Bethelsdorp resident Platje Jonker in a protest meeting against vagrancy legislation in 1834; "the white men have a screen, the colour of their skin is their screen, the 50th ordinance is our screen."[56] Such wholehearted acceptance of the necessity for freedom cemented the alliance between the LMS and the Khoikhoi, which held even through the steady disillusionment of the 1830s. At least temporarily, the millenarian vision propagated by Van der Kemp had been submerged, in the minds of the LMS converts, by Philip's gradualist vision of an improving Christian community.

Christian Sub-Imperialism: Namaqualand and Griqualand

In reaction to government discouragement of their work in the colony, many early missionaries went north to the mountains of Little Namaqualand and the Orange River valley. There they encountered people of at least partial Khoisan descent, many of whom had emigrated from the Cape Colony to escape adverse conditions. They were open to the message of the missionaries and eager for the material aspects of colonial culture, notably Western clothing and firearms.

There were two main streams of missionary activity in the north. The western stream was pioneered by Germans in the service of the LMS, but was eventually taken over by Wesleyans and agents of the Rhenish Society. The initial work in southern Namibia foundered because the missionaries could not gain purchase on what was still a very mobile society. There were a number of emotional conversions, but the permanent settlement that missionaries demanded of their converts was both socially and ecologically impossible. Missionaries became pawns in the violence of political struggle, which eventually led to the murder of the young missionary William Threlfall and his more experienced Nama assistant Jacob Links.[57] Nevertheless, Christianity remained a central part of many Namibian communities' ideology. Jonker Afrikaner, the Oorlam ruler of Windhoek, for instance, was himself a fervent preacher with an interpretation of scripture developed in isolation from the missionaries, whom he was later to accuse, among many other things, of being "blasphemous twisters of the gospel."[58]

South of the Orange the mission stations of Steinkopf, Komaggas and Leliefontein were all established before 1820. Johann Friedrich Hein, a mixed-race convert, pioneered the Rhenish mission work in the Richtersveld from the 1840s and was eventually ordained nearly half a century later. These settlements provided protection and some land at a time when Namaqualand was being divided up between white farmers. Nama converts swiftly developed tight communities with a republican form of administration under the supervision of the missionaries. Their main hope, as the captains of Steinkopf and the Richtersveld explained to the British in 1847, was that the land they had always occupied would be protected "from the Boers and others who are not from amongst us, so that we can lead a quiet, still and honest life."[59]

In the region north of the middle Orange, where the LMS was active from 1801, loose networks dominated by the Kok and Barends families congealed around missionaries and formed into new political organisations. The missionaries believed that they were creating a Christian state under their own leadership. Persuading their followers to adopt the ethnic name "Griqua,"[60] they claimed influence over the appointment of the Griqua captains, wrote the constitution and law book of the new state, and even minted coinage for it, complete with the dove emblem of the LMS. In fact, though, their direct political influence was limited. They could not, for example, persuade the Griquas to take service in the colonial army, as the British government requested. Many missionaries were forced to leave their stations after failed interventions in Griqua political and social affairs.[61]

Yet Christianity became a core component of Griqua identity. Criteria for admission to full membership of the church were strict. At least in Griquatown, prospective members had to relate the story of their conversion to the church, and one of the deacons took it down in writing.[62] Nevertheless, adherence to the church became a marker for allegiance to one or other of the political factions in various Griqua captaincies.[63] Eventually, Christianity was used to legitimate the more settled captaincies of Griquatown and Philippolis. At the same time, it was used as a weapon to expand Griqua influence to the north. Before an attack on the Ndebele, Barend Barends gave a sermon exhorting his forces "to go and murder an innocent people in the name of God and religion," as it was later cynically reported.[64] More peaceably, Griqua evangelists worked to convert the Southern Tswana, and to bring them under Griqua political influence, an aim that required the removal or subordination of the white missionaries working among them. In the 1830s the Griquas attempted to oust Robert Moffat from Kuruman and the Frenchman Jean-Pierre Pelissier from Bethulie. The failure of these moves marked the end of this episode of Christian sub-imperialism.[65]

"The Slaves of Satan and of Men"[66]

The religious revival among whites at the Cape from the late 1780s and the beginnings of the missionary movement led to a much more serious attempt to spread the Christian gospel to the slaves, the Rev. H. R. van Lier providing much of the impetus. Van der Kemp, on his arrival at the Cape in 1799, stimulated the foundation of the South African Missionary Society in Cape Town. Five years later the Society had 400 members and had established daughter societies in several Cape towns.[67]

Slave-owners did not allow their slaves to go to mission stations, which anyway were not in areas of significant slave population, except for Groen Kloof (later known as Mamre), founded by the Moravians in 1808. Slaves were preached to in Cape Town, the small towns of the western Cape, or on the farms; others were included in the private devotions on the farms or houses where they lived, as were some Khoisan in the towns or on the farms. But not all slaves and Khoisan were required, or even allowed, to attend the prayers, hymn singing, and Bible readings. When settlers felt their control over their labour force threatened, they tended to oppose Christianization of their workers and slaves. Conversely, slaves and Khoisan were more likely to convert when proselytization was opposed by the farmers, less likely when they saw Christianity propagated as a weapon of social control. One farmer told a Khoikhoi labourer who asked permission to go to Genadendal in 1794 that he could receive religious instruction on the farm, but the man replied that in his years there he had never been taught the truths of the gospel.[68] Others would recall later how their exclusion from religious ceremonies had awakened their desire to hear the Word of God.[69] Increasingly in the nineteenth century, however, the more pious white families did what they could to facilitate the conversion of all those who lived on their farms. Often, the instruction of slaves was the responsibility of unmarried girls.[70] This practice was part of the landholders' constant struggle for control over dependent labour. In 1838 many households in Graaff-Reinet ceased to provide religious instruction on their farms because, with emancipation pending, the masters did not know whether the ex-slaves (now known as "apprentices") would continue to live with them.[71]

Where a congregation of the Dutch Reformed Church (NGK) already existed, the ministers demanded to examine and baptize any converts, who would then become members of the congregation. Thus, in Cape Town, the NGK controlled the chapel established in Long Street by the South African Missionary Society, known as the *Gesticht*, under the auspices of a committee of management which arranged services conducted by available clergymen.[72] Only in 1819 was a pastor appointed and a congregation independent of the NGK established. In Stellenbosch, pious members of the congregation had been giving religious instruction to about a hundred slaves in 1799, but not until 1820 could the representative of the LMS, who had worked there since 1800, administer baptisms, signalling the beginnings of a new mission congregation.[73] LMS missionaries also began work in Paarl and Tulbagh, funded largely by contributions from the local missionary society, and in Port Elizabeth, Uitenhage, and Grahamstown. From around 1830, the Rhenish mission took over the work at Stellenbosch, Tulbagh, and Worcester, and in 1829 the Paris Evangelical Missionary Society founded a church in what is now Wellington. The Methodists, at least in towns of the colony, made no distinction between mission work and ordinary pastoral care of settlers, nor did the many churches in Cape Town, including the Presbyterians, the Union Chapel of the Congregationalists and, indeed, the NGK.

Missionaries working among the Cape's slaves were dependent upon the slave-owners both for access to the slaves – a master could forbid his slave to go to services, or refuse to allow a missionary to enter his farm – and very often for his salary. Indeed, some early missionaries, like some NGK clergy, were themselves slave-owners.[74] The message the slaves received was generally one of the necessity of obedience, of resignation to one's fate in this world, and of the hope for glory in the world to come. Missionaries justified their work to the master class by claiming that Christian slaves made more trustworthy servants, but the relations between missionaries and the farmers were often tense all the same.[75]

Before final emancipation in 1838, few slaves were converted. Their rejection of Christianity, the religion of their masters, was, in a sense, a rejection of slavery. In missionary eyes they remained "slaves of Satan and of men." Christian congregations did not welcome slave converts as equals, nor did Christianity provide any improvements in their lives. Islam was generally more attractive to slaves than Christianity, at least until 1838 (see chap. 16). Yet for a number of slaves Christianity provided a modicum of solace in an otherwise harsh and hopeless existence. As one ex-slave commented to a missionary, "Sir, the world is hard, but heaven is beautiful."[76]

"The Lord is Known To Be Unfriendly to Injustice": From Ordinance 50 to the Kat River Rebellion

Mission Khoikhoi celebrated Ordinance 50 as the guarantee of their liberties.[77] Descendants of the eastern Cape Khoikhoi thereafter tried to ally themselves with missionary liberalism to gain access to the white-run, legally encoded land tenure system that had so pointedly excluded them. The Khoikhoi were not granted the amount of land they claimed as the remnants of their ancestral homelands. In 1829, Andries Stockenström nevertheless helped persuade the administration to grant plots to individual Khoikhoi settlers in the well-watered Kat River valley, in order to create a buffer between the white settlers and the Xhosa. It was necessary to expel the Xhosa leader Maqoma, who was living there, although the Gona Khoikhoi claimed prior ancestral right dating back before Xhosa conquest.[78]

The settlement was independent, but long remained associated with the LMS and its quest to establish the Khoikhoi as acculturated and fully equal members of a racially integated society. This association was emphasized when the Philipton church called the missionary James Read senior to be its independent minister. Many of the early settlers had been among the most successful inhabitants of LMS mission stations, notably Theopolis, Bethelsdorp, and Hankey, though the majority had been previously scattered throughout the colony. There was some tension between the two groups.[79] The newcomers provided a pool of potential Christian converts; soon Read was describing religious revival in Kat River. By 1834 some 5,000 inhabitants were settled in villages throughout the area; some thirty villages, with three-quarters of the population, had LMS congregations. Another group, led by some eighty families of "Bastards," mostly of mixed white and Khoisan parentage, accepted the government agent William Ritchie Thompson as their minister. They tended to have lived with Dutch farmers and to have done well out of the relationship, bringing with them substantial property in stock and tending to claim superiority on class and ethnic grounds over the poorer "Hottentots."[80] The arrival, in addition, of many ex-slaves and Xhosa-speaking

Mfengu, as well as intermarriage and sexual relations between whites and Khoikhoi, was changing the ethnic composition of the congregations. The LMS claim became less convincing that missions were defending the "ancient possessors of the soil" from exploitation.

The settlement was important not only to the LMS in South Africa but to the entire British abolitionist movement. Between 1829 and 1834, in the final stages of the emancipation of slaves, abolitionists were arguing strongly for the desirability of free black labour. After abolition they needed to prevent the reimposition of *de facto* slavery under stringent vagrancy and apprenticeship regulations.[81] The Kat River was used as an example of a prosperous and "civilized" free black community in which men were able to assume the true independence essential for manhood, and women, implicitly, to fulfil the gender roles appropriate to "civilized" society.[82] Free labour replaced free grace in a new version of the conversion narrative, the Kat River Khoisan portrayed as a regenerated community saved by economic independence. "As soon as they were enabled to emerge from conscious degradation, and the door of manly ambition was flung open to them," the Khoisan could undergo an "entire change of character."[83] The Khoikhoi themselves used such arguments to defend civil equality during the struggles of the 1830s.

The LMS advocates of the Khoikhoi were briefly powerful in the late 1820s and early 1830s when the abolition of slavery, free labour, and the management of the poor roused passions and dominated parliamentary debate. The LMS also had personal contacts in the Colonial Office. Under evangelical influence, the British government overturned a Cape vagrancy ordinance, on the grounds that it conflicted with Ordinance 50, and returned land conquered in the 1835 war to the Xhosa.

In such circumstances, it is not surprising that many Khoikhoi within the LMS ambit were convinced that Christianity could bring power to the oppressed and peace to the land. During his 1835 visit to Britain, with John Philip and the Reads, to give evidence before a parliamentary committee on the colonial status of aboriginal peoples, Andries Stoffels, a Gona from Bethelsdorp who had moved to the Kat River, proclaimed before the 1836 annual public meeting of the LMS that "the Bible charmed us out of the caves and from the tops of mountains. The Bible made us throw away all our old customs and practices, and we lived among civilized men." The Bible brought peace: "the only way to reconcile man to man is to instruct man in the truths of the Bible." Stoffels affirmed: "we are coming on; we are improving; we will soon all be one," a reflection of the LMS's assimilationist rhetoric as well as an implicit claim to the right to political participation (see *Missionary Chronicle*, June 1836, pp. 550–52).

The LMS successes of the 1830s proved the apogee of the LMS's political power. Khoisan and ex-slaves were by now amalgamating as Coloureds. Friction between missionaries resurfaced. John Philip and the Read family continued to cooperate with the Kat River and Griqua leadership in the development of an aggressively missionary church under control of local congregations, in a pattern analogous to that of Congregationalists in Britain. In the Kat River a core of at least eight "native agents" were developing an expansionist culture of evangelism. The Philipton church established mission stations in response to appeals from Thembu,

San, and Mpondo leaders,[84] the political implications disturbing both the Wesleyans, who thought the LMS was poaching, and conservatives within the LMS, notably Robert Moffat and Henry Calderwood, who wished to maintain missionary control over church life. The result was another attack on the Reads, father and son, which left them increasingly isolated.[85] At the same time, the Khoikhoi churches, which seemed to offer the same career ladder for ministers as the white church, often failed to do so. Over half the Kat River teachers resigned in the early 1840s over the issue of inadequate pay, while "native agents" were remunerated at considerably lower rates than their white counterparts and rarely accorded equal social status.[86] The early LMS vision of Africa Christianized by Africans had begun to founder.

The rising economic expectations of the mission communities and the heady promise of the early years of the Kat River Settlement were increasingly unfulfilled. The destruction caused by the frontier wars of 1835 and 1846–47, in which many Khoikhoi served on the colonial side, was exacerbated by the avaricious malad-minstration of successive magistrates.[87] The price of collaboration was growing and its rewards shrinking. The perennial problem of overcrowding and the lack of an agricultural base on the mission stations was not solved, despite large-scale and expensive projects, notably the construction of a water tunnel to irrigate Hankey. The economic integration and prosperity Philip had once offered did not material-ize. The economy remained racially segregated and European settlers looked with jealousy at such land as the Coloureds did possess.

When "Mlanjeni's war" broke out in 1851 many Khoikhoi refused to turn out once again for the colonial army. A smaller number, led by a half-Xhosa half-runaway slave, Hermanus Matroos, joined the rebels. Khoikhoi flocked to the rebel standard from throughout the colony, most, "particularly the more violent of them," in the elder Read's words, "young giddy Men," though, on his visit to a rebel encampment, Read also reported seeing "very many women and children together."[88] A number of rebels came from Theopolis and from the Moravian sta-tion of Shiloh. Missionaries claimed that the majority of rebel Khoikhoi were from white farms rather than mission stations or Khoikhoi settlements, which may have been partly true, since the farmworkers had less to lose than those with access to their own land, no matter how unclear the title. Many rebels expressed hatred for the English settlers and distrust of the forthcoming establishment of the (white-dominated) representative assembly at the Cape. They combined an ideology of "Hottentot nationalism"[89] with the fervent millenarian Christianity their fathers had learned from Van der Kemp. Indeed, many rebels said prayers and sang hymns before battle, and a letter written by their leader Willem Uithaalder stressed "trust … in the Lord (whose character is known to be unfriendly to injustice) … and he will give us prosperity – a work for your motherland and freedom, for it is now the time, yea the appointed time and no other."[90] Christianity was well out of control of the missionaries who had brought it.

The war was a disaster for the LMS mission. Although both the Read family and many of the Kat River Khoikhoi actively sought peace, the white colony accused the Kat River Settlement, as a whole, and many other mission Khoikhoi of rebel-lion. Captured rebels were hanged, sometimes summarily;[91] rebel property was confiscated and sold to white settlers. The Theopolis mission was broken up; Philipton was burned to the ground; the Kat River Settlement was devastated and much of it purchased by white settlers. In a display of colonial vindictiveness, Andries Botha, a veldcornet and community leader in the Kat River, who had fought for the British in several wars, was condemned to death for treason after a show trial, although the evidence suggests his innocence.[92] The rule of law, for which the LMS had fought so hard, was turned against the Khoisan.[93] Philip had died in 1851; the elder Read died four days before Botha's trial began. Andries Botha himself was eventually reprieved, but the death sentence he had received symbolized the death of a great deal more.

"Spiritual Liberation" and "Civil Liberty"[94]

In the different context of the western Cape many of the same themes were being played out. After a four-year period of so-called apprenticeship, the slaves of the Cape Colony were finally freed on 1 December 1838. In the years that followed, many slaves received Christian instruction. Many moved to Genadendal, Groen Kloof, and Elim, in particular, whose combined population rose from about 2,500 to about 4,000 between 1838 and 1840. The missionaries had not encouraged new settlement, but the freed slaves often went to join friends or even relations living in the mission villages.[95] Here, they were under pressure to form nuclear families. Housing was not provided for single women on most stations. Nevertheless, many ex-slaves welcomed the opportunities given to women and adolescent girls to withdraw from the formal labour process altogether, or to return home each evening from their places of employment.[96] Children, too, could be saved from the "apprenticeship" to farmers that was often used to bind a complete family to the farm.[97] As with the Khoikhoi before them, missions also provided former slave women with some defence against sexual exploitation by farmers, an integral part of the "old system."[98]

Many of those who came to the missions left again after a few years, discouraged by the difficulty of finding work and by the rules of the mission.[99] Yet by 1848 22 per cent of the Coloureds in the rural western Cape, most of whom had been slaves, were living on the mission stations;[100] many more were maintaining ties with the missions while living and working elsewhere; and still more had spent some time there. In the first decade after emancipation, farmers considered the mission stations likely to tie up labour in useless idleness; therefore attempts were made to close them down, but increasingly missions were defended by neighbouring farmers who benefited from the flexibility they allowed in the utilization of labour.[101]

Many adult former slaves living near a mission began to frequent the evening and Sunday schools and services; the enrolment of children in the mission day-schools also increased sharply. St. Andrew's Presbyterian church in Cape Town had adults at the reading classes.[102] The core of the LMS's work in the town shifted to the school in Dorp Street, with the chapel there almost a subsidiary of the school.[103] The mission work of the Dutch Reformed Church (NGK) in Cape Town was substantially similar.[104] So, too, the Rhenish missionaries and their wives in the country towns were as much schoolteachers as pastors. In 1841, for instance, the mission in Stellenbosch was teaching about 200 children and as many adults (slightly more than half of these in the evenings), in addition to more than 250 at Sunday school. In Tulbagh and Worcester, the numbers were smaller, but not in relation to the size of the towns.[105] In 1838 a school for the training of teachers was opened in Genadendal. Its graduates spread throughout the colony.[106]

One old lady, finding herself too old to learn to read, had to be reassured that illiterates could enter the Kingdom of Heaven.[107] Other converts no doubt had a more secular approach to schooling and religious instruction, the mission stations providing some measure of escape from the harshness of farm life, even though many of their inhabitants continued to work as agricultural labourers, on short contracts. Whether or not literacy and baptism gave the residents of Stellenbosch who flocked to the Rhenish Society's schools any tangible short-term benefits, their achievement was a symbolic challenge to their erstwhile owners, and they also allowed their children the opportunity to escape the quasi-bondage imposed on many rural ex-slaves after emancipation. From such educated groups, the Coloured elite would emerge.[108]

Unlike their fellows in the east of the colony, the ex-slaves and Khoisan of the western Cape did not build a political radicalism on the basis of their Christianity.[109] They had experienced social advance on the basis of religious teaching, and indeed some feared that their children, born in freedom, would take this advance for granted.[110] They did not feel betrayed by unkept promises. Many acquired the vote in 1854 for the first elected Cape assembly. Literacy was one of the conditions of the franchise, which gave them a degree of power and recognition, and they used it. In the constituency of Caledon, the inhabitants of Genadendal and Elim made up three-quarters of the electorate in the 1850s. The old reliance of mission Christians on informal missionary influence was now replaced by formal representation of their interests (though not by one of themselves) in parliament.[111] In the countryside, more so than in Cape Town,[112] this entailed an exaggerated loyalty towards Britain in the abstract and political antipathy towards the representatives of the Dutch and English farmers,[113] who often claimed that the ex-slaves and Khoisan were the pawns of the missionaries. It is probably truer to say that Christianity had given them the means and the confidence to be independent of their erstwhile masters.

Full emancipation also gave these church members the confidence to demand control over the life of their churches. In some churches, notably in the Gesticht and St. Stephen's Presbyterian church in Cape Town,[114] and in the Rhenish missionary chapel in Stellenbosch,[115] ex-slave congregations insisted on the right to choose elders and deacons from among their own number. In both Grahamstown and Cape Town LMS congregations seceded in protest at the removal of their pastor.[116] These schisms were not theological in origin,[117] but derived from Coloured Christians' success in gaining ascendancy, in partial compensation for their inequality within the wider society.

From the 1850s, the LMS in Europe itself encouraged such tendencies. After the defeat of Christian radicalism with the Kat River Rebellion, and with the Society financially stretched, missionary control became less important than the Congregationalist ideal of financial self-support. Many Cape church members seemed better off than the potential donors in Britain. Charity from overseas was seen as "a real evil rather than a benefit." The Griqua Church in Philippolis became self-supporting in 1855, and in the 1870s almost all the LMS churches in the colony followed suit.[118] Legislation was passed in 1873 by which plots on the LMS mission stations could be transferred to individual ownership. The sanctions buttressing missionary paternalism thus disappeared.

In contrast, the Moravian missionaries maintained control over their villages. Their right to expel those they considered a danger to the villages' discipline was confirmed in court.[119] This caused some resentment, but the villagers' attachment to their birthplaces was producing a specific Moravian sub-culture, maintained even when numerous migrants from Genadendal, Elim, Mamre, and Pella moved to Cape Town. There they maintained their connection through the church at Moravian Hill, in District Six.[120]

The other churches, Methodist, Anglican and Roman Catholic, had no place in their ecclesiastical structures for a separate mission church. The standard structure of parishes, priests and bishops was thought sufficient.[121] The NGK, in contrast, sanctioned segregation of Coloureds within local churches, but this did not initially lead to the creation of mission stations.[122] In consequence, from the 1850s onwards, it is more reasonable to speak of the Cape's various denominations, not its missions.

"Secondary Blessings": The Quest for "Civilization" and Respectability

From the very beginning, the idea of converting the "heathen" was, for almost all European missionaries, whether Dutch, German or British, inextricably linked to that of "civilizing" them. The romantic reactionary view of civilization as intrinsic to sedentary peasant communities was always strong, particularly among the Moravians.[123] Like many of his fellows in the LMS, John Philip, under the influence of the Scottish Enlightenment – and recent Scottish history – stressed the rapidity whereby changes in consciousness could both lead to spiritual salvation and provide the "secondary blessings" of social and economic progress.[124] Other missionaries, such as Henry Calderwood, saw the "civilizing process" as protracted and directly linked to European political domination of Africans.

At all events, even allowing for missionary exaggeration of both pre-conversion barbarity and their own achievements, significant cultural transformation accompanied Christianization.[125] By the 1830s and 1840s converts and others were wearing Western clothing, learning to read, speaking a Dutch creole, arranging their villages according to missionary wishes in squares and straight lines, aspiring to cash wages, and (at least, superficially) adopting Western marriage patterns.[126] When James Read married Elizabeth Valentyn, he wanted her to wear her kaross to the wedding, but she compromised by wearing a Western petticoat kaross-style, around her shoulders.[127] Still, many people of Khoikhoi descent resisted the notions of work discipline, capitalist time, and individualism that missionaries sought to impose upon them; they maintained old patterns of clientage and shared with clients, friends, and relatives in hard times to the point of destitution.[128] Even though missionaries were justifiably proud of their networks of schools, often run by young Khoisan men and women, parents pulled their children out of school when their labour was needed and resisted English-style restrictions on their children.[129] There were regional and class variations in the adoption of Western cultural forms. Ironically, among the most willing to adopt aspects of Western culture were the motivated settlers of Kat River, so much despised and feared by their white neighbours, while more dependent farmworkers had little incentive to acculturate. Most did so in the end, most dramatically, in the disappearance of the Khoikhoi language in the Cape by the end of the nineteenth century.[130]

William Elliot complained in 1841 that his baptism class in Uitenhage was unnaturally large because "a profession of Christianity is considered among the coloured people of these parts, a necessary badge of respectability." By the 1840s, this was a typical response. British members of the social strata from which missionaries tended to come regarded temperance, work, self-discipline, and chastity as powerful weapons against degradation. Respectability was also part of a formidable upper-class arsenal of social control.[131] The Khoikhoi and slaves had known real degradation, and their concepts of shame and honour had been exposed to severe pressure.[132] For some, the result was self-hatred.[133] Under such circumstances, Christian respectability was indubitably, for some, a means of gaining self-respect, of reconstructing community, and of restoring the honour lost by servitude. It was also a means of assuming the cultural anxieties and values of another people.

Respectability was often, also, quite brutally, an instrument of survival. Before Ordinance 50, for example, those who looked "disreputable" were unable to travel without danger of arrest and impressment into contract labour. A number of women were so afraid of the consequences of becoming pregnant out of wedlock that they concealed the birth and were later tried for infanticide. The government had to request the missions no longer to expel such women.[134] Inhabitants of Hankey were permitted to use newly irrigated land only on condition of remaining respectable in the eyes of the resident missionary, William Philip. In the 1850s, the Rev. A. Robson had full control over the "Hottentot Location" in Port Elizabeth, receiving applications for settlement and arranging the expulsion of squatters.[135] Mfengu in Uitenhage in 1842 were saved from eviction only because the resident LMS missionary, William Elliot, intervened by testifying in detail to their respectability.[136] The *South African Commercial Advertiser*, just before emancipation, noted that the newly freed slaves would be "dependent on employment for food, and on character for employment."[137]

Nowhere is the use of "respectability" to regain control over a fragmenting community clearer than in rhetoric about drinking and temperance.[138] Church-based temperance societies, a non-conformist import with a considerable history in Britain,[139] acquired new political meaning in a society where many Khoikhoi blamed whites for the devastating introduction of alcohol among them. "The Canteens were brought here by the English settlers to ruin us," protested Venzel Mins in 1834, "and are to be found in almost every street, by which they are made rich, whilst we are now poor vagrants."[140] "Tell your children to what brandy has reduced the Hottentot nation," urged Andries Stoffels at the second anniversary of the Kat River Temperance Society, also in 1834. The same speaker demonstrated the razor-thin line between respectability and ruin:

In November last, I went on a visit to the Bay [Port Elizabeth] and Bethelsdorp; in riding past a canteen my attention was attracted by a vast number of people standing before it. I stopped and watched the persons who went in and out; I saw an English girl going in to take a soopie [i.e. a dram]; after her two of the king's soldiers went in and took each a soopie. The canteenman gave them the best kind ... A Hottentot went in to take a soopie, but he got the very refuse, for it looked so dirty that I thought it would be impossible to drink such stuff. Well, thought I, this is one way of killing the people of my nation ... Just as I rode past the bridge I met two of my acquaintances, who had once been two of the most respectable Hottentots I ever knew – lying drunk in the street and fighting with each other; I pitied them, but would not stop, for I rode past them as fast as I could; I was afraid to be seen talking with such people. I thought again the Hottentot nation is now going to ruin![141]

By 1842, the Kat River "Total Abstinence" society had more than 700 members. The Philipton church would accept only "total tea drinkers" as church deacons.[142] At the same time, alcoholism remained a pressing problem for the Coloured community, and the system of paying workers partly with a "tot" of wine remained prevalent.[143]

The interaction between notions of gender and notions of respectability showed the same combination of the defensive and the constructive. Women used mission stations and the ideology of respectability to gain protection and to strengthen themselves in relationships with men, or to escape them altogether. One unnamed ex-slave woman came, "with several others of her relatives and friends," to Kat River on the completion of her apprenticeship, and shortly thereafter converted. Her common-law husband lived in a "place of much wickedness" but left her at Kat River "to enjoy the means of grace." When he finally insisted that she return, she said "she would rather die than go to witness what she had formerly done and seen and to be exposed to Temptation," but, according to the elder Read, she had "no alternative." In return she requested that her spouse enter into a Christian marriage. Unfortunately, while waiting at Kat River for the banns to be published, she had an accident with a loaded gun and shortly thereafter died of tetanus, proclaiming, "If I die 'tis what I wished [and] prayed for – I shall only go to Jesus sooner than I expected."[144]

After emancipation, large numbers of ex-slaves had their common-law marriages legalized, although the requirement that "Christian" names be used delayed matters on Moravian stations, since converts only received such names at baptism, after a lengthy period of preparation.[145] The Christian ideology of marriage and monogamy does not appear to have been accepted fully by all congregational members. Rather, the patterns of easy marriage and divorce seem to have been replaced by informal marriages in which the formal blessing of the church was not sought: perhaps church marriages were held to be harder to dissolve and thus less readily entered into. A dispute arose at Grahamstown after the minister, Nicolas Smit, to bring the sinning to an end, followed the wishes of the Coloured congregation in marrying a couple who had been living together. His shocked superior, John Locke, believed that some period of repentance and proof of a changed life was required before a wedding was celebrated. In such a situation, one can imagine that appeal to the formal missionary power structure was a resource open in particular to women, but that much congregational sexual behaviour was self-policing.

On the other hand, the Christian ideology of separate spheres reduced the access of women to the power structures of Christianity from early to mid-century. "Enthusiastic" women could preach in unorthodox settings in the early days of missionary activity, and doubtless continued to do so. Unmarried young Khoikhoi women took charge of missionary schools and may well have had considerable authority as the only representatives of missionary societies in remote areas. Women's prayer groups and "personal experience" groups provided women with venues for action and spiritual expression. But the formal structures of all the missions, as they solidified into churches towards mid-century, were male-dominated. As the Read wing of the LMS fought to institutionalize and professionalize "native agency" and to create a salaried body of native schoolteachers, women were squeezed out: they do not appear on the LMS payroll and were not presented in the lists of "native agents" available for sponsorship by British congregations and individuals. Just as female missionaries were reduced to the role of wives from the 1810s on (before the late-century feminization of the European missionary movement), Khoikhoi women now went out to mission stations and into the African interior as the wives of native agents.[146] In this, they were part of a general move by Khoisan converts to Christianize, to civilize, and generally to teach other African groups supposedly beneficial economic behaviour. For example, the people of Kat River churches raised subscriptions to buy seed for nearby San, while a number went to the mission station they had founded with ploughs to demonstrate agriculture.[147] Some also adopted the language of civilization to make an explicit contrast between themselves and neighbouring Bantu-speakers.

In general, the claim to be "advanced" could be, and was, used by spokespeople of Khoisan or slave descent to back up demands for greater political power. Perhaps even more crucially, Christianization and the widespread adoption of new norms of respectability were, for some Coloured groups, building blocks for the re-invention of community. This pattern stands in vivid contrast to Mfengu or Xhosa communities, which felt attacked by the sporadic conversion of disaffected individuals. For Coloured churches, whose membership included most local people, church rituals (for example) expressed a new order and a shared history, based on the idea of the purified and reborn community, a process that became all the more important as the community itself became more ethnically diverse.

By the later nineteenth century – with the exception of the Muslim community of Cape Town and its environs – the missionaries' work had been done. Throughout the Cape Colony the mass of those whose grandparents had been slaves or dispossessed Khoisan had become Christian. For many, conversion had led to a sharp improvement in their social status; for the majority, probably, what the missionaries saw as liberation in matters spiritual was not accompanied by the promised temporal improvement. The implications of this failure had still to be worked out.

3

Settlement, Conquest, and Theological Controversy: The Churches of Nineteenth-century European Immigrants

RODNEY DAVENPORT

A New Diversity: Beliefs and Practices of the Settler Churches

The authorities in nineteenth-century South Africa saw the Christian churches as a subordinate but important element in colonization. The colonists themselves saw the churches rather as reassuring cultural props in an unfamiliar environment. Church leaders faced crucial decisions: to accept state dominance or resist it, to serve the needs of the settler community or to reach beyond it, carrying out the Biblical injunction to "preach to all the world." If they chose the missionary alternative, they had to decide whether to focus sharply on the propagation of the gospel or to present Christianity as part of a wider cultural package, including literacy and technical skills, the suppression of "pagan" customs and beliefs, and the defence of subordinate peoples against injustices perpetrated by the state or the colonists themselves.

During the 1790s the Reformed Church in the Netherlands, in the wake of a French invasion, lost its established position; the newly secularist state professed neutrality in religious matters, and Lutherans and Arminians successfully gained recognition as a result. At the Cape the VOC had already readmitted the Moravian missionaries in 1792 and permitted Lutherans to practise their religion in public. The Cape church was attuned to a new, more flexible dispensation. When the British arrived in 1795, they recognized the Reformed Church (NGK) as in *de facto* possession of the field and paid stipends to the NGK clergy. Yet they also encouraged the work of the Moravian missionaries, and extended the right of public worship to Cape Muslims for the first time.[1]

The Batavian occupation in 1803–6 brought French revolutionary deism to the Cape, with Commissary-General J. A. de Mist's church ordinance of 1804 providing equal protection of the law to "all religious associations which for the furtherance of virtue and good conduct respect a Supreme Being."[2] The NGK, as the dominant church in the Colony, accepted financial assistance for clerical salaries and capital expenditure and surrendered power to the state over the regulation of public worship. The consistories (or meetings of elders) of all Dutch Reformed congregations were required to have a government official, the political commissioner, in attendance, to keep political discussion within bounds. The political commissioner controlled NGK funds. The link with the Classis (Synod) of Amsterdam was broken, and the Cape NGK was granted the right to set up its own synod. No synod actually met until 1824, eighteen years after British rule had returned for a second time, when it began to draft its own regulations. It took De Mist's Church

51

Order and the General Regulation drawn up for the Reformed Church of the Netherlands in 1816 as a basis, rather than the rules laid down at the Synod of Dort (1618–19), which would have set bounds to state dominance.[3] The agendas and resolutions of NGK synods were subject to state censorship; referred to London, they were often confirmed only after long delays.[4] In 1842 the NGK synod redrafted its General Regulation, its main features being embodied in Governor Napier's general church Ordinance of 1843; but this did not bring the independence from state control many desired.[5] Further bureaucratic inefficiency, and the state's insistence that an affirmation of political loyalty be included in the liturgy, continued to rankle.

The established church in England, though undermined in the seventeenth century by Independency, and in the eighteenth by the growth of Methodism, had protected its privileges by laws restricting the political rights both of Free Church members and of Roman Catholics. When the British retook the Cape in 1806, the Church of England acquired semi-official status there, with the Governor authorized by the Bishop of London to exercise general control and to legalise marriages and baptisms for all denominations. The Test and Corporation Acts, which denied public office and the franchise to non-Anglican believers in Britain, were inconsistently enforced at the Cape. One Catholic government official was forced to resign because of his faith, but after 1826 his church received a government subsidy. Meetings of the small Methodist community were banned, but Governor Somerset nevertheless gave full encouragement to their Lilyfountain mission.[6] Visiting Scottish and Irish regiments, meanwhile, arrived accompanied by Presbyterian and Roman Catholic chaplains.

The Church of England's structure was initially so slight that it felt state pressure rather less than the NGK. After the return of the British in 1806, there was more of a clerical presence at the Cape when George Hough and Robert Jones loosely organized their English compatriots for worship in the (Reformed) Groote Kerk. Two Anglican priests accompanying the 1820 Settlers to the Eastern Cape were subsequently appointed as clergymen, but Anglicans were still unable to sustain a parochial system, despite a semblance of parish life in Grahamstown and Port Elizabeth. Under an ordinance of 1829, the first Anglican churches were built by joint-stock corporations of shareholders, including St. George's Church in Cape Town and a number of other churches in the colony.[7] Not until the arrival of Robert Gray as Bishop of Cape Town in 1848 was an attempt made to give the Anglican church an administrative system – ultimately, as it turned out, with the object of creating a church independent of the state. Unlike the free churches, the Anglican Church in South Africa held fast to rule by bishops, not only for theological reasons, which ruled out an attempt to amalgamate the Church with the NGK in 1870, but also because it shaped the organized expansion of Anglicanism throughout the whole of southern Africa – to the eastern Cape and trans-Kei, Natal and Zululand, the highveld, Kimberley and the Rhodesias, St. Helena and Damaraland, all by 1924.[8]

English non-episcopal churches, which began to arrive with the second British occupation, were initially distinguishable from the NGK and the Anglicans by a greater emphasis on missionary activity. First to arrive after the Moravians was a society set up mainly on Independent (Congregational) initiative. Known as the London Missionary Society (LMS) after 1816, its pioneer was J.T. van der Kemp, a Dutch scholar and courtier, who arrived at the Cape in 1799. Non-denominational in origin, the society became the missionary organ of the Congregational church.[9] Its effectiveness owed much to John Philip, director from 1819 to 1848, intent on spreading western culture as a vehicle for Christian conversion. It gained a wide following among the indigenous peoples because of Philip's efforts to protect them from forced labour (see pp. 34–39).[10]

The ranks of the LMS were divided over the virtues of centralization, especially after the outbreak of the Kat River rebellion in 1851 (see pp. 42–45). Philip's retirement in 1848 opened the way for major structural changes, and strengthened a proposal to the directors that the LMS missions, in accordance with the principles of Independency, should become self-supporting and cease to rely on overseas funding. By 1855 most missions had cut their ties with London, with new Congregational churches taking them over in Somerset East (1856), Grahamstown (1871), Port Elizabeth (1874), and Bethelsdorp (1880).[11] To sustain these bodies an Evangelical Voluntary Union was formed in 1855, but financial independence proved too difficult.[12] The Union was re-formed as the Congregational Union of South Africa (CUSA) in 1877.

A handful of Presbyterians arrived with the second British occupation as members of a Scottish regiment. George Thom of the LMS drew a small Calvinist Association, founded in 1808, into an embryonic Presbyterian Church in May 1813; when he later decided to join the NGK, the Presbyterians came under the pastoral care of Philip, who boosted their membership with stirring sermons. Philip's assumption that they were, in fact, merging with the Congregationalists was commemorated in the naming of their first place of worship as the "Union" chapel, but the Presbyterians broke away to form their own church in 1824, with the approval of the Edinburgh presbytery. Their first church, St. Andrew's, which opened in Cape Town in 1829, became the centre of a close community under notable ministers like John Adamson, George Morgan, and a breakaway Lutheran, Georg W. Stegmann. In addition to white colonials, they attracted Coloured people and ex-slaves, in part by provision of poor relief, health care, and biblical instruction. Their inclusive community split partially on ethnic and linguistic lines when Stegmann set up a separate Coloured, Dutch-speaking congregation.[13]

With the arrival of the 1820 Settlers the Presbyterians set up new churches on the Cape's eastern border. Members of the Church of Scotland and the Scottish Free Church also founded more than twenty mission stations, and started the remarkable institution of Lovedale (named after a minister of the Glasgow Missionary Society), which was to play an influential part in the spread of Western education through sub-Saharan Africa. The growth of Presbyterianism during the rest of the century was dramatically revealed at a meeting in Durban in 1897 to establish the Presbyterian Church of South Africa; representatives came from the Presbyteries of Cape Town, Natal, and the Transvaal, the Free Church of Scotland's Synod of Kaffraria, congregations of the United Presbyterian Church of Scotland falling under the Presbytery of Adelaide, and two independent congregations from Port Elizabeth and Kimberley. The reach of Presbyterianism had already extended across the Limpopo and Zambezi rivers with the foundation of missions, notably at Livingstonia in the future Malawi.[14]

Some "pious soldiers" of Methodist background had arrived in the early days of the British occupation, but not until two years after the founding of the Wesleyan Missionary Society in England in 1813 was Barnabas Shaw, a missionary, dispatched to the Cape. Shaw could hold services only by defying the Governor's ban, and he did so, building an effective ministry, first among the Nama in the northwestern Cape and from 1826 in Cape Town itself, extending his work to Simonstown, Stellenbosch, and Caledon by 1832. The Methodists established themselves firmly not only as pastors for white immigrants but also as missionaries among the blacks. Shaw worked in South Africa almost continuously until his death in 1854, by which time missionaries had gone from the western Cape to establish Methodist bases in trans-Orangia and north of the middle Vaal, and across the Kei as far as the borders of modern Natal. Among the 1820 settlers only Sephton's party of London Methodists accepted the government's offer of a clerical stipend. Their pastor William Shaw lived in Grahamstown from 1829 to 1856, except for four years in England. Chapels in Grahamstown and Salem were opened in 1822, earlier than those in the western Cape,[15] their work organized by missionary districts, of which there were five by 1863 (the Cape of Good Hope, Grahamstown, Kaffraria, Bechuanaland and Natal – the names would change over time). Bloemfontein was added in 1882. Districts established in the Transvaal and Swaziland were attached to the British Methodist Conference, and the question of separation from that conference, raised in the 1860s, was settled with the convening of a South African Methodist Conference in 1882, with the British Conference nevertheless retaining control over legislation and the election of the president until 1927.

English Baptists arrived with the 1820 Settlers five years after the first Methodists and some fourteen years after the first members of the Church of England. They established themselves first in Salem and then in Grahamstown, and in 1854 put up a church building in Port Elizabeth. German Baptist communities growing among the German settlers in the Border area were constitutionally separate from English Baptists but the two groups came closer by degrees, as the German churches began to use English in their services over the span of two generations. Elsewhere, too, the spread of the Baptist faith developed along ethnic and racial lines. In 1867 an Afrikaanse Baptiste Kerk was founded, and a number of Coloured churches were established in Port Elizabeth from 1888 and in the western Cape, particularly on the Cape Flats, from 1891. Indian and African Baptist churches followed after the turn of the century.[16]

The Unitarians of South Africa, like the Protestant churches, traced their distinctive stances – in their case a rejection of trinitarian orthodoxy and formal creeds – back to the Reformation. At the Cape their Free Protestant Church, set up in 1867 by an Afrikaner, D. P. Faure, (and still in existence), promoted strong humanitarian values: its membership was always modest and it sponsored no missionary activities.

Statistical details about the colonial churches in the early nineteenth century, are very unreliable and far from complete. They make it possible for some conclusions to be drawn, but also raise big problems of interpretation for which there is no space here. The various categories of membership throw light, for example, on different emphasis within the Anglican and NG churches, reflecting in particular the rural balance of the NGK, with its deflated attendance figures and the importance of the periodic *nagmaal*. For the principal churches the figures under three headings in 1898 were as follows:

Cape Colony Churches in 1898

Denomination	Nominal membership	Communicants	Average attenders
NGK	225,517	73,826	44,721
Methodist	203,067	35,048	78,954
Anglican	89,650	24,152	33,202
Presbyterian	30,679	12,231	16,351
Congreg./LMS	41,409	14,153	24,111
Lutheran	44,111	17,031	22,733
Roman Catholic	17,508	6,761	7,071
Baptist (German and English)	6,777	2,491	4,435

An ethnic breakdown of membership, linked to the distribution of "stations," throws light on the relative involvement of churches in mission, in which the roles of the Methodists, Lutherans, and Congregationalists remained outstanding. Most Roman Catholic missions were outside the Colony:

Denomination	White	Coloured*	Main stations	Outstations
NGK	145,831	23,662	159	211
Methodist	23,189	179,878	118	2,179
Anglican	34,416	41,739	172	303
Presbyterian	9,055	13,526	42	149
Congreg./LMS	3,749	38,539	67	161
Lutheran	5,108	40,428	61	90
Roman Catholic	14,965	2,543	46	64
Baptist	5,237	390	29	18

* Presumably used to define all people other than whites

The most striking development in the decade after the Anglo-Boer war was an unexplained fall in the nominal membership of the NGK from 225,517 in 1898 to 164,607 in 1907, for which an obvious explanation is lacking. In the same period the membership of the Rhenish (Lutheran) mission dropped from 15,643 to 3,681. New developments by then were the appearance of low figures for American Methodist Episcopals, the Apostolic Union, and rather higher ones for the Salvation Army (15,321 nominals, of whom one third were "coloured").

Theological Disputation in a Colonial Society

Divisions between Christian denominations in Europe, and between church and state, were compounded in the nineteenth century by intellectual challenges that apparently undermined fundamental Christian beliefs. As a result, the nineteenth-century churches sometimes sounded a less certain note than their authoritarian predecessors in the eighteenth-century and their theologically and politically assertive successors in the twentieth. Moreover, the rift between Catholicism and Protestantism widened in the era of Pope Pius IX (1846–78) and the first Vatican Council (1870); episcopal church government, contrasted with the congregational calling of ministers, remained a hard line of division among Christians, in South Africa as elsewhere.

In the Nederduitsch Hervormde Kerk,[17] the state church of the Netherlands, sectarian divisions proliferated after the Revolutionary era. The church ordinance of 1815 retained much of the rationalist character of the Enlightenment, and some theologians guided the church's thinking along Erasmian humanist lines, with Christ held up as an example rather than a saviour, and Calvinism eyed suspiciously as an alien intrusion.[18] But the influence of such thinking on the Cape was slight. The overall movement of the church, even in the Netherlands, was towards evangelicalism instead. In 1827 the *Reveil*, a Bible-orientated movement from Switzerland, working through an organization at Utrecht University, *Secor Dabar* ("Remember the Word"), encouraged personal conversion among theological students, including a number of Cape trainees. One of these, Andrew Murray, son of a Scots minister of the same name, who resisted the rationalism of his philosophy professor in favour of an intensely personal religion,[19] was to start and lead an evangelical revival at the Cape. He was the doyen in the Cape NGK until his death in 1917.

A biblical movement with a similar but more radical orientation was led by the Rev. H. de Cock, who, having been expelled from the NHK, set up his own Christelijke Afgescheidene [i.e. Separated] Kerk in Nederland in 1834, which denounced a versification of the Psalms accepted in 1773 by the Dutch Church, preferring a much earlier version. De Cock, who described the NHK's devotees as "spellbound and drunk with the intoxicating wine of the Sirens' love-songs," thus promoted a marginal liturgical feature to a status of doctrinal orthodoxy.[20] His separate church inspired the breakaway Gereformeerde ("Dopper") Kerk among a few close-knit families on the isolated Cape frontier. The Doppers practised daily religious exercises based on a reading of the States Bible and singing of psalms. Pious and disciplined, they were neither politically radical nor unusually racist.[21]

Another movement in the Netherlands influencing southern Africa was associated with Groen van Prinsterer, whose intense opposition to rationalist influences led to the publication of his *Unbelief and Revolution* in 1847. A philosophy known as "Neo-Calvinism" was developed by his disciple, Abraham Kuyper, founder of the Free University of Amsterdam in 1880 and later prime minister of the Netherlands. It accepted the duty of the state, through the parents, to ensure the Christian upbringing of children. Kuyper substituted a Congregationalist pattern of church government for an all-powerful national church, each community and each corporate body to be "sovereign in its own sphere." In South Africa his ideas found support in the 1870s in the first Afrikaans cultural movement, the Genootskap van Regte Afrikaners, and, in the 1890s, in the Kruiskerk movement led by the Rev. S. J. du Toit, and among the Doppers of Potchefstroom.[22]

In Britain at the same time, the granting to Dissenters and Roman Catholics of political rights and admission to higher educational institutions, and the granting of organizational rights to the Methodist and Catholic churches, removed important supports of the established Church of England, which, like the Reformed Church in the Netherlands, was now on the defensive.[23] Some of its members became Tractarians, seeking security in conservative doctrines looking back to Rome and away from biblical inspiration as a source of authority: their influence would strongly affect the Cape Church during controversies of the 1860s. As in the Netherlands, some members of the Church of England moved towards an evangelical stance, closer to the Dissenters in emphasizing personal conversion and supporting humanitarian social movements. At the Cape this Anglican evangelicalism, which often brought Methodists and Anglicans together in liturgical practice, was significantly diluted after Robert Gray became bishop of Cape Town in 1847, and precipitated a shift toward Anglo-Catholicism.

The theological world in Europe had meanwhile been shaken by the work of liberal theologians of the German Tübingen school, and by scientific advances, principally in geology and zoology.[24] It was still possible to be a staunch churchman and a humanitarian at the same time, or to be a "Bible Christian" without rejecting the new scholarship, but old assumptions had to be tested in the light of the new challenges, especially the Unitarian Charles Darwin's *Origin of Species* (1859), and a volume edited by Benjamin Jowett and Frederick Temple, *Essays and Reviews* (1861). The controversies resulting from these and other writings affected Dutch thought as well through the writings of scholars such as C.G. Opzoomer and Abraham Kuenen,[25] and in consequence, the leadership of the NGK in the Cape determined to combat the new liberalism, whose influence was taking root among recently graduated clergy returning from Holland.[26] T.F. Burgers, who went to Holland to complete his theological studies at Utrecht in 1853, set out as a pietistic young man, as is apparent from his letters home, but responded enthusiastically to the rationalism of Opzoomer's lectures in logic and metaphysics, and to the work of Kant on the moral imperative.[27] A predikant at Hanover in the Karoo in 1859, he spoke out against revivalism, which his opponents prized as an inoculation against heresy. At the NGK synod of 1862 a member of his congregation accused Burgers of being tainted with rationalism.

The synod itself began to close its door against "alien" influences, and in 1859, established its own seminary at Stellenbosch. The great majority of NGK trainees passed through Stellenbosch during the remaining decades of the century.[28] A new process of formal interrogation to screen the orthodoxy of clerical novices, the *colloquium doctum*, was introduced. In 1862 the judicial committee of the synod heard charges accusing Burgers of rejecting the personality of the Devil, the sinlessness of Christ's nature, the resurrection of the dead, and the continued existence of the human soul after death.[29] He was found to have erred on the Devil and on Christ's sinlessness, and was dismissed from his charge two years later.

In 1853, the year when Burgers went to Utrecht, John William Colenso was consecrated as the Church of England bishop of Natal. Five years later he delivered a series of sermons that his dean, a strict Anglo-Catholic named James Green, regarded as heretical, and which Bishop Wilberforce of Oxford thought dangerously vague.[30]

In 1861 he published a commentary on that watershed of theological controversy, the Epistle to the Romans, before embarking on an even more radical study of the Pentateuch, which appeared in seven volumes between 1862 and 1879, echoing some of the controversial ideas of Jowett's and Temple's *Essays and Reviews*. A dedicated missionary bishop with a well-trained mathematical mind, Colenso tried to offer precise interpretations of problematic biblical texts to interested Zulus he desired to convert.[31]

Christian theologians in due course adjusted their thinking to the new intellectual challenges, but public theology was slower to do so. For many, particularly in the evangelical and Dutch Reformed traditions in South Africa, "evolution" and "creation" remained polar opposites. Some people were bowled over by Darwinian arguments; others, like F. C. Kolbe, a Protestant turned Catholic priest, took them seriously but held fast to aspects of Christian belief untouched by evolutionary theory.[32] The debates would continue to unsettle the beliefs of many South Africans until into the twentieth century.

From Establishment to Voluntarism: Church–State Conflicts

The most immediate consequence of the intellectual and theological controversies in Europe and in South Africa, however, was less in the area of belief than in that of law. Church–state disputes in Europe from the 1850s to the 1870s had a direct legal impact on southern Africa, above all in the Anglican Church and the NGK. After 1833, appeals from ecclesiastical courts in Britain no longer went to higher ecclesiastical courts under Chancery, as had been the case since the Reformation, but to the Judicial Committee of the Privy Council, a predominantly lay body to which bishops who were privy councillors could be summoned in ecclesiastical cases.[33] In 1850, the Judicial Committee decided that the controversial views of a Cambridge theologian on baptism were not repugnant to Anglican formularies broadly conceived.[34] Many clergy now demanded a revival of the convocations of Canterbury and York, inactive since 1717. These recovered their debating rights in 1850. A clerical demand that bishops have collective and binding authority in matters of doctrine came to fruition with the establishment of the Lambeth Conference in 1867.[35] Earlier, in 1852, the churches in self-governing colonies like the Cape were declared to be fully competent to handle local ecclesiastical cases, with appeals only to the Crown through the Privy Council.[36]

When Colenso, as Anglican bishop of Natal, began to teach heterodox views, Bishop Robert Gray of Cape Town convened a synod which deposed him in 1863. Colenso, claiming that his appointment to Natal antedated the letters patent that placed his diocese under Gray's overall control, refused either to appear before the synod or to resign his office. He was then excommunicated by Gray, whose decision was later upheld by the Convocation of Canterbury; whereupon Colenso appealed to the Judicial Committee, which ruled in his favour on the ground that he could only be required to obey Gray's injunction if he had already submitted voluntarily to his authority. Ignoring the doctrinal issues, the Committee treated the issue as a civil liberties matter (see also p. 96).

Shortly afterwards, in 1864, the synod of the Cape NGK dismissed the Rev. T.F. Burgers from his charge, and set up a commission to examine the views of the Rev. J.J. Kotze, minister of Darling, accused of heretically questioning the Heidelberg Catechism's teaching that humanity is "continually inclined to all evil."[37] Both Burgers and Kotze appealed to the Cape Supreme Court, and both won on the technical ground that the synodal committee had ignored its own procedures. The synod appealed to the Judicial Committee of the Privy Council, which, in 1867, upheld the Cape court, also on procedural grounds. So both Anglican and Dutch Reformed churches had clearly failed to meet the common-law requirements of respect for civil liberty and the need to operate according to their own rules. But the courts had advanced sufficiently close to the forbidden territory of theology to create a case for strengthening the discipline of the churches over their own members.

The churches were divided over the strongest bond that held church and state together, clerical salaries, for which the state had retained a measure of responsibility under the Ordinance of 1843. Between 1854 and 1875 a sustained movement developed, under the inspiration of the Congregationalist parliamentarian, Saul Solomon, and his friend William Porter, the "New Light" Irish Presbyterian attorney-general of the Cape, for turning all churches into voluntary associations.[38] Porter argued that if churches received state aid, so also ought synagogues and mosques. The Congregationalists contended that the financial responsibility for a church devolved properly upon its own members, not upon the government, though, ironically, even the LMS, the missionary wing of the Congregationalist church, found it impossible to survive without state assistance after the middle years of the century (see pp. 44–45).[39] Substantial state money had gone into Anglican and NGK salaries,[40] and smaller amounts to other Christian denominations. A majority in the NGK synod found this a valid reason for rejecting voluntarism, and "Onze Jan" Hofmeyr, the middle-of-the-road editor of the NGK's *Volksvriend*, feared the "ruination of the country" if the Voluntary Bill were to be passed.[41] Thus the NGK, but not its liberal and neo-Calvinist wings, consistently opposed the bill, which nonetheless became law in 1875. The Anglican Church in South Africa took a different course, for Bishop Gray's rebuff in the Colenso affair strongly inclined the church to demand independence from the state, which necessarily involved the right to financial as well as juridical independence.

Colenso lost his position of strength in Natal with Gray's appointment of his own bishop to the see of "Maritzburg" in 1867. Colenso's congregations were eventually absorbed into a renamed "Church of the Province of South Africa" (its formal title after the Synod of 1870), once the church, under Gray's leadership, had defined its status as in communion with, but in no way subordinate to, the Church of England.[42] Between 1860 and 1870 the local Anglican bishops turned their church into a voluntary body, in terms of a resolution by the Lambeth Conference, by drawing up articles of association promulgated in January 1870 by a provincial synod.[43] When the provincial synod accepted the Lambeth resolutions it did so under certain conditions, the most important of which, known as the Third

Proviso, was a total rejection (in language designed not to offend) of the jurisdiction of the Privy Council as a spiritual court.[44]

Relations between the Church of the Province and the secular authorities in Britain and South Africa, despite this promising start, ran into a thicket of extraordinary litigation, arising mainly out of the difficulty of defining the legal rights of bishops with a dual obedience to Canterbury and Cape Town. The highlight was a dispute between Bishop Nathaniel Merriman and Dean Williams of Grahamstown in 1876–82, in the course of which the bishop successfully appealed to the Privy Council, "not as the final court of appeal in ecclesiastical causes, but as the court of appeal for cases tried in colonial courts."[45]

The relationship of the NGK to the colonial state was less turbulent than that of the Church of the Province. The NGK adapted to, so did not contest, the privy council judgment in the cases of Burgers and Kotze.[46] Its immediate problems related rather to the church's jurisdiction outside the Cape Colony. The NGK clergy, in general, had opposed the movement of Dutch-speaking settlers into Transorangia known as the Great Trek. How could the colonial synod support rebels against the colonial government? The Voortrekkers, for their part, angered by being cold-shouldered, looked to the Netherlands to provide them with clergy for a Nederduitsch Hervormde Kerk of their own.[47] The NGK had also established itself in the Transvaal, later to become the strongest of the churches there. The Cape synod soon became wary of the influence of its northern co-religionists, and, in 1857–62, H.H. Loedolff, a member of the Cape Parliament, repeatedly objected to the exercise of voting rights by ministers from outside the Colony. He won the support of the liberals, whose criticism of republican ministers seems to have stemmed from theological differences. Loedolff tried but failed, in 1863, to obtain a Cape Supreme Court ruling to invalidate resolutions of previous synods on this technical point; the orthodox succeeded in having the restriction removed, but not until 1898.[48]

In the 1870s NGK synods were caught up in an internal debate over the issue of the "free election" of ministers and members of the church councils by the congregations. "Free elections" became a slogan of liberals' protest against the common self-perpetuating renewal of church councils. When a successful parliamentary motion by P.E. de Roubaix in May 1861 raised the issue, the governor thwarted it with blocking tactics.[49] Liberals continued to challenge the power of the orthodox party on questions of doctrine and clerical rights in the secular courts, losing in the end when a younger group among the evangelical orthodox (the "Hofmeyrs, Murrays and Neethlings," in Du Toit's phrase), with forensic skills as subtle as those of the liberals, diverted the debate towards the cultural and economic needs of the Afrikaners – their language rights and farming interests – and hence towards political action.[50]

Afrikaner nationalism, in its early explosive phase during the 1870s, took its inspiration less from evangelical orthodoxy than from the thinking of the Dutch neo-Calvinist, Abraham Kuyper. The Programme of Principles Kuyper drew up for his Christian National Anti-Revolutionary Party in the Netherlands was taken over and adapted by the Rev. S.J. du Toit as guidelines for his projected Afrikaner Bond. Nonetheless, Kuyperian ideas did not take hold at the Cape, where "Onze Jan"

Hofmeyr outmanoeuvred Du Toit's attempt to "Calvinize" the Bond in the early 1880s and again a decade later when Du Toit attempted a come-back on his return from the Transvaal.[51] Kuyper's movement did, however, strengthen the orthodox centre party by providing a counterweight to the liberals. The main body of Cape Dutch Reformed opinion, orthodox but not neo-Calvinist, stayed with the Hofmeyrs, Murrays and Neethlings, whose clergy were close to their often isolated communities and sensitive to their concerns, whether on the issue of mixed-race services or of dancing and secular musical entertainment. They were as suspicious of innovations (*nuwighede*) as the Kuyperians were of "*methodisme*," concerned to maintain middle-of-the road doctrines, and resistant to any weakening of key trinitarian and christological doctrines, biblical authority, or belief in heaven and hell. They were as hostile to the Dutch-trained liberals' criticism of the Bible and rejection of conversion as they were of the Kuyperians' fragmenting of the historic Church in the name of an austere congregationalism and stress on the grim doctrines of total depravity and predestination. They were laying a basis for what would become the *volkskerk* (church of the people) of the twentieth century.[52]

Another ethnic and cultural issue affecting the relationship between the churches was the public use of language. In 1822 English superseded Dutch as the official language of the Colony. English had earlier been acceptable for religious worship in the NGK, especially for the Scottish clergy who arrived after 1814. But a movement for the recognition of Dutch in public life developed in the western Cape in 1875,[53] and thereafter, the use of English in NGK services diminished, to give way, in turn, to a dispute between rival claims of Dutch and Afrikaans, which the NGK only resolved in favour of Afrikaans later in the twentieth century.[54]

Language was also an issue in disputes over religion and education, as the church had had a dominant role in the control and content of education since VOC days. Two clerics had even sat on De Mist's secular school board of 1805, and provision was made for religious instruction of the young in the faith of their parents.[55] This precedent of state control helped the British to remould the cultural life of their new colony, with a view to the establishment of "English schools, to make that language the general one among the inhabitants."[56] In 1839 the government subsidized a public department of education; but, when these first public schools failed to attract many Cape Dutch children, the government decided to set up state-aided schools under NGK management, thus ensuring the survival of Dutch as a language of instruction until its use was formally legalized in 1882.[57]

Language rights had now become closely linked to religious practice. When the philosophy of Christian National Education (CNE) took hold in Holland in 1860, and was introduced at the Cape by the Rev. G.W.A. van der Lingen of the Paarl Gymnasium, Du Toit promoted it in his book *De Christelijke School in hare Verhouding tot Kerk en Staat* in 1876. Du Toit aimed to restore the principle of denominational instruction in schools (in contrast to lessons based on the Bible alone), and sought to guarantee that values learnt at home and in church would be promulgated in school as well.[58] During the mid-twentieth century, CNE would acquire strong political overtones linked to an assertion of Afrikaner cultural dominance; its earlier manifestations in the Cape, and in the northern colonies after the Anglo-Boer War, were, however, essentially reactive (see pp. 136–37).[59]

THE TRANSPLANTING OF CHRISTIANITY

"A Majestic Tree": British Imperialism and the Churches

Inter-state political tensions also affected the relationships between the churches. Especially significant were the departure of the Voortrekkers from the Colony in 1838, the escalation of frontier violence in a century (1778–1878) of warfare and conquest, with expropriation of the defeated Africans, revolutionary social changes attendant upon the discovery of diamonds and gold between 1867 and 1886, and the resultant collapse of good relations between Britain and the Boer republics, culminating in the Anglo-Boer War of 1899 to 1902.

The Great Trek, in part a protest movement, might have allied Briton and Boer against the liberal humanitarianism of missionaries and the Colonial Office in London, and at one level it did, especially on labour relations or frontier issues. But the Trek also strengthened the loyalty of the settlers to the Crown and against the rebel exiles. Not that the Voortrekkers lacked English-speaking admirers: William Thompson's gift of a Bible to Jacobus Uys on Uys's departure for the interior drew applause from English-speaking settlers, while Canon A.T. Wirgman found Piet Retief's manifesto of Voortrekker grievances an expression of "quiet dignity" and described the Voortrekkers at the battle of Blood River as "imbued with the spirit of Cromwell's ironsides."[60] Yet the division of South Africa into British and Boer states after the Trek created a deep divide over the legitimacy of British imperialism. Britain played an indecisive role north of the Orange between 1836 and 1870, seeking in 1836 to retain judicial control without administrative commitment, then reasserting political authority by force (Natal 1843, Trans-Orangia 1848–54, Transvaal 1877–81), then throwing the Queen's blanket over the Sotho in 1868 and southern Tswana in 1885 ostensibly to protect them against territorial invasion and enserfment. But British humanitarianism, already watered down by a concern to lighten military and political commitments, became further diluted by a compulsion to intervene in the Boer republics in response to the discovery of diamonds and gold. Church people tended to seek reassurance in the benign intentions of British rule to keep the peace, prevent slavery, and promote civilization, as William Shaw put it, "like a majestic tree spreading forth its branches far and wide, and thus affording shelter under which white and black ... may repose in peace, safety and enjoyment."[61] Even the exercise of tough punitive authority could be condoned with such credentials.

The mineral discoveries in Griqualand West and on the Reef from the late 1860s to 1880s led the churches to see the African workers housed in compounds (see pp. 242–46) as new opportunities for evangelism. By 1883 the Congregationalists were installed at the Kimberley mine and Du Toit's Pan; by 1885 the Methodists had seven clergy and nearly 200 members on the mines, while the Anglicans, Dutch Reformed, Roman Catholics, and Lutherans soon followed. Mine managers sometimes encouraged missions, because they were thought to engender conformist behaviour. By 1904 in the Rand compounds more than 18,000 Africans had church affiliations. The Anglicans had catechists in forty-three compounds, to the NGK's ten.[62] But to evangelize among black mineworkers on short-term contracts, without at the same time attracting opposition from white mineworkers, was not easy.

The confrontation between Boer and Briton, exacerbated by the mineral revolution, led to British annexation of Griqualand West in 1871 and of the Transvaal, temporarily, from 1877 to 1881, and to a movement of English-speaking and other European settlers into the towns of the Boer republics. British charges, beginning in the 1850s, that Boers were enslaving children and youth captured in war, echoed the earlier anti-slavery campaign of the 1820s and 1830s. LMS missionaries like David Livingstone, John Mackenzie, and John Moffat, reminiscent of Philip in the 1820s, urged emancipation of enserfed blacks in the name of human freedom and the right of workers to sell their labour in the best market. In the 1850s Mackenzie, in Bechuanaland, urged the British government to consolidate its hold over the African interior, and even to seize the gold mines, in order to preserve black chiefs' territorial autonomy and to protect missions.[63] Moffat, then a British South Africa Company agent at the court of Lobengula, engineered a treaty by which the British company could annex Mashonaland in the future Zimbabwe.[64] After the outbreak of the second Anglo-Boer War in 1899, the British Colonial Secretary Joseph Chamberlain observed that the government was fighting the Boer republics because "the ministers of religion in South Africa ... to whatever denomination they belong ... are heartily on our side."[65] His observation was fairly accurate with regard to British clergy, but not for missionaries from the countries of the European continent such as Germany and Scandinavia.

Most Anglican opinion in both South Africa and Britain was uncritically in support of the war. Church of England bishops, with few exceptions, endorsed it as a just war, arguing that the demands of English-speaking residents of the Transvaal (uitlanders) were fair and that blacks must be rescued from the Boers. The bishop of Liverpool even justified British burnings of Boer farms. There were minority voices, especially among "children of Anglican rectories" like Emily Hobhouse (noted for her campaign against the British "concentration camps") and her champion, the Bishop of Hereford.[66] But support for the Imperial cause was common among Cape bishops (all graduates of Oxford and Cambridge), whether, like Bransby Key of Umtata, they advocated fighting for black rights for "holy" reasons, or whether, like Dean Green of Pietermaritzburg, they thought it necessary to support the views of their white constituency.

Congregationalist opinion, as represented by the LMS and the Congregational Union of South Africa (CUSA), a significant body with 72 churches and 1,421 outstations, agreed on the importance of protecting black interests through the ending of Afrikaner control.[67] But one petition opposing the war, launched by a Congregationalist minister in Britain in 1900, drew 700 clerical signatures, while an appeal for a just peace, with autonomy for the Boers, was signed by 843 in the same year.[68] The LMS foreign secretary, on a visit to South Africa from London, applauded Boer treatment of non-combatants, but LMS missionaries at the Cape reacted so strongly that he reversed his stand. Boer misbehaviour (however much the British also misbehaved) evoked a robust defence of uitlander rights among Congregationalists, in which John Moffat was conspicuous.

So, too, were Methodist and Baptist opinions divided. Much fiery pro-war comment flowed from Methodist preachers in Britain like Hugh Price Hughes (described in one paper as "a twopenny-halfpenny Peter the Hermit") and from the Methodist Times, but other Methodists were strongly pro-Boer. So was the Baptist minister John Clifford, portrayed by Mackarness of the South African Conciliation

Committee as evincing "all the burning conviction and fanatical courage of the Old Puritan"; but H.J. Batts, a South African Baptist leader, who had been allowed to remain in Kruger's Republic after the outbreak of war, took a stand on "the big broad platform of British patriotism."[69]

The members of the British Society of Friends,[70] true to their traditional pacifist stance, opposed the war in principle, backing the formation in February 1900 of the Conciliation Committee. A Quaker journal did indict the Boer leaders for provoking war, but also published articles highly critical of the British high commissioner, Sir Alfred Milner, and the concentration camps. The principal focus of the Quakers, as in the World Wars to come, was on the provision of relief. Lawrence Richardson's post-war missions to the two Boer colonies were Quaker projects.[71]

In the nineteenth century, Christian churches had not yet begun to display a coherent response to the socio-economic problems of a modern, and interracial, South Africa. Some did demonstrate a growing sensitivity to African customs, of which they were, none the less, generally ignorant, as revealed, for example, in the perceptive comments of clerical witnesses before the Cape Native Laws Commission of 1883.[72] But two recent historians, M. Nuttall and J.R. Cochrane, have both noted that records from the period – for example four Anglican synods in the Cape – include few references to the great issues of the day that affected the subordinated blacks severely: the pass system, migrant labour, and the compounds, and that they manifest only "ideologically limited tolerances" for resistance movements such as the Zulu rebellion of 1906.[73] A formal colour bar was beginning to take shape, at a time when social Darwinism dominated the thinking of the business classes, yet the conscience of English-speakers was aroused more by the plight of the defeated Boers than that of the oppressed blacks. Only a few, like the radical daughter of missionary parents, Olive Schreiner, sensed that the future was not the whites' to control.[74]

"On Account of the Weakness of Some": Patterns of Segregation in the Churches

Moral condemnation of slavery and serfdom had hardened in Europe during the eighteenth century. All servitude was regarded as debasing, with serfdom considered the harsher status because the serf, not being property, was more exploitable. The notion that Cape slavery was more benign than slavery elsewhere has been upset by historians pointing, above all, to the low rate of slave emancipation in the Cape.[75] Yet opposition to slavery and serfdom was difficult to act upon, especially for churches ministering not only to blacks but to whites who, as employers, relied on Coloured labour. It was primarily LMS missionaries, who worked mainly among Coloured and African communities, who took the lead, in close association with reformers in Britain, in the campaign against both slavery and serfdom (see pp. 4–6, 17–19, 25–6).[76]

Missionaries were also drawn into the debates over frontier policy, especially after the start of the frontier war of 1834–35. No hard line of principle divided the churches, though the LMS and the Methodists clashed over the establishment of the Kat River Settlement in 1829. In that controversy, the LMS, concerned with the rights of Khoikhoi mission residents on the Cape's eastern frontier, promoted the Settlement, with its provision of land rights for many Khoikhoi, as a logical sequel to the emancipation of Khoikhoi from vagrancy controls. The Wesleyans focused rather on land rights acquired by whites, although a number also objected to expropriation of the Xhosa. Some, like William Shrewsbury, supported expropriation of the Xhosa warriors for punitive reasons; others, who wanted to protect African land rights, saw the Kat River Settlement as provocative. Yet others, like William J. Boyce, changed their minds in line with shifts in British policy.[77] In a public debate between Shaw and Philip in 1838–39, each found grounds to mistrust the bona fides of the other.[78]

Canon A.T. Wirgman of Port Elizabeth and Archdeacon Nathaniel Merriman of Grahamstown (both Anglicans) expressed anger over Xhosa lawlessness, Wirgman referring to the Kat River Settlement as "a hotbed of treasonable talk," and Merriman, new to South Africa in 1849, recommending jail for absentee indigenous farm labourers, and "branding or flogging" or worse for Fingo sheepstealers. When Khoikhoi read their Bibles, prayed, and even received holy communion the day before they were to commit "rebellion and wayside murder," Merriman asked, "what was a man to think?"[79] The same question might have been posed of a number of whites.

Inter-racial contact within churches was a different matter, and of great import for South African Christianity. In the nineteenth century relationships developed which would later provoke a world-wide denunciation of religious apartheid. Yet the origins of segregated worship were varied.

Methodists, who straddled the two racial cultures over a wider geographical area than any other denomination, were accustomed to separate white and indigenous congregations from the start, although they commonly considered it only a temporary expedient. Separate and adjacent buildings housed white and Xhosa worshippers at Salem, the first 1820 Settler church, and John Ayliff, the missionary at Butterworth, was "pleased" at being able to preach there in 1828, to "a small company of Dutch farmers and Hottentots ... in the same place," having previously preached to the English separately. Barnabas Shaw rejoiced over a "general prayer-meeting for the benefit of English and Dutch Christians, and Heathens bond and free," held in Cape Town in 1822, and over a gathering of seven worshippers of different nationalities in Simonstown, mainly ex-slaves, ten years later.[80]

Cultural incongruity, linguistic differences, and residential separation contributed to the general practice of segregated worship. Methodists, like almost all whites, assumed that white culture was radically superior to black, most missionaries considering that African converts should abandon undesirable cultural practices. Methodists set up different circuits for black and for white churches but without sufficient integration at the clerical level. In the end, they paid a price for this, being subject more than other denominations to the turmoils of black separatism. Although the Methodists ordained African ministers beginning in 1871, Nehemiah Tile's Thembu Church broke away in the 1880s, followed in 1892 by Mangena Mokone's Ethiopian Church. The unifying trends of shared spiritual experiences in South African Methodism were overwhelmed by blacks' desire to attain higher status than their white colleagues in a nominally non-racial church would allow, linked to a growing conviction that there were proven resources in African

Christianity which allowed blacks to pioneer new directions of their own (see pp. 82–88).[81]

For the Anglicans, too, racially separate worship was customary if not mandatory. Apart from the missionary diocese of St. John's (Transkei), all dioceses had both predominantly black and predominantly white parishes, but all were represented in the same synods. This structural unity at the top discouraged secession, and, by a strange irony, provided flexibility sufficient both to absorb the prejudice of some believers against mixed worship and to enable the Church to incorporate the Ethiopians in their fold in 1900 as a separate religious order (see pp 212–14). Episcopal structures, it could be argued, safeguarded the unity of the Anglican Church – as well as the Roman Catholic – under circumstances that might otherwise have resulted in an ethnic divide.[82]

In Baptist circles the maintenance of common worship across the colour line appears to have been relatively unimportant, at least for the Afrikaanse Baptiste Kerk. A mixed congregation was established at Stutterheim in 1867, but the Kerkraad (church council) minutes of 1924 make it clear that over a period of time separation had occurred because it was "necessary that general public opinion on race relations be taken into account" if an effective ministry among whites was to continue.[83]

It was not a foregone conclusion that worship in the NGK would be segregated. In Boer homesteads early nineteenth-century travellers found the farmer's (Coloured) *volk* often participating in the routines of family worship, although conversions were rare and those who did convert gained little status.[84] Thus the NGK synod's decision in 1857 to legitimize the custom of separate churches for the races "on account of the weakness of some" had a more decisive impact than it would have had in other denominations. It had arisen out of widespread, and fairly longstanding, discomfort within white congregations at the presence of black worshippers. Thus principle came to be abandoned, as Susan Ritner notes, "in the one vital area hitherto unbreached by white prejudice."[85] The decision was not based on language differences or on the inconveniences caused by residential segregation. In the Dutch Reformed tradition of "internal holiness" (chap. 1°), infant baptism was considered to bestow "covenantal holiness" only on children of believers. Christian and non-Christian communities were, in consequence of this theological distinction, regarded as "two static groups between which no movement was likely, if even possible."[86] An additional rationale, which the NGK shared with English-language churches, especially the Presbyterian, argued that blacks would feel more at home in their own churches than as subordinates in white churches. The decision of 1857 was followed by another in 1881 to set up the separate Nederduitse Gereformeerde Sendingkerk (NGSK, or Mission Church), thereby giving institutional shape to the previously informal relationship of separate church structures, with the "mother" NGK in a controlling position over both – a role it was to maintain for more than a century.

Presbyterians' original premise was that the races should not be segregated, and they were not in fact segregated in the early Cape Town congregation.[87] The movement leading to a separate Bantu (subsequently, Reformed) Presbyterian Church of South Africa in 1897, began in the year when the Presbyterian Church of South

Africa (PCSA) was founded to bring together most of the separate Presbyterian congregations on the subcontinent. The missionaries of the United Presbyterian Church of Scotland joined the new body; but those in the Free Church of Scotland were divided, a minority of the Free Church missionaries opting for the new multi-racial church, the majority for an autonomous African church. James Stewart, principal of Lovedale, feared that whites would leave the new united church if blacks gained control; also that a predominantly black membership would stymie a possible union with the NGK; and again – in conformity with a prevalent view in the Scottish church – that the function of mission was to support new Christian communities until they could stand on their own feet, and then let them go.[88] Others in favour of separation argued in favour of cultural autonomy for black and white. Opposition from black leaders, often for status reasons, reached a climax after the rise of Ethiopianism among the Methodists, and Pambani Mzimba's movement out of the PCSA in 1898 caused a rift that did not easily heal. A proposed compromise of 1914, which included a decision by the PCSA to continue to organize "Native Presbyteries" linked to an autonomous Kaffrarian synod whose members could participate in proceedings of the General Assembly, failed to remove the taint of subordination for blacks who wanted real freedom; nor did it satisfy whites who saw the proposal as racist. When the Bantu Presbyterian Church (BPC) was set up in 1923, the debate had not been resolved: whether to stand by the unity of the church at all costs, and risk further splits, or rationalize the position and let the BPC go.[89]

The story of how the various churches wrestled with cultural cleavages in a society that found it hard to apply the doctrine that "in Christ Jesus there is neither Jew nor Gentile, rich nor poor, bond nor free" thus betrays a tension between the pull of ethnic preferences on the one side and a sense of ethical obligation on the other. This tension was more painful in southern Africa than in most other parts of the world, because when the big issues had to be faced in the twentieth century, especially in the debates over racial parity and human freedom, the starting point was clouded by ambiguous assumptions about the meaning of baptism and notions of individual rights inherited from the earliest days of contact.

4

A Battle for Sacred Power:
Christian Beginnings among the Xhosa

JANET HODGSON

During the nineteenth century the Xhosa–Cape frontier was moved eastwards step by step, following conquests by the British Imperial and Cape Colonial forces. By the 1880s, after one hundred years of war, the Xhosa-speaking people, from the Zuurveld in the Eastern Cape to Pondoland, had been incorporated under British sovereignty, suffering dispossession of their ancestral land, destruction of their polities, and displacement and domination by alien rulers. Every aspect of their daily lives, their customs, and their beliefs had come under sustained attack from missionaries. But while the Xhosa lost the struggle to retain their political and socio-economic independence, "the colonisation of consciousness"[1] itself was never complete, even among the Western-educated black elite. The battle for sacred power between the intruding culture and the indigenous cultures continued unabated. Over the years, a number of Christian symbols and rituals were appropriated into the African worldview, providing a spiritually liberating potential with profound political implications.

The spread of Christianity into Xhosaland in the nineteenth century is roughly divided into three periods. The first, from the end of the eighteenth century to the 1820s, encompasses a time when the sacred symbols of the different groups were still freely available to one another and with mutual borrowing across the cultural divide. This phase corresponds with the "open frontier," a period in the history of frontier zones when several polities occupied the zone without one clearly dominating.[2] The second period, from the 1820s to around 1860, coincides with the coming of the 1820 British settlers, the gradual missionary advance into Xhosaland, and the African response to the closing of the frontier, that is, the conquest of the zone by Cape Colonial or British Imperial power. These colonisers tried to claim exclusive ownership over sacred symbols, with Christianity interpreted as the norm and African symbols as pagan and evil. In the third period, the high Imperial era of the closed frontier, from the 1860s to 1910, white dominance emerged unquestioned in many zones, and African people began a concerted attempt to liberate their indigenous symbols from an alienated past and to integrate them with an African understanding of Christianity.

Exchanging Sacred Symbols: Preachers and Prophets on the Open Frontier
    While archaeological evidence suggests that Xhosa-speaking people might have migrated as far as the Transkeian coast by the eighth century, the only present certainty is that they settled south of the Mthatha River before the end of the sixteenth century.[3] Two centuries later they comprised a heterogeneous group of polities,

known as Mpondo, Mpondomise, Bomvana, Thembu and Xhosa. The Xhosa nation consisted of those who recognized the royal Tshawe lineage and were divided between the Gcaleka, east of the Kei River, and the Rharhabe to the west. The Rharhabe, in turn, were split between followers of Ngqika and of Ndlambe, Ngqika having taken over from his regent uncle in 1795. As the age-old process of Xhosa expansion continued westward and clashed with an eastward-expanding white settlement, the dynastic feud among the Rharhabe opened the way for colonial advance. During the extended migration of the Xhosa, interaction with the Khoikhoi and some San had resulted in an uneven process of mutual assimilation comprised of trading, intermarriage, some conflict, and patron-client relationships. Mixed Khoikhoi–Xhosa communities were recorded from the eighteenth century on, adding to the complexity of the indigenous polities, especially on the borders of the colony.[4]

The primal religion of the Xhosa-speaking people made no distinction between natural and supernatural. All was pervaded by divinity. The ancestors, the spirits of the dead members of the lineage, who were thought to take a continuing interest in the living, were the focus of ritual activity in daily life. Religious specialists, such as homestead heads, political leaders, rainmakers, and diviners, competed for ownership of sacred power. The background God of Xhosa religion was impersonal and approached only in times of national disaster, such as drought, war, or epidemic disease. The ancient Nguni God-names – uDali, uMdali, uMenzi, uHlanga, iNkosi yezulu – express two principal concepts of deity: the one relating to origin and the other connected with the sky and natural elements. Implosive consonants or clicks in the Xhosa language indicate extensive borrowing from the Khoisan, as in the Xhosa God-names Qamata and Thixo. The gods of Khoikhoi and San, who were regarded primarily as raingivers, were appropriated into the Xhosa worldview during their migrations to fill a world extended in scale and social interaction.[5] Later, the biblical God of the missionaries would be similarly borrowed, and for much the same reasons, to fill an even bigger world with an ever more complex web of social relationships.

Survivors from shipwrecks, travellers, and visiting colonial authorities were part of the first peripatetic white population in the border region; but it was the Dutch-speaking frontiersmen who penetrated the Xhosa polity more extensively as traders, hunters, and fugitives from colonial justice. As the trekboers (mobile stock farmers in the Cape Colony) moved steadily eastward in search of grazing for their stock, white agrarian settlement followed in their wake consolidating territorial expansion. Inevitably the competition for land and cattle between two pastoral peoples expanding in opposite directions led to friction. From the 1770s intermittent border conflict escalated into full-scale war. The struggle between indigenous groups for rapidly diminishing resources added to the political fragility in the border area.[6]

When, in 1799, J.T. van der Kemp was sent by the London Missionary Society (LMS) as the first missionary to the Ngqika Xhosa, the frontier region was ablaze in rebellions by both whites and blacks. The colonial authorities initially favoured Van der Kemp's mission as strategically important but later accused him of propagating radical "Jacobin" politics. Van der Kemp's life was often in danger. Some trekboers plotted to kill him because of his preaching on the equality of all people regardless of colour. Nqgika, though suspecting Van der Kemp of being a British spy, none the less acquired prestige through his presence and the possibility of gaining access to a new source of power.[7] Van der Kemp's imagery of Christ as Conqueror empowered him to fight the good fight of faith clothed in the armour of God. It was a religion for a chaotic time when "Satan roared like a lion."[8] After Van der Kemp's departure in 1800 no missionaries were allowed to settle in Xhosaland for fifteen years.

In line with evangelical theology of the time, Van der Kemp emphasized personal conversion and faith in the saving gospel of Christ rather than good works. For him "the Word," expressed in preaching and prayer rather than in sacraments administered by priests, was the central channel of God's grace. He told how, in a sermon which made a deep impression on Khoikhoi women,

> I had described the horrors of the first and second death, and considered both as the wages of sin. To this I opposed the nature of everlasting life, and how it might be obtained by those who were weary of the service of sin, not as the wages of righteousness, and good works, but as a free gift of God's grace through Jesus Christ, who is willing to confer it on everyone that sincerely desires to accept it as such from his hands.[9]

Although Van der Kemp was a brilliant linguist, among the Xhosa he relied heavily on a Khoikhoi interpreter.[10] When he first settled with the Xhosa he reported that they had no religion and "no word to express the Deity by," that they had borrowed the name and concept of Tuikwe (Thixo) from the Khoikhoi. He condemned their "barbarous" customs, but he never tried to alienate them from their culture or to replace it with European values and consciousness.[11]

The borrowing of sacred symbols was a two-way process between Xhosa and missionary. Unable to identify Xhosa names for God, Van der Kemp appropriated the term Thixo and set about filling it with Christian content. Learning that "Utikxo" was considered the maker of all things, he said, "I bring that very one (that is, all that relates to or concerns him) to you of this country."[12]

The ritual words of the Xhosa in invocation or song were believed to have power in themselves and in transactions with the beyond. A Xhosa ruler's "word" had to be implicitly obeyed on pain of death. The seemingly magical power of white people's literacy, reinforced by their more efficient technology and military power, endowed Van der Kemp's teaching of the "Word of God" with even more powerful mystical associations among the Xhosa. His presentation of the Word in the form of prayers, hymn-singing, reading, and writing, led to his status among the Xhosa as a rainmaker.[13] When Ngqika's raindoctors failed during the great drought of 1800, he begged Van der Kemp to ask his God for rain. The missionary called the drought a divine punishment for the Xhosa's sins, a stance consistent with Xhosa thought patterns. Finally persuaded to pray for rain in the name of Jesus, Lord of Heaven, Van der Kemp's reputation was assured when it rained the next day and continued for a week, in fact, washing away Ngqika's own residence. Van der Kemp was asked whether Thixo had also given him "a power to raise dead people to life again," and to pray for the healing of the sick.[14] The Xhosa, who believed in a closed system of cause and effect that excluded chance, had this-

CHRISTIAN BEGINNINGS AMONG THE XHOSA

worldly needs: for rain, food, prosperity, fertility, healing, strengthening, protection from evil and misfortune, as well as restoring and maintaining of harmony and balance between people, their ancestors, and nature. Like Van der Kemp, most missionaries treated African people as blank slates, failing to understand that, far from inserting Christianity into a religious vacuum, they were competing for sacred power with indigenous worldviews, which appeared to serve immediate pragmatic concerns such as rainmaking and survival.

The competition for sacred power began in earnest after the British expelled the Xhosa from the Zuurveld in 1812 to make way for white settlement. For the first time the Xhosa experienced warfare leading to the occupation of their territory and seizure of the land, their means of survival. Apart from its economic importance for agriculture, cattle, and hunting, land was important to the Xhosa, too, because of its mystical attachment to their ancestors, and their sacred burial places. The ritual space of the cattle enclosures was also sacred; people could not leave them without fear of losing the blessings and protection of the ancestors, the guardians of the land.

In response to colonial aggression, Nxele and Ntsikana emerged as prophets offering Xhosa new sources of symbolic meaning and power in a rapidly changing world. They appropriated and mobilized Christian symbols: Nxele for militant resistance, Ntsikana in an evolutionary model, that allowed black people to direct their own transformation. Throughout the century these two models dominated the response to the missionary presence, among those Xhosa who neither remained rooted in ancestor ritual, nor acquiesced in the missionaries' scheme of total cultural reconstruction.

Nxele, also known as Makhanda, was of Gona parentage; he grew up on a Boer farm in the Zuurveld, where he learned Dutch.[15] Early on, Nxele showed signs of being a diviner. Contact with whites allowed him to incorporate Christian concepts into his teaching, warning people to forsake witchcraft and bloodshed. Around 1812 he came under Ndlambe's protection and began to preach like a missionary, citing as his authority a vision of Christ delivering him from being tossed into a huge fire. In addition to preaching orthodox Biblical themes such as the Fall, the Flood, Christ's crucifixion and resurrection, and the concept of salvation versus eternal punishment, he spoke of Mdalidephu, creator of the deep, and his son Tayi, and claimed to have the same mother as Christ.[16]

Following persistent frontier unrest, exacerbated by the concentration of Xhosa west of the Fish River, the Cape government allowed Joseph Williams of the LMS to establish a mission to the Ngqika Xhosa at Kat River in 1816, in the expectation that Williams would also represent colonial interests. Nxele felt rejected, having invited Williams to settle with him instead. At the same time he was aware of the increasing threat of the colonial advance. In an address to his people sometime between 1816 and 1818, he warned, "There they come! They have crossed the Qagqiwa (Zwartkops River) and they have crossed the Nqweba (Sundays River); only one river more, the Nxuba (Fish River), and they will be in our land. What will become of you then?"[17]

Nxele now developed a new message, plugged into new sources of power, but grounded in the Xhosa worldview. He depicted the world as a battleground

71

between the God of the whites, Thixo, and the God of the blacks; the whites, he said, had been punished for murdering Christ, the son of their God, by being pushed into the sea but had returned to claim their land. As the younger brother of Tayi, Nxele had been sent from out of Uhlanga, the mythical source of origin,[18] as Mdalidephu's agent to destroy the whites and to bring to life their ancestors together with their cattle.[19] "People do not die," he said; "they go to that chief [of Heaven and Earth]."[20] The missionary believed that Nxele's teaching of the corporeal resurrection of the dead was appropriated from Christianity,[21] but Nxele legitimated it by placing it within the Xhosa creation myth. He taught that the ancestors would rise from the grave but follow the same route the first African people had taken from below, a resurrection to be effected by a ritual sacrifice of cattle. Nxele now began to function as a traditional diviner and war doctor, gaining a large following in the process.

The feud between Nqgika and Ndlambe, exacerbated by a severe drought, reached a climax at the battle of Amalinde in 1817, when Nqgika was decisively beaten. He sought help from the colonial authorities, who responded by sweeping off 23,000 Ndlambe cattle. Nxele and others then mobilized a confederacy of clans to seek revenge against the authorities and, in May 1819, Nxele headed a large force in an attack on Grahamstown, assuring his people that "he was sent by Uhlanga, the Great Spirit, to avenge their wrongs; that he had power to call up from the grave the spirits of their ancestors to assist them in battle against the English (Ammamglezi), whom they should drive, before they stopped, across the Zwartkops River and into the ocean, 'and then,' said the prophet, 'we will sit down and eat honey!'"[22] These events, part of the Fifth Frontier War of 1818 to 1819, led, in turn, to punitive British reprisals. Nxele surrendered, hoping to spare more bloodshed. He was imprisoned on Robben Island off Cape Town and died a year later trying to escape. His people, considering him immortal, looked confidently for his second coming during the next three frontier wars from 1834 to 1853.[23] Nxele had incorporated apocalyptic Christian concepts within a Xhosa world of reference, drawing upon the power symbols of the new tradition to promise salvation here and now, but under the aegis of an African deity.

Ntsikana, Nxele's contemporary and rival, was the son of an hereditary councillor to Ngqika, renowned as a singer and orator. According to oral tradition around 1815 he saw a vision in his cattle byre and interpreted it as a calling from God; thereupon he collected a small band of disciples to meet twice daily for prayer, praise, and instruction in the Word of God. As a boy, Ntsikana is said to have heard Van der Kemp preach and may also have initially followed Nxele; he certainly visited the Kat River mission between 1816 and 1818, and his biblical teaching reflects Joseph Williams's influence.[24]

In contrast to later converts, Ntsikana continued to live among his own people. He adopted new beliefs and practices, such as the doctrine of salvation in Christ, and new practices, such as regular meetings of non-kinship groups for worship and prayer. He maintained cultural continuity by filling elements of the Xhosa tradition with Christian content, most notably in his Great Hymn, the first in Xhosa, which drew its symbols and images from everyday life.[25] The music of the Great Hymn was based on a Xhosa wedding song, now sung in a Christian context.[26] The words are in the form of a praise-poem, with the praise given to God as creator, defender, and protector, not to the ancestors or a ruler, and couched in the imagery and style of Xhosa oral poetry: shield of truth, stronghold of truth, forest of truth, creator of the stars, hunter for souls, the big blanket (see also p. 320). Makapela Noyi Balfour recalled attending Ntsikana's services as a boy:

> When he starts this song the people would stand or sit along the wall of the church [Ntsikana's hut] waiting for the Word of God . . . then he would start telling them what has befallen him which thing he hates, this thing called sin. And he would explain to them how they had sinned in their daily lives, point- ing at things in them which God does not like. He would then preach until others would find themselves sitting outside because it was so full . . .

His preaching brought the people to tears.[27]

Ntsikana's disciples remembered that he talked about Adam, Noah, David, the Lamb of God, and the coming of the Messiah. The last lines of the Great Hymn refer to Christ's sacrifice on the cross:

> Those hands of Thine, they are wounded.
> Those feet of Thine, they are wounded.
> Thy blood, why is it streaming?
> Thy blood, it was shed for us.
> This great price, have we called for it?[28]

Ntsikana's Christianity emphasized grace for gradual change within the histori- cal order. Although his following was small, it included those like Old Soga, coun- cillor to Ngqika, who held hereditary power. His pacifist teaching may well have owed much to the political circumstances of his patron, Ngqika, but his disciples paid a high price in persecution from blacks and whites alike. Prophecies attributed to Ntsikana warned Ngqika against warring with Ndlambe and against collabo- rating with the whites, and to accept the Book (Bible) but to beware of the button with no hole in it (money). His apocalyptic vision, clothed in African imagery, focused on the last days, the coming of God's Kingdom, and the expectation of a Messiah who would inaugurate a new era of peace:

> Then the end will come – the beginning of peace for which there has been no preconcerted council, or arrangement, of man. The reign of Broadbreast (Sifuba Sibanzi) will commence and continue in the lasting peace of the Son of Man.[29]

After his death in 1821, Ntsikana became a symbol of evolutionary change and non-violent Xhosa nationalism, while Nxele became a symbol of militant resistance grasped at again and again in times of crisis. Both prophets provided overarching African symbols of sacred power independent of white control.

"I Felt As If I Had Two Hearts": The First Permanent Missions

The coming of Joseph Williams to the Kat River in 1816 marked the beginnings of permanent missions among the Xhosa. Williams, like his Bethelsdorp colleague James Read, was a carpenter with modest education and fervent single-minded energy.[30] The nuclear mission enclave he established followed the Moravian model and was to be replicated and elaborated on throughout Xhosa territory: a square house, a church with a schoolroom, a dam and irrigation furrow, enclosed lands ploughed by oxen, and experimentation with new crops and vegetables. Williams's wife, in charge of the girls, taught them to sew dresses and weave bonnets from split rushes. A core group of Christian Khoikhoi families accompanied Williams from Bethelsdorp, providing a prototype for future mission planting through cellular division.[31] Dyani Tshatshu (Jan Tzatzoe), son of the Ntinde leader and a Khoikhoi mother, and trained as a carpenter and evangelist, acted as Williams's interpreter.[32] Like many missionaries of the first generation, Williams never mastered much Xhosa. This double translation of sermons, teaching, and parishioners' responses occurred in all pioneering mission work, making the re-interpretation of messages at every stage in the process inevitable.[33] Indigenous evangelists also made a powerful impact; Ngqika was amazed to hear Tshatshu pray in Xhosa: he had always assumed the Dutch language was part of the white's privileged access to their God. Williams was uncompromising in his condemnation of African customs like the use of red ochre for decorating the body, the paying of lobola (bridewealth), ancestor ritual, dancing, and the killing of suspected witches. He was equally rigorous in trying to introduce western clothing, the Western division of the day, respect for the Sabbath, and the "gospel of work." Christianity was equated with western civilization. Ngqika, complaining of missionary cultural interfence, said:

> You have your manner to wash and decorate yourselves on the Lord's day and I have mine the same in which I was born and that I shall follow. I have given over for a little to listen at your word but now I have done for if I adopt your law I must entirely overturn all my own and that I shall not do. I shall begin now to dance and praise my beast as much as I please and shall let all who see who is Lord of this land.[34]

Williams was in an invidious position as an unpaid government agent: in return for being allowed to run his mission he was required to give information about stolen cattle and the machinations of the Xhosa rulers. He could never satisfy all the government demands as a go-between, and Ngqika justifiably suspected his motives. Nevertheless, some LMS missionaries in the eastern Cape had become advocates for the rights of black people, incurring not only the ire of the colonial authorities but also the enmity of white settlers. The antagonism of both Boers and British soldiers was expressed in their refusal to provision Williams and in their castigation of the Xhosa as thieves and murderers destined for extinction: "Nothing but powder and ball could do to bring such savages to their senses. After they had sent a good lot of them to hell, then would be the time to go and preach salvation to them and not before."[35]

The displaced and dispossessed Kat River residents, mainly Khoisan, but including a few Xhosa, sought land and security from white exploitation on the mission stations but at the cost of severing their ties with kith and kin and also alienation from their indigenous spirituality. For the Xhosa, the uncompromising Christian evangelical demands for a change of heart clashed with their self-understanding as Africans who subscribed to a holistic worldview. Matshaya, a Zuurveld refugee, told of his own struggle in coming to terms with the cost of a personal Christian faith that was at risk from Ngqika's wrath:

> The Sabbath was made known, and we were called to attend the worship of

74

God. At the time I knew nothing of the Word, and was unwilling to enter the church. By listening to the Word a struggle commenced within me, and I felt as if I had two hearts, the one loving the Word and the other hating it. After I began to attend to the Word, I became sorry for my friends, who were living in the pleasures of the world and did not see the dangers to which they were exposed. I saw that it was desirable for me to go and remain constantly at the missionary's station.[36]

After Ntsikana's death, the Kat River Xhosa, in 1820, moved to the Chumie (Tyhume) mission at Gwali, founded by John Brownlee, another government missionary agent. The refugee Matshaya, among the first group to be baptized, became one of the first black evangelists. A women's group in Scotland raised funds for his support.

On the Closing Frontier

The coming of the 1820 Settlers from England caused the centre of gravity of the English colonial constituency to shift to the east. White appetite for land and labour grew voracious until the Cape Colony's boundary finally reached that of Natal in 1881. All Xhosa-speaking people were brought under subjugation through a three-pronged attack: military might, administrative measures, and the exploiting of indigenous rivalries. Missionary expansion kept pace with these developments. A more aggressive strategy propelled the various Protestant societies to open up new areas for the "peaceful occupation" of the country alongside traders. In doing so they became increasingly dependent on government protection.[37]

The LMS leader John Philip dominated much of this period in what the settlers deplored as "philanthropy gone mad."[38] The Wesleyan Methodist missionaries, by contrast, charged to work closely with the government and to keep out of politics, tried to minister to settlers, soldiers, and indigenous people at the same time, inevitably producing a conflict of interest. William Shaw, the only clergyman with the 1820 Settler party, envisaged an unbroken chain of "Christian fortresses" reaching to Natal.[39] Methodist personnel came largely from settler stock: Wesleyville was founded among the Gqunukhwebe in 1823, with five more stations following within seven years. At Mount Coke, Stephen Kay flew the British flag each Sabbath leaving the Ndlambe Xhosa in no doubt of the link between cross and crown.[40]

The Methodist emphasis on organization, with its system of classes and local preachers, mission-planting, and agriculture, was matched by the Scottish Presbyterians' enthusiasm for education. William Thomson and John Bennie joined Brownlee at Chumie in 1823 to begin work for the Glasgow Missionary Society (GMS), followed shortly by John Ross with a printing press. The Scots' mission mushroomed into Lovedale, Burnshill, and Pirie stations, with schools, linguistic work, translations, and publishing their priorities.[41] The Moravians made a short-lived entry into the Eastern Cape in 1823; and J.L. Döhne opened the way for the Berlin Society in 1836, becoming renowned as a Xhosa linguist.[42]

The majority of missionaries were artisans and tradesmen who made up for a lack of formal education with religious zeal and a determination to better themselves through disciplined application of the Protestant work ethic. Doctrinally, they were united in regarding the Scriptures as their sole authority for belief and practice, their missionary message focusing on the "grand doctrine of salvation": the fallen state of man, the wages of sin, and redemption from eternal damnation.[43] They commonly depicted the Xhosa as "a rude and warlike people" with barbaric customs and practices – "Gross darkness and superstition prevailed in the land," said a Scottish visitor – with the Xhosa denigrated as "worshippers of demons." The GMS missionary, Chalmers, who was "nearly overpowered" by African nudity, offered his supporters censored accounts of licentiousness.[44] But all of the missionaries demanded an inflexible standard of personal morality as the mores of European society defined them.

Mission strategy was to locate a station near a "chief," and African rulers had many pragmatic reasons for complying. Missionaries could be used as go-betweens with colonial authorities, as diplomatic agents, as political allies in intra-African disputes, as traders, as teachers of new technologies and literacy, as medical specialists, and as ritualists who could enhance rulers' prestige and give them new access to sacred power.

The early station residents were, mainly, the marginal people of black society: outcasts, misfits, political refugees, the physically disabled and aged, and those fleeing violence, or settler demands for indentured labour, or a ruler's wrath, or unwelcome marriages, or accusations of witchcraft.[45] Consequently, the people of the mission stations were varied in ethnicity, occupation, political allegiance, and association with the outside world.[46] Because people came largely for utilitarian reasons, converts were won with difficulty, though less so among the Khoikhoi than the Xhosa.

The mission station was the symbolic power base through which a reordering of time, space, structure, and content was achieved. At Chumie the bell was rung at sunrise for devotions; its ringing continued to punctuate the day, creating a discipline of time for the regimentation of physical labour. "Honest industry" was regarded as a moral virtue, idleness a besetting sin. The institution of the Sabbath, the working week, and the calendar year, contributed to a move from cyclical time, defined by seasonal agricultural pursuits, to linear time, with its eschatological sense of divine intervention in history and an end to the present order.

The Glasgow missionaries were proud that Chumie resembled a Scottish village. Houses on mission stations were built in "colonial style," square and with at least two rooms to allow marital privacy, and laid out along orderly streets. Round African huts were relegated to back rows. Doors and furniture were fashioned from local hardwood, but glass windows were brought from Grahamstown. Gardens were enclosed and burial grounds laid out. (Up to this time only Xhosa rulers had been buried, commoners' bodies being left in the open.) The mission house, church, and school formed the pivotal triad of the new Jerusalem, a circumscribing of sacred space, as alien to Xhosa culture as the events going on inside the buildings.[47]

Station residents were compelled to attend church regularly. Often services were enlivened with loud weeping, dancing, or uncontrollable laughter in unexpected response to the missionary message. On occasion war cries emptied the building in mid-service, as did the counter-attraction of oxen being raced by. Itinerant preaching allowed for a wider outreach, with "preaching places" located at cattle posts and homesteads scattered over vast distances. Here, too, missionaries struggled against great odds, including open hostility and acute discomfort: Shrewsbury recorded preaching in a hut while lying on his back, his eyes closed, to escape the pungent smoke.[48]

The missionaries' wives taught women to knit, sew gowns and shifts, and plait straw for hats. The missionaries regarded the adoption of Western clothing as residents' acceptance of "the thoughts and feelings of civilized life."[49] So, too, Christian names were symbols of new identities, biblical names or names of the august leaders of mission societies being favoured, among them, Joseph Butterworth, John Love, Richard Watson, Richard Balfour, John Barr.

Missionary religion centred on the written word, school being synonymous with church, and education a requisite for conversion. The Wesleyans used the Sunday School system. By 1825, "school people" were an identifiable class among the Xhosa.[50] Scottish missionaries led the way in reducing the Xhosa language to writing; with the arrival of the printing press, in 1823, they began to produce grammars, spelling and reading books, catechisms, hymn books and biblical texts. Other societies followed suit. Missionaries of various societies met together in 1830 to "fix the rules" of Xhosa orthography. But it was the discovery of the "euphonic concord" by the Methodist, William Boyce, that unlocked the key to Xhosa grammar: that a sentence was made up of a group of words thrown into alliterative form (the prefixes of the adjectives, verbs, and adverbs in a sentence are determined by the prefix of the subject noun). Mission teams from diverse societies published the Old and the New Testaments in Xhosa.[51]

On one level the missionary incursion into translation was bound to be significant, even integral, to colonizing African consciousness by co-opting Xhosa words to express European concepts of Christianity. This was the reverse of what Ntsikana had done when he had interpreted aspects of missionary belief and practice in terms of his Xhosa worldview, thus incarnating Christ in his African context as an African expression of Christianity. Methodist translators had difficulty in finding Xhosa equivalents for Christian terms like love, forgiveness, atonement, salvation, purity, and heaven. Xhosa words approximating their meaning were "purged of their base contents and allusions, and filled with a new and spiritual meaning."[52] But ultimately missionary use of the vernacular was a radical step forward in the inculturation of the gospel. Significantly, Ntsikana's disciples, as some of the first literate Xhosa, played key roles in providing appropriate and idiomatic expressions for biblical translations,[53] setting in motion a dialogue between faith and culture that not only came to be largely controlled by black Christians but also became an important part of their spiritual liberation from white domination.[54]

Tiyo Soga, son of Old Soga. was the first black South African to be ordained. He represented the United Presbyterian Church mission on the ecumenical team that began revising the Xhosa Bible in the late 1860s. Although Soga described his contribution as "Saxon Kafir," his Xhosa texts were lauded as pure and idiomatic, based on his wide knowledge of Xhosa custom, folklore, and history. During this same period Soga participated in the emergence of black consciousness among

THE TRANSPLANTING OF CHRISTIANITY

Xhosa Christians.[55]

Following their move to Chumie, although Ntsikana's disciples were soon absorbed into the missionary context, they continued to retain a unique identity as "the congregation of the God of Ntsikana" and regularly sang the Great Hymn in mission services. As the white presence became more oppressive, that hymn became associated with the survival of a wider Xhosa national identity. Ntsikana's disciples compared his vision in the cattle byre to Paul's conversion on the road to Damascus, providing a direct link with divinity outside missionary control. Before his death Ntsikana had commanded them to remain united in the same way as a ball of scrapings from a tanned hide, *ngenje mbumba yamanyama*, is cemented together when dry in an unbreakable mass. This phrase, interpreted as "unity is strength," became a powerful integrating force in the development of African consciousness. The test of a prophet is in offering a viable way forward, and this Ntsikana achieved for future generations.[56]

Colonizing the Sacred Power on the Closing Frontier

Economic expansion in the Colony had created pressure for more land. The Xhosa were suffering overcrowding aggravated by recurring drought, and internal divisions. The War of Hintsa (1834–35), or the Sixth Frontier War, was crucial in the closing of the frontier. After the war, intensified colonial penetration into Xhosa territory had profound economic implications.[57] With the increased use of money in the cattle trade with the Colony,[58] traders experienced a growing demand for British manufactured goods, such as spades, saddles, blankets, and clothing, while the introduction of new farming methods catalyzed an agricultural revolution.[59] The resulting transformation of the Xhosa economy led to a corresponding transformation of politics and ideologies.

Old Soga (c. 1790–1878), hereditary councillor to Ngqika and a leading disciple of Ntsikana, prospered by taking hold of the new world; he was the first Xhosa to plough, irrigate his lands, pay his followers wages, and participate in production for the colonial market. Yet he remained on the fringes of Gwali mission, attending Sunday services, but also holding daily worship in his homestead where only Ntsikana's hymns were sung. Soga refused to part with any of his wives and he consulted diviners and gave tacit support to his people's involvement in ancestor rituals. He continued also to function in Xhosa politics, taking a leading role in three consecutive wars; he was a transitional figure seeking to integrate an independent peasant movement with a new-found nationalism. Ntsikana provided the integrating symbols.[60]

From the late 1820s the Xhosa had absorbed a large influx of people, called Mfengu, refugees from the political upheavals. After Hintsa's war, the Methodist missionary, John Ayliff, led the Mfengu west to settle among and work for the colonists. This migration provoked some ethnic hostility between Xhosa and Mfengu, deepened in subsequent wars by Mfengu collaboration with the colonial forces. The War of the Axe (1847), or the Seventh Frontier War, saw a drastic erosion of Xhosa land and independence, with the area between the Keiskamma and Kei Rivers being proclaimed the crown colony of British Kaffraria. Xhosa rulers were placed in reserves under magistrates, and the Mfengu were settled on their

CHRISTIAN BEGINNINGS AMONG THE XHOSA

former land as a shield for the Colony. Conversions come slowly at first among the Mfengu; but their threefold vow, to be faithful to God and the British Crown, to support their missionaries, and to receive education, reflected a readiness to absorb Western culture, participate in the modern economy, and in due course to become involved in the political life of the Cape.[61]

With each successive frontier war, the animosity of Boers and British settlers towards black people gathered a momentum that drew the missionaries into dispute. In 1837–38 a large group of Boers left the Cape Colony, in part out of hostility to missionary influence on British colonial policy, but also in part to maintain "proper relations between master and servant" in accordance with their identification with the chosen people of the Old Testament. These emigrants, the Voortrekkers, viewed black people as "children of Ham and Canaanites," and the British as the oppressive Pharaoh. The God of the Boers, they believed, would lead them safely through the wilderness, beset by heathen, into the Promised Land.[62]

The antagonism of the English settlers to the Xhosa had been exacerbated by the war of 1834, begun, the English said, by "an unprovoked irruption of savage hordes, upon a peaceful European settlement." They made common cause with the Boers in vilifying the missionaries, who were considered to have alienated the British public from the settlers. A hostile frontier press kept the issue on the boil.[63]

Polarization between settlers and missionaries intensified cultural prejudice, hardening into racism as the settlers sought to establish power and control over black polities. In 1844, John Mitford Bowker articulated the prevailing opinion that Xhosa development in Christianity and civilization should be under settler tutelage. The missionaries, he maintained, had only encouraged them as "a nation of thieves,"[64] referring only to those missionaries who had been outspoken in defence of the rights of black people. The pivotal issue was the extent to which a particular missionary identified with or opposed the settlers' standpoint and Xhosa subjugation.

With the exception of significant converts, the large majority of Africans, at this stage, resisted the missionaries' religious message. Initial attempts by Xhosa rulers to assimilate missionaries as raindoctors were soon abandoned, as the struggle for the ownership of sacred symbols became entwined with military conquest.[65] While African socio-economic and political systems remained intact, mission agents could be ignored or their message rejected as "a killing word." An outbreak of smallpox was cited as evidence of a wrathful white God who killed sinners.[66] The failure of missionaries to incarnate the gospel as an African expression of Christianity also discouraged early conversions. Early converts were mainly peripheral to Xhosa society and could be and often were dismissed as "the mad people."[67]

As mission stations began to develop into rival power bases, and Xhosa rulers became consciously aware of an invasion of their sovereignty, resistance became more hostile. One ruler complained, "when my people become Christians they cease to be my people."[68] Indeed, Dyani Tshatshu and the Gqunukhwebe leader Kama were the only hereditary rulers to become Christians. Kama told a Grahamstown audience: "I am a black man, but I have a white heart; the Saviour who died for you died for me."[69] His decision put intolerable strain on his people.

By 1845 most rulers had become alienated from missionaries, not only because

79

of colonial wars but because of the polarizing effect of Western education. The formation of an educated black elite began in earnest in the 1840s. At the opening ceremony of the Lovedale Institution in 1841, the Rev. James Laing defended the principle of "allowing and enabling the educated native to drink at the English fountains of literature, science and practical godliness," these fountains to be dispersed through the vernacular.[70] The curriculum came to include mathematics, Greek, Latin, English, and geography, as well as religious instruction. Under William Govan, Lovedale offered a Christian and liberal education equal to any in Britain, enabling a select group of Africans to be integrated into colonial life. The undenominational seminary was open to black and white alike, although the two groups slept and ate separately. They were thus said to have been brought into a "true relationship with each other" without being "mixed up," as in an officers' mess.[71]

Girls were educated separately, the purpose being to raise them "from the degradation to which they were subjected"[72] – "slaving" in the fields, being "sold" as wives, and lacking a choice of whom to marry or whether to marry at all. Agricultural technology had changed the division of labour, but Western education provided new models of gender relationships, whether in a mission sewing school or in the more elaborate girls' department at Lovedale. The emphasis was on training African females as Christian wives and homemakers, and for domestic service in settler homes. Role models were provided by missionary wives, single woman missionaries,[73] and trained African women. The mission ideal of Christian family life made no concession to Xhosa culture.

> The clean native hut; the decently-clad inmates; the one wife, honoured and relieved of much of the heavy field drudgery; the husband taking his share of the labour of providing for the wants of the family; the children going each day to school, half naked at first, but ere long neatly dressed and learning to read, to the wonder and envy of many; the New Testament in Kafir Xhosa occupying the place of honour among the household goods, and read probably slowly but eagerly each day.[74]

In the late 1840s, Governor Sir Harry Smith combined his efforts to subvert the Xhosa rulers' influence with coercive measures to promote "Christian civilization," whether for labour recruitment, encouraging of peasant production for the market, or promoting a money economy. His policies had enthusiastic missionary support. The difficulty lay in gaining Xhosa cooperation. The Methodist, W.C. Holden, saw the need to create artificial wants, which would eventually take on the force of real wants and so inspire "constant labour" in realizing them.[75] A colleague, Stephen Kay, rejoiced that "Christianity laid the foundations of Commerce."[76] Missionary wives also helped introduce the market system: in 1832 the missionary's wife at Pirie taught "the fair principles of trade" not only by persuading people to barter their corn but to sell it by measure. At Kwelegha, Mrs. James Weir purchased corn from schoolchildren, in exchange for buttons, needles, thread and handkerchiefs, and then cooked it to feed them.[77]

Militant resistance became the only option for most Xhosa in response to increasingly intrusive settler demands. In a war precipitated by a severe drought in 1850, resistance was mobilised through the war doctor Mlanjeni. The conflict spread to Thembuland. Mlanjeni followed Nxele in appropriating Christian symbols as vehicles of power within his traditional worldview, and in developing the apocalyptic vision in which the ancestors rose to drive whites into the sea. Mlanjeni's followers believed that the missionaries' God was dead, but that their own still lived, manifested in the war doctor's miraculous powers. He was thought to possess the "secret of Eternity" and to be able to conquer death itself, with his medicines protecting the warriors from bullets. But even the support of Khoikhoi from the Kat River Settlement failed to stave off military defeat, and ever more punitive colonial measures followed, with dispossession of yet more Xhosa land, and legislation to coerce black people into the labour market.[78]

Sir George Grey, appointed the first non-military governor of the Cape Colony in 1854, and armed with a large grant from England, implemented a policy of pacification of the Xhosa through a long-term programme of socio-economic and cultural transformation. In their rush to support Grey, the missionaries risked mixing their religious aspirations with policies of colonial domination. Believing that mission education was too bookish, Grey made industrial education a cornerstone of his policy.[79] Xhosa response was minimal until the cattle-killing of 1856 to 1857 broke the rulers' power and shattered the infrastructure of their polities.

The cattle-killing was a call for supernatural aid. A lung-sickness epidemic had wiped out large numbers of Xhosa cattle. It prompted the revival of the Nxele tradition, and the development of a message of an inward-looking redemption, by a mass sacrifice of cattle and the destruction of crops. Communication with the ancestors was believed to be channelled through the visions of a teenage girl, articulated through her uncle, a councillor of Sarhili, the most influential ruler. Another young girl, Nonkosi, had similar visions. Apocalyptic expectations centred on a mass rising of the ancestors together with their sacrificed cattle from the bowels of the earth, with a return to a mythical time of peace, prosperity, and eternal life.

The prophets of the cattle-killing drew on Xhosa thought-patterns and beliefs, while using Christian symbols as carriers of sacred power.[80] The calls to rid the polluted earth of witchcraft, and to restore purity through ritual slaughtering of cattle, were religious resources used in the past to re-establish unity and recreate social harmony. The expectation of aid from Russia, at war with Great Britian in the Crimea, expanded the extended family to include other enemies of the British, supposedly also black. But the emphasis on an apocalyptic resurrection of the dead showed how millennial concepts in Christianity, linked with the second coming of Christ, were realigned with Xhosa concerns.

African cosmologies were short on speculation about life after death, the hereafter being seen as a mirror image of this world. The Christian concept of a final destiny, which incorporated everlasting happiness for the saved in the world to come, made a great impact,[81] except that non-Christian Xhosa people wished to have entry to heaven under their own control, not the missionaries', and to realize it now. The way to eternal life seemed to be as jealously guarded by the missionaries' rules and regulations as were their rights to control Xhosa entry into the colony through a pass system that sought to control the flow of those seeking work.

Xhosa accounts of the cattle-killing referred to two mysterious figures,

"Napakade" (the Eternal One) and "Sifuba-sibanzi" (the Broad-breasted One), who would inaugurate the rising of the ancestors. Through these figures God and Christ were appropriated by the Xhosa as powerful sacred symbols to support their struggle against the whites. God was now on their side. Both the Nxele and Ntsikana traditions claimed ownership of Sifuba-sibanzi, the Broad-breasted One, as a praise-name for Christ. The term could be either of Khoikhoi derivation or identified with a young chief in Xhosa folklore.[82] The expectations in time of conflict of a righteous warrior–saviour appealed as much to non-Christians as to Christians.[83]

Napakade, the Eternal One, had stronger Christian associations. The word *napakade* (meaning "ever," "of a very long time," or when used emphatically, "never"),[84] was by 1822, being used in the Lord's Prayer as *ngunapakade* to express the Christian concept of "for ever and ever," "everlasting," or "eternity."[85] Napakade may well have come into Xhosa usage during the cattle-killing through Mhlakaza. Known as William Goliath, Mhlakaza seems to have been, at one time, employed by Nathaniel Merriman, the Anglican archdeacon of Grahamstown; he was the first Xhosa to be confirmed as an Anglican. Scorned in his ambition to be "a Gospel Man" rather than a servant, he had left the Merrimans in 1853 to settle in Sarhili's country.[86] For him it was but a short step from creedal beliefs in "the resurrection of the body, and the life everlasting" to claiming eternal happiness here and now, when the need was so great, rather than waiting for the afterlife. Napakade became a new praise-name for God; with his son, Sifuba-sibanzi, he would lead the ancestors back into the world. To bring this about, the "believers" in the cattle-killing had only to follow the prophets' instructions.[87]

But the hoped-for resurrection of the ancestors failed, and thousands died of famine. Xhosa society disintegrated almost overnight. Destitute parents had little choice but to hand over their children to missionaries' care, a consequence Bishop Gray regarded as "God's providential dealings," a sentiment shared by Sir George Grey.[88] Independent Xhosaland was dead.[89] White colonization of the Xhosa culture and worldview now seemed irreversible.

Liberating African Symbols: Imperialism and Independency on the Closed Frontier

Whites in general – frontier officials, settlers, traders, missionaries, and labour recruiting agents – all had stakes in colonial expansion. Militant African resistance in the late 1870s and early 1880s had failed to stem the white advance. By 1894, the annexation of the remaining independent Xhosa polities in the Transkei was completed, when Pondoland was brought under colonial rule.

In this High Imperial era, from 1860 to 1910, missionary involvement in the process of conquest and colonization was justified by the rationale of the "white man's burden," that is, a duty to rule black people for their own good. Missionary activity did result in the emergence of a small Western-educated African elite, but in this heyday of Social Darwinism, evolutionary thinking arising from the natural sciences reinforced convictions of racial superiority. The concept of white "guardianship" influenced missionary as well as imperial political and social thinking. The ideal of an independent African church would take time to mature.[90]

From the late 1860s, missionary educational policy shifted from an elitist

Christian liberal ideal – a policy intended to widen opportunities for a black elite in colonial society that was later undermined by political pressures – toward a more practical "industrial" education for the masses. At Lovedale, with a change in direction brought about by James Stewart in 1870, only theological students continued with classics and mathematics.[91] Other African institutions, like Healdtown, the Grahamstown Kafir Institution, and Zonnebloem College in Cape Town, followed suit.

At the same time, some of the educated black elite sought to recover African symbols and integrate them into a faith both African and Christian. Tiyo Soga (1829–71), the first ordained black minister, epitomized the "ambiguities of dependence" of the "new African."[92] Educated at Lovedale and in Scotland at the Glasgow Free Church Seminary, he established the Mgwali mission for the United Presbyterian Church of Scotland (which had already incorporated the African section of the Glasgow Missionary Society) among his own Ngqika Xhosa in 1857. He married Janet Burnside, a Scotswoman. Soga's composition of Xhosa hymns, and secular and religious translations into Xhosa remained largely within the Western mould,[93] but his writing in the Xhosa press, and his lead in collecting Xhosa folk-lore and history, reflected a growing cultural nationalism together with a wider consciousness of African culture that owed much to Ntsikana's legacy.[94] In addition to the publication of Ntsikana's Great Hymn in the first hymn books, vernacular accounts of his life appeared in mission publications. For Ntsikana's disciples and descendants, his symbolic value as the father of African Christianity became increasingly important as the century progressed. Soga gathered Ntsikana's followers together at Mgwali, and the singing of Ntsikana's Great Hymn became an emotive symbol of cultural nationalism.[95] In addition, by drawing on oral sources to augment the written Ntsikana tradition, Ntsikana's followers reappropriated his story as a living legend to support their nationalist aspirations as African Christians.[96] With the publication of a secular Xhosa newspaper in the 1860s, Soga, William Kobe Ntsikana, and others formulated a black consciousness that flowered much later in African political mobilization.[97]

According to Wallace Mills, the mass conversions of the Taylor Revival in 1866, coming in the wake of the cattle-killing, represented a move from primary to secondary forms of resistance to colonialism.[98] The revival began with a Californian Methodist evangelist, William Taylor, but Charles Pamla, his Xhosa Methodist interpreter, made the powerful symbols of revival accessible to his countrymen through African imagery. The ecstasy and unleashed emotion of the revival provided tangible evidence that new sources of power were available. Its postmillennialism, stressing the salvation of the world before the second coming of Christ, supported the optimistic view that black Christians who trained as clergy and lay leaders, could advance within a "Christian civilization," and win acceptance in colonial society.[99] Adopting the moral rigour of the temperance movement, the converts sought to progress along "the narrow way" to eternal life as understood in Western theology. Still, a renewed attack on Xhosa customs was a logical corollary.

Western music and sport became part of the aura of respectability of a middle-class African identity. Church choirs depended on organ or harmonium accompaniments in competitive renderings of the Hallelujah chorus; brass bands beat out mission hymns in Western rhythms; concert recitals were offered by black Victorians on concert platforms; liquor-free tea meetings provided sober Saturday night socializing.[100] John Knox Bokwe's transcription of Ntsikana's Great Hymn in tonic sol-fa notation, and its adaptation to Afro-Western *makwaya* (choir) style singing, preserved African symbols in a more culturally acceptable contemporary form (see p. 323).[101] Debating societies flourished as an acceptable medium for expressing conflicting opinions, as did the right of some Africans to vote at the ballot box,[102] and the functioning of a black press.[103] Cricket, hunting, and horseracing offered sporting opportunites for Africans who aspired to British middle-class values.[104] In 1870 at a "friendly" cricket match hosted by the Queenstown Club for a racially mixed team from St. Mark's Anglican mission in Emigrant Thembuland, a local reporter noted that although the visitors were trounced, the match was played in "fine spirit": "there was no temper shown, no impatience, no complaints on the part of any one; every one behaved himself as a gentleman." He deplored the "abominable prejudice" of some "supposedly intelligent" spectators who had spoken as though "the Europeans were demeaning themselves in playing such a game." The African players were "far removed from the raw Kafirs, in fact they are men who, as far as book learning goes, are far better educated than many of their opponents. Several of them have been to England, and others have lived in Cape Town."[105]

Bundy has documented the role of mission stations as "foci of change" in the Transkeian territories, with Methodists in the lead and Mfengu peasant communities, newly settled on land confiscated from the Xhosa, targeted in fostering class formation.[106] Individual land tenure, improved farming methods, new cereal crops, and a flourishing wool trade expanded economic growth among the "progressive" Mfengu. Missionaries attended Mfengu Agricultural Society meetings and offered prizes at livestock shows.[107] For independent African farmers accumulation of wealth became a means of mobilizing political influence and power; this, in turn, deepened ethnic cleavages and class differences between "school people" and "red people," who remained rooted in their African worldview. The colonial policy of "divide and rule" achieved its aim with the annexation of the last independent chiefdoms in the 1880s.

The church was a significant conduit of upward mobility in class formation, with African clergy and laymen, such as John Tengo Jabavu, Elijah Makiwane, John Knox Bokwe, Pambani Mzimba, Peter Masiza, Boyce Mama, Nathaniel Mhala, and Isaac Wauchope, key figures in leading the educated elite.[108] In contrast, with few exceptions, Western-educated black women had only shadowy roles in what remained a male-dominated society. A growing number became teachers, with mission residents forming powerful associations for mutual support as mothers, and for evangelizing. In 1906, Cecilia Makiwane, a Lovedale graduate, became the first qualified African nurse, after receiving training at Victoria Hospital, Fort Hare, identical to that of white nurses.[109]

The story of Emma, eldest daughter of the Rharhabe leader, Sandile, is a good example of how the ideological marriage of church and empire could come close to destroying its own products.[110] From 1858 to 1863 Emma was educated at

Zonnebloem College, an African school for the children of African chiefs in Cape Town. When her father negotiated a marriage for a bridewealth of sixty head of cattle, Bishop Gray claimed for her the rights of a British subject. There was much relief when a match was negotiated on behalf of Qeya (Ngangelizwe), newly installed head of the Thembu, who had attended school and shown interest in Christianity. The proposed alliance thus had both political and religious significance. The couple met and "fell in love." Governor Wodehouse gave the match his blessing, and the church made plans for the wedding. But the Thembu would not agree to a monogamous marriage. Emma was whisked away to become infant teacher at the Anglican mission school in Grahamstown. Two years later she left, having been "ruined by a man of Colour." She became the senior wife of Stokwe Ndlela, a minor Mqwathi leader in Emigrant Thembuland. Later she went back "to the red clay": to wearing Xhosa dress, using red ochre, and participating in ancestor rituals. She used her Western education primarily in writing letters for her husband.

Methodism gave rise to some of the first women's prayer unions at the turn of the century, the fruit of revivalist preaching. "Purity lodges" were set up on mission stations, with Christian African women, the model of Victorian respectability, banding together to visit "heathen" homesteads to conduct services lasting sometimes through the night and over a number of days. These women evolved a spirituality uniquely their own, becoming strongly bonded as Methodist church women. The singing was enthusiastic, the prayers fervent, and the expression of emotion high. They visited the sick and bereaved; they urged teetotalism, refused to make beer, and discouraged polygamy and other African customs.[111] Anglican women, too, were active in many similar ways in parts of the Transkei, forming the Mothers' Union at St. Cuthbert's in 1903 (see also chap. 15).[112]

A reordering of African society accompanied a dramatic rise in conversions. The first generation of Christians, needing to replace a sense of belonging that had been supplanted or lost, became as fiercely loyal to their new denominations as they had been to their clans. According to Tiyo Soga, "Our people declare they would go a distance to drink the milk of the word out of the milk sack from which they had been accustomed to drink it, and if they could not get it from that, then they would take the milk that was likest that of their own cherished milk sack."[113] But, for some converts, national identity remained paramount. In 1877, fighting, which began in Transkei between Mfengu and Gcaleka, escalated into war with the Cape Colony. Dukwana, a son of Ntsikana and a leader of the Scottish mission people for nearly fifty years, scandalized white society by leaving Mgwali to fight on Sandile's side. The colonists blamed his defection on missionaries having "made too much of the blacks."[114] Dukwana was not only the first elder and first printer at Chumie, but an authority on Xhosa lore and custom and a renowned orator. In successive earlier wars, while he remained overtly neutral he had relayed messages to Sandile. For him the Christian gospel became part of the Xhosa struggle for liberation. With Sandile in the bush he held regular prayer meetings, where his followers sang Ntsikana's Great Hymn and the twenty-third psalm.[115] Long critical of colonial seizure of Xhosa land,[116] he said: "I am not fighting civilization or Christianity, they have brought me great benefits: and most of all they have taught me how I may be saved. But I am fighting against the English who have robbed us of our country, and are destroying us as people."[117]

White settlers' hostility to education of Africans, which, they said, made "many of the natives restless and ambitious," intensified in the 1880s.[118] Settlers had simply wanted mission education to produce workers. Lovedale responded that it had trained constables, telegraph messengers, teachers, evangelists, interpreters, printers, and blacksmiths. But blacks' competition with white artisans was now undermining the force of this practical argument from the colonists' point of view.[119]

The Cape school people reached their zenith politically and economically in the last three decades of the nineteenth century.[120] By the 1890s, however, the African "modernizers" were finding it increasingly difficult to realise their goal of equal social, economic, and political opportunities within the colonial system. They wanted to acquire all the benefits of whites while preserving their cultural and territorial integrity. A new political assertiveness, part of the wider process of African mobilization from the 1880s on, was apparent in the emergence of new political organizations, in a rise in electoral interest, and in an increasing criticism of the role of the church and education. Xhosa literature of the time reflects the tension between Christian teaching and Xhosa folklore, history, and traditions that the "modernizers" were assiduously collecting.[121]

A growing nationalism was evident in the new black political movements, beginning with the Native Educational Association in 1879.[122] Political groupings developed largely along ethnic lines, for example, the "Association for the Advancement of the Ngqika" at Kentani in Transkei,[123] and the Fingo Association at Peddie in the Ciskei,[124] founded in 1885. Both Xhosa and Mfengu sought to incorporate religious symbols into what became competing civil religions.

In the years leading up to the Unification of South Africa in 1910, the Mfengu lead among the school people was challenged by a rising group of young Xhosa politicians. Ethnic divisions in African elitist politics took shape in support for rival political parties backed by rival African-run newspapers, although these differences were never absolute.[125] In 1907, the Mfengu instituted an annual Fingo Emancipation Day commemoration; the milkwood tree near Peddie, where they had made their three-fold vow, became their shrine. The Xhosa responded two years later with a rival celebration honouring Ntsikana that became the Saint Ntsikana Memorial Association (SNMA). While still firmly committed to "progress" through Christian education, the SNMA sought to mobilize symbols of Xhosa cultural nationalism by recovering past customs and traditions. They wore national dress at celebrations and used the Great Hymn as their anthem. Ntsikana provided an authoritative symbol to legitimate their movement: "the blessing of God for the Xhosa nation."[126]

A shift ocurred from denominations inherited from the West to ethnicities defined by Africans, all within an essentially non-violent tradition of evolutionary change. No sooner were the two Mfengu and Xhosa organizations under way than the threat to African political rights, embodied in the draft constitution of Union, demanded a wider African nationalism in response. SNMA office holders held executive posts simultaneously in successive national bodies – the South African Native Convention (1909) and the South African Native National Congress

(1912), which later became the African National Congress.[127] They saw Christianity as an integrating force in developing a supra-ethnic African nationalism. Ntsikana became a saint for all Africans.

White mission leadership was greatly alarmed by the rising politicization and religious independency of the educated black elite, and its potential threat to mission imperialism. In 1897 Stewart denounced the new Ethiopian Church as a "Cave of Adullam."[128] Like the early political movements, Ethiopianism in the eastern Cape had an ethnic orientation. Nehemiah Tile, a member of a chiefly family, had led the first breakaway, in 1883, from the Methodist mission church in Thembuland, in an effort to achieve political and religious liberation from colonial domination. The national Thembu church he established translated Thembu cultural symbols into Christianity[129] and created a model of black-led Christian participation in African nationalist politics.

In 1898, the Rev. Pambani Mzimba, influenced by the formation of an Ethiopian church in the Transvaal, led the first secession from the Free Church of Scotland, taking his large, and principally Mfengu, Lovedale following with him to form the Presbyterian Church of Africa.[130] In 1900 the Rev. James Mata Dwane, son of an Ntinde ruler, a Methodist, after playing a leading role in various Ethiopian churches, formed his own Order of Ethiopia, primarily comprising Xhosa, within the Anglican Church.[131] Another small Xhosa breakaway from the Free Church, in 1906, was headed by Burnet Gaba, great-grandson of Ntsikana and founder of the Ntsikana Memorial Church at Pirie in 1911.[132]

The Western form of the institutional church remained foreign to Xhosa. Denominational loyalty among them was strong, reminiscent more of competition between African rulers than based on theological preference. When racial divisions within the church became increasingly oppressive, Xhosa had no difficulty in slipping the bonds of white-dominated mission loyalties and re-forming around independent black leadership.

Some Xhosa remained rooted in ancestor religion and continued to adhere to pre-colonial symbols. Their strategy of resistance to white oppression was to remain protected from colonial society within their closeknit communities. Over the years, urbanization, migrant labour patterns, and mission education gradually fed new symbols into their religious practices as well; but when, somewhat later, their Christian brethren began to reappropriate symbols from their African past, this group provided a living model of Xhosa life.

Throughout the nineteenth century, the religious interplay between Xhosa and missionary conceptions was intimately connected to political and socio-economic developments in the region. But whereas the Xhosa became increasingly oppressed by white domination in their physical lives, spiritually they found a measure of liberation in that they were inspired to create new ways of expressing their Christian faith that resonated with the totality of their African experience.

Religion has been defined as the "cultural process of stealing back and forth sacred symbols," with such symbols being seen to function as "vehicles of power to be appropriated, owned and operated."[133] In the battle for sacred power on the Xhosa–Cape frontier, Xhosa initiatives followed either Nxele or Ntsikana in appropriating Christian symbols. By the end of the century, Nxele's tradition of militant resistance had manifestly failed to achieve its political objectives. But even the forming of an independent African consciousness in the Ntsikana mould was flawed, since the educated black elite failed to exchange the triumphalistic Christology of their conquerors for a liberating Christology in which Christ is seen to identify with the poor and the oppressed.

Ex-slaves celebrate their freedom, 1838: the moment when many turned to Christianity

5

Kingdoms of This World and the Next: Christian Beginnings among Zulu and Swazi

NORMAN ETHERINGTON

A Dancing King and a Naval Captain: First Conversations about Christianity

Captain Allen Gardiner, recently retired from the Royal Navy, had reason to tread carefully on his solitary journey to the Zulu kingdom in 1835. Faku, paramount ruler of the neighbouring Mpondo people, had warned that the Zulu were "an angry people" who would kill Gardiner if he entered their country.[1] He was not to be put off. Representing no society or church organization, backed by no government, like a latter-day St. Patrick, Gardiner simply intended to meet the Zulu king, Dingane, and win him to Christ. The king turned out to be no "angry" tyrant. Nor were his people ready to kill. Everywhere Gardiner found laughter, music, poetry, and dance. Dingane was a connoisseur of the arts: he had designed the costumes of the women he led into the dancing ring "with much natural grace" and with "no ordinary ease and agility." The songs chanted were "chiefly of his own composition," for he had "a good ear and a correct taste."

"Are we not," the king asked Captain Gardiner, "a merry people? What black nations can vie with us? Who among them can dress as we do?" He took a keen interest in European fashion, from Gardiner's dress uniform to the sweeping gowns of the women he saw in pictures walking arm in arm with gentlemen of the English court. "What?" he exclaimed, "is this how you walk with women in your country?" He inspected watches, beads, an eye-glass, the naval officer's ceremonial sword, a pair of scissors. The king turned a demonstration of literacy into a contest for the women of his court who would "not believe that you can do the things that are written down, unless you were present when the directions were noted – but I tell them you can." Entering into the fun, Gardiner stood outside the fence while his interpreter wrote in pencil the names of several concealed objects, then Gardiner triumphantly plucked them from their hiding places, as Dingane roared with laughter.

Gardiner told the king that "the Book" he carried with him contained the words that had made the Britons "a great people." The Zulu were also a great people but he wished "them to know the words that they might become greater." Dingane replied suspiciously that he must consult his advisers. Gardiner dicovered that Jacob, an African interpreter who accompanied the first white settler to the court of Dingane's predecessor, had warned the Zulu court "that a white man, assuming the character of a teacher or missionary, would arrive among them, and obtain permission to build a house; that, shortly after, he would be joined by one or two more white men; and in the course of time, an army would enter his country, which would subvert his government, and, eventually, the white people would rule in his stead."

Several European houses already stood on the shore of the natural harbour at Port Natal, and white settlers had already asked for "a Missionary Establishment at Natal, whose object would be to inculcate industry and religion." How could Gardiner plant a church among the settlers without compromising his great object of evangelizing the kingdom? Relations between the Zulu king and the settlement were not good. Refugees from the kingdom whom Dingane regarded as dangerous criminals had gathered around the settlement.

Gardiner decided to undertake a perilous commission . He would escort a party of recent refugees back to Dingane (where they faced certain death) and secure a treaty binding the white settlers to return future refugees in return for the king's promise not to attack the port. So delighted was Dingane with this arrangement that he led the court in songs to mark the occasion, hailing Gardiner as a "great chief" who, as the king's headman at Port Natal, would be welcome to start a mission among the refugees there. Teaching at his court might follow.

Gardiner struck up theological conversations whenever opportunities arose. The Zulus, who believed in a creator of the universe, thought the creator took little interest in the daily affairs of the world, beyond commanding that "lamentations should be made over the dead." They had no priests, no idols, no castes. "Where is God?" they asked. "How did he give his Word? Who will be judged at the last day? What nations will appear? Will mine be there? Shall I live for ever if I learn his Word?" Among the most metaphysically curious people Gardiner met were some visitors from the neighbouring Swazi kingdom. Some day they, too, he said, should receive "the glad tidings of salvation." He saw fewer obstacles to Christianity among the Zulu than in most other dark places on earth: they had prior knowledge of God, but also no priests, idols, or castes.

Gardiner converted no one, and Zulu authorities met his teaching with suspicion or indifference, though they were interested in the technological and diplomatic services missionaries could provide. Missionaries could reach refugees, criminals, and outcasts more readily than the Zulu court, yet to identify with them imperilled the dream of mass conversions. The white settlers at Port Natal posed another difficulty. Expecting churches to minister to them as well as to the heathen, they assumed that, in confrontations with Zulu authority, the missionaries would come to their side. Yet any missionary who did so ran the risk of fulfilling the translator Jacob's prophecy: first the missionary, then the conquest. Meanwhile, other potential converts lived beyond the reach of Zulu power, especially the Mpondo and Swazi.

Missionary Visions and Strategies

As Gardiner hurried back to England in 1836 to recruit more evangelists he "had the pleasure of meeting Dr. Adams, and Messrs. Grout and Champion," the advance guard of the American Board of Commissioners for Foreign Missions, a Boston-based organization of Presbyterians and Congregationalists.[2] A fellow Congregationalist and superintendent of the London Missionary Society in South Africa, John Philip, had commended the Zulu and Ndebele nations to the American Board.

The first American missionaries mixed enthusiasm for foreign evangelism with a keen sense of personal sin. Silas McKinney, for one, confessed he had until late-ly been "exceedingly hardened in sin and impenetrable to the truth as a rock of adamant."[3] Hyman Wilder, for another, declared his beliefs "in the *total* and *native* depravity of every human being and that they all justly desire eternal death."[4] The Board approached its work with a Calvinist sense of God's Providence. Though Christ would not come again till the word had been preached to all the world, the work of conversion must come in God's own time. When Board Secretary Rufus Anderson heard that thousands of heathen had perished in a Zulu civil war, he said their deaths confirmed that they "would not have believed had the gospel been sent to them."[5]

Tempering this dark predestinationist thought was the fiery spirit of frontier revivalism. Several of the early American Board missionaries to South Africa came from the so-called "burnt-over districts" of western New York and Ohio, where the revivalist Charles G. Finney had shown that God's grace descending upon the elect could quickly transform multitudes of sinners. American Board missionaries in Hawaii believed they had proved that what had happened among frontier farm-ers could happen among the "naked heathen." The Board hoped that entire Christian nations would be raised up not only to personal salvation but also to independence and freedom. When its first missionaries reached Natal, the Rev. Hohn Codman told the annual meeting of the Board that its foreign missions par-alleled the secular mission of the United States itself:

> How can we better testify our appreciation of her free institutions, than by lab-ouring to plant them in other lands? For where the Gospel goes in its purity and power, there will follow in its train the blessings of civilization, liberty and good government. And, although it will not be the object of the devoted missionary to interfere, in any way, with civil government ... coming himself from a land of freedom, he will naturally spread around him an atmosphere of liberty.[6]

No sooner had the Americans set up fledgling missions in Natal than these doc-trines were put to the test. When the tide of white migration known as the Great Trek swept across the Highveld and down into Natal, the Americans, in appre-hension, recalled the impact of frontiersmen upon Native American societies. Were the Nguni of Natal and Zululand destined to suffer the fate? Back in Boston, the secretary of the Board lamented that "the inevitable tendency of a white colony among a black people, is *to extend*."[7] Daniel Lindley in Natal warned, at a time when whites in Natal still numbered only hundreds, that "this is already a white man's country."[8]

Had Zululand not remained independent under Dingane's successor, Mpande, the mission might have been closed because of the dim prospects of success in a land overrun by white settlers. While Lindley undertook to serve the Voortrekkers as *predikant* (minister), thus inaugurating the first settler church in Natal, his col-league Aldin Grout pursued the dream of converting the Zulu nation *en masse*, an enterprise which soon foundered, the king insisting (as with Gardiner earlier) that refugees from his authority should not be allowed to huddle together under the white man's protection. For Grout the issue was as simple as republican institutions and liberty; he could not turn away any people who gathered round him. For

Mpande the issue was sovereignty.

> The missionary came to me, and I welcomed him, and allowed him to select a location where he pleased. He built there. I told the people to go to meeting and attend to his instructions. But the people soon began to call themselves the people of the missionary, and refused to obey me ... The missionary should have told the people in the beginning that he could not be their captain. I have been obliged to kill several of those people, and much mischief has resulted from the mission established there.[9]

Grout had no choice but to withdraw, leaving behind a lasting impression that the missionaries' aim was to subvert the state.

Meanwhile, sovereignty had shifted in Natal as the British moved, after 1842, to extinguish the Voortrekker republics. As the only considerable missionary body on the spot, the American Zulu Mission (as it now called itself) was well placed. Backing up Theophilus Shepstone, Britain's newly appointed diplomatic agent, in his contention that large regions of Natal should be set aside for the African population, the Americans staked out key positions for themselves along the coast. They pursued a scaled-down version of their original vision, no longer anticipating raising up independent African Christian nations but still hoping to raise up self-governing, self-supporting African Congregational communities. For a few decades, they pursued this ambition, untroubled by outside pressures. They left others to batter at the door of the Zulu kingdom.

And others came, in a torrent of Christian missionary enterprise. Zululand was readily accessible by sea and lacked the deadly fevers that made other parts of Africa perilous. So long as the monarchy survived, missionaries might dream – as Gardiner and Grout had dreamed – of winning the king to God, and with the king, his people. Next to try was Hans Schreuder of the Norwegian Lutheran church, who arrived in South Africa in 1844, fired with vision and armed with great talents and great weaknesses. Grout recognized Schreuder's intellectual brilliance and facility in the Zulu tongue. But his personal appearance was "bad, at least not good, and when he has been living alone he has been more filthy in his person and apparel than a native." Schreuder, said Grout, was "a very passionate man" with an "iron will."[10]

For years Schreuder waited his chance on the Natal side of the Tugela River. In 1851 it came when Mpande sent for medicine for an illness. The king recovered and, during the next decade, Schreuder consolidated his position as adviser and physician, gradually planting Norwegian mission stations throughout the kingdom. No friend to the British Empire, he tried his best to avoid the diplomatic role that had seen Gardiner torn between the Zulu and the settlers. Throughout the great Zulu civil war of 1856, he sent reports to the government of Natal, but begged to "be excluded from all further connections with the political affairs between the two countries."[11] In 1872–73 his "iron will" split the Norwegian missionary society and he hived off in his own "Norske Misjonsselskap ved Schreuder."[12] Like other Norwegians, Schreuder connived with Natal officials against Cetshwayo from 1873, but did not wish to smash the kingdom, hoping until the very last minute that a negotiated peace with the monarchy under a British protectorate would provide fertile soil. He did not abandon his vision of an independent Christian Zululand until British armies invaded in 1879, whereas others had concluded that only the extinction of the Zulu state could open the way for Christ.[13]

Schreuder won few converts, but he did bring another Lutheran missionary society to Zululand. When Mpande, weakened by the civil war of 1856–57,[14] agreed to the founding of more new mission stations than Schreuder alone could supply, Schreuder invited the Hermannsburg Missionary Society, and later Swedish missionaries, who worked briefly with him prior to setting up their own stations (see pp. 177–78).

The Hermannsburgers, influenced by the romantic, chiliastic prophecies of a Hanoverian rural preacher, Louis Harms, brought a different kind of Lutheranism from that of the forward-looking Norwegians. Harms preached unorthodox and speculative sermons on the millennium and the relationship of church and state. According to Harms, the church in Europe was about to go into an eclipse which would continue until the Second Coming of Christ.[15] The church must secure a sanctuary in Africa to survive the approaching era of darkness. The sooner the work of winning the heathen was accomplished, the sooner the Second Coming. To implement the plan, his entire village of Hermannsburg enlisted in missionary work, intending, like the tightly knit communities of the Middle Ages, to devote their meagre resources entirely to the church. Harms planned to create an order of missionaries who would model their lives on those of the Christian missionaries who first carried the light to Saxony. Evangelists from Hermannsburg, accompanied by farmers and artisans, would plant self-sufficient communities in heathen lands.[16] The missionaries' lives would be communal; all would share equally in the fruits of their labour. The communes would serve a threefold purpose: provide a model of Christian community life for the heathen, function as supply posts for itinerant evangelists, and spawn new centres.

Backed by Hanover merchants, Harms fixed on East Africa as a mission field after reading of light-skinned Galla people living there. His vivid imagination saw them as descendants of Teutonic Vandals of classical times who had mated with the Ethiopian subjects of the biblical Queen Candace.[17]

In 1853, his ship *Kandaze* (Candace) made a spectacular entrance into Durban harbour with all the missionaries on deck, Luther's hymn *Ein Feste Burg Ist Unser Gott* blaring from trombones and trumpets.[18] A few months later, the *Kandaze* was back in Natal, its bold company defeated by East African climate, disease, and topography. As a staging post for a later assault, the mission established itself in Natal, in part because Harms laboured under the misconception that the Galla language was related to Zulu. A flourishing German settlement grew in east-central Natal. After Harms's death in 1865, East African dreams faded along with the more colourfully medieval aspects of the mission. Priestly celibacy was abandoned in favour of a scheme to marry male missionaries to hand-picked daughters from Hermannsburg. Communal living gave way to the conventional model of scattered mission stations run by married couples.[19] Self-support through village industry gave way to small-scale trading to African consumers. And, discouraged by the barren prospects for Christianity in the Zulu kingdom, the Hermannsburg missionaries were the first to withdraw to Natal in anticipation of an Anglo-Zulu war.

Another casualty was the mission launched by the Oblates of Mary Immaculate, a Catholic missionary society from southern France, established by Eugène de Mazenod, an aristocrat responding to the anti-clericalism of the French Revolution.[20] The rules drawn up for the Oblates were intended to repair the faults of the church under the *ancien régime*. Priests and lay brothers met regularly for sessions of self-criticism almost Methodist in intensity. They were exhorted to cherish "scorn for worldly honours, the abandonment of vanities ... distaste for riches, the mortification of the flesh and spirit ... and above all, the work of missions."[21] After their first choice of a mission field, French Algeria, proved unsatisfactory, the Oblates welcomed a call from the Vatican to begin work in southeast Africa.[22] Their first bishop arrived in Natal in 1852 to foster existing white Catholic communities and to launch new missions. Four years later he opened a mission at St. Michel, near Richmond, only to abandon the site after five years of struggle in the face of indifference from the local people and their chiefs. He went off to Lesotho in search of "a simpler, poorer people".[23]

The distrust of British imperial expansion shared by American, Norwegian, and Hermannsburg missions did not trouble others who had learn to work within the imperial framework elsewhere in South Africa. In 1847 Carl Posselt of the Berlin Missionary Society readily accepted an invitation from the Natal government after his work on the eastern Cape frontier was blasted by the "War of the Axe." The society joined the Americans in staking out desirable positions in the reserves. Seldom in the public eye, the Berliners skilfully managed their large land holdings so as to attract even more converts than the more favourably situated Americans.

So, too, Wesleyan missionaries arrived in Natal. Their leaders were a model of the advice given in William Arthur's *Tongues of Fire* (1856),[24] a popular tract that maintained that modern preachers needed no more book-learning than the fisherfolk and other disciples who followed Jesus.[25] The Methodist clergy in Natal included two storekeepers, two printers, a joiner, a moulder, an upholsterer, a roper, a wool stapler, and a manual labourer.[26] Ministers who gathered for the first eighteenth-century Methodist Conference in England had said the best method for spreading the gospel was "to go a little and a little farther" from established centres, so that "help would always be at hand."[27] In South Africa this strategy expressed itself in a plan to found a chain of stations along the coast from the Cape Colony, through Natal, all the way to Delagoa Bay.[28] In 1841 James Archbell planted the first operation at Durban and within a few years Methodist chapels had sprung up at all the principal centres of white settlement; from these centres Wesleyan preaching radiated into the African countryside. As the Natal Synod grew, it acquired supervision of the previously established Methodist stations among Faku's people in Pondoland. At the base of each Methodist "circuit" were "bands" and "classes" who met regularly to strengthen each other in faith and to collect money to support the clergy. Each quarter an ordained minister called on the members and sold tickets for class attendance. Special events helped to keep new members in a state of spiritual elation and restore flagging spirits. So did sessions of searching mutual criticism, "watch nights," and "love feasts," at their most intense creating a frenzy of spirituality. When William Taylor, the Methodist "street preacher of San Francisco," swept through South Africa in 1866, neighbours of Natal's Wesleyan congregation at Edendale suspected the minister had gone mad.[29] This vigorous programme of meeting and preaching was supported by Methodism's recruitment of lay indigenous preachers. As converts multiplied they spread a web of black evangelism over the landscape long before other denominations began to accept Africans into the Christian ministry.

Wesleyans were ambitious to preach in Swaziland but a mission to the Swazi launched in 1844 soon encountered problems similar to those that plagued the Zulu mission of American Aldin Grout.[30] Accused of allying himself to the Swazi king's enemies, the missionary James Allison scurried away to Natal, along with most of his flock. He hoped that the new station he founded at Indaleni would enable Swazis "like the Jews [to] keep up and preserve their national identity however widely they may be dispersed amongst strangers."[31] This they did when Methodism returned to Swaziland in 1881, led and supported by African Christians, somewhat to the dismay of white missionaries.[32] However, Allison defected with some of his converts to the Presbyterians, thus bringing another denominational player into southeast Africa.

While the Methodists were employing working men to found churches, the Church of England was sending missionaries from the top stratum of British society, who, under John W. Colenso, first Bishop of Natal, took an unashamedly imperial approach to evangelization. Contemplating British dominion in 1854, Colenso remarked how far it surpassed "the empire of ancient Rome in the days of its grandeur" and discerned in this vastness "God's Providence working to Christianise the world."[33] As "every English Christian" was, "in an especial sense, a Missionary," Colenso welcomed white settlers to Natal. The province wanted only "an addition of some 10,000 English people of the right stamp, to be one of the finest and productive in the whole world."[34] As the Queen's chief ecclesiastical representative in Natal, Colenso looked to the State as his natural partner in the work of evangelism, and the State rewarded him with extensive land grants. Natal's Secretary for Native Affairs, Theophilus Shepstone, abandoned the Methodism of his missionary father and assumed a prominent position among Colenso's lay supporters.

Colenso looked forward to founding government-funded industrial schools among all "the most important tribes."[35] At his own station he built a boarding school, Ekukanyeni, where sons of chiefs should learn Christian leadership along with grammar: "a Public School where the sons of chiefs would conduct themselves as any young nobleman would at Eton or Harrow."[36] Africans would, he observed in 1856, "make excellent Cricketers, and even now pitch and catch a light ball, as if they had been used to it all their lives."[37] Boys who defied their teachers were to be flogged by the bishop, without regard to their rank or parentage.[38]

A prize-winning scholar at Cambridge and author of one of Britain's most widely used mathematics textbooks, Colenso also proved to be a gifted linguist. He was helped in his Zulu studies, for a time, by W.H.I. Bleek, the German philologist who first called attention to the Bantu language group.[39] His first archdeacon, Charles Mackenzie, was a well-connected young man of independent means who went on to be first bishop of the Universities' Mission to Central Africa. Henry Callaway gave up a society medical practice in London to join Colenso in Natal.[40] Robert

Robertson, a recruit from the Scottish Episcopal Church, in 1859 launched the first Anglican missions in the Zulu kingdom.

Such resources should have given Church of England missions a decisive edge over other denominations in Natal. However, within a few years of Colenso's arrival, the Anglicans were hopelessly embroiled in internecine controversies whose reverberations reached right round the world.

Polygamy, Prelacy, and the Pentateuch

Colenso, like Gardiner, had seen parallels in Zulu culture to many elements of Christian belief and practice. The Zulu acknowledged a High God, whose name, *Unkulunkulu*, Colenso promptly incorporated into his own services.[41] Unlike missionaries of other denominations who emphasized the inherent depravity of all unconverted peoples, he insisted that a strong ethical foundation underpinned existing African relationships. Like his English theological exemplar, F.D. Maurice, who sought to build Christian ethics upon the family, he advocated conversion of family units rather than of individuals,[42] carrying this to its logical extreme of accepting polygamists as converts. A pamphlet war broke out with American missionaries, who were already shocked by Colenso's denial that sinners would suffer eternal punishment in hell.[43]

Colenso was immensely stimulated by theological discussion at his mission with Africans who brought a fresh perspective to old problems.[44] He treated two employees William Ngidi and Magema M. Fuze as collaborators, acknowledging their contributions to his translation of works into Zulu and to a series of groundbreaking treatises echoing the higher criticism of the Bible represented by Ernst Renan in France and the contributors to *Essays and Reviews* in England. A spirited commentary on St. Paul's Epistle to the Romans in 1861, followed by two books on the Pentateuch that denied Moses' authorship of the first five books of the Bible, and even worse, their literal truth, was bound to cause a stir, especially in the High Church party, whose leader, Dean James Green, had accused him of heresy as early as 1857, and now defied his authority.[45] On Colenso's victory, Dean Green barricaded himself in the Pietermaritzburg cathedral and, when Colenso's party battered down the door, flooded the building. Green fled, spiriting away the baptismal register. In the aftermath of the controversy, the governance of the worldwide Anglican communion outside the British Isles was revolutionized; no longer would the State be permitted to constitute bishops on its own authority. Meanwhile, the Church in Natal split into two factions, each headed by its own bishop. Cut off from financial support from the Society for the Propagation of the Gospel, Colenso might have had to fight on alone but for the help of his old ally, Shepstone, and the resources of the Native Affairs Department. Taking advantage of government grants for mission schools, he paid clergy who taught black children for a few hours a week and kept up Sunday services for white parishioners.[46] He suggested to Shepstone in 1869 that further revenue could be raised by collecting rent from Africans living on mission reserve lands in his care, and leasing reserve African lands to whites.[47] By such subterfuges Colenso managed to command the attention of enthusiastic white congregations, flattered to find themselves for a time at the centre of an international furore.

Ostracism and Capital Accumulation: The Rise of the Kholwa

The black population, in general, appears to have taken little interest in theological dramas. Surrounded by one of the world's densest concentrations of missionary talent and denominational diversity, most resisted conversion until the economic and political foundations of pre-colonial Nguni institutions began to crumble. Neither the friendly blandishments of Colenso nor the hell-fire preaching of the Americans and Wesleyans nor the medieval communalism of the Hermannsburg Lutherans proved specially effective. In the first five decades of evangelization material factors were far more important than spiritual ones in drawing adherents. Converts, or *kholwa* as they were called in Zulu, came in dribs and drabs rather than waves. By the time Cetshwayo succeeded his father Mpande as king in 1873, missionaries in ˙Zululand had little to show for three decades of evangelism. Norwegian church members numbered fewer than 300, most of them drawn from Natal.[48] Forty-three baptised Christians lived on Hermannsburg stations; five of these stations had no converts at all, and on others *kholwa* had been imported from Natal to serve as examples.[49] Anglican stations were more or less the same.[50]

Conditions in Zululand remained difficult for missionaries so long as the independent kingdom survived. After Grout's expulsion, African Christians were hemmed about by restrictions[51] since, from the moment they took up residence at a mission, they ceased to be Zulu citizens. Forbidden to *khonza* (give allegiance to the monarch), they lost the right to farm or hold land beyond the boundaries of the station.[52] Male converts could not serve as soldiers or maintain their regimental identification. To their old associates they were dead men or strangers.[53] Black neighbours addressed them with the sneering epithet whites applied to all Africans: Kaffirs.[54]

Beyond the southern boundary of Natal in independent Pondoland, restrictions on evangelism were less stringent but results not much more impressive. Methodists had the field to themselves until the 1870s. Faku, who lived on thirty years after Gardiner's visit, formed a special friendship with the missionary Thomas Jenkins, but remained steadfastly indifferent to his teaching.[55] Mqikela, Faku's son and successor, continued the policy of refusing to allow services more than a few miles away from the established stations – a severe restriction on the Wesleyan circuit preaching strategy.[56]

Within British Natal, chiefs lacked the power to enforce restrictions. Still, only two important chiefs showed more than a grudging tolerance for missionaries before the final decade of the nineteenth century: Mnini of the Thuli and Mqhawe of the Qadi.[57] Men and women of all social strata supported the general resistance. As a result, as the Anglican missionary Henry Callaway observed, "it is not the elite of Kafir society, which first gathers around a missionary; it is not even an average specimen of the natives."[58] Allen Gardiner had sacrificed the lives of refugees, hoping to win Dingane to his faith; his evangelical successors turned their backs on chiefs and tried to fill their churches with refugees.

Many who lived on mission stations had followed missionaries from previous postings in distant parts of South Africa; some had drifted into Natal as servants of Afrikaner farmers; not a few came on the run from their own people. Of a sample of 177 persons whose reasons for station residence were recorded by missionaries of all denominations between 1836 and 1885, 12 per cent were said to be attracted by religion, 26 per cent by prospects of employment, 15 per cent by the presence of relatives, and 14 per cent by a personal attachment to a missionary; 33 per cent were seeking refuge, including 3 per cent who had been accused of witchcraft and 10 per cent who wished to escape unpalatable marriages.[59] Of course, the more that mission stations appeared to be the haunts of misfits, aliens, and generally unsavoury characters, the less chance they had of attracting the problem-free, let alone the community leaders.

That black Christianity eventually broke out of this pattern of self-perpetuating isolation certainly owed something to external factors which were undermining the viability of pre-colonial economic and political structures. So, too, the *kholwa* themselves, despised and persecuted, found the resources on mission stations, most significantly land and education, to be powerful lures. As white settlers steadily cut back on Africans' capacity to hold or acquire land, Natal's many mission reserves and farms became appreciating assets. Missionary societies with land at their disposal won more adherents than those that did not, regardless of theology. Thus, the Berlin missionaries, who undertook a deliberate policy of buying land, succeeded where the land-poor Oblates of Mary Immaculate failed. When a second Catholic effort was launched by the Trappists in the 1880s, their ambitious land acquisition policy brought them large resident populations.[60] Later, as the *kholwa* became aware of opportunities for capital accumulation, land underpinned the prosperity of a rising Christian black middle class. The veteran American missionary, David Rood, penned a vivid description of the transition:

> They get the spirit of trade and speculation in their small ways. You will find them with bundles of the skins of the wild cat or monkey, or blankets which they have probably purchased on credit, travelling through the length and breadth of this country and even those bordering on it, bartering for hides, goats, sheep, young cattle, and then selling these to each other or to the white people. After a few years some will succeed in obtaining a few oxen and a cart or wagon, when they will engage in purchasing mealies and take to the towns for sale, or will draw sugar from the sugar estates to market, or perhaps transport merchandize [sic] from the Port to the upper districts, going sometimes as far as to the Dutch Republics or even to the Diamond fields or Goldfields five hundred miles distant.[61]

In time, some small traders became big traders. By 1864, for example, at the American station of Umvoti, where a sugar mill had been established, two members of the community calculated their personal net worth at more than 1,000 pounds.[62] Twelve years later at Ladysmith the Anglican mission was home for several residents with incomes exceeding 400 pounds per annum, about three times the salary of their missionary.[63] As incomes rose, *kholwa* invested in more land; forming themselves into syndicates, they often bid at public auctions all over the colony.[64] Men from Methodist Edendale accumulated vast holdings in central and northern Natal. Methodist offshoots of Edendale, starting in 1867 with a syndicate of more than thirty families who purchased Driefontein farm near Ladysmith, spread in all directions. There is no telling where the process might have ended had colonial governments not stepped in to limit African purchases.

In the early years it was commonplace for missions to pay parents for their children's attendance at school.[65] Later the tables were turned. Wealth bought power to *kholwa* communities – power to pay for their children's education, to evangelize, and to challenge missionary authority. Parents proved themselves to be knowledgeable consumers of education. When dissatisfied with the schools of their own missions they moved their children to rival institutions. At the higher levels of education, quality counted for much more than denominational loyalty, as the Methodist missionary H. M. Cameron found in 1879 when he "tried to press the claims of Edendale" against those of the American Congregational high school, Adams College.[66] The American missionaries, in their turn, were dismayed when their more affluent converts sent children to Anglican schools in Cape Town.[67] Poorer families were equally particular. They sought practical education for their children in the rudiments of literacy and arithmetic. The literacy they craved was in English, not in Zulu, a demand that ran directly contrary to the aim of several of the missions to produce a Zulu version of the Scriptures to supply a self-propagating African church. A major quarrel arose over curriculum in 1876 between Wilhelm Illing and the parents of children at his station near Ladysmith. Illing and his wife instructed pupils in English, German, Latin, Greek, and Hebrew, in four-part harmony, geography, and European history.[68] The parents were mainly interested in elementary English literacy and arithmetic. When the Illings refused to bend, the station people threatened to withdraw their children and hire their own teacher. Illing continued to teach advanced subjects, but eventually agreed to appoint a young African teacher at three pounds a month to take elementary subjects.[69]

By the 1880s government surveys reported that as many 3,000 African pupils were in classes, almost all of them in mission schools, many supported entirely by parents' contributions.[70]

Missionaries, constantly exhorted by their parent societies to raise up black churches that were "self-governing, self-supporting, and self-propagating," were frequently disappointed when worldly success diverted many able men from the ministry.[71] It was even difficult to recruit teachers, William Ireland lamented in 1877, "except at the more eligible and desirable posts, or unless they can receive considerably larger salaries."[72] Yet, in the long run, it was precisely the material success of the *kholwa* that made truly self-supporting churches possible.

Ironically, when Africans began to mount their own evangelistic efforts, white missionaries often greeted them with as much suspicion as enthusiasm. Black Methodists at Edendale founded the first self-supporting enterprise, *Unzondelelo*, in 1875,[73] staffed by lay preachers developed by the Wesleyan circuit system and financed by wealth accumulated through agriculture and trade. Methodist clergy were profoundly discomfited to hear from their converts that "missionaries in the past prevented them from aggressive work" and that had it not been for this impediment, "most of Africa by this time would have been evangelised."[74] However, once *Unzondelelo* leaders pledged that they would remain "entirely under" missionary supervision and "Methodist rule," the synod gave its blessing. An early triumph for *Unzondelelo* was Daniel Msimang's expedition of 1881, which removed the longstanding royal prohibition against Methodist missions in Swaziland. Yet within two years Owen Watkins was complaining that "the Edendale men wish to act in Swaziland without reference to their white missionaries."[75]

Conversations about the High God, Christ, and ethical conduct had by this time moved well beyond the dialogues of Gardiner and Dingane, Colenso and William Ngidi. They had become a babble throughout the land, laying invisible foundations for the massive advances of Christianity in the twentieth century. Methodist itinerants in the bush acquired the Zulu name *Nontlevu*: "people who talk too much."[76] A few accounts of itinerant African preaching survive in reports by missionaries. Some of these show clear evidence of an independent spirituality not readily attributable to any missionary. For example, Ira Nembula, who had been taught by his American mentors to draw harsh distinctions between heathen and Christian beliefs, tended towards universalism, in this surviving fragment of a sermon:

> He told them that he held the faith of their own people. They believed in righteousness and conscious existence after death. He believed the same truths as brought into clearer light in Christ. They believed that the spirits of the departed were sometimes hungry, and required beef of their friends who are still living; he believed that abundant satisfaction was provided for the departed in the glorified Saviour.[77]

A short prayer by the lay preacher John Langeni combines cultural originality with Methodist orthodoxy:

> Thou has sent thy Missionaries after Thy Son died to preach Thy Word, and it is a large fold of cattle in which every man may enrich himself; but we speak not of cattle of the common kind; O no! – of something far superior. O Lord Thy word is sweet-delicious things, sugar cane, *amasi* (curdled milk) are nothing to its sweetness! Open our eyes that we may see; open the eyes of *all*. And now Thy servant is about to go away rejoicing having spoken to us Thy Word and given us our tickets. O bless him! And bless our Queen on the other side of the sea. May she give herself to Thee, and not delight in earthly splendour! ... bless Mpande; bless Ketswayo ... bless all![78]

From the 1860s alternative interpretations of what it meant to be Christian were producing breakaway movements in missionary churches. A general revolt against missionary authority broke out at the American station Umvoti in the late 1860s. In the 1880s Mbiana Ngidi, a cousin of Bishop Colenso's collaborator, broke away from the American Zulu Mission, eventually founding the Zulu Mbiana Congregational Church. Others followed his lead: Ira Nembula formed the African Christian Union; Joel Msimang formed an Independent Methodist Church in Swaziland; Mangema Mokone moved to the Transvaal from Pietermaritzburg and founded the Ethiopian Church in 1892.[79]

Although the very name Ethiopian was to raise nightmarish visions of African self-determination for Natal settlers at the turn of the century, none of these separatist movements departed very far from denominational orthodoxies. (Only in the twentieth century would Zionist churches appear, blending African prophetic voices with Biblical teaching.) Questions of leadership were central to the Ethiopian breakaways. All the mission churches were slow to ordain Africans as ministers and, when ordinations did begin to multiply among Congregational and Methodist churches in the 1880s, full admission to the fellowship of the missionary clergy was denied.[80]

How Men Walk with Women: Christian Ethics, Marriage, and Family

Missionaries had struggled to get the Bible translated into Zulu, but Africans drew quite divergent conclusions from their reading. Inevitably the conversations raised thorny questions about proper Christian behaviour, most contentiously on polygamy, bride wealth (*lobola*), beer drinking, and *hlobonga* (a form of sexual activity without intercourse).[81] David Rood complained in 1869 that "native Christians when conversing upon religious topics are I think too apt to let the habit and love of discussion interfere with the simple love to know the truth ... Take such questions as polygamy or the demanding of cattle for daughters when given in marriage, they will go back to the Old Testament history, to Jacob and others, and they will say that they find these customs were approved by God ... They may say the same of the practice of beer drinking, of dancing and other evil customs."[82] An inventive searching of Scripture led other African Christians to conclude that *hlobonga* was sanctioned by 1 Corinthians 7:25, where Paul writes, "Now concerning virgins I have no commandment of the Lord."[83]

However much missionaries and their male converts may have differed about sexuality, they generally agreed about appropriate gender relationships. Had he lived long enough to witness the development of colonial Natal, Dingane's astonishment at how European men walked with women might have given way to an understanding that two strongly patriarchal societies had met at the Zulu frontier. White missionaries seldom acknowledged this, often speaking as though an important part of their mission were to free Nguni women from the thrall of male subjection. Christian matrimony, they argued, was a woman's fulfilment, while Nguni marriage most missionaries characterized as a passage from freedom to slavery.[84] As Thomas Kirkby argued in 1866:

> The position of the females in their girlhood is one of comparative ease; though even then the more arduous duties are done by them, and the boys, for the most part, go free, but female life is far from being irksome then ... and it is not until the man has purchased his property for a considerable sum, that the woman sinks to the condition of a slave.[85]

Most missionaries believed that Nguni fathers married off their daughters to the men who could give them the most cattle. The Christian family, by contrast, was praised as a state of holy liberty.

All missions, except the Catholics and the early Hermannsburg Lutherans, encouraged the recruitment of married clergy to serve as models for "the heathen." The first American missionaries selected for service in South Africa were not allowed to leave America without first finding a wife. "You should be married," wrote a Board official, "and it is of the utmost importance that you have a wife, that will make a happy and useful missionary."[86] "Family schools" usually offered some instruction by missionary wives in simple cooking and sewing.[87] The model offered by the missionary family was not especially persuasive for "the heathen," as Laura Bridgman somewhat forlornly confessed in 1869: "As for myself I am not much of a missionary. I have three little ones under six years of age. I am trying my best with God's help to make missionaries of these and if I live till they are grown up, I have hope that I shall then be a missionary too."[88] Many women broke mentally or physically under the strain of their isolated lives. For most it was unthinkable to challenge their husband's dual role as head of the church and head of the family.

Challenges to male domination did come from time to time from unmarried women and widows released from vows of obedience. Even for missionary societies that lauded the family model and derided celibate sisterhoods as popery, the employment of single female agents had attractions, no doubt, in part, because the wages of single female teachers were a fraction of those offered to male missionaries (salaries that were themselves very low except for higher clergy in the Church of England). Some of these teachers were employed at rates as low as two pounds per month in the 1870s.[89] Widowhood brought a very different type of independent womanhood. In the American mission the most troublesome widow was Katherine Lloyd, daughter of a leading Manhattan physician who arrived in Natal half-way through the American Civil War as the wife of the missionary Charles Lloyd. A fervent abolitionist, she had done volunteer work among the African–American population of New York City for several years. Once in Natal she expressed strong doubts about the Zulu Mission. "Mr. Treat, I at least had thought that when I got to Africa I would not find any – what shall I call it – well, traits of character such as people have in New York. Perhaps I rather expected the missionaries to be angels and when I found my mistake it required struggles great and long to feel that even missionaries were men and sometimes very much men."[90] Much to the consternation of older members of the mission she stayed on in Africa after the death of her husband in 1865 as a school teacher at Umvoti station, dispatching caustic comments back to the Board in Boston. Worse was to come when she, a woman, challenged the mission orthodoxy that *lobola* was a form of female slavery. With her abolitionist background, Kate Lloyd knew slavery when she saw it, and, in her opinion, *lobola* was no such thing. In a private letter to her mother she canvassed the issue in relation to Scripture and women's rights:

> It is true that those of our mission who are so strong in saying "women are slaves" and "the mission shall be broken up and go home before this horrible custom is allowed," these can bring up a few solitary cases that seem very horrible – just as I can tell of cases in America where daughters were forced to marry against their will an old and rich man instead of some one they loved who was poor ... I fear our missions have not been willing to hear the natives on the subject and so some of them really "speak evil of a thing they know not," as Paul said ... the women are no more slaves than you are to father or I was when Mr. Lloyd was living.[91]

Her own view was that most of the missionaries were glad to be rid of her "as they think me 'too kind' etc."[92] But after remarrying in 1870 to Daniel Lindley's son Newton, she lost the independent voice that widowhood had briefly conferred upon her. At about the time she left, another widow, Mrs. Mary K. Edwards, arrived to develop the Inanda Seminary for Girls. A former factory girl, she showed the capacity to challenge missionary authority on more than one occasion.[93] One of her subordinate teachers, Fannie Morris, was also critical of patriarchal rule in the mission. "Women's work outside the schools is much needed in Natal. They can do a work among the women that it is impossible for a man to do, but until this fact is recognised by the brethren, it will be much better not to send any more single ladies."[94]

What African women thought about missionary programmes for their regeneration is harder to discern. None in this period occupied positions higher than assistant teacher or "native helper," so letters from them are scarce in the archives. Although Nguni society was as patriarchal as the societies from which European missionaries came, the two patriarchal codes did not overlap at all points. Women who wished to change their partners fled to missions.[95] Young girls who feared the onset of puberty, or formed romantic attachments outside the realm of permitted alliances, could also count on finding refuge on a mission station. Missionaries, citing the principle of "religious liberty," protected such women from angry relatives and occasionally defended them in the colonial courts.[96]

A serious consequence of defining Christian marriage as liberation for women and Nguni marriage as bondage was that missionaries were quite unprepared to face Christian women who encouraged their husbands to take new wives, or who went to live with their eldest son after menopause, or insisted on picking marriage partners for their daughters.[97] Paradoxically, missionaries who complained that African marriages enslaved women also found themselves resisting the exertion of women's agency within Christian marriages.

Land and Labour; Church and State

Allen Gardiner had hoped that he might serve both the Zulu king and the settlers of Port Natal, but neither he nor any nineteenth-century missionary achieved that feat. The white population climbed from a handful in Allen Gardiner's day to about 60,000 in 1910, constantly demanding more land and more cheap labour than could easily be prised away from an African population that grew to nearly a million during the same period. The church was perpetually ground between these two millstones.

Over time, some of the white population managed to acquire exclusive access to their own ministers. Presbyterian, Dutch Reformed, and (until the coming of the Trappists to Mariannhill in 1882) Catholic clergy concentrated on whites.[98] White Christians of most other denominations had to share their clergy with African converts, but by segregating churches, services, and cemeteries they preserved as much distance from Africans as possible.

Settler politicians frequently displayed open hostility towards all missionary work. The Rev. Benjamin Markham once encountered a colonist who announced he would only contribute money to missions if it was used for "blowing Kafirs' brains out."[99] Similar sentiments, if usually more temperately expressed, cropped up frequently in the Natal press. Settlers felt a particular grievance about land. The Native Commission of 1852 commented that it had been a tragic mistake to appoint missionaries to the commission that had laid out the first African reserves.[100] Missionaries naturally resented such attacks but relied on the State in so many ways that they seldom replied in kind.

Settler legislators were difficult masters for the missionaries, but preferable on balance to independent African rulers. One by one, missionaries working in

Zululand followed the Hermannsburg Society in turning against King Cetshwayo. Robert Robertson of the Anglicans, like Hans Schreuder of the Norwegian mission, provided military intelligence on Zulu affairs to the Natal government on the eve of the Anglo-Zulu war.[101] One of the few clergy to condemn that war and call for the restoration of the king was Bishop Colenso – the man who had once been the staunchest believer in the expansion of the British Empire. His change of mind had been effected by the disillusionment he felt with Natal's administration of Africans after the brutal treatment of Chief Langalibalele and the Hlubi people in 1873–74.[102] Pursuing justice as relentlessly as he had once pursued Biblical scholarship, he reluctantly concluded that his longtime friend and supporter Theophilus Shepstone was a whited sepulchre. Pronouncing Natal's entire system of African administration to be evil and corrupt, he alienated the State, his only prop after his heresy trial. By tarring Natal's settlers with the same brush, he decimated his white congregations. Cetshwayo won Colenso's heart by offering to shelter chief Langalibalele, and the bishop was determined that he should not share the Hlubi chief's fate. Colenso devoted the ebbing years of his life to a campaign for the restoration of the Zulu monarchy,[103] a campaign that partially succeeded. Still, subsequent Zulu kings never danced as Dingane had danced for Gardiner. After Colenso's death in 1883, his devoted daughters Agnes and Harriette carried on the cause of the Zulu royal house until well into the twentieth century. Their efforts, as much as their father's, ensured that the name Shepstone had chosen for the bishop – *Sobantu*, or father of the people – would be enshrined in African memory.

Other clergy in Natal lacked Colenso's stubborn, lofty courage. But, willy nilly, many of them were likewise torn between reliance upon, and hostility to the State. Things got tougher for them as settler influence began to preponderate over officials responsible to Britain. All the principal missionary societies depended to some extent on government support: societies lucky enough to have arrived before 1860 received substantial grants of land.[104] Also, Natal's Charter dictated that £5,000 per annum must be set aside for purposes connected with African welfare, and in 1865, nearly 40 per cent of this reserve fund went to mission schools.[105] For organizations perpetually short of cash and under instructions to make themselves self-supporting, this money was a godsend. Under Governors Pine and Scott mission schools were supported in the 1850s and 1860s. Sir George Grey, as High Commissioner for South Africa in 1855, strongly supported both Bishop Colenso's "school for chiefs' sons" and "practical" industrial training in concentrated village settlements such as he favoured for the eastern Cape.[106] As time passed, the preference for industrial schools grew; Dr. Mann's Report on Industrial Training and Education for 1864 listed six, all run by missionaries, where instruction included such crafts as wagon-making, carpentry, brick-making, cabinet-making, sewing, stone masonry, and ploughing.[107] Responding to an opportunity, missionaries rushed into those industrial schemes that would attract grants, even when they were dubious about their educational value.[108]

Thus, just as Africans were beginning in significant numbers to seek secondary and higher education, pressures from settlers and government combined to force the publicly funded institutions into narrow channels. Catholic missionaries of the Trappist monastic order put the state industrial education policy to the test in the

1880s. Here was a mission virtually tailored to suit the demands of white settlers. Their foundation settlement at Mariannhill dispensed industrial education on a grand scale, training stone masons, "carpenters, cabinet makers, blacksmiths, wheelwrights, wagon-makers, plumbers, tinsmiths, tanners, boot-makers, harness-makers, tailors, printers, and even professional photographers."[109] The abbott of Mariannhill was equally practical in his approach to female education, writing that "it is neither good nor necessary that the girls make such an extensive study of book subjects as boys. To form and train up useful girls and honest wives is the aim."[110] Nonetheless, when the Trappists applied for large government grants, they met strong opposition from colonists who insisted they wanted "to make the natives good labourers, but not farmers or skilled artisans."[111]

Natal's achievement of Responsible Government (or internal self-government) in 1893 – under an arrangement ensuring that virtually all voters were white, set the stage for a head-on confrontation between missionary educational aspirations and the white colonists' insistence on the lowest possible standards.[112] Although the actions of the colonial state affected every mission in Natal, the American Zulu Mission was singled out for special attention, its large land holdings and Congregational goal of raising up self-governing African churches making them an object of suspicion in an era when the first Ethiopian churches were alarming the authorities. By 1907 the American mission was administering 59 primary schools, three boarding schools, and a theological college, all of which totalled 3,964 pupils.[113]

Since the middle of the last century, the government had supported schools from the £5,000 Reserve Fund. Under new legislation, all mission reserves were required to collect rents from African residents, part of which was to be spent on education and other welfare services. This not only served the old settler objective of pushing Africans into wage labour, but also gave the Natal government leverage over mission schools. Once again the principal demand was that schools provide basic education in agricultural and mechanical skills. Once again the missions, beholden to the government for land, knuckled under.

The colonial state could not secure the total victory on the educational front it won in relation to land and civil rights. So long as Africans were willing to pay for higher education, and foreign missions were willing to support elite schools, a small coterie of such schools was able to achieve equality in academic qualifications, if not in social status. The first African university graduate returned to Natal in 1876 with a degree from America's Howard University. Others followed: doctors, lawyers, teachers. From that group emerged such notable leaders as John L. Dube, H.S. Msimang, A.W.G. Champion, Saul Msane, and Albert Luthuli. Significant as these achievements were, they were a far cry both from the aspirations of the nineteenth-century missionary pioneers and the insistence of African communities on education for equality and freedom.

Still, by 1900, a network of black evangelists, many of them educated and self-supporting, had spread over the land. No longer facing opposition from chiefs and kings, the Christian gospel could be freely preached everywhere. The crisis of the old order had so shaken the foundations of old faiths that, for the first time, converts began to flow to the churches in large numbers. Numerically, Christians were still a minority of the population, but as the old missionaries had taught, the field was now "white to the harvest."

6

Monarchs and Missionaries
among the Tswana and Sotho

ROGER B. BECK

The nineteenth-century experiences of Sotho and Tswana with Christianity differed, in some significant ways, from those of the Nguni-speakers (like the Zulu, Mpondo, and Xhosa) to their east and southeast. When Christian missionary activity began among them, at the beginning of the nineteenth century, Sotho and Tswana lived in towns or villages ruled by a chief. Some of these chiefs showed greater interest in Christianity than their Nguni counterparts, enabling the implantation of Christianity among them at least for a time.

Despite the early start and high profile of the London Missionary Society (LMS) throughout southern Africa, no one denomination monopolized any region, and Sotho and Tswana successfully played off one missionary society against another. Both attracted zealous missionary translators who produced some of the first vernacular Bibles in Africa, providing both societies with written texts at an early date. So, too, both groups quickly recognized the advantages of European schooling and promoted it among their people.

The "Sotho–Tswana," – a closely related cultural and linguistic group consisting of a number of political sub-groups, including the Kwena, Thlaping, Kgatla, Rolong, Ngwato, Ngwaketsi, Tlharo and the Southern Sotho – occupy a large region of southern Africa bounded by the Orange River to the south, the Drakensberg or Maluti Mountains to the east, the Zoutpansberg Mountains to the north, and the Kalahari Desert to the west.[1]

The split between the Sotho and Tswana, first created by disruptions in the highveld in the 1820s known as the Difaqane, were reinforced when the Great Trek of the 1830s left a wedge of Boer settlement between independent Sotho societies to the east and independent Tswana societies to the west.

"What Have You Brought for Barter?": Chiefs and the First Missionaries to the *Tswana*

Among the Tswana, Christianity spread in four phases in the nineteenth century, each closely identified with the activities of one of four LMS Scottish missionaries: the LMS's early director and traveller, John Campbell (1812–14, 1818–21); a patriarchal preacher and translator, Robert Moffat (1821–70); an explorer, physician, and missionary, David Livingstone (1841–52); and a missionary imperialist, John Mackenzie (1860–99).

The first two missionaries to the Tswana, Jan Matthys Kok and William Edwards of the LMS, settled in 1801 among the Tlhaping near their capital at Dithakong (Lattakoo), the southernmost Tswana city. Kok and Edwards preached the gospel on their own, having little contact with each other, and with meagre support from the LMS, living apparently in abject poverty, slightly alleviated by small profits from the ivory trade. Kok was slain by two Tlhaping men in 1806. Edwards, who had travelled as far north as Kanye, the Bangwaketse capital, left as his most important legacy his work near the site of the future Kuruman mission station, where he died in 1842.[2]

In 1812 the LMS sent the Rev. John Campbell to the Cape to inspect its settlements, establish order, and encourage "conversion of the heathen," keeping in view at the same time the promotion of their civilization.[3] Campbell, accompanied by two missionaries, James Read and William Anderson, travelled from Griqua Town to Dithakong. He tried to persuade the Tlhaping chief, Mothibi, to accept missionaries, but Mothibi refused – his people had no time for such distractions, he said – and "besides, the things which this people teach are contrary to all our customs, which the people will not give up." Campbell countered with an offer of missionary teachers who would stay out of Tswana internal affairs, and Mothibi grudgingly consented to let them teach Dutch to the children, if the teachers stayed some distance from Dithakong. Campbell recorded Mothibi's instruction in bold letters: "SEND INSTRUCTORS, AND I WILL BE A FATHER TO THEM."[4]

Mothibi wanted missionaries to facilitate trade with the Cape, especially for guns and ammunition, and not to try to convert his people to Christianity. When four LMS missionaries[5] arrived in 1816, expecting a joyful reception from people eager to receive God's word, Mothibi's first words were, "What have you brought for barter?"[6] They returned to Griqua Town, their initial attempt a failure, but James Read and Robert Hamilton established a permanent mission in that same year. Mothibi granted permission for them to remain among the Tlhaping. The next year they moved to his new capital "New Dithakong," later known as Kuruman. The chief required presents and trade goods in exchange for permission to preach. The LMS established stations throughout Tswana country and over the years converted many Tswana to Christianity as Campbell had envisaged and Mothibi had feared.

In 1821, the Rev. Robert Moffat joined Hamilton at Kuruman, soon to become the centre of missionary activity in southern Africa from which Christianity would spread throughout the interior. Many newly arrived missionaries served there for some time and most made a pilgrimage to Kuruman before continuing on to mission stations farther north. African ministers also were trained in Kuruman.

Moffat's initial successes were in part a consequence of the part he played in the battle near Dithakong in 1823 when, according to his own account, with the support of armed Griqua he held off an attack by starving marauders and subsequently took part in the rescue of the victims and their distribution as labourers in the Colony.[7] In late 1829 Moffat met with the Ndebele chief Mzilikazi, who had moved from northern Natal to the highveld during the troubles of the 1820s, and maintained a friendship with him over thirty years, helping to defuse conflict between the Ndebele and the Tlhaping. His enormous energy, strong character and singleness of purpose sustained him through forty years at Kuruman, where he lived till 1870, preaching the gospel, and though a "mere gardener" by training – translating the whole Bible into Setswana.

Political and military activities became a point of great contention among the missionaries, and resulted in a bitter, public dispute between Moffat and John Philip, the director of the LMS in South Africa. Moffat's attitude, despite his own actions, was simple: the one important task for a missionary was the conversion of the heathen to Christianity. He totally opposed Philip's view that a missionary should concern himself with the plight of the indigenous peoples and fight against oppression and exploitation by white settlers. He disapproved, for example, of Campbell's involvement in the internal affairs of the Griqua and strongly rebuked Philip for his efforts to gain political and legal rights for the Cape Coloureds in the Cape Colony. Isaac Schapera explains Moffat's attitude as a product of his isolation in the interior among a people who had not yet suffered colonial domination, land alienation, and loss of civil rights, a pattern of oppression Philip had witnessed among the Khoisan at the Cape.[8]

From 1821 to 1829 the Tswana were unresponsive to Moffat's evangelistic message; and Mothibi and his followers slowly drifted away from the church and then from the mission settlement. But Mothibi's departure was a blessing in disguise for Moffat; it allowed him time to establish a mission at Kuruman on his own terms without control by any chief, baptizing his first converts in 1829. His following grew slowly, his congregation never exceeding about a hundred members, doubtless a response to his strict demand of exceptional moral behaviour and Christian commitment, for he excommunicated any who fell short. His honesty and his refusal to become involved in local Tswana politics earned him the respect of the Tswana, and as a consequence made the way easier for later missionaries. Yet in his private journals Moffat described the Tlhaping as souls to be saved from degenerate behaviour; he repeatedly referred to them as liars, beggars, and thieves.[9] His published works rarely referred to the Tswana at all, and then only to contrast their failings with Christian virtues;[10] he told his readers that descriptions of Tswana practices or customs would prove "neither very instructive nor very edifying" to them.[11] The Tswana, he believed, had no religious beliefs, despite their reverence for ancestral spirits, and for their supreme spirit, *Modimo*. Of Mzilikazi, the Ndebele leader who showed deep feelings of friendship and devotion to him, Moffat wrote coldly that he was no more than "a heathen soul to be pitied and to be saved, and an instrument through whom the Christian virtues might be spread."[12]

The physician, David Livingstone, like Moffat a Scot, but more highly educated, arrived at Kuruman in 1841 to begin his great African adventure and settled at Kolobeng among the Kwena. The Tswana liked Livingstone because he cured their illnesses and he learned their language; also, he was Moffat's son-in-law, and, unlike Moffat, appeared sympathetic toward Tswana culture and customs. But Livingstone could not endure the daily routine of mission station life, and, in the mid-1850s sent his wife and children back to England and set off to explore central Africa. He opened up new markets for British commerce, believing that trade and conversion went hand in hand, and converted a few Africans to Christianity as he passed through their lands. In southern Africa his one convert was the Kwena chief Kgosi Sechele I, who abandoned his faith six months after his baptism. Livingstone's work among the Tswana was, he said, a "failure";[13] his greatest contribution to the missionary effort among the Tswana was his exploration and opening up of northern Tswana regions to European missionaries.

The Rev. J.J. Freeman, who visited all LMS mission stations in 1849–50, painted a rather bleak picture of the progress of Christianity among the Tswana. After fifty years of evangelization in southern Africa, the Kuruman station did thrive – particularly its school and printing press – but other stations either no longer functioned or showed only negligible results for decades of labour.[14]

"The Finger of God Was Clearly Visible": Missionaries and Moshoeshoe of the Sotho

The history of Christianity among the Sotho began in 1833 with the arrival of missionaries from the Paris Evangelical Missionary Society (PEMS).[15] Paris missionaries would later describe its first phase, to 1848, as a "Golden Age" of mission advances. Its second phase, to 1854, following the disruption of the Sotho kingdom by Boer, Kora, and Griqua intruders, witnessed a counter-reaction to Christianity among many Sotho. After 1854 came a long period of consolidation, with other faiths and denominations, particularly the Roman Catholics, Anglicans, and Methodists, challenging the PEMS for supremacy among missions, while traditional religion also experienced a strong resurgence.

The PEMS in 1829 received an invitation from the LMS director in southern Africa, John Philip. It promptly sent three newly ordained missionaries to the Cape. One of these, Isaac Bisseux, remained in the western Cape, working in the Wagenmakers Valley. Samuel Rolland and Prosper Lemue settled at Mosega among the Hurutse Tswana, but, abandoning this mission when Mzilikazi's depredations scattered the Hurutse, they moved back near Kuruman and founded a new station called Motito.

Three more PEMS missionaries, Eugène Casalis, Thomas Arbousset, and their aide, the non-ordained artisan/missionary Constant Gosselin, arrived at the Cape in 1832, and were on their way to Motito when a Griqua hunter, Adam Krotz, told them that a powerful Sotho chief, Moshoeshoe, had asked for missionaries to live and teach among his people. They agreed to go: "The finger of God was clearly visible; it pointed out to us the road which we should take."[16] "The road" led into country unknown to most Europeans. Moshoeshoe's subjects, a core group of Sotho/Tswana descent, with a mixture of Nguni peoples, lived under his protection from the horrors of the *Difaqane*. Moshoeshoe's capital, an impregnable fortification on an immense flat-top mountain called Thaba Bosiu, provided water, grass, garden space, and shelter during sieges; from its heights rocks could be hurled down upon Zulu, Griqua, and Boer attackers.

Casalis, Arbousset, and Gosselin, needing more space for their mission station, on Moshoeshoe's advice, settled on a site about twenty-five miles to the southwest. The missionaries were disappointed that Moshoeshoe chose not to live among them, but probably fared better without him – like Moffat at Kuruman. As Ellenberger said: "The missionaries were thus not at the chief's, but at home; that made a very big difference."[17] For Moshoeshoe the mission station could be a buffer and outpost against attacks from the Koras, a Khoisan group; also the missionary presence would symbolize his own authority in the southern part of his kingdom. The Morija site soon became a thriving station with a church and a school. Moshoeshoe sent his two oldest sons, and a contingent of other younger men to Morija.

In 1837 Casalis moved into a stone house at the foot of Thaba Bosiu, and soon became the king's closest European adviser and confidant. Unlike Moffat, who never reciprocated overtly Mzilikazi's signs of friendship and respect, Casalis formed a close relationship with Moshoeshoe, who called him "my teacher, my father, my mother ... a true MoSotho."[18]

In contrast to the early LMS missionaries among the Tswana, the PEMS missionaries initially found the Sotho receptive to Christian teachings. They saw Moshoeshoe as a brilliant and thoughtful leader who enjoyed conversing and debating with them. Still, their criticism of Sotho customs, such as polygamy, social stratification between chiefs and commoners, dress, architecture, circumcision, and rituals,[19] angered many of Moshoeshoe's people, and, by the late 1830s, they were warning against public Christian ceremonies that ignored, or opposed, traditional practices. They believed that angry ancestors would wreak vengeance on their entire society. The early Paris missionaries always occupied a tenuous position among the Sotho, their influence limited essentially to the mission station's boundaries.

Moshoeshoe himself allowed the missionaries to bury converts in a Christian cemetery on Thaba Bosiu.[19] He stopped convening initiation schools, renounced the killing of witches, and agreed to divorce those of his many wives who converted to Christianity, while permitting them to keep their land and cattle.[20] However, most of his counsellors, many among them members of the royal family and powerful members of his own generation, distanced themselves from the missionaries, or displayed outright hostility toward them. In response to these fears among his people, Moshoeshoe delayed his own conversion until the moment before his death; he was never baptized.[21]

During this "Golden Age" for missionary activity, to 1848, the PEMS missionaries founded stations serving both Sotho and Tswana at Bethulie, Beersheba, Mekoatleng, Berea, Cana, Bethesda, Hermon, and Hebron. It took nearly six years to win the first convert, but after 1838 they made rapid progress. They enjoyed a relative peace, a freedom to work, and a position of influence later missionaries would never know. In 1844 Arbousset took five of Moshoeshoe's kinsmen, including three of his sons, to Cape Town for further Christian study. By 1848 the PEMS had established nine active mission stations among the Sotho; they had baptized over 2,000, and had prepared another 1,000 for baptism. Nearly 2,300 were attending their Sunday services, and more than 600 students were enrolled in the mission schools run by missionaries' wives.[22] The dangers of the *Difaqane* were, on the whole, over, and the Sotho began to form into a nation.

Voortrekkers, Missionaries, and British Protectorates

Boer settlers in the 1830s began their Great Trek out of the Cape Colony, and crossed the Orange River, heading northeast toward areas of higher rainfall. One party met and defeated Mzilikazi in present-day Transvaal, forcing him to flee. Another party looped north around Moshoeshoe's kingdom, then defeated

Dingane and his Zulu army at Blood River in Natal. The Boers had not trespassed on Moshoeshoe's territory and had rid him of two of his greatest enemies. But some Boers began to settle in the rich Caledon River valley, where Sotho and Tswana farmers had settled around mission stations. Soon the Boers had built permanent homes and claimed ownership. The resulting land disputes soon forced the missionaries into political roles they had sought to avoid. In 1843 Moshoeshoe called upon British authorities in the Cape Colony to help block the Boers from preempting any more of his territory. With the advice and assistance of the missionaries – Casalis and Philip – Moshoeshoe and Adam Kok, leader of the Griqua community at Philippolis, signed a treaty with the Cape governor, Sir George Napier, that recognized Moshoeshoe's sovereignty over all the lands between the Orange and Caledon rivers, and a strip of land west of the Caledon. Wesleyan missionaries,[23] two days after the treaty's signing, protested to the colonial officials on behalf of other chiefs in the Caledon valley, most of whom lived on Wesleyan missions. Litigation heightened the tension between the Wesleyans, who supported the other chiefs, and the PEMS missionaries, who endorsed Moshoeshoe's land claims.[24] In 1849 Captain H.D. Warden, British resident in the Orange River Sovereignty recently proclaimed by Governor Sir Harry Smith over territory between the Orange and the Vaal rivers, laid down fixed boundaries between the rival claimants in the Caledon valley, alienating some territory claimed by Moshoeshoe in the process.

During the second phase of PEMS missionary activity among the Sotho, from 1848 to 1854, relations between the PEMS and the Sotho rapidly deteriorated. Traditionalist Sotho, who had always mistrusted missionaries, now began to press Moshoeshoe to rid his kingdom of them. They viewed all Europeans as intent on stealing their lands and forcing them into subservience, with Christianity as their chosen means. Only a return to their traditional religion and practices, they thought, could save Sotho society.[25]

In all the land disputes with the Boers and British the Paris missionaries had argued in favour of Sotho rights. Casalis, indeed, became something of a foreign secretary for Moshoeshoe, but the Paris missionaries' pacifist position angered many Sotho. In contrast to the assertive Moffat, the Paris missionaries preached Christian pacifism, took Biblical injunctions against killing and stealing literally, and extended these prohibitions to include killing in war, theft of cattle, and retaliation against marauders. They told their Christian followers to disobey Moshoeshoe's calls to arms, refused to take part in a revenge raid on the Tlokoa to the north, and denied communion to those who did take part. To many Sotho this stand seemed weak and cowardly, and came to typify Christianity itself.[26]

As supreme military leader, Moshoeshoe regrouped all the Sotho under his authority, and away from the missionaries and their influence. Reviving African religious traditions, he dutifully performed the necessary purifications and rituals of warfare. Previously, the links between Christianity and European civilization had favoured the missionaries. Now it was a definite hindrance.[27]

Over the period 1848 to 1854 the Sotho continued to lose portions of territory in a series of wars. The public reactions against Christianity began late in 1848 when Molapo, Moshoeshoe's second son and the most prominent Christian convert, renounced Christianity. By 1852 all five of Moshoeshoe's Cape Town-educated Christian kinsmen had abandoned their acquired faith. As the numbers of Christian believers declined, the prestige of traditional diviners and prophets rose, including the Xhosa prophet Mlanjeni (see pp. 80–81), whose millenarian message against all whites, including Christians, found a sympathetic ear among the Sotho in 1850–1.[27] Moshoeshoe, following the mood of his people, made contact with Mlanjeni. Defying missionary teaching, he refused to divorce any of his wives and he married a number of new ones; he performed traditional ceremonies and rituals, reconvened initiation schools, and listened to the portents of the female Sotho diviner Mantsopa.

France's February Revolution of 1848 added to the woes of the PEMS, whose directors, faced with their first deficit, closed the Paris Mission House, refused to pay the bills of their missionaries, and abandoned the three newest stations of the Sotho mission. Over the next twelve years the Sotho mission received no new missionaries and no funding.[28]

From the 1830s, Moshoeshoe had remained loyal to successive British governments, but when the British invaded his territory in late 1852, his forces defeated them and forced them to withdraw. The Bloemfontein Convention of 1854 ended British sovereignty over the Orange River territory and recognized the Boer-controlled Orange Free State. It did nothing to rectify what Moshoeshoe saw as the injustice of the Warden Line or to protect him from land-grabbing attacks by his neighbours, particularly the Boers on his western border. The British, in essence, left him to fend for himself. And although PEMS missionaries continued to offer advice and support, Moshoeshoe lost access to his two oldest and most respected European friends when Casalis returned to France in 1855, and Arbousset in 1860.[29] From 1858 to 1884, the third phase of the Sotho mission, the Sotho were almost constantly at war and endured several invasions and temporary occupations. Boer invaders from the Orange Free State destroyed the PEMS stations at Morija and Beersheba during the first war in 1858. Seven years later the Boers burned all the mission stations and expelled all French missionaries from Sotho country for advocating the Sotho cause. None returned until 1868, when England declared Basutoland a British protectorate. "The Lesotho Church slowly recovered," wrote Perrot; "life on the stations returned to its old order, but without the enthusiasm, or the magnificent promise of the earlier years." By now many Sotho viewed Christianity as an agent of disintegration rather than a factor of social consolidation as in the early years. They chose to maintain the traditional order and sought to breathe new life into their own religion.

When in 1871 the British handed the protectorate over to the Cape Colony, the new authorities tried to break up the Sotho political organization and weaken the power of the chiefs, with the support of some missionaries. Cape officials also sought to disarm the Sotho, whom the Paris missionaries advised to turn in their guns. Refusing to submit to the Cape officials, the Sotho fought the three-year War of the Guns, which they won, keeping their independence, and their guns. In 1884 the British once again made Basutoland a British protectorate, allowing the Sotho chiefs almost total freedom to rule.

Among the Tswana, too, missionaries had been drawn into triangular conflicts between African rulers, Voortrekker republics, and British imperialism. Living far beyond the Cape borders, early missionaries to the Tswana had necessarily refrained from active involvement in Tswana internal politics. They depended on the Tswana for food, shelter, and protection from African chiefs. With increased European penetration of the African interior, which began with the Great Trek and gathered momentum through the remainder of the century, missionaries, feeling less obligation to show respect to African rulers, could ask colonial authorities to remove those leaders who thwarted their efforts.[30] But, as among the Sotho, missionaries were often counsellors, interpreters, and secretaries to Tswana leaders and often acted as their liaisons with European officials.

Moffat's successor in the second half of the nineteenth century, John Mackenzie, the last great Scottish missionary to the Tswana, was almost as involved in Tswana and Cape politics as in missionary work itself. He arrived in Kuruman in 1860, then moved to the Shoshong station among the Ngwato, where he remained for fourteen years.[31] With the help of the most famous Tswana convert, Kgama III, then the eldest son and successor to the Ngwato chief, Sekgoma, Mackenzie built a new and larger church in Shoshong. He trained a generation of teachers and native ministers to carry the gospel among their own people. As an unapologetic British imperialist, Mackenzie favoured British dominion in southern Africa as the most likely agent for spreading the Gospel message, and lived to see his dream fulfilled with the establishment of a British-controlled Bechuanaland Protectorate in 1885.

Rising Competition: Africanist Reaction and More Missions

When, in the War of the Guns, the church counselled the submission of the Sotho, those who remained loyal to the church were seen as traitors by Sotho nationalists. The victory of nationalism in the war weakened the church while reinforcing traditional beliefs. Economic conditions, too, advanced the traditional society at the church's expense. An enormous market developed for African livestock, produce, and labour after the discovery of diamonds in 1867 and of gold in 1886. The Sotho with surplus grain, other foodstuffs and livestock, entered into the capitalist monetary system around and within their borders. Wealth and abundance destroyed any idea that only the Christian God could bring happiness and prosperity to the Sotho. Years of famine and hardship had favoured Christian evangelization; prosperity favoured the religion and cultural practices of the ancestors. No longer did Sotho automatically associate Christianity with European civilization.

The practice of giving "marriage cattle" flourished during this period of prosperity, Sotho seeing Christian marriages as outside the law, contracted behind the bushes.[32] Although the PEMS missionaries never abandoned their opposition to marriage cattle, the Catholics and Anglicans came to tolerate the practice and, thus, made some inroads among the Sotho.[33] The Anglicans gained another advantage because they held their services in English, which the Sotho believed to be the key to the wider world.[34] Polygamy remained the accepted and preferred form of marriage among Sotho, some of whom, with knowledge of the Bible, quoted the Old Testament in its favour. Many Sotho believed in an all-powerful God – not one who judges right and wrong and punishes sinners, but a neutral or amoral God who extends temporal protection and eschews judgment.[35] African cults took various elements from Christian ceremonies, especially the more elaborate and mystical ceremonies, such as holy communion from the Anglicans and Roman Catholics.

When large numbers of Sotho moved away from the most heavily Christianized areas in the south and central regions of the country to the mountains north and east to plant their crops away from colonial authorities and missionary influence, disruption and loss of continuity occurred on the mission stations. PEMS missionaries saw those Sotho who moved away as the most pagan and the most hostile of all to civilization and Christianity.[36] They continued to serve Moshoeshoe and later chiefs as interpreters and as liaisons with other Europeans, but no other PEMS missionary ever enjoyed the privileged and respected position that Moshoeshoe earlier bestowed on Casalis.

The arrival of Roman Catholic, Wesleyan, and Anglican missionaries among the Sotho, as well as traders, settlers, government officials, and other whites, brought further competition for the PEMS missionaries. The Roman Catholics posed the most significant threat. Father François Allard, Bishop of Natal and the interior, and Father Joseph Gérard, both members of the Oblates of Mary Immaculate, first visited the Sotho in early 1862 and met with Moshoeshoe's son Molapo. Allard's earlier Zulu mission had nothing to show for nearly a decade of labour (see p. 196) but he was hopeful about the potential of a mission among the Sotho, already familiar with Christianity, albeit in Protestant form, and the Bible. Here he could fight two enemies at once, the Protestant "heretics" and the "heathen." Moshoeshoe granted permission for a Catholic mission station, under the direction of Gérard, about twenty miles south of Thaba Bosiu, near modern Roma. Certain doctrines and practices of Catholicism proved particularly attractive to the Sotho, the concept of the Holy Virgin and the saints seeming to parallel the "intermediary" spirits of the traditional religion. The elaborate rituals of Catholicism, with ornate vestments, statues, crucifixes, candles, incense, music, and stately and mysterious pageantry, appealed to many Sotho. And, unlike the PEMS missionaries, who had sometimes opposed Moshoeshoe's policies, seeing themselves as his superiors, Allard and Gérard rarely questioned Moshoeshoe's authority.

The Anglican church's missionary effort began in the 1870s when the Rev. Edmund Stenson founded a mission in southern Basutoland and the Rev. John Widdicombe began a mission in the north in the Leribe District.[37] After Widdicombe supported the Cape government during the War of the Guns and advised his congregation to turn in their weapons, Sotho attacked and destroyed both stations. Stenson moved back to Wepener in the Orange Free State, but Widdicombe rebuilt his station at Thlotse and remained another twenty-five years, establishing one of the most successful mission stations, with a school, a training college for teachers, an industrial school, a mission house, and a chapel.

A critical moment in relations between the missionary societies and the Sotho occurred in 1888 when a Christian woman asked for a divorce from her polygamous husband, whereupon the Sotho called a *pitso* (national assembly) to discuss, among other topics, the question of the legitimacy of Christian marriages that were contracted without marriage cattle, inviting all three mission societies to comment. The Paris missionaries refused to yield their position on this or any other question;

the Catholics and Anglicans said they accepted the custom of marriage cattle. No statistics exist for Anglican growth at this period, but the Catholics clearly gained in prestige and influence at the PEMS's expense. Progressing only slowly after their arrival in 1852, they had converted only 230 adults by 1871 and only 700 by 1879. They made as many conversions in 1887 as they had in the previous twenty-one years; after 1887 they averaged about 350 conversions a year. Still, the 24,500 Sotho Christians belonging to the Paris Mission in 1907 far exceeded all the 6,000 of other groups combined.[38]

The number of Sotho converting to Christianity grew at a faster pace than that of the Sotho population at large, particularly from 1874 to 1892, when the population rose from around 80,000 in 1857 to around 218,000 in 1892. The Paris mission had 1,788 adult Christians in 1857 (the same number as in 1847, before the setback); 3,550 in 1874; and 12,460 in 1892. However, as Perrot points out, while the number of Christian adults increased by 9,000 between 1874 and 1892, the number of non-Christians increased by about 72,000.[39] Paris missionaries estimated that, of the total Sotho population in 1892, 9 or 10 per cent called themselves Christians, a number that did not change significantly until well into the twentieth century. At the turn of the century the PEMS missionary Hermann Dieterlen admitted that the "overwhelming majority of the Basotho nation are still resistant to Christianity."[40]

The LMS dominated the Tswana missionary field, but other mission societies also operated successful missions among the Tswana in the nineteenth century. Once a Tswana community had allowed a particular society to establish a mission station in its midst, it generally denied other societies permission to settle. Thus, some communities refused LMS missionaries because other societies had got there first: for example, Dutch Reformed missionaries from the Transvaal among the Kgatla Tswana in 1860 around Mochudi in Botswana, and Anglican missionaries principally among the Hurutshe in the Tati District. The Ngwato originally had accepted Hermannsburg Society Lutheran missionaries in 1860 until they withdrew, and sheer chance led Mackenzie to Shoshong, where he served the most famous Tswana convert to Christianity, the Ngwato chief, Kgama III. The Methodist Missionary Society began work among the Rolong Tswana, establishing an important station at Thaba Nchu in the future Orange Free State. The Roman Catholics, until well into the twentieth century, had no permission at all to carry on mission work in Tswana country.

By the 1880s each major settlement had a resident missionary of some kind, except in the far north, where African Protestant missionaries predominated. Although Livingstone and others had made contact, in the 1840s and 1850s, with the most distant Tswana people, the Tawana in the northwest corner of modern Botswana, African preachers carried out most of the missionary work in this field after the late 1870s and into the twentieth century. A European missionary and some Ngwato Christians began a mission in Ngamiland in 1877 but the European soon left. An African evangelist, Khukhu Mogodi, with little support from the LMS, served the Ngamiland mission until his retirement in 1905, when another African evangelist, Somolekae, who had assisted him from the 1890s in starting the first church and school, took his place. By accepting baptism in 1860 while still a prince, Kgama of the Ngwato had turned his back on the traditional rites and rituals his father Sekgoma I still strongly supported. This prolonged struggle between father and son ended with Sekgoma's flight into exile and Kgama's assumption of the chieftainship in 1875. Kgama proceeded to create a Christian state in which alcohol was forbidden, traditional ceremonies and practices were discouraged, and Christian education enjoyed a high priority. Kgama was also concerned to unite his people (a mix of Ngwato, other Tswana, and San peoples) into a nation and to preserve his territory from alienation and attack. Soon after assuming power, and with the full support and encouragement of Mackenzie, Khama asked for British protection of his eastern boundary against Boer incursions from the Transvaal. His land lay along the famous "Missionary Road" that led from Cape Town north into modern Zimbabwe. By 1885 this was the most important trade route into the interior; hence the British were anxious to prevent a union of Transvaal Boers with Germans in Southwest Africa (modern Namibia) or East Africa, or with Portuguese in Mozambique, that would cut off this vital artery. Kgama gave his wholehearted support to the establishment in 1885 of the British protectorate over Bechuanaland. Like Moshoeshoe, Kgama was a skillful diplomat who made a pragmatic and realistic appraisal of the forces poised to take away his independence. His loyalty to the British crown and pragmatic attitude toward his colonial neighbours obliged him to compromise traditions such as land tenure but allowed him to hold his people together and maintain a relative independence.[41] Kgama ruled until 1923. Because of his responsiveness to the advice of Mackenzie and other missionaries, and his sincere and deep Christian belief, Europeans saw him as the model Christian African ruler.[42]

Translation, Literacy, and Education

The first Christian missionaries to the Tswana and Sotho were charged with spreading the Gospel and shepherding their listeners to eternal salvation. To fulfil that commission, these missionaries, some would say, imposed not simply their Christian beliefs but also their cultural, political and commercial values. It is, for example, clear that missionaries brought modern agricultural aids like ploughing with oxen, irrigation, and wagons. Moffat introduced new methods of vegetable gardening and crop irrigation. Missionary wives taught domestic skills such as knitting, sewing, baking, nursing, and midwifery. But religious and language texts produced in African languages by missionary translators may well prove the most important legacy of the Christian missionaries.[43] Lamin Sanneh, in his book *Translating the Message*, argues that the process of translating the Bible and other texts into an indigenous language, such as Tswana and Sotho, compelled missionaries to study every aspect of the society. Indeed, by learning the name for things in African languages and recording them in a form that could be passed on from generation to generation, Sanneh says, missionaries saved these cultures from extinction and made possible, when independence finally came, a revival of African cultures, languages, and traditions.[44]

Early missionaries to the Tswana had preached in Dutch with Khoikhoi translating their message, but Moffat set out to learn Tswana. After five years of effort he published, in 1826, his first translation, a Tswana spelling and reading book.

For the next thirty years Moffat worked on a translation of the Bible, aided by fellow missionaries Roger Edwards and William Ashton, and, in 1857, published the first complete Bible translation in a South African indigenous language.[45]

Although the translation tradition began with Moffat and the LMS at Kuruman, missionaries elsewhere quickly took up the translation effort, and books and other literature soon appeared in most of the Tswana dialects. Each missionary society published materials intended for the Tswana group among whom they lived, the Methodists in Serolong, the Dutch Reformed in Sekgatla, the LMS in Setlhaping, and the Lutherans in Sekwena. However, as a consequence of such disparate efforts no single orthography for Tswana was adopted, a problem that plagues Tswana writers to the present.

Samuel Rolland of the Paris Missionary Society translated some parts of the New Testament and several hymns into Sotho and, in 1843, set up the first printing press in Basutoland at his mission station at Beersheba. A second generation Paris missionary, Adolphe Mabille, published a Sotho–English dictionary and, after 1863, on a small printing press at the Morija mission station, he produced *Leselinyana* (Little Light), the oldest still existing vernacular newspaper in southern Africa. He had also translated the entire Bible into Sotho by 1879.

A literature requires people to read it; hence, for the LMS missionaries of post-Enlightenment Britain, "evangelism was inseparable from education."[46] The LMS started the first schools among the Tswana, with Kuruman serving as the centre of LMS education. Kuruman-trained evangelists and preachers taught and established schools in the most distant villages. Except for the Tawana in the isolated Ngamiland region, most Tswana had access to European schools by the 1860s. Primary schools, staffed with Tswana teachers, existed by 1880 in all major Tswana villages, primarily focused on religious instruction but also teaching reading, writing, arithmetic, history, geography and some domestic science (sewing, baking, and ironing) for girls. Teachers taught almost entirely in Tswana, although some parents objected because they wanted their children to learn English in order to understand the European culture. Mission schools in this region, always short of funds, received little support either from their missionary society or from colonial governments. Low salaries attracted few good teachers, and the level of education remained generally poor. Not until 1904 did the Bechuanaland Protectorate provide any funding for education.

PEMS missionaries promoted Sotho education as fervently as did the LMS among the Tswana. During the Golden Age schools were started at all the mission stations, including the first mission at Morija. The schools were usually run by the missionary or his wife, although Arbousset established some evening schools managed by African assistants in the villages. Samuel Rolland's wife ran the school at Beersheba serving over three hundred students. In 1846 the missionaries decided to establish a secondary school or seminary for Sotho catechists and teachers. Events of the late 1840s and 1850s delayed these plans, however, and the Boys' Secondary School at Morija did not open until 1866. Schools suffered during these rough years of the second phase of missionary activity but began to recover in the late 1850s with the arrival of the second generation of PEMS missionaries. By 1871 there were 1,876 "scholars" studying in mission schools.[47]

MONARCHS AND MISSIONARIES AMONG TSWANA AND SOTHO

In 1871–72 the missionaries and the Basutoland administration reached an agreement whereby the missionaries would be responsible for public education. In return for government subsidies, including all or the greater part of teachers' salaries, the schools had to offer instruction in reading and writing in Sotho, and some English and arithmetic. The missionaries also had to provide school buildings and to allow an official inspector to visit each school once or twice a year. Otherwise they had complete control over the schools, including appointment or dismissal of teachers, and were able to offer Bible instruction as the centrepiece of instruction. The Boys' Secondary School became a Normal School in 1875 for teacher training. In 1873 a Preparatory School was started for younger pupils preparing to attend the Normal School and then was converted in 1880 into a Bible School. A Girls' School was founded in 1871 and had seventy students by 1879. According to Ellenberger, the school sought to "form Christian women who would have a good influence on their families and round about them. It was less a matter of giving them a good education than of developing their character, teaching them order, cleanliness and home duties."[48] An Industrial School was established in 1878 for boarding students, and soon supplied the country with carpenters, masons, saddlers, and shoemakers.[49] These four boarding schools, together with the elementary education system furnished by the missionaries, provided Lesotho with a solid educational foundation that continued into the twentieth century. Yet, in part because of resistance to Christianization in this period, as late as 1892, only 12 to 15 per cent of school-age children were enrolled in mission schools.[50]

As the nineteenth century ended, missionaries throughout southern Africa faced yet a new threat from African Initiated Churches (AICs). Less widespread among Sotho and Tswana than elsewhere in southern Africa, AICs attracted African Christians for a number of possible reasons. A few rulers saw these churches as a means to weaken missionary influence, while sustaining African customs and maintaining their own chiefly powers. Some African ministers were offended by the failure of mission churches to grant them positions of leadership in their churches, some by the racist attitudes and behaviour of a number of missionaries. Some believed that God called them to establish a new church proclaiming the true message.

But generally, in the nineteenth century, Sotho and Tswana rulers preferred European missionary societies, which they could control to some degree. They viewed AICs – break-away bodies led by dynamic spiritual leaders – as threats to their own authority. Whatever form they took, these churches were alien to the African societal structure dominated by the chief; they were accordingly discouraged and repressed and made little headway among the monarchically dominated Tswana and Sotho.

It was the disposition of Tswana and Sotho rulers that determined success or failure of Christian missionary activity. The rulers invited the missionaries in and determined where they could settle, what activities they could perform, what benefits they must provide, what members of society they could influence, and when they must leave. Missionary fortunes shifted with the political, social, and economic forces at work among the Sotho and Tswana, forces over which the missionaries had little control. The rise of a powerful prophet, the threat posed by other Europeans seeking African land, or a dearth of funding from the metropole could reverse years of missionary effort. But it was the African ruler who allowed the mission, if not to thrive, then at least to maintain its presence. Moshoeshoe continued to protect the PEMS missionaries, for example, even when the majority of the Sotho aristocracy and many commoners wanted them sent away.

Rulers and missionaries had, for the most part, different agendas. The rulers believed that missionaries could bring guns and other trade goods, provide knowledge of the European world, protect their people from outside interference, and offer Western medicine and education. Later, when white settlers were encroaching on their lands, the same rulers relied on missionaries to help them attain their autonomy. Moreover, with varying degrees of diplomatic skill, Moshoeshoe being perhaps the most adept, the rulers played off one missionary society or church against the others to gain the benefits they sought. The missionaries, for their part, did everything possible, within the parameters set by the rulers, to advance their own, very different, agenda. But while the missionaries' ultimate goals of conversion and lifelong membership in the church met, in this period, with only limited success among the Sotho and Tswana, their most enduring legacies may well be those for which the rulers originally invited and later tolerated them – health care, education, certainly a written language, and two independent nations.

E. Lemue, Paris Evangelical Missionary, holding evening service

7

The Spread of Christianity among Whites and Blacks in Transorangia

IRVING HEXHAM & KARLA POEWE

At the beginning of the nineteenth century Europeans in the Cape Colony saw the southern African interior as a vast and uncharted expanse. In the region they knew initially as Transorangia lived various African peoples, including the Sotho–Tswana as well as the Venda, Pedi, Ndebele, and a few Swazi and Zulu. Some of these African communities were settled, others in a state of constant flux. During the 1820s and early 1830s African societies in Transorangia experienced intermittent warfare, often called the *Difaqane*, a consequence of incursions from the Cape frontier region and Natal.[1] In the 1830s the white settlers from the Cape Colony, known as Voortrekkers, swept into the region stretching from the Orange River in the south to the Limpopo River in the north, and between the Kalahari desert in the west and Natal in the east.

African societies of Transorangia practised different patterns of habitation: individual homesteads (Zulu), villages (Sotho, Venda, and some Tswana), and towns (Tswana). While all groups engaged in hunting, agriculture, and herding, techniques and implements varied considerably, as did clothing and footwear. All were patriarchal, but kinship systems differed as to the role and ranking of wives, the function of bridewealth, the acceptance of levirate and sororate marriages, and so on.[2] Many of these factors directly or indirectly affected religious practices and, taken together, explain, up to a point, the varying responses to the arrival of Christian missionaries and subsequent conversion rates.

It is remarkably difficult to reconstruct "traditional African religion" in Transorangia before 1910, since almost all our information about African beliefs comes from missionary sources. Early missionaries, like Robert Moffat of the London Missionary Society,[3] looked for church-like buildings, temples, or other structures serviced by an organized priesthood with regular worship services. For them, religion meant cultic practices like those of Christianity, Islam, Judaism, and Hinduism. By contrast the beliefs and practices of Africans in Transorangia seemed to have centred not on worship or church organization but on practical matters, like the planting of crops, childbirth, and, most of all, healing. Not surprisingly, therefore, missionaries found it necessary to adapt their approach. Robert Moffat, for example, devoted much attention to the provision of a water supply at Kuruman Mission, while David Livingstone's relationship with traditional healers has attracted considerable attention in an area where both sides had something to contribute.[4]

Moffat stated that "among the Bechuanas, the name for God, adopted by the missionaries is *Morimo*" (now rendered *Modimo*). He went on to say that in its traditional usage "Morimo did not, then, convey to the mind of those who heard it the idea of God." Moffat explained that when he first arrived in southern Africa he was convinced all men believed in God; eventually he gave up this view in the light of contrary evidence. After repeated attempts to talk about God to numerous Tswana, he reluctantly came to the conclusion that they had no concept of God whatsoever.[5] Disagreeing with this view, the modern Tswana theologian and historian of religion, Gabriel M. Setiloane, argues that missionaries like Moffat failed to recognize the true dynamics of Tswana religious beliefs because they looked for a personal God similar to the God of Western Christianity.[6] He concludes that the High God of the Tswana, *Modimo*, is the force of life itself and, as such, is correctly referred to by the impersonal IT, similar to the *mysterium tremendum et fascinans* of Rudolf Otto's *The Idea of the Holy*.[7] Once this basic fact is recognized, Setiloane argues, many confusions in Moffat's account of his struggle to understand Tswana beliefs can be resolved, because, despite his weaknesses, Moffatt was an astute observer of Tswana religion.[8] Setiloane points out also that the Sotho–Tswana do not appear to have had a creation myth, but that the Ndebele, like the Zulu, did.[9] The available evidence suggests that Zulu traditional religion centred on ancestors and did not involve a belief in a high God, while the Sotho–Tswana recognized an overarching, impersonal force, similar to a high God.[10] Yet, despite differences in beliefs and ritual practices, they shared many beliefs, for example, in witchcraft, prophecy, and a concern for healing powers.[11]

Sympathetic Healing and Witchcraft: Folk Religion among the Boers

As a result of unsettled conditions on the Cape frontier attributed to the "tyranny of British imperialism," along with disputes about the treatment of non-European servants, the abolition of slavery and sundry other local grievances, between 5,000 and 14,000 frontier Boers and their servants migrated out of the Colony between 1836 and 1845, in what came to be known as the Great Trek. These Voortrekkers packed their belongings into covered wagons and crossed the Orange River to move into largely uncharted territories, where they eventually founded two independent republics, the Orange Free State and the South African Republic (Transvaal).[12]

The Afrikaner poet and theologian J.D. du Toit (1877–1953) encapsulated a popular Afrikaner version of the story in these words:

> But see! the world becomes wilder;
> the fierce vermin worsen,
> stark naked hordes,
> following tyrants.
> How the trekkers suffer,
> just like another Israel,
> lost in the veld – by enemies surrounded,
> but for another Canaan elected,
> led forward by God's plan.[13]

Before the Great Trek, ran the myth, the interior of the continent was inhabited by "wild tribes" totally cut off from "the civilizing influence of Christianity." But the Boer "freedom seekers," who preferred the dangers of an unknown frontier to injustice, brought civilisation and Christianity to them.[14]

The available evidence about Voortrekker religion is fragmentary and open to conflicting interpretations. The argument that Calvinism played a central role in Boer society, once taken for granted but more recently challenged, remains open.[15] The Dutch Reformed Church at the Cape (the NGK) condemned the Great Trek as an act of open rebellion.[16] The majority of Voortrekkers retained a residual if strained loyalty to the NGK but had to obtain occasional ministrations from men like the former LMS missionary Erasmus Smit[17] and the American missionary Daniel Lindley.[18]

There is considerable evidence that Voortrekker society was a typical frontier society where folk religions flourished in a climate of relative religious isolation.[19] The frontier society established by the Boers was in some respects similar to that of their Nguni, Sotho, and Tswana neighbours. A few Boers lived in small towns, the majority on relatively isolated farms well away from other Boers, well removed at first from the vices, the literary culture, and the pace of settled urban life. Like the Africans of the region, the Boers loved their cattle. Like Africans, too, they married, to some extent, within clan-like groups identified through common ancestors, and they shared religious beliefs and practices. For example, after various churches were established in the region, almost all Murrays, Gerdeners, Malans, and Marais's remained loyal members of the NGK, while after 1853 the Engelbrechts, Van der Hoffs, Jouberts, and Brands in the north tended to join the newly formed Nederduitsch Hervormde Kerk van Afrika (NHK). Similarly, Venters, Van der Walts, Potgieters, and De Klerks were members of a distinct Boer sub-culture generally known by the name "Dopper," most of them eventually joining the Gereformeerde Kerk (GK) in 1859.[20]

Between these family and church clan formations there was little or no contact. Inter-marriage between them was frowned upon and often led to excommunication from the local church, and social ostracism. Couples who ignored local prejudices often ended up moving to the larger towns like Bloemfontein, Johannesburg, or Pretoria.[21] Even within a given religious tradition sub-clans seem to have existed. Thus within the GK a clear division existed along family lines between the orthodox Calvinists and others more inclined to folk beliefs, and even practices such as polygamy.[22]

Before the evangelization of frontier communities by representatives of these three Dutch Reformed churches, the majority of frontier Boers seem to have lacked much meaningful commitment to Christianity. In 1839 the American missionary Daniel Lindley, who was generally sympathetic to the Boers, wrote that they were in need of evangelization, conversion, instruction, and guidance in developing a pious Christian way of life. In a letter of 17 July 1839 he said of the Transvaal Boers: "In most of their houses you will find a Bible ... But this good book is, with a *few* exceptions, little read and less understood ... They are deplorably ignorant." Lindley closed by saying, "I do sincerely believe that the cheapest, speediest, easiest way to convert the heathen here is to convert the *white ones* first."[23] A year earlier, Prosper Lemue, a French missionary to the Sotho, noting the hostility of the Boers to missions, described the Voortrekkers as "a scourge which threatens the Basuto nation and the neighbouring tribes ..." and "a source of anxiety to the true friends of missions."[24]

Ten years later a Cape Town-born adventurer, James Chapman, who spent many years living on the frontier as a trader, noted that among "the Boers ... education and general knowledge is very limited," and added that "the majority of Boers are superstitious ... [and] believe in omens."[25] In Chapman's view it was their lack of respect for formal religion that led many Boers to oppose missionary work and to "take no interest in the souls of [Africans]."[26] American, French, and German missionaries throughout Southern Africa tended to agree with these assessments.[27]

There is, moreover, considerable evidence that the Boers brought into Transorangia many folk beliefs and practices far removed from the orthodox Calvinism of the Cape Church. Central to the beliefs of frontier Boers in the nineteenth century were folk medicine, spiritual healing, herbal remedies, and sympathetic magic. In his autobiography, Paul Kruger tells how, after a shooting accident, he amputated his thumb. When "the wound healed very slowly [and] ... gangrene set in ... [the local Boers] killed a goat, took out the stomach, and cut it open. I put my hand into it while it was still warm. This Boer remedy succeeded ..."[28] Kruger went on to note that the goats grazed on a river bank where many herbs grew. This he thought explained the success of the cure. The use of animal innards was common in Boer folk medicine, as in African traditional healing.[29] For example, a common remedy for influenza was to skin a sheep or lamb and lay the fresh hot pelt on the chest of the sufferer. Animal dung and plants were used for the treatment of wounds. Certain leaves were rolled into herbal cigarettes believed to cure a variety of ills; leaves were thrown on smouldering fires with the patient inhaling the fumes, a practice reminiscent of African healing practices, the smoke possibly thought to drive out evil spirits. Similarly, to cure influenza the skin was lacerated, possibly with the intent of releasing demons.[30]

One practice that clearly involved a belief in sympathetic magic was the traditional cure for a rupture. A young sapling tree was split down the middle with an axe, the two halves held forcibly apart, and the patient passed through between them. Then the split tree was bound together with strong twine: if the tree recovered and lived, the patient was cured, but if it died the treatment would prove of no avail.[31] African or "Slamaaier"(Malay) witchdoctors were sought when other means had failed, as well as to hex enemies.[32] A number of charges of witchcraft were brought before GK church councils in the late nineteenth and early twentieth century.[33] In some cases the reason cited for consulting a witchdoctor was clearly medical, in others patients sought "charms" or revenge. A church council would explain to a person charged with witchcraft that such practices, being unChristian, must cease. One man argued that "some people have powers which they can use to puzzle others"; he declared that he could find no statement in the Bible against such powers, which, he was sure, had helped him. Disciplined by the church, he remained unrepentant.[34]

In 1910 and 1911 the Synod of the GK in the Orange Free State held discussions of the problem, as did other provincial synods. As a result the GK commissioned two elders to write a booklet outlining the biblical position on these issues and alerting church members to the "dangers" of witchcraft beliefs. Within a few years of these events witchcraft was referred to only occasionally in church documents.[35]

Probably the most important and widespread traditional religious belief was the belief in second sight and the gift of prophecy, usually attributed to individuals born with a caul, considered to possess extraordinary psychic powers. Such people were said to be able to foresee droughts and disasters as well as weddings and births. Telepathic gifts were attributed to certain farm people. Thus, one prominent professor emeritus reported that in 1909 he had witnessed a fellow student communicating with his brother by telepathy over several hundred miles. Such a gift, the professor maintained, had been common among country people in his youth, although few urban Afrikaners, he said, possessed the gift of telepathy today.[36] Sometimes, as in the writings of Herman Charles Bosman, Afrikaner ghost stories have definite religious connotations, many such stories warning of impending death or the activities of malevolent spirits.[37] Some Afrikaners took magical precautions to protect themselves from the spirits, of which the most popular was the *tokkelossie*, African in origin, a small, hairy man said to possess immense strength and sexual power.[38]

"Converting the White Ones First": Missions to Whites in Transorangia

Because it opposed the Great Trek, the NGK was slow to establish congregations beyond the Orange River. Its first regular evangelists in Transorangia, during the 1840s, were Andrew Murray Sr., J.H. Neethling, and P.K. Albertyn. From 1849 to 1851 Andrew Murray Jr. (1828–1917), in a series of extensive preaching tours like those of American Methodist circuit riders, set up a number of small churches, usually on the farms of pious farmers. A few church buildings were also erected in small towns like Bloemfontein, Potchefstroom, and Rustenburg.[39]

The religious situation changed dramatically in 1852 when Dirk van der Hoff arrived from the Netherlands to minister to the people living in the South African Republic (Transvaal). A number of other able, Dutch-trained ministers, including A.J. Begemann and G.W. Smits, followed him and together established the first indigenous Reformed church in Southern Africa.[40] The name of Van der Hoff's church, De Nederduitsch Hervormde Kerk van Afrika (*Hervormde* means literally "re-formed") or NHK, reflects his nationalism and the desire of many Transvalers for political independence. Van der Hoff played an important political role in the young Republic, in 1853 helping develop its first educational policy. Later he became chairman of the Republic's Board of Education. Together with others, he drafted the Constitution, adopted in 1857, designed the state's flag, the Vierkleur, and wrote a national anthem and other patriotic songs.[41]

An advocate of "modern thought," Van der Hoff was regarded as a "liberal" or "modernist"[42] by his religious opponents. He accepted the biblical criticism of the period, questioned many traditional Christian beliefs, and generally adopted the latest European fashions in theology.[43] Apparently Van der Hoff did not at first contemplate a complete separation from the NGK in the Cape.[44] For him an independent church in the Transvaal was a matter of political pride rather than doctrinal purity.[45] As time passed, however, the NHK developed into the People's Church (*Volkskerk*) of the South African Republic, similar to the type of church structure found in the various independent German states of the period. The NHK's attempt to become the state church of the South African Republic led, in 1863–64, to a desultory two-year civil war, in which members of the NHK, with supporters of the establishment, fought against members of the GK and other dissidents led by Paul Kruger. Eventually, in a political compromise, the NHK was assigned a place as one church among many.[46] Because the NHK made no attempt to spread beyond the Transvaal until relatively late, it encouraged a narrow Transvaal, rather than a broad Afrikaner, nationalism.

The second independent Reformed church to be founded in Transorangia was the Gereformeerde Kerk van Zuid-Afrika (Reformed Church of South Africa, or GK), founded in 1859 by the Rev. Dirk Postma. In the Netherlands Postma had been a member of the secessionist Afgescheiden Christelijke Gereformeerde Kerk (Separated Christian Reformed Church, or ACGK), which sought to uphold traditional Calvinism against the inroads of theological liberalism.[47] In 1857, a well-known Orange Free State politician, J.J. Venter, wrote to the ACGK in the Netherlands, complaining about the evangelical and liberal influences in southern Africa and appealing for a minister loyal to the teachings of Calvinism as formulated in the Synod of Dort (1618–19).[48] In response, Postma was sent to Cape Town in 1858 and from there to the Transvaal, where he sought to work in harmony with Van der Hoff. Shortly afterwards, in a visit to Rustenburg, he made contact with[49] the Doppers, adherents of traditional Calvinist beliefs and practices. About 6,000 in number, 8 percent or so of the Boer population, the Doppers were led, in the early part of the nineteenth century, by the Voortrekker Potgieter, and in the 1830s and later by Paul Kruger, the president of the South African Republic. With Postma they disliked evangelical hymns, as well as Van der Hoff's liberal theology.[50]

When, in 1859, the synod of the NHK decided to enforce the singing of modern hymns in all its congregations, the Doppers, considering such hymns doctrinally impure, argued that only the Psalms of David should be sung. A group of Doppers led by Paul Kruger left the Rustenburg congregation of the NHK and invited Postma to become their minister, thus forming the GK, which quickly established congregations throughout the whole of southern Africa.[51] From the beginning this conservative church claimed to be the true representative of Calvinism in the region.

Postma, like Van der Hoff, played an important role in Afrikaner history, encouraging education and a sense of national identity among members of the church in the Cape, the Free State, and the Transvaal.[52] Before 1899 members of this church, notably Kruger, were prominent in Transvaal politics. Postma's able assistant Jan Lion Cachet, among others, encouraged the development of Afrikaans and the growth of a pan-Boer, or Afrikaner, identity. After the Second Anglo-Boer War its members took a leading role in the Second Language Movement (see p. 302), in Christian National Education (see pp. 136–37), and in the development of Afrikaner nationalist ideology. Yet the GK itself was inactive politically, until, between 1902 and 1915, it lent support to the rising Afrikaner nationalist cause, allowing, for example, its various publications and synods to support J.B.M. Hertzog, the leader of the National Party after 1914.[53]

The work of the NGK beyond the Vaal was at first overshadowed by the newly founded NHK and GK, but in the 1860s was slowly re-established by a new breed of evangelical ministers strongly influenced by the piety of John Murray,[54] the first-professor of theology at the new seminary in Stellenbosch, and his brother Andrew Murray Jr. Because of their emphasis on the evangelization and education of blacks, and on interdenominational prayer and holiness meetings,[55] and because of their willingness to work with English-speaking ministers and congregations,[56] representatives of the NGK in the Transvaal were often regarded as traitors to the Volk.[57]

The possibility of uniting the NGK churches in the Transvaal and Orange Free State with the NGK in the Cape foundered in 1862 when theological liberals, in their campaign to gain control of the Cape synod from the evangelicals, appealed to the civil courts to exclude from the NGK synod representatives of regions outside the Cape (see p. 60).[58] To the dismay of evangelicals, the courts did so, and evangelical influences within the synod were drastically reduced. The NGK remained divided into a number of geographically defined churches, weakening any sense of a common identity, and limiting its potential for fostering nationalism among its members. However, the evangelicals, through their control of Dutch Reformed theological education in southern Africa at the seminary in Stellenbosch, and aided by divisions among the liberals, eventually gained complete control of the NGK in the Cape and elsewhere.[59]

The Reformed Churches were not alone in Transorangia. Anglicans in the 1850s made repeated abortive attempts to establish a congregation in Bloemfontein. In 1863 a bishop was consecrated for the Orange Free State, and Anglican work began in earnest. Later, in 1879, the Anglican Church extended itself northwards, founding a new diocese in the Transvaal. Anglican clergy north of the Orange ministered to English-speaking white farmers and traders. Later they added a growing population of miners and other fortune hunters; but only slowly developed missionary outreaches to blacks.[60]

The first Catholic work in the north began with visits by an itinerant priest, Father Hoendervangers, in the 1860s. By 1869 two priests were stationed in Bloemfontein and itinerant preachers were beginning to enter the Transvaal. Following the First Anglo-Boer War (1879–1881) more than two-thirds of all Roman Catholics, largely miners and prospectors, left the Transvaal. Not until 1886 was the decision taken to establish a Roman Catholic mission to the Transvaal, and even then it catered mainly to whites.[61] During this time various other smaller Protestant groups, such as the Plymouth Brethren,[62] and even some members of the Greek Orthodox Church, entered Transorangia.[63] Some Pentecostal groups were also active,[64] and various other sectarian groups such as the Swedenborgians, Mormons, Jehovah's Witnesses, and Theosophists, entered the area.[65]

By the late nineteenth century a network of small Christian churches had been established among all white groups in Transorangia. Ministers were particularly successful in recruiting Boers to the Reformed churches, especially after the Boer defeat in the Second Anglo-Boer War (1899–1902). The cultural and political gap between English-speakers and Dutch-speakers intensified as each group was attracted to different denominations.[66]

Boer religion appears to have been far more complex in Transorangia than in the Cape, where, by the end of the century, evangelicalism triumphed. In Transorangia three dominant religous strands existed: residual rationalism, which co-existed alongside folk beliefs, a more traditional Calvinism, and a growing evangelicalism. The rationalists found a religious home in Van der Hoff's NHK, the Calvinists in the GK, the evangelicals in the NGK or in one of the English-speaking evangelical churches such as the Methodists, and from 1900 in various Pentecostal groups.

Two reasons may be advanced for the growth of a strong religious culture among whites in Transorangia. First, from 1860 onwards a series of evangelical revivals, led by Andrew Murray in the Cape, spilled over into the northern regions,[67] leading to a gradual increase in church attendance among whites, and to the formation of inter-denominational prayer meetings and para-church organizations devoted to personal holiness and the advance of missions.[68] Second, following the Boer defeat in the Second Anglo-Boer War,[69] the three Reformed Churches provided the demoralized Boers with what is today called social security.[70] Given the British failure to solve the problem of Transorangian poverty during the period of reconstruction, 1900 to 1905,[71] the Reformed churches gained the loyalty of the Boers by providing them with practical aid,[72] and, as a result, the majority of Afrikaans-speakers in Transorangia were attending church regularly by 1910 and considered themselves committed Christians.[73] At the same time, although in lesser numbers, English-speaking whites were gradually drawn into a variety of churches that were spreading slowly throughout southern Africa.

Competition and Compromise with Colonialism: Missions to Blacks in Transorangia

Early in the nineteenth century various Christian and semi-Christian groups ventured beyond the uneasy borders of the more settled Cape Colony into the interior of central southern Africa. Groups of mixed racial origin, originating in the Cape, and later known as Griquas, began to circulate and settle beyond both the Orange and the Vaal.[74] The first whites to venture north were adventurers and missionaries, like Jacobus Kicherer, some of whom later became traders. The early travellers ranged over a vast area and, although they spread some knowledge of Christianity among Africans, they established no permanent mission stations.[75] At the end of the Napoleonic Wars in 1815, the Congregational London Missionary Society (LMS), soon to be followed by the Methodists and other societies, renewed efforts to establish a permanent missionary presence in central southern Africa; the systematic evangelization of African societies north of the Orange had begun (see also chap. 6). Thus, missionaries and not the Voortrekkers were the first Europeans to settle in central southern Africa; and the first white born north of the Cape was the child of a missionary.[76] Soon afterwards, however, the relative isolation of the frontier ended for ever with the arrival of large numbers of Voortrekkers.

Wesleyan missions, the South African origins of which are difficult to pinpoint precisely (pp. 54, 75), existed in Transorangia from the 1820s, though the first Wesleyan church in the South African Republic was founded by David Magata, an African, at Potchefstroom in the late 1860s. Little is known about Magata. As a young man he was enslaved by the Matabele; while in captivity, he heard the preaching of two American missionaries and converted to Christianity. After Boers attacked his captors, he escaped to the Wesleyan mission at Thaba Nchu, where he studied with William Shaw and was commissioned to preach. An enthusiastic and successful preacher, he spread Christianity among Africans on the High Veld and in Natal.[77]

Other Methodist missions, both formal and informal, were highly successful in Transorangia, and as a result by 1913 there were 51 Methodist missionaries, 36 black ministers, 2,091 black local preachers, and 21,300 African members of the Methodist church in the Transvaal,[78] an impressive growth from the 3,401 converts they reported in 1883.[79] The Scottish missionary statesman James Stewart commended the Methodists' "great evangelistic fervour, energy, and spiritual warmth," as well as their "unswerving belief in the power of the simple preaching of the gospel of Jesus Christ."[80] He praised Wesleyan efforts to use "native ordained preachers and native evangelists ... [and for devoting] much time and effort to native education ..." Nevertheless, the aggressive evangelism of the Methodists, and their great reliance on poorly trained black lay preachers and evangelists – virtues in Stewart's eyes – made their work controversial among other mission agencies.

The noted German missiologist Gustav Warneck, professor of theology at the University of Halle, charged that Methodist missions "intrude discourteously into the fields of other societies, while the maturity of their Christians and the education of their native helpers leave much to be desired."[81] The Boers, too, took a strong dislike to "Methodism," identifying it with the growth of political consciousness among Africans,[82] a view supported by the Dutch prime minister, theologian, and philosopher, Abraham Kuyper, who blamed English religion, especially Methodism, for imperialism in general, and for the Second Anglo-Boer War in particular.[83] His South African disciple, J.D. du Toit (Totius) would later follow his teacher's example, denouncing Methodism as the cause of innumerable ills, particularly the erosion of distinctions of race and class.[84]

There were few Anglicans in Transorangia before 1910 and their impact on Africans was small. In 1883, for example, only 948 Anglican converts were reported, although eight mission stations had been established in the Orange Free State and two in the Transvaal.[85] The missionary activity by the Roman Catholic church in the Boer Republics was insignificant, and inhibited by government decrees until 1905. Only after 1910 did Anglicans and Roman Catholics begin to have a significant influence among Africans in northern areas.[86]

Various other English-speaking missionaries were active in Transorangia throughout the nineteenth century. They belonged to relatively small societies or were independently financed, and their contribution to the history of Christianity in Transorangia is poorly documented. There is, for instance, no history of the missionaries sponsored by the Plymouth Brethren, who produced many highly motivated converts with a significant impact on other Africans.[87] The role of African-Americans as workers, missionaries, and evangelists especially in the Ethiopian and Zionist movements, however, has been well documented (see pp. 212–16).[88] Around the turn of the twentieth century other smaller missionary societies

129

became active, especially in the shanty towns around Johannesburg, among them the South African Compounds and Interior Mission, a local missionary society founded in 1896 by a Natal lawyer named A.W. Baker (see p. 244); the Presbyterian Church of South Africa Mission, founded in 1904; and the Suisse Romande Mission, founded in 1869 by the Reformed churches of the canton of Vaud, Switzerland, a mission supported by various French churches and, in 1883 by the Free Churches of Neuchâtel and Geneva. The Suisse Romande society worked in Transorangia from its inception, its most famous South African member the missionary anthropologist Henri Junod. All these missions played an important role in the evangelization of Africans, but their work is often underestimated, as noted, because of a lack of detailed information. The mission work of the Dutch Reformed Church in Transorangia began in 1857 but was slow to develop before 1910. The evangelical ethos of DRC missions made them very similar to the English-speaking missions and to Methodism, as the more conservative Calvinists were quick to point out.[89]

British missionaries had many advantages over their continental counterparts. They spoke the language of one of the dominant powers in the region and could always appeal for help if necessary. They could also depend on much stronger financial support from their home bases: in the latter half of the nineteenth century even the worst-paid British missionaries were far better off than the best-paid German ones.[90] Far less dependent on farming, hunting, or trading for the necessities of life, British missionaries enjoyed greater freedom to act independently in the face of opposition from Boers than did the German and other continental missionaries.

German speakers were the most important group of missionaries in this area prior to 1914,[91] but, like members of the smaller societies, they are largely ignored in English-language literature. The first German missionaries to arrive in Transorangia were members of the Rhenish mission, founded by a German pietist group in the town of Elberfeld on the Rhine in 1799 and largely dependent on lay support. Its first missionaries reached South Africa in 1829. Rhenish missionaries operated on the borders of Transorangia from 1836 onwards, originally crossing the Orange as itinerant preachers on scouting expeditions. In the 1840s the mission began its permanent operations on the borders of Transorangia.[92]

The Berlin Missionary Society was established in Berlin in 1824 by a group of pious scholars, including Johann Neander (1789–1850) and F.A.G. Tholuck (1799–1877), with support from the German Lutheran churches. It sent out well-educated missionaries who attempted, often with great success, to establish viable Christian communities of local converts who learned trades and received a thorough education. It established permanent stations in Transorangia from 1834.[93]

Members of the Hermannsburg Mission, founded in 1849 by Ludwig Harms in Hermannsburg, Germany, and supported by the Lutheran churches of Hanover, arrived in 1858 (see p. 93). Its first missionaries went out in groups to found "mission colonies," to teach European skills to local peoples and to provide an example of Christian living. In general, their missionaries were poorly educated persons drawn from the German working-class. Following the death of Harms in 1865, a schism in the state church of Hanover led to the establishment of the Free Church of Hanover, to which most of Hermannsburg missionaries adhered, but a smaller group continued to support the state Church. As a result of these theological disputes several Hermannsburg missionaries in South Africa left the mission in 1890, to form a new one, the Hanoverian Free Church Mission, with Free Church support.[94]

Precariously positioned in the Voortrekker republics, the German missionaries tended to be circumspect in criticizing the Boers. They received meagre financial support from their home churches – under a policy designed to encourage self-reliance – and hence were vulnerable to local pressure.[95] Among themselves, the German missionaries asserted candidly that the Boers were a hindrance to the spread of the gospel. They complained about Boer mistreatment of blacks, particularly about the arbitrariness of Boer law, which, they claimed, changed whenever convenient. They reported to their headquarters in Germany that blacks were being cheated out of their land and driven to accept serfdom or worse.[96] Before 1880 the Berlin missionaries were more cautious in their criticisms than either the Rhenish or Hermannsburg missions, which had strong bases in British territory and were therefore less dependent than the Berliners on the goodwill of Boer authorities.[97] The Germans despaired at what they saw as a lack of true piety and Christian virtue among the Boers, and were full of praise for British rule.[98] Yet for pragmatic reasons, German mission policy, especially in the South African Republic, accepted subservience to Boer authorities.

In theory, German missions were expected to establish self-sufficient communities supporting their missionaries and many converts,[99] and to train blacks in modern agriculture, preparing some others for skilled trades; but these training schools and communities, effective in the short run, eventually failed, as seen most strikingly in the history of Botshabelo,[100] a mission town that grew from 867 baptized Christians in 1868 to 2,747 in 1892. It featured modern farming, a church school, a store, a printing press, a smith, and a wheelwright. Richter describes it as a "cultural oasis," because of the many admirable achievements of African converts in education and the arts.[101] Soon, however, succumbing to external pressures and the failure of its people to find acceptance outside the mission, it was plagued by secessions and the creation of what are now known as African Initiated or Independent churches (AICs).[102] The most famous of these secessions was led by Johannes Dinkwanyane, who separated from the Botshabelo mission in 1873 to form an independent Christian community.[103] As a result of this break, external pressures, and other conflicts, the remaining African population at Botshabelo returned to African farming techniques and cattle, bringing to an end a bold educational experiment.[104]

In the Boer republics all missionaries were viewed with suspicion, although German missionaries less so than English. The German missionaries were under constant pressure to take out local citizenship, or in some cases to act as government agents. When they yielded they won favoured treatment, but at the cost of alienating blacks. They found it almost impossible to acquire land for their farm settlements, and the use of the land they did obtain was strictly limited by government insistence on oaths of loyalty. Later they discovered that African converts whom they had trained in a trade were often denied the chance to practise their new skills off the mission station. White employers either insisted on employing only white tradesmen or paid black tradesmen the same rates as unskilled labourers.[105]

After the First Anglo-Boer War (1880–81) German missionaries became more sympathetic to the Boers, in part because they felt betrayed when the British abandoned the Transvaal in 1881. But they also responded to increased pressure from the Transvaal government, because they were infuriated that a Hermannsburg missionary, H. Fuls, with a group of other witnesses, had testified to the British about Paul Kruger's allegedly sadistic treatment of blacks. Fuls eventually resigned from the mission.[106]

During the Second Anglo-Boer War (1899–1902) German missionaries were in a particularly vulnerable position, often suffering greatly because each side suspected them of being in league with the other. In general, German missionaries regarded British methods of warfare as "barbaric," the brutal murder of the missionary Daniel Hesse by Australian troops lending a personal edge to their alienation from British rule.[107] Many families of German missionaries were interned as enemy aliens in British concentration camps, where they observed epidemics ravaging the Boer community, and developed a strong, if guarded, sympathy for the Boer cause.[108] It should also be noted that the war had the unintended effect of spreading Christianity among blacks in the camps and through the dispersal of many Africans from the mining centres back to their rural homes.[109]

Among their African converts, the Berlin missionaries encouraged a patriarchal society with the missionary taking the place of the chief. African customs and experiences were welcomed within limits and African spirituality valued. The Berliners mastered African languages and encouraged the use of the vernacular in worship. They did not question the reality of dreams and visions in African conversion and Christian life: on the contrary, like the Anglican Henry Callaway in Natal, they regarded such experiences as genuine expressions of the work of the Holy Spirit, and encouraged their converts to report such phenomena. The other German missionaries were less enthusiastic and more conventional in their piety, but all German missionaries respected the testimony of converts, regarding them as genuine Christians and responsible persons, capable of personal growth through education.[110]

The pattern of conversion to Christianity among Africans in Transorangia differed somewhat from the pattern among Zulu in Natal. In Transorangia, especially in German mission areas, mass conversions sometimes occurred with the encouragement of chiefs, while Zulu converts were often individuals alienated from their society. Almost from the beginning, missionaries in Transorangia discovered that African converts broke away to form their own churches.[111] The wrenching experience of schism quickly led church leaders to believe that religious diversity was hindering church growth, a view repeated later by historians such as Peter Hinchliff, who saw "competition to 'sell' rival brands of the Christian faith" as "the great curse of nineteenth century missionary expansion."[112] Yet as Stark and Bainbridge have shown, there is considerable evidence that religions and religious movements thrive on open competition.[113] Where churches are established by the state, and public worship is strictly controlled, religious commitment tends to be low, but in a religious "free market" people flock to the religions of their choice.

Rather than hindering the growth of Christianity, as the missionaries thought, religious diversity actually encouraged the growth of African Initiated Churches (AICs) and the rapid spread of Christianity to all African groups in southern Africa.[114]

By the early 1900s British colonial administrators considered "Ethiopianism" (see pp. 211–15) a major threat to the peace of the entire region,[115] and as late as 1924 the influential Christian writer Edgar Brookes described Ethiopianism in highly negative terms.[116] Only after the publication of Bengt Sundkler's *Bantu Prophets in South Africa* in 1948,[117] did white attitudes towards AICs begin to become more favourable.[118] Although AICs had begun to develop almost as soon as missionaries arrived in Transorangia,[119] the first independent African religious movement to take the name the "Ethiopian Church," was founded in 1892 by the Rev. Mangena Mokoni, a Wesleyan minister based in Pretoria.[120] The example of his church, with its creative use of the Bible and explicit African imagery, inspired a host of imitators, including the Zulu "prophet" Isaiah Shembe, who was born in Transorangia,[121] as well as the founder of the Zion Christian Church of the Transvaal, Ignatius Lekganyane.[122] By 1910 AICs were slowly beginning the phenomenal growth that makes them the largest Christian movement in southern Africa today.[123]

From the beginning of the nineteenth century, when few Christians were to be found in Transorangia and those few, black or white, lived in essentially pagan societies, Christianity had spread steadily until 1910, when the majority of whites and about a quarter of the blacks were committed Christians; for many Christianity formed a central part of their identity.[124] Rarely in the history of the church has Christianity spread so quickly under such difficult circumstances as in nineteenth-century Transorangia.[125] Especially amongst Africans, growth was far swifter and more effective than the first Christian efforts to evangelize Europe, particularly Germany,[126] and compares well with the growth of Christianity in America.[127] In a twenty-five-year period, from 1875 to 1900, fewer than a hundred missionaries and their wives were directly or indirectly responsible for the conversion of about 25,000 African converts.[128] At the same time a handful of Reformed ministers managed to draw the majority of the Boers living in Transorangia into one of the three Dutch Reformed churches. Most English-speaking whites professed some attachment to Christianity. These impressive results contradict the view of many scholars that evangelism in the nineteenth century was a colossal failure.[129]

Christianity adapted to local cultures, both black and white. An interest in healing and folk medicines was shared by both communities, as was a belief in prophecy. Traditional practices, such as polygamy and rituals for blessing homesteads, seem to have been accepted by many black and Afrikaner Christians.[130] Even though the majority of blacks chose to become Lutherans, and most whites joined a Reformed church, among both groups the notion of a *Volkskerk* (Peoples Church) embracing the entire culture was influential. Independent church movements developed among both black and whites, as AICs, Apostolic, and other Pentecostal movements began to make an increasing impact at the turn of the twentieth century. Despite the growing separation between black and white Christians

in Transorangia, the history of Christianity in both groups was surprisingly similar.

8

Modernization and Apartheid: The Afrikaner Churches

JOHANN KINGHORN

In 1970 the principal of the Afrikaans-speaking University of Pretoria told an anecdote to a massive gathering of students. Just after the turn of the twentieth century a Dutch *meester* (schoolmaster), brought at great expense to teach children in the flat and isolated western Transvaal, created a crisis by teaching that the earth is round and revolves around the sun. After much deliberation the parents put it to the meester that, while they accepted his superior knowledge about other regions, where conceivably the world might be round and turning, his teaching was demonstrably false in the western Transvaal, especially because it clashed with the authority of the Bible. He was requested, in future, to teach the pupils only biblical science. This story caused the University of Pretoria students to roar with laughter. Their earth was no longer flat or static. Nor did they live any longer in the western Transvaal; they had become urbanized, upwardly mobile, thoroughly modernized. Twenty years later that generation of students would participate enthusiastically in the demise of apartheid, the system their forebears had so resolutely devised. Between these generations lies a fascinating history of twentieth-century social and intellectual transformation.

During much of the twentieth century South Africa was swept over a cataract of social revolution. The century had begun with the bitter war between the Voortrekker republics and British imperialism, a visible symptom of a social and economic upheaval begun with the discovery of diamonds in 1867, and of gold in 1886. The Transvaal and all of South Africa, hitherto a remote outback, was suddenly catapulted into the global market economy, becoming an indispensable chip in the international politics of industrializing Europe. As if overnight, European and African farmers, rural in lifestyle, feudal in mentality, and most of them illiterate, were compelled to deal with industrialization, urbanization, the pluralization of society, the intrusion of international politics into the region, and the clash of competing ideologies. There followed a century of confusion, conflict, and massive social engineering instituted by Afrikaners.

Political, ideological, or economic perspectives, though valuable, cannot alone penetrate to the core of the matter. Only by including the perspective of religion can we understand those value judgements that led Afrikaners to mobilize themselves so as to draw most South Africans, over most of the twentieth century, into the magnetic field of their politics. It then becomes clear that this process is best described as Afrikanerdom's slow and agonizing adaptation to modernity. The Afrikaner churches joined other institutions at the centre of the Afrikaner dynamic, profoundly shaped by it and shaping it in turn. The social history of these churches (at least up until the 1970s) overlaps largely with the social history of South Africa itself.

The churches involved in this chapter are: the only nationwide church of the group, the Dutch Reformed Church or NGK (first established at the Cape in 1652 and spreading to the northern interior from 1836 onwards); the very small Hervormde Kerk or NHK (established in 1855 with its base in the Transvaal); the even smaller Gereformeerde Kerk or GK (established in 1857, also in the Transvaal); the Dutch Reformed Missionary Church or NGSK (established in 1881 with its nucleus in the Cape) and the Dutch Reformed Church in Africa or NGKA (established in 1963 by uniting various missions principally in the Free State and northern Transvaal). The last two, the NGSK and NGKA, were founded by the NGK, respectively for Coloureds and for Africans; in 1994 they united into the Uniting Reformed Church of Southern Africa (URCSA). By far the most powerful church in the political and cultural history of South Africa has been the all-white NGK.

Despite cultural, and to a lesser degree, the logical, differences among these churches, they share two important features. They distinguish themselves from all other churches in South Africa by their historical roots in continental European traditions of Protestant theology and piety, particularly Dutch and German Calvinism (cf. pp. 16–24); and their histories are bound up with the history of the Afrikaners, who were the dominant political force in the first seven decades of twentieth-century South Africa.

Predictably the Afrikaner churches initially reacted against modernization. Not so predictable, however, was the strength of that resistance or the length to which Afrikanerdom would eventually go in an attempt to ward off modernity.

Battling Modernism in Education and Science, 1900–1935

The first organized expression of Afrikaner resistance to modernity came early in the century in the Transvaal, led by the Gereformeerde Kerk (GK). Given its exceptional stress on self-determination, its patriarchal concept of authority structures, and its literal adherence to the Reformed confessions of the seventeenth century, it is understandable that the idea of sovereignty (*sowereiniteit*) was central to the GK's theology. God was sovereign, and so were all the spheres of life (*sowereiniteit in eie kring*).[1] One such sphere was education, which from the GK's point of view had to be Christian or it was not education. Before the Anglo-Boer War, with the establishment of an independent theological school at Burgersdorp (which eventually moved and, later, became the Potchefstroom University for Christian Higher Education), a tradition of Christian education based on the Reformed confessions of the seventeenth century had already been established.

Following the pattern of conservatives in the Netherlands, advocates of Christian education saw education as the study of all the sciences based on the doctrine of the sovereignty of God, the creator and maintainer of all things. This perspective was deemed necessary in view of the perceived ungodly challenge of "humanism" to the sovereignty of God, the root of eighteenth- and nineteenth-century disorders such as the French Revolution, Darwin's evolutionary theory, campaigns for human rights, and so on.[2] The "Lockean" ideas imported by the

British into the Transvaal schools after the Anglo-Boer War were, in the view of many Afrikaners, an unacceptable indoctrination into humanism, and they launched a campaign of resistance. On 22 October 1902 the Commission for Christian National Education (*De Commissie Voor Christelijk-National Onderwijs*) was organized with wide support, even by certain moderate political leaders like General Jan Smuts. The title "national" was significant, implying that humanist ideas were by definition alien. After a mere three years there were 300 Christian National schools in the Transvaal, but, by 1907, when state money was withdrawn and funding for the schools from the Netherlands ran out, they were closed.[3]

The campaign for Christian education was renewed when the churches convened a conference in 1918 at Pretoria to formulate an education policy that would accord with the ideals of Christian National Education. Nothing came of it, but the churches persevered, organizing parents' bodies for the cause. In 1934, at a conference at Potchefstroom, the churches formulated a Programme of Action and Principles and appointed a board to promote it. In 1948, when the National Party won power, Christian Nationalism became the official education policy for South Africa, implemented, particularly, in the Bantu Education Act of 1953 that introduced into black schools, as in white schools, compulsory religious instruction (that is, Christian, Reformed evangelization) at all levels.

Meanwhile another ideological battle broke out in the Cape Province, where communities had not been severely disrupted by the Anglo-Boer War. Though many Cape Afrikaners sympathized with the northern Afrikaners, they had no serious problems in accommodating to the presence of the British. Outwardly a climate of moderation and open-mindedness prevailed, helped along, no doubt, by the relative affluence of the Cape and the presence of two universities strongly promoting classic European vaules. But behind the genteel veneer trouble was brewing in the evangelical heart of the Afrikaner churches. Reformed in essence but modified by German pietism, Scottish puritanism and a touch of American conservatism,[4] Afrikaner evangelicalism was characterized by an emphasis on individual religious experience; on the virtues of modesty, diligence, and sobriety; on intellectual and moral education; on a highly motivated missionary movement; and on a somewhat mystical piety. Its perspective was nurtured by the NGK theological seminary at Stellenbosch (established in 1859 and the only NGK seminary in South Africa until 1939), and also by the intellectual and pastoral leadership of the younger Andrew Murray.[5]

During the 1920s the outer calm of the Cape church was shattered by an intellectual storm around Johannes du Plessis, a professor at the seminary at Stellenbosch,[5] best known for his books describing his three extensive tours through Africa. Du Plessis was deeply drawn to Africa, which he believed ripe for cultural and intellectual renewal through Christian missions. He became known as the doyen of the missionary cause, for which he was held in high popular esteem. But he was also attracted to modern trends in theology, and, impressed by modern science, was convinced of the need to reconcile the Bible with it. To address such issues, in 1923, he established a journal *Het Zoeklicht* (*The Searchlight*), vehemently opposed by a former student, D.R. Snyman, who, in turn, began to publish

Die Ou Paaie (*The Old Ways*) in 1926. A battle royal soon spilled beyond the boundaries of the NGK, and, in 1930, Du Plessis was relieved of his teaching duties at the seminary. Numerous church hearings and two Supreme Court cases followed, in which the Kuyperian theologian from the GK, J.D. du Toit, was invited from Potchefstroom to testify against him. Du Plessis won the court cases but was never again reinstated by the seminary.

Many of the Afrikaans elite, including General Jan Smuts, then leader of the opposition in the South African parliament, sided with Du Plessis, to them the voice for a new openness to the world of modern reason. The final court case was followed closely by the daily newspapers.[7] Senator Dr. F.S. Malan, a leading political figure in the Cape and an elder in the congregation of Cape Town, in his book *Our Church and Prof. du Plessis*, put his finger on the core issue, the (future) relationship of "our church and the scientific developments and progress of our time."[8]

Arguing from traditional theology, the church accused Du Plessis of transgressing Christian doctrine by questioning, for example, Christ's omniscience during his earthly existence, as well as Moses' authorship of the first five books of the Bible, the infallibility of the Reformed confessions, and the divine inspiration of the Bible. They also challenged his acceptance of Darwin's concept of evolution. To Du Plessis it was clear that human reason had to be liberated from preconceived conceptions; to the NGK such a view capitulated to the ideas of the Enlightenment. Revered as he was, Du Plessis simply had to be charged with "modernism."

The Du Plessis affair, though essentially theological, was to have immeasurable impact on the churches' ability to deal with the socio-economic crisis that engulfed Afrikaners from the 1920s. In the paranoia that followed the court cases and for many years thereafter the NGK guarded imperiously against any appointment at its seminaries (including, after 1939, the University of Pretoria) that might conceivably promote the cause of "modernism." This policy meant staffing the church's intellectual leadership either with conservative pseudo-Kuyperian neo-Calvinists or with romantic nationalists, and, as a consequence, from the mid-1930s the NGK became the intellectual bastion of resistance against modernization.

"Holding Course in the Crisis": Economics, Politics, and Social Theory, 1932–1950

Indicative of the all-pervasive mood were the monumental three volumes edited by F.J.M. Potgieter (professor at the seminary at Stellenbosch), H.G. Stoker (philosopher at Potchefstroom), and J.D. Vorster (NGK pastor in Cape Town, brother of the later Prime Minister Balthasar J. Vorster) and published between 1935 and 1941 under the title *Koers in die Krisis* (*Holding Course in the Crisis*). All the editors were later to play decisive roles in the unfolding of the apartheid culture. Eloquent in their presentation of the "Calvinist" solutions to humanity's ills, these volumes reflected the conviction that the crisis was total, threatening the foundations of Afrikaners' value system. It also reflected a resolve to deal with the threat by taking total control of South African history – a resolve about to be implemented politically, economically, and, eventually, militarily. The threat had three distinct but related facets: poverty (economics), the pluralization of society (politics), and a breakdown in what were deemed Afrikaner values (social theory).

A 1932 report, funded by the Carnegie Corporation[9] of New York, on the so-called "poor-white" problem, documented the depth of social transformation under way in South Africa. After the Anglo-Boer War the Afrikaner community (except in the Western Cape) had become increasingly impoverished, particularly after 1929 and the great depression, followed by a severe drought. The Afrikaners were compelled to migrate to the cities in search of work, abandoning their rural way of life. Before 1925 the urbanization of Afrikaners was a gradual trickle, but after 1925 it became a flood. Within one generation the social profile of the Afrikaner community changed, as Afrikaners lost the freedom of the countryside, along with their self-image of independence and liberty. More important they suffered a drastic decline in class status, as erstwhile landowners became labourers. Job opportunities in the cities were also scarce, particularly because rural Afrikaners, with no sophisticated skills, were capable only of manual labour. The Carnegie Commission classified 300,000 South Africans as "poor-whites," that is, living below subsistence level. The majority of them were Afrikaners. One out of every three Afrikaners lived in severe deprivation.

The churches, chiefly the NGK, responded with practical steps to support and develop the Afrikaner community but more importantly became involved in the formation of public policy. The comprehensiveness of their approach is evident in their views on white poverty: the causes of poverty – material and mental, self-induced or structurally enforced – had to be discovered and remedied. The churches did not find it difficult to pinpoint the root sources: the city, the British *geldmag* (money-power) and the *swart gevaar* (black peril).

A report in 1947 by the NGK's secretaries for poverty relief in the various provinces, issued under the title *Kerk en Stad* (*Church and City*), rather romantically contrasted rural with city life: God-centred versus human-centred; identity versus plurality; thrift versus waste; integrity versus recklessness. The city was said to devalue labour; it created a host of problems such as divorce, sexual immorality, crime, oppression, and gambling. Liberal capitalism, aided and abetted by democracy, was at the heart of all these disorders. It was time, the report said, to throw off the yoke of the "tyranny of private interest," particularly of capitalists in South Africa who did not "belong to our [Afrikaner] nation and, thus, did not feel any obligation to our ideals, language and religion."[10]

Not that the churches were going to do it alone. They could slot into broader initiatives in combating the inequities of the "foreign" capitalists. Between 1915 and 1918 an Afrikaner press, one insurance company, and the Cooperative Winemakers Union were established in the Cape; and at about the same time the Afrikaner Broederbond (an elite organization which soon decided to operate in secrecy) was founded in Johannesburg – all with the express aim of rehabilitating Afrikaners. Over the years a significant number of pastors were members of the Broederbond. New initiatives followed in the 1930s, among them, the establishment of the Volkskas bank (literally, Cupboard of the Nation) and the convening, in 1939, of the first Volkskongres (Congress of the People) on economic matters, an enormous gathering whose goal was to perform a *reddingsdaad* (deed of salvation).[11] It is extremely difficult to ascertain the churches' actual role in these efforts. It is safe to say, however, that the purposes of the churches and of the various organizations overlapped, as did their value systems, and that to a great extent the same individuals were active in each. As late as the 1960s and 1970s a moderator of the general Synod of the NGK and pastor at Stellenbosch was chancellor of the University of Stellenbosch and a board member of some of the Afrikaner companies as well. And when the dynamic behind the above enterprises led to political power for the National Party in 1948, the churches, whose members now dominated parliament, benefited directly from generous state donations to their social work programmes.

But the churches did also act on their own. Among their more imaginative initiatives were the two attempts by the Cape Church to establish "work colonies." Interest in such ventures began in 1894 and, after some help from the Cape Government, a piece of land was bought at Kakamas. In 1919 a similar venture was attempted at George. Both failed and soon had to be abandoned. The churches' non-commercial ventures were much more numerous and successful. Over the years the NGK was heavily involved in providing boarding houses for poor pupils (growing from nine in 1917 to 178 in 1927); it spent considerable sums and energy in establishing industrial schools until they were eventually recognized and taken over by the Union government in 1925; it established a school for the deaf, blind, and mute at Worcester in the Cape; it founded orphanages (25 in 1947, including one in Salisbury, Rhodesia) as well as homes for the aged and a few hospitals. Some para-church organizations were established, particularly from the 1930s onward, most important among them, the Christelike Maatskaplike Rade (Christian Social Boards) which, with lay participation, coordinated various social work activities. Various women's organizations also came into being, the best known the ACVV (Afrikaner Christian Women's Movement). These organizations' contribution to the general advancement of Afrikaner society was quite astounding.[12]

Even so, the practical steps to provide temporary relief to the poor were not the central contribution of the churches. They sought to cooperate with other forces in the political task of transforming society, a task, as the churches saw it, inextricably linked to the "black peril." Like whites, blacks were flocking in great numbers to the cities and ending up in the poorer areas. Blacks in the cities sold their labour at a considerably lower cost than whites, thus exacerbating the poor-white problem. J.W. Macquarrie,[13] commenting on the Carnegie report, had put his finger on the sore spot: "The problems of the native and the Poor White, where they are not identical, are inextricably interwoven."

Faced with this problem the churches opted for a segregationist solution. In its "missionary policy" statement of 1935 [14] the NGK said:

> The Afrikaner's traditional fear of "Equalization" of black and white was born from his abhorrence of the idea of racial admixture. The Church therefore declares unequivocally that this admixture is undesirable and rejects anything which might lead to such a situation, but does not begrudge the native and the coloured a social status as honourable as he could achieve ... Where the Church declares her opposition against ... the disregarding of racial and colour differences of whites and blacks in the course of everyday life she

would like to promote social differentiation and spiritual or cultural segregation to the benefit of both sections.

Or as D. Lategan, Du Plessis's successor at the seminary at Stellenbosch, put it in 1939:

> The policy of segregation as advocated by the Afrikaner and his Church is the holy calling of the Church to see to the thousands of poor-whites in the cities who fight a losing battle in the present economic world. This policy will entail the removal of unhealthy slums, the creation of healthy suburbs where a sound Christian family can be developed, the undesired moral conditions can be overcome, and therefore as a consequence a healthy state, nation and Church can be developed. The application of segregation will furthermore lead to the creation of separate healthy cities for the non-whites where they will be in a position to develop along their own lines, establish their own institutions and later on govern themselves under the guardianship of the whites.[15]

Two of the essential characteristics of the policy of apartheid are already evident in Lategan's statement: group areas and white supremacy. In the next few years various commissions of the NGK, no doubt keeping an ear to the ground of Afrikaner politics, refined and expanded them. Soon a committee was set up to petition the government (after 1939 the generally pro-British administration of Prime Minister Smuts). From October 1942 onwards they repeatedly asked for prohibition of racially mixed marriages, for curbing of extra-marital racial mixing, for the establishment of residential group areas and, finally, for racially separated factories.[16] Smuts assured one delegation that his government shared their aims, the differences between them lying only in the choice of method.

Public emotion ran particularly high about mixed marriages, and the churches were quite vocal on the issue. A rather crude, but by no means exceptional, example of the prevailing attitude was given by the GK minister, Philippus J.S. de Klerk:

> Equalization leads to the deterioration of both nations. Mixed marriages between higher, civilized and Christianized nations with lower races militate against the Word of God ... This is nothing less than a crime ... The Voortrekkers constantly guarded against such admixture and through their act of faith our nation was saved as a pure Christian race in this our land.[17]

No wonder that the first apartheid legislation enacted by the National Party after taking over power in 1948 was the Prohibition of Mixed Marriages Act. Soon afterwards the new government enacted a stiffened Immorality Act, against interracial sex, and the Group Areas Act, which imposed urban segregation.

The role of Afrikaner churches went deeper than political activism. They nurtured the underlying values, the very soul of Afrikaner mobilization. Two core values were stressed: the family and hierarchical authority, neither of which, of course, is peculiar to Afrikaners. In the case of the Afrikaners, however, these values were undergirded by religious traditions (inherited, through a complicated history, from medieval theology) enshrined as doctrine. Any situation or context, therefore, in which they were perceived to be under threat was to be interpreted as a threat to religion as well. This connection between religion and social values later made it possible to elevate secular apartheid policies to the status of faith and to turn a modern-day inquisition loose on anyone of alternative mind.

The keystone of the Afrikaner value system was the religious presupposition of a cosmological hierarchy headed by God, the ultimate source of all being, consisting of an all-encompassing descending structure of authorities over all of human existence. Of course, modernity, in general, and natural science, in particular, fundamentally challenged this presupposition. In the twentieth century human rights and democracy became the benchmark for social manifestations of this challenge. The model of a society based on the principles of equality, liberty, and fraternity – and driven by the profit motive – is in most respects contrary to a society modelled on the premise of hierarchical authority; it calls for a profound redefinition of human value, authority, and status.

The clash became consciously conceptualized in the churches during the 1930s and 1940s. The social context grew more and more plural while the "equalizing" of people in urban environments and the breakdown of the extended family structures and hierarchies of rural societies increased. Thus the conditions in the cities (or "the exile of modernism, liberalism, humanism and evolutionism" as the editors of *Koers in die Krisis* described it)[18] were seen to threaten terminally the values of family and authority, threats experienced not merely as socio-political problems, but as challenges to religion. But, except for vague feelings and intentions, neither the churches nor Afrikaner politicians had any clear solutions. A conceptual framework and definite policies were needed, and these eventually did emerge from the fusion of the core Afrikaner values with three different currents of thought: nationalism, the neo-Calvinism of Abraham Kuyper, and racism. This fusion was mediated by the churches.

Nationalism redefined the concept of "family" to denote a shared language community among genetically related people. "Nation" was taken as the outer or socio-political manifestation of such a relationship. Nations became personalized entities and acted historically as individuals writ large. Hence expressions such as "the Afrikaner," "the British," and so on. The fusion of nationalism with the value of family was a powerful means of policy formulation. The traditional assumption that the primary unit of human existence was the family could now be applied to the question of human social order.

In Afrikaans literature the classic intellectual expression of nationalism came in 1936 from the philosopher Nico J. Diederichs, later to become state president:

> In the first place nations must be seen not as human creations but as ordinations and institutions of God Himself ... The individual being ... is an abstraction ... Outside the membership of the nation no-one can ever achieve his full being. Only in and through the nation the human being becomes himself ... Participation in the realization of the nation's calling means participation in the fulfilling of the plan of God. Service to my nation is thus part of my serving God. But also my love for my nation is love for my God, because the love of a nation is not in the first place love of people or countries or states, etc. but the love of the universally applicable values on which the nation is based.[19]

Contemporary reality was perceived as moving in the opposite direction. Liberalism, communism, and Roman Catholicism appeared to be bent on integrating all of humanity into one single human entity. From a nationalist perspective this was a formula for disaster.

But why was this happening? It was at precisely this point that the Kuyperian neo-Calvinism of the Netherlands was grafted onto the nationalist paradigm. It provided the interpretive tools with which the impending collapse of the moral and social order could be understood as a consequence of modernity's rejection of the structure of a religious hierarchy of authority.

In the Kuyperian tradition the fundamental error of European history was a consistent erosion, since the French Revolution, of the sovereignty of God in favour of the autonomy of the individual. The neo-Calvinist movement of South Africa built on this conclusion, arguing that to maintain the hierarchical structure of authority and order in society was a God-ordained duty, as was also resistance to its opposite, "anthropocentric humanism."[20] As D. Lategan put it at the annual opening of the Stellenbosch seminary in 1944 (extrapolating from the prophet Elijah's resistance to Canaanite religion):

> The spirit of Elijah was not a simple Humanism which rests on a natural basis and is the product of the prophet himself ... It entailed in the first place the view of the world of a prophet-statesman and in the second place the way in which he applied his view of life and the world in practical circumstances ... Over and against this Baalism he posed the absolute sovereignty of God, over and against naturalism he posed the pure supranaturalism which emphasizes both the transcendence and immanence of God. Over and against Materialism he accentuated the proper Spiritualism ... Over and against Humanism he posed that pure Calvinism which puts God and his honour number one in his life and activities. Over and against Atheism he posed pure Theism ... Over and against Totalitarianism Elijah placed the counsel of God through which God ordains and ordinates everything in His divine predestination.[21]

When, after the National Party's electoral victory of 1948, resistance to exclusive white power escalated among blacks, and the South African Communist Party in particular struck at the heart of the ideological roots of apartheid, communism became the primary enemy for Christian nationalists. J.D. Vorster, the leading anticommunist, wrote in 1947:

> It is particularly the fact that communism is becoming more and more the view of life and the religion of the coloured peoples which makes a peaceful solution to this problem almost impossible ... The Creator alone can explain the purpose of the different races and the proper relationship between them ... and what the Book says can be abbreviated in the words of Acts 17:26: "from one blood all the nations of humanity were made to live all over the earth, while He previously ordained the times and the boundaries of their domicile."[22]

To Vorster it was apparent that apartheid was the only social order consistent with the hierarchical structure of authority. Anything else, anything tending towards egalitarianism, could only be evil.

By the early 1950s all of this had already fused into a complex and rather sophisticated theory on society and social order, well summarized in a report to the synod of the NGK of the Transvaal in 1951:

> The human attempt to restore unity, the internationalism and cosmopolitism which emphasizes ... the absolute fraternity of all people, is not derived from the Christian teachings ... but is produced by pure humanist tendencies which decree that the human being should be the centre and measurement of all things. Different principles of binding [i.e. foundations of collective entities – J.K.] are advanced to support this. From the French Revolution the principle of binding of international solidarity is the slogan of freedom, equality and fraternity. Communism on the other hand emphasizes class division ... Humanism again proposes that the level of Western civilization is powerful enough to eradicate all the differences between the races and nations. The total failure of all these attempts shows once again that we will find no solution at the international level ... Unity, says Kuyper is not derived from the world. Only the word of God can indicate the infallible principle of binding.
>
> It is evident that God had ordained national governments in order to maintain law, order and justice but never did he institute any international government ... Thus the division of nations is to be directly derived from the authority of God and represents the social embodiment of the divine structure of authority. But this structure of authority extends further: The humanistic claim to equality is unscriptural because it does not take into account the fact that God has decreed structures of authority within every society. As the child cannot be equated with the parent, the labourer cannot be equated with the employer nor the subject with the authorities, so there are also differences in status within the nation. According to the Word of God the idea that Christianity ought to diminish differences in race, nation and status is most certainly wrong ... There is a just, God-pleasing hierarchy of power in the family and the state and between nations, as well as a God-ordained obedience to authority. According to God's Word, therefore, social justice does not mean the equal treatment of all people but rather ... *that everyone receives what God had ordained for him according to his own status level* (my emphasis).[23]

How did this complex theorizing affect the social history of the country? It all hinged on how the concept of the hierarchical structure of authority would be translated into real social structures. Two possibilities existed that were seemingly consistent with the core Afrikaner values: a nationalist approach or a racist approach. The end result, after much wrangling, was a racially defined nationalism – known to the world as apartheid but to Afrikaner nationalists as "separate development," a concept in which, however, one of the core values of modernity – the equality of people – was implicitly affirmed. By opting for a fundamentally nationalist (as opposed to racist) approach the NGK contributed in a contorted way, and contrary to its own intentions, to the introduction of a universal franchise in 1994.

Both nationalism and racism are models of societal hierarchies, the latter defining hierarchy according to assumed biological differences between groups of people. Inequalities are, in consequence, shared collectively. They are furthermore immutable and cannot be changed, even gradually. Nationalism stresses the same differences racism does but sees them not as immutable but as the outcome of var-

144

ied stages of the development of nations. In principle, therefore, for the nationalist all nations are potentially equal, and at the end of time all will reach the same level. Before then more developed people have the task, or "calling," to educate the lesser developed. Paternalism, called then in South Africa "guardianship," becomes the embodiment of the ethical norm of justice. By contrast, racism assigns no responsibility to "higher" nations regarding the needs of "lower" ones. For it, justice is not an issue. The difference between nations is not a moral issue, simply a genetic fact.

Until 1948 the nationalists and the racists seemed to be pursuing the same goals. According to both, the initial step had to be the physical and geographical separation of races. But when it came to practical policy formulation, the differences became evident. Slowly the nationalist group grew in strength and began to assert its position more emphatically; it found in the NGK a support system. Significantly, in 1949, the influential opening address by the chairman of the Federal Council of the NGK included these words:

> [The aim of apartheid is not ...] oppression but development, growth, upliftment, more privileges and rights according to one's own abilities, talent and potential ... The Bible does not instruct us to have apartheid but it does not prohibit us from doing so either. However, the Bible decrees Christian guardianship. And our entire history leads in this direction too. Whether we like it or not, we are the guardians of the coloureds and the natives too and we shall have the right to give reckoning to God about our guardianship. Of course we have the right to guard our own interests. But if we do this at the expense and against the interests of the coloured races then we will be disloyal to our guardianship.[24]

The decisive moment came in 1950, when yet another people's congress, this time on the "native question," was held in Bloemfontein. The driving force behind this initiative was G.B.A. Gerdener, professor of missions at the seminary at Stellenbosch. The congress itself was a national event, attended by overseas observers. The opening address was broadcast on the radio. Afrikaner anthropologists, economists, educationists, linguists, political scientists, and sociologists participated in the preparations. The agenda was nothing less than a blueprint for the entire social restructuring of South African society. In the congress the concept "race" was replaced by "separate development." South Africa was described as a cosmos of *nations* (i.e. not races), each with a unique character and culture but at different stages of development. The only Christian way to safeguard every culture and to avoid friction and abuse was to separate the nations, thus providing room for the organic development of each according to its special needs.[25]

The concept of a South African community of autonomous states was born at this congress. Soon the term apartheid ceased to be used, being regarded as negative and racist. In the ensuing years the resolutions of the Bloemfontein congress were debated and refined. Hendrik F. Verwoerd, when he became prime minister in 1958, began to implement those which appeared to him to be practical politics.[26] As for the churches, until the late 1980s, the NGK, HK and GK carried forward the ideal of separate development, which to them was the embodiment of true biblical justice under South African conditions.

Debates within the Afrikaner churches between 1950 and the mid-1970s were to become increasingly abstract and doctrinaire. On the basis of Kuyperian thought, scholastic distinctions were made between concepts such as unity and uniformity, plurality and pluriformity, and so on. In the end an impenetrable edifice of learning evolved which served to solidify the hegemony of Afrikaner power. It was complemented with a puritan ethic imposed on the entire society through the cooperation of the lawmakers, who were mostly members of the NGK, HK, and GK. Thus, for example, when Neil Armstrong set foot on the moon, South Africans were unable to watch the event, because television as a "foreign" and "perverse" pastime did not yet exist in South Africa. But the most provocative social manifestation of sin, in the view of church leaders, was the intermingling of nations, either at the individual or at the state level. In the modern world such mingling was manifest in the United Nations, the World Council of Churches, and also in the demand of those in South Africa who wanted a unitary interracial state and a single parliament.

By about 1950 the previously scattered manifestations of anti-modernism had consolidated themselves into a self-confident political force. Mainly through the churches it had developed a theoretical basis which legitimated the use of political power to enforce on society policies largely designed to restore the country to a non-plural and non-modern way of life. Nonetheless, in the anti-modernist theories, there was an element of ambivalence, which was to become transparent as a result mainly of Christian missions.

The Trojan Horse: Reformed Missions and Development

The motivations for mission work in the Afrikaner Reformed churches were mixed. While most were driven by purely evangelistic considerations, more than a few people supported or engaged in missionary work in order to keep blacks black, to freeze them in their own, albeit somewhat Christianized, traditions. Yet, by its very nature, missionary work propelled African societies in the direction of modernization. This, coupled with the interpretive framework implicit in nationalism, led to a focus on development questions. Thus, at the People's Congress which met in 1950 in Bloemfontein, initiated by the NGK's Commission for Missions, the principal theme was social and economic development.

Mission work had begun in the Cape Reformed church in the the middle of the nineteenth century. At first, the Cape Church looked to the north, since the Methodists and the Anglicans had already established themselves in the Cape interior. The NGK's first station was founded in the northern Transvaal in 1863. Soon work was undertaken in present-day Kenya, Malawi, Mozambique, Nigeria (under the auspices of the Sudan United Mission), Sri Lanka, and Zimbabwe. Only from the mid-1930s did NGK churches in other provinces and the GK in the Transvaal begin to warm to missionary work.

In the early 1950s, in particular, an explosion of missionary zeal occurred in the northern provinces. By then international doors were closing to South Africans because of apartheid, and the explosion of missionary energy had to be directed internally. Not that that was a problem. The missionary upsurge coincided with the optimistic moment when apartheid was being redefined as separate development.

Pastors resigned from their comfortable suburban congregations and started mission stations in rural black areas of South Africa. The various synods appointed full-time mission secretaries. Money started to pour in. By 1974 the NGK spent 6.6 million rands per year on internal missions, an amount equal to three per cent of the average gross monthly income of all its members.[27]

This movement, in some respects, can be compared to the mission movement in the USA toward the end of the nineteenth century: thoroughly evangelical, socially conscious, and politically triumphalist. The main difference, of course, was that the new generation of missionaries took separate development very seriously indeed. They established schools and hospitals even before they built churches; they started handiwork classes for women and craft schools for men; they organized youth clubs (in 1992 80 per cent of all South African youth belonged to church clubs, only 15 per cent were members of political parties); rejoiced with their black members and cried with them; baptized and buried them. But all along they insisted on being called "boss" and "madam." In those few cases where blacks were allowed through the front door of a pastor's house, they were served tea, if at all, from special tin cups, the china being reserved for "Europeans." Blacks were supposed to develop, to be sure, but separately.

Probably the most enduring consequence of this church-sponsored spurt in development was the concerted drive to translate the Bible into a variety of African languages. To do that, the church had to create grammars, and invested enormous skill and effort in the task. More spectacular was the building of schools and hospitals. Compared to the English-speaking churches and the Lutherans, the NGK did not build or maintain many schools in South Africa (as opposed to Malawi and Zimbabwe, where its achievement was enormous). Yet, because of its late start inside South Africa, the NGK turned to building schools precisely at the time when the Verwoerd government nationalized the entire school system for fear that church schools would undermine the ideals of apartheid. In compensation, a group of missionaries from the Reformed churches were allowed to draw up the syllabus for religious instruction, a compulsory subject at all levels. In this way the Reformed churches retained some influence over state black schools without bearing the administrative burdens.

The NGK outshone other churches in the field of medicine. Its mission hospitals mushroomed from the 1950s, and scores of young medical doctors and nurses spent the first part of their career in them. At first the church paid for all of this, but later the state began to subsidise. In Transkei alone, an area where the NGK was not even particularly active, in 1969 a total of 63,298 patients received treatment at its hospitals. In 1978 the missionary arm of the NGK had (inside and outside South Africa) forty hospitals, six schools for the deaf and six for the blind, nine old-age homes, seven homes for victims of chronic diseases, eight orphanages, eight reformatories, four youth hostels, and assorted other institutions.[28]

The net result of all this missionary effort was that, in 1978, the white NGK had 1,531,000 members and the various black churches born from their missionary work had grown to 1,892,000. The history and the outcome of the missionary work of the NGK depict like nothing else the ambivalent character of the idea of separate development. Once it was agreed that the purpose of segregation was development, an ironic process of gradual "equalization" ensued. The centripetal power of Afrikaner mobilization drew more and more blacks into its orbit. There were many examples of life-long friendship and mutual respect between Afrikaners and blacks, even if clothed in the confining garb of paternalism. Taken together with similar ventures by other churches, though not on the same scale or under the same banner, the bonding over decades between blacks and whites in missions perhaps helps explain a perpetual mystery about South Africa: why, despite all the problems, it has refused to lapse into Armageddon. From the perspective of the mid-1990s it is amazing that so many Afrikaners, especially church leaders, really believed in separate development. Perhaps some of them already realized – but if so they didn't say it then – that the assumption underlying the emphasis on development was a belief in the inherent equality of all people.

It was not until the 1980s that the policy implications of such an assumption were to become clear. That moment of truth was, however, preceded by the darkest days of apartheid.

Ambiguities and Modernization, 1950–93

The apartheid ideology did not prevail in the Afrikaner churches without resistance, at first from whites in the NGK, but later from blacks in the NGSK and NGKA. The best known among the early NGK objectors was Beyers Naudé, who was stripped of his office as pastor and moderator of the Transvaal NGK in 1964 because of his involvement with the Christian Institute, a multiracial, ecumenical body that did much to promote the cause of Black Consciousness and Black theology during the 1970s (see pp. 386–87). Shortly after the murder in detention of Steve Biko, the Black Consciousness theorist closely associated with the Institute, and the 1976 Soweto uprisings, Naudé was put under house arrest that lasted until 1984.

Two other prominent figures in the NGK, Benjamin B. Keet (professor in systematic theology at Stellenbosch) and Barend J. Marais (professor in church history at Pretoria) also spoke out strongly against the churches' unequivocal support for the political programme of apartheid.[29] Partially as a result of the protests of these three, a number of Afrikaner church leaders by the end of the first decade of National party rule began to doubt the feasibility and moral legitimacy of the policies of the time. When, in 1960, police killed 68 women and children who were protesting the pass laws in Sharpeville near Johannesburg, these doubts were reinforced. Afrikanerdom was rocked to its foundations by the Sharpeville massacre. How could a policy designed to reduce friction lead to such violence? In December 1960 the World Council of Churches (of which the Cape and Transvaal NGK churches and the NHK were still members) organized a consultation on the South African crisis at Cottesloe in Johannesburg (see pp. 162–63).

The consultation, later seen as a symbolic watershed, caused one of the most acrimonious debates in the history of the Afrikanerdom between 1950 and 1980.[30] Although the consultation did not plead the cause of general integration, its resolutions conflicted with Prime Minister Verwoerd's policy of a total, territorial separation of nations in South Africa. Most important it recognized all racial groups as "indigenous" and as citizens of South Africa and demanded equal rights for all to participate in the life of the country and to share in the responsibilities, rewards, and privileges of citizenship. It asserted that there were no scriptural grounds for the prohibition of mixed marriages; it acknowledged that wages received by the "non-white" majority were below subsistence level, and affirmed that the right to own land "wherever he is domiciled, and to participate in the government of his country, is part of the dignity of the adult man."

From the perspective of the ruling establishment these resolutions were bad enough. Worse, however, was the fact that the majority of the resolutions originated from the Cape NGK. To Verwoerd and others this could only mean treason from within Afrikaner ranks. In his New Year's radio message Verwoerd called on the churches to rid themselves of their betrayers, and they did. At the various synods convened soon thereafter all delegates to Cottesloe were severely reprimanded and stripped of their synodical duties. Almost in one go, opposition in the NGK and the NHK was eradicated. Even so, the nagging doubt of many church people had been clearly stated, and was to resurface after the Soweto uprising of 1976. The submission of the Cape church to the Cottesloe consultation remained the classic statement of that doubt. Dealing with the "ethical formula" required to solve South Africa's problem, it said:

> Inasmuch as the Bantu grow in Christian principles and civilization and develop the sense of duty and responsibility, all rights and privileges as well as duties and responsibilities must be awarded them on either one of two premises: either along with the whites, or together as Bantu. This [choice entails] either the way of eventual total integration ... or the way of territorial separation between white and Bantu. This is the crossroads where South Africa stands today ... As far as the NGK is concerned, the proper way to go is the one of independent development of white and Bantu in their respective areas ... [but] if it becomes evident that all the Bantu can not be housed in their own areas on the basis of full development, *the church accepts that those Bantu who will then be in the white sector of South Africa will be dealt with according to the above ethical formula, i.e.* [they will integrate] *with the whites.*[31]

Thus separate development was reaffirmed, but the backdoor to integration was left open. Perhaps, the delegates implied, apartheid would fail to deliver its promises. If so, the ethical implications measured against the claim of justice were spelled out. To Verwoerd, however, and to the majority of the members of the Afrikaner churches, the mere idea of failure was unacceptable; everything had to be done to ensure that apartheid would succeed. Pressure had to be applied politically, and alternative ideologies had to be exorcised. In this process the new leadership of the churches played an important role, particularly in the censoring of ideas. Yet the doubt lingered.

The issue of justice was again and more urgently raised after the uprising of 1976 spread from pupils in Soweto to the entire country. For the first time church leaders conceded that government had made many mistakes, and, in line with the prevailing mood of reorientation in the Afrikaner community at large, the synod of the NGK decided in 1982 to revise its 1974 official document on socio-political issues. At the next synod in 1986 a new policy document was accepted, and refined in 1990. The 1990 document dealt at length and without hesitation with "apartheid," rather than with separate development. The discourse was no longer doctrinaire on socio-political issues. Concepts such as "modernism," "godless humanism," etc., disappeared altogether. Peace with modernity had been made. "Principles" were still mentioned but systematically subordinated to ethical concerns:

> In principle the right of nations to the liberty to safeguard and develop their own cultures and values must be acknowledged as an inherent right of the human being as long as the rights and freedoms of others are not impeded and the Biblical claim of love for the neighbour ... not nullified ... Only over time it became evident to the NGK that the policy of apartheid ... [went] further than acknowledging the right and freedom of all people and cultural groups to remain true to their own values ... [It functioned] in such a way that the majority of the population of this country experienced it as an oppressive system which ... benefited one group unjustifiably above the others.

> In this way the human dignity of fellow human beings was affected and apartheid had come in conflict with the principle of love and justice ... [This] is unacceptable in the light of Holy Scripture and Christian conscience and must be rejected as sinful ... *The NGK ... rejects all forms of discrimination and sincerely desires that all should be free to participate in their fatherland and should receive equitable and equal opportunities to achieve prosperity and wealth.*[32]

Contrast this with the almost contemptuous rejection in 1951 of the Universal Declaration of Human Rights by the Transvaal synod of the NGK:

> The point of departure of the declaration is totally wrong ... Only according to the anthropocentric way of thinking can one speak of "the inherent dignity ... of all members of the human family" ... According to the theocentric way, which is our church's way of thinking, the human being receives what is justly his when God gives him his God-ordained share ... The rights and privileges of people [are] very different according to God's free will ... *Justice in the world does not depend on whether each and every one is treated equally but on whether one is treated according to what God has ordained for him in the light of the inequalities which He Himself has created* ... Freedom and peace in the world are also not dependent on so-called human rights but on the human being's obedience to the laws and decrees which God has instituted for human beings ... Evidently the declaration breathes the spirit of "freedom, equality and brotherhood" of the French Revolution which was just as God-forgetting and anthropocentric in its essence ... The adoration of the power of the United Nations is an outrageous transgression of authority.[33]

In 1974 there was already some restraint. The NGK could not "accept rights in as much as they are claims which the human being in his own right has." Even so, "human rights are those rights that God gives to his image, the human being, enabling him to fulfil his duties and his calling." In 1990 it was stated that "... although the concept 'human rights' is not found in the Bible, the issue is found all over."[34] This statement represents a remarkable change of direction. Human rights were now accepted as in accord with biblical justice. This could only happen because the mainstream of Afrikaners was no longer resisting modernity. In fact, the erstwhile monstrous "city" had proven to be the "salvation" of the Afrikaner community. Because of apartheid's affirmative action in favour of whites, the poor-white problem had been solved by the 1960s, and Afrikaners, and their churches, had grown prosperous and at home in the world of markets and finance. Earlier activism was replaced with a kind of self-centred piety, and anti-modernist theology disappeared. In 1990 the NGK synod even adopted a resolution that modern dancing was, after all, not sinful.

From Submission to Defiance: The Black Reformed Churches, 1950–1994

Meanwhile, taken as a whole, the Afrikaner churches were growing more and more black and less and less Afrikaans as the missionary work bore fruit. In 1951 the NGK Bantu Church of SA was established in East London – ironically, but in keeping with the ideal of "guardianship," presided over by an all-white moderature. In 1963 it became the NGKA, under black leaders who at first were well disposed to benevolent white paternalism, particularly since the white congregations paid most of their bills and almost all of their salaries. The NGKA is exceptionally difficult to typify. Perhaps because of how it began, it was always in the shade of self-proclaimed "guardians," always cast in the role of grateful beneficiaries of white benevolence. During the years of its existence it never developed a distinct religious mode or contributed creatively to the Africanization of Christianity. Such debates as there were on these issues took place between white pastors deemed to be seconded to the NGKA by the (white) NGK. On the whole, then, the NGKA was a shadow image of the NGK. When a distinctive character did emerge it was entirely for political reasons.

Compared to the NGKA, the NGSK had a distinctive character. Closely linked, since its establishment in 1881, to what was known as the Cape Coloured community, it represented most of the values of that community: strict puritan rules for the lives of individuals (made even stricter by the constant transgressions of these rules and the consequent severe censure by the church) in conjunction with a romantic but not pentecostal pietism. The largest church in the Western Cape, the NGSK was an anchor of the Cape Coloured community in the decades of apartheid, providing not only social cohesion to the community but self-esteem to individuals.

The NGSK seminary was absorbed, in 1971, into the University of the Western Cape, a university established for the Coloureds in the 1960s. Soon the new theology faculty became the base for the ideas, then radically new in South Africa, of Black theology. Yet the driving force remained outside the faculty, with Allan Boesak, the campus student minister who returned from studies in the Netherlands in the mid-1970s. About 1975 things began to change; a love–hate conflict between Reformed blacks and whites broke out in the mid-1970s in rough coordination with the growing political and military conflict between the white government and the liberation movements.

Typical of the attitudes and practices before 1975 was the activity of the Standing Commission of the NGKA for Liaison with Government, whose meetings with government officials were always very courteous, with both sides expressing mutual appreciation despite possible differences. The commission never failed to state the burning issues of black society at such meetings, but, because of the NGKA's close ties with the NGK and thus with the ruling establishment, and because the majority of the NGKA commissioners were white pastors temporarily seconded by the white NGK, not until 1976 did the commission raise such issues confrontationally.

This ambivalence is well illustrated by the discussion about black servants who lived at night in backyards in "white" neighbourhoods. In 1971 the NGKA synod told the commission to "urge the state, at its earliest convenience, to give effect to the policy that domestic servants live within their own family circles in the Bantu suburbs and to spend the nights there." This request was in line with apartheid policy and reflected the view of white ministers predominating in the synod. However, when the commission met on 15 October 1971 to prepare for a meeting with the government, its members, two out of three of whom were black, differed substantially from the synod. The meeting with the government never took place. Instead, a survey of opinions was taken among those "who slept in the backyards," on the basis of which it was reported to the synod in 1975 that black servants were happy to live in backyards, where it was much safer and cheaper, and where there was less immorality than in the townships. In any case they had no families in the townships, and it was more important for them to earn money for the upkeep of the children than to starve together in the townships. "What then is the problem in the backyards? There is no problem about sleeping in the backyards. It is only advantageous to white and black people." The synod, still white-dominated, was in a difficult position: How to defuse the issue without offending either their black parishioners or their ideological superiors in the NGK? They resolved their dilemma with a typical sleight of hand: "Servants should be left in the backyards ...," they said, "until conditions have improved to such an extent that their service would not be needed any more ... " That is, the bantustans had to be developed so that blacks themselves would decide to return. Thus "influx control must be administered in such a way that the homelands first be developed until blacks themselves opt to go back there."[35]

Such sleight of hand was to no avail. By 1976 relations between the NGKA and the NGK progressively soured as the younger generation of black ministers became increasingly unwilling to play the game of courtesy. Serving in the townships and not in the "mission fields," they had been shocked out of submissiveness by the Soweto uprisings of 1976. Shortly before, the NGKA had decided to affiliate with the South African Council of Churches (SACC), thereby openly siding with the enemy in the view of the white Afrikaner churches and the government. The battle lines were drawn: on the one hand the Afrikaner churches (which, in practice, meant the NGK); on the other, the churches affiliated with the SACC, which were sympathetic to the cause of liberation as embodied in the African National Congress.

Now the NGKA slowly began to change its character. Up to this time the piety and rituals of the black congregations were mirror images of those of the whites. Now, for the first time, "struggle" and the "theology of struggle" pervaded all spheres of life and piety. The NGKA, and its Coloured equivalent the NGSK, became havens for a growing number of white ministers and theologians disillusioned with the mainstream of Afrikaner thinking. One, Nico Smith, a former professor at the University of Stellenbosch, attracted much attention when he decided to live with his black congregants in Mamelodi, a township near Pretoria. Such white pastors, together with blacks returning from studies abroad, had discovered legendary martyrs such as the American civil rights leader, Martin Luther King Jr., the Latin American liberation theologians, Bishop Romero and Camilo Torres, and Kaj Munck, the anti-Nazi theologian in Norway. They soon coalesced into a razor-sharp opposition to the NGK.

The first onslaught, both verbally and emotionally, came from the NGSK, led principally by the dynamic pastor and theologian, Allan Boesak. During the 1980s Boesak was a towering figure, first in his capacity as moderator of the NGSK and later also as president of the World Alliance of Reformed Churches (WARC). Having studied in the Netherlands and having spent considerable time at Grand Rapids, Michigan, Boesak realized early on that international interest in South Africa could be an important leverage in the national debate. In 1982 at the Vancouver meeting of WARC he significantly influenced the discussion on South Africa; in the end the WARC voted to suspend membership of the white Afrikaner churches and to declare a *status confessionis*, a state of affairs in which the very essence of Christianity is threatened and a new confession of faith is called for.

One month later, in South Africa, the synod of the NGSK adopted a confession preceded by these words: "Because the secular gospel of apartheid fundamentally threatens the reconciliation in Christ as well as the unity of the church of Jesus Christ, the NGSK in South Africa declares that for the church of Jesus Christ a *status confessionis* exists." The synod then drafted a confession finally ratified four years later in 1986, known as the Belhar Confession after the suburb where the synod had convened.

The Belhar Confession dealt with three themes. First, the unity of the Christian church was affirmed: "Any teaching ... obstructing or shattering the active unity of the church or which might even lead to the formation of separate churches is rejected." Second, the essence of the Christian message was interpreted as reconciliation (as opposed to sovereignty), with any form of enforced separation of people rejected. Third, the principles of justice and peace were declared to be rooted in a God who reveals himself "in a world full of injustice and enmity, [as] in a special way the God of the suffering, the poor and the aggrieved ..." Belhar rejected "any ideology which legitimates any form of injustice and any teaching which refuses to resist such an ideology in the light of the Gospel."[36]

By the time of the Belhar Confession South Africa was under a state of emergency and State President P.W. Botha was combating what he called a "total onslaught" on South Africa. Nationalist ideologues interpreted the third part of Belhar (like the Kairos Document published in 1985 by the Institute of Contextual Theology: see pp. 375, 392) as liberation theology, which they considered a religious veneer of communist indoctrination. But Belhar was taken seriously in white church circles, nonetheless. It had struck at a sensitive nerve in the official white apartheid theology: the nagging conscience. The theme of justice had been an integral part of the theological legitimation of apartheid. Now Belhar had taken up the same theme, drawing conclusions diametrically opposed to apartheid. In the 1950s grand apartheid was still not much more than an experiment in its initial stages, but by the mid-1980s it had become a reality and to many, particularly blacks, a grim reality. Belhar reinforced the already considerable doubt in many white Afrikaner minds.

The NGSK and the NGKA went ahead to unite in 1994. Significantly, the new church is called the Uniting Reformed Church of Southern Africa (URCSA). It sees itself as the kernel of a united Reformed church in southern Africa into which all Reformed churches, above all the white NGK, are invited. In 1995, discussions concerning the shape of such a union were in progress.

The context had, however, changed almost beyond recognition. The roots of URCSA lay in the days of fierce total onslaught against apartheid and attempts to repress it totally. By 1995, the underlying problems of South Africa had overtaken the agenda of the apartheid era. The almost total politicization of civil life during the late 1980s quickly made way for concerns about poverty and development. In the mid-1990s it was far too early to attempt an assessment of the churches' role in the new era.

Robert Moffat preaching to a Tswana audience

9

Grappling with a Colonial Heritage: The English-speaking Churches under Imperialism and Apartheid

JOHN W. DE GRUCHY

When, in 1986, Desmond Mpilo Tutu was enthroned in St. George's Cathedral as Anglican Archbishop of Cape Town, the sanctuary was crowded with memorabilia of South Africa's colonial past. The service, too, was a remarkable blend of Anglican tradition and African spontaneity, a portent of hope during a "state of emergency" marked by accelerating resistance and violent repression. It exemplified the painful yet inevitable transformation of the English-speaking churches, once the spiritual home of white English-speaking South Africans, into a vital spiritual vanguard of the black-led struggle against white racism and apartheid, and of the transformation of white-ruled South Africa into a non-racial democracy.

"Loyal Messages": The Churches, Imperialism, and the "Native Question"
The "English-speaking church" denominations included the Anglican Church of the Province (CPSA), which was the church of the British colonial establishment, and had become a separate province of the Anglican communion in 1870, and the Church of England in South Africa (CESA).[1] Baptist, Congregational, Methodist and Presbyterian churches, which had also arrived in South Africa at the beginning of the nineteenth century to minister to British settlers, also belonged to this group.[2] Associated with each were missionary societies that sought to evangelize the indigenous peoples of the sub-continent. Settler and mission congregations developed along parallel lines; in due course these separated lines would begin to converge, but not until well into the twentieth century.

From the arrival of the 1820 Settlers, English-speaking communities reproduced the parochial life of Great Britain (see chapter 3). Anglican parish churches co-existed with Baptist, Congregational, Methodist, and Presbyterian congregations, as did their emerging denominational structures. Church architecture, liturgy, and hymnody reminded the church members of "home." The majority of their ministers were trained in Britain until the middle of the twentieth century. The traditions that divided the churches there kept them apart in South Africa as well. The Anglicans treasured episcopacy and the Book of Common Prayer, eventually producing their own South African revision in 1954,[3] and again in 1989. The Presbyterians, many of them previously members of the established Church of Scotland and suspicious of Anglican episcopacy because of historic conflicts in Scotland, found more affinity with the Dutch Reformed churches, with whom they shared a common Calvinist heritage. Baptists, Congregationalists, and Methodists, all Free Church by tradition, too, shared something of the Presbyterian wariness of Anglican hegemony. Theologically they were evangelical and pietist in orientation, laying stress on Biblical authority and the experience of personal conversion, yet with some conservative Calvinists and some liberals among them. But distinct traditions of belief and governance gave each a separate character. Baptists and Congregationalists, both zealously committed to the autonomy of the local church, were divided on the issue of baptism, the Baptists baptizing only adults who had come to faith, the Congregationalists baptizing the children of believers as well. The Methodists, who treasured their hymn-singing tradition, local "class" meetings, local preachers, and youth guilds, expanded to become the largest of the English-speaking denominations.

On issues of social behaviour the churches also differed. Temperance, which preoccupied all churches and reform groups in the early decades of the twentieth century, in South Africa as in Britain and North America, was a matter of concern to Methodists and Baptists more than to Anglicans, a reflection to some extent of class distinctions among the settlers. Yet as the English-speaking community in South Africa became more affluent, and as race became the key to social stratification, class distinctions among English-speaking South Africans, while still significant, were less determinant than they were seen to be "back home."

The English-speaking churches were united in their loyalty to the British Empire, and their missionary societies, wittingly or not, enabled the spread of colonialism and the consolidation of imperial power. The English-speaking churches rallied to the British cause in the Anglo-Boer War (1899–1902), praying for the day when the entire sub-continent would be under the rule of the British sovereign (see pp. 63–64). "Loyal messages" were regularly sent to the Governor-General, the British monarch's representative in South Africa, from synods and conferences, a custom which even continued some time after the National Party came to power in 1948.

At the end of the Anglo-Boer War, when the English-speaking churches were beginning to consolidate their denominational structures, control firmly remained in the hands of the white membership. These churches generally supported the racially discriminatory constitution of the Union of South Africa adopted in 1909, despite opposition from many African leaders who were members of their churches. Segregated also at the local level, they adopted a somewhat liberal, paternalistic stance on the "native question," purporting to speak on behalf of blacks, especially "civilized" blacks educated at mission schools. At the same time they attempted to engender a spirit of unity between English and Afrikaner, inspired by the conciliation policy adopted by the British colonial office after 1905.[4]

The government census of 1911 revealed that more than a quarter of the African population was now Christian.[5] Since many of these had received a colonial-style missionary-based education, it is not surprising that black political leaders were often active members of mission churches with strong British connections. Such leaders, together with those drawn from the Ethiopian churches (see p. 215) protested against the racial discrimination built into the constitution of the Union; their outrage, which they justified both by nationalist aspirations and by Christian ideals, found further expression in the inauguration of the South African Native National Congress in Bloemfontein in 1912, renamed the African National Congress (ANC) in 1923. The principles adopted by the Congress affirmed the liberal Christian values, such as individual rights and freedom, which had been taught in the mission schools.[6]

Yet, the English-speaking churches, aligned with the South African Party government and, more generally, with white South Africa, were often unable, and usually unwilling, to act in concert with their African memberships in the struggle for equality and justice.[7] Nevertheless, when the introduction of land and labour legislation, beginning with the Mines and Work Act of 1911, effectively reduced blacks to the roles of migratory labourers and in some respects serfs, legislation denounced by black Christian leaders like the Methodist Zaccheus Mahabane as unredeemably evil,[8] some English-speaking churches did speak out against it. Still, their response was ambiguous and qualified, indicative of their endeavour to serve the interests of white congregations while at the same time trying to adopt a more liberal stance on the "Native Question." The English-speaking churches' sometimes meagre and almost always wary response to African nationalism provoked considerable cynicism among blacks. The first president of the ANC, the Congregationalist leader John Dube, charged that Christianity "had an offensive smell to a large number of Natives."[9] Nonetheless, Christianity was expanding rapidly amongst the African population, and despite denominational fragmentation, it provided a unifying ethical basis for African nationalism. The ANC, for its part, encouraged unity amongst the churches.[10]

With some exceptions, the English-speaking church leadership had little grasp of the plight of the black rural communities and the black workers caught up in the rapid urbanization and industrialization of the early decades of the century, especially during the First World War. White members of the churches, part of the growing and expanding mercantile class, generally identified more with bourgeois society than with labour.[11] The funding of church programmes and the erection of church buildings and private church schools were dependent upon their capital. But some qualifications are necessary. In the early part of the century, for example, there were strong ties between Methodism and Cornish miners settled on the Reef, while some church leaders showed considerable insight in their analysis of the issues that sparked the white miners' strike in 1922.[12]

The English-speaking churches were in fact caught between Afrikaner and African nationalism. They continued to seek good relations with the Dutch Reformed Church (NGK), but the NGK's alignment with the interests of Afrikaner nationalism and its advocacy of racial segregation, increasingly during the 1920s and 1930s, made such an entente increasingly difficult. Aware that the church could not remain forever divided by race and still be Christian, certain leaders of the English-speaking churches began to take cautious steps toward the endorsement of a multiracial society, rather than of the segregationist vision emerging in Afrikanerdom and the NGK.

"No Insuperable Barrier": The Elusive Search for Union

In cooperation with their parent denominations in Britain, the English-speaking churches took an active interest in the ecumenical movement that gathered momentum after the end of the First World War. Small in size compared with the NGK, the white English-speaking community recognized that union could be advantageous. Indeed, soon after the ending of the Anglo-Boer War, negotiations had begun between the Presbyterians (PCSA) and Congregationalists (CUSA) and between Congregationalists and Baptists. Although both efforts failed, plans for co-operation among missionary societies were more successful.

In 1903, the first of many South African Missionary Conferences brought together English-speaking and Dutch Reformed missionary leaders to discuss common problems and formulate policy and strategy (see chap. 23). A visit to South Africa in 1906 by John R. Mott of the United States, the leading ecumenical statesman of the time, spurred moves toward common endeavours, just as it helped to heal some of the hurts left over from the Anglo-Boer War.[13] Mott organized the International Missionary Conference in Edinburgh, in 1910, which launched the modern ecumenical movement.[14] World-wide pressure from foreign mission fields, inspired by the Edinburgh Conference, now encouraged churches in Britain to work towards union. In South Africa, where settler and mission congregations co-existed, it was only a matter of time before denominations whose overseas counterparts were engaged in union negotiations should take similar action in South Africa. At its 1927 General Assembly the Presbyterian Church of Southern Africa (PCSA) received a report on discussions with the Wesleyan Methodist Church noting that "there appears to be no insuperable barrier in the way of such closer organic union either in the doctrines held by the two churches or in their systems of government."[15] These were remarkable statements, given that Presbyterians and Methodists differed substantially in doctrine and polity. Yet the Presbyterians resolved to confer with the Wesleyan Church "to consider ways of approach to a closer affiliation ..."[16] Union negotiations among Presbyterians, Congregationalists, and Wesleyan Methodists progressed by fits and starts until the outbreak of the Second World War in 1939. Attempts to unite the PCSA and the Bantu Presbyterian church (established by the Church of Scotland Mission), beginning in 1934, failed, but three branches of Methodism united in 1931 to form the Methodist Church of South Africa.[17]

A second visit by Mott in 1934 gave new impetus to the ecumenical movement, and two years later the Christian Council of South Africa was established,[18] with the English-speaking churches and the Cape and Transvaal synods of the NGK as founding members. The other two NGK synods refused to join the Council, and in 1941 the Cape and Transvaal NGK synods withdrew, claiming that the Council was biased towards the use of the English language and because they fundamentally differed with the other churches on the "native question."[19]

In 1942 the Christian Council of South Africa convened a conference at Fort Hare to discuss the task of the churches in "Christian Reconstruction" after the Second World War. There was hope in the air, at least among liberal English-speaking and more moderate black Christians, that a concerted effort to build a more just South Africa would follow the war. Instead there came a new era of Afrikaner nationalist domination and the beginning of apartheid.

Ecumenical relations between the Congregational, Methodist and Presbyterian churches did develop after the war, despite continued division and even competition. In 1947, these churches established the first ecumenical faculty of divinity in the country, at Rhodes University. When government policy insisted that it enrol whites only, the churches acquiesced. Ecumenical co-operation in black theological education had existed at Lovedale Bible Institute since 1885, and from 1920, at the South African Native College at Fort Hare. But, in 1959, the government took over Fort Hare and instituted legislative action against other theological institutions. As a consequence, the Methodists, Presbyterians, Congregationalists, and Anglicans in 1960 set up the Federal Theological Seminary (FEDSEM) at Alice near the Fort Hare campus, for the training of black clergy.[20] The government's 1975 expropriation of the Alice campus eventually led to the relocation of FEDSEM to Imbali near Pietermaritzburg. The segregation of theological education reflected the reality of segregation in the churches themselves, but FEDSEM was a symbol also of the churches' resistance to apartheid.

In 1967 the United Congregational Church of Southern Africa (UCCSA) emerged from efforts of the predominantly white and Coloured Congregational Union (CUSA), the Bantu Congregational Church (formerly the American Board Mission) and the churches of the London Missionary Society (largely in Botswana and Zimbabwe). The new church was only ten per cent white. A similar attempt to unite the largely white Presbyterian Church of Southern Africa (PCSA), the Tsonga Presbyterian Church (formerly the Swiss Mission), and the Bantu Presbyterian Church was unsuccessful. But conversations between the Congregationalists and the PCSA, in abeyance for some years, resumed shortly after the UCCSA came into being in 1967, and considerable progress was made before the 1984 defeat, by a slender margin, of a proposal to unite.[21]

The use of the designation "Southern Africa" in the title of most English-speaking churches from the late 1960s indicates that they had become international churches. Not all of them have dioceses, synods, or regions in every southern African country, but most spread from Mozambique to Namibia, and some are in Zimbabwe and Botswana. Equally important are their links with international ecumenical bodies, such as the World Council of Churches, and with their own worldwide confessional families, as for example, the Anglican Communion, the World Alliance of Reformed Churches (Presbyterian and Congregational), and the World Methodist Conference. All of these links were to prove significant in the struggle against apartheid.

The Anglican Church had explored union with the Dutch Reformed church in 1870 (see p. 52), but kept aloof from union negotiations with the other English-speaking churches until the early 1960s. After the 1958 Lambeth Congress of the world-wide Anglican communion urged Anglicans to become involved in church union negotiations, the Bishop of Grahamstown, Robert Selby-Taylor, took the initiative to begin discussions with the Presbyterians and Methodists. With Presbyterians and Congregationalists already in the process of union negotiations, the Church Unity Commission (CUC) was set up in 1967 to seek the union of these churches (including the Bantu and Tsonga Presbyterian churches), and other denominations were invited to participate as well. The Lutherans and Roman Catholics attended as observers, but no other churches participated.

The CUC proceeded with its work, gathering annually to discuss the issues separating the churches. A major step towards union was taken in 1974 with acceptance of a Declaration of Intent that made intercommunion possible between the Anglican and the other churches. Union itself, however, remained elusive. The principal theological problem was episcopacy (rule by bishops), unacceptable most of all to the Presbyterians. There was also considerable apathy about the idea of union amongst black clergy, and, more generally, in local churches.

Grass-roots support for church union varied considerably from place to place, depending on the interest and commitment of local clergy and regional leaders. Church union was seldom regarded as a priority, but the CUC did enable many significant steps to be taken, including the formation of united parishes and congregations, and the mutual recognition of baptism. An attempt to take the process further through establishment of a "covenant relationship" between the churches was submitted to the church courts in 1982, but failed to obtain the necessary support of the Anglicans.[22] Episcopacy was still the major stumbling block, but another was ordination of women, practised in all the churches except the Anglican. The church leadership committed itself to the continuing work of the CUC, a commitment reaffirmed in 1992.

By the late 1970s it appeared that the movement towards church union had largely run its course in many parts of the world. In South Africa, the fact that the CUC effort involved only the English-speaking churches inhibited union at the local level, since congregations engaged in ecumenical cooperation there were not necessarily all members of the CUC. This was particularly so within the black community where, in any case, denominational loyalties were particularly strong and the priority was not church union as such but ecumenical solidarity in the struggle against apartheid. Nevertheless, in 1996 a major step towards church union was taken when the CUC denominations resolved to recognize each other's ordained ministry, thus making it possible for non-Anglicans to preside at the eucharist in Anglican parishes and vice-versa.

A Growing Unity and Resolve: The Churches Confront Apartheid

In 1949, the Christian Council of South Africa convened a conference at Rosettenville, focusing on the theme "The Christian Citizen in a Multi-racial Society." By now the mood was far more sombre than at the Fort Hare Conference in 1942; it had become clear that the newly elected National Party government was bent on implementing its ideology of apartheid. The conference condemned the proposed policies, as did successive conferences of the Christian Council.[23] Conferences convened by the NGK, though some were attended by representatives of the English-speaking churches, were far more cautious (see pp. 151–54), dominated as they were by supporters of government policy.[24]

All the English-speaking churches criticized apartheid in principle, and passed resolutions against related legislation. Those with a larger black membership (Anglicans, Congregationalists, Methodists, and, though not explicitly handled in this chapter, Roman Catholics) were relatively outspoken, those with a smaller black constituency (Presbyterians, Baptists) relatively restrained. The failure of the English-speaking churches was not in the passing of resolutions, but in their implementation.

The English-speaking churches were not segregated into racially separate synods or denominations, as the Dutch Reformed, Lutheran, and Baptist churches were, but there was considerable racial discrimination in their common life and practice.

Congregations and parishes were almost invariably segregated. Their leadership was virtually all white. Also, salary scales for clergy remained higher for whites. An attempt to segregate the Methodist Church, advanced at its annual Conference in 1954, was narrowly avoided by a counter-motion won by a slender majority that claimed that the church was "one and undivided." It is scarcely surprising, then, that while black church members tried to ensure that their churches kept up pressure on the government, they did not expect a great deal from them; they pinned their hopes far more on political bodies like the African National Congress.

The divisive issue among white church members was not so much the condemning of apartheid legislation in principle, but the political role their churches, and especially some ministers and priests, were increasingly playing. In the Anglican church several expatriate priests, in the decade after 1948, played active public roles, among them Michael Scott, Trevor Huddleston of the Community of the Resurrection, and Bishop Ambrose Reeves, of Johannesburg.[25] Archbishop Geoffrey Clayton, Metropolitan of Cape Town, was concerned that the church as an institution, and especially its priests, should not be actively engaged in politics.[26] Huddleston and Reeves, however, after working closely with the black community, came to the opposite conclusion;[27] it was, they argued, insufficient to pass resolutions, since the white minority government was illegitimate and Christians were called upon to take sides in the black struggle for liberation, and, therefore, to join forces with the ANC. Most churches stood aloof from the Congress of the People at Kliptown in June 1955, at which the Freedom Charter was adopted, though Huddleston and a few other clerics were present.

A particularly critical moment for the churches came in the early 1950s, when the Bantu Education Bill, to withdraw state financial assistance from mission schools, was introduced in parliament. Mission schools had a long and distinguished tradition in South African education. While, in normal circumstances, it might have been appropriate for such schools to be taken over by the state at this stage, these were not normal circumstances. With Bantu Education designed to keep blacks subservient to white interests, the churches were now caught in a dilemma: if they handed over their schools to the state, the schools would keep their government subsidy; if they did not and lost their subsidy, most mission schools would be forced to close. Bishop Reeves, like other leaders of the English-speaking churches, spoke out strongly against the bill, but without making any impression on the government. The Roman Catholic Church tried to retain its schools, but it had great difficulty in doing so.[28] The Anglicans surrendered their schools under protest but retained the hostels. The Methodists and Presbyterians recognized that, whatever the dangers, certain financial benefits for the churches and black pupils could result from the assumption of responsibility by the state over a matter which was arguably one of mandatory public concern. Black opinion was divided, not least within the ANC.[29]

The churches were able to wrench some minor compromises on the matter from the government, such as keeping their hostels at Fort Hare, but in the end they capitulated, losing control of some of the finest educational institutions in the country, and also their influence in black education. The Bantu Education Act, passed in 1953, left the field to the apartheid educational ideologists, with increasingly tragic consequences for all concerned.[30] The cost of defying the act and maintaining the church schools would have been considerable. But the churches did not heed their prophets, who called for such a step despite the cost. In general, the English-speaking churches, in responding to the implementation of apartheid, generally found it difficult to know when to draw the line and take a decisive stand or when to yield and compromise.

In 1957 the government promulgated the "church clause" of the Native Laws Amendment Bill, in an attempt to achieve what Prime Minister Hertzog had tried to do in 1937, only to be defeated convincingly by the churches.[31] In a blatant move to force apartheid upon the churches, this new bill made it difficult for black people to attend worship in white group areas. There was an outcry from all the English-speaking churches, including the Roman Catholic, while even the NGK was perturbed. Several church leaders, notably Archbishop Clayton, called on their clergy to disobey the law. Eventually the bill was passed, in a slightly revised form and became law, though it was rarely implemented.[32] It had, at least, created a new unity among the English-speaking churches in opposing the government and, for the first time, brought the Roman Catholic church to co-operate in an ecumenical protest against an apartheid policy.[33]

In 1960 the massacre at Sharpeville required a prompt response. Archbishop Joost de Blank, Clayton's successor, demanded that the World Council of Churches (WCC) expel the Cape and Transvaal NGK synods from its membership for the sake of the future of Christianity. Although the WCC refused to do so, it did assist in organizing a conference of its South African member churches. The Cottesloe Consultation, held in Johannesburg in December 1960, was one of the most significant events in the history of the church in South Africa (see p. 148). Eighty delegates of the WCC's South African member churches, primarily from the English-speaking churches, and including eighteen blacks, along with representatives of the NGK and other Afrikaner churches, debated their response to apartheid, and with the exception of the Nederduitsch Hervormde Kerk delegates, reached consensus.[34] The statement that emerged from the conference affirmed that all racial groups were eligible for the responsibilities and privileges of citizenship. It rejected segregation in the church and the government's prohibition of racially mixed marriages; it criticized the migrant labour system and job reservation (the reservation of certain jobs for particular races); and it affirmed the right of all people to own land.[35] In doing so it challenged some of the fundamental tenets of apartheid policy. Yet it clearly did not go as far as black English-speaking church delegates wanted; nor was it an unequivocal rejection of "separate development" as such.[36] The statement asserted there was "no objection in principle to direct representation of Coloured people in Parliament,"[37] but said nothing about representation for Africans, who had been removed from the common voters' roll in 1936. Nonetheless, the implications of the statement were far-reaching, and, significantly, it had the support of the NGK delegates.

Political pressure from Prime Minister Hendrik Verwoerd led to the rejection of the Cottesloe Statement by the NGK synods shortly afterwards, and to the withdrawal of the NGK from further ecumenical ventures. This split among the churches led Beyers Naudé, Moderator of the NGK's Southern Transvaal synod, and some

English-speaking delegates at Cottesloe, to establish the Christian Institute of Southern Africa (CI) in 1963.[38] The initial aim of the CI was to provide ecumenical support for dissident NGK members and ministers in opposing apartheid. It soon attracted members from the English-speaking churches who felt that their own churches were not taking a sufficiently strong stand. A further consequence of Cottesloe was the strengthening of ecumenical relations between the English-speaking churches within the Christian Council, which now began to take on a new lease of life.

Both the CI and the Christian Council were dominated by whites. Indeed, there were still virtually no blacks in the national leadership of the English-speaking churches. The first Coloured chairman of the Congregational Church, C.W. Hendrickse, was elected in 1945; not until 1960 did Anglicans appoint their first black bishop, Alphaeus Zulu, who became suffragan bishop of Zululand; the first black president of the Methodist Church, the Rev. Seth Mokitimi, was only elected in 1964. The first black moderator of the Presbyterian Church (PCSA) was the Rev. James J.R. Jolobe, inducted into office in 1971.

Two major international ecumenical events of the 1960s decisively influenced the churches in South Africa. The first was the Second Vatican Council of the Roman Catholic Church (1962–65), the second was the Geneva Conference on Church and Society sponsored by the WCC in 1966. Vatican II brought the Roman Catholic church in South Africa into much more direct contact with the English-speaking churches, and encouraged a far stronger and ecumenical commitment to social justice than had previously existed. The Geneva Conference on Church and Society took an even more radical position than Vatican II, calling on Christians to participate directly in the struggle for justice in situations of oppression and revolution.[39] This led directly to the establishment of the WCC's Programme to Combat Racism (PCR), which was established to provide support for organizations fighting racism, as well as liberation movements that were combatting settler governments in southern Africa.[40] This programme was to have a decisive impact on the English-speaking churches, who comprised the majority of the WCC's South African membership.

Black–White Polarization and Cooperation

In 1967 the Christian Council changed its name to the South African Council of Churches (SACC), and a year later, in co-operation with the CI, published *The Message to the People of South Africa*,[41] its central theme the rejection of apartheid as a false gospel. The government reacted strongly and immediately; so did sections of the member churches of the SACC. But in due course, and with some reservation, the English-speaking churches, with the exception of the Baptist Union, did endorse *The Message*, as did several thousand individuals. The Baptists withdrew their membership of the SACC and became "observers."[42]

The next phase in the church struggle against apartheid, and one which led to growing polarization in the churches, was a response to the black political renaissance of the Black Consciousness Movement (BCM) and the rise of Black theology (see also pp. 371–72, 386–87).[43] At the heart of Black Consciousness lay the conviction that white liberals, who had spoken on behalf of blacks especially after the government in 1960 banned the ANC and the Pan-Africanist Congress (PAC), could not truly represent the black oppressed. Blacks themselves must direct their own struggle for freedom. Black students then withdrew from the liberal National Union of South Africa Students (NUSAS), and formed SASO, the South African Students Organisation in 1969, with Steve Biko as its first president. The birth of SASO can be traced to the emergence of a black caucus at the national conference of the University Christian Movement (UCM) held the previous year in Stutterheim.[44] Many BCM leaders were theological students or ordained ministers, or at least had some contact with the church.

The UCM was an ecumenical alternative to the segregated and theologically conservative Student Christian Association, the principal student Christian organization on university campuses. The SCA had been multi-racial, but pressure from the NGK in the late 1950s and early 1960s led to its fragmentation along ethnic lines, the SCA serving white English-speaking students, with parallel organizations for Afrikaners, blacks (the SCM), and other groups. When the World Students' Christian Federation (WSCF) demanded that the SCA adopt a stronger stand against apartheid, the SCA refused, forfeiting its membership in 1964. A few years later it adopted a conservative evangelical statement of faith. As a result, the English-speaking churches found it difficult to identify with the SCA and sought to establish an ecumenical student movement. In this they were overtaken by more radical Christian students, who took the initiative and, with the cautious blessing of the churches, established the UCM in 1967. Within a short time the majority of its membership was black and located on the campuses of universities and colleges founded by the government for blacks. New black theological voices began to articulate a theology of protest against apartheid strikingly different from the liberal message of their churches.[45] During the next few years the movement adopted an increasingly radical style of worship, theology, and political activism, and, for that reason, eventually lost the support of most white leaders within the English-speaking churches.

Nonetheless, Black Consciousness and Black theology had considerable impact on the life of the English-speaking churches as a whole. Younger black ministers, many of them trained at the FEDSEM, where Black theology was particularly influential, asserted increasing pressure on the churches. With the exception of the PCSA, all the English-speaking churches now had a majority of blacks, but only now did this fact begin to influence church policy in any concerted way. That none of the churches withdrew from the WCC over the controversial Programme to Combat Racism was an indication of this growing black influence, though the ambiguous synodical responses on the subject indicate growing polarization within the churches. For many blacks, the issue of membership in the WCC became an important yardstick by which to measure the extent to which the churches were committed to the struggle against apartheid.

When the SACC National Conference met at Hammanskraal in 1974 a mood of desperation was in the air. Every attempt to resist apartheid by the BCM, the CI, and the SACC, as well as by the churches, had been severely countered by state security action. Many church people had been arrested, banned, or deported. Apartheid legislation was being implemented speedily and ruthlessly. To make matters worse, South Africa was about to become embroiled in the civil war in Angola. Delegates to the conference knew that the pressure cooker was boiling in the black townships and that the lid might burst soon with terrible effect.

In trying to determine what response white Christians could make to the growing conflict, some white delegates raised the possibility of conscientious objection to military service, an issue not directly affecting blacks, who were not subject to the draft. It was a direct challenge to the moral authority and legitimacy of the state, and to the patriotic assumptions of most whites.[46] The controversial Resolution on Conscientious Objection, which argued that the war in Angola was unjust and that Christians had an obligation not to participate in it, put member churches of the SACC at odds with by far the majority of white South Africans, who supported the government and the military. The majority of blacks opposed the war. Throughout the ensuing years this issue remained a major point of contention, heightened by the government's jailing of increasing numbers of young people, both Christian and others, for refusing to do military service.

South Africa was thrust into a new political era by an uprising initiated by young black students in Soweto in 1975, and strongly influenced by the BCM and SASO. The Soweto uprising, rapidly imitated by uprisings throughout the country, changed the course of South African history.[47] The churches in Soweto and other black townships often fulfilled a crucial, though sometimes reluctant, supportive role in this uprising. As casualties mounted, funeral services became political events in which the churches and community organizations co-operated, marking the beginning of a new phase of church involvement in the struggle within the black community. Soweto was the prelude to more than a decade of intensifying black resistance, state repression, church-state conflict, and struggle between conservative and radical groups within the churches. During this period the Afrikaans Reformed churches, with the exception of some leading individuals, continued to consolidate and rationalize their support for apartheid and government policy,[48] while the English-speaking and Roman Catholic churches, torn apart by the conflict between white and black interests, sought to speak and act more prophetically. English-speaking church opposition to apartheid, especially in synodical resolutions, remained constant, but leadership in the struggle was largely assumed by the Christian Institute, and, especially after it was banned in 1977, by the SACC, under its general-secretary Bishop Desmond Tutu (see p. 387). By 1978 the predominantly black staff of the Council had grown considerably, and its programmes had diversified and extended to meet the urgent needs spawned by apartheid and the struggle against it. Moreover, the SACC took the lead in calling for an intensification of international sanctions against South Africa as the only peaceful strategy remaining.

The SACC and its member churches were constantly under surveillance and attack from the government for their opposition to apartheid and, especially, for their stand on the Programme to Combat Racism (PCR). Foreign priests and missionaries were deported, leaders and publications banned, and frequent raids occurred on the SACC offices. In this pursuit the government had the full use of the state-controlled radio and television services, and much support from the rest of the media, as well. It also funded, or established, right-wing religious groups and organizations for this purpose, as was revealed in the Information Scandal that rocked South Africa in 1978.[49]

The government exploited the tensions between the SACC and whites in its member churches to the full, aware that the latter were antagonistic towards the PCR and the SACC's resolutions on such issues as conscientious objection and the war in Namibia, as well as on the SACC's general political direction. Indicative of this was the fact that the Baptist Union terminated even its observer status in 1976.[50] Some whites also left their churches to join politically more conservative denominations, notably the evangelical Church of England in South Africa. Most remained faithful to their own churches, concentrating their efforts on local church and parish concerns.

Charismatic, Confessing and Prophetic Movements

While some of the more politically conservative churches may be labelled evangelical, they were only part of a much broader evangelical community in South Africa, which spanned the political spectrum. Virtually all Protestant denominations, including the NGK, sections of the Anglican church, and many black churches would regard themselves as evangelical. By this they mean that they derive from the Protestant Reformation and that the evangelical doctrines on faith, grace, and scripture are fundamental to their theology and practice. The term evangelical has taken on new meanings in the twentieth century, when it has often been equated with fundamentalism; but in South Africa, evangelicals range from those involved in ecumenical endeavour and more progressive in their theology and politics to those who are fundamentalist and eschew cooperation with churches of other convictions. From 1973, when the Congress on Mission and Evangelism was jointly sponsored by the SACC and Africa Enterprise, an evangelical para-church organization led by the Anglican evangelical and evangelist Michael Cassidy, some evangelicals played an increasingly important political role in working for national reconciliation.

A significant number of evangelicals, and others within the mainline churches, were attracted to the charismatic movement. After its beginning in the United States,[51] it spread widely in South Africa among ministers and lay people, particularly within the white and Coloured constituencies of the major denominations. By the 1970s significant charismatic groups existed in all the English-speaking churches, as well as in the Roman Catholic Church, and even in the NGK. The charismatic movement was strengthened greatly when Bill Burnett, the Anglican Bishop of Grahamstown and later Archbishop of Cape Town, together with several other bishops, became part of the movement.

Various reasons have been given for the emergence of the charismatic movement. Globally it was in large measure a reaction against the social and political activism of the mainline churches, and symptomatic of a universal hunger for transcendence and spirituality evident in the 1960s and 1970s. In South Africa the political situation after the Soweto uprising and the war in Angola had created a climate of despair and anxiety especially among white church members. In response, the charismatic movement offered them a new sense of community, of personal meaning, and of spiritual assurance, just as the AICs did among blacks.

But the movement also created dissension and led to the formation of independent charismatic churches which broke away from the English-speaking churches.

By the mid-1980s much of the earlier dynamic of the movement had come to an end within the English-speaking churches, though its influence was still apparent in many individual parishes and congregations, especially in new forms of worship, and in a renewed stress upon spirituality and the ministry of healing. In general, worship within many English-speaking congregations became more open and flexible, and a concerted attempt arose to develop a holistic spirituality in which social witness was integrated with prayer and worship. There was also a growing concern to produce liturgies embodying not only traditional, but also contemporary, and indigenous South African elements. Already, in 1975, the Anglican Church had produced its experimental "Liturgy '75," which was replaced in 1989 by a new *South African Prayer Book*, published in all the languages used in the church, a mammoth undertaking. As its general preface indicates, the new prayer book sought to locate the liturgy within the context of the southern African crises and to stimulate further development of indigenous forms of worship.[52]

The polarizations which had developed so markedly during the 1970s and 1980s indicated the extent to which the English-speaking churches were divided within themselves by differing perceptions of social reality and differing understandings of the task of the church in society. While the SACC and other more activist Christian organizations confronted the state and the structures of apartheid prophetically, other initiatives concentrated on spiritual renewal, and on programmes of evangelism. Among divisive theological issues were the legitimacy of the state, Christian support for the armed struggle against apartheid, and the relationship between racial reconciliation and the demands of justice. In February 1980 the SACC convened a consultation at Hammanskraal on racism, which issued an ultimatum to "all white Christians to demonstrate their willingness to purge the church of racism." The black delegates at the consultation went on to declare that if, after a period of twelve months, no evidence of repentance was shown in concrete action, they would have no alternative but to witness to the Gospel of Jesus Christ by becoming a confessing church.[53]

The idea of forming a confessing church in South Africa, similar to that born during the church struggle in Nazi Germany, had long been debated in South Africa. It had inspired Beyers Naudé to launch the Christian Institute.[54] Now, however, blacks declared that a confessing church in South Africa should be black conceived and led, and that it might well break away from the white dominated churches if they did not change significantly. No such breakaway occurred, but it was now clear that since the emergence of Black theology, a "black ecumenical church" had taken shape within the churches, uniting black Christians and theologians across denominations in a common struggle against apartheid and discrimination in their own denominations. The black "confessing church" did not come into being, in part, because denominational loyalties were too strong; also, in part, because many of the churches were by now led by blacks. Also, the idea of a confessing church was more congenial to English-speaking churches within the Reformed tradition (Presbyterian and Congregational) than it was to Anglicans and Methodists. It was among the churches of the Reformed tradition, and especially in consort with black Dutch Reformed theologians, that the debate about "apartheid as a heresy" began in the early 1980s, leading the Dutch Reformed Mission Church (NGSK) to produce its Belhar Confession in 1982, declaring apartheid to be a heresy. The Presbyterians and Congregationalists later took a similar stand. The theological legitimation for apartheid which the white NGK provided was now rejected by those standing within the same broad Reformed tradition (pp. 153–54).[55]

The escalating protest against the government's proposed "tricameral" constitution in 1983 overtook the "apartheid is a heresy" debate. The church struggle now focused specifically on the struggle for the liberation of South Africa.[56] Churches debated the legitimacy of international pressure against apartheid through sanctions and disinvestment, and through organized protest, even participation in revolutionary violence and the armed struggle.[57] During 1985–86, as the war in Angola and Namibia intensified, a new wave of resistance and protest surged in the black townships, often led by the trade unions. The government responded by proclaiming States of Emergency (the second of which, beginning on 21 July 1985, lasted until after State President P.W. Botha's resignation in 1989) and used its massive security power to crush all opposition at enormous cost. An undeclared civil war was in progress forcing Christians and the churches to take an unambiguous stand.

Church leaders from the English-speaking churches, such as Bishop Tutu, played a crucial leadership role in the absence of the recognized black political leaders, many of whom were in prison or exile. On 16 June 1985, the tenth anniversary of the Soweto uprising, the SACC called on the churches to pray for the end to unjust rule.[58] In retrospect, this was a decisive moment in the church struggle. The SACC had now publicly declared the state to be a "tyrannical regime" and was praying for its removal. In this tense context the internationally celebrated Kairos Document was published by the Institute for Contextual Theology.[59]

The Kairos Document was a response to the spiral of violence in the years of unjust rule implemented by police and military force. Its dominant theme was the illegitimacy of the South African government, indeed, its tyrannical character, which had to be resisted through civil disobedience. While the Kairos Document did not overtly justify the liberation armed struggle, it was a radical rejection not only of the "state theology," which supported the status quo, but also of the more liberal response to apartheid of the English-speaking churches through the years, "church theology":

> We have analyzed the statements that are made from time-to-time by the so-called "English-speaking" Churches. We have looked at what Church leaders tend to say in their speeches and press statements about the apartheid regime and the present crisis. What we found running through all these pronouncements is a series of inter-related theological assumptions. These we have chosen to call "Church Theology" ... The crisis in which we found ourselves today compels us to question this theology, to question its assumptions, its implications and its practicality.[60]

"Church theology," in the view of the Kairos Document, was a false understanding of reconciliation, that is, a notion that reconciliation between black and white in South Africa could be achieved without the transformation of social and political structures and without the establishment of a just, democratic order (see also pp. 376–79).

The Kairos Document heightened the tension within the English-speaking churches that had been growing in intensity since the WCC initiated its Programme to Combat Racism, and widened the gulf between those committed to the struggle against apartheid and those who supported the status quo. In general, the English-speaking churches found it difficult to accept the challenge to civil disobedience presented to them by the Kairos Document, though some responded more positively. The United Congregational Church, for example, established a task force to work out a meaningful response, and this led to a far-reaching Pastoral Plan for renewal and mission. The tendency was to identify more fully with the National Initiative of Reconciliation, established by Africa Enterprise to provide a "third way" to approach the issues.[61] Nevertheless, it was the Kairos Document that gave theological direction and impetus to those political activists, including a growing number of "concerned evangelicals," seeking to be Christian in the struggle against apartheid.[62]

Women's Struggle for Equality in the Churches

The Kairos debate brought more decisively to the fore, among other issues, the question of the role of women within the churches, a matter in South Africa generally subordinated to the interests of the struggle against racism, but one which the churches could avoid no longer. As in most other countries and denominations, women in the South African English-speaking churches remained in largely supportive roles even though they comprised the majority of church members. Until recent years women were seldom included in the courts of the churches; they were seldom present at major conferences; and they were usually not eligible for ordination. The question of the role of women had been a subject of discussion much earlier in this century, as, for example, in the debate at the Anglican Provincial Synod in 1924 on whether women should be admitted as delegates.[63] Not until 1960 were they admitted. The first woman was ordained in the Congregational Church in 1934, and the first woman chair of the Congregational Union, Emilie Solomon, was elected in 1937. The Presbyterians did not allow women to be elected elders until 1967, and did not approve their ordination to the ministry until 1973, followed by the Methodists a few years later.

The debate on the ordination of women to the Anglican priesthood became a major issue within the Anglican Church from the 1970s onwards.[64] The Lambeth Conference, in 1968, had requested that consultations on the matter be initiated throughout the Anglican communion, and a 1970 report to the CPSA suggested that the church was coming to the acceptance of women in the priesthood, although with considerable uncertainty and opposition. A number of commissions and consultations led to a decision in 1982 to ordain women to the diaconate, but not yet to the priesthood, a proposal narrowly defeated at the Provincial Synod in 1985. Opponents feared that, had the vote been in favour, the church would have split. In 1992 the CPSA, by a significant majority, voted to ordain women for the first time.

Anglican women's religious orders, such as the Community of the Resurrection of our Lord, in South Africa since the end of the nineteenth century, had fulfilled a vital role in education and in ministry to the poor.[65] All the churches also had women's organizations. The Mothers' Union, which had a long tradition in England, was particularly strong in the Anglican Church. The Methodist Manyano, or Prayer Union, the first Methodist women's organization in South Africa, was founded at the beginning of the century; the red, black, and white uniforms of its members became distinctive symbols within the black community (see chap. 15).[66] Black women's organizations emerged in other churches, each with their own uniform, though they were matters of contention during the debates on church union. In 1904 the Presbyterians had formed a women's association of women of all races, though groups at the local level were usually racially segregated. The union of the various racially segregated women's organizations in the Congregational Church took place in 1967, but the black Isililo insisted on not disbanding. In the Methodist church, both black and white women's organizations voted against unity.

The role of women in the churches reflected their role in society broadly. Women, particularly black women, have borne the brunt of discrimination on a wide range of issues, not only ecclesiastical, in South African society. But they did not always take discrimination passively. In 1913 black women protested action against the Pass Laws; the Bantu Women's League, formed later that year, with links to the newly established ANC,[67] undoubtedly included many black women members from the English-speaking churches. But the most notable women's protest against apartheid was a 1956 march by 20,000 women on the Union Buildings in Pretoria. Again, it may be assumed that a large number of women from the English-speaking churches were present: Helen Joseph, the well-known Anglican activist, was involved.[68] The march set a pattern for subsequent political protest action, including the events leading to the shootings at Sharpeville, and in the escalating mass actions of the 1970s and 1980s. Throughout these decades women took the initiative in boycotts against boosts in rent in black townships, and in the costs of electricity, transport, and consumer goods. The women's movement in South Africa was divided between black and white women. The struggle for white women's suffrage in the 1920s led to white women's receiving the vote in 1930, but not black women. With the formation of the Black Sash in 1955, liberal and largely English-speaking white women did become directly involved in the political struggle against apartheid. Many of them were also members of the English-speaking churches.[69] In the 1980s, distinctly South African forms of feminist theology reflecting these issues emerged in some theological faculties and ecumenical organizations.[70] It is clear that when South Africa began to break free from the shackles of apartheid, the concerns of women began to receive greater prominence on the political agenda, and also within the English-speaking churches.

"Midwife to the Birth of Democracy": The Churches at the End of Apartheid

After the state of emergency the government proclaimed in 1986, the Mass Democratic Movement, a broad alliance of anti-apartheid organizations, including church-related groups, was often led by clergy from the English-speaking churches such as Archbishop Desmond Tutu, and co-ordinated by the South African Council of Churches and its regional branches.

President F.W. de Klerk's speech in parliament on 2 February 1990, announcing the unbanning of the ANC, the Pan-Africanist Congress, and the South African Communist Party, and shortly thereafter, his release of Nelson Mandela and other political prisoners, set in motion a train of events which were to transform the social and political life of South Africa, and bring about change in the political role of the churches and of church leaders. The time had come to give way to political leaders now released from prison or returning from exile. Church leaders, particularly those whose anti-apartheid record was unquestioned, found themselves in the forefront of efforts to mediate between warring factions in the townships. Notable amongst them was a former political prisoner on Robben Island, Mmutlanyane Stanley Mogoba, General Secretary and Presiding Bishop of the Methodist Church.

Two events signalled the beginning of a new phase in the political involvement of the churches in South Africa. The first was the National Conference of Church Leaders at Rustenburg in November 1990, which brought together leaders from Roman Catholic to NGK to AICs, from the English-speaking to the Pentecostal and independent charismatic churches. For the first time Christian leaders of wide diversity, many in strong political opposition to each other over the years, sought to reach a common mind on the witness and role of the church in the shaping of a new and just South Africa. While tensions remained, the conference moved towards consensus on some key, previously polarized, issues. The Rustenburg Declaration, adopted at the conclusion, was, in many respects, a compromise document.[71] The second significant event was the Consultation organized by the SACC and the WCC for their member churches held in Cape Town in October 1991. It was the first time, since the Cottesloe Consultation, that a WCC delegation had visited South Africa.[72] Unlike Rustenburg, the Cape Town Consultation achieved consensus on all core issues.

Concluding Comments

The face of the church in South Africa has changed dramatically since the beginning of the century. In 1900 only two church blocs, the Dutch Reformed and the English-speaking, were involved significantly in the public arena, though many black Christians were providing leadership within emergent African nationalism. This has now been transformed. The AICs are now the largest of all church groups (p. 211), though not as politically active in an organized way as the mainline Christians. The Roman Catholic church, larger than any other single denomination, is active in ecumenical projects. Pentecostalism (chap. 13), together with the independent charismatic-style churches, has become an important social force; indeed, a former general secretary of the SACC, Frank Chikane, is a black pastor of the (Pentecostal) Apostolic Faith Mission, and the current general secretary, Hlope Bam, is a black Anglican woman.

A year after the Cape Town Conference, Nelson Mandela, a member of the Methodist church, in addressing the Ethiopian Free Church in South Africa, said: "The church in our country has no option but to join other agents of change and transformation in the difficult task of acting as a midwife to the birth of our democracy and acting as one of the institutions that will nurture and entrench it in our society."[73]

How the English-speaking churches will respond to this challenge remains to be seen.

This chapter has not discussed many aspects of the day-to-day life of the English-speaking churches, such as worship, youth work, the work of hospital chaplains and chaplains in the military, programmes of evangelism and revival, institutions run by the churches for the disabled, lay preaching, and training courses on spirituality and mission. These better-known activities form the backbone of church life. Without them there would be no English-speaking church witness – ambiguous, halting, and cautious, as it has been, yet sometimes prophetic – on racism and apartheid, within the social history of South Africa.

10

Lutheran Missions and Churches in South Africa

GEORG SCRIBA WITH GUNNAR LISLERUD

Of some 60 million Lutherans in the world in 1994, 7.6 million lived in Africa. Of these, some 842,000 (including Moravians) were in South Africa, where Lutherans comprise only a small proportion of the South African population – down from 4.1 per cent in 1960 to 2.1 per cent in 1990.[1]

More than a century earlier, however, Lutherans had run more than a third of the mission stations in southern Africa – 70 per cent of those in Natal and Transvaal – and had provided almost a half of the missionaries in the region.[2] Among many black communities in Natal and Transvaal, Lutheranism became the majority expression of Christianity by the early twentieth century, though it was later overtaken in some regions by other denominations. Black Lutherans have long outnumbered white Lutherans, and by 1991 accounted for 97.6 per cent of the total.[3]

Missionaries from Germany, Norway, and Sweden brought the Lutheran faith to South Africa, planting churches among Africans and white immigrants. The missions were divided by nationality, form of church governance, liturgical traditions, and by their degree of emphasis on the Lutheran confessions and the extent of their willingness to cooperate with non-Lutherans. German missions, in particular, aimed to plant specifically national churches (in German, *Volkskirchen*), in which Christianity would be expressed in the language and culture of individual African and immigrant peoples.[4] As a result, a patchwork of distinct Lutheran churches spread through Southern Africa.

In the twentieth century Lutherans devoted considerable energy to overcome these divisions by grouping disparate congregations and missions, first into synods, then into regional and ethnic churches, and most recently into federations and South Africa-wide churches. With the exception of members of the Lutheran Free Churches and other Lutheran splinter groups, most black Lutherans are now united in the Evangelical Lutheran Church in Southern Africa (ELCSA), founded in 1975, and most white Lutherans in the United Evangelical Lutheran Church in Southern Africa (UELCSA or the United Church), founded in 1965. Efforts to produce a more organic union between white and black Lutherans have so far not succeeded.

All Lutherans – and the closely related Moravians – are united by allegiance to distinctive features of the Lutheran strand of the Protestant Reformation. They continue to find inspiration in the life and teachings of Martin Luther and in the confessional writings of Luther's time, especially the Augsburg Confession of 1530, which stress God's unconditional love, and justification and salvation solely from

God's grace through faith in Jesus Christ. In Lutheran theology the Bible is the authoritative source of doctrine, both as Law, which judges a sinner before God, and as Gospel, which proclaims God's justification or acceptance of a sinner by grace alone. Lutheranism retains more from pre-Reformation Christianity than do Calvinism and other branches of Protestantism. More than many Protestants, Lutherans stress that God works in his church through the sacraments as well as the preaching of the Word. Altar and pulpit have equal emphasis in their church buildings, and their liturgical life is organized around the church year. Lutherans envisage God as imparting the Holy Spirit through Word and Sacrament, and therefore do not emphasize the direct intervention of the Spirit, as in visions.

A distinctive Lutheran doctrine – often blamed for Lutherans' hesitance to challenge the apartheid state – is the belief that the Christian is subject to the authority of "two kingdoms" – the spiritual and the civil – both ordained by God and neither with power over the other. Also important in the highly fragmented ecclesiastical situation in South Africa is the Lutheran doctrine of church unity. Lutherans believe that for the Christian church to be truly united it is sufficient that the gospel be preached in conformity with a pure understanding of it and that the sacraments be administered in accordance with the divine Word. Ceremonies of human origin need not be observed everywhere, although they are seen as helpful for outward peace and for overcoming disparities.[5]

Lutheran Beginnings in South Africa

Many of the early white settlers in Cape Town were German Lutherans, who, as early as 1665 and again in 1719, were granted permission to participate in the services of the Dutch Reformed Church and to take Holy Communion under clearly defined conditions. By the mid-eighteenth century about 28 per cent of the white settlers were Germans, and most of these were Lutheran.[6] From 1741 onward the Lutherans repeatedly asked the ruling Council of Policy to let them establish their own congregation. In 1774 they erected their own church in Strand Street, Cape Town, and received permission to hold their own services there in 1779. The Dutch Reformed authorities imposed restrictions; the Lutherans could have no altar, their order of service had to be that of the Reformed church, and the language of the services was Dutch. The singing alone could be in German. Some eighty years later the "language issue" became cause for a split in the Strand Street Congregation; those demanding services in German founded the St. Martini congregation. In the nineteenth century, after some 40,000 Germans emigrated to South Africa, more German-speaking Lutheran congregations were founded in the western and eastern Cape.[7]

Formal mission work among the indigenous inhabitants of South Africa, namely the Khoikhoi, began with the Moravians, a nondenominational community established in Germany in 1722 by Count Nikolaus Ludwig von Zinzendorf, adopting the Lutheran Augsburg Confession as its confessional basis. The Moravians, proclaiming the gospel in combination with an ethic of hard work, founded self-supporting and close-knit communities both in Europe and in the many mission fields they occupied. In July 1737 Georg Schmidt, a 26-year-old Moravian missionary, settled at Baviaanskloof (later renamed Genadendal),[8] and erected there a simple hut, laid out a garden, and began teaching the nearby Khoikhoi. A few years later he baptized five or six converts, thereby offending the Dutch Reformed clergy, who had him expelled from the Cape in 1744 (see p. 28).[9] Almost a half century later, in 1792, three Moravian missionaries arrived at Baviaanskloof, discovering to their joy that one of Schmidt's converts, Lena, an old blind woman, was having others read her passages from the Dutch New Testament that Schmidt had given her. The pear tree that Schmidt had planted was still blossoming.[10] The new missionaries built a dwelling-house and church, began a garden, and opened a school. Khoikhoi flocked to the mission. The colonial rulers encouraged the establishment of further stations: Groenekloof (later renamed Mamre) in 1808 and Elim in 1824. A leper asylum founded by the Moravians in 1817 at Hemel-en-Aarde near Genadendal was moved by the government to Robben Island in 1846. Before long Moravian mission work extended from the western Cape to the eastern frontier into the Transkei.

In the nineteenth century representatives of nine Lutheran mission societies arrived in South Africa. All these German and Scandinavian societies were founded in the revivalist movements of the early nineteenth century. One such society, the United Rhenish Missionary Society (RMS), was founded in 1828 by twelve pious laymen in Elberfeld, Germany, and by participants in similar groups in other Rhineland towns. They included members of Reformed and United (Reformed–Lutheran) churches, as well as strict Lutherans. The first Rhenish missionaries came to the Cape under the guidance of Dr. John Philip of the London Missionary Society, seeking to create settlements on the Moravian model that would be self-subsistent and independent of funds from overseas. In 1829 they started to work in the Cape Colony, founding missions at Wuppertal – where J.G. Leipoldt began gardening, milling, tanning, blacksmithing, and carpentry – at Stellenbosch, and at Tulbagh. Starting in 1840, the Rhenish Society transferred its principal missionary engagement to the north, where it worked among the Nama, Damara, Herero and Rehoboth in present-day Namibia, and also founded and supported some white German congregations. Together with the Finnish Mission Society the RMS was so influential there that Lutherans today are the largest denomination in Namibia. In the Cape Colony RMS missionaries cooperated effectively with the (Dutch Reformed) Suid-Afrikaansche Zendinggenootschap, founded by local colonists, and in time took over its work. In the 1930s and 1940s, when the RMS suffered severe financial retrenchment, it turned over all its stations in the Cape Province to the Dutch Reformed Church, except Wuppertal, which it eventually transferred to the Moravians in 1966.[11]

Another of the German mission societies, the Berlin Missionary Society (BMS), was founded in 1824, in response to an appeal from prominent Berliners, among them university professors and members of the Prussian upper classes. More urban in tone than the other Lutheran missions, it was destined to work in the growing towns and cities in southern Africa. Although the BMS existed in the context of the Prussian Union Church (a Reformed–Lutheran union), it regarded itself as Lutheran. It emphasized a higher standard of academic training for its missionaries than many other societies. Its work, which would eventually spread widely throughout southern Africa, started among the Kora in the Orange River Sovereignty (at Bethany) in 1834. Other stations were soon established among the Tswana in the Cape Colony (1837), the Xhosa in British Kaffraria (1837), the Zulu in Natal (1847), and in the Transvaal (1860), Mashonaland (1892–1906), and Swaziland (1930).[12] By far its largest field was the South African Republic (Transvaal), which the BMS entered after consultation with Boer authorities, founding stations among the Southern Sotho, Pedi, and Venda. Its most important station was Botshabelo ("City of Refuge"), where the BMS built a school, shop, mill, and a printing and bookbinding department.[13] The BMS was the largest of the Lutheran societies in southern Africa. In 1955 it ministered to over 111,000 African Christians on 73 stations and 1,069 outstations[14]

Another German society, the Hermannsburg Mission Society (HMS), was founded in 1849 in the small town of Hermannsburg, near Hanover in Germany. Its founder, Ludwig Harms, was a strong critic of rationalism and the eighteenth-century Enlightenment; his preaching sparked a revival among the farming community that made up his congregation. Harms set up the HMS on strict Lutheran confessional principles. HMS missionaries and lay "colonists" were to establish a string of congregations in Africa modelled on the medieval communities that had evangelized the German borderlands east of the Elbe River. They were also to create a mission church identical in doctrine, liturgy, discipline, and organization to the church at home. Harms believed that the "heathen" would be attracted by three distinctive features of Lutheran missions: "the glory of our divine service, the pure teaching and divine sacrament of our church and the power of our singing." Emphasizing the rural nature of the mission, Harms came to embrace the epithet assigned to it by some of its opponents – *Bauernmission*, or Farmers' Mission.[15]

The HMS founded its first mission station at "Hermannsburg" in Natal, in 1854, and from there daughter stations spread throughout Natal, and later into the Zulu kingdom. At the second station, Ehlanzeni, the mission set up the first seminary for indigenous evangelists in 1870.[16] In 1857 it took over a station, Liteyane, begun by David Livingstone, and used it as a base for mission work among the Tswana, which proved more successful – in numerical terms – than the HMS Zulu mission.[17] In 1866 the HMS agreed with the Berlin society to divide the Transvaal along a line drawn due north from Pretoria: the Berliners would work east of the line, and the Hermannsburgers to the west.[18] By 1955 the HMS mission operated 23 stations among the Zulu, and 21 among the Tswana.

The German mission societies also initiated the establishment of Lutheran congregations among white settlers in the Cape, Transvaal, and Natal. In some cases, missionaries working among blacks would begin a parallel ministry among German settlers; in others, the settlers would form a congregation and ask the mission to send a missionary to be their pastor. Though served by missionaries, most of these German congregations maintained their financial and administrative independence from the mission, and in time formed German synods separate from the black churches.[19] For example, New Germany was established in 1848 when settlers called the BMS missionary R. Posselt to be their pastor, who at the same time remained a missionary and founded Christianenburg among the Zulu. The "Friedenskirche" in Johannesburg originated in 1888 when some German settlers, who were holding a memorial service for Emperor Wilhelm I, asked H. Kuschke, a Berlin missionary, to become their pastor. Other German congregations were established in Pretoria, Kimberley, Pietermaritzburg, and numerous smaller locations in the Transvaal, the eastern Cape and Natal – some with German names like Berlin, Potsdam, or Heidelberg.

Within the HMS, missionaries and "colonists" formed the core of a congregation in which blacks and whites at first worshipped together, but with the arrival of women and children, services and schooling evolved along language lines. By 1869 most "colonists," no longer feeling needed by the mission, left the direct service of the HMS to become independent settlers in Natal or Transvaal. The HMS accepted pastoral responsibility for other German-speaking congregations,[20] such as New Hanover, which was established in 1858 by some Germans who, having left the Berlin settlement of New Germany, called an HMS pastor. Several other HMS congregations were established in southern and northern Natal and the Transvaal. The German congregations, unlike the black mission churches of the HMS, were financially independent from the mission and therefore had the right to elect their own pastor.[21]

After the death of Ludwig Harms, a dispute arose between his brother, who was mission director and pastor of the Hermannsburg congregation in Germany, and the official church of Hanover, about influences from the Prussian Union Church. The establishment of the Hanoverian Free Church was the result. In South Africa this dispute prompted four pastors of German-speaking congregations and two missionaries, all dedicated to upholding the Lutheran confessional writings, to secede from the HMS in 1893, taking with them the congregations of Kirchdorf, Lüneburg, and Bergen. From this secession emerged a German-speaking Free Evangelical-Lutheran Synod in South Africa (FELSiSA) consisting of some eleven congregations, as well as a separate Hanoverian Free Church Mission, which, with American and German aid, conducted missions in the same areas as the Hermannsburg Mission Society. Because of their strict emphasis on the Lutheran Confession, these bodies did not join other Lutheran bodies in the ecumenical undertakings and Lutheran mergers of the twentieth century.[22]

Norwegian missions, like their German counterparts, were founded in early nineteenth-century revivals and influenced by the precedents of Moravian missions. One revival, begun by the farmer and merchant Hans Nielsen Hauge, emphasized Bible study, prayer, conversion, and repentance. Another, partly influenced by the Danish pastor-poet N.F.S. Grundtvig, emphasized the pastoral office and divine worship and made an impact upon Norwegian pastors. Haugian and Gruntvigian representatives, along with Moravians, came together in 1842 to found the Norwegian Mission Society (NMS), which developed as a church-oriented, and democratic organization within the state church of Norway.[23]

The first NMS missionary to South Africa, Hans Palludan Smith Schreuder (see p. 92), arrived in Port Natal (the future Durban) on New Year's Day 1844. Denied access to the Zulu Kingdom of Mpande, he founded an influential mission station at Umphumulo north of Durban in 1850. After he had healed Mpande's rheumatism, he was granted land at Empangeni within the Zulu kingdom, where he served as the king's physician. By the time of the Anglo-Zulu War (1878–79) 22

Norwegian mission stations had been established in Zululand. Schreuder, appointed as bishop in 1866, quarrelled with the NMS over his episcopal powers, and resigned in 1873. He aligned himself soon after with the Schreuder Mission, which gained support especially amongst the clergy in the Church of Norway, and established friendly contacts with the newly founded Church of Sweden Mission (CSM). The two missions shared a high view of the bishop's office; they also believed that missions should be fully integrated into the structure of the church and not dependent upon voluntary missionary societies, even those that worked within the church.[24]

Americans of Norwegian descent developed close ties with the Schreuder Mission. P.L. Larsen, the first President of the Luther College in Decorah, Iowa, married the sister of Schreuder's successor in South Africa, Bishop Nils Astrup. In 1928 the Norwegian Lutheran Church in America took over the management of the mission, and later founded missions in the goldfields of the Orange Free State. The Americans contributed outstanding managerial and administrative skills to the Lutheran missions.[25]

The Swedish missionaries who came to South Africa were not members of the evangelical, interdenominational Swedish Missionary Society, but rather of the more orthodox and "high-church" Church of Sweden Mission (CSM), which was founded in 1874, and had the archbishop as its president. The first Swedish missionaries, O. Witt and C.L. Flygare, who arrived in South Africa in 1876, went to Schreuder's station at Entumeni to study Zulu language and customs. Soon, however, they split with Schreuder and opened their own missions in Natal and Zululand. In 1878 the Swedish Home Board established its first mission station, Oscarsberg, at Rorke's Drift. Its first indigenous worker, Joseph Zulu, a refugee from the Zulu royal house, received his training in Sweden and returned to Natal as an evangelist and teacher; in 1901, during a second visit to Sweden, he was ordained.[26] In 1902 the CSM began to minister to Zulus in Johannesburg, many of them Lutherans, who had found employment in the Witwatersrand mines. Thus Lutheranism did not remain entirely attached to its rural roots.[27]

During the last part of the nineteenth century Scandinavian seamen, storekeepers, carpenters, wagon-builders and farmers settled in South Africa. Like the Germans, many of them turned to missionaries of their own nationality to minister to them as their pastor. Scandinavians in Durban founded an interdenominational church, which by 1890 had become a purely Lutheran congregation known as St. Olav, with Norwegian as the language of worship, a Norwegian missionary as pastor, and the superintendent of the NMS as trustee. In 1882 another congregation was established at Marburg in Natal by farmers and fisherfolk from the west coast of Norway. The settlers brought their own minister from Norway, but their inability to pay his salary later forced them sometimes to rely on an NMS missionary from Durban. In Johannesburg, with more than 2,000 Scandinavians by 1900, a joint Scandinavian congregation was founded in 1897 under an American Lutheran pastor, Paul Gullander. The church split in 1907, the Danes and Norwegians remaining in the "Scandinavian Evangelical Lutheran Congregation in Johannesburg" the Swedes and Finns forming the Gustav Adolf Congregation, which relied on CSM missionaries and the Swedish Seamen's Mission until 1970.

In the 1980s the St. Olav congregation split and as an independent congregation has no ties at present with a Lutheran church body. In 1994 the Gustav Adolf congregation at Kelvin joined the ELCSA (Natal–Transvaal).[28]

Uniting the Fragments of Lutheranism: Early Synods and Federations

The fragmentation of South African Lutheranism had resulted in part from the diversity of Lutheran countries sending missionaries and settlers to South Africa, and in part from intra-Lutheran disputes about the proper relationships between churches and mission societies and between Lutheran and other churches. In South Africa the establishment and consolidation of congregations according to national (cultural and linguistic) background led to ethnic and racial divisions – particularly between white and black – and often to resistance against ecumenical efforts. The same missions had founded and initially cared for both black and white congregations, but unification and consolidation among black and white churches proceeded on separate, if parallel, tracks in the twentieth century.

In the beginning the administration of a mission lay in the hands of the home mission agency in Europe. Money it collected from donor churches and congregations was used to acquire Christian literature, buy land for the mission, and pay the salaries and pensions of missionaries, evangelists, and African pastors. The mission director or his representative inspected the mission field from time to time, and the mission agency appointed a superintendent or "propst" to supervise the work on site. The constitutional structure of the home church was introduced on the mission field; missionaries met locally in mission conferences to discuss common matters and to elect their office-bearers. Once congregations were properly established, they relied on income from the economic enterprises of the mission stations and on contributions raised from their members. Administrative powers were gradually decentralized, especially when, during the two Anglo-Boer Wars and the two World Wars, overseas financial support was cut off. In time it became necessary to establish synods consisting of representatives of various congregations, in order to elect local leadership and adopt a constitution.

After the First Anglo-Boer War of 1880–81, for example, the Hermannsburg mission in the Transvaal set up a synod among the Tswana, which met first in December 1882 at Emmaus, although the Superintendent of Natal voiced his opposition. Though the synod had no executive powers, two representatives from each congregation discussed the office and duties of the elders. The next synods took place in 1885 (Kana), 1889 (Saron) and 1893 (Rustenburg). However, with rising tension between the English and the Boers, the ensuing Anglo-Boer War, and the establishment of the Union of South Africa, conferences of missionaries were re-established in place of synods.[29]

Among whites, the first impulses toward consolidation came from the church members themselves. German-speaking settlers, who had assembled their own congregations and erected their own church building, parsonage, and schools, and asked a mission society or home agency for a minister, became accustomed to a more congregational form of church government. Prompted by the desire to co-operate with other congregations in common endeavours, such as liturgy and church life, to attain financial independence from a mission society, and to strengthen German culture through schools, the settlers took the initiative in the early founding of synods. Each congregation was represented by its pastor and a layman, the German schools by their principals; the synods discussed theological issues, agreed on rules for pastors' salaries, and elected office-bearers.

The first German Lutheran Synod in South Africa was established in St. Martini, Cape Town in July 1895 as the "Deutsche Evangelisch-Lutherische Synode Südafrikas" under the supervision of the Royal Regional Consistory of Hanover in Germany. Comprising six congregations in the Cape Colony, with three others present as guests, the synod elected Pastor Wagener as chair of its executive and accepted as its basis "the specific confessions of the Evangelical Lutheran Church." Later it was divided into an East and West circuit.[30]

Similarly, in 1911 eleven German-speaking congregations connected with the Hermannsburg mission, mostly in Natal, established the German Evangelical–Lutheran Synod of Hermannsburg, with an emphasis on the Lutheran confessions. It encouraged German-language schools and sought to gain more independence from the mission, though it maintained the spiritual heritage of Hermannsburg and drew its pastors from among the missionaries. Its first präses (president) was the Hermannsburg mission director Egmont Harms, the nephew of the mission's founder.[31] A third German synod, the German Evangelical–Lutheran Synod of Transvaal, which originally comprised eleven Berlin-related congregations, was constituted in March 1926, its two pillars German custom and Lutheran faith.[32]

Responding to blacks' aspirations for more autonomy, the Berlin mission, in 1911, constituted five black synods: Northern Transvaal, Southern Transvaal, Zulu–Xhosa–Swazi, Orange, and Cape. Factors behind this decision were mainly the Ethiopian movement and the financial hardship experienced by the BMS during and after the Second Anglo-Boer war. The synods proved a blessing during the two World Wars, when the mission was completely cut off from its German base and deprived of staff and finances.[33]

The next wave of synod formation among blacks occurred during the 1950s with the founding of the Norwegian Zulu Synod, the Swedish Zulu Synod, the (Norwegian) Mankankanana Synod, the Hermannsburg Zulu Synod, and the Hermannsburg Tswana Synod in the Transvaal. Thereby the missions' original goal of establishing autonomous and indigenous churches was being achieved. Long before this, however, the Lutheran missions gradually began to cooperate with one another. Concerned to counter the "active propaganda" of other denominations, the Norwegian, Swedish, and Berlin Mission Societies decided in January 1910 to establish the Co-operating Lutheran Missions (CLM). Initially the CLM was to last for ten years, but fifty years later it had become the driving force for formation of a united Lutheran church in Natal and for closer cooperation of Lutheran missions throughout southern Africa.[34]

The CLM established a combined teachers training college at the Norwegian Missionary Society station at Umphumulo. The South African government had given notice that it would support only four training centres and the Lutherans wanted to ensure that one of the four was Lutheran. In addition, the cooperating mission societies trained pastors in a common seminary at the Swedish Church

Mission station at Oscarsberg and evangelists at Emmaus, the training centre of the Berlin Mission. In 1949 a Zulu High School with an educational programme designed to appeal to Lutheran students was set up in Eshowe by the CLM. It also set up a pre-seminary school at Untunjambili in 1955 (moved to the Umphumulo campus in 1962) to enable students to obtain seminary entrance qualifications at the matriculation level.

The CLM also founded a Lutheran Publishing House to issue materials in Zulu, particularly the Small Catechism and Hymn Book. In 1928 it inaugurated *Isitunywa*, a Lutheran magazine, and the Zulu *Almanac*, which included a directory of the hundreds of CLM missionaries and black pastors. *Credo*, a bilingual Lutheran theological journal for southern Africa, was published by the CLM, beginning in 1954.[35]

In 1928 the American Lutheran Mission (Schreuder Mission) joined the CLM, followed, in 1938, by the Hermannsburg Society, which, however, maintained its own centre for training evangelists at Hermannsburg and a printing press in Moorleigh. From 1949 the CLM worked for a united regional church in Natal, Swaziland and Transkei to be called the "United African Lutheran Church in South Africa" but at the same time opted for a larger council that would include other Lutheran synods, both black and white. Within the CLM itself, work continued towards uniting the five synods in Natal into one regional church. The Hanoverian Free Church became an observer in the CLM from 1952 to 1962, but did not join the merger and became an independent church in 1967. The CLM also engaged in mission work among Indians in Natal.[36]

In 1953 CLM missions joined with the Moravian, Rhenish and Finnish Missionary Societies (the latter operating in South West Africa) to form the Council of Churches on Lutheran Foundation in South Africa (CCLF). In 1958 two German synods in South Africa and one in South West Africa joined, while two others became observers. The CCLF's principal task was to promote cooperation between Lutheran missions and synods within the larger southern African region. In 1960 the CCLF in cooperation with the Lutheran World Federation established a radio station, "Radio Voice of the Gospel," in St. Ansgars, Roodepoort, which would later broadcast from Addis Ababa across most of the African continent and also in Asia.[37]

Consolidation: The Emergence of South Africa-Wide Lutheran Churches

Beginning in the 1950s, the Lutheran missions, synods, and churches of southern Africa began a complex period of consolidation and restructuring, which consisted of three phases. First, they established regional "black" churches (which included Coloureds and Indians, the other two racial categories of the apartheid era, along with some whites, mostly from missionary families). These regional churches were finally merged in 1975 into ELCSA, a large, relatively centralized church. Second, in 1964, several German ("white") churches united into UELCSA, a rather decentralized church. Third, in 1966, most of the Lutheran bodies in South Africa, white and black, along with Lutheran churches from neighbouring countries, grouped themselves into a Lutheran federation (FELCSA, re-formed as LUCSA in 1991). The desire for larger churches ran parallel to the attainment of

THE CHURCHES OF MODERN SOUTH AFRICA

independence from the mission societies; the idea of *one* Lutheran church in southern Africa had been one of the aims of missionary work in South Africa all along.[38]

Spurred by the general thrust for independence in much of colonial Africa, and promoted by the 1955 All-African Lutheran Conference in Tanganyika (now Tanzania), a movement for closer cooperation and formation of a united Lutheran church emerged in southern Africa, particularly Natal. The movement for Lutheran unity gained ground particularly among the missions and synods that cooperated in the CLM and the CCLF. In 1957 representatives of missions, black synods, German synods, and the Moravians met in a Preparatory Assembly in Durban to discuss two alternate forms of Lutheran union: a federation of regional churches, and a united Lutheran church. Within the black synods, which represented some 700,000 members in South Africa and South West Africa, many pushed for a single united church, while within the white synods, representing about 50,000 members, many argued that the spiritual unity that already existed among the synods made a constitutional merger unnecessary. The German synods, in particular, stressed that their special responsibility to maintain German culture and language made a merger with the black synods difficult, and it is likely that many of their members were also motivated by their support for the government's apartheid policy. In the end, despite white opposition, the Preparatory Assembly recommended that Lutherans strive to create a united Lutheran church.

As the first step in this process, the Lutheran mission societies, along with black and white synods from South Africa, South West Africa, and Rhodesia, met, in 1958, in a Constituent Assembly at Christianenburg near Durban. This body, pressed in particular by black delegates, decided to form a "Regional Church for the Zulu–Xhosa–Swazi Region," which would then federate with similar churches that would be founded in other regions.[39] The decision to form a federated church did not reflect the apartheid ideology of racial separation, since the regional churches would have no clauses stipulating membership by race or ethnicity, and each would be able to register members, and call pastors, from different groups. Yet, as long as the white synods declined to join, the federative process would tend to create churches in each region that were closely identified with one or several African ethnic groups.[40]

The first such regional church was created in Natal, where the five Lutheran mission societies were already cooperating in the CLM. Representatives of the Zulu–Xhosa–Swazi Synod (Berlin mission), the Norwegian Zulu Synod, the Swedish Zulu Synod, the Mankankanana Synod (Schreuder Mission), and the Hermannsburg Zulu Synod met at Kwa-Mondi (Eshowe) in 1960 to conclude discussions on constitutional issues of unification. At a key point in the deliberations a sudden peal of thunder persuaded some delegates that "heaven has spoken" in favour of the union, and the conference concluded by pledging to merge into "the new Evangelical Lutheran Church (Zulu–Xhosa–Swazi Region)."[41] Thus the first regional church was constituted on 7 July 1960, when four of the five synods agreed to unite into a single church, but the Hermannsburgers held back until 1963. The 1961 assembly adopted the "United Testimony," which, closely following the merger document of the American Lutheran Church, established the confessional basis of the new church, in particular its interpretation of the office of bishop, which the Zulu Synod of the Church of Sweden Mission and some black clergy favoured as the presiding officer rather than a president. It was made clear that the office of a Lutheran bishop is not linked to the apostolic succession nor is the bishop a powerful chief to rule over the Church but rather he is a minister, together with all other ministers, in the Church. This clarification was necessary because members from the background of German and American missions were not familiar with the episcopal office.[42]

The words "Zulu–Xhosa–Swazi Region" in the proposed name of the new church emphasized, in line with the Volkskirche ideology, its basis in (Nguni) language and culture. In 1961, however, the name was changed to "Evangelical–Lutheran Church in Southern Africa, South-Eastern Region," (ELC-SER) to reflect the emerging view, which countered the government's apartheid ideology, that the Lutheran church was to be geographically, not culturally based. Some hoped to build on the constitution and liturgy of the South-Eastern Region to create a non-denominational, ecumenical "All African Church" using English as lingua franca at its general meetings and assemblies. But this ambitious idea gained little support. The first leader of the ELC-SER was Bishop Helge Fosseus (1960–1972) of the Swedish Mission. His successors, P.B. Mhlungu (1972–78), L.E. Dlamini (1978–88) and S.P. Zulu (1988–96) were all African.[43]

After ELC-SER, regional churches were also founded in the Transvaal (1962), in the Cape–Orange Free State (1963), and in several surrounding countries. At roughly the same time the Moravians created two independent churches in the eastern and western Cape, and, by 1966, thirteen Lutheran and Moravian churches, white and black, existed in southern Africa.[44] Each became independent from the mission society that had created it. Some blacks feared that the missions would desert them, leaving them to their own spiritual, financial, and administrative resources. Some older Africans, who identified the church with the missionary, doubted that the indigenous clergy were ready to assume responsibility. But to other blacks the time seemed ripe for church independence, which would coincide both with the independence of African states from colonialism and with the South African government's policy of separate development.[45]

Missionaries in the newly independent churches were not expected to serve as pastors in a congregation but, rather, to participate in mission and evangelization, diaconal work, production and distribution of literature, stewardship, and Christian education.[46] In the 1970s, however, the churches began to call missionaries from overseas mission agencies to serve as pastors in parish work. Such missionaries were expected to recognize the regional church as a self-governing body. Even though they worked in these churches, they were paid by their mission societies, and were representatives of the Lutheran "mother church" in America and Europe. The new churches, in consequence, remained remarkably dependent on the overseas churches.

While the African Lutherans were consolidating into regional churches, the German-speaking churches in southern Africa were also moving closer together. Aware that many German settlers were assimilating into English or Afrikaans cultures and were losing their Lutheran identity, the leaders of the German-speaking churches, in cooperation with the Lutheran World Federation (LWF), formed, in January 1958, a Board of Trustees for Lutheran Extension Work in South Africa to minister to English- and Afrikaans-speaking Lutheran congregations. The Board was to produce Christian literature in these languages, and to investigate the possibility of establishing a chair of Lutheran theology at a South African university with the help of the LWF. Non-German congregations such as Welkom, Durban, St. Peter's by the Lake (in Johannesburg), and Eshowe were founded. These, together with the Strand Street Church in Cape Town, were affiliated to the Board of Trustees.[47] In training their theology students, the Lutherans were cautious about cooperating with Reformed theological centres at universities such as Stellenbosch and Pretoria. They accordingly decided to establish their own theological training centre, which was opened in 1972 by Dr. G. Wittenberg and Dr. W. Kistner, in the department of divinity of the denominationally neutral University of Natal at Pietermaritzburg.

Union of the German Lutheran synods had been delayed by the Hermannsburg church's insistence that the Transvaal and South West African churches should, like the Hermannsburg and Cape churches, adhere strictly to all the Lutheran confessional writings. When the non-Hermannsburg churches stated that they were not in principle against the Formula of Concord but that historically this document was not part of their heritage, the Hermannsburg demands were moderated. The church leaders of four churches[48] and two affiliated congregations came together, in 1964, to found the Clerical Council and thereby the United Evangelical Lutheran Church of Southern Africa (UELCSA). The new church held its first general synod the next year in the Strand Street Church, Cape Town, the oldest Lutheran congregation in South Africa. German, English, and Afrikaans were stipulated as official languages, but German was generally used in the meetings of the general synods for nearly thirty years. UELCSA has a fairly loose structure; it is "in essence and in its confessional ties a *church*, in organization more a *federation of churches*," whose component parts retained legislative and administrative autonomy.[49] Its clerical council stated in 1965 that UELCSA was to care for the spiritual needs of immigrants and youth; to educate pastors; to develop common arrangements for congregational life, liturgy, and church music; to undertake closer cooperation with the black churches; and to develop the Christian Academy, an institute of adult education founded in 1955 at the Cape with aid from the Evangelical Church in Germany (EKD).

The consolidation of black and white churches proceeded simultaneously with moves to strengthen federal structures that would embrace both groups. The Federation of Evangelical Lutheran Churches in Southern Africa (FELCSA), founded in 1966 as successor to the CCLF, embraced thirteen Lutheran churches in South Africa and surrounding countries, including the regional black churches, as well as the Moravian churches, and the white UELCSA (but not the Zulu and German Hanoverian Free Churches). Its combined membership was about 750,000.[50] Though it enjoyed only those powers transferred to it by the member churches, FELCSA was nonetheless a public symbol and voice of Lutheran unity and the Lutheran churches' channel to ecumenical bodies inside and outside southern Africa. It also supported programmes and institutions for theological training, mission, evangelism, literature, and diaconal work, and fostered closer fellowship among the thirteen churches. Moreover, its conferences issued declarations on behalf of southern African Lutherans on political and social issues (see pp. 190–4).

Many Lutherans sought to transcend regional churches and loose confederations by creating a church embracing different races, classes, and cultures on a common confessional basis. As congregants of the four regional churches moved to the industrial area of the Witwatersrand and Pretoria, pastors and missionaries, aware of overlapping of work, proposed a new church that would incorporate members from diverse language and cultural backgrounds. But others objected that lopping off parts of existing churches would appear to add to Lutheran divisions even as it fostered fellowship among different African linguistic groups. In consequence, in 1973, FELCSA's committee on unity and merger matters, along with the bishops of ELC-SER and the Transvaal and Tswana regional churches, initiated merger conversations with one another and with the Cape–Orange Regional Church. A draft constitution of the new church was discussed in 1974 at Tlhabane and a Constituent Assembly was convened in 1975. There was so much readiness, indeed longing, for unity in a single nationwide Lutheran Church that delegates resolved to proceed with union even before resolving some outstanding questions concerning the establishment of a Rand Regional Church which had caused tension among the constituent churches. An invitation was issued to the white churches to join the merger, and an executive meeting of FELCSA decided to go ahead with the merger whether the white churches agreed or not.

Acid bombs thrown into the Constituent Assembly's meeting hall – those who threw them were never arrested by police – only strengthened the delegates' resolve to unite. On 18 December 1975 they established the Evangelical Lutheran Church in Southern Africa (ELCSA). It was organized into four dioceses: the Cape–Orange (chiefly Coloured, Afrikaans in language), the South-Eastern (chiefly Zulu), the Northern (chiefly Northern Sotho and Venda), and the Western (chiefly Tswana); a fifth (Rand or Central) diocese, to embody the multilingual ideals of the church proposed earlier, was established the following year. Each diocese was to retain much of its identity in ELCSA under the leadership of an elected bishop. The Indian Lutheran congregations and the St. Olav Norwegian congregation were to be included in a Durban Circuit.[51]

ELCSA decided to become a member of the Lutheran World Federation (LWF), FELCSA, the South African Council of Churches, the All Africa Council of Churches, and the World Council of Churches.[52] It is the official organ for relationships with overseas partners and other church bodies, and serves as the voice of the church in negotiations with the government. It formulates the policies of the church, initiates pastors' retreats, and co-ordinates the work of men's, women's, youth and Sunday School groups in the dioceses. ELCSA also handles the finances of the church, including grants from overseas partners, contributions of the congregations, and proposes equal salary scales for church workers (although paid by the diocesan treasuries). ELCSA is organized into dioceses, circuits, parishes and congregations, as well as three administrative bodies – the General Assembly, which meets triennially, the Church Council with a full-time Treasurer and General Secretary, and the Presiding Bishop. In addition to the four original dioceses, the

Central Diocese, encompassing the Witwatersrand–Pretoria area, was constituted in 1977. The Botswana Diocese was established in 1982, after a split in the Western Diocese in 1979 in which a large section became independent as ELC Botswana under Bishop Robinson. The Eastern Diocese (Swaziland and Eastern Transvaal) was established in 1988 as a sub-division of the South-Eastern Diocese. In the drive towards a merged church some congregations split off, some to form RELUCSA, a Reformed Lutheran Church in Southern Africa without any links to other Lutheran bodies.[53]

It was not clear whether the white churches of UELCSA would fit into the new ELCSA structure, and if so, how. Theological conferences of UELCSA, in 1975 and 1976, on the theme "Confession and Unity of the Lutheran Churches in Southern Africa," discerned three possibilities: churches of UELCSA separately joining ELCSA dioceses; UELCSA accepted as a "floating" (not geographically based) diocese of ELCSA; or UELCSA and ELCSA intensifying their cooperation under the FELCSA umbrella. Leaders of UELCSA agreed, in principle, that one Lutheran church in South Africa was needed, but they found this prospect threatening to their autonomy and chose the third option, of increased cooperation with ELCSA.[54]

The reluctance of the white churches to join ELCSA, like their resistance to an unequivocal rejection of apartheid, was soon interpreted by leaders of ELCSA and overseas partners as support, whether indirect or direct, of the government's policy. In the wake of political unrest of 1976 and 1985, ELCSA in 1988–89 withdrew from FELCSA, despairing of its value in promoting unity. It later rejoined the restructured Lutheran Communion of Southern Africa or LUCSA in 1991.[55] Prompted by pressure from overseas Lutheran churches, and particularly by the suspension of two white churches by the LWF Assembly in Budapest 1984, a Unity Committee was established in 1985 between ELCSA and the two South African components of UELCSA – ELCSA (Cape) and ELCSA (Natal–Transvaal) – to discuss the unity of the Lutheran churches in South Africa. But first they had to confront the problem of the deeply divided Lutheran response to apartheid.

People's Churches and the Black Pastorate
Ever since Martin Luther translated the Bible into German and wrote a "Deutsche Messe" including hymns in German, Lutherans – in Scandinavia also, where Norway, Sweden, Denmark, and Finland each established a national Lutheran church – stressed vernacular languages for expressing the Christian faith. Lutheran missions in South Africa accordingly stressed the importance of learning African languages and of developing vernacular forms of worship. They also contributed zealously to Bible translation. Berlin missionaries pioneered translations in Northern Sotho and Venda; a panel mostly of Hermannsburg missionaries revised Robert Moffat's translation into Tswana for use in the Central Tswana region; and in 1867 the Berlin missionary J. Döhne helped the missionaries of the American Board in the first translation of the Zulu New Testament. Schreuder of the Norwegian Mission Society also translated the Norwegian Altarbook, the lectionary, Luther's Small Catechism, and parts of the Bible. The HMS published a Zulu translation of the New Testament based on the Textus Receptus in 1922, and

the whole New Zulu Bible was revised and published in 1959 by a CLM commit-tee of both black and white members chaired by Pastor O. Sarndal, a Church of Sweden missionary.[56]

A natural outgrowth of the vernacular emphasis of Lutheranism and its history in national churches in Europe was that Lutheran missions stressed creation of national or ethnic churches on the mission field. German founders of Lutheran mis-sions, such as Harms, opposed the pietistic concept held by Von Zinzendorf of con-verting individuals rather than nations. After World War II the missiological debate on the task and aim of mission intensified in ecumenical circles, as theologians deliberated on the rise of National Socialism in Germany and the role the church-es and missions had played in it.[57]

Despite their commitment to the vernacular and the idea of national churches, Lutheran missionaries – and often the black clergy they trained – tended to dismiss African world views and African practices in Christian worship and spiritual life. In 1961, for example, the "Church Practice and Discipline" section of the merger document of the South-Eastern Region asserted that an adult seeking baptism must reject polygamy and ancestor worship (as well as all rites and feasts connected with it), and must be married only by Christian rites. A number of abuses of lobola (the payment of bride price prior to marriage), were condemned, along with the prac-tices of smelling out sorcerers and consulting witchdoctors. Christians, the merger document declared, should not fear the dead or try to influence their return through the use of medicines.[58]

During the 1960s, a survey conducted by Hans Florin under the auspices of the LWF prompted serious rethinking of Lutheran stances on some aspects of African culture, particularly at the Missiological Institute established at the Lutheran Theological Seminary, Umphumulo, in 1965. In 1969, for example, the Institute re-evaluated African funeral rites, attempting to appreciate the philosophy that under-lay them and to understand behaviours previously considered superstitious or even absurd. For example, death in African reasoning is not the end of life but a transi-tion to a new stage. The Institute called on churches to rethink from a Christian perspective their approach towards the departed and the ancestors and their rela-tionship to the family and ethnic group.[59]

Although worship in all the Lutheran churches follows roughly the same pat-tern, a considerable variety of forms and practices has emerged from the variety of cultures in South African Lutheranism. Worship stresses fellowship and celebra-tion; in black churches, especially, there is dancing and singing when the collection is brought up the aisle. Hymns in black churches are often sung in parts (soprano, alto, tenor, bass), without written scores, though seldom accompanied by drums. Most congregations of European background use an organ or guitars, and those of Hermannsburg heritage, a brass band. In 1995 the member churches of LUCSA declared that indigenization of the liturgy, of African church music, and of other forms of expressing and interpreting the gospel should be encouraged and shared in combined services.[60]

Lutheranism puts great emphasis on devotions and prayer in Christian homes. In South Africa domestic devotions typically consist of praying, singing and Bible-reading, or reading the Moravian Watchword for the day, i.e. a 250-year-old tradition of having a text chosen by lot each day. Pastoral counselling may be sought during phases of change in family and personal life, but among Africans coun- selling, for example on marital problems, is often done in a customary way by the clan. At crucial stages of life the church is supportive: at birth with baptism; at puberty with confirmation; at the establishment of a family with marriage; and at death with the funeral.

African leadership, which was one precondition for successful national church- es, often emerged quite early, and sometimes without much direction from the mis- sions. David Mokgatle Modibane, for example, converted around 1839 by Methodists at Thaba 'Nchu, preached with enormous success in cooperation with many missionary groups, including the Lutherans. He founded several congrega- tions, including one at Bethany, near Pretoria, which, on the invitation of the peo- ple, was taken over by the Hermannsburg missionaries in the early 1860s and built into one of their chief stations in the Transvaal.[61]

Well into the twentieth century African evangelists with formal training were crucial in congregational work, but in exceptional cases Lutheran Christianity was spread by evangelists with no formal training. Paulina Nomguqo Dlamini (ca. 1858–1942), for example, known as the "Apostle of Northern Zululand," had served the Zulu king, Cetshwayo, in her teenage years. Later, while working on a white farm, she was visited twice in dreams by a figure in white robes who told her, "Paulina, arise and accept this Bible. Go forth to where the sun rises and teach my people, the old and the young." After her employer, Gert van Rooyen, persuaded her that the person was Jesus, she was baptized by Hermannsburg missionaries in 1887.[62] In obedience to the white figure's command she became an evangelist, working with various missionaries, and other African evangelists, in the founding of many congregations in Zululand. "I began with the work of the Lord while stay- ing with the van Rooyens," she recalled. "I kindled a fire in the hearts of the peo- ple; this spread and grew in intensity. I then saw for myself that the word of God is Truth. Yes, this fire from the word of God spread and set many a heart alight."[63]

Within the mission structure, missionaries slowly began to nurture African lead- ership. They supervised the African churches in the election of their church elders, who would attend to the orderliness of worship and assist the missionary in run- ning the congregation and visiting the sick and needy. Other African assistants, after receiving instruction from the missionaries, preached sermons and taught cat- echism classes. Each mission taught and trained co-workers to assist, for example, in Bible translation. As their congregations grew and out-stations were established, the Lutheran missionaries realized the necessity of training black school-teachers, evangelists, and pastors.

Timotheus Sello and Martinus Sewushane, the first two Africans to become Lutheran pastors, were ordained by the director of the Berlin Mission Society, Dr. H.T. Wangemann, in 1885. In the Pedi persecution of 1864 Sewushane had been one of the confessing Christians, and Sello was a helper of Superintendent Knothe, who started a "National Helpers' School" in Mphome/ Kratzenstein in 1881. As pastor at Lobethal, Sewushane, angered by what he regarded as the paternalism, authoritarianism, and excessive strictness of the missionaries, joined the mission- ary Johannes Winter, who, in 1890, broke with the Berlin mission to found the

Bapedi Lutheran Church with the support of Cholokwe, the Pedi chief. Winter, who was a son-in-law of director Wangemann, wanted to be an African for the Africans. Against the order of the mission leadership, he ordained some "national helpers" who had been trained as evangelists at Botshabelo and is said to have married a second wife, a Pedi, according to African custom.[64] The Bapedi Lutheran Church, which preceded the better known "Ethiopian" secessions from other missions, attracted many followers of the Berlin mission, including the whole congregation at Nain. The mission, fearful that the new church would ordain its own pastors, tried to inhibit its growth by asking the government of the South African Republic to suppress it by law. Director Wangemann, convinced by these events that the mission had been too hasty in ordaining Africans, postponed further ordinations. The Lutheran missions determined to tighten their institutional control of the training of pastors. Each society founded its own institutions: the Berliners at Botshabelo in the Transvaal (1878) and Emmaus in Natal (1905), the Norwegians at Umphumulo (1893), the Swedes at Oscarsberg at Rorke's Drift (1908), and the Hermannsburgers at Ehlanzeni (1870, moved to Hermannsburg in 1928–29). At Untunjambili the Schreuder Mission established an evangelical school in 1890; but, as already noted, the Co-operating Lutheran Missions in 1912 rationalized Lutheran education by training teachers at Umphumulo, evangelists at Emmaus, and pastors at Oscarsberg.[65]

The Lutheran Theological Seminary (LTS), established at Oscarsberg, was crucial in the education of an indigenous clergy.[66] It opened in 1912 with nine students and CSM missionary J.A. Hellden as principal.[67] After the Second World War, it expanded its constituency beyond Natal, by training pastors for Lutheran synods throughout southern Africa (including Namibia) and the Eastern Province of the Moravian Church. As a centre for pastoral conferences and refresher courses for clergy, it bridged numerous Lutheran bodies, and, in 1960, moved to NMS land at Umphumulo, where the government allowed it to admit students of different racial backgrounds, but no whites. This was a controversial decision, because plans were under way to create a broader ecumenical seminary (the Federal Theological Seminary, or FEDSEM) at Alice in the eastern Cape.[68] Although invited to join this seminary, the Lutheran synods and missions preferred to concentrate on a closer union within the Lutheran family and followed LTS to Umphumulo.

The training institution of the Hermannsburg mission for Tswana-speaking evangelists and later pastors was at Bethel in the western Transvaal. In the process of forming a regional church the training institution was moved to Marang near Rustenburg in 1958 as a joint effort of the Sotho-speaking missions with the help of the Lutheran World Federation. Pastors were trained there until the end of 1992, when a decision was made to have only one theological seminary, this institution to be situated at Marang in the Transvaal. The seminary would, however, continue to operate at the Umphumulo campus until the financial situation of the Church made it possible to extend the buildings at Marang.

UELCSA, for its part, founded the Lutheran Theological Training Centre at Pietermaritzburg for theology students from its four German-speaking member churches, with substantial help from the LWF. In 1985 it became a joint venture of ELCSA and UELCSA.[69] Presently all ELCSA students study at Umphumulo for a diploma, some continuing for a post-graduate degree in Pietermaritzburg.

The commitment to an African pastorate and the growing centralization of theo-logical study helped produce an African leadership that was more or less of a com-mon mind. The Lutheran African pastors are not, however, without their critics. They were often accused of denying the laity free expression of their God-given gifts. Only the pastor may stand near the altar, and though women are in the majority in most congregations, they have not been encouraged to participate in the critical decisions of the congregation's life. Congregants under 25 have also been neglected, in the view of some critics. The church has recently made efforts to respond to such criticisms by involving youth, women's groups and the laity more deeply in congregational and church life. Whatever its failings, however, the black pastorate has provided a strong impetus to the unification movements and, also, to the broad struggle against apartheid.[70]

Lutherans, South African Society, and Apartheid

Lutheran mission roots lie largely in the values of pre-industrial Europe, with a mistrust of urbanization and modernization, and in a tendency (in the nineteenth century) to cooperate with the Boer authorities in the Transvaal. In contrast to many Anglo-Saxon missions, therefore, Lutherans were slow to adapt to the new conditions of twentieth-century South Africa and reluctant to follow their parish-ioners from the countryside to the city. In a sympathetic but critical portrayal of the "Lutheran Image" (1967) the German theologian Hans Florin suggested that "those who are Lutherans in urban churches have as a rule come from rural areas. Such people are proud to be Lutherans, proud to be members of 'an honest church.' As attributes of this 'honest church' they name dignity of worship, a definite doc-trine and (as far as the Transvaal is concerned) a cohesive Lutheran hinterland." However, Florin found that many other Africans of Lutheran background avoided the Lutheran church in town because of a "lack of an appealing program, lack of prestige, and an indistinct socio-political identification."[71]

By 1925, 37,687 or 18 per cent of African missionary school pupils were in Lutheran schools, but only 5 per cent of aspirant teachers were in Lutheran train-ing colleges, and there were no Lutheran secondary or "industrial" schools. Only one of the twelve missionary hospitals in 1925 was Lutheran, and only one of the twelve missionary doctors.[72] As a consequence Lutherans were slow to develop an African elite attuned to modernity; Florin noted in 1967 that "the number of intel-lectuals in the Lutheran Church is today smaller than in the Anglican and Methodist churches."[73] As the Lutheran churches entered the era of apartheid they were consequently less prepared to grapple with questions of structural justice and national policy than some other mainstream Protestant churches.

Lutherans' lack of experience in what would later be called "prophetic" Christianity had been intensified by their comparative isolation from ecumenical bodies. Lutherans had participated in meetings of the Natal Missionary Conference, founded in 1886, and in the eight General Missionary Conferences, which were open to all Protestant missionaries, held between 1904 and 1932. However, they played little role in shaping the discourse and activities of the General Missionary Conferences, being responsible for only 3 of the 73 papers given at the eight meetings.[74] Lutherans protested any drift into an emphasis on social issues and politics; this attitude was epitomized in *Zwischen Nil und Tafelbai* (1931), a book written by Siegfried Knak, director of the Berlin mission, which included a critique of Anglo-Saxon missions in Africa.[75] Lutherans were also slow to join the Christian Council of South Africa (later South African Council of Churches or SACC), which was established in 1936.[76] Since the formation of ELCSA in 1975, however, black Lutherans participated actively in the SACC; President Habelgaarn of the Moravians and Bishop M. Buthelezi of ELCSA served terms as SACC president,[77] while the Rev. W. Kistner served as director of the SACC's department on Justice and Reconciliation.[78]

The slowness of the Lutherans to challenge the Nationalist government was widely seen as a consequence of the Lutheran Volkskirche policy. Harald Winkler, for example, charged that "the Lutheran churches have divided along racial lines, in conformity with the policies of separate development and apartheid."[79] The continued existence of all-white churches was particularly problematical. Some argued that, though South African Lutheranism was a plant with "two stems," both stems came from a single "root" imported from Europe. More radical critics, such as Winkler, charged that even the root was divided, and that European Lutheranism was responsible for the divisions within South African Lutheranism and for its weak response to apartheid.[80] Critics were convinced that Lutheranism's divisions were closely related to its feeble social and political witness and called for, in Winkler's words, a "prophetic Lutheran ecclesiology ... a vision of a united church with a bold social witness."[81]

In 1963 the ELCSA-South-Eastern Region (ELC-SER), in an early Lutheran response to apartheid, affirmed the church's unity as the body of Christ and rejected church segregation and discrimination as contradictory to God's will and the gospel.[82] In the same year, in association with the Transvaal and Tswana regional churches, it called on the Lutheran World Federation to sponsor a survey of Lutherans in South Africa. The 1964–65 report by Florin attributed the Lutherans' political silence to their rural, conservative, and Volkskirche tendencies, but also to their narrow interpretation of Luther's doctrine of the two kingdoms – the one spiritual, the other civil, each strictly separate, with neither free to dictate to the other. Florin hinted broadly that the doctrine was neither based on Scripture nor relevant in the modern situation "where most secular nation states would not be prepared to acknowledge [the] paternal authority of God." Florin urged South African Lutherans to rethink the two-kingdom doctrine and to consider the "pragmatist-biblical" approach of the Calvinists, which had provided the church "with a ready justification for action and effective witness."[83]

The formation of FELCSA in 1966 was seen by many black Lutherans as a step toward a united church and also toward more radical social witness. Influenced by Florin's report, FELCSA invited members of Lutheran churches to a pastoral conference at Umphumulo in 1967 on the "Lutheran Teaching on the Two Kingdoms."[84] The delegates concluded, in the Umphumulo Memorandum, that the two kingdoms, though separate, both belong to God; the structures and imperatives of the two kingdoms cannot therefore contradict one another, and the church must be active and render service in political and social life. They also declared that "we ... reject the Policy of Separate Development." The Umphumulo Memorandum, intended for internal distribution to Lutheran churches in South Africa, was, by mistake, published prematurely by the LWF press association, causing a stir especially among German-speaking Lutherans.[85] The next year, another FELCSA conference on "Church and State" declared that Christian witness and action should not be confined to the realm of the church, but extended to all social and political structures requiring correction and reform.[86] In yet another FELCSA gathering, at Swakopmund in 1975, Lutheran leaders called on all Lutherans "to withstand unanimously the alien principles which threaten to undermine their faith and to destroy the unity in their doctrine, in their witness and their practice." The most dangerous of such alien principles were identified as the emphasis on ethnic churches, the belief that unity among Christians could be purely spiritual, and the belief that the political and economic system of South Africa was a product of natural laws and hence could not be judged in the light of the Bible.[87]

Florin's report also influenced the missiological courses at the Lutheran Theological College (LTC) at Umphumulo, which served as a platform on which the dialogue between denominations "on this multi-racial subcontinent could be carried out in a relaxed and peaceful atmosphere."[88] The Missiological Institute at LTC conducted a series of courses on the South African situation, including such overtly political subjects as migrant labour (1970), church and nationalism (1974), affluence and poverty (1977), and capitalism and Marxism (1978). In most of these courses, which were subsequently published, LTC students, theologians, and laity of all major denominations participated. Lutheran opinions on the South African situation were also expressed through FELCSA's journal *Credo*.

After 1975, with the formation of the united but black-dominated ELCSA, there was a new platform for Lutheran witness against apartheid from a church that transcended ethnic boundaries. Since the inception of FELCSA, Lutherans had responded to the socio-political situation mostly through the FELCSA office, but ELCSA itself now took a more open stand. In 1984, at Rosettenville in Johannesburg, the Church Council of ELCSA affirmed "her stand against apartheid and that it is a heresy. It is oppressive against the majority in our country." The Council condemned the new constitution that would give Coloureds and Indians, but not Africans, some limited power in governance.[89]

Although the German-speaking "white" Lutheran churches often argued that the church must avoid political involvement, their response to the "Message to the People of South Africa," distributed by the SACC in 1968 (p. 163) and to the Umphumulo Memorandum on the Two Kingdoms in 1968, demonstrated that they supported the government's policy of protecting cultural and ethnic identities. However, as the South African churches became independent and as overseas mission partners withdrew, new affiliations with overseas partners, such as the Evangelical Church in Germany and the Lutheran World Federation, had to be found. This, in turn, led to a struggle within the "white" churches, whose traditional foundations and beliefs were under fire. In 1972 a group of conservative Lutherans, the Greytown group (NELCSA), broke away from the ELCSA (Hermannsburg) mainly for political and church-policy reasons, and in 1973 joined the Free Church (FELSiSA).

Overseas pressures pushed South African Lutherans, but particularly whites, toward a stronger stance against apartheid. During and immediately after the First World War the General Lutheran Conference in Europe and the National Lutheran Council in America launched a comprehensive aid programme which, after the Second World War, was intensified; it led, in 1947, to the establishment of the Lutheran World Federation (LWF) in Lund, Sweden. The LWF, with headquarters at the Ecumenical Centre in Geneva, has regarded itself as a free association of Lutheran churches, a means of serving the international Lutheran community; its member churches regard themselves as in "pulpit and altar fellowship" with one another.

The LWF's stance against apartheid became increasingly forceful in a series of world assemblies. In 1970, at Evian in France, it called on member churches to develop programmes to abolish racism and injustice in church and society, and decided to send delegations to report on churches' compliance with these goals, after which it would distribute its financial aid accordingly. In 1977, at Dar-es-Salaam in Tanzania, it addressed South African Lutheran churches explicitly, declaring that the South African situation was a "status confessionis," in which the essence of the church was imperilled unless it rejected apartheid. In 1984 the LWF assembly in Budapest, convinced that the white South African Lutheran churches had rejected the offer of black Lutherans for fellowship at congregational level, and concluding that the white Lutherans would not aid blacks in their struggle against apartheid, voted to suspend two white churches from membership: the Evangelical–Lutheran Church in Southern Africa (Cape Church) and the German Evangelical–Lutheran Church in South West Africa/Namibia. In 1990, the LWF assembly at Curitiba in Brazil called on all member churches to press the South African government for fundamental change; the LWF pledged to support financially an intensive programme for a peaceful transition to democracy, and with repatriation of exiles. These promises were only partially fulfilled because of financial constraints.[90] In 1992, in view of the ongoing unity discussions, the suspension of the two white Lutheran churches was lifted by the executive of LWF, and ELCSA (Natal–Transvaal) was accepted as a new member of LWF.

The Evangelical Church in Germany (EKD), which had a contractual agreement with the German churches in South Africa for regulating appointments of pastors from overseas, also supported the battle against apartheid. It applied pressure on the "white" churches to accelerate unity negotiations with the "black" church and to take a clear and open stance against apartheid. Members of the "white" Lutheran churches regarded this as unwarranted interference in their affairs; tensions consequently arose between these churches and pastors from overseas.[91]

In response to intensive pressures from black South African Lutherans and from international Lutheranism, the white Lutherans in South Africa began to forge a theological response that was neither defiant nor repentant. In 1983, in a study paper on unity and political responsibility, UELCSA said that, although the church did have a political responsibility, it should not seek to bring about change through revolution. It rejected both the conservative evangelicals' "ethic of restoration" and the liberation theologians' "eschatological" or "revolutionary" ethic, and advanced, instead, an "ethic of the cross," for continuous reformation without revolution. In its 1986 "Word of Hope," UELCSA, reacting to the suspension of two of its members at the LWF Assembly in Budapest, rejected apartheid and confessed its failure to heed the requests and complaints of "our black brothers."[92] In 1987 the synod of one of the constituent churches of UELCSA, the ELCSA (Natal–Transvaal), adopted a resolution stating that apartheid must be abolished, though it blamed South African problems, not on apartheid alone, but on the difficult relations between the First and Third Worlds which were reproduced in microcosm in South Africa. It also rejected the use of violence, whether to achieve change or to maintain the status quo.

The dismantling of apartheid and the election of Nelson Mandela as president of South Africa in 1994 eased the conflicts between the white and black churches." Despite ongoing disputes over apartheid, a Unity Committee had been established in 1985 between ELCSA and the two constituent churches of UELCSA – ELCSA (Cape) and ELCSA (Natal–Transvaal) – to discuss unification of the Lutheran churches in South Africa. This Unity Committee generally met twice each year and all three participating churches agreed to work on a proposed constitution for the new church. A new draft constitution worked out by the Unity Committee sought to assimilate ELCSA's more hierarchically structured constitution,[93] with the more congregational structure of ELCSA (Cape) and ELCSA (Natal–Transvaal), where individual congregations own property and have the right to call their own pastors.[94]

Remaining questions still under discussion, as of 1996, are: whether to delimit dioceses solely along geographic lines or to accommodate historical (that is, cultural and linguistic) preferences as well; how much power to grant congregations to own property and elect their own pastors; whether to "consecrate" or "install" bishops and whether to elect them for life or a fixed term; and how to equalize pastor's salaries between the more wealthy white and poorer black congregations.[95] During the current negotiations members of the three churches have been encouraged to come together in pulpit exchanges, combined services, and other kinds of joint meetings.

The distinctive features of the Lutheranism brought from Europe to South Africa, especially its conservatism and its emphasis on national churches, at first made it an appealing choice for Africans. But it became increasingly less attractive in the twentieth century, as it was slow in offering either the tools for dealing with modernity (such as schools, urban churches, and theologies of political protest) or the bridges to African culture that the Pentecostals and Zionists offered. Lutheranism has, nonetheless, put down deep roots in black culture while at the same time retaining its role as preserver of several white immigrant cultures. The core message of Lutheran theology has not been silenced in the South African context, even if it has been diverted for many years into separate ethnic and racial spheres: that God's love for a fallen world, given by grace, is received solely by faith in Jesus Christ.

11

Moving from the Margins to the Mainstream: The Roman Catholic Church

JOY BRAIN

A Late and Slow Start

A history of the Christian Church in South Africa before 1860 might well have ignored the Roman Catholic Church altogether, so limited was its contact with other denominations and so small the number of its adherents in South Africa. It lagged far behind the Protestant churches and missionary societies, at first because of the religious policies of the Dutch East India Company, which excluded all who did not accept the tenets of the Reformed Church, and, later, because of the disarray of the Catholic Church in Europe in the wake of the eighteenth-century rationalist movement, the French Revolution, and the Napoleonic wars.[1]

Some Catholics did live at the Cape before 1795, but, because of the Company's law, they were obliged to conceal their faith. Although the *Kerk-Orde* (Church Ordinance), passed by the Batavian Republic in 1804, made it possible for a handful of clergy to come from the Netherlands to minister to Catholic soldiers, they were repatriated with the garrison in 1806 when the British reoccupied the Cape. Catholic chaplains were sent out after 1817, but there was no resident bishop or established Catholic presence until Easter Saturday 1838, when the first Catholic bishop, Patrick Raymond Griffith, an Irish Dominican, arrived in Cape Town. Bishop Griffith found there the ruins of a chapel that had been washed away in a flood a few months before, and a small and scattered congregation with meagre funds. During his busy twenty-five years in South Africa he visited the eastern districts of the Cape Colony, established parishes at George, Grahamstown, and Port Elizabeth, and opened a school for boys, the Mercantile and Classical Academy, the first of many Catholic schools to offer a broad education to Catholic and non-Catholic pupils. He also erected St. Mary's Cathedral in 1841, still one of Cape Town's principal places of worship.

In 1846 Bishop Griffith applied to Rome for a separate vicariate[2] for the Eastern Cape, a request approved the following year. Father Aidan Devereux, consecrated bishop of the Eastern Districts of the Cape of Good Hope, brought the first community of religious sisters, the Assumptionist Sisters of the diocese of Paris, to open a convent in Grahamstown. He started the first Catholic newspaper, *The Columnist*, to reach his far-flung congregation.[3] He brought in a group of Dutch-speaking Flemish priests, one of whom, Father Jacobus Hoendervangers, became the pioneer priest of the Orange River Sovereignty, later the Orange Free State. After Devereux sent a priest to visit Catholics in Natal, another vicariate was created, centred on Natal but including virtually half of South Africa, from the Kei River to Quelimane, and inland along the Tropic of Capricorn, including the

Orange Free State, the entire Transvaal, Lesotho, and Swaziland. The French-speaking Missionary Oblates of Mary Immaculate (OMI) were put in charge of this immense territory, under Bishop J. M. F. Allard, who arrived in Port Natal, the future Durban, in 1852.

By the middle of the nineteenth century, the ratio of Catholic priests to territory was so small that only the main towns had a resident priest. Over vast areas there were no priests at all and Catholics travelled to the towns to receive the sacraments or, as Griffith's diary shows, joined a Protestant church.[4] Griffith and his successors faced a chronic shortage of priests and of funds for expansion at a time when the major pontifical missionary societies[5] were funding new missionary enterprises all over the world.

The first task of bishops opening up new territories was to trace the Catholics across the countryside, bring them together into communities or parishes, provide churches, build schools for their children, and instruct adults about their faith through Catholic newspapers and periodicals. Catholic lay people were so few that it was unrealistic to expect them to provide these facilities for themselves, particularly since most were families of Irish or Dutch soldiers, or discharged soldiers living in poverty. Some small Catholic churches were built with the assistance of British soldiers stationed in the towns, for example, in Grahamstown, Bloemfontein and Kroonstad; others were built by priests and parishioners, or by lay brothers. All the buildings were small and simple, with the minimum of decoration. After the mineral revolution of the 1870s and 1880s, many Catholics emigrated to South Africa, mostly struggling artisans and blue-collar workers. Catholics of the professional class, traders, and farmers were always in the minority.

Education was a fundamental part of the Catholic mission until recent times and, in every diocese religious brothers and sisters were brought in to run Catholic schools for boys and for girls. Religious communities working in South Africa were the Dominican Sisters of King William's Town, the Dominican Sisters of Cabra, and the Holy Family Sisters of Bordeaux (teachers), the Augustinian Sisters, the Filles de Jésus de Kermaria, and the Sisters of Hope (nursing), the Sisters of Nazareth (homes for orphans and the old), the Marist Brothers, and the Christian Brothers (teachers). In the eastern Cape the dynamic Bishop James David Ricards (1871–93) brought the Jesuits to Grahamstown to open St. Aidan's, a college for boys. From here the Jesuit Zambezi mission was launched in 1879.[6]

Social welfare and charitable work have long been part of the Catholic apostolate. Bishop Leonard of Cape Town brought in the English Sisters of Nazareth to open homes for the aged and orphanages, and established the Grimley Institute for the Deaf and Dumb. Bishop Jolivet brought the Augustinian Sisters from Brittany to Natal to open private hospitals, as well as a home for orphan and destitute coloured and Indian boys. The Sisters of Nazareth extended their work among old and abandoned people from Cape Town to Durban, Johannesburg, Kimberley, Pretoria, and Port Elizabeth.

The number of urban and white Catholics grew slowly through natural increase, through immigration, and by conversion. There was no attempt to convert Protestants, although enquiries were welcomed and instruction given on request, many converts coming as a result of marriages to a Catholic. In such marriages the non-Catholic was required to marry in the Catholic church and to bring up the children as Catholics.

Throughout the nineteenth century the Catholic Church was regarded as a foreign institution in South Africa: many of its priests were not English-speaking, its liturgy was in Latin, and a number of its rituals, such as the use of incense and the wearing of colourful vestments, were seen as exotic. Prejudice against Catholics existed in many quarters. The talented and highly educated Colonel Christopher Bird, on the Cape governor's staff from 1807 to 1824, was convinced that his failure to achieve promotion to high office was a consequence of his Catholic faith. His son John, well known in colonial Natal, also believed that his religious beliefs held him back.[7]

The Catholic bishops, aware that many of their adherents were poorly educated, tried to provide Catholic reading matter in the form of periodicals and newspapers. Bishop Ricards, the first editor of *The Colonist* (from 1850 to 1859) also founded the *Catholic Magazine of South Africa*, the only Catholic periodical in English for more than thirty years. He wrote several books, most notably *The Catholic Church and the Kaffir*. Father F. C. Kolbe, a convert to Catholicism, was the most prominent of the editors of the *Catholic Magazine*, and a lecturer who rebutted anti-Catholic outbursts from what he called "a narrow clique" of Dutch Reformed churchmen.[8] When a Transvaal paper referred to priests and nuns as "liars, murderers and doers of everything that is abominable," Kolbe complained of "an active propaganda of personal libel against Catholics which ought to be incredible."[9] He gave as good as he got, with humour. Efforts were also made in some dioceses to obtain books in Dutch and in English to help Catholic lay people counter criticism and accusations against the Church, such as those in scurrilous publications like Maria Monk's *Awful Disclosures of the Hotel Dieu Nunnery in Montreal* and *Roman Catholic System* by William Hammond, one of the most energetic anti-Catholic preachers.[10]

After the discovery of gold on the Witwatersrand in 1886, the economic and political centre of South Africa moved from Cape Town to Johannesburg, and many Catholic families settled there. Separated from the Natal diocese in 1886 and formed into a separate prefecture, the Catholic Church in the goldfields began to grow rapidly and to acquire property for churches and schools. The Sisters of Hope, the nursing branch of the Holy Family Sisters of Bordeaux, took charge of the Johannesburg Hospital; the Marist Brothers opened a school for boys; the Holy Family Sisters established a convent school in End Street. The Sisters of Hope remained in Johannesburg throughout the Anglo-Boer War, looking after wounded soldiers from both armies.

"Not to a Few Heretics": Beginnings of the Black Mission

The Catholic Church's prime objective in South Africa was to open mission stations among the African people. Bishop Allard had been told clearly in 1857 that he had been sent to Natal "not to a few heretics who inhabit your towns but to convert the Zulus."[11] But unfamiliarity with the language held his French-speaking clergy back. The bishop also found that it was not easy to ignore the legitimate requests of white Catholic colonists who had been without a priest for almost a decade. In 1854, when reinforcements came, Allard assigned two young priests to learn English and Zulu before he dispatched them to open the first mission to the Zulus. They lived in a Zulu settlement, picking up the language as best they could.[12] Allard tried twice, but in vain, to evangelize the Zulus in southern Natal; and then, urged on by his superior-general, he decided to look beyond Natal. At Thaba Bosiu in Lesotho, he met Moshoeshoe, founder of the Basotho nation; and Moshoeshoe granted him a site for a mission station – why, it is not clear, since the Paris Evangelical Missionary Society had already been active in Lesotho since 1835 and had given Moshoeshoe excellent service in a variety of ways.

The first Catholic mission in Lesotho, Motse-oa-'M'a-Jesu, was opened in 1863 and thereafter Bishop Allard spent most of his time there, leaving the Natal work to the parish priests of Durban and Pietermaritzburg, Fathers Sabon and Barret. After a difficult start, the Catholic party at Lesotho made many converts. Allard brought Holy Family Sisters from Bordeaux in 1864 to improve the life and prospects of Sotho women. The missionaries disapproved of the practice of forcing young girls to marry old men who could pay a substantial bride price. Moshoeshoe's support for the Holy Family Sisters allowed them to continue despite opposition from Sotho traditionalists. They set out to teach the women to read and to write, to sew, to grow and prepare flax and hemp, and to spin wool for the weaving of cloth. They encouraged them to hone their traditional crafts and to experiment with new designs. Allard believed that eventually many polygynists would be converted to Christianity and that the sisters would care for the abandoned wives, as they did later at Mariannhill in Natal.[13] In fact, many Sotho women were converted to Christianity long before the men, for whom the prohibition on polygyny was an obstacle to conversion, and only a handful of abandoned wives actually sought refuge at the missions.[14] The Catholic mission effort in Lesotho grew steadily in the nineteenth century and prospered in the twentieth.

Mission work among the indigenous people in the western Cape was concentrated in Namaqualand, a geographically inhospitable area on the Orange River. In 1873, a priest of the Society of African Missions, who had worked at Springbok for a time, moved on to Pella, to take over after a Lutheran missionary had been murdered by San. Five years later the Oblates of St. Francis de Sales, sent to manage the Pella district, found the priest living in "apostolic poverty."[15] The Oblates, under direction of the energetic French-speaking Bishop Simon, made determined efforts to evangelize the residents of Pella. They planted date palms and tropical fruit trees, and built a substantial church and school, establishing an oasis in the desert that still continues to astonish travellers.

In the eastern Cape, Bishop Ricards expressed his strong views about mission work among the blacks in his vicariate publicly and often controversially. He criticised the London Missionary Society by implying that it did not sufficiently promote hard work and a sense of responsibility. On a visit to Europe, in search of a congregation willing to work in his new diocese, he heard about the agricultural colonies in Algeria set up by the Trappists, who lived a life of prayer and manual labour. He promptly invited a group of Trappists to establish a model farm in his vicariate, where blacks could be instructed both in the Christian faith and in efficient farming.

The Trappists, under Father Franz Pfanner, settled on a farm near the Sundays River in 1880, but at a time of serious drought, and in the inhospitable thorn veld. Unable to make a living there, the Trappists informed Ricards two years later that they had decided to leave and move to Natal. Ricards was left with debts they had incurred and a useless property.[16]

In Natal, Bishop Jolivet, who succeeded Allard in 1874, had already accomplished much before the Trappists arrived – he was to build churches, schools, hospitals, and homes for orphans and the elderly, and established a number of stations, offering to each family a plot of land on which to grow vegetables and graze their animals. St. Francis Xavier mission at the Bluff, Durban, Oakford mission, near Verulam, and Maryvale, outside Pietermaritzburg, were successful examples of such communities.[17] His decision to bring the Trappists to Natal was the most far-reaching of his episcopacy: Franz Pfanner would lead the Trappists in an extraordinary growth of Catholic missionary work in Natal and the Transkei. Pfanner bought a large farm near Pinetown, which he named Mariannhill, developing it with the help of skilled lay brothers and erecting substantial buildings in German style. Within eighteen months Pfanner had a staff of two priests, thirteen choir monks, and sixty-four lay brothers. By 1898, with 285 monks, Mariannhill had become the largest abbey in the world, both numerically and in the number of its extensions.[18] In addition, a party of five lay women helpers, the forerunners of the Sisters of the Precious Blood, arrived from Germany and Austria in 1885. Pfanner established an extensive series of stations throughout southern Natal, each one day's ride from the other, each intended to be self-sufficient. Under his successors, properties were bought in the Transkei, northern Natal, and Rhodesia (now Zimbabwe).

In establishing mission stations on large farms, Pfanner intended to develop their agricultural potential, while nurturing the spiritual and educational development of the Africans living on the properties. He planned to divide the properties eventually among the African tenants. Africans were drawn to the mission schools to observe intensive farming methods and their results.[19] Gradually the work of evangelization grew. However, soon it became obvious that the Trappist rule of silence and religious discipline was not reconcilable with mission work, and Pfanner resigned in 1892.[20] His successors experienced the same problems, and, in 1909, the year of Pfanner's death, the Mariannhill missionaries broke away from the Trappists, to form their own congregation, the Religious Missionaries of Mariannhill, now the Congregation of Missionaries of Mariannhill. Pfanner's objective, of subdividing the mission farms among the Christian communities living there, was not attained. The migratory labour system lured the younger males to the towns while the various Land Acts, notably those of 1913 and 1936, made it illegal to sell or lease land to Africans in "white areas." As the number of lay brothers declined, it became more difficult to farm the mission land efficiently.

By the close of the nineteenth century, the position of the Catholic Church in South Africa had changed considerably. It had many more adherents, priests, and religious than fifty years earlier, as well as excellent schools, hospitals, homes for the aged, and orphanages. The bishops had succeeded in breaking down some of the prejudice against the Church and, for white Catholics at least, all the facilities to support typical Catholic community life were now available. Nonetheless, after sixty years of Catholic presence in South Africa, there were few black Catholics and few facilities for them. The Catholic missions in the Transvaal were adversely affected by the Anglo-Boer War; in Natal the Zulu missions of the Missionary Oblates of Mary Immaculate served urban Africans around the principal population centres; in Zululand, Catholic missions had been in existence only since 1895. However, the Trappist stations in southern Natal, with 96,879 acres of farm land, were growing steadily, with 2,200 Africans baptized in 1895 and about 1,500 children attending school at various stations.[21] By 1903 the number of Africans baptized in Natal, the Transkei, and Zululand had risen to 10,000.[22] In the Cape, Namaqualand, and the Orange Free State, missions among blacks were progressing slowly, but only in Lesotho, where 8,000 had been baptized by 1904, was there reason for satisfaction after the years of effort. And when one of the chiefs, Griffith Lerotholi, was received into the Catholic Church in 1912, he was followed by numerous converts.

Depression and Financial Disaster

The Anglo-Boer War, which had ended in 1902, was followed by a period of optimism and prosperity, especially in the Transvaal. Real-estate values rose sharply, and the Catholic temporary administrator in Johannesburg decided to sell many of the properties bought in the 1890s to use the proceeds, first to buy other sites, which were then mortgaged and still more land was bought throughout the Transvaal. However, the speculation led to a collapse in prices; mortgages were called in, and the Catholic Church in the Transvaal lost all its properties. By 1910, the church found itself as it was in 1886, with no property, but now with a large Catholic population requiring churches and schools.[23] In Natal, plans to pay for a new cathedral that depended on selling valuable Durban church land on the post-war market were in abeyance; in 1903, after Bishop Jolivet died, his successor discovered that the economic depression made the properties impossible to sell.

Both Catholic dioceses entered the post-war era with serious financial problems. The depression lasted until 1909, impoverishing Catholic parishioners as well. When the depression began to bottom out, plans were well advanced for unification of the four South African colonies. Only after unification was achieved in 1910 did the economic gloom really lift.

A few Catholic missionaries had returned to Johannesburg in 1901, eager to save what they could of the pre-war mission work, some of which had been organized by the Trappists. Their first project was the Railway Mission opened in Doornfontein. Its services were attended mostly by domestic workers, for whom a night school was opened. This little mission grew steadily, especially after large numbers of migrant labourers returned in 1904; it proved to be the nucleus of a much more extensive Catholic evangelization in the townships and mine hostels around Johannesburg and on the East and West Rand.[24]

During the First World War, French priests were called home to the European front and many German priests and brothers were interned or restricted to the interior by the South African government. The mission effort was consequently reduced. Still, Cardinal van Rossum, the Cardinal Prefect of Propaganda, whose task it was to monitor progress in evangelization around the world, was dissatisfied with the rate of growth of Catholic missions, particularly in Africa; and while the war was still under way, Pope Benedict XV issued the encyclical *Maximum illud* on the need to train indigenous clergy in the mission countries and to extend existing missions by the creation of new vicariates and prefectures. Cardinal van Rossum saw an urgent need to evangelize the Africans in South Africa. The first apostolic delegate, Archbishop Bernard Gijlswijk OP, appointed in 1922, had instructions to remove all obstacles and to accelerate the mission drive, as well as encouraging vocations among the local people, especially blacks. Existing vicariates were divided and new ones created.

New communities and religious orders, particularly from the former German colonies, were assigned areas of jurisdiction. Among these were the German Benedictines of St. Ottilien, who had been working in Tanganyika since 1888, the German-speaking Benedictine Missionary Sisters of Tutzing also from Tanganyika, the Pallottine fathers (Society of the Catholic Apostolate), the German Congregation of the Sacred Heart Fathers, and the Missionary Sons of the Sacred Heart (MFSC). These changes brought in not only more missionaries but fresh ideas and approaches, and led to the opening up of new districts to the church, and at present there are thirty dioceses in the Republic of South Africa, Namibia, Swaziland and Botswana.[25]

Although evangelization was organized and directed by the bishops, the initiative for expansion was sometimes taken by Catholic lay people who saw a local need for a church or a school. One example is that of the liberated slave Saturnino do Valle, who inducted his fellow ex-slaves and their families at Durban's Bluff, bringing them to the priest for baptism in 1873.[26] Another occurred at Ladysmith, where a group of Africans walked twenty-five miles to town to ask the priest to say Mass for them separately from the whites, since they could not understand the English homily and instruction.[27] The priest had not been aware of their existence since they lived far out of town; later he was able to establish a mission site for them there with sanction from the local authority. In the Transvaal and Orange Free State similar African initiatives were common. While five men and women at Nancefield, near Johannesburg, waited for twenty-five years for a church to be built for them, they kept a mission going there seven days a week, with Mass said by a priest every Sunday in one of their homes. Father Leo Muldoon, an outstanding and overworked missionary, listed twenty-five similar groups of lay men and women who pioneered missions in the impecunious days of Catholicism in Johannesburg in the 1920s and 1930s.[28]

The encouragement of religious vocations among Africans was another of Cardinal van Rossum's priorities, as was the setting up of novitiates and seminaries. The first South African black candidates had been sent to Rome in the 1880s and the 1890s for training as priests.[29] South African congregations ran modest seminaries and novitiates of their own, but not until 1948 did a national South African seminary open for the training of diocesan priests. Initially based in Aliwal North, St. John Vianney seminary, for the training of white priests, opened in 1952 in Waterkloof, Pretoria, under Irish Franciscans. Because the Group Areas Act forbade black and white students to be taught together, the Church was obliged to provide separate facilities. These were set up for blacks at St. Peter's major and St. Paul's minor seminaries in Hammanskraal, outside Pretoria. In 1976 both seminaries were closed in the wake of political unrest, with black students admitted to St. John Vianney seminary to study with whites. St. Paul's reopened in 1981, and moved to Cape Town in 1993, when St. Peter's moved to Garsfontein, Pretoria. Both St. John Vianney and St. Peter's seminaries now accommodate students for the priesthood of all races.

In the 1930s the mission drive accelerated, especially in Natal and the Transvaal, as more priests arrived from Europe and from the United States. Efforts were made to open mission stations and schools in the urban locations. In the rural districts numerous outstations opened near mission stations, supervised by catechists and visited by a missionary priest once or twice a month. The outbreak of the Second World War brought a temporary disruption, with many young South African-born priests volunteering as military chaplains, and with German, Austrian, and Italian clergy and religious interned for a time. Others, for example the German Franciscans in the Kokstad prefecture, were sent to Johannesburg and put in the care of Bishop O'Leary. German and Italian missionary congregations, which depended on their homelands for funds and replacements, found their outside support gone in the wake of the war and the post-war disruptions. Funding did not resume until well after the war's end.

"Better Fields, Better Homes, Better Hearts": Mobilizing the Laity

In the 1920s efforts were undertaken to encourage closer involvement of the Catholic laity in the Church's life. Catholic Action, introduced by Leo XIII and the subject of Pius X's 1906 encyclical, *Il fermo proposito*, was defined by Pius X as "the sum total of apostolic work, distinct from spiritual undertakings and the associations set up to promote them." Two decades later, Pius XI saw an urgent need to bring the laity together because of the universal shortage of priests; also, an increasing number of Catholic associations with similar objectives were weakened by competing for candidates.[30] The Transvaal took the lead with formation of an umbrella Catholic Federation to represent all Catholic societies (or sodalities). The most prominent of these were the St. Vincent de Paul Society, founded in 1904, to care for the poor and needy of all races, and the St. Peter Claver Society, with similar objectives, run by black Catholics, active in the late 1930s. Catholic Action also included societies for men and women, youth and students, as well as associations designed to encourage spiritual growth, such as the Grail and the Legion of Mary. Professional groups, among them Catholic teachers and nurses, formed their own societies, and in Durban, Indian Catholics formed societies for men and boys. Branches of the Belgian Abbé Joseph Cardijn's Young Christian Workers, which opened across South Africa, became predominantly black and still exist. But numerically the Guild of St. Anne for black women and the Sacred Heart for men far exceeded all others in popularity. The former, also known as Women of St. Anne, originated in Canada and from there was introduced into Lesotho. It provides both a religious and a social function for women as well as providing leadership opportunities. The Sacred Heart sodality does the same for men, who also assist the priest with various parish duties.

The Catholic African Union (CAU), another form of Catholic Action, was formed in 1928 by Fathers Bernard Huss, Emmanuel Hanisch, and Jean-Baptiste Sauter, all of them members of the Congregation of Missionaries of Mariannhill. Huss, an educationist and lecturer on agriculture, became aware that Clements Kadalie's Industrial and Commercial Workers' Union, an organization with a membership of 100,000 at its peak, was attracting Catholic workers. Responding to the social teachings of Leo XIII and Pius XI that any organization working for justice and better conditions for workers called for support, the church set up the CAU "to develop a social welfare programme for Catholic Africans and to offer a political alternative to the ICU,"[31] because the ICU included a number of Communist Party members strongly opposed to the Christian churches and particularly to missionaries. With its slogan "Better fields, better homes, better hearts," the CAU concentrated on agriculture, water supplies, improved crops, and co-operative savings and credit banks. It ran courses, organized conferences, and had the support of the majority of the bishops. It attracted a substantial membership, but exact figures are not known, probably because it was organized at parish rather than at national level. It continued long after Kadalie's ICU had collapsed, and disappeared only in the 1970s. Its savings bank was supported by members until the 1970s, when building societies, each with their hundreds of branches, took over its functions.

South African Catholic lay spirituality followed the models of England and Ireland, from where so many of the clergy originated. Catholic doctrine was taught at schools, at special catechism classes, and from the pulpit. There was an obligation to attend Mass every Sunday, to refrain from meat on Fridays and to fast during Lent, to contribute to the support of priests, and to send children to Catholic schools.[32] Devotional life centred on the Mass, Benediction of the Blessed Sacrament, First Friday devotions, the praying of the rosary, and family prayers. Processions celebrated major feast days, particularly Corpus Christi, which brought Catholics together in a display of solidarity. In 1929 the International Eucharistic Congress, in Durban brought thousands of Catholics from all over Southern Africa to worship together.

"All This Is Done in the Name of Christian Civilization": The Catholic Church in the Apartheid Era

In 1948 the National Party, under Dr. D. F. Malan, won the general election by a narrow majority, and for the first time the word "apartheid" surfaced in the nation's political vocabulary. Apartheid's intent, according to the Sauer report, was "to maintain and protect the purity of the white race by means of territorial segregation, by regarding the presence of the urban black as temporary, by labour control, by the suppression of trade unions, by separation of political representation," but also by the imposition of Christian National Education (see p. 137).[33] The *Southern Cross*, the Catholic weekly newspaper,[34] took issue with the National Party view that Indians were "temporary sojourners" in South Africa who should be repatriated as soon as possible. Bishop Hennemann, Catholic bishop of Cape Town, who had drawn attention to the dangers of racial segregation as early as 1939, crossed swords with the new government on the issue of segregation of trains, aimed at Coloured commuters, which he described as a "noxious, unchristian and destructive policy." Hennemann sent a letter entitled "Crisis in the Life of the Nation" to all Catholic clergy in his diocese to be read in all churches the following Sunday. In it, the segregation of train passengers was condemned as "an obvious intrusion on the liberty and dignity of non-white citizens" and, what was worse, "all this is done in the name of Christian civilization." Hennemann directed that the "holy hour" the following Sunday be devoted to a plea "that our country may be guided by God to find a solution to its racial problems in peace and with justice."[35]

Relations between the National Party and the English churches were uncertain at best and Malan's statement to parliament that his government did not recognize the rights of people who "undermine the principles of apartheid, who preach equality and who propagate foreign ideologies"[36] was seen as a warning that those churches should tread softly. Hennemann's critical remarks had been unusual for a Catholic bishop and, at the time, were considered rash by many Catholics, because anti-Catholic feeling was running high in certain Dutch Reformed Church circles and the bishops feared being declared "undesirable." In 1949 a National Party provincial congress proposal to exclude Roman Catholics from holding office was defeated, but another proposal to appoint a committee to investigate Catholicism in South Africa succeeded; its findings were printed and distributed, and, shortly before the 1953 elections, published in *Die Kerkbode*, the official organ of the NGK. Its proposals would provide for all Catholic schools, hospitals, and other Catholic institutions to be brought under direct government control; for a prohibition against further entry of Catholic religious, teachers, or immigrants into South Africa; for the banning of any Catholic priest, teacher, or lay person who attacked Protestants or tried to undermine the government or the Christian National Education system; and for a prohibition on the importation of Catholic "propaganda literature" into South Africa, and any printing or distribution of such literature inside South Africa. The report urged the next synod to take up the matter with the government and to establish a full-time secretariat to combat *die Roomse gevaar* (the Roman peril).[37]

The Vatican's apostolic delegate to South Africa nevertheless set a conciliatory tone for relations with the government, assuring Malan that the Catholic Church, and its spokesmen, "would always act firstly by memoranda and consultation," and not in "an underhand manner."[38] In general, Catholic leaders' caution proved effective in the early years of apartheid, ensuring that Catholic mission and parish life could go on as usual, but after a year in office, the National Party government introduced and passed by overwhelming majorities a number of laws that directly affected the churches and their institutions: the Prohibition of Mixed Marriages Act (1949), the Group Areas Act (1950), the Bantu Authorities Act (1950), the Bantu Education Act (1953), and the Immorality Act (1957, amended 1967, 1969).

The Bantu Education Act of 1953 affected the African mission schools sponsored by all Christian denominations, 17 per cent of them by the Catholic Church. Over the years, the subsidy given by government to approved schools had been used to pay the salaries of teachers, with the mission authorities themselves paying for buildings and equipment. Under the 1953 Act, the subsidy was to be withdrawn over a four-year period. In addition, all schools were to register with government departments, and only pupils belonging to the denomination that controlled each school could be enrolled there. The Catholic bishops, who saw the schools as the centre of the entire Catholic missionary endeavour, accordingly launched an appeal for funds, both in South Africa and abroad, to keep the schools running without subsidy. Other Christian denominations decided to close their schools at the beginning of the year.[39]

An American priest and experienced fund-raiser, Fr. Peter Ruffel, now undertook to organize the campaign to keep the schools open. Pledges of a million pounds were received and £756,540 was collected[40] – a remarkable achievement for this small Catholic population, few of whom were well-to-do. Support came from overseas, too, especially from the German society Misereor, which provided funds over many years. Nevertheless, these were stopgap measures, since R228,000 would be needed every year. Teachers were asked to accept a salary lower than the government schools paid for equivalent qualifications and many agreed, but, over the following years, the most qualified teachers moved on to government schools or out of teaching altogether. In addition, a number of Catholic primary schools closed as a result of relocation of black families and the barring of non-Catholic pupils under the Bantu Education Act. In 1972 the bishops decided to close all primary schools or hand them over to the government. Some secondary schools stayed open, with teachers' salaries at the level of salaries in government schools. As of 1995, there are still in existence a few Catholic high schools of high standard for black pupils, in great demand by parents for their discipline, their solid education, and their record of excellent examination results.

The bishops' decision to keep the schools open was a matter of controversy. On the positive side, Catholics were drawn together in common sacrifice and became aware of the importance of mission education to the development of the church. The bishops' decision gave the Church fifteen or twenty years to work out and implement a new missionary approach, and it did so with great effect. But some experienced observers, including Professor Adrian Hastings, who believe that the concentration on education in the mission field was in itself an error and that the family, not the school, should have been the centre, considered that the closing of the schools would ultimately benefit the Catholic Church.[41]

The churches were also greatly troubled by the Group Areas Act, which uprooted and dispersed black people from their homes, and led in consequence to the closing of a number of community institutions. The Act prohibited white religious and lay teachers from living and working as missionaries in "non-white" areas; churches and schools were left empty and unsaleable in the former "black spots."[42] There was an urgent need to build new facilities where the people were resettled, even though white missionaries could no longer serve there.

Catholic bishops protested repeatedly against the injustices of apartheid, but without result, and sometimes with the disapproval of white Catholics themselves. For example, Archbishop Denis Hurley of Durban, who as a native of South Africa could not be deported like so many foreign clergy, and others were criticized by their flock or a small section of it. A South African (Catholic) Defence League was formed in the Transvaal to voice lay Catholics' criticism of the Southern African

Catholic Bishops' Conference (SACBC) and its "disloyalty."[43] Overseas, however, the SACBC was held in high esteem and attracted considerable support. When Khanya House, the Pretoria headquarters of the SACBC, was destroyed by fire under suspicious circumstances, offers of assistance came from several overseas sources, with the cost of rebuilding met by the Irish bishops.

Initiatives from the Top: The Second Vatican Council and the Southern African Catholic Bishops' Conference

For the worldwide Catholic Church Pope John XXIII's announcement of the Second Vatican Council, held from 1962 to 1965, was of enormous and lasting significance. Among the 2,625 bishops at the final session, 311 were from Africa and, of these, 60 were black.[44] Among the significant decisions taken were the replacement of the Latin Mass with the vernacular, and plans for greater participation in the Mass by the people. The Council's document *Ad Gentes* favoured dialogue with non-Catholics about Christian unity, and an increasing role for Catholic laity.

Vatican II prompted efforts in South Africa to bring about, or at least talk about, Christian unity: Catholic bishops began to send representatives as observers to Protestant conferences and meetings, and to invite Protestant churches to theirs. An Ecumenical Research Unit was formed, based at St. John Vianney seminary, to carry out socio-religious research on Christian unity. Cooperation was initiated with theological institutions, including the University of South Africa and, more recently, the University of Natal. Catholic and Anglican bishops have met regularly to discuss matters of common concern, including political matters and common action for justice and peace. Consultation and cooperation between scholars engaged in translating the Bible into African languages, long under way, have continued. But although some conversations have been held on relations between the Dutch Reformed and Catholic churches, no serious progress has been made on closer contacts.[45] Only very recently has real progress been made when the Catholic Church was accepted as a full member of the South African Council of Churches.

No study of the history of the Catholic Church in this century can ignore the role of the Southern African Catholic Bishops' Conference (SACBC) and its thirteen commissions.[46] The first informal meeting of bishops in South Africa took place in 1895, the second in 1924 after the appointment of the first apostolic delegate, and a third in 1928. In 1948 the SACBC was established, representing all the bishops in the Union of South Africa, Botswana, Swaziland, and Namibia, meeting each year in plenary session.[47] Six pastoral regional conferences are convened yearly to discuss problems, especially those of language groups. The general secretariat, situated in Pretoria, is responsible for communicating the SACBC's decisions through publications and through the Catholic media. One of its priorities was to inform Catholic lay people about Vatican II, to implement its decisions, and to encourage ecumenism. Press statements on controversial topics such as criticism of the government, the police, and the treatment of political prisoners ensured that the bishops speak with one voice on matters of public policy. In recent years the work of the secretariat has to some extent been taken over by Lumko Missiological Institute.[48]

THE ROMAN CATHOLIC CHURCH

The Catholic Church, particularly its German missionaries, has an enviable record in the publication of grammars, dictionaries, catechisms, prayerbooks, and educational aids in African languages.[49] The first Zulu catechism was produced by A. T. Bryant (then Trappist Father David), active in Zulu language studies from the time of his arrival at Mariannhill in 1883, and the first full edition of the New Testament was translated into Zulu by Catholic missionaries and produced by Father Gerard Wolpert in 1890.[50] Missionaries were in the forefront of serious study of African culture, and Bryant's books on the Zulu, based on his research while a mission priest in Zululand, are still in use.[51] Bryant prepared phrase and work books for use by his colleagues. One of the most eminent Mariannhill-educated Zulus, Benedict Vilakazi, collaborated with Clement Doke to produce the Zulu–English, English–Zulu dictionary in current use.

The SACBC's pastoral institute, the Lumko Missiological Institute, runs intensive courses on African languages and provides teaching and reading material for catechesis. It also fosters African liturgical music and gives musical training (pp. 321–22). It has studied the formation and function of Basic Christian Communities in Brazil and promoted their use in South Africa,[52] filling both a religious and a social need in the rural areas and townships. In the late 1990s the effectiveness of these communities was reduced by violence in the townships, where people hesitated to leave their homes at night for meetings.

The Catholic Institute of Education, established by the SACBC in 1985 to replace the Department of Schools, reassessed the Catholic school situation when government reform made interracial schools possible again. The majority of schools had continued without interruption, despite the Bantu Education Act and its restrictions, in educating black and white pupils separately. Some of the African schools such as St. Francis College at Mariannhill, St Joseph's College at Inkamana, Pax College at Doornspruit outside Pietersburg, and a few others have become well known for their educational standards and have produced a number of contemporary black leaders.[53] The necessity to engage lay teachers, paid at far higher salaries, to fill the places left empty by a decline in vocations among the congregations of sisters and brothers who had done most of the teaching, forced an increase in school fees and to some extent watered down the traditional Catholic spirit in the schools. Many parents then turned to co-educational government schools, where fees were lower, sending their children to after-school religious classes. In the 1990s the schools the bishops worked so hard to establish before 1960 are disappearing. Catechists and parents, rather than Catholic schools, have instead had to serve as the prime religious educators of young Catholics.

Mission hospitals began to be directly affected by government policy in 1970 when, beginning with the Transkei, the state Health Department took over control of all health services. By 1973 mission hospitals in other "homelands," including the Catholic mission hospitals at Nongoma and Glen Cowie, were brought under government control.[54] Catholic hospitals have also been affected by the shortage of religious sisters, and by the costs of modern medical equipment, the smaller ones closing or being bought up by private companies. Many religious sisters who served in them retrained as pastoral assistants or counsellors, and now work in urban parishes or are attached to rural mission stations. Those in the homes for the aged and children have continued with their apostolate.

Rising Voices: Women and Blacks in the Church

The Catholic laity, first encouraged to participate more actively in church affairs in the 1920s, and recognized by Vatican II as having co-responsibility with the clergy for growth of the church, are represented by the Commission of the Laity and the South African Council of the Laity, with advisory powers.[55] Lay men and women are active in a large number of sodalities and associations, including youth movements; they sit on parish councils and voice their opinions in the Catholic press and to the SACBC through their bishops.[56]

A burning issue of the present time is the place of women in the Christian churches. Although the ordination of women has been accepted in the Anglican Church in South Africa, and in other countries, the Catholic Church has held out against it. Many Catholic women, unhappy with this stand, are protesting strongly, especially in the United States. The position of women in the Catholic Church differs from that of women of other faiths and denominations because of the role of its religious sisters in the educational, pastoral, and medical spheres, the role of contemplative nuns in the prayer life of the church, and the substantial number of sisters working in mission fields all over the world. The mother-general or superior of the large communities has always had considerable authority and, with her counsellors, decides all the everyday, and many of the long-term, affairs of her sisters. Though she is under the general jurisdiction of the local bishop, a strong-willed superior can appeal over the bishop's head to the Sacred Congregation for Religious in Rome, as has happened several times in South Africa.[57] Similarly, the matron of a Catholic hospital has responsibility for the smooth running of the institution and control over all her nurses. As one sister remarked, "I enjoy my work and, after all, we cannot all be standing at the altar saying Mass!" At a consultation between the laity and the bishops in 1975, the international year of the woman, the president of the Catholic Women's League in South Africa, Medea Hussey, listed the following points in reply to the question, What do women want? "They want equal opportunities to participate in pastoral work and in the ministries, a greater awareness of their role as Christians, education for their new roles in family, in work and in leisure, that the Church speak out against injustice and discrimination against women on the grounds of sex, especially African women who have to contend with discrimination because of tribal customs in addition to the legal disabilities that all South African women suffer. Finally they would like their organizations recognised and provided with consultative status on matters of public concern e.g. abortion and family planning."[58] There is a long way to go before this is put into practice in any South African church organization.

One of the most significant changes in the Catholic Church in South Africa has been brought about by demands for Africanization, which followed the remarks of Pope Paul VI on a visit to Africa in 1969: "You [African bishops] can give the Church the precious and original contribution of negritude which she needs particularly."[59] On 23 January 1970, five black priests issued a manifesto, published in the liberal Johannesburg newspaper, the *Rand Daily Mail*, charging the Church with discrimination against black priests and toleration of racial segregation in its ranks. Complaining that they were often treated like altar boys, they demanded that "new avenues be opened up for our priests, such as a specialized apostolate, serving on the so-called national commissions, playing a meaningful role in the administration of the diocese." They demanded that the hierarchy expedite Africanization, adding "for instance, why can't Soweto have its own bishop?" They suggested "that a department of African Affairs be created on a national level chiefly to look after the interests of Black Catholics," and concluded with a declaration of faith: "We firmly believe that Christ's church is one, holy, catholic and apostolic. We hope to live, work and die as true sons of our beloved Brother and Saviour Christ."[60]

Wide publicity was given to the black priests' manifesto, and it prodded the hierarchy into action. The first and, until 1970, only black bishop, Pius Dlamini, had been appointed to the newly established Umzimkulu diocese in 1954. After the manifesto was published, black appointments came rapidly: Bishop Peter Buthelezi was appointed auxiliary to Bishop Boyle of Johannesburg in 1972, was transferred to Umtata in 1975, and three years later consecrated as Archbishop of Bloemfontein. In Durban, Bishop Dominic Khumalo was appointed auxiliary to Bishop Hurley with residence in Pietermaritzburg; while in Cape Town, Bishop Stephen Naidoo became auxiliary to Cardinal McCann, succeeding him as archbishop in 1984. In 1997, of South Africa's 26 dioceses, 7 have black bishops or archbishops.[61] In the last ten years young black priests have being appointed to some of Johannesburg's white parishes, something unimaginable ten years ago, and blacks are now represented on all the commissions of the SACBC.

A Growing, More African Church

In the twenty years from 1970 to 1990 there was a remarkable growth in the number of black Catholics in South Africa. The Catholic Church now has more black members than any other mainline Christian Church, and nearly half as many as the Protestant churches combined: approximately 80 per cent of Catholics in South Africa are black, up from 74 per cent in 1980, a consequence of energetic Catholic mission drives after 1922 and in the years after the Second World War. In every diocese dedicated missionaries, mostly from Europe, opened mission stations, built churches, and opened schools. The changes after Vatican II, particularly the vernacular Mass, and the Church's unwavering hostility to racial discrimination may also have played a part. So did the growth in the number of African clergy and the opportunities for promotion to bishop, archbishop, and even cardinal. After the Nationalist government took over the mission schools, the Catholic church was forced to develop new methods of evangelization, with laity involvement encouraged in voluntary evangelization, catechetical programmes, and supervision of small chapels erected near mission stations. There was more emphasis on reaching the people, on deepening their understanding of the faith, and on visiting them in their homes to discuss problems and to foster community leadership. The general change in attitude towards blacks within the Church, the large number of "foreign" missionaries untainted by apartheid, and the fact that the Catholic Church has no connection with Afrikaner nationalism may be partly responsible for the appeal of the Catholic Church among Africans.[62]

Emigration and a tendency toward small families have slowed the growth in the number of white Catholics. Since Vatican II there has been no pressure for conversions from other denominations. Missionaries from overseas still continue to work in the African missions across South Africa, and financial assistance is still received from Europe and North America for educational and other facilities for impoverished black communities. A turning point in Catholic mission policy came in 1928, when Bishop (later Cardinal) Hinsley, an expert on Catholic education, visited South Africa, reporting back to Rome on the position of Catholic missions. Concluding that the future of Catholicism in Africa lay with the blacks, he was instrumental in "bringing some sort of system into Catholic education in the missions"[63] and in obtaining the first grants for Catholic mission schools.[64] As a result of his efforts, and those of the many mission congregations active in South Africa, the Catholic Church began to move away from the image of the "oppressed, marginalised and foreign church" it had hitherto been.[65]

12

"A Branch Springs Out":
African Initiated Churches

HENNIE PRETORIUS & LIZO JAFTA

A New Kind of Church

Alongside the churches planted by missionaries in South Africa runs a remarkable strand of African Christian churches born of the interchange between Africa and the West. An indigenous contribution to Christianity in South Africa, these diverse churches by 1991 embraced at least 9.2 million people and 47 per cent of all black Christians, up from 40 per cent in 1980, a dramatic increase compared to all other religious groups.[1] More people in South Africa belong to African Initiated Churches (AICs) than to churches originating in European and American missions.[2] Many AIC members call these mainline churches *iicawe zomthetho* (churches of the law, recognized by the government) and their own churches *iinkonzo zoMoya* (spiritual churches). The AICs do not regard mainline churches as standard or ideal churches and find their own norm in early Christianity, as the frequent use of Biblical church names demonstrates: for example, Apostolic Nazareth Jerusalem Corinthians Church in Zion, Bethlehem of Judia (*sic*) Church of South Africa, Ephesians Mission Church, Cush Nineveh Church. David Bosch considered the AICs to be the most important recent development in the global history of Christianity:[3]

> Few students of the African religious scene today would doubt the importance and significance – also for the future of Christianity on this continent – of the African Independent Churches. These churches, together with similar Christian movements among other primal societies ... may indeed be seen as the fifth major Christian church type, after the Eastern Orthodox churches, the Roman Catholic Church, the Protestant Reformation, and the Pentecostal churches.

The various groups belonging to this fifth kind of church are distinguished from non-Christian religious movements in Africa, on the one hand, and from indigenous movements within the mainline churches, on the other.[4] The names by which this movement has been called, some of them dubious or derogatory, reflect primarily the attitudes and perspectives of church and government officials and scholars. They have been called native, separatist, heretical, proselytic, quasi-Christian, millennial, magico-religious, neo-pagan, syncretistic, and cultic.[5] In this chapter the term "African Initiated Churches" is used to focus on the churches' distinctive African origins. The churches' self-reliance and refusal of foreign financial support or leadership has also led to an alternative description, "African Independent Churches." Paul Makhubu, a leader of a group of these churches, comments: "An African Independent or Indigenous Church means a purely black-controlled

211

denomination with no links in membership or administrative controls with any non-African church ... the AICs are churches that have completely broken the umbilical cord with the western missionary enterprise."[6] L.N. Mzimba, the son of the founder of the African Presbyterian Church, stated that Ethiopianism aimed "to plant a self-supporting, self-governing and self-propagating African Church which would produce a truly African type of Christianity suited to the genius and needs of the race, and not a black copy of any European Church."[7]

Their search for independence and their rootedness in the native soil is a positive development of the Christian faith in a South African context and not merely a rejection. They left much intact: for example, the Bible in the vernacular. Bengt Sundkler says that the AICs show "what the African Christian, *when left to himself*, regarded as important and relevant in Christian faith and in the Christian church."[8] Inus Daneel notes that they are "largely adapted to the needs, life-view and life-style of Black people. The use of the term 'church' is ... apposite and technically correct since the leaders all see their movements as churches of Christ and wish to be recognized as such."[9] The AICs share an emotional and ideological affinity for individuals, communities, and localities of Old Testament and New Testament times. They have in common a quest to "indigenize," to establish a new African Christian identity.

The AICs number at least 6,000 churches, each with its own history.[10] At this stage the pieces of the provisional AIC mosaic are still being uncovered, collected, and assessed. The AICs are highly diverse, and have been categorized according to a variety of typologies. Some major ones have been summarized as bridges back to African culture, or as revolts against colonialist oppression, or as searches for supernatural power, above all for physical healing.[11] Typologies range from Sundkler's Ethiopian–Zionist–Messianic distinction to Makhubu's more recent evaluation. Such typologies should be regarded as archetypal categories, for they can scarcely deal fairly with changing historical factors in a complex context. Ethiopian and Zionist churches, for example, each have distinctive social origins and goals and arise from dissimilar historical backgrounds. This chapter handles first the Ethiopian type, then the indigenous spiritual (with Zion City and Zion-Apostolic as sub-types). (A third group, also initiated by Africans, but close to international forms of Pentecostalism, is sometimes called "modern revivalist" or "pentecostal" and is discussed in chapter 13.) Our typology makes a distinction between "*spiritual*" churches (a widely used self-description suggesting Pentecostal origins which echoes much of the praxis of these churches); "*indigenous*" rather than "independent" churches (suggesting a desire to be rooted and contextualized in the African soil rather than merely independent of western churches, especially as the epithets "indigenous" and "initiated" are preferred in recent literature); and "*modern revivalist*" churches, of which Nicholas Bhengu's large Assembly of God is a well-known example (covering a fast-growing type of independent black-initiated church which has not abandoned the western Christian tradition, particularly the American Evangelical from which it originates (see pp. 229–30).[12]

The Ethiopians: "We Come to Pray for the Deliverance of Blacks"

The Ethiopian church arose in the late nineteenth century under ecclesiastical and colonial circumstances described in previous chapters. By the beginning of the twentieth century about twenty had been founded; however, their roots reach far back into the history of white settlement in southern Africa. Janet Hodgson has argued that the tradition of the Christian prophet Ntsikana foreshadowed and inspired the formation of AICs. Ntsikana had evolved a Christianity rooted in his people's traditions, and his followers developed his gospel creatively, in ways that were undoubtedly Christian.[13] As the nineteenth century progressed, manifestations of latent "Ethiopian" sentiments appeared. That thousands of Christians sided with the rebels during the last Frontier War in 1879, as they had not in earlier wars, was a harbinger of later ecclesiastical protest.[14] Along with some minor or temporary withdrawals, three noteworthy secessions took place in the 1880s: the Thembu Church, founded by the ex-Wesleyan Nehemiah Tile in 1884; the Lutheran Bapedi Church, formed in 1889 by the Berlin missionary Johannes Winter, who clashed with his fellow missionaries' paternalistic and discriminatory attitudes toward the Pedi Christians; and, also in 1889, the African Church established in Pretoria by an Anglican evangelist, Khanyane Napo.[15] All three remained tied to particular ethnic groups and hence were not the seeds of a national movement. According to the literature on Ethiopianism, some of the principal causes of the movement were: the frustrated desire of many Africans to become church leaders; colour prejudice practised by missionaries and their failure to live by the Christian brotherhood they proclaimed; disputes over church discipline rooted in differing moral standards; the precedent of schism and denominationalism in Western Christianity; personal ambition among Ethiopian founders and their conviction of a divine calling; the denial to black women Christians of adequate means of self-expression in church; and the availability of Scripture as the basis for a critique of mission Christianity.[16] Ethiopianism was a direct expression of resistance against the missionaries, white settlers, and the colonial government. The consciousness of oppression was distinctly marked in these churches and required no "agitation" by African–Americans, as white opponents often claimed. From the complaints of numerous Ethiopian leaders it is apparent that spiritual matters were not the primary issue, but rather Africans' dispossession from the land, the dispersal of groups from their homelands, the lack of legal resources, unemployment, starvation wages, poor education, poor urban housing, and police mistreatment of Africans.[17]

Norman Etherington has shown that, although some of these factors were present in parts of South Africa by 1860, no independent churches appeared before 1880. He argues that some African Christians were pushed over the edge into independency in the last decades of the nineteenth century, as a prospering black peasantry saw its secular opportunities for leadership and material advance crushed by growing economic and political oppression.[18]

Why "Ethiopian"? George Shepperson has shown how many former African slaves in British North American and Caribbean colonies, even prior to 1871, came to recognize their lost country and heritage in Biblical references to Ethiopia and Ethiopians.[19] So, too, in southern Africa, such texts as Psalm 68:31, "Let Ethiopia stretch out her hands to God," and the baptism of the Ethiopian eunuch by Philip (Acts 8), provided a direct ideological link to the ancient church, without mediation of Western churches. The name Ethiopia, with its mystical connotations, was soon interpreted to refer to all black Africa, and a longing arose to plant authentic, indigenous churches across the entire continent. By 1902 "Ethiopianism" was used to refer to the entire indigenous church movement, even by hostile whites, who attached political connotations to it. Whites' fears that the movement would lead to a universal black uprising were reflected in a flood of press articles against the "black peril," and John Buchan's novel, *Prester John* (1910), echoed the anxious colonial attitudes toward independent African preachers. The Selborne memorandum of 1907 urged political union among the South African colonies, among other reasons because unaccustomed and disturbing activities among blacks, including the rapid spread of Ethiopianism, were causing much anxiety among whites, particularly in Natal and the Transvaal.[20] By 1893 Ethiopianism was outgrowing its earlier ethnic particularism and was developing a pan-African vision. Ethiopianism had become "a generic term to describe a whole range of the black man's efforts to improve his religious, educational, and political status in society."[21] At the turn of the century it was influential, not only among African rulers, such as the chiefs and headmen, but also among the growing African bourgeoisie and wealthy peasantry. Ethiopian sentiments spread, too, among the thousands of African labourers on the Witwatersrand and took root among laity and pastors of various ethnicities. Newly founded churches sometimes merged with one another, while others experienced fresh dissension and schism.[22]

In 1892, the Rev. Mangena Mokone resigned from the Wesleyan Church in Pretoria to form, together with 57 followers, the first nationwide indigenous church in South Africa, the *Ibandla laseTiyopiya,* or the Ethiopian Church, which eventually provided the broader movement with its name. In 1892 two formerly Anglican groups under the leadership of Samuel James Brander from the northern Transvaal and Joseph Khanyane Napo from Pretoria joined Mokone, who then journeyed to the South African Republic and the Orange Free State, where he recruited Jakobus Gilead Xaba and Marcus Gabashane with large numbers of their followers. Mokone had much success in Johannesburg, where a congregation was organized in 1893, led by three migrants from the eastern Cape. In 1896 James Dwane became the leader of the church. In this year Ethiopianism also became a comprehensive movement in South Africa when the Ethiopian Church sought affiliation with the black African Methodist Episcopal Church (AMEC), founded in the U.S.A. in 1816 by African–Americans.[23] The Ethiopian Church became the Fourteenth District of the American AMEC, its work consolidated and expanded to 10,800 members by a visit of Bishop Henry Turner to South Africa. The unity of the church was broken when Dwane, doubting the validity of the AMEC's episcopal orders, left in 1900 with a flock of 3,000 to found the Order of Ethiopia as part of the Anglican church. The majority of the church members remained loyal to the AMEC, which strengthened its ties with the parent body, the first resident bishop arriving from the U.S.A. in 1901. In 1904 a further schism occurred in Pretoria when Samuel Brander, dissatisfied with African–American missionaries, established the Ethiopian Catholic Church in Zion.

Parallel to and independent of these secessions, a number of influential churches were founded: the Zulu Congregational Church established by Samungu Shibe

(1897), the African Presbyterian Church by P.J. Mzimba (1898), the Cushites by Johannes Zondi (1899), the African Native Baptist Church by William Leshega (1905), and the African Congregational Church by Gardiner Mvuyana (1917). More than seventy churches were in place by the first decade of the new century, while around 1904 the movement had a following of some 25,000.[24]

As Shula Marks has shown, the apparent complicity in the Bambatha Rebellion of 1906 by some members of indigenous churches, such as the African Presbyterian Church, reinforced the fears of Natal whites that Ethiopians had fomented the disturbances.[25] But the South African Native Affairs Commission of 1903 to 1905, which recommended political and territorial separation between black and white, declared that the Ethiopian movement was not subversive and should operate free of government supervision.[26]

The Ethiopian leaders did not see their work as directed to political ends, although they did seek answers to the question of liberation within the Christian faith, and they did foster a new consciousness of African dignity and self-reliance. The movement was also political in the sense that it complemented the activities of the African political elite by raising, in the church sphere, issues of African equality and rights.[27]

The indigenous church leaders could distance themselves from mainline churches, but African political leaders, if they wished to be effective, could not stand aloof from white politics.[28] The formation of the Union of South Africa in 1910 practically enshrined the principle of South Africa as "the white man's country." The increasing alienation of Africans' land, culminating in the Native Land Act of 1913, and the general decline in the status of Africans led to the formation of at least seven political organizations in which Ethiopians were prominent. Most important, in 1912 a number of secular and religious leaders banded together to establish the South African Native National Congress (later, the African National Congress or ANC), the first national political organization of Africans. Some Ethiopians rose to prominence in the ANC, among them Henry Ncayiya, the senior chaplain of the ANC, president of the Ethiopian Church; Charlotte Maxeke, founder of the ANC Women's Section, an active AMEC laywoman; Dr. A.B. Xuma, ANC president, also of the AMEC; and R.W. Msimang, drafter of the ANC constitution, and a leader in his father's Independent Methodist Church.[29]

The rise of the ANC contributed to the waning of the influence of the Ethiopian movement. By 1926 whites regarded secular not religious forces as the principal threat to their domination; in that year of labour unrest, fears of Ethiopianist intrigue were replaced by fears of plots against white supremacy by the international labour movement and by the powerful African labour organization, the Industrial and Commercial Workers Union.[30]

Though the classical period of Ethiopianism had ended, the movement itself by no means disappeared. By the 1930s, while schism and fragmentation among Ethiopians continued, the movement produced a new dimension through the efforts of black petty bourgeoisie intellectuals to develop the notion of spiritual nationhood as part of the broader ideology of African nationalism. "Increasingly they tended to view the independent churches in a political context, both as a celebration of Africanness and as a practical experiment in black self-determination."[31] Some new churches were founded, among them in 1933, the Bantu Methodist Church (nicknamed by its members the Donkey Church). Much of the pathos of this church, and in a sense of the entire Ethiopian movement, is reflected in these lines by the church's historiographer:

AN EXULTANT SONG OF THE DONKEY CHURCH

We are children of black Africa,
We rise from all the lands south of Africa.
We are the black Wesleyans – we come from all nations.
We approach our God while offering our prayers.
We are children of black Africa.
We come to pray for the deliverance of the Blacks.[32]

The relative decline of Ethiopianism is further explained by the fact that some white missionaries launched autonomous churches with continued missionary links, such as the Bantu Presbyterian Church (1923) and the Bantu Baptist Church (1927). Until the middle of the century the Ethiopian-type churches possibly still formed the majority of AICs, but, though census figures do not distinguish between types of indigenous churches, an analysis of the 1970 census by David Barrett suggests that by then the indigenous spiritual churches (often called Zionists) were almost twice as numerous as Ethiopians.[33] The ratio has probably grown significantly since.

Nonetheless, though relatively less prominent today than formerly, the older Ethiopian churches have had an uninterrupted history, steady growth, and continued influence.[34] The AMEC, for example, in 1916 had 108 ordained ministers, 216 preachers and lay helpers, some 20,000 members, more than 1,000 students in primary education, and 500 students in its three secondary institutions.[35] As of 1995 it had more than 125,000 full members and is one of the largest of all churches among South African blacks.

In general, the Ethiopian churches have retained the liturgies, hymn-books, teachings, organization, vestments, Bible interpretation, and much of the spirituality of the traditions from which they originated, and are, in this sense, less obviously African in ethos than the indigenous spiritual churches. However, they tend to be more tolerant of indigenous custom than mainline churches. Some, too, have moved toward Zionist forms,[36] as indicated by the names and practice of such churches as the Ethiopian Church in Zion, the Ethiopian Zion Church of South Africa and the Charismatic Ethiopian Church.

"A Branch Called Zionism": The Indigenous Spiritual Churches

Another factor in the relative decline of the Ethiopian movement was the emergence of a new type of indigenous church that challenged the pan-African vision of some of the leaders of the Ethiopian churches. Unorthodox leaders of "Zionist"-style" churches were eager to preserve the patrimony of their particular people from the greed of the whites.[37] In 1904 an African author in the *Native Eye* lamented: "Where are the proud rulers of Natives? They have fallen ... Where is the great Ethiopia, the great teacher of Kafirs? She is divided and today springs out of her a branch called Zionism!"[38]

The "branch called Zionism" had – as with the Ethiopians – an important root in the U.S.A. Variations of the name of the Christian Catholic Church in Zion, founded by the American John Alexander Dowie, are still common in South Africa. Many churches trace their origin to Zion City, in Illinois, where Dowie founded a theocracy in 1896 with schools, stores, and factories, all controlled by Zionists, a safe haven for the faithful. In 1897 his church appointed its first official in South Africa, the Rev. J. Buchler. Pieter le Roux, a missionary in the Dutch Reformed Church with his wife Andrina, left this church in 1902 for doctrinal reasons, bringing 400 Africans into the church he had helped to call into existence at Wakkerstroom. By 1905 it had 5,000 members. In 1904 a group of twenty-seven Africans were baptized in Johannesburg by another Zionist pioneer, Daniel Bryant.[39] American Pentecostal groups, such as the Apostolic Faith Mission, the Full Gospel, and the Church of God, arrived during the first decade of the century (see pp. 229–30). Notable, too, was the work of Edgar Mahon, "the one European in South Africa who managed to establish something akin to a 'Zion City' of his own."[40] These pioneers together with their African converts provided the initial impetus of what was to become one of the fastest-growing church movements in Africa.

Unlike the origins of the Ethiopian movement, where doctrinal differences with other churches played a negligible role, certain biblical teachings were decisive in the founding of Zionism. The principal teachings of the Dowie tradition were: divine healing, baptism of adults by immersion in the name of the Trinity, and a belief in the imminent return of Christ. When, through the influence of Le Roux and others, the movement was gradually influenced by Pentecostalism, baptism by the Holy Spirit and speaking in tongues were added to its practice.

There seemed to be an intrinsic affinity between traditional African conceptions and Pentecostal religiosity, particularly in the Zionist emphasis on healing through the power of faith and the indwelling Spirit, which resonated with the traditional belief that witches, sorcerers, and the spirits of the ancestors caused illness. Yet Sundkler concluded that the beginnings of black Zion were not as exclusively "African as one might presume or would like to believe. The first decade of the movement echoes with the hearty and happy – and sometimes not so happy – relationship between White commitment and an emerging Black charismatic community."[41]

Zion Cities: The Founding of a New Community

An early type of Zionism, Zion City churches, arose in the years between the two World Wars, in a period in which the living conditions of Africans were deteriorating, with most urban workers living in mine compounds, overcrowded locations, or slum-yards, and the majority of Africans in the rural areas with limited access to land. Along with the influential African National Congress and the Industrial and Commercial Workers Union, religion provided a channel for struggling with such conditions: new, self-supporting Christian communities arose on the land with the name "Zion" in their titles, a symbol of the New Jerusalem. Zion City churches also appeared in urban areas (where most AICs were Ethiopian) but the movement remained mostly rural, concentrated in the Transvaal and Natal.[42]

A whole series of Zion City churches emerged from the first group of black Zionist leaders around Le Roux at Wakkerstroom. One of these leaders, Daniel Nkonyane, was responsible for the local work of the Christian Catholic Apostolic Church in Zion, and, before he broke away, he introduced certain elements in worship: white robes, bare feet, holy sticks, and Old Testament symbolism, all visible hallmarks of Zionism today. In 1911 Nkonyane was able to obtain a site at Charlestown (an important junction on the border of the Transvaal and Natal) to build his headquarters, a prototype of many Zion Cities in this period.

The Dowie model can also be recognized in some of the names of other notable churches founded at this time: Church of Christ (1910); Church of the Light (1910); Zion Apostolic Church of South Africa (1911); AmaNazaretha (1911); Church of the Spirit (1916); Church of the Saints (1919); Christian Apostolic Church in Zion (1920); and the Zion Apostolic Faith Mission (1920), from which Engenas Lekganyane's Zion Christian Church (ZCC) seceded in 1925.[43] Few of the founders and leaders of these churches were well-educated, but like the Ethiopian leaders, they were sometimes related to or had links with the traditional African ruling class, and were eager to maintain close connections with traditional royalty. The early leaders and their followers were predominantly male.[44]

Engenas Lekganyane's ZCC at Moria near Pietersburg has developed into the largest, best-known, but by no means most typical indigenous church in South Africa, financially self-reliant and exceptionally strong. Its spiritual life is not separated from its successful business enterprises, the two conceived together as facets of the wholeness of Christian life. Church funds bought farms, provided loans to business people to build shops run by the church, and bought gifts for secular authorities.[45]

The AmaNazaretha (Church of the Nazirites) also has a mass following, but, unlike the ZCC, did not spread throughout the country. It, too, has combined spiritual and material success. It is organized hierarchically along the lines of Zulu social structure, its leader or high-priest addressed and treated as *Inkosi* (chief or king), or as *Ubaba* (father), and assisted by well-trusted ministers who form a council, among them, evangelists, preachers, and leaders of groups for people of different gender, marital status, and age. Many Zionists would not regard this church as part of their own movement, yet "Shembe has realized what most Zion leaders could only dream of creating, but never managed to turn into reality: to found a *Zion* centre for his Church, preferably on a Holy Mountain."[46] Absolom Vilakazi has characterized the AmaNazaretha as both different from and similar to other "separatist" churches: while it is deliberately and unapologetically Zulu, encouraging distinctive Zulu modes of dress and dance in worship, and accepting polygamy, its aim, like that of other Zion City churches, is "the founding of a new society, and the inculcation of new social and economic values."[47]

Another Zion City figured prominently in the political history of South Africa. In 1921, the government decided to use force to evict members of Enoch Mgijima's Israelites (or Church of God and Saints of Christ) from their holy city at Ntabelanga (near Bulhoek), a city erected without permission on crown land. In the attack, 183 members were killed or fatally wounded. Nelson Mandela has stated that "almost every African household in South Africa knows about the massacre of our people at Bulhoek in the Queenstown district where detachments of the army and police, armed with artillery, machine guns, and rifles, opened fire on unarmed Africans."[48] Since the appearance of Halley's Comet in 1910, Mgijima had had visions of the end of the world. In 1919 black Israelites from many parts of South Africa gathered at his home to await the Lord's coming. They believed that they were the real Jews and the chosen people of Jehovah, who would deliver them from white bondage. They kept the Sabbath and the annual Passover festival and rejected the New Testament as a fiction of the whites.[49]

A further Zion City church, the Ibandla lika Krestu (Church of Christ) of James Limba, has like the AmaNazaretha, many features not typically Zionist, particularly its urban base. In Port Elizabeth, between 1929 and 1949, it developed an alternative and exclusive community. Its organizational structure was hierarchical and closely resembled traditional Xhosa society. Its doctrines and code of behaviour promoted group solidarity, and it encouraged church members to limit social interaction to fellow believers. Limba served on the New Brighton Advisory Board, the only channel of communication for Africans with the local authorities. His disciplined, law-abiding members were regarded as a moderating influence on many township inhabitants. Their focus on church activities; their promotion of family life; their abstention from smoking, drinking, and overtly political activities; their observance of the Sabbath; their residential clustering of members; and their large-scale employment by the head of their church made them into a close-knit and distinctive community in the township. Nonetheless, they could find in their urban setting no sanctuary as complete as Shembe's Ekuphakameni village or Lekhanyane's Moria. Their church, while not of the world, was still very much in it.[50]

A Healing Ministry and "Lady Bishops": Zionist–Apostolic Churches

After the Second World War, though Ethiopian and Zion City churches continued to grow, a third type of indigenous church, the Zionist–Apostolic, arose, chiefly among the rapidly growing black working class. In the words of one of their spokesmen: "The members of our Churches are the poorest of the poor, the people with the lowest jobs or with no jobs at all. We are what they call the 'working class.' When people become highly educated and begin to earn big salaries they usually leave our Churches."[51] James Kiernan, who has investigated Zionism at KwaMashu in industrial Durban, confirms that "In this population of poor people, Zionists stand out as poorer than poor."[52]

Deteriorating conditions on the land forced large numbers of Africans off the land and into the cities.[53] Between 1939 and 1952 the South African urban black population almost doubled: the comparatively high wages in town did not keep step with increasing costs of rent, food, transport, fuel, and clothing; the urban community suffered from insufficient housing, inadequate municipal services, and malnutrition, especially of children. Under such conditions indigenous spiritual churches expanded rapidly. Typically the Zionist–Apostolic churches took the form of small healing bands gathering in a room or garage as their "temple," in open fields, or at a riverside. From 1951 to 1958, a period of massive urbanization, churches in the cities sought to maintain unity with their "mother" centres in the rural areas; but after 1958 small churches were required to get government recognition to attain legal privileges, such as the right to church sites. Amalgamated into larger churches whose administrative offices were in the cities, their spiritual leadership usually remained in the countryside.[54]

The Zionist–Apostolic churches are thus neither exclusively rural nor urban, but products of a complex interchange between both sectors, largely brought about by migrant labour.[55] In the mid-1960s, after the government's system of recognizing churches was abandoned, the number and size of Zionist–Apostolic churches increased. Large, overarching organizations were formed, such as the Assembly of Zionist and Apostolic Churches and the African Independent Church Association. Umbrella organizations still active in the 1990s include the Christ the Rock Indigenous Churches, the African Spiritual Churches Association, the Council of African Independent Churches (affiliated to the South African Council of Churches) and the Federal Council of Indigenous Churches.

While in Ethiopian and Zion City churches women have tended to play a marginal role, in some Zionist–Apostolic churches they have come into their own. Mia Brandel-Syrier has shown how the popular *manyanos* or women's organizations are havens providing friendship, a sense of belonging in a lonely world, and reinforcement of self-respect. The manyano is "a vessel for communal outpourings of pent-up feelings and frustrations, but also a source of fervour, of love of devotion, and even ecstasy."[56] Manyanos are very common in the Zionist–Apostolic churches. Sundkler estimated in 1976 that this "white-dressed crozier-carrying army of Zionist women" numbered at least two million and comprised two-thirds of AIC membership.[57] Kiernan's more recent study confirms that "The ratio of women to men in any Zionist group is roughly three to one. Not only that, but the women of various groups meet together every week at an all-female gathering. This means that women are a formidable force within Zionism, in both weight of numbers and unity of purpose. It follows of course that Zionism as an organization tends to serve female interests predominantly."[58]

In Zionist–Apostolic churches female prophets are common, and usually in the majority, as was the case among traditional healers. In the mainline churches, by contrast, black women are generally denied self-expression in the prophetic and healing ministry. Prophets' visions, predictions, and healing carry considerable power even when few have formal positions in the established, male hierarchy of the churches. Their authority complements that of the male officials, who do not generally see them as threatening. Some women, however, have become the heads of individual churches as prophet-leaders or "Lady Bishops," the best-known among them the prophet Christina Nku, founder of the Saint John's Apostolic Faith Mission. Ma Nku, as she is popularly known, experienced what is a rather common spiritual pilgrimage for a founder of an indigenous spiritual church. She had been a member in an established church, the Dutch Reformed Church, and then of the Apostolic Faith Mission. Treated for poor health by a Zionist healer, she had visions that she understood to come both from God and from the Devil. One visitation instructed her to build "God a Church with twelve doors," at Evaton, near Vereeniging, which was an urban area then reserved for whites, but later, in a rare decision, set aside as an African freehold area. The mission Ma Nku built in 1939 became a huge undertaking, and is today possibly the fourth-largest indigenous church in all South Africa. After the death of her husband Lazarus, who had assisted her in her work, her son Johannes was given the senior male position. By 1970, her control over her church was beginning to wane, and the church chose Petros Masango as Archbishop over Johannes Nku. By then, when Saint John's had accommodated itself to the general pattern of male leadership, it had some 50,000 members. Yet, in addition to the provision (found in most AICs) whereby a woman may hold office because of her husband's position, Saint John's provided for a deaconess (to minister to female patients) and also for ordained female ministers.[59]

"Holy Living Through the Power of the Indwelling Holy Ghost": The Theology and Spirituality of the Indigenous Spiritual Churches

The emphasis in the indigenous spiritual churches is on the Holy Spirit. The Son, the second person of the Holy Trinity, is sometimes superseded by the Holy Spirit. Healing and exorcism are central to their spiritual life, in contrast to the focus of most of the mainline churches. Discourse on the doctrines of salvation, the person of Christ, the nature of humanity, and the Trinity itself, which have occupied the Western churches for centuries, are not emphasized. All the indigenous spiritual churches assume the existence of a Supreme Being – otherwise, there would be no Spirit nor any spirits. Still, they see little need for theological reflection on this Supreme Being's nature or gender. They take for granted that God creates and provides, just how is never at issue. That God is good, just, holy, and merciful is accepted without speculation.

The credo of the *AmaNazaretha* (Shembe's Church), for example, reads:

> I believe in the Father
> And in the Holy Spirit
> And in the Communion
> of Saints of the Nazarites.[60]

The Son is omitted – since in Zulu culture a son is not equal to his father – and superseded by the Spirit.

In the *Izihlabelelo zamaNazaretha* (Hymns of the Nazirites) Isaiah Shembe wrote of the Holy Spirit:

> Let the Holy Spirit descend upon me, my Lord
> So that I may be made new in Spirit
> Be like unto the Saints
> Who are before you.[61]

The baptismal formula of the Christian Catholic Apostolic Church in Zion (CCACZ) states: "All those who accepted Jesus Christ as their personal Saviour and having confessed their sins will be baptized in the name of the Father, the Son and the Holy Spirit,"[62] a formula similar to that of the mainline churches, but, in the indigenous spiritual churches, only adults are baptized, after the confession of sins, and the role of the Holy Spirit is emphasized. In the ordination certificates of the clergy of the CCACZ are the words: "Zion's Gospel is … Holy Living through the power of the indwelling Holy Ghost, by whom the sons and daughters of Zion are being prepared for the coming of Zion's King." The power of the Holy Spirit is expressed in charismatic gifts and in visible signs and powers; at baptism each believer is expected to receive the gifts of the Spirit, in some more than others. Gifts like the ability to perform exorcism or to have visions or to speak in tongues are often interpreted as a direct consequence of the second baptism by the Holy Spirit.

Most leaders of these churches are charismatic, some supposedly able to perform miracles. Most are convinced that they have been raised up by the Holy Spirit. B.E. Ngobese's description of Isaiah Shembe is typical: "All the biographies about Shembe recount various incidents during which he had personal experiences of the Holy Spirit. There were also occasions when people received the power of the Holy Spirit through his preaching and ministry."[63] The Spirit is believed to seize and possess the person concerned, in what is called the indwelling of the Holy Spirit. But alongside the Spirit, some churches also recognize "the spirits" – ancestral beings who appear in dreams to convey messages for the living. The relationship of these multiple spirits to the Holy Spirit is not always clear. The "syncretism" of these churches is most evident in their incorporation of traditional African religious concepts into their worship. Ancestral spirits mediate between the Supreme Being and human beings, between the Creator and the creatures. W.B. Vilakazi, who has done extensive research work on the Zulu concept of the spirit, says that the "conception of the amadlozi/amathongo (spirits) and their world inspires the living with the desire to be part of that world and give them hope and courage in facing the present world." The world of the ancestral spirits is one "closely modelled on our present world, but happier, peaceful and more desirable."[64] The ancestral spirits once lived in this world as visible, identifiable human beings, loved, honoured, respected guardians of their families. As spirits, they are gone and yet not gone, invisible yet visible in dreams and visions. In times of danger, they give advice. The living are excited by the hope of being with them again in everlasting enjoyment.

In the unpleasant circumstances under which these churches emerged, the spirits offered solace and support. When the poll tax imposed on the Zulus in Natal led to the Bambatha Rebellion of 1906, Zulus resisted the tax, convinced that the ancestral spirits were on their side. Some members of the indigenous churches readily took up arms to fight, while members of the mainline churches, discouraged by missionaries, rarely did so. An unbroken continuum between past, present, and future is more evident in the indigenous spiritual churches than in the mainline churches. The African concept of *ubuntu* (humanness) is central: one *is* because one *belongs*. One's community stretches from the past through the present into the future; the future, as part of an unending cycle, belongs to the past. *Ubuntu* does not cease with death, but continues in another form. The mediatory role of the ancestral spirits is a principal source of vitality and dynamism in some indigenous spiritual churches. More recently established spiritual churches, for example, the Gospel Church of Christ, with some two thousand members, allows no room for ancestral spirits but does rely on the direction of the Holy Spirit. Members of mainline churches sometimes accuse churches that emphasize spirits of worshipping their ancestors and not God or Christ. The churches reply that they do not worship but merely venerate ancestors, placing them in the context of the "communion of saints," which the mainline churches also recognize.

The services of the indigenous spiritual churches have a much livelier liturgy than mainline denominations, another source of their vitality. Their liturgical forms are not imposed from above, or foreign to the worshippers. Extempore prayers, the wearing of uniforms, the use of drums, dancing, and symbolic instruments, and innovation in worship are central to their life. Walter Matitta, leader of the Nazarite Association of Lesotho, developed a fellowship meal as part of the Nazarite service that is not Biblical, or a legacy of African spiritual tradition, but, in Stan Nussbaum's words, "an innovation, differing in nature from the usual Christian forms of eating together. It is not a substitute for holy communion, which all Nazarites were to partake of in their respective churches. It is not modelled on the New Testament love feast or any particular Old Testament feast, though it brings together some features of various meals."[65]

Indigenous spiritual churches are rich in symbolism, varying from church to church according to the availability of natural and manufactured resources, such as water, trees, mountains, stones, clothes, and candles. Symbols are meant to enrich spiritual experience and to point beyond the visible to the invisible. Lekganyane's call to the leadership of the ZCC was symbolized by an episode concerning his hat, which blew away and settled under a tree where falling leaves filled it. The leaves, Lekganyane saw as symbolic of the gathered community of Christians he was to lead.

Almost all the indigenous spiritual churches use uniforms that also have symbolic meanings. Khaki symbolizes that human beings are dust and to dust shall return. White is a symbol of purity, red of the blood of the Lamb. Christian identity is most often symbolized by cloth crosses, worn by members, or wooden crosses carried in processions.

Rituals are also symbolic. In some churches purity is exemplified by the act of taking off one's shoes, as God instructed Moses to do when approaching a sanctuary. In healing, *impepho* (incense) and candles are used; incense is also used by traditional healers to invoke the presence of the ancestors, and candles by the prophets to symbolize the presence of God.[66]

The ministry of healing, common in most of these churches, is probably the most profound aspect of their spirituality. The CCACZ offers healing services twice each week. In healing, the spiritual and material dimensions of religion are brought together: while the head of the healer is in the spiritual world, his or her feet are deeply rooted in the natural world, especially in the use of water, mixed with green (or sometimes dry) plants, leaves, salt, or lime as medicinal resources (*iziwasho*).

The healing ministry is conducted within the traditional African view of the world as permeated by both good and bad spirits. The *iminyama* (bad spirits) are believed to attack innocent individuals constantly. Faith healers counter-attack these bad spirits through prayer and *iziwasho*. The constitution of the CCACZ says: "Our Lord commands in the book of James that hands are to be laid on the sick in prayer and through their faith they shall be healed."[67] E.K. Lukhaimane estimates that in the ZCC, 80 per cent of its followers joined because of an experience of illness or similar trouble, 15 per cent through the influence of relatives or close friends, and 5 per cent because they believed that the ZCC was raised by God and was serving a good purpose.[68]

Not only can individuals be healed, but so can the environment. Indigenous spiritual churches, for example, have reflected on the issue of ecological liberation, including the responsibility of protecting the earth.[69] Diviners believe that *umnyama* (darkness, evil) is the result of the pollution of the air by evil spirits. Sometimes the healing of a person takes place concurrently with healing of the environment, water being the principal agent. Some indigenous spiritual churches' emphasis on the soil, plants, trees, air, and water encourages the practice of keeping the environment clean.

But the foundation of spirituality for the indigenous churches is the Bible, regarded as the Word of God, in most cases requiring, for interpretation, neither formal theological training nor commentaries. The Bible is seen as providing the ethical standards needed to guide worshippers in the conduct of their daily lives. The indigenous spiritual churches see themselves as closer to the Bible than the mainline churches, and closeness to the Bible is interpreted as closeness to God. Practices in the mainline churches that have no clear Biblical base, such as infant baptism, are often condemned as machinations of the devil. Prophecy, the ministry of healing, the seeing of visions, the conveyance of messages through dreams, are all believed to be based on the Bible, channels through which God speaks to the people today, as in ancient times.

"In the Front Line of Suffering": The Political and Social Impact of the AICs

It is widely believed by scholars and journalists that AICs are apolitical and, as such, socially insignificant, or even that they have supported the oppressive status quo against the black freedom struggle. For example, some commentators cite the case of Isaiah Shembe, who, in the 1920s, instructed the Nazirites to turn in their Industrial and Commercial Workers Union membership cards. Others note the invitation issued, at the height of the 1985 disturbances, to the State President, P.W. Botha, to attend the 75th anniversary of the ZCC. However, assessments of the ZCC as conservative, apolitical, or antipolitical had to be reassessed seven years later when not only the state president but also the leaders of the African National Congress and the Inkatha Freedom Party attended a mass meeting of the ZCC at Moria, the church's headquarters. Indeed, as one 1992 report noted, this church "with an estimated five million members can be an important support base for any political party."[70] Although the membership claim of five million is grossly exaggerated, as is the membership of several other AICs – 2 or 3 million affiliated members would be a more realistic estimate – the argument holds good, especially if the approximately 10 million potential voters in all the AICs are considered.[71]

The Ethiopian churches, in their origin, had an indirectly political character that contributed to the rise of black consciousness. In most indigenous spiritual churches, however, after their multiplication in the 1930s, political concern waned. Today the ZCC's attitude of urging its adherents to be obedient citizens represents much political opinion among AICs. Yet, indigenous church leaders themselves and researchers have demonstrated the influence of millions of AIC members on socio-political developments. The churches may not practise active politics, but they often recognize the right of individual members to take part in political organizations of their choice, such as trade unions, civic associations, or even political parties.

The former South African Government generally adopted a policy of reluctantly tolerating the AICs and not interfering directly in their church affairs. The churches, however, had a continuous struggle to win government recognition, which entailed several privileges. In 1940, at a synod of the Bantu Dependent Church in Bloemfontein, the following resolution was adopted: "That this synod ... deeply deplores the attitude of the Government in refusing the sanction of the recognition of this church and more especially as this is opposed to the pronounced policy of the former Minister for Native Affairs, the Hon. General J.B. Hertzog, that the Natives should be allowed to develop on their own lines."[72] The hostility of local white authorities, chiefs, and established missions, as well as the low educational level of the AICs and their penchant for schism, all shaped the government's attitude to indigenous churches. Efforts to gain recognition often met with paternalism, racial prejudice, and bureaucratic obstruction. Even collective bargaining proved fruitless. By 1945 only eight of 800 AICs – and not a single indigenous spiritual church among them – were recognized.[73] Since 1963 registration of churches has ceased, except for the purpose of noting the names of churches and eliminating the duplication of church names, but this change in policy has done little to help the AICs and has encouraged new breakaways.[74]

Noting that political organizations over the years have tried to recruit AICs into their constituencies, a prominent indigenous church leader explained that such efforts have failed because:

> The AICs are found mostly among the rank and file: "The man in the street." These people are the first to be hit by whatever happens politically or economically. When prices of bare necessities like bread, mealie-meal [maize], oil, rent or transport are increased they get hit first. They are well-informed of what is happening politically. They may not express their views directly, or openly, but when strikes or boycotts happen, they find themselves in the front line of suffering and even death. They are at the cutting edge of life. The AICs find themselves involved politically in this sense.[75]

The change in political atmosphere in South Africa, with the release of Nelson Mandela in 1990, affected traditional AIC views. Political awareness was raised, particularly in some Ethiopian churches, as well as among youth in indigenous spiritual churches and residents of squatter settlements. Recent research on Soshanguve near Pretoria indicates that many AIC members there are eager supporters of black nationalistic organizations but that the political views among most AIC members do not differ perceptibly from those of the overall population.[76] One event may be a trend-setter. When the authorities of the "homeland" of Ciskei massacred protestors at Bisho in 1992, a delegation of the African Spiritual Churches Association boldly approached the Ciskeian authorities. Archbishop N.H. Ngada, the president of the Association, reports: "On September 15, our 9 person delegation ... met Brigadier Oupa Gqozo in his office. On the way we stopped at the place of blood to pray ... We had also made our demands quite clear: 'Ciskeians want a democratically elected government.'"[77]

Not much notice has been taken of the unpretentious, often inconspicuous, but immense influence AICs have played in shaping the contours of the new South Africa. These churches, although seldom directly active in organized political movements, have, through their forms of spirituality, their simple life-style, and their work ethic moulded a new socio-political consciousness. They have insisted on an ethic of self-restraint and thrift; they have prized personal discipline and integrity; they have taught their followers to be industrious; they have offered them liberation from evil powers, and psychic, spiritual, physical, and social healing. Their impact on society, and hence indirectly on politics, has been tremendous. As G.C. Oosthuizen has said, "The AIC is thus a movement towards adaptation to a modern secular society without discarding the deep religious disposition which was basic to the African world view."[78]

These churches have wholly cut the umbilical cord with the churches of Western origin. They are the largest and potentially the single most important religious group in South Africa, and, in spite of weaknesses and divisions, their vitality, their rootedness in the African traditions, and their capacity for innovation will most likely have a decisive influence on the history of the church and society in the changing South Africa. No re-joining of the cord is possible, only a novel ecumenical relationship between the different strands of the same faith. How the mainline churches respond to the AICs may be one of the most significant ecclesiastical issues for the next century.

13

The Segregated Spirit:
The Pentecostals

ALLAN H. ANDERSON & GERALD J. PILLAY

Fewer than one hundred years from their origins, Pentecostals, along with charismatics, form the largest Christian group in the world after the Catholic church, and the fastest-growing Christian movement, estimated at over 372 million in 1990.[1] In 1991 Pentecostals and members of African Initiated Churches (AICs) with affinities to Pentecostalism (referred to here as Pentecostal-type Indigenous Churches)[2] accounted for more than 40 per cent of the South African black population. This amazing growth is the result partly of the ability of Pentecostalism to adapt itself to specific cultural contexts; partly of the enthusiasm, spontaneity and spirituality of Pentecostalism; and partly of its ability to address core problems of South Africa: ill-health, poverty, unemployment, loneliness, sorcery, and spirit possession. The growth of these churches is much more rapid than, and often at the expense of, the older churches.[3]

At least 6,000 churches in South Africa, comprising some ten million people, can be identified with some form of Pentecostalism, especially in the emphasis on the Holy Spirit and on practices such as divine healing, exorcism, prophecy, revelation, and speaking in tongues. These churches invariably follow the Pentecostal preference for adult-believers', not infant, baptism.

Little has been written on the history of black Pentecostals in South Africa, and some histories of white (especially Afrikaner) Pentecostals are written as if they represent the entire Pentecostal movement. White Pentecostals often assume, in consequence, that the growth of the Pentecostal movement is wholly the result of the labours of whites. In fact, Pentecostalism has developed spontaneously among the African population, usually (in the case of African Initiated Churches) without any assistance from white churches, and sometimes (in the case of Pentecostal mission churches) despite it.

Zion City, Topeka, and Azusa Street: The North American Legacy

The roots of twentieth-century Pentecostalism can be traced to eighteenth- and nineteenth-century Methodist and Holiness movements, especially to John Wesley's concept of "Christian perfection" or "entire sanctification,"[4] imparted to the believer in a "second blessing" crisis subsequent to, and separate from, an initial conversion or justification (confession and forgiveness of sin).[5] Interest in Holiness and "Christian perfection" experienced a revival during the nineteenth century, particularly through the ministry of Phoebe and Walter Palmer in the U.S. But there was a significant shift in emphasis on the nature of the second blessing, from seeing it as an imparting of "perfection" or "holiness" to a "baptism of the Holy

Ghost," which would give the believer "power for service." At the end of the century at least twenty separate Holiness denominations seceded from the American Methodist Church, all claiming to be true followers of Wesleyan teaching. Non-Methodists also were interested in the Holiness movement; revivalist evangelists, like Charles Finney and Asa Mahan of Oberlin College, and, later, Dwight L. Moody, and his successors R. A. Torrey and Ira Sankey, did much to popularize the teaching of Spirit-baptism. In Britain, the Holiness Movement spawned the annual Keswick Conventions, which emphasized "baptism for service." Significantly, one of the leaders of this movement was Andrew Murray, Jr., several times Moderator of the Dutch Reformed Church (NGK) in South Africa. Dayton observes that by 1900 the shift in the Holiness movement, "from Christian Perfection to Baptism of the Holy Spirit was nearly universal."[6] A large section of the Holiness movement was also now beginning to espouse divine healing as a central tenet.[7]

John Alexander Dowie, the healing preacher in Illinois, had considerable influence on South African Pentecostalism, far greater than his influence on American Pentecostalism. Dowie, who may have been an exponent of Keswick holiness views,[8] extracted teachings on divine healing from their Holiness context and gave them slightly different theological grounding, with healing as a manifestation of Pentecostal power.[9] In Zion City, Illinois, Dowie reigned as "First Apostle" and had assumed the role of "Elijah the prophet" over a movement he founded and called the Christian Catholic Apostolic Church in Zion (CCACZ). This church, which claimed to have 20,000 members by 1905, emphasized divine healing, threefold baptism of adult believers by immersion, and the active pursuit of holiness.[10] Several of the early leaders of the Pentecostal movement in North America were associated with Dowie and both pioneer Pentecostal leaders Charles Parham and William Seymour visited Zion City; moreover John G. Lake, a Pentecostal missionary to South Africa, was an elder in Zion City. Dowie's death in 1907 led to massive defections from his church to the new Pentecostal movement.

"Speaking in tongues" was a widespread phenomenon in several holiness churches, but Charles Parham was among the first to focus on tongues as an external sign of the baptism of the Spirit. The first recorded incidence of tongues speaking as "initial evidence" was in Parham's Bible school in Topeka, Kansas, in January 1901. Just as the disciples had "spoken in tongues" after their "conversion," so these Christians claimed it as their "second blessing."

William Seymour, an African American, became a student at Parham's Bible College in Houston, Texas, in 1905, although by "special" arrangement he had to sit outside the door of the classroom. In 1906 Seymour went to Los Angeles, invited by a Holiness church, where he preached the new message in a former African Methodist Episcopal church building turned livery stable. Here the worldwide Pentecostal revival began. People flocked to his, mostly black, church in Azusa Street, received the Spirit, and carried the message of Pentecost to fifty nations within two years.[11] Although the Azusa Street revival did not originate the distinguishing traits of Pentecostal theology, it did capture the attention of many Christian leaders and popularized the Pentecostal experience in an unprecedented way. At Azusa Street, people of all races and social backgrounds "achieved a new sense of dignity and community in fully integrated Pentecostal services."[12] Synan states that "directly or indirectly, practically all of the Pentecostal groups in existence can trace their lineage to the Azusa Mission."[13] The earliest Pentecostal pioneers to South Africa, John G. Lake, for example, were influenced by the Azusa Street revival, and much of the early theology of South African Pentecostalism was imported from the U.S. Lake revisited Azusa Street at least once to report to Seymour on events in South Africa.[14]

After about 1910, however, North American Pentecostalism had no further direct influence on the progress of Pentecostalism in South Africa.[15]

Wakkerstroom: The South African Azusa Street

Many Pentecostal and indigenous Pentecostal-type churches in South Africa have their roots in events in Wakkerstroom in the south-eastern Transvaal – events which, in turn, were influenced by Zion City and later by Azusa Street. Pieter L. le Roux, a Dutch Reformed missionary working in Wakkerstroom, joined the Zion movement in 1902 or 1903, together with some 400 African co-workers and converts. Le Roux had been a student of Andrew Murray and was especially interested in Murray's views on divine healing. Le Roux and his followers had become aware of the Zionist movement through Dowie's magazine *Leaves of Healing*, and had requested membership, inviting Dowie to send a representative to South Africa. In 1904 Daniel Bryant, Dowie's appointed overseer of the CCACZ, arrived in South Africa[16] and, soon thereafter, Bryant baptized 141 converts at Wakkerstroom, including Le Roux. From the Wakkerstroom group of "Zionists," which grew to 5,000 members by 1905,[17] a whole series of Zionist and similar Pentecostal-type churches eventually emerged.[18] Wakkerstroom was to South African Pentecostal-type churches what the Azusa Street revival was to the worldwide Pentecostal movement. The continuity between the early Zionist movement and the Pentecostal movement in Southern Africa is crucial to our understanding of subsequent developments, and places indigenous Pentecostal-type churches within their correct historical and theological context.[19]

In 1908 several Pentecostal missionaries arrived in South Africa from the United States, led by Thomas Hezmalhalch and Lake, apparently having set out on their own initiative. Le Roux learned from them that "Zion taught immersion and divine healing, but NOT Pentecost."[20] Lake and Hezmalhalch soon took over the "Zion Tabernacle" in Johannesburg for services,[21] and were largely identified with the Zionist movement. A number of other Pentecostal missionaries soon arrived, mainly from North America and Britain, and independently of each other, among them, Charles Chawner, Henry and Anna Turney, and Hannah James, who were to play significant roles in the formation of the Assemblies of God (AOG).[22] George Bowie, of the Pentecostal Mission, arrived in South Africa in 1910. Archibald Cooper, an immigrant to South Africa, and Le Roux joined Lake's new Pentecostal movement called the Apostolic Faith Mission (hereafter AFM),[23] and soon themselves became leaders. Cooper did not remain long in the AFM, and was soon holding independent services.

The theology of the early Pentecostal churches (including what were to become the Apostolic Faith Mission, the Assemblies of God, and the Full Gospel Church of

God) was determined largely by these white Pentecostal missionaries. Their position remained compatible with the theology of Dowie's Zion church in its principal features of faith healing, exorcism, personal piety, and spiritual revival. The quest for direct spiritual experience and a sense of revival made these early congregations vibrant communities of worship, prayer, and evangelism. By comparison to more staid Christians in the traditional churches, these Christians were ebullient, and their churches grew rapidly.

The Pentecostals, in addition to their Holiness theology, emphasized the baptism of the Spirit as a second experience, the proof of which was the gift of "speaking in tongues." The evidence of being filled with the Spirit was, in Holiness theology, the sanctified life. In Pentecostalism the evidences were more dramatic.

After Le Roux moved to the AFM, his African fellow-workers at Wakkerstroom continued to regard themselves as "Zionists," but like Le Roux they also embraced the Pentecostal doctrine of the Holy Spirit and still considered Le Roux a leader. A meeting between representatives of the North American-based "Zion Church" and the AFM executive in 1909 agreed that Le Roux was in charge of the Zion mission work in the Transvaal, and that these two organizations would "mutually acknowledge each other's certificates" of membership and ordination.[24]

The Pentecostal movement in South Africa initially grew among the disenfranchised black people and the poor-white Afrikaners reeling from the aftermath of the Anglo-Boer War.[25] As in most other churches in South Africa, leadership was kept firmly in the hands of white men,[26] resulting, eventually, in the separation of the black Zion churches from the Pentecostals. An issue of the AFM magazine *Comforter* in 1911 noted that "the vast majority of native work is being conducted by natives themselves without white assistance"[27] ... but, limited to leadership in their local constituencies, Africans were not permitted to emerge on a national level in these churches, even though they were largely responsible for the spread of the Pentecostal message throughout the country. At first there was no perceived schism between Le Roux (and the AFM) and these African Zionists. Pentecostalism apparently did not take the place of Zionism, but was simply added to it. In 1910 the AFM executive committee decided that "whereas the natives deem the name of Zion so essential that this portion of our Mission be known henceforth as the Zion Branch of the Apostolic Faith Mission."[28] The Zion church in Johannesburg became the AFM's first headquarters. Many of the AFM's first white members were also former members of Zion.[29]

The first Pentecostal services in Johannesburg, held in the Zion church in Doornfontein,[30] were racially integrated. Burton reported that "all shades of colour and all degrees of the social scale mingled freely in their hunger after God."[31] The white Pentecostals, however, decided soon after the missionaries arrived, to separate the races in baptisms,[32] and, like other churches in South Africa at this time, yielded to the pressures of white society to develop segregated churches.

White Robes, Beards, and Healing: Pentecostal Roots of the "Zionist" AICs

The Pentecostal churches consisting solely of Africans – like the Zion Apostolic Church – continued to work together with the white Pentecostals,[33] and early white Pentecostal leaders actually encouraged independent African groups to join the AFM.[34] Estrangement between the black and the white Pentecostals was to happen gradually. Although it appears that one of the Zulu Zion leaders, Daniel Nkonyane, may have broken with Le Roux and the AFM as early as 1910,[35] the earliest clearly recorded secession took place in 1917, when Elias Mahlangu (one of the Wakkerstroom group) broke from the white-controlled Pentecostals to found the Zion Apostolic Church of South Africa. By then it is likely that numerous other black Pentecostalist churches existed.[36] Out of the Zion Apostolic Church, Edward Motaung's Zion Apostolic Faith Mission (ZAFM) seceded in 1920 (the name showing an obvious desire to maintain continuity with the AFM). Engenas Lekganyane's Zion Christian Church (ZCC), in turn, seceded from the ZAFM in 1925 and is now one of the largest churches in South Africa.[37] The white AFM did not recognize these later secessions nor was it probably even aware of them.

Not only did African Zionists retain most of the doctrines and practices of the Pentecostals but they tended to favour the name "Apostolic" as well as "Zion," demonstrating a desire to be identified with the new Pentecostal movement. In 1932 the General Secretary of the AFM, I.D.W. Bosman, stated that "112 of 400 Zionist groups could be shown to be offshoots of the Apostolic Faith Mission."[38] Hollenweger speaks of "hundreds" of independent churches deriving from this source.[39] The AFM retained Dowie's threefold immersion, as did most of the black Zionist churches, and the practice is widespread among African Pentecostals in southern Africa today. Speaking in tongues and prophesying, introduced not by Dowie's movement but by the Pentecostals, were also retained and practised by most Zionist and Apostolic indigenous churches. The differences that emerged – at least originally – were mainly external. Le Roux and other white Pentecostals, for example, objected to blacks' use of external symbols such as staffs and the wearing of uniforms and robes.[40]

Engenas Lekganyane (c.1885–1948), founder of the Zion Christian Church, encountered Le Roux and the AFM in Johannesburg in 1908.[41] Lekganyane, who had suffered from an eye disease for many years, had a vision in which a voice said that if he went to Johannesburg he should join the church that baptizes by threefold immersion in water, and thus find healing for his eyes.[42] He was "baptized in the Holy Spirit," by Elias Mahlangu, before Mahlangu's Zion Apostolic Church seceded from the white Pentecostals in 1917, and his eyes were healed.[43] Lekganyane joined a congregation near his home, which at that time was called the Zion Apostolic Church (ZAC). Lekganyane maintained contact with Le Roux, who gave him his preaching credentials in 1916.

When a split arose in Lekganyane's home congregation over the name of the church, Lekganyane favoured the name "Zion" rather than Apostolic Faith Mission, an indication of his preference for identification with the black Zionists rather than with the white-led Pentecostals. Lekganyane started his own congregation in Thabakgone. A powerful preacher and evangelist, he soon became leader of the church in the northern Transvaal, continuing for a short while with Mahlangu after his break with the AFM, until differences between them emerged. Wearing white robes, growing beards, and removing of shoes before a service were customs promoted by Mahlangu that Lekganyane found objectionable. Encouraged by a revelation that a multitude of people would follow him, he determined to found a church of his own. When, in 1917, he prophesied that Britain would defeat Germany, and this prophecy was fulfilled a year later, his prestige among his people grew. His final break with the ZAC came in 1920, when he went to Basutoland (Lesotho) to join Edward Motaung's Zion Apostolic Faith Mission (ZAFM), which had also seceded from the AFM. There he was ordained as a bishop in the Transvaal. Once again differences emerged, chiefly over administrative matters, and at the end of 1924 or the beginning of 1925, he returned to found the Zion Christian Church (ZCC).[44] Lekganyane's marriage to a second wife was a contributing reason for the break with Motaung, who opposed polygamy, but Lekganyane remained his strong admirer, and named his second son, Edward, after Motaung. At this time reportedly more than 900 members of the church followed Lekganyane.[45] The church grew at such a pace that, by 1943, only eighteen years later, there were more than 40,000 members, making it one of the biggest African Initiated churches in Africa.

From the beginning of his ministry Lekganyane emphasized divine healing by the laying on of hands. As the church developed he also began to bless various mundane objects, such as strips of cloth, strings, papers, needles, walking-sticks, and also water, to be used to confer healing and protection. Several miraculous incidents are attributed to Lekganyane in the latter part of his life; in this respect, he was a true Pentecostal.

Today the ZCC is one of the biggest denominations in South Africa. Like most other AICs, the ZCC does not have a written "dogma," its theology, in the Pentecostal tradition, emphasizing healing, exorcism, and prophecy. But in its distinctive prophetic healing practices and its adaptations to African life and rituals, it developed beyond its Pentecostal roots (see also pp. 217–19).

The St. John Apostolic Faith Mission, a prominent indigenous church in the Transvaal, also has its roots in the AFM. It was founded by Christina Nku, known to her followers as Ma (Mother) Nku,[46] who was born in 1894 into the Dutch Reformed Church (see pp. 220–21). As a young girl she had the first of many visions. At twenty she became seriously ill, but in visions God told her that she would not die. Ten years later, now married to Lazarus Nku, she became ill again; in another vision of a big church with twelve doors, she was told to follow the baptism of John and Jesus. She and her husband were baptized in the Apostolic Faith Mission that same year (1924), when they became acquainted with P. L. le Roux.

Christina Nku did not remain long in the AFM. Apparently, P. L. le Roux had objected to "some of her more elaborate displays of prophetic rapture."[47] In another "vision" she was shown the exact place where she was to build her church with twelve doors, near Evaton (south of Johannesburg). Ma Nku became well known as a healer and, within a few years, gathered thousands of people into her church, whose name, St. John Apostolic Faith Mission, like that of Edward Motaung's Zion Apostolic Faith Mission, showed a continuity with the AFM and the Pentecostal movement. Some of her practices (particularly her healing practices) brought increasing distance between St. John and the Pentecostal movement. For instance, she prayed over water in thousands of bottles and buckets, which was believed to have healing power, for use by her members.

These African Initiated Churches (AICs), particularly of the Pentecostal type, mushroomed from some 30 churches in 1913 to 3,000 in 1970, and to over 6,000 in 1990. The proportion of the African population who are members of these churches dramatically increased, from 21 per cent in 1960 to 30 per cent in 1980, to 46 per cent in 1991. Some ten million South African blacks are now members of AICs, the majority in those of Pentecostal-type.[48]

The different church groups described here have common historical, liturgical, and theological roots in the Pentecostal and Zionist movements at the turn of this century. All emphasize the working of the Holy Spirit in the church with supernatural "gifts of the Spirit," especially healing, exorcism, speaking in tongues and prophesying – although there are sometimes pronounced differences in the practice of these gifts. All these churches also practise adult-believers' baptism by immersion. These features distinguish them from most other Christian groups and justify their inclusion under one generic category, "African Pentecostal churches." The use of the term "Pentecostal-type" to describe those AICs that make up the bulk of African Pentecostals in South Africa is an attempt to avoid generalizing or overlooking the obvious differences that exist, acknowledged by the church members themselves. Referring to these churches as "Pentecostal" does not in any way overlook their distinct liturgies, healing practices and particularly their different approaches to African traditional religion, and their unique contributions to Christianity in a broader African context.

Pentecostals and Racial Segregation

While most African Pentecostals are members of Pentecostal-type AICs, a large number remain in the interracial Pentecostal mission churches, especially the Assemblies of God (AOG), the Apostolic Faith Mission (AFM), each with about a quarter of a million members, and the somewhat smaller Full Gospel Church of God (FGC). Others are in much smaller independent Pentecostal mission churches, and in a number of new and large independent Charismatic churches. Pentecostal churches have continued to grow in South Africa, having overcome their pariah image in the white community by sucessful evangelistic and healing campaigns. By the early 1990s these Pentecostal churches together constituted over 10 per cent of the total South African population.

The Apostolic Faith Mission or AFM[49] prospered especially amongst African people and Afrikaans-speaking whites. Among blacks it grew in these early years partly through the remarkable work and healing ministry of Elias Letwaba. Much of the growth among the white Afrikaners was given impetus by the "Central Tabernacle" in Johannesburg, regarded as the "mother church" of the movement. Le Roux was made president in 1913, when the AFM was officially registered with the government. By 1918 it had about 13,000 black and 5,000 white members, most of the latter Afrikaners. Ten years later these figures had trebled. In 1928 Maria Fraser, accusing the AFM of having departed from its holiness roots, seceded from the white church and founded the Latter Rain Mission, a group characterised by separate community living and by blue dresses worn by its women.

In 1955 G. R. Wessels, a senior pastor in the AFM and its vice-president, became a senator in the ruling National Party, contributing to a serious schism in the white church, with liturgical disputes and the question of academic qualifications for ministers also playing a part. The white AFM, eager to improve its image with the National Party government and the dominant Dutch Reformed Church, dispensed with liturgical practices such as exuberant services with hand-clapping and "dancing in the Spirit," that tended to estrange them from the established white Afrikaner community. They also agreed that pastors were to have formal theological training and a minimum of twelve years' schooling. A minority, convinced that the church had "lost the Spirit," like Maria Fraser before them, seceded, and formed the Pentecostal Protestant Church. The white AFM was to become increasingly identified with and subservient to the apartheid policies of the government.

The AFM is a striking example of the differences in outlook of white and black members.[50] From the founding of the church in 1908, white members determined the constitution, and power was vested in an all-white executive council. The African, Coloured, and Indian sections of the AFM were controlled by a missions department and a missions director appointed by the white church. None of these three sections had any legal standing. Until 1991 only white persons could become "legal" members of the AFM.

In 1985 the white Executive Council called the three other sections together to discuss the future of the AFM. A proposed Document of Intent declared that the AFM "accepts the Biblical principles of unity; ... rejects the system of apartheid based on racial discrimination as a principle in the Kingdom of God and within the structure of the Church; [and] ... accepts the principle that the Church should operate as a single structural unit ..." By June 1986 the Declaration had been approved by the four racially distinct Workers' Councils (conferences of representatives from local churches) and a committee was appointed to work towards unity. But it soon became apparent that the majority of white AFM members interpreted "unity" to mean "equality" before God in separate church structures. In ensuing negotiations the white Workers' Council unilaterally changed the wording of the phrase "rejects apartheid" to "rejects all systems of discrimination." A Committee for Unity drew up an interim constitution for a united AFM, which the three black sections accepted; the white section proposed two divisions in which the white section would remain segregated from the black church. A stalemate resulted, since the white church still controlled the finances and supported many pastors, and it was the only section legally recognized in the church constitution. In 1990 the three black sections combined to form the Apostolic Faith Mission, Composite Division. In 1991 the Workers' Council of the white church accepted the new umbrella constitution, with two sections in the AFM. Thus the white churches remained separate, but for the first time in the eighty-year history of the AFM, black peoples were legal members. There are now two presidents of the AFM: in 1993 Frank Chikane was elected by the Composite Division of the church, and Isak Burger by the all-white section or Single Division. Politics, not theology, has kept the two sections apart. In April 1995 the Single Division accepted the constitution for a united AFM, and the biggest stumbling block towards unity was resolved.

The second of the major Pentecostal mission churches, the Full Gospel Church of God, or FGC, has more English-speaking members than the AFM and a large

Indian constituency (pp. 290–92).[51] It began with the arrival, in 1910, of the North American missionary George Bowie, sent by the Bethel Pentecostal Mission of Newark, New Jersey, and soon joined by other missionaries, most notably Archibald Cooper, who immigrated to South Africa from England in 1902. This mission in the white community divided into two factions under Bowie and Cooper in 1916, but reunited in 1921.

The FGC's work among black people was largely dependent upon financial assistance from the Bethel Pentecostal Assembly in the U.S., but in 1936, during the Depression, this support dried up, and the mission to black people suffered greatly. Among the Indians in Natal, however, J. F. Rowlands, in 1931, founded the Bethesda Church; it became the largest church in the South African Indian community. In 1951 the Full Gospel Church united with the Church of God (Cleveland, Tennessee), named thereafter the Full Gospel Church of God in Southern Africa. Finances again flowed to South Africa from the U.S. In 1952 the FGC bought land at Irene, where it built its headquarters and erected the Berea Theological College, opened in 1965 for whites only.[52]

Several unsuccessful attempts were made by the white sections to unite the FGC and the AFM, a union that would have included the many thousands of black members in these two churches, but without consulting them. Attempts at union apparently foundered, principally on the mode of baptism (the AFM practising a threefold immersion and the FGC single immersion), the autonomy of local churches (more pronounced in the FGC than in the AFM), and the issue of language, for the numerous English-speakers in the FGC feared that a united church would be dominated by the Afrikaner majority among the whites.

The first open agitation for unity within the FGC began in 1975, initiated by the three black constituencies.[53] The FGC, with its large Indian membership, was approximately 80 per cent black, but the white section, as in the AFM, controlled the legislative body and had the sole right to change the constitution. Negotiations stumbled on for eleven years, until the formation of an umbrella legislative body, the Ordained Ministers' Council, purportedly non-racial, in 1986. But the black churches continued to exist as separate bodies, and black leaders, especially Africans, were inadequately represented, as a consequence of the academic and theological qualifications required for membership. A "General Moderature" was then elected of representatives from all four racial groups, but still under the control of the whites. Pressure by the black churches against white control increased, with May 1990 set as the date for establishment of a united church; but in February 1990 the majority of white churches requested an indefinite period of time to "prepare" their members for such unity. In May 1990 two separate associations were formed: the three black church organizations along with eight white churches formed the United Assemblies Association of the FGC, and most of the white churches with a few black churches created a separate association, called the Irene Association. Effectively these two associations formed separate church bodies, though legally constituted as one FGC. The black churches gave the white FGC until February 1994 to resolve the differences, but as of mid-1995 they were not yet resolved.[54]

The Assemblies of God (AOG), the third major Pentecostal mission church, was originally a church of blacks only, though, as usual, under white control. In 1925, various missionaries from North America and Europe were organized into the South African District of the Assemblies of God in America.[55] By 1932 the AOG in the U.S. had recognized the AOG in South Africa as a separate national church. Until 1935 there were no white congregations in South Africa, but in 1938, provision was made for different church sections under different leaders, each with complete autonomy. In 1938, when Nicholas Bhengu joined the movement with his associates Alfred Gumede and Gideon Buthelezi, the stage was set for future participation of black leaders in the Assemblies of God national executive, a unique feature among Pentecostal churches in South Africa.

A leading figure in the church, James Mullan, a white, moved to Port Elizabeth in 1944, followed a year later by Bhengu. The revival that followed Bhengu's ministry, first in Port Elizabeth, but more especially in East London, lasted until the late 1950s, and resulted in the AOG's becoming the fastest-growing Pentecostal church at that time, particularly among black South Africans. In 1950 Bhengu launched the "Back to God Crusade," an evangelistic and church planting body that developed quite independently of the white missionaries. The black churches that sprang up from this movement soon constituted the majority in the AOG; they were autonomous, self-governing, self-supporting, and especially self-propagating. Inevitably, conflicts arose between expatriate missionaries and indigenous leadership (particularly in the Bhengu group), with the missionaries disturbed by what they perceived as Bhengu's autocratic leadership style. James Mullan and John Bond, two white AOG leaders, supported Bhengu against the missionaries. In 1964, a group of black leaders (mainly in the Transvaal) and the missionaries associated with the AOG in the United States withdrew from the AOG to form the International Assemblies of God (IAG).

The AOG withdrew from the Fellowship of Pentecostal Churches (to which the AFM and the FGC belonged) because of dissatisfaction with the conservative stance of the other Pentecostal churches.[56] Nevertheless, some of the tensions described in the other two churches existed here, too, albeit to a lesser degree. Unlike the other principal Pentecostal churches, the AOG was not divided into "mother" (white) and "daughter" (black) churches. It was, as Watt points out, "a black church before any white congregations were formed."[57] Its division into autonomous associations or "groups" was the result of the work of leaders and missionaries. Bhengu, for example, was the founder and head of the largest group, the Back to God Crusade. Black churches that had come under Bhengu's leadership became known after 1990 as the Assemblies of God Movement.

The AOG "groups" are mostly divided along racial lines, although some of the leaders will contest this statement. Watt, for example, calls this a "simplistic view," though he concedes that, "some groups were limited to a racial group" but that others were not.[58] In fact, almost all of these groups are racially separate, reflecting the divisions in South African society.[59] The Coloured and Indian churches make up the overwhelming majority of a group called the Assemblies of God Association.[60] The white churches, generally known as "the Group," are led by John Bond. This division into "groups" lends support to racial division, the main criticism of the AOG by its younger black leaders.

At present the AOG has one general executive, elected by one General Conference (biennial). "Groups" meet separately at conventions in the interim years and nominate their own candidates for the General Executive. The Assemblies of God Movement (Bhengu's group) has twelve of the twenty-two seats on the General Executive, the other ten chosen from the other groups, five to represent whites, and five to represent the Coloured and Indian groups. Nevertheless, for much of its history the General Executive has had a majority black leadership, presided over by a white chairman, John Bond, leader of the white "Group," who has held the position of chairman since 1967, when he was elected by an 85 per cent black general conference. The new position of vice-chairman was created at the October 1991 conference, and Isaac Hleta from Swaziland was elected to this post.

The New Pentecostals

In the 1950s, when two well-known North American Pentecostal evangelists visited South Africa, thousands went to hear them who had never been in a Pentecostal service before. First came William Branham, who stunned many whites with his revelations and miracles; next came Oral Roberts, whose large tent meetings set a standard for evangelists of all races for many years to come. Tent crusades have since been an integral part of South African Pentecostalism, Nicholas Bhengu and Richard Ngidi (in the AFM) using them with particular effectiveness in the black communities. In the 1980s Reinhard Bonnke, a German evangelist, started "Christ for all Nations," with an emphasis on evangelism in the black townships of South Africa.

Many others joined new Charismatic or "Neo-Pentecostal" churches, especially those in the International Fellowship of Christian Churches (IFCC), founded in 1985 and led by Edmund Roebert of the Hatfield Christian Church (Pretoria) and Ray McCauley of the Rhema Bible Church (Johannesburg). These churches, which grew rapidly in the 1980s and 1990s (particularly among whites), are strongly influenced by megachurches in the U.S. The Hatfield church, originally a Baptist church, has some five thousand members, and the Rhema church, modelled after an independent Pentecostal church of the same name in Tulsa, Oklahoma (home also of Oral Roberts), has more than ten thousand in the Johannesburg area. A church in Soweto, at first a Rhema church, now called Grace Bible Church and led by Mosa Sono, has three thousand members, and is the largest black church in the IFCC. The IFCC now forms one of the largest Pentecostal–Charismatic bodies in the country. In 1992 a controversy within the IFCC erupted over the leadership's decision to become observers at the South African Council of Churches. The white conservatives in the group objected to what they perceived as an unholy alliance with "liberals" and supporters of the "interfaith" movement, and a small number left the IFCC as a result.

There are other smaller cooperative groups of (mainly white) Charismatics and independent Pentecostals in South Africa. Fred Roberts heads an association of "Christian Centres" called Christian Fellowships International; Derek Crumpton heads Foundation Ministries and Dudley Daniels (now based in Australia) leads New Covenant Ministries. Several of these associations have joined in a loose association called Christian Ministries Network. In addition, since the 1970s there have been active Charismatic movements in many of the mainline churches (see pp. 166–67).

"The Mission Stands for Segregation": Pentecostalism and Apartheid
Though the first Pentecostal meetings in South Africa were racially integrated, only four months after the founding in 1908 of the AFM, the Executive Council referred in its minutes to "the necessity of getting adequate accommodation for the holding of services in Doornfontein especially for the coloured people."[61] Less than two months later it decided that "the baptism of Natives shall in future take place after the baptism of the white people."[62] In 1910 separate national conferences for white and black people were held, and a "Native Council" was formed of three white and three black members, whose decisions had to be ratified by the all-white Executive Council.[63] In 1917 a resolution adopted by the Executive Council demonstrated clearly the prevailing prejudices:

> We do not teach or encourage social equality between Whites and Natives. We recognise that God is no respecter of persons, but that in every nation he that feareth Him and worketh righteousness is acceptable to Him. We therefore preach the Gospel equally to all peoples, making no distinctions. We wish it to be generally known that our white, Coloured and Native peoples have their separate places of worship, where the Sacraments are administered to them.[64]

In 1925 the Executive Council decided that all black districts should be under the control of a white overseer or district superintendent.[65] Decisions made for black people by whites had to be obeyed, or they had to leave the church.[66] In April 1944 the following resolutions revealed the white AFM's support of the emerging apartheid philosophy of the National Party, governmental policy after 1948:

> 1) Race relations: The mission stands for segregation. The fact that the Native, Indian and Coloured is saved does not render him European ...
> 3) Native education: The mission stands for a lower education [for black people] but is definitely against a higher education.

In a revealing article on "The Church and Racism" in the AFM's magazine *The Comforter* in September 1955,[67] C.P. du Plessis affirmed his belief in the mental, emotional and spiritual superiority of the white race, all based on the Scriptures.

African leaders in the Pentecostal mission churches seem to have accepted this pattern of racism. The AFM pioneer Elias Letwaba, like many Africans of his time, raised no objection to the indignities placed on him because of the colour of his skin.[68] Towards the end of his life he wrote this in Afrikaans in the AFM magazine, the *Trooster*: "I pray for our benefactors, the White people, who have brought the Eternal Light to us. My nation must learn to love our benefactors ... and be obedient to them, because there would be no heaven for us poor Blacks if it were not for the White man."[69] Letwaba's attitude was a principal reason why he remained in the AFM for the rest of his life. His contemporaries Motaung and Lekganyane, and many other blacks chose to leave and found their own churches. Letwaba had the dubious distinction of being one of only two black district overseers ever to be appointed in the AFM's first 50 years; he had even been allowed to speak at white conferences. Similarly, in the 1970s, the Zulu AFM leader Richard Ngidi would not allow any discussion on what he perceived to be political matters, probably because of the prevailing view in the AFM, and in most Pentecostal circles, that involvement in politics was sinful.[70]

Some Africans in the Pentecostal mission churches did struggle against apartheid, most notably the General Secretary of the South African Council of Churches, and President of the AFM's Composite Division, Frank Chikane. Despite his activism, Chikane considers himself a Pentecostal in every sense of the word.[71] As a young man, he was very active in the AFM church in Soweto, and at the age of eighteen was already secretary of the church board. At university, he followed Cyril Ramaphosa as chairman of the radical Student Christian Movement. He joined the evangelistic organization "Christ for All Nations" led by Bonnke, then enrolled for theological studies by correspondence to train as an AFM pastor. In 1976, while serving a congregation near Krugersdorp, Chikane was involved in a community project to alleviate the suffering of the black people in Kagiso, and formed the Interdenominational Youth Christian Club for this purpose in 1978. Between 1977 and 1982 he was detained four times by the police, although never convicted of a crime. In detention he was tortured, once by a white deacon of the AFM.[72] In 1980 he was ordained an AFM pastor, on the condition that he should not participate in politics. But his continued involvement in the freedom struggle and community projects got him into trouble with the AFM leadership. In August 1981 he was suspended by the West Rand district council, on the ground that he had broken conditions of his ordination.[73] Only intense agitation by the Reinstate Frank Chikane Campaign, an unofficial organization within the AFM, forced the lifting of his suspension in 1990. In 1992 Chikane was appointed advisor to the new AFM Composite Division interim Executive Council formed by the unification of the African, Coloured and Indian sections of the AFM that year. On 20 May 1993 he was elected president of this division, having come a full circle from suspension in a church to its highest office bearer.

Unlike Chikane, Nicholas Bhengu, who pioneered the Assemblies of God's transformation to an indigenous African church, rarely made socio-political pronouncements,[74] but according to Watt, he was quite clear "that black people would be brought to liberation from political and economic oppression through the gospel. He believed that, by coming back to God, blacks would be prepared for nationhood and political power."[75] He and other black AOG leaders "refused to allow the prevailing social context to separate them from Whites and to shape the Church."[76] Still, in spite of this view, he did not challenge the status quo, believing that political activity was futile, and forbidding his members to affiliate politically. He was described by some African nationalists as a "sell-out" and received several threats to his life. Liberation would only come through God, he said: in Dubb's words, "through non-violence, good relations with Whites, obedience to the laws of the land and, above all, through faith in God rather than in political action."[77] In this respect Bhengu followed the stance of most Pentecostals.[78]

In the 1980s the struggle for unity in the Pentecostal churches, encouraged more outspokenness against apartheid. For example, Pentecostals comprised at least half of the signatories of "The Evangelical Witness," drawn up by the Concerned

Evangelicals in 1986 as a reaction to the perceived political conservatism of Evangelicalism.[79] In 1988 a group of Pentecostals from Natal (mainly Indians) drew up "The Relevant Pentecostal Witness," a more specifically Pentecostal statement against apartheid that stressed the non-racial origins of the Pentecostal movement and a theology of the Spirit motivating a preference for the poor and oppressed.

Pentecostalism and the Dawn of a New South Africa

White South African Pentecostals do not always acknowledge their inter-racial beginnings. The former President of the AFM, Francois Müller, referring to the black origins of the Pentecostal movement in America, commented: "Later Seymour was replaced by more able people and the different races ceased worship together."[80] Isak Burger, the current (1995), President of the white "Single Division" of the AFM, also described the notion that Pentecostalism originated in a black church as a "warped, one-sided conclusion," saying that the Pentecostal movement developed a "natural and spontaneous segregation." He attributed the segregation in the AFM "to the fact that some Afrikaners who understood the history, nature and the attitudes of race relationships in South Africa better than the Americans [Lake and Hezmalhalch] were elected on the Executive."[81]

The South African Pentecostal movement thus acquiesced in the social system of apartheid South Africa. Its early integration and fellowship were short-lived. Black people were denied basic human rights in the very churches in which they had found "freedom" in the Spirit. In consequence, many African Pentecostals withdrew to the AICs or found comfort in their new-found Pentecostal "spirituality" and remained for the most part "other worldly."

South African Pentecostalism, despite denials of some, has its roots in a marginalized and underprivileged society struggling to find dignity and identity. It expanded among oppressed African people who were neglected, misunderstood, and deprived of anything but token leadership by their white Pentecostal "masters," who had apparently ignored biblical concepts like the priesthood of all believers and the equality of all people in Christ. And yet the ability of Pentecostalism to adapt to and fulfil African religious aspirations was its principal strength.

African Pentecostalism, of which the indigenous Pentecostal-type churches are its predominant demonstration, has grown in the past thirty years to such an extent that it has become the major force in South African Christianity. The indigenous Pentecostal-type churches, in turn, made their own distinct contribution to African theology, having developed along quite different lines from the more Western Pentecostal churches. These churches demonstrate what happens when Pentecostal pneumatology encounters the traditional spirituality of Africa, and what African people, when left to themselves, do with Pentecostal pneumatology. The overriding African concern for spiritual power from a mighty God to overcome all enemies and evils that threaten human life, results in an extensive ministry of healing and exorcism. African Pentecostalism created a Christian liturgy in a free and spontaneous way that does not betray its essential Christian character, but liberates it from the foreignness of European forms.

Holistic, ecstatic, and experiential religious practices are still found in Pentecostal liturgy throughout the world, because they were borrowed from the nineteenth-century African–American Holiness movement, which, in turn, had some of its roots in traditional African religion – the shout, antiphonal singing, simultaneous and spontaneous prayer, and dance. Early Pentecostals emphasized the freedom, the equality, the community, and the dignity of people in the sight of God. Later Pentecostals acquiesced in the societal forces that tended to divide them, finding spiritual comfort in separate spiritual spheres. Whether the egalitarian or separatist tendencies of Pentecostalism will triumph in the new South Africa is a major question for the next century.

Pentecostal baptism in the sea

14

The Struggle for Sunday: All-male Christianity in the Gold Mine Compounds

TSHIDISO MALOKA

The discovery of diamonds at Kimberley in 1870 and of gold on the Witwatersrand in 1886 put South Africa on the path to industrialization with the help of cheap African labour recruited throughout the sub-continent. African men worked on the mines for four to twelve months, returning home when their contracts expired. African women working in the fields in rural areas supplemented the earnings of the migrant workers, hence helping to subsidize the profitability of the mines. The mine workers were housed in rectangular all-male barracks known as compounds, an institution developed in the Kimberley diamond mines that later spread to the Witwatersrand gold mines. Whereas Kimberley diamond workers could leave the premises only at the end of their contracts, Witwatersrand gold miners could visit nearby locations (segregated urban neighbourhoods for Africans) and compounds on weekends, with special passes. The number of African workers in the gold mines increased in round figures, and with some fluctuations in times of war, from 15,000 in 1890 to 184,000 in 1910, to 202,000 in 1930, to 305,000 in 1950, to 364,000 in 1969.[1] Illness from nutritionally poor diets, inadequate sanitation, and rampant respiratory diseases, resulted in high mortality rates.

The gold mines of the Witwatersrand (a region that stretches from Springs through Johannesburg to Randfontein) were seen as a prime field for Christian missions. Catholics, Anglicans, Baptists, Lutherans, Presbyterians, Calvinists, Methodists, and Congregationalists regarded the gold fields as an opportunity to convert Africans (see p. 62), who would then carry the faith back to their home areas. Missionary efforts in the gold mine compounds began as early as the 1890s and increased after the Anglo-Boer War ended in 1902. By 1904 more than 18,000 Africans were in one way or another associated with Witwatersrand Christian churches.[2]

African Pioneers and Missionary Supervisors

The propagation of Christianity in the compounds and locations was the consequence not only of missionary activity but also of the zeal of African Christians who did their best to spread their faith among their mates. African converts gathered fellow Christians in the compounds for frequent prayer and religious services. A number wrote letters to missionary newspapers celebrating their progress but lamenting the lack of support from white missionaries. An African Christian arriving in a compound looked about for a suitable church, and if he found none, might well set up his own. At the turn of the century, Thomas Lutseke, an African assistant engine-driver on a mine near Germiston, used his own hut both for Sunday services and for weekday school classes for children and adults. From his own savings and from collections among his people he built a small iron church building in the location; the Anglicans later helped him add a roof. Eventually, he abandoned his work on the mine, sacrificing a salary of six pounds a month to work full-time for Anglican missionaries at a mere two pounds a month.[3]

A number of Africans converted at the mine were employed as full-time evangelists by the missionaries; some of these, restless for autonomy, set up their own churches. One such was a Mozambican, James Ngonyama, who was converted in 1896 by the South African Compounds and Interior Mission (SACM) at the City and Suburban mine in Johannesburg, and hired as one of the SACM's first African evangelists. By 1913 Ngonyama was running his own "Gazilandi Socide" on the Reef and in southern Mozambique.[4] Ethnic and language differences were not barriers to such efforts, since many Africans spoke more than one language and could translate for those who could not understand the services. At Knights Deep mine in Germiston in 1916, for example, the Sotho and Shangaan held a joint Christmas service. Christian work at the Premier Diamond mine near Pretoria was headed by Africans as late as 1928, despite the arrival of numerous missionary societies on the Witwatersrand. At Dutoitspan in Kimberley in 1937, Sotho Christians were still holding services on their own, and also together with the Xhosa.[5]

Over time most African-led religious initiatives came under the control of white-led missionary societies, in part because African leaders who regarded themselves as attached to a particular denomination frequently sought out contact with that denomination's white missionaries. Africans might, for example, conduct their own religious feasts and festivals, teach literacy classes, and arrange communal support for victims of accidents; yet they might invite missionaries to conduct the special Christmas and Easter services, administer baptisms, and the Holy Communion, in light of the congregations' doubts that Africans had the authority to undertake the most important rites and celebrations. Missionaries, for their part, endeavoured to attract these independent African groups to their denominations and societies. Africans' need for funds for books and writing materials, communion vessels, and other items the miners could not afford was a clear inducement to link up with a missionary society. In the mid-1890s, for example, it cost the SACM about £473 to build a hall and cottage at its City and Suburban site, £135 for a pump and well at its New Primrose site, and more than £40 for the installation of electricity at its Simmer and Deep cottage and hall.

Missionary societies with buildings on the mine property sometimes also had to pay employers for rent and electricity.[6] Gaining permission and appropriate venues for religious services in the compounds required good relationships with mine authorities, especially compound managers, and here the white missionaries had more influence than the Africans, who had no "surface rights," that is, no right to use land leased by the mines. Missionaries could also help workers get employers to sign the "travelling passes" they needed to leave the compound.[7] Contact with missionary societies thus could give formerly independent African groups privileges they otherwise would not have, including more influence with authorities, more access to facilities such as chapels and churches, and fellowship with a much broader community of Christians.

CHRISTIANITY IN SOUTH AFRICAN SUBCULTURES

"Something Should Be Done for the Heathen": Strategies and Methods of Compound Missions

Although missionary societies regarded the Rand as an important and strategic site for their work, at first most neglected the compounds to focus their attention instead on Africans in the urban slums, whom they regarded as more "civilized" and hence easier to evangelize than the transient mine workers. The South African General Mission (founded in 1889 with headquarters in Cape Town) and the Wesleyan Methodists did begin to work in the compounds soon after the discovery of gold, but offered nothing more than Sunday visits. The American Board, which came to the Witwatersrand in 1894, concentrated on Zulu workers outside the mines.[8] Not until 1896, when Albert Baker (who had abandoned his law practice in Natal for evangelical work) established the interdenominational South African Compounds Mission (SACM), did comprehensive missionary work in the compounds begin. Concerned that "something should be done for the heathen who were being demoralized by strong drink and card playing, and other vices of civilization,"[9] Baker requested and received a building site at the City and Suburban gold mine. That same year he was joined by Ernest Mabille, who had been expelled from the Paris Evangelical Missionary Society in Lesotho in 1894 for adultery with a Sotho servant, and a man named Angus Black of Boksburg. Within two years, Baker's SACM expanded its activities to four other mines, establishing halls for worship, schools, and cottages for evangelists to live in. They scheduled regular visits to nearby compounds and hospitals.[10]

Baker's methods became a model for evangelizing the compounds. He located his buildings, which included a missionary cottage and a hall for services and literacy classes, near the compounds. He trained African evangelists to assist the white missionary staff, convinced that Africans converted on the Rand would transmit the Christian message to their families in the rural areas. He saw the mines as the most strategic point in the country, the place that brought together Africans from diverse regions who then dispersed, conveying the gospel with them. Other missionary societies soon adopted Baker's model.

The Anglicans established their Rand Native Mission under Latimer Fuller, a priest of the Community of the Resurrection, and Herbert Bennet in 1903; within three years their operations covered more than seventy centres on the Reef, among them, twenty-seven churches.[11] The Paris Evangelical Missionary Society established itself among the Sotho miners in 1922. By 1923 about twenty-six missionary societies (representing nine denominations and seven nationalities) were operating along the Reef, almost double the fourteen there in 1912.[12]

Strategies for evangelizing in the compounds depended not only on the specific doctrines of a denomination, but also on its choice of a group among whom to evangelize, and on the number of personnel it had available. The Anglicans, the Wesleyans, and the SACM directed their efforts to all Africans in the compounds, translating their sermons into two or even three languages. Other missions sought to convert miners from a particular rural region where the mission was already operating, and hence used the language of the region. Thus, the American Board and the Swedish mission selected the Zulu of Natal; the Berlin mission, the Sotho-speakers from the Orange Free State and the Northern Transvaal; the African

244

Methodist Episcopal (AME) church, the Shangaan of Inhambane; the Swiss Mission, the Shangaan of the Lourenço Marques district and the north and eastern Transvaal; and the Paris Evangelical Mission, the Sotho of Lesotho. Baker could speak Zulu and Ernest Mabille spoke Sotho. The Anglicans sent Bennet to Natal to learn Zulu, and urged Fuller to improve his rudimentary knowledge of Sotho. The Swiss introduced the use of Shangaan. Indeed, missionaries were occasionally dismissed for failing to learn the African language of the people to whom they were to preach.[13]

The importance of learning African languages was illustrated by Bennet's story of one zealous English visitor who asked to preach to those "dear black souls":

> A good interpreter was found for him and the visitor made an eloquent discourse. But the interpreter, knowing the people whom he was addressing and their besetting sins, turned all the preacher's unctuous phrases about "love," and "excuse for ignorance," into the strongest denunciations of wrath upon evil doers and warnings to his hearers about the danger of disregarding the manifold calls which God had vouchsafed to them. When the interpreter was told afterwards that this device of his had been noticed, he said that he knew the preacher wished to help the people and, therefore, he had felt bound to interpret his pious wish rather than his unwise words.[14]

In the earliest years of the SACM, Baker would stand in the compound courtyard, playing hymns with his portable harmonium to attract an audience, and would then begin to preach. After cottages and halls had been erected, and more white missionaries and African evangelists employed, the SACM adopted a more sophisticated two-tier approach: on weekdays missionaries and evangelists would visit the compounds and on Sundays lay preachers would meet for prayer and then divide into groups of about twenty to forty to preach from morning to evening in the compounds. By the 1920s more creative methods were used to attract the miners' attention. Visual aids were commonly used to enhance sermons; for example, black, red, and white hearts to illustrate, respectively, "sin," the "blood of Jesus," and "salvation." Leaflets were handed out to workers, in the hope that they would later be taken to families back home. Salvation Army brass bands attracted audiences to the sermons; Anglicans processed into the compound courtyard preceded by an uplifted wooden cross and led by missionaries in cassocks and surplices, chanting hymns. The American Board in the 1920s organized sports activities and showed motion pictures, with the support of mine and city council officials, as leisure time activities that could provide the "natives" wholesome alternatives to "vices," such as crime and beer-drinking.[15]

The courtyards used for services were readily accessible to the workers living in the surrounding dormitories. On Sundays in summer, workers engaged in their own varied activities in the courtyards such as dancing, singing, and playing of games, and the missionaries saw them as potential congregations. In winter, missionary visitors tended to concentrate in the dormitories, where workers huddled around fires. In 1906 Baker visited some workers underground during working hours for hymn-singing and prayer, but such visits to the mine, doubtless discouraged by mine authorities as an interruption of work, were apparently rare. By the 1940s, churches had tended to shift their priority again to "locations," the segregated housing areas in the towns.[16]

The importance of African volunteers and African lay preachers in missionary work is shown, for example, by the policy of the SACM and the Paris Society, which sent lay-preacher miners to assist the African evangelists on Sundays, eventually offering some of them full-time employment. Missionaries grouped the mines into sectors, allocating certain evangelists and volunteers to each, and coordinated and monitored the evangelists, who conducted most of the visits to the compounds, counseled miners about their personal problems, and performed funeral services. As with white missionaries, African assistants' family members, especially wives, shared their evangelistic responsibilities.[17]

Procedures for selection of evangelists varied from one mission to another. The Paris Society, after reports of "bad" conduct by some of its African evangelists and volunteers, tightened up its selection procedure. The task of training and producing evangelists for its Rand mission was assigned to the Bible School and the Leloaleng Industrial School in Lesotho.

"Religion and No Nonsense": Mine Owners Come to Appreciate the Missions

Mine authorities might have welcomed the missionaries as allies in instilling a work ethic and discipline in the miners, but, in fact, most employers were hostile in the beginning. In the Kimberley diamond mines De Beers did supply its workers with Bibles in various languages, but mine and compound managers on the Rand were initially dubious of the pragmatic value of the gospel. Indeed, like many other whites they feared that "educated natives" would develop political aspirations and ideas about collective bargaining; some thought workers would refuse to work on Sundays. A compound manager told Bennet that "if I find any nigger going to Church, I shall know that he is not giving all his time and attention to his work, and his work will be increased. And if your native preacher attempts to enter the compound to visit the Church boys, I shall put him in the stocks."[18]

As a result of white owners' and managers' opposition, "policeboys" on the same mines had clear instructions to keep missionaries and their evangelists away. One compound manager who found workers assiduously learning to read in a dormitory, tore up their books, and threatened to punish them if they were caught again. In one compound, a visiting chief ordered the sjamboking (beating) of one of his people who had insisted on preaching in the courtyard despite orders to desist.[19]

Missionaries patiently engaged mine authorities in discussions and debates about access to the workers. Baker, in efforts to gain permission for his evangelists to enter the compounds, agreed to numerous restrictive conditions: to teach only in African languages; to confine literacy lessons to reading the Bible and communicating in writing with missionaries; to require abstinence from drugs and alcohol as a condition of church membership; to teach that the restitution of stolen goods was necessary for repentance and spiritual growth; and to refrain from interfering in employer–employee disputes over wages and working conditions. Baker's contract for a building site gave mine authorities the power to evict him with a one-month notice if they were dissatisfied with his work.

The insistence on the restitution of stolen goods was, in effect, a spiritual threat used to enforce a secular order. One Barnabas, confessing to Baker that he had stolen a pair of Wellington boots from his compound manager, returned to the mine to earn money to pay back the owner.[20] In 1911 the SACM could report that, "Since this work began over 2,500 converts have been tested and baptized among these miners, and £300 of stolen money has been paid back to employees as a result of the encouragement which is given to converts to make public confessions of sin."[21] It is not surprising that the compound manager of the City and Suburban mine praised Baker in 1920 as "a good disciplinarian" who "taught religion and no nonsense."[22]

No law in South Africa provided for granting of building sites, or "surface rights," to missionaries until the passing of the Township Amendment bill (Act 34 of 1908). Some mine officials themselves took the initiative to facilitate mission work on the mines, having come to appreciate the usefulness of the missionary gospel in instilling discipline in workers and in insisting that the workers abstain from alcohol. Halls were made available for church programmes and financial donations were provided.[23] At the third annual meeting of the Transvaal Compound Managers Association in September 1921, as the Chamber of Mines newspaper *Umteteli wa Bantu* reported, "duly accredited missionaries are now authorised to hold religious services in Native Compounds."[24] Mine authorities, impressed by the disciplined behaviour of converts, even arranged for them to be put in separate dormitories according to denominations. On some mines employers "ganged" converts together for work under their white "boss boys" and offered facilities for worship and school.[25] By the end of the 1920s mine authorities, in response to the 1923 Urban Areas Act, arranged with municipal authorities to release some of their African employees to look after the mission cottages and halls during the absence of an evangelist or the missionary.[26]

But missionary activity in the compounds was not only an incentive to discipline and subservience. There were disputes among mission societies that had to be arbitrated by the police. Sometimes a compound manager had to provide separate dormitories for up to fifteen competing sects and denominations.[27] Conflict among societies working among the Shangaan was particularly rife because so many groups were involved, with much duplication of efforts and squandering of resources. Often separate groups competed for an audience in the compound courtyard, trying to outbid the other with hymns and preaching, and creating a lot of noise and disorder, and even violence. Preachers would sometimes attack each other verbally in sermons in the other's presence; converts often prevented other denominations from visiting their room in the dormitory. One group of Christians, trying to evangelize another group in the dormitory, "went to stand in front of the door, and as the door was locked they started chanting and announcing the 'true' Gospel; they accused the other of eating pork and smoking, this being proof of their paganism. The Christians who were being attacked could no longer tolerate this and came out of their dormitory with sticks to disperse this group."[28]

Attempts to neutralize such competition were discussed at the South African General Missionary Conferences in 1904, 1906, 1911, 1912, 1921, and 1925. By 1940, about ten societies were working peaceably together in the compounds, undertaking joint visits, and sharing platforms. Still, separatist churches, outside these arrangements, continued to compete with preachers of mission societies for space and a hearing in the compounds. "They throw themselves on the ground," wrote the Swiss missionary Samuel Bovet, "lying on their backs, they repetitively make some utterances to their fellow brothers, or rise unexpectedly and accompany their preaching with big jumps, reminding one of war dances and especially invocations of pagan diviners."[29]

Mine officials eventually grew wary of granting building sites, fearing to open the way to innumerable applications from other bodies.[30] In fact, it was not uncommon for ten or more church buildings to be concentrated on a single site, the adherents of each group seeking to explain and justify their differences to potential converts. As a result, sometimes it took societies more than two years to get their application processed. Some mine owners took back land allocated to churches for a development project of their own, razing the church buildings on the site. Twenty churches at Randfontein in the 1930s lost buildings in that manner.[31]

"We Are Not for Missionaries, Man"; Miners Resist Christianity

The miners in the compounds formed, of course, not a natural community, but an artificial community organized around work alone. Only on Sundays or special days like Easter and Christmas were they freed from work. Isolated in the compounds from their families, without women, they were driven to rely on beershops and brothels in the nearest urban locations. The missions, in propagating the gospel on Sundays to this mine community, had to compete with these other leisure-time activities. One Paris Society missionary commented, in 1950, on the missions' difficulties in reaching the Sotho miners:

> Out of over 200,000 Basutos from Basutoland living in the Transvaal, we hardly minister to 30,000, whereas in Basutoland out of five Basutos, one belongs to the Church. "Why so many lost for the kingdom?" will you ask. Because evil and sin are prevalent in those quick grown urban areas. Strong drink pulls down both the brains and bodies of thousands. Immorality and prostitution break down many families, which, in most cases, were only built up yesterday. Crime, burglaries and faction fighting are notorious at Johannesburg and it makes our heart bleed to realize that, in many cases, Basutos of Basutoland are involved in those … [his dots] To those who have chosen to serve the Devil, church and religion have but a meaning of distrust.[32]

Missions like the Paris Society failed to understand the role that beer-drinking, prostitution, and dancing played for Sotho migrants, and the significance that miners in the compounds attached to their few holidays, especially to Sundays.[33] One Paris Society minister complained that "though these Basuto workers on the Rand get so interested in the Word of God, they take it that the usefulness of the Gospel is only to dispel their sorrows and to comfort and console them in times of need and difficulty. On days of happiness and sunshine they do not bother to go to Sunday services; they would rather go to location beer-halls or visit friends on a Sunday than go to church."[34] Beer, prostitution, and dance expressed group and kinship solidarity and cultural ties with home, as well as offering escape from the dehumanizing and alienating conditions on the mine and in the compounds. In the locations and slums, miners could visit *marabi*[35] shebeens (taverns). Sotho preferred to visit urban Sotho shebeens to enjoy themselves with *famo* and *focho*[36] dances and music.[37] One Paris Society pastor lamented that:

> Men do not go to church on Sundays but join one drinking circle after another to the accompaniment of the piercing ululation of the women. Their language takes on hard tones and is associated with a fierce blood-thirsty nation. They pride themselves in singing church hymns over pots of beer; they take verses from the Holy Bible and twist them to serve their own ends. "Abide with me" becomes a prostitute's plea.[38]

Missionaries, in their contest for Sunday, would begin their visits early, around 10 a.m., before workers left for the locations or began their drinking sessions (if they had not begun already on Saturday night). But many Sotho who wanted to join the church also wanted beer; many dropped out of the church because of its strict policy of teetotalism. At Sunday services some of the congregants were in a stupor from drinking, some drowsy, others passing out and collapsing in front of the preacher.[39]

Some workers resisted efforts to draw them into the orbit of Christianity. The most common form of open resistance was attempted sabotage of a church service or a meeting.[40] When one evangelist visited Sotho in their rooms, "[R]ight here [in the room], words of contempt and mockery are thrown at this servant of the Lord ... Eventually some ask him: 'Who are you, what do you want here?' He does not answer and carries on."[41] The miners often did not understand what missionaries were doing there, since they themselves were there only to work: "... you will hear somebody say 'This man is here with his things of missionaries. We are not for missionaries, man; we are here only for work!' When we say this we then sing our *mohobelo*."[42] An evangelist who gathered his group at a corner in the compound courtyard described a pattern of resistance:

> a passer-by shouts his war song, as he goes past the group. Some of our people ask him to keep silent and off he goes. He is soon followed by another who sings his own praises ... They persuade him to lower his voice. Here come two fellows cursing each other. They restrain them. Some are playing Bantu chess [*morabaraba*], others dance. The evangelist preaches in the very midst of noise, clapping of hands and curses.[43]

The playing of drums and other noisy instruments by workers disrupted the proceedings of a number of meetings or services: "We were announcing our meeting by moving about the courtyard of the compound, singing hymns, with our group of christians," one missionary reported, "but young heathens, armed with their drums, also moved about the courtyard, causing a big disturbance; on this day we preached in vain."[44] Even attacks on converts were not uncommon; the dormitory mate of one of Baker's early converts, who had ceased to take part and help pay for the beer-drinking sessions, found his books ripped, his writing slate smashed; when all these acts of intimidation failed to dissuade him, his mates tried to bar his way to a Sunday service, but he managed to escape.[45]

Choirs, Schools, and a "Shelter Against Temptation": Miners Accept Christianity

Nonetheless, conversion to Christianity had some attractions and advantages for miners. To attain these privileges a miner could pretend to be pious during week-days, then revert to his own ways and venture out to the locations on weekends. Some workers preparing to go on a shift and fearing working underground, might be more receptive to Christianity than at other times.[46] Membership in a church provided access to popular forms of leisure activities, such as the church choirs. Choirs and fund-raising concerts or "tea meetings" had been taking place in slums and locations on the Reef since the beginning of the century, introduced from the eastern Cape and later Natal, by Christian converts.[47] The Paris Society organized Sotho mine choirs under the auspices of *bahlanka* (young men) involved in evangelical work and Bible studies. Their "Rambling Vagabonds" and the "Basutoland Shooting Choir" were reported to be among the most popular Sotho choirs in Sophiatown in 1921; among the most popular Sotho choirs in the compounds during the 1930s were the "Dinare" and the "Roaring Tigers" of State Mines near Brakpan. Such choirs sang secular songs as well as hymns. Many choirs had a large popular following. In 1936 "Miss Moipato, Ngoan'a Malome" (Lady Moipato, My Cousin Sister) competed with "*Chuchumakhala*" (Steam Train) as the favourite Sotho choir song in the compounds and the locations. Concerts provided platforms for contests among choirs; the audience would bid money for such and such a person or group to sing such and such a song. At one concert, in a hall at Village Deep in March 1926, the "Roaring Tigers" and the "Racooks" performed in response to the bid of one E. Malimabe; just under £12 was raised in addition to the money collected from the sale of entrance tickets.

But African miners were attracted most by the literacy classes the missions ran in the mine dormitories and halls. An average of fifteen pupils attended each Paris Mission school in the 1930s. Some schools run by the American Board had up to thirty pupils in 1918. Teachers focused their lessons on reading and writing skills, using blackboards or wall charts, slates and pencils, and the Bible for reading. In some schools, classes learned to sing hymns, and held prayer meetings. It took two to three months for an average worker to gain basic literacy skills.[48] To encourage sustained attendance, compound managers sometimes placed pupils together in one dormitory, perhaps along with miners who avoided alcohol. In one compound, in 1924, two Sotho paid a dormitory mate one shilling per month to teach them to read and write. When they returned home, some miners opened night schools to teach their kinsfolk.[49]

Well-to-do societies like the SACM were able to build special halls for schools, but the less affluent Paris Society faced difficulty in expanding its literacy work. It charged pupils between one shilling and one shilling and sixpence in the 1930s. The SACM charged two shillings, more than the average one shilling and eight pence earned by an African miner on a shift. If some pupils delayed in paying or left at the end of their contract, the teacher could not get paid. The collapse of many Paris Society schools in the compounds was blamed on "lazy" teachers and the drop in student attendance, but teachers, too, may have also left after the expiration of their mine contracts.[50] School fees, after all, had to compete with other expenses of the miners like beer, *dagga* (marijuana), extra food, gambling, or money to be sent home.

One Paris Society missionary was convinced that "the most real advantage of these schools for those who participate in them, is to provide them with an effective shelter against all temptations that they are subject to [on the Rand]."[51] Miners attending day and night SACM schools "would be taught to read and write, and, after careful testing, would be baptized."[52] The SACM school at Nourse Deep in 1915 was said to be "too small for the pupils and congregation, and they are clamouring for enlargement and offering to pay part of the cost."[53] Missionaries, exploiting this opportunity, required all pupils to attend prayer meetings and church services. They sold quantities of books, especially cheap Bibles supplied by the Foreign Bible Society at a price of one shilling and sixpence for a New Testament and two shillings and sixpence for a complete Bible. In 1927, the Paris Mission sold more than £400 worth of books, among them 156 Bibles. Some missionary societies ran their own printing press; the Paris Society, for example, had its own Morija Book Depot, which published *Leselinyana la Lesotho* (established in 1863) and other interesting material that literate miners could read aloud to their mates in the dormitories. The SACM's printing press at New Primrose, which issued its newspaper *Izwi Lentokozo*, also supplied the society with leaflets for regular distribution in the compounds; other printed materials were sold at the book depot at Crown Reef.[54]

By the end of the 1920s, popular night schools existed in every gold mine compound. Mine officials themselves now sought to systematize these schools by employing and paying a teacher who would include "subjects designed for the refinement of Native home life."[55] By the 1940s mine owners were taking an even more active interest in the education of their African workers, providing classrooms with benches, chalk, and blackboards; arithmetic was now being taught, in addition to reading and writing.[56] Missionary societies continued to teach miners, but some mines employed their own teaching staff and provided services and facilities free of charge.

Knowledge of reading and writing was a source of power and influence for workers in the compounds. Scribes received one shilling from dormitory mates for writing a letter. Literate workers stood a chance of getting white-collar jobs outside the mine or clerical and other better-paying jobs at the mine itself. Such work provided married workers with the right to live in the married quarters instead of the single-sex compounds. Competition for such jobs was keen. A Sotho who went to the mines in 1916, Stimela Jingoes, for example, was forced to abandon his training as a teacher for work at a mine, but a compound manager, convinced that he was too young to go underground, offered him a "desk job" instead; thereupon his jealous Sotho *induna* (boss-boy) tricked him out of getting this job, and he was forced to work underground after all. One miner looking for a job at Kimberley was singled out from a crowd outside the mine by a compound manager who "gave me a pen, book, a small box, [and] a desk." But the miner could not write. "I was so hurt when I remembered how my father tried to send me to school, being so ignorant, I preferred to look after the animals [as a herdboy]." The miners' association of literacy with desk, pen, and book, suggests that literacy was considered to be a way of gaining a comfortable and better-paying job, and one not physically demanding. It seemed better to sit and work with a book than to engage in the hard and dangerous physical labour of digging for gold underground.[57]

As miners accepted the Christian religion, many took it with them to their homes in the rural areas. One Sotho migrant returning to the Maluti (the mountainous eastern part of Lesotho), said of the Paris Mission to his compatriots: "This is truly a mission ... In Johannesburg I met a white missionary of the Protestant mission of Lesotho, who spoke Sotho well, and again, today, back at home, in the midst of mountains, there is again a white missionary of the same mission that I met. I now believe in their work ... It is a solid and true one."[58]

After World War II, as noted above, in response to increasing African urbanization, missions shifted their principal base to urban townships. By 1962, for example, the Paris Society's Rand mission was divided into four parishes, which stretched from the east to the west of the Witwatersrand, and from the north in Pretoria to Klerksdorp in the south and Welkom in the Free State. With focus now directed to the townships, miners were expected to attend services there.[59] Evangelizing stable and permanently settled African communities seemed to missionaries to promise better results than working among the artificial and single-sex mine communities. Thus missionary presence on the mines went into a long process of decline, and churches, cottages, and schools on the mine property were moved to the locations.

Missionary work in the mine compounds facilitated the spread of Christianity not only in the black urban locations but also to some rural communities. Migrant workers converted on the mines returned home with leaflets, Bibles, literacy skills, and the new religion; they were then followed by mine-based missions, such as the SACM, which extended their work to the rural areas.

Yet, for all their successes, the missionaries on the compounds, failing to appreciate the complex nature of compound life and the significance of mine holidays for workers, had devised evangelical strategies that antagonized many potential converts and slowed the spread of Christianity. Missionary work in the compounds was, in this sense, a struggle over the miners' precious leisure time, particularly the way they spent their Sundays.

15

Power in Prayer and Service: Women's Christian Organizations

DEBORAH GAITSKELL

Organized women's church groups flourished among both black and white South Africans in the early decades of this century, but they emerged earlier and grew more rapidly among blacks. African women's Christian organizations (*manyanos*, to use the Xhosa word for these prayer unions) existed in many areas well before the First World War, while the white Methodist Women's Auxiliaries, for example, did not emerge until the war itself. By 1940, more than 45,000 black Methodist churchwomen supported a movement ten times as large as the movement supported by their white co-religionists.[1] The Anglican Mothers' Union (MU) in South Africa had close to 34,000 members by 1970 – triple the size of MU in either west or central Africa – and of this membership few were whites or Coloureds.[2]

Mia Brandel-Syrier in the 1950s called manyanos "the oldest, largest and most enduring and cohesive" of all African women's organizations in South Africa.[3] The large size of the manyano movement is perhaps no surprise, considering that at least two-thirds of South Africa's population in the 1910–60 period was African, and only around one-fifth was white.[4] But the disparity in membership figures between black and white women's church groups suggests that black women valued such groups far more than white women did.

Reports from the early days of two different organizations convey the characteristic flavour of each. In 1919, African women of the Johannesburg Primitive Methodist Church held a series of revivalist recruiting meetings in the Orange Free State. Although each was formally opened by black male evangelists, women leaders then took turns to pray and exhort their hearers to repentance.

> Mrs Kumalo took the first chance, she sang Hymn No 175 in Xosa, then Mrs Tsewo was asked to pray; after the prayer Mrs Kumalo read from St John the 3rd Chapter (about Christ teaching Nicodemus the necessity of regeneration). This became a very strong sermon. Mrs Soni prayed, after her prayer Hymn No 27 was sung in Xosa. Here 8 joined ... On Sunday the 23rd ... Mrs Tsewo took the turn and read from St Luke the 13 Chapter 24 verse. This sermon became a piercing sword to the people. In this morning service six joined ... On the 24th, we took another Sermon ... here many people were moved. 3 repented as new members, 7 joined. Total from Saturday evening to Monday evening we got 33.[5]

The next year, the white Women's Auxiliary (WA) Annual Meeting convened at the Methodist Conference in Grahamstown. In this centenary year of the arrival, in 1820, of British settlers in that region, the presidential address included a tribute to the "heroism" of the British women pioneers. "There is much work for women to do in the Church, other than the collecting of funds," the meeting declared, urging more female teaching and leadership. The "glad news" was announced that a mission pioneer's female descendant had just been appointed the WA's "own missionary." Branch reports were read, and the General Committee "spent much thought and time in drafting a revised and enlarged Constitution."[6]

The women's groups in South Africa, then, showed contrasting styles. The African groups evinced an activist, evangelistic fervour, with much "praying and preaching."[7] The English-speaking white women were, by contrast, avid fundraisers, aware of their British heritage, relatively restrained and staid in worship, organizationally formal but generally nonparticipating in their conference proceedings, though happy to support the evangelistic efforts of others. The spiritual life of the manyanos seems to have been more creative and vital than that of the white women's groups.[8]

But any stereotyping of these African women's church groups as spiritually active but socially passive, and of white female organizations as socially active but spiritually passive would be inaccurate for this early period, even though in later decades Lilian Ngoyi of the African National Congress (in the 1950s)[9] and Thoko Mpumlwana, of the National Education Crisis Committee (in the 1980s),[10] decried those who wept over their burdens but did nothing apart from waiting for God to act. Earlier in the century, manyanos undergirded popular resistance on key occasions, such as the 1913 female anti-pass demonstrations in Bloemfontein,[11] the Herschel store boycott of 1922, the Natal beer protests of the 1920s,[12] and perhaps even the mobilization of the Potchefstroom women's protest of 1929 against residential permits.[13]

That African women's spiritual strength was not necessarily at odds with political power in the first half of the twentieth century was acknowledged by the spirited Xhosa woman poet Nontsizi Mgqwetho in her rallying-call of 1924 to the "Die-hard" African women protesters of Herschel[14] to recognize their common cause with the manyano women and the protective solidarity of the prayer group movement:

> Manyano and Die-hard!
> Why look askance at each other?
> You each command a flank in battle,
> Break rank only when victory's ours.
> Peace!
>
> Manyano's for you a mighty stem,
> Roots in the earth, touching the sky;
> Right from the start, Manyano's the shield
> To ward off the white man's arrows.
>
> What misfortune's befallen Manyano?
> We no longer know how to sing its praises:
> It's like fog-ridden cattle out on the plains,
> Yet it binds congregations together.

What's more powerful than Manyano?
Must I continue proclaiming this truth?
If someone rose from the grave to tell you
You might hear, but for now you're deaf.
So listen!![15]

Motherhood, Sexual Purity, Service, and Fund-Raising: Contrasting Ideologies

In the Methodist case particularly – and Methodism seems to have had a pervasive influence on the style of all African women's groups – the contrasting rationale of African and white women's groups was highlighted in their very names. African women founded a Prayer Union, white women a Women's Auxiliary – not, it appears, a trivial difference. Although both groups saw themselves as helping their local churches, and although both took pride in their important fund-raising role – the African women within a few decades had amended their name to "Prayer and Service Union" to encompass this – African women's focus on prayer was a clear difference, one praised by white Methodist women who knew both groups.[16]

In pre-Christian South Africa, motherhood was the cultural destiny of adult African women. But mission Christianity set out to restructure gender relations completely, and through its twentieth-century organizations for African women, to propagate European Christian ideals of marriage, wifehood, and motherhood.[17] By and large the African Christian women joined groups explicitly as *mothers*, and, particularly under the influence of missionary supervisors, assumed a vital role in safeguarding female chastity, marital fidelity, and maternal and domestic responsibilities.

Although Victorian missionaries in South Africa repeatedly deplored the "slavery" of African women as "beasts of burden" in agricultural production, they agreed with Africans that women's most important roles were reproductive. Though some stressed preparing girls for domestic service to settlers,[18] none regarded a lifetime of wage labour as desirable for female converts. They saw African girls primarily as future wives of Christian men, mothers of Christian children, makers of Christian homes. In their ideal of a transformed sexual division of labour, men would perform the heavy farming with ploughs, and women would sew the clothes that signified conversion; a Christian wife would be a "helpmeet" not a "slave." Early mission education of African girls, both formal and informal, had these notions as its bedrock.[19]

Still, the first women's prayer unions seem to have evolved not from the mission schools but from devotional meetings started by white missionary women for "uneducated" adults. Such women first met in weekly sewing classes, which were a feature of mission stations among the Tswana and Zulu, for example, from the 1830s, because to be "dressed" or "clothed" in Western rather than African fashion was identified with seeking Christian instruction or baptism. This widespread emphasis on sewing probably, from the earliest years, brought women together in church groups in a way that men never were. The gendered assumption that clothing was predominantly a female responsibility thus served to create a distinctively Christian group solidarity among women in virtually all the Christian denominations. Those who sewed together then prayed together. From at least the 1880s in the eastern

Cape, missionary wives brought baptized African women together in associations for regular, if unstructured times of shared "testimony," exposition of Biblical passages, and spontaneous prayer that are the lifeblood of church groups for thousands of African women more than a century later. While, by the early 1900s, such gatherings aimed to help women assume new responsibilities as Christian wives and mothers, they also seem, as in the case of Mrs. A. Waters's meetings in Engcobo from the 1880s on into the 1920s, to have been an outlet for energetic and successful female evangelization of "heathen" women, and also for denouncing African beer and exhorting members to total abstinence.

As mission schools and churches spread from outlying regions to town in the late nineteenth century, women's movements followed. In the first half of the twentieth century, motherhood remained central to the three most prominent prayer movements of mission churches in the Johannesburg area: those in the Methodist and Anglican churches and in the American Board Mission. Mrs. S. Gqosho, wife of an African minister in Potchefstroom, started the Wesleyan Methodist Prayer Union in the southern Transvaal in 1907. She brought a small group of women together to pray "for their families and for the common unity and for their sins," as well as for the safety of husbands and sons working on the mines, and for the uprooting of witchcraft and superstition. This manyano's goals were "to cultivate the habits of praying and to consolidate Christianity among the folks,"[20] but after the white chairman of the district installed his wife, Esther Burnet, as president in 1910, the focus on the domestic virtues of the devout wife and mother sharpened. Mrs. Burnet urged the delegates at the 1915 convention to "show the power of their religion in the way they care for their husbands – many of whom are not Christian – and in an increased effort to train their children for the Lord."[21] The first constitution stressed the need to keep house and family clean, to clothe children, and to instruct them in the Christian faith.[22]

Mrs. Burnet's daughter Lilian set out the Union's aims more formally in 1913, with an emphasis on moral self-improvement, and on home and children (most crucially, daughters): to secure due recognition of the place of a Christian home in a people's life; to inculcate the moral duties of industry, honesty, truthfulness, cleanliness and kindness by example and precept in the home; to train younger women and girls to take their places as Christians in the national life; to encourage individual missionary effort among women not yet evangelized; and to consider any questions that affect the life of the native home and the morals of the people.[23]

Domestic education for African women was emphasized throughout the subsequent decades, as, for example, in the sessions at the 1923 manyano conference on "Health in the Home" and "Duty of a Christian Mother to Her Children."[24]

The Anglican Church was the second most important Witwatersrand church for Africans in that era. Deaconess Julia Gilpin, a white missionary from the Society for the Propagation of the Gospel (SPG), started the Women's Help Society (WHS) in 1908 to help African Anglican women communicants develop regular devotional habits and a Christian standard of life, under conditions in the African mine locations which, she said, made it "almost impossible for a decent woman to retain her purity and self-respect," since so many couples living there were not married.[25] Gilpin's core founding ideals seem to have focused on prayer, hymn-singing, and marital respectability. She linked African women with the WHS rather than with the other alternative in England, the Mothers' Union, because the MU's prohibition of membership to divorcees and unmarried mothers might exclude some women affected by the growing irregularity of African domestic life in town. (The WHS took a less scrutinizing, less punitive approach to past sexual lapses.) Because mission staff could visit only intermittently, Anglican groups evolved under African leadership, drifting somewhat – to the disapproval of white missionary supervisors – from the liturgical practices of white Anglicanism and toward the revivalistic style of many other churches.

African women of the third most important Protestant mission in the Johannesburg area in the early twentieth century, the American Board Mission (ABM), founded their women's group out of anguish over adolescent, not adult, female "purity." The Congregational ABM was centred among the Zulu in Natal, where, in 1912, after African men at a church gathering accused their wives of laxly supervising their young people's courtship practices, a women's revivalist prayer movement called *Isililo* ("wailing") sprang up, with women repenting of their shortcomings in childrearing and enlisting other mothers to take responsibility for their children's moral training.[26] In accepting this role African Christian women turned their backs on pre-Christian norms, by which female relatives other than the mother had provided sex education, with peer groups monitoring premarital sex-play.

While the ABM women – uniquely, it seems – founded their movement on the issue of adolescent sexual purity, other churches were also wrestling with this question.[27] Discussion about children at the 1912 Transvaal Methodist Manyano convention, for instance, centred "especially on the care of girls, who so often fall into evil ways."[28] By the end of the war, the Anglican women's society on the Reef was also trying to help mothers guide and direct unruly daughters. In all three churches special associations for unmarried girls were set up under the protective aegis of their mothers' manyano organizations, to guard them from "moral downfall." The initiative seems to have come from the African women in each case, although Methodists and Anglicans consulted with the white women leaders in getting the groups started. The issues of chastity and obedience surfaced in the Anglican rural Ciskei in much the same period, at a 1910 conference held at the African women's request to inaugurate the Mothers' Union in Keiskammahoek: "Very earnest was the Address about two weaknesses in Native Home Life, viz, the lack of obedience among children, and of purity among the younger people." The following year a white Anglican nun reported with satisfaction that the "native people seem to have reached so simply and straightly the dominating idea of the Mothers' Union – united, prayerful guidance in the difficult task of the up-bringing of our children by precept and by example."[29]

The manyanos are well known for their uniforms, distinctive for each denomination, adopted by the first or second decade of this century. White mission supervisors, in their drive to standardize blouses and hats for more orderly uniformity, may have unintentionally enhanced the appeal of uniforms, though later they vainly criticized the African members for "over-emphasis[ing] the non-essentials, such as badges, uniform, rules for absentees."[30] One Natal missionary primly observed:

"Considering the multiplicity of 'uniforms' seen in Native country, members of the Mothers' Union would be well advised to make their homes distinctive, and keep their clothes commonplace."[31] But special church garb came to distinguish the devout at a time when Western dress alone had lost its own significance as a symbol of Christian affiliation. Indeed, being "bloused" by the prayer union was a solemn milestone of a woman's religious commitment, a reward for upright living, a public proclamation of marital respectability. The uniform also, Epprecht suggests, has an egalitarian potential: "Even the poorest women could thus rise to positions of status and respect which were otherwise unattainable."[32] The complex cultural borrowings in the choice of outfit and the deep significance attributed to them can be traced back to the African women themselves. Methodists talked for instance, of their red blouses being inspired by British soldiers' red uniforms – they, too, wanted to be "soldiers of the cross" – but coming to symbolize Jesus' red blood washing away sin (hence black skirts) and bringing purity (hence white collars and hats).[33]

White women's organizations, like their black counterparts, were also partially rooted in the coupling of sewing and femininity. The history of the white Methodist Women's Association (later Women's Auxiliary or WA) in the Transvaal reports "companies of women here and there meeting together, perhaps to sew for a bazaar, perhaps to talk over Church affairs, often also getting down to real things, difficulties of the soul-life, blessings received, desires after greater things."[34]

But, in contrast to the manyano, the WA did not explicitly emphasize motherhood in its initial goals, even though the same Esther Burnet and Ellen Cox – both knowledgeable and enthusiastic about black manyanos by virtue of their husbands' ministry to Africans and their own leadership roles – were active in 1915 in centralizing and formalizing the few white women's groups into a WA district council. The WA defined its work as advising the various associations "as to the best ways of helping the womanhood of the Church to reach the highest and best in character and service."[35] The goals were personal growth and practical help, rather than Christian motherhood. In its first constitution, of 1918, the WA set itself the aims: "to promote the spiritual life of the members … to co-operate in assisting the various departments of Church work … to promote the interests of Missionary, Social, and Temperance work."

Although the WA ran daytime meetings for full-time housewives, and recognized the importance of the Mothers' Department to the work of the branches, the founders apparently believed that their members were less in need of help in creating Christian homes than were African converts. Recruitment of members and self-education in running an organization were the WA's priorities:

> The first year or two were spent in organising and educating our forces, rousing interest and enthusiasm in our members, training ourselves to conduct our own meetings and to do everything as efficiently and in as business-like a way as possible. We had to overcome a certain amount of prejudice and even opposition.

The Biblical admonition from Hebrews 10:24 printed on the first membership card, "Let us consider one another, to provoke unto love and to good works,"

258

underlined the importance of church activism. What initially had "first place in the duty and affection of our members" could be seen as an extension of mothering: they took responsibility for the maintenance of the Epworth Children's Homes for white orphaned children, founded in 1921 as the First World War Memorial of the Methodist Church in the Transvaal. Within a decade, 87 white children were in these homes.

In widening their circle of "good works", the WA, prompted by the (white) district chairman's wife, who presided over the Transvaal African manyano, "thought that it was now our duty to care for our sisters of another colour." The WA then raised money to support African "Biblewomen," the first working in Swaziland after 1924, to explain the Gospel to "heathen" women in their village homes, visit the sick, and hold services for them. By 1930, the WA was funding 33 such Biblewomen across South Africa, and 79 by 1961. Operating like a nineteenth-century movement, the white WA also enthusiastically supported two white women missionaries in Pondoland from 1922 to 1925, collected bottles and bandages for medical missions, and raised funds for hospitals, for support of African nurses, and for temperance education among Africans.[36]

In the big urban centres, black and white Methodist women came together on special occasions. When, in 1930, some 200 African women held their annual district manyano at Ndabeni, Cape Town, the Cape WA branches provided some funding "and encouraged them by attending their meetings and holding out the hand of fellowship." Near Pietermaritzburg in that same year, more than 90 WA and some 100 manyano women attended a missionary meeting at Edendale mission.[37]

Each triennial WA report noted the number of white branches, their members, and the total funding they had raised. But the African Transvaal Methodist manyano and the Natal *Isilelo* also organized effective fundraising, for example, to set up a domestic science school at Kilnerton (nearly £4,000 were given in annual shillings over 25 years to improve girls' employment opportunities) and to purchase a farm at Umzinto, where Zulu women said their children could live if they became destitute.[38]

WA records, too, show an awareness of responsibility for the Christian socialization of white youth. The Young Women's Auxiliary (YWA), founded soon after the First World War, had reached a membership of 564 in 31 branches by 1931. The YWA developed a flower mission to the sick, made clothes for converts, organized treats and picnics for Sunday school children, and formed groups to study books such as *The Settlers and Methodism* (after the centenary of the arrival of the 1820 settlers), *The Life of John Wesley*, and the Bible.[39] Still, unlike the drive behind the Zulu *isilelo*, neither the WA nor the YWA demonstrated anxious concern about sexual "purity" of youth. The WA leadership, in 1921, addressed, more generally, "big social problems, especially as regards child-life, and the fostering and educating of the young life of our Church."[40] By 1960, the WA widened its concern about temperance and social welfare, creating a Christian Citizenship Department to deal with issues such as "Temperance Reform, Gambling, Sunday Observance, Marriage Guidance, Race Relations and Social and Moral Welfare." Questions about sexual mores and conjugal relations were subsumed under more general topics.[41] In this relatively late and subsidiary concern about sexual issues, white church members were caught up in a wider Western movement of growing frankness about sexuality. Sex was central much earlier for the African women's groups, partly because the whites who initially helped set the agenda for these groups saw Africans as more "sexual" than whites and less disciplined in sexual behaviour. It seemed to the whites that urbanization, industrialization and Christianity were undermining African "traditional" sexual mores, whereas English-speaking whites had long ago been exposed both to the city and to the Christian moral emphases on responsible motherhood and teenage chastity. Christian movements, on this view, were accordingly crucial in relieving the stresses imposed on African women by monogamy, migrancy, rural impoverishment, urbanization, industrialization, and family and community breakdown.

African women seem to have come together for prayer, primarily as mothers with onerous new obligations as Christian home-makers. White women, for their part, organized primarily as an auxiliary, a service and fund-raising aid to the church. The overriding goal of most white Methodist women's groups, most of whose members were not in paid work, seems to have been to organize good works and find inventive ways to raise money. Thus the Queenstown WA reported in 1930, "All have shown a fine spirit, giving cheerful and happy service to every call. These calls have kept our Visiting, Social and Work Committees busy." Port Elizabeth's "many and varied activities ... included a Box Supper and Concert, a Gift Evening and Sale of Work," while Vryheid's efforts were "bring and buy, cake, and jumble sales, talent money, lantern lecture, and ping-pong tournament."[42]

Preaching, Wailing, and Quiet Devotion: The Spirituality of the Women's Organizations

Both black and white women in the inter-war period drew strength and enjoyment from meeting in church groups, but with contrasting patterns of devotional activity. Enthusiastic missionary observers of the well-attended week-long Transvaal Methodist manyano conventions stressed that the singing among Africans was "indescribable," prayer "the supreme business for which the delegates came." "These native women have a wonderful power in prayer and they use it to the full." Delegates began with dawn prayer and continued through a daily schedule of evangelistic, temperance and testimony meetings, memorial and communion services. "The meetings for testimony were ... very striking." "Unlike many Christian friends of a lighter hue, there was no unwillingness to speak. On the contrary, no sooner did one sister finish her story, than two or three were on their feet."[43]

Descriptions of stirring male preachers confirm that African women's powerful volubility was not gender-specific, but characteristic rather of African church life more broadly. An American Board deputation earlier in the century was particularly impressed by

> the native gift of speech, shall we call it of eloquence? which seems to belong to the Zulu in a remarkable degree. The ease with which they utter their thoughts is extraordinary. They do it with vigor and a power to command attention. Of course there is peril in volubility, and too much should not be

made of it. But it is refreshing to find those who have received the message of the gospel so ready to tell it to others ... There are few dumb Christians among them.[44]

Some whites explained voluble African forms of worship as similar to earlier forms of European Christianity, most notably eighteenth-century Wesleyanism. Mabel Allcock, drawing on conventional racial generalizations, described an evangelistic meeting with that comparison in mind:

The Bantu people are very emotional. They work themselves up into an almost hysterical state. It reminded one of the description of revival meetings in Wesley's day. The red-bloused women all prayed aloud and together, the heathen women rocked and moaned, the babies cried and the little boys peeped through their mothers' blankets to see what this strange sight meant ... it is wonderful how this type of revival service suits the temperament of this wild people.[45]

What missionaries sometimes put down to "wild" African emotionalism has complex roots in oral culture and the history of revivalism. Late-Victorian African Christianity in South Africa was the product of the electric encounter between these two. Its distinctiveness was kept alive into a second and third generation because of growing African leadership between 1880 and 1920. By contrast, the revivalist heritage became attenuated in the white churches, despite its enthusiastic advocacy by key British Methodist leaders in the Transvaal in the 1920s. Different theological traditions seem to have been at work,[46] with Africans more responsive to a directly interventionist, challengingly personal God who answers prayer, and whites driven by ethical preoccupations with service and more reticent about publicly articulating a personal faith in a God who seemed more remote.

Confronted with the emotional spontaneity of the praying manyano women, white missionaries mingled enthusiasm with criticism. Some spoke of the impropriety of women praying through the night. "One hesitates to quench and discourage their eagerness to pray ... yet it is so much mixed up with a sort of excitement and it is so bad for women, mostly mothers of families, to get into the habit of being out all night."[47] Mystical "high church" Anglicans despaired at the African preference for praying "corporately and vocally, not as we do, individually and silently."[48] Activist Americans sometimes lost patience with the African women's attachment to praying and preaching rather than getting down to business and taking "*definite* steps for bettering their home condition."[49]

Isabel Hofmeyr has noted, among the northern Transvaal Berlin Mission community, a surprising weakness of literate Christianity in the face of a tenaciously oral culture. Church services were "appropriated by popular taste which helped to dictate the form and style of holy worship and other mission activites. These almost invariably relied on orality, performance, festival, spectacle and image, or, in other words, the central resources of African culture."[50] The appeal of "praying and preaching" to Africans should be seen in the light of the indigenous traditions of oral expression in which women shared – oratory, folk tales, and praise poems vigorously performed to a convivially responding group.[51] Prayer in precolonial African religion was spoken, corporate, and spontaneous.[52] Africans also valued participation by as many people as possible in public communal deliberations, another emphasis taken over by the prayer groups.

The style of the manyanos, common to all the denominations, had roots also in late nineteenth-century revivalist preaching that sought to induce a kind of anguish over personal sin, with bewailing and confession, and a public commitment to a fresh start. Africans were first exposed to the highly participatory, emotional type of service led by British and American evangelists, their message translated by Africans, in the Cape and Natal in the 1860s and 1890s.[53]

The practice of all-night revival meetings spread widely among black congregations as far apart as St. Cuthbert's in the Transkei in 1896 and Pietersburg in the Transvaal in 1905. In the 1920s, revival services were Transkei Anglicans' principal means of converting the "heathen." Wailing became particularly entrenched in women's groups, perhaps because weeping was seen as more culturally appropriate for women, especially at Nguni funerals. Isililo ("wailing"), the term the American Board women chose for their movement – and clung to when American supervisors wanted them to call it "Women's Welfare Group of the American Board" – refers to the protracted ritual keening of women after a burial. It is associated with the helplessness and submission expected of women at times of sorrow; men, on the other hand, traditionally ended mourning by an aggressive act of ritual hunting.[54] Throughout black Africa, wailing is regarded as typically female, and the singers of stylized funeral laments are invariably women.[55]

In addition, the sociability and mutual support offered by prayer groups helped compensate for the isolation and monotony of the Western nuclear family held up for emulation by the missionaries. Christian ideas of domesticity, too, ensured that women would bear the primary responsibilities of home-making and child-rearing, while the Christian stress on individualism and monogamy simultaneously cut them off from some older communal supports. Although lacking formal women's groups such as those of pre-colonial West Africa, African women in South Africa performed many daily tasks communally with other women and girls, such as collecting wood, water, and thatching-grass, and stamping mealies. Women also came together for leisure activities like dancing or singing. In Nguni communities, particularly, where women married out of their lineage and went to live with their husbands away from their families of birth, solidarity with other women was a necessity. Now, African Christian women turned to other churchwomen as substitutes for kin at times of crisis, sickness, and death. Manyano women would ask their group to "give me a hand to pick up the burden." One woman in trouble said: "I must get some strength from the mothers in this chain."[56]

The devotional life of white women seems less fervent and expressive, and also less group-oriented. Although groups might report "a wonderful spirit of love and fellowship," or a regular day when, "led by one of our members most, if not all, join in discussing a given topic to the help of our spiritual life," or a special "Testimony Meeting, when all present took part," it still seemed to be a matter of note if members participated regularly, as manyano members usually did. So, for a Port Elizabeth white group, "the increasing number of members who have taken part, either in prayer, reading or giving papers" was "an interesting feature" of their weekly meetings. The emphasis was much more formal than in African groups, with "excellent addresses" which were "very much appreciated" or papers which "inspired, encouraged and helped," on such topics as "Bible Study, Temperance, Missionary and Social Work."[57] White groups generally agreed that a plethora of activity made it hard to attain "the real object of the W.A.," wondering if "the deepening of our spiritual life" had been sufficiently attended to.[58] According to a 1919 report, "All branches report work of a devotional nature, and we realise that this is our mainspring and our work will utterly fail if this be neglected."[59]

Men, Women, and Power in the Church

It seems that women, black and white, were working with contrasting notions of empowerment, drawing in part on models of male church leadership in their own traditions. For white Methodist women, it was seen as imperative to master efficient business and organizational procedures in order to gain male respect and, hence, to be taken seriously. They had to show that they, too, could run meetings "properly," and make a sizeable financial contribution to church growth. African women's priorities also reflected, in part, the well-established patterns of gender relations in the African church; women must prove that they, like male preachers, could pray extempore and sway a meeting by their eloquent preaching.[60]

African Christian women early in this century were eager to preach. A white Anglican nun wrote from the Transkei in 1916:

> We have been making great efforts to guide and control the zeal of the Christian women who were described by one of themselves as "thirsty for (the work of) preaching." There is no need for paid Bible women here, for all the women want to preach, either to the heathen or to each other. Their zeal is excellent, but their knowledge is not always equal to it, and many of them are possessed by the idea that souls can only be won through noisy ranting.[61]

Despite this hunger for preaching, only rarely did African women's zeal for oral expression of their faith lead to leadership positions in mixed public gatherings. Perhaps they were resigned to the limitations missionaries placed on their leadership and preaching role, and the opposition they might face from jealous black male clergy. Manyanos provided a segregated, "safer" sphere of female religious oratory. When a certain Mrs. Somngesi, for instance, who had organized the Primitive Methodist Prayer Union in the Orange Free State and Aliwal North, applied in 1917 to be listed on the Church Plan as an Exhorter, some African men "argued that if a woman was granted the privilege many more would want to come on because 'You know what women are.'"[62] In 1921 Rosalina Kumalo of the same denomination – it is worth remembering the tradition of women's preaching in Primitive Methodism[63] – succeeded in getting a church erected at Consolidated Main Reef on the Witwatersrand for the evangelization of "raw" compound dwellers. With a band of fellow believers, she visited there regularly, exerting "great influence" as a "born orator" with "exceptional energy," as the white superintendent reported. After union with the Wesleyans in 1931–32, Kumalo's church building for the miners was dismantled and she was driven out of her own township church "because the new parson and others did not favour vigorous women orators who surpassed them in influence."[64] Thousands of African men could, on the other hand, channel their oratorical eloquence into "local preaching," a vital arm of Methodist expansion. For example, in 1931, the Transvaal Methodists had 3,647 African local preachers, 36 African evangelists and 55 African ministers.[65]

African women not only wanted to preach but to lead evangelistic efforts, as male African revivalists had done in Natal in the 1870s and 1890s, expressing a new self-confident African Christian expansionism.[66] But the social and theological tenor of Christian communities confined these desires to the "women's sphere." Not until some fifteen to thirty years after African men were doing so, did African laywomen and ministers' wives hold evangelistic conferences and begin to preach to potential converts. Ecclesiastical authority clamped down on women's evangelism. On the Reef, for example, white church leaders took titular and constitutional control of the manyano prayer unions, installing a white female president and rewriting the movement's aims.

Black male leaders themselves were ambivalent about female autonomy and their often exuberant revivalism. Resentful African Methodist women, in the 1920s, were repeatedly reminded that each prayer group still came under the control of the local African leaders' meeting.[67] In the early 1920s, black Anglican clergy on the Reef were sharply divided on whether women's all-night prayer meetings should be blessed or banned, and suspicions of African husbands in the Natal churches in the 1930s spread scandal and slander about such gatherings.[68] Two African male ministers of the American Board, at the inaugural regional conference for the isililo in Natal in 1912, told the women that they must elect a chairman, secretary, and treasurer, and "advised the delegates to deport themselves in a proper and tranquil manner because the officers of the Durban Corporation might get upset by the excessive noise they were making."[69]

The creative, self-confident women's prayer groups stopped short of breaking away from the missions and forming independent churches, partly because they were only one aspect of the local church congregation, even if the very "backbone," as was repeatedly asserted. In their marginal position women were free to experiment, to learn from other denominations, and to make Christianity their own, unconfined by rigid conceptions each denomination had for male, but not for female, ministry. Women could preach in prayer unions, for example, without becoming literate or undergoing formal training. As a woman testified at a convention in the 1920s, "I cannot read the Book. I took the red blouse [the uniform] and daily I am out preaching to the heathen."[70] Yet what seemed empowering then, was later deplored by some women. In the 1960s, an African worker for the Mothers' Union reported with regret of a group in the Transkei, that "they cannot read or write, the only thing they can do is to preach and to pray."[71]

Considerable enterprise, vitality, and self-confidence were required for spreading the Word, and the black women's actions do not fit an image of cosy homemaking. The isililo grew because a group of women, led by Mrs. Nomali Gobhozi and Mrs. Ntolo Kaula (though joined for part of the way by some men) walked, "singing hymns and stopping for the night on the way ... like vagrant wanderers because of this great gospel of Isililo," to six American Board mission stations.[72] Mrs. Gqosho, founder of the Transvaal Methodist Manyano, spread the movement by revivals throughout the district, followed by a convention in 1908 arranged (to the admiring surprise of the white male superintendent) entirely by women. They brought "their own food or money, and many of them slept on the floor of the church."[73] The 1915 Manyano conference in Swaziland dispersed for two days to preach in the countryside to "the heathen women in the kraals." A band of some hundred women, led by Ellen Cox and five African ministers' wives and bearing a banner sent by the ladies of Nottingham, England, sang hymns at various settlements, gave testimonies, prayed with the people, and invited those who "cried for mercy" to the evening service.[74] A group of seven black Primitive Methodist women raised £25 and went by train from Johannesburg to Aliwal North and Zastron in 1919 – a round trip of a thousand miles – to thank the church for its support and hold revival services. Their secretary described with zest the effective female preaching.[75]

The Transvaal Methodist Manyano had its first African woman president by 1937. The Mothers' Union, which had a small number of white members as well (segregated by congregation), had no African vice-president until 1948, no African president until 1974. Before these dates white women missionaries had filled the highest offices in both organizations. As the manyanos spread throughout South Africa, white missionary supervisors frequently said they could not attend each weekly meeting. Most gatherings, therefore, were conducted instead by African clergy wives. And where white personnel were numerous, as in the so-called Anglican "settlements" in Sophiatown and Orlando in the 1930s pioneered by SPG missionary Dorothy Maud, the single white women staffworkers concentrated almost exclusively on children, in part because the African wives did not grant unmarried white women much authority or legitimacy in a family-focused spiritual movement.

In white women's groups devotional talks were often given by male ministers,[76] rather than by women lay members. In the black groups, by contrast, wives of African clergy seem to have had more of a guiding role, though both white and black male ministers officiated at large public meetings and at communion services for manyano annual conventions. It was crucial to manyano formation in the Transvaal that the number of ordained African ministers grew substantially among the Methodists after the Anglo-Boer War (from 17 in 1902 to 35 in 1908), since a growing number of ministers or clergy invariably meant a commensurate increase in spouses who came to be regarded as "ordained" themselves, finding in manyanos a vital outlet for their leadership. The ministers' wives' dominance of the prayer unions was highlighted in the "uproar" they made, when, in 1931, the highest manyano office went to a "lay woman." The manyanos' committees, and the offices of secretary and treasurer, both locally and regionally, gave women experience of more formal corporate organizing and record keeping.

In principle, white women in the 1920s could be Methodist local preachers, but the Transvaal country districts, especially, had "an almost unconquerable prejudice against women preachers." There was an excellent woman at Carolina, reported the district chairman, but "the people simply will not come when she is appointed."[77] Much the same ecclesiastical prohibitions and constraints on female leadership in the church at large applied to white women as well as black; yet white women seem not to have developed preaching and leadership gifts to match those of African women. The WA President in 1920 almost lamented women's fund-raising ability:

> My dream of the Women's Auxiliary all these years has been not so much of *money* power, as *woman* power ... there is much work for women to do in the Church, other than the collecting of funds; real woman's work, visiting, teaching, leading.[78]

Hence the celebration of the "outstanding ability" and verbal eloquence of the WA President for 1922–25, during whose term of office WA members addressed the Methodist Conference for the first time. Her colleagues now applauded

> her capable handling of a meeting over which she presides, and her wonderful gift of addressing a gathering of men and women at a moment's notice is known throughout our Connexion ... It was a great moment, and we felt so proud of our President, as she stood before that gathering of men and spoke with such confidence.[79]

Yet white women sometimes preached as well. Women assumed considerable responsibility for raising support for the troops and the general war effort during the Second World War, but also "many a small preaching place would have had to close down for the duration, had not W.A. members stepped into the pulpits when man-power was so woefully depleted,"[80] as a white Methodist woman observed. Still, when, like the African women, WA members came together in large annual meetings, they listened to addresses by men and a few exceptional women rather than seeking opportunities to pray and preach themselves. Their participation was primarily procedural and organizational, receptive rather than expressive. They were more "hearers" than "doers" of prayer and preaching. Both theology and culturally specific notions of appropriate gendered church behaviour seem to have been at work. Most white women expressed their faith corporately by being "doers" of good works and as well-organized fund-raisers. African women needed and desired to validate and demonstrate their Christianity by explicit personal verbal testimony, exposition, and prayer.

Churchwomen's organizations were more important to African women than to white women for three key reasons, ideological, cultural, and ecclesiastical. First, for African women much more overtly than for white women, Christianity gave a new primacy to motherhood, while posing tough new challenges to Christian mothers. Second, a culture that had been primarily oral could take more eagerly to the vocal emphasis of revivalist Christianity, while weeping and confession and repentance were acceptable among African women, who anyhow had been sidelined in traditional religious practice. Third, in the African churches planted by missions, the frustration of women forbidden to preach in mixed church gatherings coincided, at the turn of the century, with the emergence of a generation of educated ministers' wives who were eager and able to assume leadership of all-women's organizations.

African and white churchwomen's groups – among Methodists, at any rate, and perhaps more widely – seem to have exhibited curiously complementary strengths in the first half of this century. Each organization was often berated for its lack of what the other seemed to embody. Thus, African women took eagerly to praying out loud about personal and community needs and to expounding the message of the Bible and the need for repentance, while white women, who seemed to find it hard to share their private needs or to speak in public, concentrated on practical welfare projects and enthusiastic fund-raising. The African prayer unions, by contrast, though effective fund-raisers, determinedly resisted efforts in the 1950s to reshape their meetings to provide more practical instruction and community activism.

And, yet, the broader, constructive social and political impact of African women's prayer unions has been too easily dismissed. Hence one's eager seizing upon Mgqwetho's phrase about manyano as "the shield to ward off the white man's arrows."[81] The role of white women's church groups in either entrenching or challenging gender subordination, racial separation, and class division in twentieth-century South Africa awaits further research – although a case could probably be made for white groups challenging all three to some extent. For black women, one can echo Epprecht's insistence that, for all their contradictions and occasional conservative tendencies, these groups "were and remain a vital element" in the maintenance and rejuvenation of their communities. Even while "generally accepting a gender ideology based on women's subordination to men," such groups "gave women crucial support to enhance their *de facto* autonomy from men." They "helped to provide a sense of direction, accomplishment and pride" for women in "what was an otherwise demoralising and deteriorating socio-economic setting."[82]

16

Between Christ and Mohammed: Conversion, Slavery, and Gender in the Urban Western Cape

ROBERT C.-H. SHELL

Christianity and Islam both appeared in South Africa in the early years of the Dutch East India Company's settlement of the Cape of Good Hope. Numerous Europeans, most of them at least nominally Christian, visited the Cape as sailors and soldiers of the East India Company, and some stayed there as settlers. The Cape also served as an exile for political leaders defeated by the Company in its Asian wars. Most of these exiles were Muslims, as were some of the approximately 2,000 "convicts" deported by the Company from its Asian possessions. Some of the approximately 63,000 slaves imported to South Africa between 1653 and 1808 originated from areas in south and south-east Asia, and later in east Africa, all influenced by Islam. Consequently, from the 1650s, near the confluence of the Atlantic and Indian oceans, adherents of the two great universalist world religions jostled on the waterfront of Cape Town, the world's newest port, later to be called the mother city of South Africa.

In Cape Town one may speak of some real competition for souls between Christianity and Islam. Missionaries of both Christianity and Islam were active in the town by the late nineteenth century. But much earlier, the policies of the ruling Company and the labour policies of the European settlers favoured and hindered – at different times – the growth of both religions, as did complex and interlocking social processes of slavery, manumission, emancipation, and marriage. Until well into the nineteenth century Cape Town maintained a more fluid social structure than the rest of European-ruled South Africa in matters of residential mixing, inter-racial sex, and associations of race and class.[1] There was, in consequence, more room for social and commercial interaction between Christians and Muslims, a growing tolerance, and even a few intermarriages.

Settlers, Exiles, and Slaves: The Coming of Christianity and Islam

Most of the European settlers brought their Christian heritage with them to South Africa, particularly the several hundred French Huguenots who arrived after 1688. The Europeans had, however, little missionary vision. One Stellenbosch Huguenot minister, Pierre Simond, planned to convert the Khoikhoi but accomplished nothing. In 1705 the Rev. Henricus Beck received official congratulations when he converted a Muslim.[2] Yet neither the Company, which was inhibited by considerations of cost, nor the Dutch Reformed ministers, whom the Company appointed and paid, undertook any systematic missionary effort among the indigenous peoples or the slaves from 1652 to 1795, the period of Company rule. Similarly, few settlers evangelized among the slaves under their authority, in part because they came to believe they would have to free any slaves who became Christian.[3]

Though the official Dutch Reformed Church was based in Cape Town, as early as 1694 most Christian congregations were rural. Islam, by contrast, was based primarily in the port of Cape Town, and among a handful of early Muslim exiles living at outposts of the colony such as Robben Island and Constantia. It was spread by word of mouth by *hafez* (persons who had memorized the Quran), and in ceremonies conducted at night in secret mosques in Muslim homes (*langes* or *masjids*), and later, at the end of the eighteenth century, when the Muslim congregation had become larger, in the town's quarry. The secrecy was necessary: the laws of the Dutch East India Company imposed heavy penalties, including confiscation of the slave and a stiff fine, "on all who suffered their slaves to embrace the tenets of Mohammedanism."[4] Penalties were sometimes fiercer: in the 1712–13 court case of Santrij, a Muslim "*Javaans Paap*" (Javanese Pope), – who, in the judge's words, presided over a "parliament of vagabonds" – the prosecutor asked the suspect "whether under the cloak of piety, he had not brought all the slaves and convicts to his faith?" He answered that he had, "because he was their religious leader [*Paap*] and that this was a Javanese custom."[5] The court sentenced Santrij to have his tongue cut from his mouth (the punishment for his evangelizing) and to be burnt alive (the punishment for his incendiary tendencies).[6]

Among the early Muslim political exiles to the Cape was a man named Shaykh Yusuf, widely regarded as an Islamic saint. Yusuf, born in 1626 at Macassar (on Sulawesi in modern Indonesia) was a relative of the King of Ghoa, the ruling dynasty of Sulawesi. Converted to Islam, he went on *hajj* (pilgrimage to Mecca) at age 18.[7] His teachings earned him veneration, which followed him to South Africa after his banishment there in 1694. At the Cape, even his expectorated spittle was collected and revered.[8] His home, near Faure, became a gathering spot for Muslims and runaway slaves until his death in 1699. Though he was not the first Muslim at the Cape, he is regarded as the founder of Islam in South Africa.[9]

Most early Cape Muslim leaders came from the ranks of the convicts (*bandietten*), not the political exiles. Bandit *imams* (Muslim pastors) – labelled on the convict rolls "Mahometaanse priesters" (Mohammedan priests) – trickled into the Cape throughout the eighteenth century: among them, Sapoer (n.d.), Abdul Radeen (n.d.), Abdullah van Batavia (n.d.), Aloewie Said van Mokka (1744), Hadjie Mattaram (1746), Agmat, Prins van Ternate (1766), Al Jina Abdullah (1766), Imam Fakirij van de Negerij Niassinna (1746), Noriman van Cheribon (1767), Imam Abdullah (1780), Imam Noro (1780), Imam Patrodien (1780), and simply Achmat (1795).[10] Islam flourished among the convicts even after the end of Dutch rule. In 1829, the Rev. William Elliot, in charge of Christian evangelism among Muslims, was surprised to find that "there are at present eighty three convicts lodged in the battery, about half of whom are Mahometans."[11]

These early imams, who formed the core of the Cape's *ulema*, or Muslim clergy, became a hereditary class. An imam interviewed in 1824 said that his father was a "Mohammedan priest," who "came to the colony from Java when about sixteen years of age; he was brought here as a slave, and was purchased by an old Malay priest, who gave him his freedom after instructing him in the Mahometan faith, and when he died, my father succeeded him as priest."[12] This hereditary group of early imams included the first Cape Muslim to go on hajj (Hajji Hassan al-Din ibn 'Abd Allah, or as the English street directories listed him, "Carel Pilgrim") and also the first Muslim scholars to write the now celebrated religious and other manuscripts in the new Arabic-Afrikaans. Several of these nineteenth-century imams were also ancestors of the twentieth-century Muslim clergy.

In the Household of Abraham: Slavery, Manumission, and Religion

Slaves came to South Africa from the Indonesian archipelago, Bengal, the South Indian Coast, Sri Lanka, Madagascar and the Mascarenes, Angola, and the east coast of Africa, bringing a broad spectrum of religious and mystical beliefs and rites. The Dutch East India Company had a firm policy of baptizing its own slaves born at the Cape, but among the slaves owned by the settlers (the overwhelming majority) neither the Company, nor the Church, nor the settlers themselves engaged in significant proselytization. Owners who converted their slaves to Christianity were bound by vague Dutch Reformed precepts, though not by law, to bring them into the realm of legal and social equality. Most important, the right of an owner to sell a fellow Christian was circumscribed. Johann Georg Bövingh, a visiting missionary, noted, shortly before 1714, that a separate congregation could be easily formed from the few Christianized slaves, "since many have a substantial experience of Christianity from many years' contact and ask to be become Christians themselves." Yet the slaves' masters, "as I hear from many people are not willing to agree, as slaves who are baptized cannot be sold again."[13] By 1799 most slave owners believed they would lose the right to sell their slaves if the slaves became Christian.

Interestingly, Muslim slave owners were under similar, though Quranic, strictures. Both Christians and Muslims derived a similar prohibition against selling coreligionists from the Old Testament example of Abraham, who circumcised all his household, including his slaves, thus making them part of his familial responsibility. Imam Muding explained to a British official in 1824 that a "Mahometan who has purchased a slave is forbidden by the principles of his faith to sell him, and they are never sold. If they embrace the faith, they [and their children] are enfranchised at the death of their owner."[14]

In Dutch Reformed Christianity, baptism (which replaced the Old Testament rite of circumcision) was the key to both church and society. Although there is no baptism ceremony mentioned in the Quran, Cape Muslims derived a similar rite from the *Sunnah* (the practices of the Prophet), which encourages circumcision for boys, between seven and forty days after birth. In 1824, according to a Muslim contemporary, Imam Ackmat, infants had to be brought to the mosque seven days after their birth (it was eight days in the Dutch Reformed faith), and then named by the imam.[15] Little had changed thirty years later when John Schofield Mayson, a visiting British officer, observed: "With the naming of their offspring the Malays[16] have little to do. The all-efficient priest [sic] bestows a name on the infant chosen out of the nomenclature of the prophets, from the day or month of his birth, or from some other source."[17] By the twentieth century, imams had appropriated the term "baptism" itself; as one observer noted: "Mohammedans seem to have some rites, that take the place of Baptism and holy Communion, called by the same name."[18] There is some evidence that the former rite as an equivalent Muslim ceremony was termed *doopmaal* – perhaps after the Christian ceremony. This word later became *doekmal*, still part of the Cape Muslim traditions.[19]

In general, the several hundred slave men who bought their freedom or received it as a gift from their owners, did not turn to Christianity, but by the 1790s they were turning to Islam. By the 1790s there was a small Muslim mercantile community in Cape Town, described by both travellers and colonists. They used their relative prosperity to free their own slaves and set a dramatic example by manumitting others, including Christian slaves. The Christian missionary, John Philip, noticed in 1831 that many slaves once owned by Muslims had been freed: "I do not know whether there is a law among the Malays binding them to make their slaves free," he wrote, "but it is known that they seldom retain in slavery those that embrace their religion, & to the honor of the Malays it must be stated many instances have occurred in which, at public sales, they have purchased aged & wretched creatures, irrespective of their religion, to make them free."[20]

Few such acts of compassion for their fellow religionists could be found among the Christian slave owners. William Elliot of the "Mission to Moslems," in explaining why, before 1838, the majority of Cape Town slaves had turned to Islam, stressed that the "systematic benevolence" of the Muslims in manumitting slaves more readily than the Christians held out "a powerful inducement to the heathen, yea, even the nominally Christian to embrace Islamism." Even more important, Elliot believed, was "the pleasure which slaves appear to enjoy, in being of a religion different from or opposed to that of their owners ... The most prominent wish in the heart of a slave is to dissolve every connexion between himself and his master – he wishes to have as little as possible in common with his master."[21] Here Elliot points to a powerful, but little discussed, anti-colonial motivation for Islamic conversion. Converts to Islam owed no intellectual inspiration to the European presence. Every Muslim knew his or her religious identity was autonomous. A Muslim convert, *ipso facto*, was no "Uncle Tom."

Islam's authentic universalism, too, had a powerful appeal. Even a slave could be a leader in the Cape Muslim religious community. Achmat of Bengal, a slave in the eyes of the settlers, was, for example, appointed chief imam of the Dorp Street mosque in 1806. Similarly, in 1823, Abdulgaviel, also a slave in settler terms, became the Simonstown imam.[22] Muslim universalism sometimes extended into the domestic sphere; some Muslim slaves ate at the same table as their Muslim masters. By contrast, Maart van Mosambiek, a qualified and intellectually gifted slave, who professed Christianity and was owned by the London Missionary Society in the early nineteenth century, and who was eager to evangelize "among the natives," was neither baptized nor freed and enjoyed no equality in the radical LMS.[23]

When, in 1838, the British parliament abolished slavery, the complex and poisoned associations between the colonial state, the hated institution of slavery, and Christianity were dissolved. At emancipation some Cape Town Muslims wrote an open letter to the governor published in the press, expressing their gratitude for being "restored to the possession of our natural rights as men, and admitted to all the privileges of free British subjects by the magnanimity of the King and people of

England."[24] Soon after, imams holding Union Jacks led a procession of Muslims through Cape Town that would later transform itself into Cape Town's annual New Year Carnival.

Yet, in the long run, emancipation aided Christianity more than Islam. The massive machinery of Victorian missionary endeavour, freed of the immoral association with slavery, began to gain more and more Christian converts. By 1891, the census enumerator recorded several hundred "Malays" (that is, persons probably of Muslim ancestry) as Anglican, Catholic, Congregationalist, Moravian, Lutheran, and even Dutch Reformed.[25]

Claiming the Promise of Universalism: Conversions through Marriage

During the era of slavery, the Cape Muslim free black population, predominantly male and not growing by natural increase, remained small. Most slaves who converted to Islam were male, while a number of women converted to Christianity through marriage or concubinage with settlers. These women were attracted by the civic advantages of Christianity. Under the Statutes of India, which governed the Cape under the Dutch East India Company, only persons baptized in the Dutch Reformed, and later the Lutheran, churches were regarded as burghers or citizens, and only they could gain civic advantages through Christian marriage. Although by 1804 Cape Colonial law recognized all Christian (including Catholic) marriages, no slave or "heathen" could marry.

Between 1652 and 1795 some privately owned women slaves were baptized as Christians, not because of missionary efforts or evangelism, but because of the surplus of Christian male colonists who, desiring to marry, could not find suitable settler women. To the European bachelor's mind a slave bride was better than no bride. Over this period there were, on average, four European males to one European female, and, as a direct consequence, around 1,000 slave and Khoikhoi women married into Christian settler society, according to marriage records. A male settler wishing to marry a female slave had to instruct her in Christian precepts and in the Dutch language, then arrange for her to be baptized as a Christian, and pay a manumission bond to the *diaconij* (deaconry). In the case of slaves owned by the Company, the groom had to sign an antenuptial contract, providing that if he predeceased the bride, the cost of the bride's upbringing would be paid for out of the estate.

From a woman's perspective there were profound reasons for conjugal conversion. The matrilineal descent of slave and free status as set forth in Roman Dutch law dictated that children of women slaves remained slaves. Children of freed slaves, on the other hand, were born free. For a woman, the shortest route to her and her children's freedom was a Christian marriage. Marriage of a woman slave to a settler always meant Christian conversion for the bride and also civil freedom. This channel for escape from slavery through marriage was apparent from the founding of the colony. The slave Catharina of Salagon of Bengal, for example, was baptized and manumitted just prior to her wedding in 1656 to Jan Woutersz. This escape hatch applied to political exiles as well. A granddaughter of Shaykh Yusuf married into the Dutch settler Retief clan in the 1720s and thereby entered the ranks of the free. However, over the subsequent century, as the number of free women increased, the demand for slave wives declined among settler males, along with the baptism of adult slave women.

Given the high proportion of males to females in the settler population, only slave women could escape slavery through marriage to a European. Proportionally fewer slave men than women were manumitted, and none for purposes of marriage. However, slave women could also escape slavery by marrying Muslim men. Early in the nineteenth century, some Muslim males purchased and married female slaves, although these marriages were not recognized by the laws of the colony. In 1807, Frans van Bengal, the Muslim field chaplain at the Battle of Blaauwberg, applied for the manumission of his slave Marianna, whom he had married in a Muslim rite. In 1828 Imam Hadje Medien applied for the manumission of his wife and children, formerly his slaves. At roughly the same period the aristocratic Dutch missionary Theodorus van der Kemp, in a Christian ceremony, married a slave woman from Madagascar, a union whose interracial and interclass character caused a sensation throughout the colony.[26] In 1863, in a further sensational wedding, the Muslim missionary Abu Bakr Effendi married a 15-year-old Christian English woman, after a courtship which, the press uncharitably reported, was conducted with the help of an Arabic/English dictionary. These marriages and attendant conversions breaching class, race, civil status, language, and religious background were potent public demonstrations of the universalism implicit in both Islam and Christianity.

Almost no legal benefits accrued to a woman married by Muslim rite. She could not initiate divorce, while her husband had only to announce the word "divorce" three times in order to divorce her. When a Muslim husband and wife were separated by sale, the imam would re-marry the man (but not the divorced woman) since, one imam explained, Muslim men could have more than one wife.[27] A slave woman married in a Christian rite, on the other hand, was accepted as the sole wife in the Christian community, and her children would be brought up as Christians and burghers. The huge Basson clan, for instance, are all descended from Ansiela van Bengal, a household slave of Jan van Riebeeck, in the first generation of settlement.

A further attraction of Christianity for slave women was that, after 1823, Imperial legislation forbade separation of a Christian slave mother from her children, an irksome prohibition to all slave owners who wished to maintain an unrestrained domestic market in slaves. Muslim marriages (and divorces), on the other hand, were not recognized as legal and therefore did not prevent separation of mothers from their children. According to William Wilberforce, the great champion of slave emancipation, Christian Cape slave owners encouraged their slaves to turn to Islam for this reason. The owners wanted their slaves to consider that their conjugal unions had local, community significance, but equally the owners could be reassured that such unions had no legal standing. Most of all, the owners wanted their slaves to remain marketable. Slaves who had converted to Christianity directly threatened the functioning of the free market in the sale of human beings. Between 1810 and 1824 only 86 Christian slave baptisms took place in the entire colony. Remarkably, Christian slave owners were undermining the evangelical rationale of their own religion while encouraging the growth of a Muslim counter culture.

After emancipation, marital conversions to Islam continued, but for quite different reasons. A few Muslim men by the 1850s had achieved considerable status in the colony. Some were successful artisans or retailers, and a handful were substantial property owners. Abstinence from alcohol, which Islam required, had made them desirable slave overseers in the era of slavery and now continued to be an attraction to women, even to some European immigrant women. Lady Duff-Gordon, an English intellectual writing well after emancipation, saw Muslim sobriety and earnestness as the most important reasons for European female conversions to Islam: "Yes, indeed the emigrant girls from England turn 'Malay' [Muslim] pretty often, and get thereby husbands who know not billiards and brandy, the two diseases of Capetown."[28]

Thus the direction of marital conversion changed twice, benefiting Christianity and Islam at different times. In the seventeenth and eighteenth centuries some slave brides became Christians before entering into marriages that conferred citizenship on themselves and social and legal advantages for themselves and their offspring. In the nineteenth century some slave women embraced Islam because their Muslim grooms had freed them. Later, after emancipation, some women, including Christian European immigrants, turned to Islam because Cape Muslim men were not only industrious, but also sober. In principle, both Islamic and Christian marriages offered the prospect of a trans-racial community, but this promise was always constrained by the exigencies of the European-dominated colonial administration and its legal system, which reserved most privileges in the colony for people of European descent.

Town and Country: The Geography of Conversion

The first Christian mission established specifically for slaves, the South African Missionary Society, began in 1799, under the first British occupation of the Cape. Its church, in present-day Long Street in Cape Town, is a cultural landmark. The founder, Michiel Christiaan Vos, a mulatto slave owner, persuaded the Cape government to pass legislation in 1812 reassuring settlers that they were not bound to free their slaves if they baptized them. The stage was now set for Christian proselytization among slaves, since the juridical link between Christian baptism and freedom had been severed. Also, the governing authority was now more tolerant of all Christian denominations and specifically of missionary movements. But it would be an uphill battle: Islam was by then firmly ensconced in Cape Town, an embarrassment to Christian missionaries passing though on their way to the fertile mission fields of South Africa's interior.

The early Christian missions to Cape Town, though energetic, failed. By 1816 they recognized that there would have to be a generously supported, dedicated mission to Muslims if Christianity were to make any progress among the townspeople of colour.[29] This began in 1824 when a "Mission to Muhammadans" was started in Cape Town with a grant of £150 to convert 3,000 Muslims (exactly a shilling per convert). William Elliot, who helped run the mission, was disconsolate at the slow progress of his mission and resigned in 1828, noting that since 1824 "I have been occupied in the ... Mission to the Muhammadan population of Cape Town, under many discouragements arising from the determined hostility, and the insuperable reserve of Muhammadans in reference to Christians, together with their peculiar form of social life, which almost precludes the possibility of approach and the unbounded control which their priests exercise over them."[30] In 1831, John Philip wrote to the directors of the London Missionary Society (LMS): "What was the result of all this formidable apparatus for the conversion of Mahomedans to Christianity? Just what might have been expected. The closing of any door before opened for our entrance ... [only] two Mahomedan slaves had been converted ... the mission ended when Mr. Elliot could get no more children to teach and no Mahomedans to listen to him anymore."[31] Subsequently, nearly all arriving missionaries leapfrogged the heavily Islamicized town to go to much more successful rural and frontier missions among the indigenous peoples.

After the abolition of the oceanic slave trade in 1808, observers and census takers described Islam as an urban religion, and the dominant one among both slaves and freed blacks. That year, the Earl of Caledon, the first civilian British governor of the Colony, wrote to Viscount Castlereagh, the British Secretary for War and the Colonies, that "the ... slaves are mostly from Mozambique, arriving here [Cape Town] in total ignorance, and being permitted to remain in that state, they, for the most part, embrace the Mahomedan faith."[32] The Rev. John Campbell of the LMS found in 1814 about "a hundred men, chiefly slaves, Malays and Madagascars," worshipping in a Cape Town mosque. In his comprehensive 1822 survey of the Cape Colony the comptroller of customs, William Wilberforce Bird, wrote that Islam "is said to be gaining ground among the slaves and free persons of colour at the Cape: that is to say, more converts among Negroes, and blacks of every description, are made from Paganism to the Mussleman, than to the Christian religion."[33] In 1828, the Wesleyan–Methodist mission in Cape Town reported ruefully: "[b]ut, oh, what little fruit has been seen from the labours of Schoolmasters and Missionaries on the children who have been taught the principles of Christianity in this place! With but few exceptions, they follow either a base, sinful course of life, or are ensnared by that awfully prevalent delusion [of] Mohammedanism." Mission reports from the suburbs of Cape Town tell the same story.[34]

Emancipation initiated the first significant wave of urbanization in South Africa. After the British parliament's abolition of slavery in the British Empire took effect in 1838, many freed slaves left their owners in the agricultural areas and moved to town, where many embraced Islam.[35] As John Mason has pointed out, many rural ex-slaves who stayed on their owners' estates also embraced Christianity at this time.[36] Some slaves had been compelled to wait for emancipation before they were allowed to be baptized. As one such slave, Katie Jacobs, reported:

Shortly after our liberation, my husband and I went to Durban [i.e., Durbanville] to be baptized and married. The Rev. [Johannes Jacobus] Beck, who performed the ceremonies, was kept busy from morning to night, as there were hundreds of ex-slaves gathered together for the same purpose. I had often asked my master to allow me to be baptized, but he would never consent – why, I cannot tell.[37]

Since the newly freed slaves could choose between the two religions at emancipation, a double religious revival ensued. Petrus Borcherds, a Dutch Reformed minister, guessed at the relative proportions of converts at emancipation: "Some have attached themselves to Christian churches and institutions, but most, especially in Cape Town, to the Mohammedans, with whom they were previously more or less connected."[38]

But there were also a few Muslims in the rural areas, where, in the boom in wine-farming of the 1820s, Muslims – with their reputation for abstinence – were in great demand as wagon drivers and supervisors. Some white farmers encouraged conversion to Islam after 1838 for this practical reason. By 1848 the Anglican Archdeacon, Nathaniel James Merriman, reported that "the native families" who had settled on a neighbour's farm "were all of Mozambique origin, and were of course, heathens, but that all of them had at least nominally joined the Mohammedans, and loved to be considered as Malays."[39] Some rural Muslims kept their faith secret. For example, Lady Duff-Gordon, who wintered in the tiny inland village of Caledon in the 1860s, provided a telling anecdote of the one Malay tailor in the village. He was, she wrote, "obliged to be a Christian at Caledon, though Choslullah told me with a grin he was a very good Malay [i.e., Muslim] when he went to Cape Town. He did not seem very much shocked at this double religion, staunch Mussleman as he was himself."[40]

Immigration Versus Conversion

Though Islam was spreading impressively in the towns among locally born people of colour, another process began to counterbalance these gains, as European Christian immigration, from the 1820s onward, flowed into the towns and villages of the Cape Colony. By 1891, 27 per cent of all urban Christian Europeans had been born outside the colony, compared to only one per cent of urban Muslims. While both religions increased through natural reproduction and conversion, Christianity enjoyed an extra boost through steady immigration, which, by 1891, had virtually Christianized all the Cape towns, overshadowing the Muslim gains in the locally born population, even in Cape Town.[41] Islam continued to grow in absolute terms, from 3,000 in 1822 to 15,000 Muslims in 1891, but by that year Christians easily outnumbered the Muslims.

Yet it was precisely when the triumph of Christianity seemed assured that a pessimistic conviction took root among many devout Christians that "Slam's Kerk is die Zwart Man's Kerk" (the Islamic church is the black man's church);[42] here "black" was taken to mean not only the Coloureds, among whom Islam had long flourished, but the Africans as well. The Reverend Thomas Fothergill Lightfoot, in charge of the Anglican "Mission to Moslems," noticed in 1900 that "many representatives of the African tribes" had become converts to Islam. Later, during the First World War, when the Muslim Turks were enemies of the British Empire, there was further anti-Muslim hysteria and exaggeration of Muslim gains. Gustav Bernhard Gerdener, a Stellenbosch theologian and missionary, noted in 1915 that "the thousands of Moslems in the Rand [goldmine] compounds are enthusiastic propagators of their religion" and that "many of the raw natives return to their homes strongly under the influence of Islam," though he admitted that reports of "hundreds of Moslem missionaries" in the Rand compounds were manifestly exaggerations.[43]

In fact, the increase in the conversion to Islam had occurred mainly between 1770 and 1842, and, by 1900, was a phenomenon of the past. In 1913 the government printers of the new Union of South Africa published the results of its first census (taken in 1911), which showed that Christians, most of whom were white, numbered 45.7 per cent of the total population. More than half of the population was listed as having "no religion," which meant, in most cases, adherence to African religions. The new Union had only a tiny leavening of 45,904 Muslims – 0.8 per cent of the total population. Among the "Coloureds," Muslims numbered only 6.15 per cent. The disparities between Christianity and Islam have since grown even more, chiefly because of the massive adherence of Africans to Christianity. In 1990, the proportion of Christians in the total population had soared to 76 per cent, while that of Islam had increased only slightly, to 1.13 per cent, which included Indian Muslims from Natal (a separate group not discussed in this chapter).

At the founding of the colony, when the world's two great universalist religions were simultaneously introduced, the stage was set for religious conflict. It was even possible that South Africa might have become predominantly Muslim, as seemed to be happening in the late eighteenth and early nineteenth century. However, the abolition of slavery, and hence the ending of the advantages the slave regime gave to Islam, the massive success of Christian missions outside Cape Town, and the continuous immigration of Christian Europeans counteracted the spread of Islam in the towns and combined to make South Africa an overwhelmingly Christian country.

17

Ambivalence, Antipathy, and Accommodation: Christianity and the Jews

MILTON SHAIN

Ambivalence

For the most part, Jews in the colonized "New World", including South Africa, did not go through the formal struggle for emancipation European Jews experienced in the eighteenth and nineteenth centuries with all its scars. A South African legacy of systematic discrimination against non-Protestants did, however, affect relations, to some extent, between the Christian majority and the Jewish minority,[1] with Jews denied the right to settle at the Cape during the Dutch East India Company period (1652 to 1795). The Batavian administration (1803 to 1806) repealed that restriction, and their administrative heirs, the British, maintained the repeal. However, Jews did not have rights accorded to Protestants in the South African Republic (Transvaal), where Dutch-speakers settled after the Great Trek. The *Grondwet* (Constitution) of the Republic, identifying the Dutch Reformed church with the state, denied non-Protestants the right to vote, to hold military posts, to assume the offices of president, state secretary, or magistrate, to become members of the First or Second Volksraad (National Council) or superintendents of natives in the mines. Nor were Jewish children permitted to attend government schools. Government subsidies were granted only to schools conducted in the Dutch language. In the Orange Free State, whose constitution separated church and state, the Dutch Reformed Church received Volksraad recognition, and until 1877 Jews were forbidden to serve on a jury.[2]

When the constitution of the South African Republic was drafted in 1858 (and revised in 1889) there were few non-Protestants among whites in South Africa. Jews did have cordial relations with the state and even held positions within its machinery despite the structures denying their civil rights. The constitution was based not on antisemitism in particular but on the Boers' desire to retain their sovereignty in the face of British expansion. The reluctance of the Boer leaders to change the constitution to provide full rights for non-Protestants, despite substantial pressure from Catholics and Jews, was governed by the Boers' general mistrust of others and their fear of being swamped by *uitlanders* (foreigners). Periodically the government singled out Jews for praise, President Paul Kruger saying in 1892 that he respected "the Jewish and other faiths without distinction" and hinting that Jews would "attain civil rights if they proved their trustworthiness."[3]

In the Cape Colony, where the state gave financial support to churches at its discretion until 1875 (see p. 59), church and state were formally separate.[4] The British governor, Sir Harry Smith, informed the Jewish community, in 1848, that all religious denominations were "equally valid" and that Jewish interests were "as blended with the people at large, for whether a man is a Jew or a Christian, he is equally protected by the law, as I believe equally acceptable in the eyes of God."[5] An act of 1860 empowered the government to appoint Jews as marriage officers[6] and another act eight years later proscribed any discrimination or penalties based on religious affiliation.[7] Such steps reflected classical nineteenth-century British liberalism, which was rooted in respect for the Judaeo–Christian tradition.[8] Christians contributed liberally to the building of Cape Town's first synagogue in 1848[9] and subscribed to a fund for 500 Jewish victims of a devastating fire in Bawe, Poland, in 1861.[10] In Port Elizabeth they contributed towards a synagogue fund,[11] as they did also in Oudtshoorn, where a Christian, M. Black, served as honorary secretary of the synagogue building committee.[12] In 1881 Christians gave substantial support to a Jewish fund for the victims of riots in Russia. "These disgraceful acts," exhorted the *Cape Times*, "have been brought on a people guiltless of anything but a difference of race and religion."[13] The Rev. A.F. Ornstien of the Cape Town Hebrew Congregation proclaimed in a New Year's sermon in 1883 that Jews in South Africa enjoyed the "freedom to make an honest livelihood, undisturbed by the persecutions to which their race was being exposed in other parts of the world."[14] Five years later he expressed similar views while laying the foundation stone of the Oudtshoorn synagogue: "The Jew and his Christian neighbour," he told a gathering of between 400 and 500 persons, "worked together in harmony."[15] In 1891 Kimberley's Mayor, E.H. Jones, led an interdenominational protest against the persecution of Jews in Russia, in which Catholics, Presbyterians, and Wesleyans supported a resolution deploring Russia's behaviour and its failure to enshrine religious liberty among its national human rights.[16]

And yet, beneath that surface harmony, and more consistent with the earlier denial of rights, an anti-Jewish stereotype was developing among Christians, its contours clearly visible by the 1890s, when an influx of eastern European Jews transformed the hitherto essentially bourgeois and acculturated Anglo-German Jewish community. Jewish merchants began to be accused of illicit diamond buying on the diamond fields and of business malpractices in rural areas. Special targets in the larger centres were the "Peruvians" or Russian Jews, perceived in Johannesburg, in particular, as associated with the illicit liquor trade and the seamier sides of the city's social life.[17] From the 1890s there was a growing movement in the Cape Colony to curtail the immigration of the eastern European Jews.[18]

An even more sinister dimension of the negative racial stereotype was the linking of Jewish financiers with conspiritorial international networks of capital, a traditional accusation of antisemitism. J.A. Hobson captured the view in his reports from Johannesburg to the *Manchester Guardian*, attributing the Anglo-Boer War to the interests of a "small group of international financiers, chiefly German in origin and Jewish in race."[19] In the postwar years "Hoggenheimer," a vulgar cartoon caricature of a Jewish financier, with a semitic nose and fleshy lips, appeared widely in the general press, symbolizing on a higher plane the assumed machinations of the Jewish pedlar and of the illicit diamond and liquor dealer.

The anti-Jewish stereotype in South Africa was of course – at least in part – a reflection of traditional European stereotypes. But it was also firmly rooted in and enhanced by a South African historical context and a local milieu. In the South

African rural areas Jews often were creditors or suppliers to struggling farmers, who, not realizing that structural social changes were undermining their old security, now projected their feelings of alienation and displacement onto this readily available symbol of change.

In certain quarters at least, Jews were perceived through a theological more than a financial prism; sermons and religious literature and comment – mostly, but not exclusively, among pietist Dutch-speakers – often portrayed the Jews as a people who had deviated from their roots or lost their way by failing to accept Christian truth. Thus, in 1897, a certain "G," in a letter to De Kerkbode, the official organ of the Dutch Reformed Church (NGK), asserted that the Jews, having departed from their ethical foundations and having become secularists, harboured a deep-seated hatred for Christianity. Their hope for the coming of the Messiah abandoned, Jews, according to "G," sought money and power.[20] This letter provides a classic illustration of how theologically based conspiratorial views could be secularized and manipulated to suit a modern age.

The notion of Jewish deviance was cited by another correspondent to De Kerkbode in 1898, who questioned the so-called "historical mission" of the Jews. Why would Jews always live among similarly monotheistic peoples?[21] "G" had identified Jews as a subversive threat; this correspondent viewed them as a spent force. Still, both letters show that religion could be a formative influence on perceptions in late nineteenth-century South Africa. Christian responses, too, were scathing to a speech by Rabbi Joseph Hertz of the Witwatersrand Hebrew Congregation, who to a Jewish audience in 1898 had, so it was said, denigrated Jesus as a mere ordinary Jew who had been crucified for rebellion. Because the world was still divided and without peace, Hertz maintained, Judaism's challenge remained and would be ultimately fulfilled.[22]

The newspaper Land en Volk, which had, for some time, adopted an anti-Jewish stance,[23] replied to Hertz that Jews' ideals were not always "noble," that money was their idol.[24] "Een Christen," a letter writer, supported the paper's sentiments; his earlier sympathy for Jews had disappeared in the wake of Rabbi Hertz's statements. In a reference to the Jewish struggle for civil rights in the South African Republic, he recommended all to read De Joodsche Wet Onthuld: Talmud Studien (The Jewish Law Unveiled: Talmud Studies) to understand Jewish opposition to Christianity.[25]

The Rev. James Gray of Pretoria, a Presbyterian, also responding to Hertz's speech, criticized his understanding of the historical record, and argued that, since their dispersion, Jews had not "been the pilot that ... steered the world." All "higher things," he contended, had been the Christian church's work.[26] The Anglican dean of Cape Town warned his own flock on Good Friday of 1899 that Jews were gathering in their synagogues at Passover to curse Gentiles.[27] The Cape Times berated the Dean for speaking, "however unintentionally in the accents of Judenhetze that disgraces the Continent of Europe, and the anti-Dreyfus fury that degrades France." It was ridiculous, it said, to "throw up" the crucifixion at the modern Jew, "the cultivated ones at any rate," who "far from reviling profess a high respect for the ethical teaching of Jesus."[28]

Paul Kruger, a missionary-minded Christian who had endeared himself to the

Jewish industrialist, Sammy Marks, appears to have defended Jews in the "naive hope" that they would eventually come to the "true faith of Christ," "if they are properly defended."[29] He spelled out his views in a detailed 1899 manifesto explaining why Jews ought to be given citizenship.[30] Throughout the 1890s the NGK attempted to convert Jews – regular reports of their successes appeared in the columns of *De Kerkbode*,[31] – as did some missionaries from abroad;[32] yet the impact upon Jews appears to have been slight.[33] The missionary impetus toward Jewish conversion provoked the Yiddish journalist, N.D. Hoffmann, to write an impassioned defence of Judaism and the Jewish people, a comment specifically on the establishment in Cape Town of a Christian Mission Centre, headed by a Jewish convert to Christianity.[34] Jewish newcomers, it appears, went to the South African Mission for the Jews in Cape Town for free instruction in English rather than to consider its proselytizing message.[35]

The Christian world view also, however, inspired in others great respect for "the people of the Book."[36] Numerous individuals supported the call for Jewish (and Catholic) civil rights in the South African Republic. Others took up the cause of destitute Jews.[37] Against a background of mounting xenophobia the novelist Olive Schreiner, a child of missionaries, passionately supported the Jewish victims of Russian pogroms, and welcomed them to South Africa "not merely with pity, but with a feeling of pride that any member of that great much suffering people, to whom the world owes so great a debt, should find a refuge and a home amongst us ..."[38] Such sentiments were often transformed into support for the neophyte Zionist enterprise.[39]

Yet widespread negative feelings persisted. In 1914, the *South African Jewish Chronicle* made this laconic assessment: "South Africa as a whole – contrary to the expectations of the would be immigrant – does not accord a very hearty welcome and apparently is already regretting that she made it possible for them to come."[40]

Antipathy: Nazism, Afrikaner Nationalism, and Christian Opinion

During the First World War Jews were accused by some of "shirking" or avoiding military service and, in the postwar period, of identifying with radical political causes. The 1922 Rand Rebellion was popularly construed as a Bolshevik plot orchestrated by eastern European Jews. Though classic "Jew baiting" was regarded as unacceptable in mainstream opinion, a new eugenicist discourse maintained that eastern European Jews were unassimilable and were polluting the "Nordic" character of (white) South African society. From the mid-1920s on, calls for exclusion were made across the language and party divides, culminating in the Quota Act of 1930 that brought to a virtual halt eastern European Jewish immigration.[41]

Within a few years antisemitism became an influential component of strident Afrikaner nationalism, fed by an alienated and powerless "poor white" element. It was particularly evident in the rhetoric and actions of the "Shirt" movements, most notably Louis T. Weichardt's Greyshirts in the 1930s, who were inspired by Hitler's triumphs and tactics, particularly "brownshirt" thuggery and Nazi propaganda. At its peak the movement had 2,000 members, its success inspiring a number of similar organizations across the country.[42]

Anti-Jewish hostility in South Africa was further fuelled by the entry of 3,614

German–Jewish refugees in the three years after Hitler's ascent to power in 1933. The groundswell of anti-Jewish feeling included demands from the opposition National Party for Jewish quotas in the professions and other restrictions that resembled the German Nazi agenda. The United Party was prompted to introduce an Aliens Bill of 1937 designed to restrict Jewish immigration, particularly from Germany, though without mentioning Jews by name. The bill failed to satisfy the Nationalists, for whom no Jewish immigration at all was acceptable, their most articulate spokesman, H.F. Verwoerd, editor-in-chief of the far-right *Transvaler*, devoting one lengthy editorial to "The Jewish Question from a Nationalist Point of View." In it he recapitulated the whole corpus of South African (and European) antisemitic discourse: Jews dominated business and the professions, and were unassimilable, alienated from the Afrikaner, and guilty of questionable commercial morality and of use of their money to influence government through the English-language press.[43] By 1937 the "Jewish Question" was no longer the concern solely of fringe fascist groups but firmly entrenched within mainstream white politics, an integral part of "völkisch" Afrikaner nationalism.[44]

Against this background the Witwatersrand Council of Churches in 1937 passed a series of resolutions condemning the spread of antisemitic propaganda and calling on Christians to oppose it as "inimical to the welfare of the country" and as contrary to the "spirit of Christ." The Council proposed that Jews and Christians take joint action to combat movements that fomented dissension and ill-feeling,[45] a call that led to the foundation of the South African Society of Jews and Christians in 1937.[46] Leading public figures and clergymen were involved: the Rev. C.H.S. Runge was president; the vice presidents were the Rt. Rev. G.H. Clayton, Bishop of Johannesburg; the Rev. A.S. Clegg, president of the Witwatersrand Church Council; the advocate Maurice Franks; a member of Parliament, Sir Robert Kotze; the Chief Rabbi, Dr. J.L. Landau; and the Rev. William Nicol, Moderator of the NGK. The Society's objectives were to maintain and promote good relations between Jew and non-Jew and to eliminate causes of friction, through lectures, publications, and social services. Membership of the Society was open to everyone sympathetic to its objectives, and members were to promote its objectives in their own sphere. The Society spread throughout the country, issued several pamphlets and booklets,[47] and founded *Common Sense*, a liberal monthly, in July 1939, with financial support from the South African Jewish Board of Deputies.

A few months after the inauguration of *Common Sense*, antisemitism received further impetus from the South African parliament's divided decision to support the British Commonwealth's war effort against Germany. In counterattack, a powerful anti-war movement was launched, orchestrated by the *Ossewabrandwag* (Ox-wagon Sentinel), a paramilitary authoritarian movement born out of the centenary celebrations of the Great Trek. Throughout the Second World War the appeal of fascism in certain South African circles and, with it, the hate-filled rhetoric of antisemitism, remained overt. In 1940 an avowedly pro-Nazi party, the New Order, was founded by Oswald Pirow. In the early 1940s a range of major National Party publications illustrated how Mussolini and Hitler had influenced the exclusivism of insurgent Afrikaner nationalism in which the Jew had no place.[48] Nationalists and other extremists ignored stories of Axis atrocities, disguising them as allegations of British propaganda. A World Jewish Congress report on the appalling plight of eastern European Jewry in June 1942 failed to generate concern among Nationalists, whose attitudes remained unchanged even in the wake of Anthony Eden's 17 December 1942 statement to the British House of Commons that Hitler intended to exterminate the Jews. Such pronouncements did galvanize the supporters of the war effort, and a number of mass meetings, addressed by non-Jewish leaders and Christian clergy, denounced Nazi barbarism. In the words of the Minister of Labour, Walter Madeley, "the conscience of South Africa has been stirred."[49]

As the desperate struggle against Hitler continued, increasing awareness of the nature of his regime eroded the warm reception formerly accorded in South Africa to Nazi and fascist ideas. Yet nationalist newspapers even as late as December 1945 minimized the magnitude of the Jewish tragedy, concentrating instead in the postwar on the sufferings of the defeated German people, and calling it ironic that German war criminals should be judged at Nuremberg by countries that had dropped the atom bomb on Japan.[50] But pro-government newspapers welcomed the Nuremberg trials, with Prime Minister Jan Smuts expressing great sympathy for the primary victims of Nazi aggression, even though he remained opposed to large-scale immigration of Jews to South Africa, maintaining that Israel was their appropriate destination.

Accommodation: Rapprochement Between Afrikaners and Jews

The "Jewish Question" rapidly receded from the public agenda in the postwar years, as attention moved to the country's mounting black–white racial problems and the National Party's policy of apartheid. To Jews the question had not disappeared. South Africa was now ruled by a party with a long history of antisemitism and with pro-Nazis and other opponents of the war against Hitler among its leaders. Yet Jewish leaders effected a rapprochement with the National Party and settled into a working relationship with the government. Shortly after the war the Greyshirts and New Order disbanded, and in 1951 the ban on Jewish membership of the Transvaal National Party was lifted.[51] In that same year the Society of Jews and Christians and *Common Sense* both ceased operations. In 1953 Prime Minister D.F. Malan returned from a visit to Israel full of praise and admiration for the "Jewish People." The National Party seemed to wish to put the tensions and excesses of the 1930s and 1940s behind it with a united front for the apartheid campaign. In its "apartheid" system, Jews, as whites, were to have a rightful and welcome place. Rapprochement was aided by broad economic growth and, more particularly, by postwar upward mobility, so that by the 1960s, a new Afrikaner bourgeoisie – well-educated, confident, and more optimistic than its forebears – expressed little sense of competition with, fear of, or contempt for Jews.

Nevertheless, anti-Jewish sentiment persisted in certain influential quarters, directed against alleged Jewish involvement in communist as well as in anti-apartheid activities. J.D. Vorster, actuary of the NGK and chairman of the Campaign to Combat Communists, went out of his way to persuade Jews to condemn communism.[52] Despite Vorster's protest that the Church's newsletter "Antikom," which linked Jews with communism, was not antisemitic,[53] it was public knowledge that some associated with the publication were indeed notorious antisemites, among them S.E.D. Brown, editor of the *S.A. Observer*, a blatantly antisemitic and anti-Zionist monthly. In addition to repeating tales of Jewish so-called world conspiracies and Zionist plots, the *S.A. Observer* lauded Arthur Butz's *The Hoax of the Twentieth Century*, a book that denied the Holocaust, the Nazi genocide of European Jewry.[54]

Anti-Jewish hostility in South Africa in the early 1960s was compounded by Israel's support for the African bloc at the United Nations. The government, in retaliation, blocked the transfer of funds raised by South African Jews for the Jewish Agency in Jerusalem.[55] Following Israel's victory over its Arab neighbours in the Six Day War in 1967, relations between Israel and South Africa improved and, by the early 1970s, Pretoria had established close ties with Jerusalem. In 1975 a South African branch of Christian Action for Israel was founded, and in 1976 Prime Minister B.J. Vorster visited Yad Vashem, the Holocaust Commemorative Centre in Jerusalem. The irony of the visit by someone interned during the war for anti-government and pro-Nazi activities was not lost on liberal South African Jews. Yet the overriding message was clear: mainstream Afrikaners now accepted the reality of the Jewish tragedy.

Although antisemitism, in its crude and programmatic sense, was now, apparently, relegated to the past, the Jewish minority still failed to enjoy completely equal rights in the NGK-dominated South African society. In education, for example, in 1967 the government introduced the notion of Christian National Education with Christian character and Christocentric religious instruction (see chap 8., p.4), although Jewish students could withdraw from class to attend their own programmes. Then, too, Jews were threatened by demands raised in some universities to change the Conscience Clause in the founding statutes of the nine earliest universities in South Africa, which stipulated that no test of religious belief could be imposed on any university student or teacher. Groups in the Dutch Reformed Church objected to a "neutral" conception of higher education, but, in the end, only Potchefstroom University was able to modify its Conscience Clause in line with that institution's historic theological origins.[56]

The South African Jewish Board of Deputies kept a watchful eye over the Conscience Clause as it did (together with the Rabbinate) over missionary activity, especially by the Jews for Jesus, an organization established in the 1970s to propagate the idea of Jewish conversion.[57] A range of Christian statements, in books and articles, made it clear that the proselytizing imperative remained operative for many South African Christians.[58] The most obvious claim that South Africa was a Christian country came from the SABC's public relations officer, Retief Uys, explaining why rabbis had no air-time on the newly inaugurated SABC-television service.[59] "South Africa," he said, was a "Christian country," in which "only members of Christian denominations were invited to take part in regular religious programmes."[60] Such comments did not go unchallenged by those Christians who appreciated the plurality of South African religious life. Such realism, coupled with tolerance and broad-mindedness, propelled an ecumenism and an inter-faith dialogue from the 1970s on. This did not lead in South Africa to a significant increase in mixed marriages between Jews and Christians, for which estimates range between 15 and 24 per cent for the 1980s.[61] In 1976 an historic meeting of Jewish and Christian clergy convened in Cape Town to meet Immanuel Jakobovitz, Chief Rabbi of the British Commonwealth. In 1984 a South African chapter of the World Conference on Religion and Peace was formed with clergy from across the religious spectrum.[62] The new respect for religious pluralism was best exemplified in May 1992 when the Chief Rabbi, Cyril Harris, delivered opening prayers for a session of the "Congress for a Democratic South Africa II."

A newer concern among South African Jews has been a growing anti-Zionism among the black and, more particularly, among the Muslim population, informed largely by a third-world Weltanschauung, an equating of Zionism with "racism," allegations of military "collusion" between South Africa and Israel, and an empathy with the Palestinian people. More than two decades ago Melville Edelstein, in a study of a sample of matriculation students in Soweto, found that Africans experienced a greater "social distance" from Jews than from English-speakers in general, although less than from Afrikaners.[63] The students told him that an African who was loth to part with his money was "stingy as a Jew." Edelstein thought that such prejudice arose from New Testament teaching in school and church.[64] Recently Marcia Leveson has examined Jewish stereotypes in the fiction of black writers, and found that a number of blacks (including Coloureds and Indians) see Jews as exploitative and powerful.[65] A 1990 study by the Human Sciences Research Council has confirmed substantial elite African antipathy towards the Jew, compared to a virtual absence, at present, of antisemitism among white elites.[66]

It must not be forgotten that the majority of Africans in South Africa are Christians with a deep attachment to the Bible and Holy Land, a sentiment that could generate an element of' philosemitism (strong respect and sympathy for Jews) or at least a position of neutrality. In the final analysis, however, the record of Christian–Jewish relations in South Africa has been determined not by age-old religious ideas and motifs but by specific circumstances rooted in time and place. For example, the coincidence of exclusivist Afrikaner nationalism confronting Jewish upward mobility and visibility in urban settings undergirded the "Jewish Problem" of the 1930s and early 1940s. But confrontation between Jew and Christian was not inherent in the South African religious framework. No assessment of the Christian–Jewish relationship in South Africa can ignore the public prominence of a number of Jews. Nor can it deny the persistent strain of philosemitism manifested among some South Africans from earliest times. Jews, like other whites, have benefited, sometimes with feelings of guilt, from the comforts and opportunities accorded to whites in what has been a predominantly Christian society.

18

Community Service and Conversion: Christianity among Indian South Africans

GERALD J. PILLAY

A meeting held on 10 October 1851, in Durban, to discuss Natal's acute labour shortage, resolved that "the introduction of the coolies would be the salvation of the colony."[1] After protracted wrangling between the governments of Natal and of India, a first group of 350 Indians arrived in 1860 to provide muscle for Natal's agriculture, especially for the local sugar industry.[2] Within a few years of their arrival their contribution to the colony's economy was widely acknowledged, notably by the leading sugar producer, Sir Liege Hulett, in a parliamentary report.[3]

The vast majority of the 152,184 Indian migrants to Natal between 1860 and 1911 arrived as indentured labourers, most speaking Tamil, Telugu, or Hindi. A small group of "passenger" Indians, mainly Muslim and Gujerati-speaking Hindu traders, who were free British subjects – probably about 1,000 – arrived in the wake of the indentured labourers and the commercial opportunities they created.[4] The labourers had agreed to five- and ten-year indenture contracts with the option to return to India or, should they decide to stay, to exchange their free passage back to India for a piece of land.[5] Most of the first groups of immigrants, unhappy with their ill treatment in South Africa, did return to India. When, in 1872, the British colonial government of India stopped further emigration to Natal,[6] a "Coolie Commission" was appointed by the Natal government to investigate the immigrants' complaints of ill-treatment. The Commission Report led to abolition of corporal punishment of Indian labourers, and to grants of land and provision for schools.[7] Emigration was again allowed from India to South Africa in 1874, but, after a brief period of peace, the boost in the Indian population provoked strong anti-Asiatic feelings. The Wragge Commission found "the majority of the white colonists were strongly opposed to the Indian as a rival and competitor both in agriculture and in commerce."[8] Actually, the threat of Indians as commercial rivals was more perceived than real for only some 10 per cent of them were traders. The others were of the working-class. By 1891, about 60,000, or 94.4 per cent, of them were unskilled labourers, this census figure falling to only 89 per cent by 1904.

The wide antipathy to Indians led to repeated demands that immigration cease and that Indians already in South Africa be repatriated – demands that persisted until the 1960s. Thus, Indians in South Africa were beset from the start not only by socio-cultural and political insecurity, and by severe legal restrictions;[9] after 1948, their condition was even further exacerbated by the apartheid laws that took aim at them directly.[10]

By 1911, at the end of Indian immigration, 152,184 immigrants had arrived. Of these, nine in ten, some 137,099, were Hindus, 12,935 were Muslims, 2,150 (1.4

per cent) were Christians, and a few were Jains and Buddhists.

Founding Schools and Churches: Christianity and Indentured Workers

Among the 350 Indian immigrants who arrived aboard the *Truro* in 1860 were 50 Catholics and only about 4 Protestants.[11] Meeting with them shortly after their arrival, a French priest, Jean Baptiste Sabon, recorded: "They appear very intelligent and are much respectful towards a priest. Before leaving the place they knelt before me, asked for my blessing and in the streets they greet me, stopping for the purpose."[12] Sabon learned Tamil and set about gathering the Indian Catholics and the few Syrian Christians of the Roman rite into a congregation. In his first year he baptized two Indian children and on 13 January 1861 performed the first Indian–Christian wedding in South Africa – between Charles Joachim and the young widow, Catherine Curpiah.

Indian Christians brought with them forms of Christian worship new to Natal. During the celebration of Christmas midnight Mass in 1861, for example, Indian Catholics processed through the streets beating a large drum and accompanying an ornate crib as they would have done in an Indian village. More musicians joined in the singing and worship as festivities continued throughout the night. Sabon wrote of this event: "Though Indians are not perfect – far from it – there are some among them who are more zealous than many other Christians elsewhere."

The Indian Catholic numbers, 50 at the beginning, shrank when almost all who came under the first indenture contracts returned to India by 1872. When immigration commenced again in 1874, the percentage who were Catholic was smaller than in 1860. Sabon and his successors aimed primarily to establish a Catholic community, not to evangelize; but by 1892 there were 300 Catholics, in two congregations in Durban and Pietermaritzburg.

The Durban parish, St. Anthony's, was made up mainly of indentured and "free" Indians. The handful of passenger Indians who had come to teach in the Catholic Indian schools were among the few educated Indians in the colony even as late as 1890 and, as such, played a big role in the leadership of the congregation. Caste differences, though still maintained in some Christian circles in India, appear to have quickly disappeared in Natal or at least to have been subordinated to the common struggle for survival and community.

At the turn of the century, when Bishop Jolivet of the Catholic Church began to build the cathedral in Durban, he sought to integrate the predominantly Indian St. Anthony's into the new cathedral's parish. St. Anthony's petitioned to remain separate, and Fr. Radulfus Maingot, from Ceylon, arrived to take charge of it. Fluent in Tamil, he extended St. Anthony's mission to Isipingo (just south of Durban) and to Mount Edgecombe, Verulam, and Darnell on the Natal north coast. By 1905, about 400 of the 1,040 Indian Catholics in Natal attended St. Anthony's church.[14]

Protestant ministry among Indians began when the Methodist minister Joseph Jackson Jr., paid pastoral visits to the first Indian labourers on a sugar estate on Natal's north coast. In 1862 the Methodist church acquired perhaps the most dynamic of all the early missionary pioneers to Indian immigrants, Ralph Stott, an indefatigable English missionary from India, already fluent in Tamil, who learned Hindi and Telugu as well, and preached in all these languages shortly after his arrival. Over the next three years he contacted Indian employees on almost 80 estates and he found the employers who held their indentures generally indifferent to the spiritual welfare of their workers.

In 1872, after many of its members returned to India, the Methodist Mission Society considered closing its Indian mission, but Stott, then 71, protested: "I consider the mission of such vital importance," he wrote, "that I will stick to it whether you support me or not ... I shall not give up now. No never."[15] The society stood by its decision, whereupon Stott replied: "You sin against 7,000 coolies and against all India ... I am in my 72nd year; I feel strong to labour as I did 20 years ago and while that strength continues, the Coolie mission shall have it."[16] The society promptly reversed its decision. Stott spent his last years before retirement in 1879 preaching to Indian workers on the sugar estates. Four Indian catechists, Stephen, Nundoo, Josiah, and Bissesor, assumed most of the teaching responsibilities of the church in Durban. The mission spread to Pietermaritzburg through the efforts of three white laymen, C.T. Varley, W. Christie and J. Andrews. John Thomas, an Indian from India, who helped extend the work of the mission to the Natal midlands, was ordained in 1902, the first Indian to be ordained to the ministry in South Africa.[17]

The Anglican church mission to Indian settlers began long after the Roman Catholic and Methodist missionary efforts. In 1860, when Indians first arrived, the Anglican church (then the Church of England) was preoccupied, under Bishop Colenso in Natal, with its Zulu mission. Requests by the Anglican Indian Mission in Natal to the Bishop of Madras for priests in 1869, and appeals for funds to the Society for the Propagation of the Gospel fell on deaf ears until 1883, when Lancelot Parker Booth, a district surgeon who had treated Indian labourers and their families around Umzinto and become aware of the ill-treatment they endured from white employers, offered his services to the Anglican Indian Mission. Booth was ordained two years later and took charge of the Anglican Durban Mission and its 70 members.[18] He opened a dispensary in his home and, for the first two years, worked without salary. Under his superintendency the St. Aidan's church was completed and two orphanages were established. In 1889 Booth went to India to enlist the help of the Bishop of Madras in procuring Indian clergy for Natal. As a result four clergy, Solomon Vedakan, Simon Peter Vedamuthu, Subban Godfrey, and Joseph Nullathamby were recruited for Natal.

The influence of the Anglican Indian Mission on the Indian settlers was incommensurate with its small size. At a time when Indian immigrants had little or no health care from the Natal government, Booth's clinic served the entire Indian community, earning the respect of many Hindus and Muslims, as reflected in an £80 annual donation (from 1891 on) from the newly formed Natal Indian Congress. Honoured in 1900 for his services by the Indian community, Booth received an address drawn up by the secretary of the fund-raising committee, Mohandas K. Gandhi.

The first Indian Lutheran congregation was founded more than ten years after the Anglican Indian mission, when, in 1896, the Matthews family gathered in their home in a Durban suburb a few Indians who had become members of the Hermannsburg Lutheran church in India. C. Matthews, a catechist of the Indian

Methodist church, joined the Seaview Lutheran congregation in 1909, bringing with him a few Methodists from his previous church.[19]

The few Baptists among the first Protestant immigrants could join only Methodist or Anglican churches until 1903, when the Rev. John Rungiah, sent out by the Telugu Baptist Missionary Society, collected a congregation of some 62 to found the first Telugu Baptist Church in Natal. Between 1903 and 1911, when more than 200 Indian Baptists arrived in Natal, branch congregations were established on the Natal north coast and Pietermaritzburg. Baptist churches were also established in Durban by A. Reuben and on the south coast of Natal by N.E. Tomlinson. Tomlinson's congregations were affiliated with the South African General Mission, the other congregations forming the Natal Indian Baptist Association. When Telugu and Tamil Baptist congregations chose to maintain separateness, Rungiah and his followers left to form the Natal Telugu Baptist Association.[20]

By the 1920s five denominations (Roman Catholic, Methodist, Anglican, Lutheran and Baptist) had well-established if small congregations in the Indian communities along the Natal coast and inland between Pietermaritzburg and Newcastle. During the nineteenth century the churches focused chiefly on providing immigrant Christians with pastoral care and opportunities for worship. None of the five churches had significant success in converting Hindus or Muslims to Christianity. The congregations were led by white and Indian clergy and by deacons from India and Ceylon, with numerous Indian lay ministers and catechists to assist the clergy. When no professional clergy were available, small groups gathered in homes and were taught by the lay leaders. These home fellowships often became the nuclei of new church congregations. The Methodists established "chapel schools," informal schools for children that doubled as places of worship for adults.

In 1874, 2,501 white and 48 Indian children were attending school, the government that year spending £8,817 on white education and £40 on Indian education.[21] Long before the colonial government showed any serious interest in the education of Indians or even before "free" Indians acquired the means to help themselves educationally, the churches provided the only source of education for most Indians. The first church school was established by Fr. Sabon, using as his textbook the Tamil books donated by the Oblates of Ceylon. Only later did the government grant Sabon's school £25 a year. Between 1867 and 1884, with the help of a few teachers from India, the Methodist Stott established night schools with adult literacy classes. The first local textbook for Indian education in Natal – a primer in English and Hindi – was produced by one of these immigrant Indian teachers, Henry Nundoo.

Among Catholics, Methodists, and Baptists, congregations were formed first and schools later, but among Anglicans schools often preceded the founding of congregations. In the 1860s two small Anglican schools offered to teach Indian children; under Booth several new ones began. By 1883, 9 of the 21 Indian schools in Natal were administered by Anglicans, among them the first school for Indian girls run by Mrs. S.P. Vedamuthu, a teacher from India. In the next ten years, Anglicans organized 3 more schools for girls, and also Sastri College, a boys' school later to become famous. They recruited highly qualified teachers, most notably D. Koilpillai, who went on to found the first secondary school and teacher-training college for Indians in Sydenham, Durban. By 1916, his training college had prepared 66 local Indians as teachers.[22]

The schools served not only children of Christians but Hindus and Muslims, as well. They helped produce many of the first leaders among the Indian immigrants to South Africa. These schools earned the respect of all Indians for providing the first and, for long, the only available educational opportunities for Indians until the opening of community schools.

Revival and Fission: Indian Pentecostalism in an Age of Segregation

The established Indian churches grew relatively slowly after the 1920s. (See Table below.) After the 1930s other established denominations founded congregations, among them: the Presbyterian Church Mission begun by Dr. E.P. Reim; the Reformed Church in Africa, whose congregations were extensions of the mission of the Dutch Reformed Church; the Evangelical Church of South Africa, formerly the South African General Mission; the Church of the Nazarene; the Evangelical Bible Church; and the Seventh Day Adventist Church.

But by far the most significant development in the history of Indian Christianity in this period was the establishment of Pentecostal churches. Between 1925 and 1980 Pentecostals acquired more Indian members than all the other denominations put together (see chap. 13, passim). With the introduction of Pentecostalism, Christianity, for the first time, grew rapidly among Indian South Africans and began to alter the religious composition of the whole Indian community.

Church Affiliation of Indian Christians and Their Relationship to the South African Indian Population (1980)

	% of Indian population	Number	% of Indian Christians
Reformed Church (in Africa)	0.5	4,105	4.0
Anglican	1.1	9,031	8.8
Methodist	0.5	4,105	4.0
Presbyterian	0.2	1,642	1.6
Lutheran	0.1	821	0.8
Roman Catholic	2.6	21,346	28.8
Full Gospel (Pentecostal)	2.8	22,988	22.4
*Other (principally Pentecostal)	4.7	38,587	37.6
Total	12.5	102,625	

*The vast majority of the "Other" category were Pentecostals who were not "Full Gospel Church" members, i.e. Bethesda members. However, many Bethesda members who, in the 1980 census, listed their church affiliation as "Bethesda" rather than "Full Gospel," also appeared in the "Other" category.

Pentecostal churches emerged during the 1920s and early 1930s, as Indians left the rural areas to find work in the cities. Urbanization inevitably brought with it new and difficult problems. The joint-family system (*kutum*), which had provided communal stability, though still dominant up to the mid-1920s was "visibly diminishing,"[23] and well-established customs were either changing or falling into neglect.[24] The Indian elite was becoming entirely urbanized. Young Indians, forced to cope in a Western context, were slowly becoming alienated from their traditional culture.[25]

Relocated families formed new communities in and around Durban and Pietermaritzburg, and here Pentecostalism first took root. For example, Indians working for the Durban Corporation or in the railways lived in barracks north-east of the city centre, where Bethesda, destined to become the largest church among Indian South Africans, began. So, too, the Apostolic Faith Mission spread among mill-settlements on Natal's north coast.

All three Pentecostal denominations established in South Africa by the 1920s, the Full Gospel Church (to which Bethesda affiliated), the Apostolic Faith Mission, and the Assemblies of God, founded Indian congregations during the period of rapid urbanization. Bethesda with approximately 39,000 Indian members remains as of 1995 the largest of these three; the other two have about 5,000 members each.

In 1922 John Alexander Rowlands, a businessman and evangelist from Bristol, England, settled in Pietermaritzburg, where he established a mill and a stud farm while pursuing evangelistic interests. He attended the Full Gospel Church, which he found sufficiently "non-established" for his tastes.[26] With his friend Ebenezer Theophilus, an Indian greengrocer and member of the Methodist church who shared his devotion to holiness theology, Rowlands founded the United Pentecostal Mission of Natal on 17 July 1925. The Mission aimed to spread the Christian message throughout Pietermaritzburg. A.H. Cooper, the head of the Full Gospel Church in Natal, encouraged its establishment, in part because, in keeping with the segregationist sentiment of the time, he disapproved of the mixing of the races in the services of Pietermaritzburg's Full Gospel Church. J.A. Rowlands's two young sons were encouraged to teach Sunday school at the Mission, and when the older, John Francis, was 22, he set off for Durban, where with the three young Indians from the Baptist Church, D.G. Samuels, D.M. Gabriel and A.J. Williams, he gathered a congregation at the Corporation Barracks in 1931.[27]

Rowlands and his Indian friends formed a zealous band of evangelists. Just three weeks after his first meeting in Durban a group of converts travelled to Pietermaritzburg seeking baptism. Two questions became pressing: what was his ministerial status and what ecclesiastical affiliation should the new congregation seek? Rowlands's strong revivalistic stance made affiliation with any of the established churches difficult; and, with some Baptists, Anglicans, and Methodists now joining his church, his ministry was denounced as divisive from several pulpits of the established churches. Thereupon, Rowlands and his congregation joined the Full Gospel Church, and Rowlands was ordained there in 1931.

Rowlands's younger brother, Alec, later ordained, acted as his personal assistant. The two brothers remained bachelors, committed wholly to the work of Bethesda. Their mother, Edith Hartland, led the women of the church. By 1933 Rowlands had achieved a level of acceptance among Indians unprecedented for a white person in South Africa. He lived with an Indian family for a while, and later shared a room with his first Indian co-worker, F. Victor, the first of more than 40 Indians to be ordained as pastors in Bethesda by 1980.

In 1933 Bethesda launched the first of its many "campaigns" of week-long special meetings held once or twice each year. Some campaigns lasted 100 nights during the peak period of the revival of the 1940s and early 1950s. At these services Rowlands preached colourful and compelling sermons, with strong ethical and holiness emphases, and "Bethesdascopes" (slideshows) afterwards. The services almost always ended with a call to commitment to Christ and to the work and extension of the church. The Back-to-the-Bible campaign of 1953, for example, ended with many signing a covenant, before a congregation of more than 2,000, to pray and work for revival.[28] At large services as many as 300 converts would be baptized. In 1954 alone, Bethesda gained 815 new members.[29] The Bethesda revival continued well into the 1960s, followed by a period of consolidation and institutionalization, when, over the next 15 years, several church buildings and a college to train ministers were erected and, for the first time, the church considered a church policy and constitution. In November 1980, at Rowlands's death, control of Bethesda effectively passed to the Full Gospel Church with which Bethesda had affiliated 47 years earlier.

The second large Pentecostal work among Indians, the Apostolic Faith Mission (AFM), was organized in the 1930s principally by the American Pentecostal missionary, Charles Samuel Flewelling, and his wife Ida. Finding a small band of Indian AFM members in Stanger, the Flewellings provided much-needed pastoral guidance,[30] and over the next eight years AFM branches were established at Port Shepstone, Doornkop, Harding, Seven Oaks and Verulam. In 1945 a vibrant congregation was formed with workers of the mill settlement of Mt. Edgecombe. Branch congregations, many established and led by Indian lay evangelists, provided simple services of extempore prayers, singing, Bible reading, and preaching. The congregation was encouraged to give testimonies to exhort their fellow worshippers to speak in tongues, and to prophesy. By 1982 the AFM Indian membership was estimated at about 3,000, its largest congregation, at Merebank, having about 1,000 members.[31]

The Assemblies of God (AOG), the third major Pentecostal movement among Indians, has two separate movements: the Bethshan Gospel Mission, founded by the Norwegian, F.L. Hansen, and a group of churches established under Stephen Govender, an Indian evangelist, in the early 1950s. Bethshan began modestly, in 1940, in a renovated shop in Overport; over the next 14 years it recruited both Coloured and Indian families. One of Hansen's first achievements was the establishing of a "home of safety" for orphaned and destitute Coloured children, an organized social-care programme unusual for Pentecostal churches, which ordinarily stress "salvation of the soul" and care for their own members. Bethshan, like Bethesda, was for the most part under the control of its founder. Its first Indian member, David Nadesen, was ordained only in 1978. Care of the congregation and its branches in Clare Estate, Reservoir Hills, and Phoenix, remained principally in the hands of lay people. Like Rowlands at Bethesda, Hansen supervised but intervened only when necessary.[32]

Stephen Govender's congregation, "Peniel International Assembly," started as an independent church in Gale Street, Durban, and in 1954 was formally incorporated into the AOG. In 1960 the church suffered gravely, as did many of the Indian Pentecostal churches, when the Group Areas Act compelled Indian people to move out of the city centres to "Indian" areas. Govender and his helpers moved their church to the Indian area of Merebank in 1962, where within six years Peniel Assembly grew to number 250 adult members. In 1967, with more and more members moving to Chatsworth outside Durban, the largest Indian settlement, two more AOG congregations were founded there.[33]

Among all three Pentecostal movements the first congregations were established among the communal settlements in Durban, Pietermaritzburg, and in towns on the Natal coast. The initial "nucleus" of many of the early congregations of the 1930s included a few Christians from "established" denominations, usually Baptists and Methodists who were attracted to the revivalist life and worship of the Pentecostals; but, in time, the vast majority of their membership were converts from Hinduism. The churches revolved around strong charismatic, often autocratic, leaders like Rowlands, Hansen, and Govender. During the early years of revival and growth there was little or no concern with polity, constitution, or any fixed statement of belief: such concerns surfaced only in the 1970s, as the revivalist groups became increasingly institutionalized.

Among Indians there was little resistance to white missionary leadership as there had been elsewhere in South Africa among many Africans. With the level of education of the early Indian converts meagre and their ignorance of ecclesiastical matters vast, white leaders, missionaries, and visiting evangelists took over almost all authority. The alienation of Indians from an often antipathetic white colonial society partly explains their reliance on white leaders who, contrary to their experience and expectations, actually identified with them and helped and cared for them. Furthermore, the deep respect Indians had for their "gurus" dissuaded them from disagreeing with or questioning the frequently paternalistic attitudes they encountered. Still, the actual evangelism and expansion of the congregation were achieved principally by Indian laypeople, preaching as Indians to Indians. Resistance to white leadership did not emerge until the 1970s, when the successors of the founders apparently expected to assume a similar leadership simply because they were white.

Criticisms of apartheid were also rare among Pentecostal Indians until quite recently. Like other Evangelicals in South Africa, Pentecostals have tended to shy away from open political expression and from public criticism of social injustices. Rowlands was among the few Pentecostals who offered some criticism of apartheid and of racial segregation, and even he did so in a guarded and tempered form. In 1949 he wrote:

> It is our firm conviction that the policy of the present South African Government in trying to introduce "apartheid" into the country has no sanction whatever in the teachings of the New Testament ... We rejoice because our citizenship is in heaven and there is no "apartheid" there ... There is also no "apartheid" at Bethesda where we are all one in Christ ... irrespective of race or colour.[34]

Indians, under constant threat of repatriation until the 1960s, seem, in consequence, to have felt too insecure about their status to be politically outspoken; it
was deemed expedient to be cautious in criticizing the government. Furthermore,
the government maintained a careful surveillance of its critics, and even mild resistance was ruthlessly put down. By the end of the 1980s, however, the racial segregation in the established Pentecostal churches, with each racial or ethnic group in
its own separate branch, led to open rejection of the official policies of the
Pentecostal Churches led by white ministers. In some cases, black and white sections divided into separate and autonomous churches (see pp. 233–37).

Crisis, decision, commitment, and dedication were fundamental themes in the
life and worship of these Pentecostal churches. Everyone in each congregation was
called to evangelize, and clergy and laity were not readily distinguished. During the
time of socio-economic and cultural upheaval that was largely the result of
apartheid legislation, churches like Bethesda gave succour to people caught
between the old, traditional Indian life and culture, now rapidly passing away, and
the new, Western, secular life. They gave to their members a feeling of continuity
with an old culture and helped to foster their socio-psychological well-being. They
provided a level of societal cohesion sufficient to cope in difficult circumstances
and to develop a relatively large middle class despite their disenfranchisement.
Pentecostal churches inadvertently contributed to social stability by creating surrogate communities for their members.

Between the late 1950s and the late 1980s more than 41,782 Indian families
(about 278,000 individuals) were forced to leave the Durban city and suburbs
declared white areas under the Group Areas Act, and were moved to peri-urban
Indian settlements, the largest of which are Chatsworth and Phoenix, some 30 kilometres to the north and to the south of Durban. At this time, several groups seceded from the three established Pentecostal churches to found independent
Pentecostal churches, now more than 50 in the Durban–Pietermaritzburg area, and
more than 75 in the South African Indian community as a whole. The congregations range in size from 25 to around 200, with six having memberships exceeding
500.[35] The breakaways were largely a reaction to rigid ecclesiastical centralization
in the older Pentecostal churches or the result of personality clashes among aspirants
to leadership positions. In several instances members who had been censured in a
disciplinary action left with a following to establish a new congregation. Some
leaders left hoping to get a bigger stipend in a new congregation.

The independent Pentecostal churches successfully adapted themselves to the
economic situations of their poorer members in attempting to cope with the aftermath of their forced removal. The pastors were nearly always as poor as their
members, and since churches were costly to build, they worshipped instead in
homes, garages, back-yard structures, or pitched tents on private land. Indian
Christian churches, controlled by denominational headquarters and drawing on
grants and "foreign aid," did erect church buildings and on a grander scale than
local congregations could afford; yet these buildings remain relatively empty.

The new Pentecostal churches have laid stress on healing and exorcism.
Churches such as the Pentecostal Repentant Church in Chatsworth and the Bible
Deliverance Fellowship in Phoenix, both emphasizing healing and exorcism, have

grown the fastest of all denominations in recent years. Although some of the smaller independent congregations remain unstable, others have now put up church buildings and have established strong congregations; others have amalgamated or affiliated with a larger Pentecostal denomination.

Indian Churches and Their Hindu Neighbours

With the emergence of Pentecostal churches and their active evangelism, Hindu leaders became more vocal in their criticism of Christian proselytization.[36] During the 1930s and 1940s converts to Christianity were sometimes ostracized or turned out of their homes by their Hindu families. However, with Hindus' tradition of tolerance of other religions, breaches in family ties were rarely permanent. Local Indian newspapers sometimes have carried letters opposing Christian evangelism and asserting that, not Hindus, but white South Africans needed conversion from their sins of racism. Bethesda, because it gained the most converts, came under the most severe censure.[37]

Some Indians, viewing conversion to Christianity as tantamount to cultural betrayal, exposed the contradictions between the South African government's Christian claims and its policies of persecution and inequity. In 1936, when Bethesda was beginning to gain notice, Swami Adhyanandgi, a visiting guru from India, told a huge gathering of Hindus in the Durban City Hall:

> We have enough troubles in the world, in political, economic and social spheres with the materialist philosophy of greed and hatred, and the survival of the fittest ... the votaries of the different faiths should not add to that trouble by the mad run for proselytising.[38]

In 1960 a Hindu leader, referring back to Adhyanandgi's speech, complained that the advice of 26 years earlier had fallen on deaf ears and that Natal's Hindus had failed to respond adequately to the problem of proselytization.

Indeed, Christian evangelists, especially those from the independent Pentecostal churches, have often been tactless and insensitive to the religious feelings of others. In its early years *Moving Waters*, the official monthly paper of Bethesda, carried an article comparing Christ and Krishna, which drew widespread criticisms from Hindus, who accused Rowlands of "defaming Lord Krishna." Rowlands quickly apologized to the Hindu community, and the matter was put to rest. On another occasion an Indian woman convert, interviewed on South African television by a visiting evangelist from the United States and a guest of Bethesda, held her *Kamachee* prayer lamp in her hand; she testified that she had now "come to the true light" and no longer needed to light the Hindu lamp as an aid to devotion. The interview, intended for American fundamentalist audiences, drew strong criticism among South African Indians; Bethesda was accused of disrespect for the *Kamachee* lamp, the focus of daily family prayers among Hindus. Again Rowlands, seeing the implications of this incident, apologized.[39]

Except for these two public incidents, however, Rowlands gained the respect of many in the Indian community, mainly through his genuine interest in India and Indian culture, as the following letter in 1955, written by a Hindu to a newspaper, makes clear:

> It is a puzzling situation ... we know that Pastor Rowlands's chief work is to

convert as many Hindus as he can to Christianity, and while no one can quarrel with that in a free country, what is baffling is that he should give publicity to Hindu achievements ... in recent years Bethesda has been going ahead with its work without directly attacking any other religion.[40]

The loss of Hindus to Christianity, ironically, contributed to a renaissance within Hinduism itself. Movements such as the Arya Samaj, the Savaite Sungum, the Divine Life Society, the Ramakrishna Mission and the Krishna Consciousness Movement established themselves in South Africa, just as they had done in India, as part of a neo-Hindu reaction to Christian missions.[41] They promoted a more simplified philosophical form of Hinduism, with services not dissimilar to those of Christian churches. In the mid-1970s at a Back-to-the-Ramayana campaign in Pietermaritzburg (a parallel to the Back-to-the-Bible-campaign of Bethesda) the swami of the Rama Krishna Centre in Durban delivered an illustrated sermon similar to the Bethesdascopes. As early as 1935, soon after a Bethesda campaign, the Hindu Maha Sabha was reconstituted, its inaugural meeting bearing a striking similarity to Bethesda's own larger campaigns. It met in the Durban City Hall and was addressed by the mayor, centring on the problem of conversion and the need to renew Hinduism in Natal. Unintentionally, Christian churches, especially those which had attracted most converts, had contributed to a re-appraisal of Hinduism in a setting of severe social and cultural change.

Conversion to Christianity had declined by the 1980s, even in Pentecostal circles, as the most revivalist of the independent churches tended, after ten or fifteen years' existence, to become more institutionalized and increasingly to resemble denominations. Maintenance of established structures became more important to them than evangelism and church growth.

There were, then, two distinct phases in the establishment of Christianity among Indians in Natal. During the first phase, from 1860 to 1925, Catholic, Anglican, Methodist, Baptist, and Lutheran churches established missions, which, however, gained few converts and remained small. Their principal achievements lay in the education of Indians – the Natal government's provision of schools for them being tardy and inadequate – and, in the case of the Anglicans, in providing the first medical services for Indians. The second phase began with the arrival of Pentecostal missionaries in the 1920s, whose churches, especially Bethesda, emphasized evangelism, revival, and faith healing and induced many Hindus to convert to Christianity. The number of Christians among Indian South Africans consequently grew from 4 per cent in 1925 to almost 13 per cent in 1980. In a time of social upheaval resulting from urbanization and forced removals under the Group Areas Act, this evangelical form of Christianity provided Indians, especially those alienated from their traditional life-style and culture, with stable surrogate communities organized around worship.

19

The Drumbeat of the Cross: Christianity and Literature

JEFF OPLAND

English writers in South Africa have long enjoyed free access to the secular and religious press, and, as participants in a literary tradition with roots outside the country, to a wider overseas readership. They have been able to articulate Christian themes and convictions as a matter of personal taste. By contrast, when Afrikaans writers asserted the independence of their language late in the nineteenth century, they did so in the face of dominant English and Dutch cultures, and had to free Afrikaans from its demeaning image as a language of illiterates. In this struggle, Christianity was intimately involved; Afrikaans writers were circumscribed only by the religious convictions of their local public or the sensibilities of an Afrikaner government that saw itself as Christian.

Writers in black languages, like those in Afrikaans, had to establish new literary traditions but, as distinct from the Afrikaners, their encouragement to literacy came from without; writers in black languages were dependent on publishing media in the hands of Christian missionaries or other whites sometimes (though not always) unsympathetic or hostile to black culture. Black writers could either comply with the religious or political ideology of their white publishers or turn to their own oral traditions, which were an important outlet for creative artists in expressing their resistance to white control or to Christianity. Some writers, however, have succeeded in articulating Christian convictions in a literary fusion with African forms and themes.

Loosening the Apron Strings: Christian Literature in English

South African writers in English generally sought their publishers in England and their audiences in the English-speaking world at large. After the British occupation in the first decade of the nineteenth century, especially in the eastern Cape, new journals directed at local English settlers were published, carrying poems, stories, and even serial novels.[1] Early in the history of these local literary periodicals, the *South African Journal*, edited by Thomas Pringle and John Fairbairn, ran afoul of the governor, Lord Charles Somerset, for criticizing his policies toward settlers, but the issue of press freedom was engaged and soon won.[2] Thereafter, writers in English could publish either locally or in the mother country; sometimes publication in South Africa preceded publication in England. When Pringle's poems, originally printed in Cape journals, were reprinted in his book *Ephemerides*, issued by a British publisher in 1828, "several had undergone extensive elucidatory revision and were supplied with footnotes" to render them accessible to a wider English reading public.[3]

English folklore in South Africa also shows deference to England. Songs sung in South Africa, for example, tend to preserve texts current throughout the English-speaking world. Children in South Africa, as elsewhere, counted "Eeny meeny miney mo, catch a nigger by his toe," even though "nigger" had no local currency, and local disyllabic terms of racial abuse could easily be substituted. Ralph Trewhela reported in 1980 that "Some years ago the South African Folk Music Association sent Brian Babbington on a search around the Eastern Cape for songs that might have been handed down from the 1820 Settlers, but it was fruitless ... It does seem that, song-wise, our British forebears were too closely tied to the apron strings of their motherland."4

Authors in English were free to adopt secular or Christian themes in their work or not, as they saw fit. Ministers could write secular poetry, and lay people could write Christian poetry: like English poets anywhere in the world, the choice was entirely theirs. Edward Heath Crouch's *Treasury of South African Poetry and Verse* (1909) concludes with a section of "Religious and metaphysical poems" by nine poets, most of whom are featured elsewhere in the volume.

Christianity can contribute to setting or characterization in a work: Herman Charles Bosman's Marico farmers in *Mafeking Road* pray before meals and at funerals, journey to Zeerust for *nagmaal* (Holy Communion), and read the Bible in their homes. Or a work can reflect its author's Christian convictions: "The inform-ing faith" of Alan Paton's *Cry, the Beloved Country* "is unashamedly Christian lib-eral, based on Lincoln's Gettysburg speech on the one hand and the Sermon on the Mount on the other."5 Biblical idiom suffuses Paton's writing, as it does the work of Guy Butler, who claims the Bible as his principal literary influence. Or Christianity can be more deeply integrated into the literary texture, as in Pauline Smith's collection of short stories, *The Little Karoo* (1925), where Christianity is all-pervasive, not just in the piety of her characters, but in theme and symbolism. In "Ludovitje," for example, written in a style heavy with biblical repetitions and inversions, a black migrant farm labourer is impressed by the faith of the narrator's sickly young son:

> But when Ludovitje came among them, singing his psalm, they would stop in their work to listen to him. And quickly they came also to sing it. Yes, these men that did not yet believe in the Living God, the Heavenly Father, came so, as they builded our dam, to sing the 114th psalm – "Tremble, thou earth, at the presence of the Lord, at the presence of the God of Jacob, Who turned the hard rock into a standing water and the flintstone into a springing well."
>
> So they would sing, and Maqwasi, that was the head of the gang, would say to the child Ludovitje: "Tell us now! Who is this King of Jacob? And where is now this springing well?"
>
> And Ludovitje would tell him. Of the wanderings of the children of Israel he would tell him, and of God's guidance in the Wilderness. Of God's good-ness and mercy to those that love Him he would tell him, and of the pure River of Water of Life that He has given us.
>
> Maqwasi would say to him: "Where runs now this River of Water of Life?"
>
> And Ludovitje would answer: "Clear as crystal is the River of Water of

Life and close by the throne of God and of the Lamb it runs."

Yes, so it was that my darling spoke with Maqwasi the Kaffir, and always he would say to me: "Wait now! Maqwasi will yet be a pearl in my crown." When the young Ludovic takes to his deathbed, Maqwasi requests permission to stand at his door.

Gently he came, but Ludovitje heard him, and sitting up in his bed he held out his hands and cried: "Maqwasi! Maqwasi! Clear as crystal is the River of Water of Life and close by the throne of God and of the Lamb it runs. Can you not believe, Maqwasi?"

And Maqwasi, standing there with tears in his eyes, answered him: "Master! Now I believe."

Yes, God knows how it was, but from that moment Maqwasi believed.

As he dies, Ludovic has a last request of his teacher: "Sing now the 114th psalm, and Maqwasi, that is the pearl of my crown, will sing it also." After Maqwasi digs the dead child's grave, and completes his work on the dam, the narrator's husband Piet approaches him.

Piet went to him and asked him to stay. "Work now for me on the farm, Maqwasi," he said, "and surely for the sake of the child I will deal well with you."

But Maqwasi answered him: "Master! For the sake of the child to my own people I must go. To tell them of the River of Water of Life I must go, that they may also be pearls in his crown."

In this parable of the mission enterprise, the African takes up the preacher's vocation; the lone pearl in the child's crown will in turn add more pearls to that crown; the builder of dams, converted with tears in his eyes, commits himself to bring the River of the Water of Life to Africans; the hard rock has been turned into a standing water and the flintstone into a springing well. The story concludes on a profoundly prophetic note. Before he leaves, at Piet's request, the dam-digger digs the graves of his white masters alongside the grave he has already dug for the child:

So Maqwasi dug for us graves in the claystone. One on each side of the child he dug them, and left us, and went again to his own people, spreading the Word of God among them.[6]

Michael Chapman has argued that a major shift in identity took place in 1960, when South African English poetry, turning away from Europe, moved from its "traditional" to its "modern" phase. The massacre at Sharpeville in 1960 and South Africa's forced withdrawal from the Commonwealth "were clear indications to the white English-speaking citizen that the sixties marked the end of an era, a period characterized in many respects by assumptions about English culture as a civilizing force." South African English literature turned inward to exploit its local resources, a search frequently ending in despair and nihilism. "The difference between the 'traditional' and the 'modern' poet might be seen to be a difference between those for whom the ideals and hopes of a Christian liberal humanism are still valid and those for whom they are not."[7] To take two of Chapman's examples: Butler, the traditionalist, concludes "Mountain" with the lines

Frequently now I catch myself off balance,
tempted to take the wings of the morning or dive

to the uttermost parts of the sea.
Perhaps that moment which refused so firmly
to be a turning point
should be the only point
round which my life should turn;
perhaps God is neither old nor young;
in depth or in height. He simply is,
and we,
when we accept Him simply,
are.

In contrast, Douglas Livingstone, a harbinger of modernism, concludes his "Iscariot" with Judas, who rejects a Jesus for whom there is no resurrection, crouching,

kicking panoramic stars and cosmic views
in the teeth, stabbing holes in the back
of beyond, and frantic at the curse
of sentience, I roar to heaven three vows –
giving god the back of my hand

and accepting an existence devoid of consolation:

... I'll choose Earth as my rack.
Last; for prayer: my lips will spit a terse
goddam – those oddly flat and nailing vowels.

English literature in South Africa may have cast off the colonial cloak after 1960, as Chapman argues is true for poetry, but the European connection remains. However defiant Livingstone's Judas may be, he is still racked and nailed like Jesus on the cross, exploiting Christian imagery to express his revolt. South African writers have always enjoyed access to a Christian tradition common to the English-speaking world for theme, imagery, or setting; they have always been free to embrace, reject, or ignore it.

"The Language Ever Hallows Us": Christian Literature in Afrikaans

Afrikaans literature, on the other hand, took root and grew in South Africa itself, as part of a political movement explicitly Christian. With the appearance of *Die Afrikaanse Patriot*, the first newspaper in Afrikaans, on 15 January 1876, a new era began for Afrikaans writers. The inaugural issue concluded with "Die Afrikaanse Volkslied," which asserted that God provides every nation with its own land, language, law, rights, and time, and that the Afrikaner's time was coming.[8]

Throughout the seventeenth and eighteenth centuries, South African diaries and newspapers were produced in Dutch. Around the turn of the nineteenth century, Afrikaans was spoken but not yet written.[9] Its earliest literary uses were designed to sneer at it and its speakers from a Dutch perspective: the satirical *Lied ter eere van de Swellendamsche en diverse andere helden by de bloedige actie te Muizenberg* (1795) mocked the illiteracy of those who used the language. M.D. Teenstra's *Vrughten mijner werkzaamheden* (1825) illustrated the divergence of popular speech from pure Dutch. A British settler, Andrew Geddes Bain, mocked the Afrikaans patois spoken by Coloureds in his humorous monologue *Kaatje Kekkelbek*, which satirised John Philip's missionary efforts among Khoikhoi (see chap. 2, *passim*). First performed in Grahamstown in 1838, the sketch reflects an English settler attitude to mission education in Kaatje's opening statement:

> My name is Kaatje Kekkelbek,
>   I come from Katrivier,
> Daar is van water geen gebrek [There is no lack of water],
>   But scarce of wine and beer.
> Myn A B C at Ph'lipes school
>   I learnt ein kleene beetje [a little bit],
> But left it just as great a fool
>   As gekke [silly] Tante Meitje.

And Kaatje's concluding statement scorns Philip for coaching Andries Stoffels and Jan Tshatshu, who gave evidence before the Aborigines Committee in London's Exeter Hall ("Extra Hole"):

> Regt jong! I wish toch dat de *mis-denvaarheid Syety* would send me to England to speak the trut net so as oom Andries en Jan Zatzoe done in *Extra Hole*, waar al de Engels kom met ope bek om alles en te sluk wat ons Hot'nots voortel [where all the English come open-mouthed to swallow everything we Hottentots say]. I not want Dr. Flipse to praat soetjes in myn oor wat I moet say [to whisper sweetly in my ear what I must say], so hy done met Jan Zatzoe ...[10]

Following the second British occupation of the Cape in 1806, a policy of anglicization was inaugurated, especially after Somerset's Language Proclamation of 1822 made English the language of law and government as from 1827, and the School Act of 1865, which banned Dutch for school instruction. The government even tried to use the Dutch Reformed Church (NGK) itself as an agent to implement these restrictions by importing Scottish ministers. Yet the church remained the most important stronghold of the Dutch language and nationality in the country,[11] and its clerics figured prominently in the First Afrikaans Language Movement of 1875–1900, mounted in opposition to the exclusive language policies of successive British governors.

In 1872, Arnoldus Pannevis, a Dutch teacher at Paarl, concerned about Afrikaans-speaking Coloureds' ignorance of the Bible, argued in a letter to *De Zuid-Afrikaan* that the Dutch Bible should be translated into Afrikaans. Two of his students, C.P. Hoogenhout and the Rev. S.J. du Toit, pleaded in *De Zuid-Afrikaan* for a Bible translation not for Coloureds but for Afrikaners, made the case for an Afrikaans literature, and challenged the influence of English. The subsequent

301

exchange of letters between Hoogenhout and Du Toit, along with Pannevis's plea for a Bible translation, led to a meeting in Paarl in 1875, the establishment of the *Genootskap van Regte Afrikaners*, and publication of the *Patriot* the following year.

The first issues of *Die Afrikaanse Patriot* are filled with xenophobic imagery of conflict, in which religion, language, and national identity are inextricably enmeshed: the struggle for an independent language assumes the dimensions of a holy war, and Afrikaans becomes the focus of a cult. The front page of the first issue proclaims that the *Patriot* will demonstrate to the world that Afrikaners have a language in which they can say whatever they wish. Readers are exhorted to "Step outside! [*Kom uit!*] Write your language! They already write kaffir language and Bushman clicks. Why then should our language be stifled? Step outside!"[12] The Afrikaans language is blessed, a special gift of God:

> There is but one mother tongue, the language of our heart. The language in which we learnt to say *mommy* and *daddy* at our mother's breast – the language in which we received our first impressions – the language in which our devout mother taught us as children to say the beloved name of our Lord Jesus – the language in which our parents always served their God – the language in which our honest father continued to exhort us on his deathbed, the language in which our dying mother breathed her last in a prayer for us – *the language ever hallows us* – this language we can never exchange for any other in the world ...
>
> True Afrikaners, we summon you to join us in recognizing that the Afrikaans language is our mother tongue given to us by our Dear Lord; and to join us in standing for our language through thick and thin; and not to rest before our language is widely recognized in every respect as the national language of our land.[13]

Poems featured in later issues declare that Dutch and English are on a par, but that Afrikaans must be dominant ("*Afrikaans moet baas wees*"). "We must attain our Mother tongue because the Lord God stands at our side."[14] The literature of the First Language Movement exhorted its readers to write and contribute to the recognition of Afrikaans. Little influenced by Western European models, it drew markedly on folklore and consisted of protest poems, religious poetry, didactic or historical prose and drama.

With the unification of South Africa in 1910, Dutch and English became official languages, but by 1925 Afrikaans was recognized as a medium of instruction for Afrikaans-speakers. The official language struggle was over: the government recognized the equality of English and Afrikaans. By 1933 the Christian Bible was available in Afrikaans. The literature of the Second Language Movement, lasting roughly from 1900 to 1930, was less didactic than that of the First: younger writers aimed at developing Afrikaans as a language of culture (*kultuurtaal*).[15] The themes became more universal, more diverse, often influenced by Western literature. Much of the poetry stressed individualism: "With the younger generation a greater individualism is present which sometimes leads to a strongly philosophical verse, on occasion even to a strife-with-God."[16] With the struggle engaged and all but won by the First Movement, Afrikaans writers now were free, as English writers had always been, to choose secular or religious themes as they saw fit, moderated only by the religious convictions of the Afrikaner reading public.

When, after 1960, English literature freed itself from the apron strings of its mother country, Christianity had become less important a theme than politics or identity. When Afrikaans achieved a comparable independence at the turn of the century, however, Christianity provided a source of inspiration for writers, as it has to the present; there have always been Afrikaans writers who have drawn on Christianity, notably in versions of biblical narrative in all genres. J.D. du Toit (Totius) used biblical parallels between the Israelites and the Afrikaners in *Ragel* (1913) and *Trekkerswee* (1915). Eitemal's *Jaffie* (1953) tells the Christ story from the animals' points of view, especially that of Jaffie the donkey; C.M. van den Heever wrote two allegorical biblical novels based on the stories of Ahasuerus and Moses. W.E.G. Louw's poetry draws heavily on biblical characters and themes, such as Adam, Cain, the prodigal son, and Christ's passion. His poetry explores the relationship between man and God and, in *Terugtog* (1940), his personal struggle with God, a theme that also characterizes the poetry of N.P. van Wyk Louw. Many of the poems of Elisabeth Eybers draw on biblical situations – "Maria," "Hagar," "Pietà," "Job" and "Portret van 'n Vrou," in which a mother offers herself up like Christ. G. J. Beukes produced Bible dramas on Jesus, Judas, and Salome, while F. A. Venter produced two biblical novels. Adam Small has used Bible images of Egyptian slavery and Roman oppression to depict the experience of Coloureds under apartheid, and the Bible remains significant in the work of M. M. Walters, Antjie Krog, Sheila Cussons, and especially Lina Spies and I. L. de Villiers.

But just as the 1960s heralded a new phase in South African English literature, so too some Afrikaans writers of the 1960s, the *Sestigers*, broke with tradition, turning both outward to seek inspiration in Europe and also inward, as writers in English did, to seek an identity in Africa. This latter impulse, since it sought the Africanness in Afrikanerdom, brought them into conflict with apartheid ideology and with the Calvinist morality that sustained it. One Sestiger, the novelist André Brink, offered this characterization:

> It was a movement – inasmuch as the work of a small group of such widely diverging temperaments and talents can be termed a movement – with purely literary origins, starting as a revolt against hackneyed themes and outworn structures in Afrikaans fiction. But because so much of it was European in inspiration – which appealed immensely to younger readers but came as a cultural shock to the Establishment and all its agencies – the iconoclastic ardour of these writers soon caused them to collide head-on with most of the established religious and moral values of "traditional" Afrikanerdom.

Afrikaans had won freedom by establishing its own independent publishing firms; now a number of Afrikaans authors struggled in turn against Nationalist control of these presses.[17] In the mid-1970s, works by Etienne Leroux, André Brink and others were banned under the government's Publications Act of 1974. The Sestigers, however, won out in the end, outlasting ideological and political censorship to achieve local and international recognition.

"For the Upraising of the Moral Life": Christian Literature in Black Languages

The black vernacular languages of South Africa were first transcribed and printed by Christian missionaries, who laid the foundations of vernacular linguistics and literature.[18] Within two months of his arrival among the Xhosa, J. T. van der Kemp of the London Missionary Society (see pp. 34–38, 69–71) produced an elementary Xhosa grammar and a vocabulary of some 600 words. John Bennie of the Glasgow Missionary Society, who took up residence among the Xhosa at Tyhume in 1821, was the first person systematically to engage, as he put it, in "reducing to form and rule this language which hitherto floated in the wind."[19] A printing press from Scotland arrived at Tyhume in 1823, and Xhosa was printed for the first time later that year. Robert Moffat of the LMS (see pp. 107–09) established a press at Kuruman among the Tswana.[20] Members of the Paris Evangelical Mission Society (see pp. 110–13) settled among the Sotho in 1833; a catechism was printed in Southern Sotho at Cape Town in 1837; a printing press arrived at Beersheba in 1841 and issued Bible translations before its destruction by fire in 1848; in 1861 a new press was set up at Morija, which issued the early classics in Southern Sotho. These were the pioneers: other languages, such as Zulu and Venda, developed written and printed traditions later. Tswana faltered after its early start, but Xhosa and Sotho led the way.

John Bennie's initials appear at the foot of the earliest extant piece of printed Xhosa, a one-page reading sheet dated to 1823. In it, Bennie demonstrates a sensitivity to Xhosa taste, exploiting the Xhosa absorption with cattle: Bennie affirms Xhosa values, while at the same time introducing his readers to biblical narrative and to white culture. "All cattle belong to God," the sheet proclaims. "He is their owner." Cattle were given to Noah, they serve humans with God's consent, and are slaughtered (referring to Xhosa ritual sacrifice) through a covenant with God. "All the colours of cattle," the sheet concludes, "are made by God the owner."[21]

The missionaries' early efforts were devoted to transcribing languages, establishing grammars, and providing school readers and catechetical material, but soon they had to pay attention to the reading needs of school graduates. No mission press has a more venerable history in the production of such vernacular literature than the Lovedale Mission Press, and no director of the press contributed as much as did the Rev. R.H.W. Shepherd (director from 1927 to 1958). Shepherd wrote:

> In all its efforts for the spread of literature Lovedale recognised that there was a danger lest the missionary agencies, having in their schools taught vast numbers to read, should leave non-Christian and even anti-religious elements to supply the reading matter … While in school and when they left it it was imperative that they find within their reach literature suited to their every need, in order that they might have an understanding grasp of Christian life and morals.[22]

Apart from biblical translations and tracts, translations of John Bunyan's *Piligim's Progress* were published in Tswana in 1848, in Xhosa in 1867, in Southern Sotho in 1872, and in Zulu in 1895. Throughout the nineteenth century, however, the most significant progress in cultivating a black readership and encouraging vernacular writing was achieved through less formal, more ephemeral newspapers and journals.

The Wesleyans were the first to publish pieces written by native speakers of Xhosa. They issued two pioneering periodicals, *Umshumayeli Wendaba* (Preacher of the News) from 1837 to 1841 and *Isibuto Samavo* (A Collection of Tales) from 1843 to 1844. The first Scottish periodical was *Ikwezi* (The Evening Star) published at Lovedale in 1844. The Southern Sotho journal *Moboleli oa Litaba* (Communicator of the News) appeared in 1841, followed by *Leqosana la Lesutho* in 1850, printed by the Wesleyans at Platberg. The first appearance of *Leselinyana la Lesotho* (Little Light of Lesotho) in November 1863 marked a turning point in the history of Sotho literature, for *Leselinyana* fairly exploded with contributions from readers, many of them recording oral traditions. In these periodicals, and their nineteenth-century successors, written literature was nurtured, flowered, and came of age. They carried mission and overseas news, and devoted much effort to presenting the biblical story, Christian morality, and European culture in general, but the first Xhosa contributions by native speakers tended to be in modes established by oral tradition, for example discourse and legend. Like *Die Afrikaanse Patriot*, they urged African writers to write as they spoke.

Regular features in the early Wesleyan periodicals were dialogues composed by missionaries. In the seventh issue of *Umshumayeli* (January 1839), for example, Student tells Lazy that he is on his way to school to learn how to read and write.

Lazy: I can count already, though I've never been to school. But reading is something I can't do. What is it?

Student: Reading is talking to books: they tell stories (*imbali*) about things, which are put into books; when someone looks at them he sees they're there, he studies and he knows; he reads and he knows what they're all about, and then he can tell other people.

Lazy: How can they be put in books? Aren't stories things spoken with the mouth?

Student: Little marks are made, and these marks are words telling what's being said.

Student explains that news from far away can be written in books, that news from times long past can be recorded in books so that it is not forgotten; "Even God's word from heaven can be put in books and received here." Lazy is amazed.

Lazy: You're not kidding! I also want to study!

Student: You must study, so that you're not called Lazy any more.[23]

The next issue of *Umshumayeli* (April 1839) contained the first piece of published writing by a native Xhosa speaker: Jivashe's account of events during the Mfecane is told in the manner of a traditional legend, or *imbali*. The fifth issue of *Isibuto* (January 1844) included a fictional conversation imitating the style of those in which an Englishman tells an ignorant Xhosa about his country, but here a Mfengu turns the tables and informs an ignorant Englishman about *his* nation. It is the first dramatic dialogue written by a native Xhosa speaker.

The earliest generation of Xhosa authors were literally and figuratively the children of Ntsikana. The earliest known Xhosa author (as distinct from Ntsikana himself, who remained illiterate and whose compositions were memorized and later written down for the first time only after his death) was Noyi the son of Gciniswa, a disciple of Ntsikana. Noyi followed the prophet's instructions and settled on the Tyhume mission station, where he was one of the first five Xhosa baptized by John Brownlee in 1823, taking the name Robert Balfour. Noyi wrote a legendary history of the Xhosa people (which commences with the words *Embalini kutiwa*, "It is said in a legend [*imbali*]") which John Bennie prepared for publication. Had it passed through the presses, it would have been the first secular book ever published in Xhosa. In an undated 10-page tract, probably from the 1830s, appears a two-page sermon, "Ilizwi lika-Dukwana" (The Voice of Dukwana), almost certainly by Dukwana, a celebrated preacher who was a son of Ntsikana.[24] A grandson of Ntsikana, William Kobe, contributed a series of historical articles to a later Lovedale newspaper, *Isigidimi SamaXosa* (The Xhosa Messenger) in the 1880s. And Mary Ann, who was in the party of five baptized with Noyi in 1823, became the first woman to write for publication when she contributed a letter to *Isitunywa Sennyanga* (The Monthly Messenger) in December 1850.[25]

Isitunywa, published by the Wesleyans in 1850, explicitly solicited contributions from its readers, but black contributions were not always acceptable to white missionary editors. The issue of control was first engaged explicitly in *Isigidimi SamaXosa*, published by Lovedale between 1870 and 1888, initially under the firm control of James Stewart, principal of Lovedale. Responding to a black reader's appeal for *Isigidimi* to be used to preserve Xhosa customs and traditions, Stewart made his position clear in February 1871:

> There is very little in old Kaffirdom worth preserving – and we think it will be the wisdom of the natives as soon as possible to move forward into day – and secure the blessings which the present time brings to them. We make this statement even while we intend if possible to publish from time to time brief notices of Kaffir Laws and Customs. These possess a value, as enabling us to understand the native people better – and have an interest as belonging to a certain state of society. But this is a very different thing from holding up that state as worthy of imitation or preservation.

In the following month, Stewart clarified the implications of this policy in rejecting for publication an oral poem produced in honour of a chief's son at his circumcision. The poem, Stewart wrote, was "not suited to our purpose. The inducements to young men to forsake their education, and to leave their employments, for the ceremonies of circumcision are so many, that we cannot afford to place an additional one before them by throwing the halo of song and romance about the practice."[26] Stewart's scorn recalls a similarly unsympathetic attitude towards Sotho poetic performances expressed by Dieterlen and Kohler in the commemorative *Livre d'or de la mission du Lessouto* (1912):

> In a large gathering, sitting round waiting to hear a royal message, a man seems suddenly seized by an irresistible devil. He leaps forward, parades in front of his friends, his head held high, his eyes large and staring, his face contorted, his voice raised in pitch, making violent gestures; he declaims his praises but without varying the intonation of his voice, and with such a stream of words that it is difficult to understand all the words ... The white man laughs, finding this infantile, ridiculous and grotesque. As for the black man, he admires, he exults at this spectacle which for him is worthy of heroes and which responds to his most intimate ideas and to all that is virile in him.[27]

Yet the missionaries were not universally hostile to local traditions which, as Stewart argued, enabled them to understand their target population. Indeed, the first secular books printed local folklore, some of them derived from earlier publication in mission journals. In Xhosa, three booklets were isssued by the Anglican St. Peter's Mission Press at Gwatyu in 1875, 1876 and 1877, versions of tales by Aesop and of English folktales together with Xhosa folktales, and a transcription of a historical narrative (*imbali*) about the Mpondomise of Mditshwa. As early as 1841, Casalis produced his *Études sur la langue séchuana* (i.e. Southern Sotho), which contained the texts of four praise poems and eight animal praises in French translation, as well as a 50-page appreciation of "Poésies des Bassoutos." Clearly the French missionaries were more sympathetic to traditional poetry than Stewart: Casalis argued that Western and Sotho poetry shared an "admirable correspondence which is sufficient to show that poetic feeling is indeed one of the attributes of the human soul, and that art, which has so often been confused with genius, is valuable only inasmuch as it respects and encourages the development of a faculty with which God himself has endowed those whom he intends should charm or brighten the world."[28] Arbousset included the Sotho text of a poem in praise of an eland in his *Relation d'un voyage d'exploration au nord-est de la Colonie du Cap de Bonne-Espérance* (1842) accompanied by a sensitive interpretation of the poem. Azariel Sekese's extensive articles on folklore, which originally appeared in *Leselinyana* after 1887, were published as *Mekhoa ea Basotho le Maele le Litsomo* in 1893. Subsequently, articles on folklore, originally published in *Leselinyana*, formed the basis of books by Everitt Segoete (1915), Z.D. Mangoaela (1921) and J. Mapetla (1924).[29]

The publication of these early secular booklets may have been designed to promote the process of conversion through familiarity with African traditions, but the missionaries may also have been aware of the widespread "discovery of the people" in Europe in the late eighteenth and early nineteenth centuries.[30] Certainly missionaries and those associated with mission schools pioneered the collection and publication of black South African folklore: Henry Callaway among the Zulu, Edouard Jacottet among the Sotho, and George McCall Theal among the Xhosa.

Early in the twentieth century, the missionaries addressed as one of the consequences of their involvement in black education the need to publish vernacular literature in book form. D. D. Stormont appealed to the Second General Missionary Conference in 1906 for the development of vernacular literature as an adjunct to the mission enterprise: "Now a Christian Literature aiming at the setting forth of Christian morality in its relation to the Customs of the Native peoples, would be bound to do more for the upraising of the moral life, than the slow means of the present day."[31] Early in the twentieth century the mission presses started producing literature in books. Some of these pioneering works were free of reference to Christianity, like S. E. K. Mqhayi's historical novelette *Ityala Lamawele* (The Trial of the Twins, 1914), but most were clearly the products of mission readership and education. The Lovedale Press issued Mqhayi's now-lost *USamson* in 1907, and then H. M. Ndawo's *Uhambo LukaGqoboka* (Christian's Progress, 1909), a Bunyanesque allegorical novel like the early Sotho *Moeti oa Bochabela* (Traveller to the East) by Thomas Mofolo (1907), which had been serialized in *Leselinyana*.

Monono ke Moholi, ke Mouoane (Wealth is Like Mist and Fog, 1910) by E.L. Segoete was heavily moralistic, as were two Xhosa novels published in 1913 and 1914 written by Letitia Kakaza, the first black female author of note.

The mission presses exercised control over the books they issued. Although Shepherd felt that the ending of Jordan's novel *Ingqumba Yeminyanya* (The Wrath of the Ancestors, 1940), for example, indicated a triumph of traditional over school forces, he saw it through the press unaltered.[32] At other times, however, he suppressed significant work. Shepherd received the manuscript of S.E.K. Mqhayi's biography of Elijah Makiwane in 1932 and, concerned about its frank treatment of Xhosa–Mfengu animosity, he procrastinated: the manuscript remained unpublished at Mqhayi's death in 1945, and has since disappeared. Two other works by Mqhayi, the predominant figure in Xhosa literature – a biography of W.B. Rubusana and his essay *Ulwaluko*, which Lovedale's reader called "a plea in defence of the rite of circumcision" – were rejected by Lovedale. Shepherd criticized the biography of Rubusana for lacking detachment in reporting the feud between Rubusana and John Tengo Jabavu: "As a missionary press, we cannot allow ourselves to become involved in political controversy making for division among the Bantu people." In rejecting *Ulwaluko* Shepherd suggested to Mqhayi that "the right method" of advancing Mqhayi's argument "seems to be through the churches and Christian bodies rather than through a publication of the Lovedale Press." Both manuscripts are now lost.[33]

Black authors have thus been constrained to comply with the Christian ideologies of mission educators (or, in more recent decades, with the political imperatives of commercial publishers concerned to see their products prescribed for school use): the Rev. C. B. Brink's preface to the published proceedings of a conference on Christian Literature for the Bantu of South Africa, held in Johannesburg in 1956, offered the book "for information and guidance to all those who are working to subject the spirit of Africa to the spirit of Christ."[34] Black Christian authors – many of them, like the Xhosa writers John Knox Bokwe, Tiyo Soga, Jonas Ntsiko or J. J. R. Jolobe, themselves ministers – chose to write on Christian themes, comfortably within the religious ideology of the missions, and much early writing dealt with moral themes like the evils of drunkenness or the godlessness of city life, or adopted Bunyan's allegorical mode. Other writers, most prominently Mqhayi, suffered rejection, or, like W. W. Gqoba in his long poems "The Great Debate between Pagan and Christian" and "The Great Debate about Education," aired powerful anti-mission arguments, but awarded the contest to the Christian faction.[35]

"We're Plagued by Christians": Christianity in Black Folklore

Blacks have retained independence over only one major form of literary expression, the spoken word.[36] Black folklore frequently conveys a less accommodating attitude towards Christianity and the mission enterprise than published literature. The praise poem of Kreli [Sarhili], for example, testifies to the social divisions the missionaries initiated among the Gcaleka between Xhosa and Mfengu:

> The Butterworth Mfengu are so high and mighty:
> Butterworth features in missionary records.

The praises of his son Sigcawu scorn the church's opposition to polygamy: "If his home's on church land he'll bear no children."[37] Hugh Tracey recorded a Zulu song expressing the attitude of a schoolchild to a church committee's inspection visit:

> The Committee's at the school.
> We're plagued by Christians.[38]

The missionary Karl Endemann, nicknamed Little Bellows, recorded a satirical Sotho song directed against himself:

> Were I on foot and drenched with rain,
> I'd not seek shelter with Little Bellows.
> He lies – we've caught him at it:
> "I preach God's Word," he claims. Liar![39]

And Robert Sobukwe's collection of Xhosa riddles includes comparisons between a Wesleyan minister and a white-necked raven, between an Anglican priest and a stork, between prayer-meeting women in their red headgear, green blouses and brown dresses and the Cape aloe; one riddle comments pointedly, "My woman stays alone the whole week, but meets people two or three times a week – a church building."[40]

The modern Xhosa oral poet D. L. P. Yali-Manisi often exploits traditional imagery of the book and the rifle as agents of dispossession, as in an oral poem he delivered in the 1820 Settlers Monument at the Grahamstown Festival in July 1977:

> You entered bearing the Bible,
> You said, "Receive the great book,
> Cast aside your lore and custom."
> We took up the Bible and followed you,
> Preacher became soldier,
> He shouldered his rifle and fired his cannon,
> Rharhabe's mountains roared,
> Dust arose and the land flared.

In 1983, addressing divinity students at Rhodes University, Manisi referred to the English settlers as those who

> coursed the sea bearing the Bible,
> concealing a musket beneath their cassocks.

In 1970, at the climax of a performance on the cattle-killing of 1857, Manisi apportioned blame for the loss of Xhosa independence:

All of our troubles began with conversion:
we accepted conversion embracing God,
yet this very God that we embraced,
this Bible is pregnant with evil incarnate,
held by a man who faces westward,
his clerical collar prim in front,
secured behind by a butterfly stud;
at his back a hidden cannon
that looms as soon as he opens his mouth
and shatters the sinews of those before him.
When confusion assailed the land
the missionaries sliced clean through,
they sliced clean through urging peace and calm.
That hound of hounds, the child of Grey,
Big George, the son of Grey,
claimed he was just rearranging the land,
yet in this time of shame and disgrace
he stood to one side and shaded his eyes,
counting the corpses in mounting piles.
The Xhosa lay stark with not a shot fired,
clawed their way forward on their bellies,
dodging the cannon to get at their killers!
I've finished!!
I've finished.[41]

Only through the medium of his oral traditions has the black author enjoyed the freedom to express his anger at the collusion between church and state, or to mock the Christian bearers of Western civilization.[42]

Imbumba Yamanyama: An African Synthesis
  Because the various literary traditions of the region have by and large developed discretely, one should speak of literature in South Africa rather than of South African literature. Despite a common Christianity, or familiarity with Christianity, writers and performers in any one language are rarely familiar with or influenced by the literature in another. White writers have created black characters, or presented their conceptions of black culture, with varying degrees of success: in Afrikaans, N.P. Van Wyk Louw's "Raka" depicted an African trickster; in English, Guy Butler has produced a version of a Zulu praise poem in "Isibongo of Matiwane". David Darlow, long an English lecturer at Fort Hare, celebrated African heroes like Khama, Moshoeshoe, Ntsikana, and Shaka in epic poems, always from his Christian perspective. In his tribute to the members of the South African Native Labour Contingent drowned in the English Channel in 1917 (*The Mendi*, 1940), Darlow invested the tragedy with a Christian interpretation:

So to death
They went, six hundred Africans; no breath

310

Of cowardice besmirched their sacrifice.
With oozy lips they murmured: "Now. O Christ."
Six hundred Africans before the astonished world
Flaunted a banner that shall not be furled.[43]

In his epilogue, he had the victims safe in heaven:

The Great King raises his hand to salute you,
Warriors of Africa,
Honoured by your sacrifice, warmed at his fire-side.
Ye are his warriors now and for ever.

Mqhayi, too, saw Christian consolation in the *Mendi* tragedy in his poem "Ukutshona kukaMendi" ("The Sinking of the *Mendi*"):

With what else could we then have made sacrifice?
What else is a people's oblation?
Is it not the young men of the race?
Is it not the best loved of the people?
Thus speaking, we go to the root of things;
We strike deep, and we open a way.
Was not Abel the whole world's oblation,
And Messiah the oblation of Heaven?[44]

In his Xhosa epic "UThuthula," J. J. R. Jolobe also glosses his narrative from a Christian perspective. Ngqika's councillors plot to oppose Ntsikana's preaching:

Amaphakathi staid were moved with fear
When they beheld the Gospel's power at work.
They were not ready yet for any change
In ancient order, custom, life and faith.
For counsel fresh in secret some did meet
To find a way to kill this strange new thing.
Alas! this Truth for ever dogged by hate
Though muffled it shall never be by man.
At Babylon was not a furnace made?
And yet amid its flames it stalked unharmed.
To kill it Herod, too, at Palestine
By Massacre of Innocents did try.
At Calvary did they not once exult
With hope of triumph over this same Truth?
And yet it rose victorious over death.[45]

And he condemns Thuthula for abandoning her husband Rharhabe for his nephew Ngqika not on grounds of incest, as in Xhosa custom,[46] but on the grounds of Christian morality:

311

Alas! Thuthula, thou didst bring disgrace
And shame on marriage vows. Thy conscience, too,
Did witness to the violation made.
In man's associations wedlock's pure.[47]

Chris Mann's "Cookhouse Station," a widely anthologized poem, urges white travellers to see not only the smiling policeman on the platform but also the migrant workers, not only the white soldiers whistling at a girl but also the black widow, and to be sensitive to black history and culture:

And if it is a midday in December
with a light so fierce
all the shapes of things quiver
and mingle, make certain you see
the shades of those who once lived there,
squatting in the cool of the blue-gum tree,
at ease in the fellowship of the afterdeath.

And if you ever pass through Cookhouse Station
make certain you greet these shades well, otherwise
you have not passed that way at all.

Sensitive as it is to African religion, significant as it is in urging whites to perceive the African spirit in their landscape, this poem yet speaks across cultures, as do those writers who impose Christianity on African experience. Their sincerity is not in question, but arguably Ntsikana's African gospel of assimilation – that heterogeneous cultures should fuse into one tightly compacted ball (*imbumba yamanyama*) – is achieved best when African literature absorbs and integrates Christianity and speaks in its own unfettered voice, when Christ is Africanized.

South African verbal artists using the media of speech or print occasionally achieve a creative accommodation, as in Ntsikana's hymn (see pp. 72–73) or the Zulu praise poems, traditional in style and ethic, celebrating Isaiah Shembe,[48] the founder of the Nazareth Baptist Church:

The Breaker-away, we left and we set out for our own Zululand,
because he broke away with his holy message.
The New Gospel which we saw setting the mountain on fire, and preachers
and evangelists denied it.
They denied that we had just preached the gospel.
They brandished their Testaments and Bibles in unison. They said it was
written "Thus!"
Breaker-away, let us leave and let us head for our own Zululand,
because he broke away with the Gospel,
the Gospel which we saw approaching with our own royal leaders
adorned with the plumage of the red-winged loury ...

Fire which blazed at the top of Ndulinde Mountain,
it blazed on with fierce flame,
it was stoked up by Shandu of Ndulinde.
Assegai red at the holding end,
you attacked with it at Mpukunyoni,
because you attacked through the gospel.[49]

In a spontaneous performance recorded on a Sunday morning in December 1970, the Xhosa praise poet Nelson Title Mabunu depicted the crucifixion as a Xhosa ritual sacrifice, with all nations uttering *"Camugu"* (mercy), as do the Xhosa at the moment when the voice of the bull, its throat slit, is heard bellowing, signalling the ancestors' acceptance of the sacrifice, and communion between living and dead:

For the bull was sacrificed on the Mount of Calvary,
Sacrificed indeed on the Mountain of Bones,
And all the nation cried "Camagu!"
"Camagu!" for sins on earth are pardoned,
All the nations cried "Camagu!"
For God and the people are one.[50]

One of the greatest of Xhosa poets, Nontsizi Mgqwetho, was a devout support-er of the black women's prayer societies (*manyanos*) (see chap. 15, passim) but a passionate critic of the iniquity of black Christians in Johannesburg; an activist who admired Charlotte Maxeke, the Christian civil rights campaigner, but who castigated the failure of blacks to respond adequately to white oppression.[51] In her lament on the death of the Rev. B.S. Mazwi, published in the newspaper *Umteteli wa Bantu* on 23 February 1924, the ancestral shades inhabit not only the African landscape of Chris Mann's poem, but heaven, too; and she urges Mazwi to resist Satan quite as heroically as Shembe wields his gospel:

You took him from us, Lord of all!
In peace you removed your servant;
Prophets heard from shepherds
As angels bore him to you. Camagu!

Peace, Pastor Mazwi! You spoke
And all were drawn into your prayer;
And those who once mocked you, Father,
Now perceived your glory.

Walk with pride in Paradise,
Stalwart of Africa.
Create a commotion in heaven
And thrash all the creatures of hell.

Son of Mazwi, Gabriel's called you.
Go! Confer with the shades.
In death may your bones cover Africa
And shower us with light.

Walk with pride in Paradise,
Stalwart of Africa.
Blessed are those who die in the Lord
But hell is wracked by duststorms.

Walk with pride in Paradise,
Stalwart of Africa:
Monstrous Satan's hurled about
As hell blinks in fear.

Son of Mazwi, Gabriel's called you:
Shoulder your nation's cries
And mount the hill of Calvary
To the drumbeat of the cross.

Mgqwetho is as outraged as Manisi by the rapacity of whites and the emptiness of their promises, but she distinguishes between Jesus and the gospel preached to blacks. On 22 March 1924 she addressed the readers of *Umteteli*:

We, the converts, are prone to see
The mote in another's eye.
Africa, we now make a refuge of you
In which to conceal all our sins.

And yet even Jesus who bore our sins
Was a man, cracked on the cross;
He was the Word, and He became flesh:
Because of Him we wear a crown.

What do you want of Africa?
She can't speak, she can't even hear;
She's not jealous, not vying for status;
She hasn't squandered the funds of her people!

Where is this God that we worship?
For the one we worship isn't our own:
We kindled a fire and sparks swirled up,
Swirled up to European heights.

Hear the wisdom of the Europeans' God:
"Gird yourself, black man, for the treasures of heaven

While we gird ourselves for the treasures of Africa!"
Just like the sages of Pharaoh's land

Commanded the Jews: "Bake bricks with grass,"
And by sundown they stood empty-handed,
So it is for us black people now:
We're up with the sun, empty-handed by dusk.

So come on home! Remember your God
Who rescued the ship in distress,
Ancient Bone, from which they sucked marrow,
May it still yield marrow to Africa.

So come on home! Make a fresh start!
Remember the Crutch you leaned on as lepers,
Let Him lead you dryshod across this Red Sea.
Food from another man's pot makes you fart.
    Please hear me!!

In one of Mgqwetho's poems (1924) entitled "Induli kaXakeka enyukwa nguNtu" ("The Hill of Struggle the Black Man Climbs"), Jesus joins South African blacks as they strive for freedom: his Calvary is theirs too:

Steep this hill the black man scales,
Steep enough to challenge Christ;
Mouth foam-flecked, groaning in pain,
His ears rang as he mounted this hill.[52]

English and Afrikaans writers, with Europe at their backs, have been free to accept or reject Christianity in their work. For black South Africans, Christianity was only one aspect of a cultural complex imposed from without; the writing and publishing of literature remained an enterprise largely under Western control. Only through the spoken word could black opinion be expressed and communicated with any freedom. Unlike writers in English and Afrikaans, writers in black languages could ignore Christianity only at the whim of whites who controlled the presses; if they expressed their Christian convictions, for a century or more they had to do so with a Western voice through a Western medium. But the tensions and conflicts are resolved and a new cross-cultural synthesis achieved when the gospel is decked with royal lourie feathers, or wielded as a bloody assegai in heroic combat, or when Christ the bull is ritually slaughtered or mounts Calvary to the beat of African drums. The religion of the colonizer has then been colonized.

20

South African Christian Music

A. CHRISTIAN MUSIC IN THE WESTERN TRADITION

BARRY SMITH

Western religious music may well have been first performed in South Africa by Bartolomeu Dias's Portuguese sailors. In February 1488, near Mossel Bay, the all-male crew, led by an accompanying priest, may have sung a *Te Deum*, or a hymn to the Virgin, the music carrying across the rocks and dunes on the threshold of Africa. But the Portuguese decided not to colonize South Africa and thus it was the Dutch and the English who introduced the Western church-music tradition. Initially almost entirely Protestant in character, it was followed in later centuries by Catholic music, brought to South Africa particularly by the Germans in the eastern Cape and by the French in Natal.

A unifying factor for early white settlers was the Calvinist Dutch Reformed Church, under Dutch East India Company protection, for many years the only religion tolerated at the Cape. Calvinist music, unlike the Catholic choir-dominated liturgy, is essentially music for the congregation, to be sung by all. By 1655, when evening prayers were said at the Cape fort, they were no doubt accompanied by two or three verses of psalms sung from the 1566 Psalter of Petrus Dathenus, the hymnal of the Reformed churches of the Netherlands, a translation of the French Genevan Psalter of 1562. A later version of these psalms, published in 1775, became the official hymn book in the Dutch Reformed Church in South Africa, and stayed in use for more than 150 years. By the time Afrikaans replaced Dutch in services in 1920 and a new translation of the psalms became available at the end of the 1930s,[1] the original music of the sixteenth century had undergone dramatic changes. The free metre of the old Genevan tunes had been gradually transformed into the characteristic four-square, regular rhythms of modern hymn tunes, with the modal tonalities of many tunes now major or minor, and sung at a monotonously slow pace.

Music more secular in style and origin gradually found its way into the repertoire of the Reformed church, as devotional songs based on folk tunes were printed during the seventeenth century in the Netherlands and imported to the Cape. In 1883 a selection of such hymns was published under the title *Hallelujah!* A volume of Dutch translations of English and American sacred songs, entitled *De Kinderharp* and containing many revivalist tunes, had already appeared during the 1860s, and the popularity of these sometimes sentimental hymns and sacred songs resulted in another hymn-book (also entitled *Hallelujah!*) first appearing in an Afrikaans translation in 1930. These books were intended for the white Dutch

Reformed congregation, although in certain sections of the community they were considered musically *déclassé*. The Coloured mission churches of the Dutch Reformed Church had their own song-books, the first published by the Rhenish Missionary Society in the mid-nineteenth century under the formidable title *Geestelijke gezangen ten gebruike van Evangelische gemeenten uit de heidenen in Zuid-Afrika* (Spiritual Songs for Use by the Evangelical Congregations Formed from the Heathen in South Africa).[2]

With its emphasis on congregational musical participation, the Dutch Reformed Church in South Africa never developed a strong choral tradition, its musical strength lying more in its organ music, closely modelled on that of Europe. A number of Dutch Reformed churches in South Africa have fine organs of neo-classical design. In recent years, as a counterbalance to the growing influence of the Pentecostal churches among the Afrikaners, more popular music, of the so-called charismatic kind, has been gradually introduced, sometimes as a prelude to the formal service itself, and often with guitars and piano for accompaniment rather than the organ.

When Britain occupied the Cape in 1795 and again in 1806, Anglicans were permitted to hold their services in the Groote Kerk in Cape Town. Not until 1834 were Anglican services held in an Anglican edifice, the newly completed St. George's Church.[3] From 1820 on, as adherents of other denominations arrived at the Cape, Methodists, Presbyterians, Congregationalists, and Baptists brought their own musical tastes and traditions. At this time music in England was dominated by the powerful figure of Handel, whose presence stifled the national musical English voice that had flourished in Tudor times and reached new heights with Henry Purcell in the seventeenth century. The musical jewels of Tudor England would not be rediscovered until the early twentieth century, and the church music brought to South Africa by the early British settlers was often not of the highest quality.

The first English settlers in South Africa probably used some of the early collections of hymns assembled in the late eighteenth and early nineteenth centuries, the metrical Psalters modelled on European counterparts and compiled by Church of England clerics such as Sternhold and Hopkins (1562) and Tate and Brady (1696). Not until 1769 was the first Anglican hymn-book published in England, Madan's *Collections of Psalms and Hymns*. Long before the Anglicans, the Nonconformist settlers, particularly the Congregationalists, Methodists, Presbyterians, and Baptists, had produced a number of hymn books of their own, with many tunes no doubt considered by Anglicans to be somewhat frivolous and in bad taste. They were none the less sung with great enthusiasm by the early Nonconformist settlers, particularly the Methodists, proud that "Methodism was born in song." The Calvinist Presbyterians, as also the Dutch Reformed, used metrical psalms as the principal music in their congregational worship. The Lutherans imported their strong musical tradition firmly underpinned by the German chorale. In the second half of the nineteenth century, the Church of England had produced comprehensive anthologies such as *Hymns Ancient and Modern* (1861), which, like other later hymn-books, such as *The English Hymnal* of 1906, were widely adopted and continue to be in use in South Africa's principal Anglican churches. Unlike their sister churches in the United States and Australia, South African Anglicans produced no local hymnals, and instead imported their music direct from England, with little effort to cross-fertilize local musical traditions with those of Europe.

A few nineteenth-century hymns may have been part of Catholic worship, though at this stage hymn-singing had not yet become integral to Catholic services. In the early days Roman Catholic church music in South Africa probably consisted chiefly of the more accessible examples of plainsong and simple settings of the Mass such as the *Missa de Angelis*. Late nineteenth-century Roman Catholic missionaries did compile simple hymn-books in African languages, the first indigenous one printed in Pietermaritzburg in 1876, but not until 1941 was a compilation *Katolieke gesang- en gebedboek*, provided for Afrikaans-speaking, mostly Coloured, Catholic congregations.[4]

The rise of the "charismatic" movements in South Africa of the 1970s (see pp. 166–67) brought a plethora of hymn- and chorus-books, notably the American *Sounds of Living Waters* volumes – popular and "non-elitist," but sometimes bordering on the commonplace. Increasingly, guitar and piano were used instead of the organ in worship. Also through the medium of the English language, church music in general has been opened to fertilization from African–American Christians, with spirituals, gospel songs, freedom songs, and "folk-mass" music finding their way from the United States. For many years the music of the Coloured churches closely followed in the Western tradition, but more recently an increasing desire to identify with Africa has been reflected in their choice of music. By the 1980s visiting African choirs sometimes performed African music in predominantly white churches from which apartheid had once tried to bar them, and a few whites, from time to time, worshipped in black areas. Heartening indicators of musical cross-fertilization were seen, for example the use in the Coloured Dutch Reformed Mission Church of gospel and freedom worship songs.

Many churches were built during the second half of the nineteenth century, largely Victorian–Gothic in style, and modelled on English parish churches, at a time when the rise of the High Church "Oxford Movement" in England influenced parish churches to imitate aspects of cathedral worship (see p. 331). Many of the new churches in South Africa were built to accommodate choirs and organs in the chancel. Small, imported organs with two manuals were squeezed into tiny organ chambers, to accompany surpliced choirs in ambitious anthems and canticles by Victorian composers. There were sporadic attempts to establish and maintain an English cathedral-style, all-male choral tradition, but few such choirs survived after the middle of the twentieth century, two notable exceptions being the choirs of St. Mary's Collegiate Church in Port Elizabeth and of St. George's Cathedral in Cape Town, where Robert Gray, the first Bishop of Cape Town, established a choir school in the 1840s. Cape Town cathedral presented many of the great masses with choir and full orchestra. The so-called sacred cantata (often sung at Passiontide and Christmas) was popular, as can be seen from large piles of such works gathering dust in music cupboards or organ lofts around South Africa. Just as Handel had dominated English music in the eighteenth century, so Mendelssohn and Gounod dominated the nineteenth, and tastes among the settler organists and choirmasters, who had been trained in England, favoured works by composers like Ludwig Spohr, Sir John Stainer, and Sir Arthur Sullivan. It was unfortunate that second-class Victorian music long provided a model to local composers.

The influence of the Royal School of Church Music (RSCM), founded in 1927 and based in England, has been particularly important in South Africa. After 1960, when its first summer school was held in Cape Town, these important musical events have been held annually, alternately in Cape Town, Johannesburg, Pietermaritzburg, and Grahamstown under the direction of distinguished church musicians, from England or the US. In these summer schools South Africans of all races met, lived, and sang together, an experience denied them in ordinary day-to-day life. Influenced by the RSCM, standards of church music have been noticeably raised in South Africa.

Some of the most moving of recent South African choral music has grown out of the life of black people, particularly the resistance and freedom songs. Much of this music has a soaring, timeless quality retaining elements of the spirituals sung by slaves in the American South. Today, the Catholic church, closely followed by some Anglicans and other denominations, has realized the value of including such music, with instruments such as marimbas, in liturgical worship, even though white and Coloured congregations are often conservative musically, preferring to sing what they know and like. Musical education in South African schools (particularly in black schools) has been woefully neglected in the past, and a priority has now been set to establish music education programmes that replace the existing sol-fa method with staff notation. This will greatly facilitate the learning of new and exciting music, for the African choral tradition is as fine and stirring as can be found anywhere in the world. There seems no danger or threat of extinction now from any Western cultural influence.

B. CHRISTIAN MUSIC AMONG AFRICANS

DAVID DARGIE

Much earlier than their European counterparts, African communities in South Africa developed an indigenous tradition of Christian music, along with various styles that mingled African and European elements. These developments have been most thoroughly researched among the Xhosa, who are the subjects of the following analysis.

The Missionaries and Xhosa Music

There was only one way for the first Xhosa converts to be officially Christian: they had to be members of the mission church and, often, residents of a mission station. Missionaries hoped to separate these converts from much of their traditional way of life, lest they be lured "back into the bush." Conversion to Christianity thus meant being Europeanized in music, as in other aspects of culture.

The abstract concept "music" was not expressed in traditional Xhosa language, which tended to focus instead on activities: songs, dances, and the roles of singers. The word *i-culo*, defined in Kropf's Xhosa dictionary as "originally a short song, now a hymn," which today refers exclusively to church or school singing performed without bodily movement,[5] was chosen by missionaries to make clear that in church or school one does not -ombela (sing and clap in a group while others dance and sing). From this new use of the stem -cul- a vocabulary was constructed to express Western musical concepts. In time umculi came to mean a musician, umculo to mean music.

Missionaries did publish and encourage the use of one African piece of music, the "Great Hymn" of Ntsikana, the revered founder of Xhosa Christianity (see pp. 72–73). So, too, they encouraged converts to compose Christian music, but not a single hymn they composed was in traditional African musical style. Festiri Soga (1865–1906), son of "Old" Soga, Ntsikana's chief disciple, composed hymns in African style, but his father, who until his death in 1878 held Christian services in his home in imitation of Ntsikana (and not under missionary direction), would not permit Festiri's songs in the services, only those of Ntsikana.[6] Of the collections of hymns issued by the missionaries, the first edited by a Xhosa may have been that of Tiyo Soga, Festiri's younger brother, a hymnal published in 1864[7] that contains a number of the compiler's own hymns – all in Western verse form.[8]

The church music of the missionaries followed a diatonic system and carefully avoided African rhythm.[9] Traditional Xhosa harmony is based on a pattern of major triads (three-note chords), originating from the use of the overtone patterns of musical bows. In Xhosa singing and bow playing, the harmony, following the melody, shifts from one chord to another a whole tone apart (e.g. from F major to G major). The repeated use of major chords in the diatonic harmony of pieces like Handel's "Hallelujah Chorus" was appealing to the Xhosa ear. The diatonic system of scale and harmony (as in the white notes of the piano) became the musical basis for African Christian singing, even among peoples who, unlike the Xhosa, do not use major triads in traditional music, or scales of whole and half tones. Converts were taught the sol-fa notation, a system barely adequate for the simplest diatonic music, and quite unable to reflect African rhythm.

Many African Christians succeeded nevertheless in developing an African version of the diatonic system, using African versions of the chords. Especially in choral singing blue notes occur frequently, and chords are very sweet, not reproducible on piano or organ. If the tones indicated by the sol-fa notation did not fit their taste, the singers adjusted them. Just as in traditional music, where harmony parts using the same texts must move in parallel, in this "Afro-diatonic" music a parallel movement also occurs: the harmony singers tend to move in the same pitch direction as the melody, each part shifting to select the new chord-note as guided by the ear. The result is something identifiably African, even if African rhythm itself is absent.[10]

Most church music the missionaries used consisted of European hymns translated into African languages, with a sprinkling of European melodies as diverse as the German soldiers' marching song "Morgenrot," and "Darling Clementine" (sung in Latin by Xhosa Catholics to the words of "Tantum ergo"). The task of translators was complicated by the word- and sentence-tones vital in nearly all African languages of southern Africa, where each word has its individual tone, the relative pitch levels of the syllables helping to determine the meanings. Languages such as Xhosa, Zulu and Sotho have also a characteristic falling–rising–falling sentence-tone: the first phrase begins high, falls (through the steps of the word tone), and ends lower; the next phrase begins high again, but lower than the phrase before, and then falls at its end, and so on. European melodies set to African words take no account of sentence-tone, and make nonsense of word-tone, thus altering the meanings of words, or rendering them meaningless altogether.

The early missionaries seem either to have been unaware of this confusion or to have ignored it. But some missionary translators and hymn arrangers were troubled that the stress in African words fell in "the wrong place," that is, the phrases of European hymns tend to end on a strong beat, while in most African words the accent is on the penultimate syllable. Some arrangers tried to remedy this by a system of "double-knock": repeating the final note on a weak beat to accommodate the final unaccented syllable. Some Anglican missionaries (and others) sought to address the problem by abandoning rhythm altogether, using psalm tunes with no musical rhythm at all, allowing singers to put the word stress where it fell naturally.

In traditional African music there is no equivalent of the specialized church choir, since singing involves everybody in the rites and ceremonies of life.[11] The introduction of choirs, which made it easier to conduct church services in the European way, required Africans to learn to sing in European style. But such Europeanization took singing away from the ordinary worshipper. So, too, the introduction of choir competitions, in which choirs attempted more and more difficult music, resulted in the laborious production, in sol-fa notation, of complicated specialist choir pieces, engendering a spirit of competition unsuitable for worship. In recent years better understanding of African music has led some missionaries to see the choir not as a group of specialists at all but as leaders of music who can enhance worship by involving the entire congregation in the singing.[12]

Not until the early 1960s, some 140 years after the death of Ntsikana, did any missionary urge a Xhosa Christian to compose church songs in traditional Xhosa style. In that period, Catholic missionaries Oswald Hirmer and Fritz Lobinger, both later members of Lumko Missiological Institute, raised the question with the leading Xhosa sol-fa composer of the time, B.K. Tyamzashe. Tyamzashe turned to Ntsikana for inspiration; the result, "Gloria," his most successful composition of this type, was published in 1965.[13]

In the Catholic mission areas, the papal encyclical *Musicae Sacrae* (1955) encouraged missionaries to promote local music for use in worship. It led to the production of the famous *Missa Luba* in Zaire, and to the adoption of much new African church music, especially in Rhodesia (now Zimbabwe), where the people regarded it as an expression of their resistance to settler rule. In South Africa, Anglican, Protestant, and Catholic missionaries had already given impetus to such a process. In the 1950s a Swedish Lutheran missionary, Henry Weman, had tried to use local music among Zulu Christians in Natal, but many Africans were not yet ready for it. Hundreds of church songs composed in Zulu style still lie unused in archives in Natal.[14] In 1962 the Southern African Catholic Bishops' Conference (see pp. 205–8) launched Lumko Missiological Institute, then at the old Lumko mission in the eastern Cape, as a place where missionaries could study African languages, anthropology, and related subjects, learning how to adjust themselves to Africa. In 1977 at the request of Lumko, David Dargie began to conduct church-music workshops at which local people were invited – and guided where needed – to compose new church songs in African styles. From 1979 to 1989 Lumko published more than 160 music tapes, most of them African church music, in some twenty African languages. Borrowing an idea from Zimbabwe, Lumko also introduced marimba xylophones as church-music instruments; "Lumko" marimbas soon spread across southern Africa.[15]

Not all major developments in African church music, however, have involved Afro-diatonic or traditional African techniques. Many Xhosa and other African musicians have used the Western diatonic music system. The greatest achievement in this genre is unquestionably Enoch Sontonga's majestic "Nkosi Sikelel' iAfrika."[16]

Xhosa Music Outside the Missionary Realm

Ntsikana's discovery of Christianity was free from the immediate influence of European Christians, and in composing his hymn he must have relied on typical Xhosa music techniques. He had been converted in about 1814, some fifteen years after the departure of the missionary J. T. van der Kemp. According to his disciples, he received the Holy Spirit immediately upon his conversion and sat up all night creating and singing the "Helele homna" chorus of his "Great Hymn," to this day widely regarded as the summit achievement of Xhosa song.[17] For a long time the original version of this song (or perhaps songs) seemed to be lost, but in 1981 two versions of it were recorded by Dargie in the Lumko district, both versions, unlike the church survivals of the song, employing the traditional call-and-response form and African rhythm. On the tape, the first version was sung by two elderly women at Mackay's Nek mission, one of the players accompanying on the *uhadi* musical bow, the most important traditional Xhosa instrument; the second version performed in Sikhwankqeni valley, by a large group of elderly women who had not heard of Ntsikana, and did not know that the "wounded hands" of which they sang were the hands of Christ. Added lines in the Mackay's Nek performance seemed to indicate that the song was used as a freedom prayer song during the 1850–53 War of Mlanjeni against the white settlers. In 1983 Dargie recorded a third traditional version, performed by four women of Ngqoko village (two kilometres from old Lumko); and again one of the women accompanied the song with the *uhadi* bow.[18]

Using these recordings and the typical performances of other Xhosa songs as a guide, one may speculate that, in performances by Ntsikana and his disciples, the "Great Hymn" was sung to the background of the "Ahom, homna" chorus, which became the "Helele homna" line of the hymn-books. On any particular occasion perhaps only a few verse lines may be used, related to the preaching of the day and repeated over and over, and in no strict order. After Ntsikana's death his disciples joined the new missionaries at Tyhume, who took great care to write down all versions of the song. In the hymn-books these lines were published in quasi-European style, interpretable as four stanzas of five or six lines each, all to be sung in fixed order. But there is evidence that more verses exist than appear in the hymn-book version, both in missionary transcriptions and in the traditional and partly traditional versions that have come to light. From the beginning, the missionaries at least partially shaped the Great Hymn into a Western hymn form.

J.K. Bokwe (1855–1922), the first Xhosa ordained minister of religion, devoted much study to Ntsikana's hymns, which he knew not only from church performance, but also through his parents and grandparents, who were disciples of Ntsikana. Bokwe published a series of transcriptions of Ntsikana's hymns between 1878 and 1914. In the end, he distinguished "four hymns" of Ntsikana: the "Bell," the "Life-Creator," the "Round Hymn" and "Great Hymn,"[19] perhaps all four originally parts of the one song.

The Mackay's Nek performance indicates that by the mid-nineteenth century Ntsikana's song already enjoyed the status of a national song and freedom song among the Xhosa. Its continuing influence is attested by Tiyo Soga, the first black South African Christian minister to be sent overseas to study. Soga married a white woman, but, taking great pride in his Africanness, was an apostle in South Africa of the black consciousness already finding expression in West Africa. Again and again Soga reports how he and others used Ntsikana's song in worship, and what effect it had on the congregation, frequently moving them to tears. This was the period when the British were tightening their grip on the Xhosa. Tiyo died in his early forties, before his father, "old" Soga. Father and son had both preached Christianity, but not the subjugation of their people to the British (see pp. 77–78).[20]

The majestic hymns of Ntsikana, as sung in church versions today, take their place beside the finest Christian anthems, but they lack African rhythm and African call-and-response form: all their verses are organized to be sung to the same melody, which is typically European. Still, their power should not be underestimated, for they retain a sense of Xhosa melody and Xhosa harmony, especially the "Round Hymn" and the "Great Hymn". It is easy to understand how they must have moved the hearts of Xhosa people when their nationhood was suppressed and their land alienated.

The "Ethiopian" churches, founded since the 1880s in opposition to white domination, have generally continued to use mission hymns and songs, but the "Zionist" or "indigenous spiritual" churches (see pp. 216–17), created since the early twentieth century by leaders anxious to express Christianity in an African way, have been much more innovative musically, joyfully embracing African rhythm and ignoring the missionary taboo on drumming. The use of the drum and other rhythmic instruments, such as rattles and bells, has long been, for conservative mission Christians, the most objectionable characteristic of Zionist worship, one that puts the Zionists in the camp of the diviners or "witch-doctors," too close to pre-Christian African religion for comfort.[21] Also, since many adherents of African religion, and of Zionist Christianity, are "uneducated" (i.e. have not attended school in the Western way), and since many are from the "lowest" social groups, worship with a drum has been seen as a sign of low status by those who regard themselves as educated or of higher social rank. This prejudice against drumming was a constant stumbling-block in the early years of the work of the Lumko music department. On two occasions, nearly two thousand kilometres apart in South Africa, church and choir members threatened to burn down their (Catholic) church if the missionary introduced the drum.

Another missionary taboo, the ban on dancing, has had an interesting impact on worship in some Zionist churches. In traditional Xhosa rites, the faithful stand around and sing and clap, while the diviners and other inspired people dance in the areas in the middle. Similarly, in Xhosa Zionist services in rural areas, people stand in a circle and sing and clap. When the Spirit comes, people have to move, but since dancing is taboo, they do not dance, but rather walk or run in a circle amid the singers. This circular movement – sometimes including running at high speed – occurs also in Zionist worship in urban townships. At a service in New Crossroads in 1986, the presiding Archbishop T. Kukisi of the Bantu Christian Asiria Church in Zion of South Africa referred to it as "i-merry-go-round"[22] In some Zionist churches dancing is permitted only at the end of the service, when people dance out from the place of worship, singing the final chorus.

The Zionist churches looked to African religion for inspiration in the conducting of services. For example, in Ngqoko village near old Lumko, the function of the diviners (all of whom in Ngqoko are women) is to put the supplicants in touch with the spirits of the ancestors (and through them, ultimately, with God).[23] While dancing, the diviners each carry a stick as a symbol of their authority, and a drummer (or more than one) beats the drums in a triplet rhythm. The diviners in Ngqoko wear leg rattles, consisting of reeds woven around the lower legs and allowed to dry in place. These rattles support the drum rhythm. When the singing stops, the diviner proclaims the divination. If those present agree, they say "Camagu!" (which is also the diviner's title) or "Siyavuma!" (we agree).

In Zionist church services in the same village, the minister, as the authority figure, carries a stick, but in the left hand, while in his right hand is the Bible. The songs in the service may use traditional or Afro-diatonic techniques, but all employ the same characteristic rhythm of the diviners' songs and are accompanied by the type of drum the diviners used.[24] Dancing is forbidden, though people move and run in a circle. To support the drum rhythm, at least two women use rattles of wire and metal. When the singing stops, the minister declaims his sermon, which frequently deals with the Holy Spirit, and members of the congregation respond by saying – not "Camagu!" – but "Amen!" In the cities, Zion Apostolic churches may use only songs in Afro-diatonic style, many of which are used by mainline churches as well. These hymns, too, are accompanied by the drum, rattles, and bells in a forceful rhythm, but not necessarily the rhythm typically used in villages such as Ngqoko.[25]

Perhaps it was the renewed discovery of pride in being African that, in the early twentieth century, fostered a feeling of freedom in worship. One early focal point of musical change, including the mainline churches, was the *manyano* groups – the women's unions and sodalities (see chap. 15 passim) – and the young men's groups, such as the *amadodana*. Meeting outside the formal worship and often in the absence of clergy, such groups used body movement, clapping, restrained dancing, and rhythmic beating of hymn-books. The entry point for a more African music is frequently the end of the service. As the minister processes out of the church, clapping and body movement begin. A similar spirit of rhythmic joy can suffuse the mood of pilgrimages, when one may see buses "dancing," as the pilgrims inside dance to their hymns and choruses.

In the recent "mainline" tradition of a wider freedom of worship, perhaps the freest of all have been those Christians who could be considered as both "main-line" and "independent" at the same time – a difficult role to maintain because of discriminatory policies in white-dominated churches in former years, as a result of which many African Protestant groups were cut adrift from their white parent churches. Most notable among these black churches are the A.M.E., the Bantu Methodists, and the Transkei Methodists. Among churches like certain African Methodist groups, singing may be somewhat more restrained than the "Zionist style" – that is, church songs with drum and African rhythm, called in Xhosa *iin-goma zaseZiyoni* "songs in Zionist style" – but without drums or rattles, and per-haps less exuberant. This singing nonetheless uses African rhythm – clapping, body movement, and beating of hymn-books with the open palm. Many songs are not hymns arranged in verses but choruses of frequently repeated single-line texts or simple verses more closely related to the cyclic songs of African music than to the stylized structures of Western hymns. Such songs, called *"amakorasi"* or choruses, are sung with beating of hymn-books (and also, the beating of cushions held in the hand), with clapping and some body movement: they are frequently called "Methodist songs" in Xhosa, *iingoma zamaWesile* ("songs of the Wesleyans").

A single song may, in fact, be considered both a Zionist song and a Methodist song, depending on the method of performance. What was originally a mission song – or even something very High Church out of the Anglican *Hymns Ancient and Modern* – can be totally transformed by the method of performance. A "Methodist" transformation of a song, it must be stressed, can, like a Zionist ver-sion, boil over with exuberance. During chorus singing people may jump into the air, especially when, as on pilgrimage, they feel released from usual constraints. The use of rhythm and body movement does not imply any specific emotion; indeed many African congregations sing choruses using Christ's agonized words on the cross in such a way that a European visitor might imagine they are expressing the joys of Easter, when in fact they are identifying the sense of forsakenness of Christ with their own sufferings under apartheid.[26]

The Freedom Struggle and Christian Music Today

Today choral singing, with clapping, body movement, and even drumming is entering worship in the mainline churches more and more often, perhaps most of all in those churches and areas where the spirit of resistance to apartheid has been strongest. Especially in urban African congregations church singing today sounds much the same whether the congregations consist of Xhosa, Zulu, Sotho, or other people of South Africa. Whatever the stylistic differences in their precolonial music, urban African populations have largely absorbed and interpreted Afro-diatonic music techniques in the same way. In urban situations there is still a strong tradi-tion of diatonic composition and of the use of choirs; choir leaders compose spe-cial choir "show-pieces" by the hundred, writing the music out painstakingly in sol-fa notation, to be performed under a conductor's baton by uniformly robed choirs. And yet, at the same time, the chorus singing movement has given a new opportunity to all worshippers to celebrate together in a more African way.

In the twentieth century, when resistance to white domination grew in the urban areas, where Christians were heavily concentrated in the large black townships, freedom songs grew out of the style of the mission songs. Most notable among them was "Nkosi sikelel' iAfrika". In the renewed resistance after the Sharpeville massacre of 1960, powerful and dignified resistance songs like this bound people together in the face of violent repression. But, by the mid-1980s, the musical style of the freedom songs was moving closer to traditional music, some employing traditional scale and harmony, many employing rhythm through dancing. New expressions of African rhythm developed to suit the spirit of the times, for example the "war dance" called *itoyitoyi* of the young cadres of the African National Congress and the United Democratic Front.[27] The struggles for political freedom found expression in worship, and encouraged the bringing of traditional African musical elements into the church. The use of drums, marimbas, and other instruments in church music in Zimbabwe in the 1960s and 1970s, as well as the use of new church songs composed in Zimbabwe in African styles, inspired similar developments in South Africa and Namibia.

In recent times many Africans still feel torn between the European standards set by church and school, and their spiritual needs as Africans (and often their responsibilities as patriots as well). While mainline clergy frequently complain that their church members also attend Zionist church services, some clergy see no threat in this desire to participate in ancestor rituals and in other practices of African religion.[28] Many worshippers see no difficulties in attending two church services of different types on the same Sunday, or in consulting figures such as the faith-healer of Cancele – as long as the clergy do not find out.[29] People are worshipping across denomination lines as well, and musical cross-pollination is the inevitable result. Mainline church people are borrowing and spreading "Methodist" and Zionist songs,[30] Zionists in Xhosa rural areas are using songs in neo-Zulu musical style (and some Zulu texts).[31] Western hymns are Africanized in performance in many Zionist congregations and also in many mainline, traditionally mission churches by the use of drumming, rhythmic instruments and body movement.[32] Religious music is alive and flourishing, a harbinger, perhaps, of a future ecumenical unity.

21

South African Christian Architecture

DENNIS RADFORD

Colonial Preaching Boxes: The Classical Style

The practice of religion at the Cape under Dutch-East India Company rule was monopolized, with rare exceptions, by the Dutch Reformed Church (NGK). The small size of the settlement and the Calvinist preference for unadorned settings and simplicity of worship meant that there was little incentive to construct many or large places for worship. In 1795 there were still only five churches in the colony, but the influence of these few buildings was to last well into the nineteenth century, in part because the low level of technology inhibited innovation, in part because the religious sentiments and cultural tastes of the white settlers were conservative.

The first church services were held in 1652 in a room in the wooden fort built by the first commander at the Cape, Jan van Riebeeck, on the site of the present Grand Parade.[1] In 1666 a wooden church was built within the new stone castle, which still stands. No illustrations of the church have been found. In 1678 the foundations of a permanent church were laid in what was then a churchyard at the top of the Heerengracht, now Adderley Street, opposite the Great Hospital, but the church was only completed in 1704. Later known as the Groote Kerk or Great Church, it is thus the mother church for all the Dutch Reformed churches in the country. It took the form of a Greek cross (in which the arms of the cross are of equal length to its trunk) or two interlocked thatch-roofed rectangles with gables at each end (Fig. 1). Its most obvious models were the Dutch churches dominated by a pulpit such as the Nieuwe Kerk (1645) in Haarlem.[2] The present tower, placed at the north end of the church, dates from this period. The gables, a distinctive feature of Cape Dutch architecture, were neo-classical. Between 1779 and 1781 the church was enlarged by removing the re-entrant walls and placing large circular columns at the old corners. The illustration shown here (Fig. 2) gives some indication of the size and shape of the new interior. Fig. 1 shows the extension with the new gables and also shows the prominence of the tower, which is confirmed in contemporary views and panoramas. From 1835 to 1841 the church was rebuilt yet again to give it a rectangular form with a clear span of about 25 metres (80 feet). It remains today substantially as left by Herman Schutte, its architect and builder, in a curious combination of classical gables and Gothic windows.[3]

Slightly earlier (1687) but much less grand was the first church at Stellenbosch,[4] the forerunner of many later, equally humble, Dutch Reformed churches. It was a simple rectangle with a hipped thatch roof and set in a small walled churchyard. After it was destroyed by fire in 1710, its successor was built in 1719 on a Greek cross plan. It was in fact a smaller version of the Groote Kerk. In 1814 the wings were extended and neo-classical gables built at the ends. The illustration (at p. 30) shows the front gable, also very typical of this period. The church was substantially rebuilt in 1863 and survives in that form today.

From 1774 a small community of Lutherans in Cape Town used a warehouse in Strand Street for services.[5] In 1780 they received permission to worship there, and in 1791 and 1792 added to it a church-like façade designed by Anton Anreith, the Cape Town sculptor who had previously designed and constructed the pulpit. After 1818 the present tower was added. Both internally and externally the Lutheran church is probably the finest surviving early church in the country, particularly noteworthy for its grouping with the two flanking houses (Fig. 3).

The Moravians had started mission work at Genadendal in 1737, which, after a long hiatus, was resumed in 1791 (see p. 34).[6] By 1803 there were about a thousand people at the mission, and around 1800 the first large church was built (Fig. 8). It had a steeply pitched thatched roof with crow step gables at each end, something novel at the Cape and obviously of North German inspiration. Fig. 9 shows the interior in 1811, which Burchell described as "plain and neat; the walls were white washed and the ceiling was supported by two strong though rather clumsy pillars of masonry."[7] In Cape Town the first Sending Gesticht, the mission to the Coloured community, built its church at 40 Long Street in 1799, with a façade that strongly resembles that of the Lutheran church, but without the tower.[8] The simple, rectangular building survives today as a national monument.

The five churches built at the Cape by 1795 had similar liturgical purposes: they were preaching boxes built to give as many worshippers as possible good sound and sight lines to the centrally located, elevated pulpit. Elements such as sounding boards, elaborately carved and located above the preacher, helped the acoustics and often made these pulpits into very grandiose affairs. Those at the Groote Kerk and the Lutheran Church still survive. Galleries at the back, or even at the side, were often added to bring more of the congregation close to the preacher. Internal ornament was sparse, owing both to theological inclination and a lack of able artists. The illustration (Fig. 2) of the interior of the Groote Kerk typifies this period. Externally what is most noticeable is the thick walled construction; most openings are apparently cut into the building's envelope. White-washed plaster covered the church and was also used on the gables. Other ornamentation – initially restricted to the doors and windows during this period – derived from the classical vocabulary of mouldings and orders, with European styles such as baroque, rococo, and neo-classicism influencing the artisan's work.[9]

The most difficult technical problem facing the early church builder was to achieve a large compact and unobstructed space. Long lengths of wood were in short supply, as was the technical ability to span wide spaces without columns. Also problematic was the ability of the rough stone and clay walls to absorb the heavy point loads which a truss system would impose. Consequently, the average builder was restricted to a clear span of about of 8 metres (about 25 feet) and a plan in the form of an I or T. Since bell towers were also structurally unsafe, for the ringing of bells created a dangerous momentum that could cause the walls to collapse, bells were hung in small free-standing structures situated in front of the church.

Other good examples of early churches survive at Tulbagh (the old NGK church, 1748–95) which no longer corresponds to its pre-1795 form, and at Paarl (the Strooidak church, 1805).[10]

Although the British first occupied the Cape in 1795, not until the 1820s did they influence church architecture. With the new government came new religious denominations and thus the need for additional churches. As the established church in England, the Anglican church sought a prominent position for itself in Cape Town, just as it did in other colonial capitals. To this end it was granted a site at the bottom or town end of the old Company's gardens, near the British governor's residence, where it rivalled the nearby Groote Kerk.[11]

In 1829 a design for the new church, St. George's, was complete and the building was finished four years later (Fig. 62). It could hold 1,150 people. The cathedral, as it shortly became on the arrival of Bishop Gray in 1848, was based almost exactly on St. Pancras, London (1819), a much-admired church in the fashionable Greek Revival style – a style derived from specific Greek prototypes like the Parthenon and Erechtheum in Athens and characterized by Doric columns and sparsity of ornament.

St. George's front façade had a large Ionic portico, topped by an hexagonal steeple freely derived, like that of St. Pancras, from the Tower of the Winds in Athens. (Missing were the two side porches supported by caryatids – columns in the form of Greek women – a prominent feature of St. Pancras.) Internally it was bare, a simple rectangle with a gallery: like the Groote Kerk, a preaching box modified slightly for low-church Anglican worship with a central altar or communion table and a side pulpit. This form had been introduced by Christopher Wren, the influential British Renaissance architect. The local architect, John Skirrow, adapted it to local conditions. Robert Gray, the first bishop of Cape Town, and his Anglo-Catholic successors disliked the building's preaching-box characteristics, and it was demolished early in the twentieth century to be replaced by the present cathedral on the same site.

Another, more modest example of the Greek Revival is St. Andrew's Presbyterian Church (Fig. 61) built in Cape Town in 1827–28 fairly close to the Lutheran church.[12] Designed by Henry Reveley, son of a prominent English Greek Revival architect, it has, like St. George's, a simple rectangular plan, seating 500 together with 300 more in a gallery. Its chief feature is the Doric-temple front façade, which, unusual for its type, covers half the width of the church, its columns being half exposed rather than fully round – probably a concession to economics. The church is surrounded by its own churchyard, as were its Scottish predecessors.

Outside Cape Town the neo-classical innovations were gradual and most new churches were still essentially barns with Cape Dutch gables. The Dutch Reformed church at George (Fig. 64), an exception, is probably based on a design by Herman Schutte, the builder of St. George's. Though the foundation stone had been laid ten years earlier, it was completed only in 1842.[13] The body of the church is in an entirely traditional T-shape, and its only distinguishing feature is the tower, which looks like a robust version of St. George's. The base with its temple front shows superficial influence of St. Andrew's Presbyterian church.

After the arrival of the British 1820 Settlers in the eastern Cape a number of churches were built in the new towns and in the countryside, most of which have since been rebuilt. A good example still surviving, in almost its original condition (Fig. 60), is St. John's Anglican Church in Bathurst near Grahamstown.[14] Designed in 1829 by Major Michell of the Royal Engineers and surveyor-general of the Cape Colony, it was completed in 1838. Built in the local sandstone, the church is the usual simple rectangle focused on a central altar and side pulpit but with a small porch and a short tower. The sides and back elevation are bare, so that the chief interest lies in the western front, which, rather than being inspired by the Greek Revival, harks further back to the Renaissance architecture of Nicholas Hawksmoor (1661–1736), an associate of Christopher Wren. The Rev. William Shaw recorded "that this village church, together with the character of the surrounding scenery and buildings, serves to remind an Englishman of many a rural spot in his own country of surpassing beauty."[15]

In the early nineteenth century many mission societies began their activities in the hinterland, often beyond the formal boundaries of the Colony,[16] and founded stations or settlement where both converted and unconverted Africans might live under their control. They determined the physical layout of the mission and directed the erection of buildings. The church at Kuruman, a typical early nineteenth-century mission, founded in 1821 (Fig. 31),[17] was T-shaped like many other rural churches. It was also thatched with hipped ends and appears to have had a small turret at the junction of the ridges. It was scarcely bigger than the small two- to-three-room cottages beside it, with separate entrances on both wings, probably to divide the congregation by sex. Like virtually all the early missions, it was not inspired by elite European architectural trends and had almost no architectural ornament, internal or external.

On the eve of the Victorian era, church building in and around Cape Town had become much more sophisticated and varied in its styles and had undergone technical advances. Progress was often achieved through great struggle, as is witnessed by the frequently long periods it took to build the churches. The style of all the buildings discussed so far remained classical, their function to accommodate Protestant ritual, with an emphasis on the pulpit or a combination of pulpit and communion table.

Cathedrals and Country Churches: The Gothic Revival

Church architecture in South Africa during the Victorian period, like its counterparts elsewhere in the Anglo-Saxon world, was dominated by the Gothic Revival – an emphasis on stone construction, the form of the Latin cross, pointed windows and doors, and a strong commitment to reproducing actual medieval prototypes.[18] Classically inspired buildings continued to be built, but usually out of ignorance or in defiance of the vogue for the Gothic. Yet the Gothic Revival, widely as it was accepted, still had to be tempered by the ritual needs of the various denominations, especially through a manipulation of the principal interior elements such as the pulpit and altar. The earliest Gothic Revival churches actually predate the Victoria era, one of the earliest being the Roman Catholic chapel near the Castle in Cape Town, built around 1821.[19] It was a tiny rectangular building about three bay buttresses long, its Gothic style being apparent mainly in the pointed windows, battlements, and pinnacles. As such it is a good example of eighteenth-century Gothic – a frilly, slightly decorative form of the style not based on any precise historical precedent. The later, more serious-minded Gothic revivalists would have termed it "debased."

A somewhat larger version, far from Cape Town, was St. Paul's Church, Durban.[20] Now replaced by a later church on the same site, St. Paul's was started in 1851, eight years after the British annexed Natal, and completed six years later according to the design of R.S. Upton, an architect–surveyor. Like so many of the early Gothic buildings it was a simple rectangle divided by buttresses into five bays. It also had a small square chancel at the east end. Under the steeply pitched slate roof the plastered walls were accentuated by some simple Gothic mouldings and Gothic pointed windows with tracery, one large one in the west elevation being particularly elaborate. As originally designed, it was intended to have a large square tower with battlements and pinnacles, but since the tower was costly and not strictly necessary, it was omitted, as happened with so many Victorian churches.

Robert Gray, who arrived as the first Anglican bishop of the Cape in 1848, and his wife Sophy were principally responsible for bringing a more serious-minded version of the Gothic Revival to South Africa. Inspired by Anglo-Catholicism they sought to restore many of the early rituals and settings to the Anglican church. Sophy Gray's involvement in the design and construction of many Anglican churches throughout South Africa remains a little obscure, but she apparently did design drawings at least, basing each one on a set of "model" churches she and her husband brought with them. All the "Sophy Gray" churches are similar and fairly doctrinaire in their form and details. Scores of small Anglican chapels built late in the century, each with a long nave separated by an arch from a deep chancel or sanctuary, show her influence. The sanctuary contained a raised altar while the pulpit, in accordance with Anglo-Catholic ritual preference, was de-emphasized, placed in the nave and to the side. Chapels and baptisteries were sometimes added later. A little parish church, St. Mary the Virgin in Woodstock,[21] Cape Town (Fig. 66), although not well known, is a good and typical sample. The first portion was built in 1852, with piecemeal additions over the next few decades. Each section is separately roofed and articulated so that the building has a picturesque quality to it. Buttresses are heavy and appear to be structural. The simple ornamentation, based meticulously on medieval prototypes, is mainly confined to the doors and windows.

The Anglican Cathedral of St. Michael and St. George in Grahamstown (Fig. 68) is a professional version of the more literally minded Gothic Revival. Designed by the English architect Sir Gilbert Scott and his son John Oldrid Scott, the cathedral gradually replaced the previous church of St. George's; its impressive tower and spire were finished in 1879.[22] The church is constructed of local stone that carves poorly; hence the windows are simple pointed openings with little tracery and plain mouldings, and the spire itself is not of stone but of precast concrete blocks. Standing in the centre of the town's main square, the Cathedral helps endow Grahamstown with the qualities of an English county town.

So pervasive was the idea that Gothic was the only proper style for churches in the latter half of the nineteenth century that many denominations ordinarily favouring a more austere setting eventually capitulated to it. The Methodist church on Greenmarket Square, Cape Town (Fig. 69), based on the design of Charles Freeman, a well-known local architect,[23] fills most of its prominent urban site. Basilican in form, it also has a short chancel and a conspicuous tower and spire. It has possibly the most complete surviving Victorian church interior: its elaborate finishes and fittings, including an organ, choir, pulpit, and communion table grouped together at the chancel end, restate the essentials of the preaching church and distinguish it from Anglican or Roman Catholic churches of the same style.

With the discovery of diamonds near what became Kimberley in 1867, and the subsequent discovery of gold in the Transvaal, the whole southern African region received a great economic boost; its towns grew rapidly and new ones were founded.[24] The consequent need for new churches for all the various denominations was mostly satisfied by fairly modest buildings, wood-framed churches clad in corrugated iron and lined internally with wood boarding. Almost all the materials were imported and sometimes the entire building was itself prefabricated and sent out from Europe as a kit,[25] but most churches were built on the spot quickly and cheaply. Covered with corrugated-iron sheeting, the buildings were mostly regarded as temporary expedients in a pioneering situation. Many have survived, nonetheless.

The example shown in Fig. 72, originally built for the Lutheran mission in Kimberley in 1875 and transferred to the De Beers Museum in 1963,[26] is typical of many hundreds of such churches. A simple box with the vestry placed behind as a substitute chancel, it has a steep pitched roof with a small porch and pointed Gothic windows. Because of the structural lightness of the building, the bell was hung in a separate steel-framed structure to the right of the building.

During the nineteenth century, especially after the opening up of the hinterland, many Dutch Reformed churches were rebuilt, sometimes twice. The original T-shaped thatched buildings were pulled down and replaced by grander structures, inevitably Gothic in style, but so varied in detail that none is really typical. The one shown in Fig. 67, located at Ladismith in the Cape, dates from 1872–74, replacing an earlier church of 1850.[27] Still the basic preaching box, though on a much larger scale than heretofore, it is a good example of the work of Carl Otto Hager (1813–98), a German-born architect and master builder in the western Cape. Many small towns in the region are still dominated by Hager's churches. The façade of the Ladismith Church cleverly combines buttresses, pinnacles, pointed arches, and niches, which together give it a vertical quality and disguise the great breadth of the front. Many of these churches preserve the nave/chancel pattern, in which the nave is dominant and the chancel is often really a vestry, a room used for church meetings, and not part of the space for worship. The ornament is all in plaster and the details fairly commonplace. Sophy Gray would not have regarded it as "correct."

Not all the new rural churches were Gothic. A fine example of a classically inspired design is the Dutch Reformed church at Cradock in the Cape built in the local free stone between 1864 and 1867 on the design of St. Martin-in-the-Fields, London (Fig. 63).[28] The rural town churches were often carefully sited, usually in the centre of their own square so that their principal feature, a fine façade, or tower, or combination of the two, would have an axial relationship to the principal street. The interior, although now much larger, followed the basic layout inherited from the eighteenth century, with the focus on the combination of pulpit and communion table. A new feature was the organ, its impressive collection of pipes set up against one of the walls, usually above the back gallery, or in combination with the pulpit, as in the Greenmarket Methodist church.

By the end of the Victorian era and the conclusion of the South African War (1899–1902), the two British colonies and the two former Boer Republics had moved far beyond their modest circumstances of some sixty years before. Whereas there were probably fewer than fifty churches in the region in 1838, most of them fairly humble, at the end of the century there were hundreds, many as sophisticated in design and execution as churches elsewhere in the colonial world.

Local Materials and Exotic Styles: The Early Twentieth Century

The most important church architect at the beginning of the twentieth century was Herbert Baker (1862–1946), who designed and built a few churches in Cape Town in the 1890s. After his appointment as Anglican diocesan architect in the Transvaal after the Anglo-Boer War he developed concepts that influenced most new churches in the first thirty years of this century.[29] Baker stressed simple forms and insisted on the use of "honest" traditional materials like stone and wood rather than iron and plaster, and leaned towards Early English Gothic as an appropriate stylistic model.

His first large-scale design in Cape Town was for the proposed rebuilding of St. George's Cathedral (Fig. 70). Obviously inspired by Norman churches, the original plan had a nave with side aisles, a crossing, short transepts, a chancel flanked by chapels, and a chevet (rounded east end). The new building was set out along Wale Street at right angles to the old. To replace the tower of the old St. George's, which had terminated the vista up St. George's Street, Baker planned to erect a large free-standing Gothic tower. The main entrance to the cathedral is effectively that of the north transept, an unusual feature in a cathedral. The architect, aware both of the hot climate and the difficulty of obtaining good local freestone, chose to light the building with small lancet (pointed) windows. The stone of the church is mostly Table Mountain quartzite, and the roof is covered with red clay tiles. The roof structure is timber without vaults, another concession to lack of requisite materials and skilled labour. Unfortunately St. George's has never been completed to Baker's design, and most of the nave and the splendid tower are still missing.

In the Transvaal Baker and, later, his partner designed a large number of Anglican churches, mostly quite small, of which St. Michael and All Angels, Boksburg, is typical.[30] Built in 1911, just two years before Baker left South Africa, it is widely regarded as the finest of his parish churches. The plan consists of an aisled nave of seven bays, plus a chancel and an apse roofed by a concrete semi-dome. To the south is an adjoining chapel, and to the north a vestry. The stone interior is dominated by a dark-stained wooden ceiling supported by a wooden superstructure. The long, low simple mass of the exterior is pleasantly contrasted with the handsome tower in the north-east corner, the local light-coloured freestone of the walls set off by the red tile roof. The extensive use of round arches, rather than the pointed Gothic arches, throughout the building indicates Baker's leaning towards the Romanesque, a style that preceded the Gothic in medieval Europe. St. George's church, Cullinan, near Pretoria, represents one of the most humble of the Baker churches (Fig. 71). Built in 1904 as the parish church for the nearby diamond mine, it is a simple rectangle built of the local stone but with a corrugated-iron roof – a material not greatly valued by the architect. The west end has a plain gable surmounted by a small belfry.

After Baker's departure from South Africa, both the firms he left behind in Johannesburg and Cape Town continued to design and build churches, a notable example being the former Church of Christ the King in the African township of Sophiatown, Johannesburg, consecrated in 1935.[31] Designed by Frank Fleming, Baker's former partner, in 1933, it was, from 1943 to 1949, the parish church of Father Trevor Huddleston, which he immortalized in *Naught for Your Comfort* (1955), his influential denunciation of apartheid. Now somewhat altered, the church is built of blue stock bricks and is basilican in form with a central aisle lit by a clerestory and side aisles, subsequently raised to accommodate galleries. Perhaps the most distinctive feature, the bell tower, is a landmark in the area, very like that at St. Michael and All Angels, a simple unadorned shaft incorporating some subtle set backs, completed by an inset belfry and capped with a steep pyramidal tiled roof.

During the 1920s and 1930s the Afrikaans architect Gerard Moerdyk and his partner produced a great number of Dutch Reformed churches characterized by a mixing of historical elements. Moerdyk's work is eclectic, highly sophisticated, and generally of a high order in the choice of materials. Moerdyk grafted on to a Byzantine-inspired, domed central plan both neo-classical and Gothic elements, as well as eighteenth-century Cape Dutch gables. He also used traditional materials such as stone and insisted on high-quality interiors, with details such as the hand-made pews individually designed for each church. Examples of his work are found in smaller towns throughout the Orange Free State (e.g. Reddersburg), Natal (e.g. Ladysmith), and the Transvaal (e.g. Volksrust), as well as in Bloemfontein, Johannesburg, and Pretoria.[32]

Moerdyk's Dutch Reformed church at Sunnyside, Pretoria, dating from 1927, is dominated by a large tiled and ribbed dome capped by a cupola (Fig. 65). By contrast, the tall adjacent stone tower, though solid and virtually undecorated for the lower two-thirds, blossoms into a small octagon temple form complete with dome, flèche, and weathervane. Noticeable secondary elements are the large gables at each end. Their plain, monumental character is set off by the large upper semicircular windows almost certainly derived from Roman structures such as the Baths of Caracalla.

Some of the most interesting buildings of this period were inspired neither by Baker nor by Moerdyk; for example St. Patrick's, Bloemfontein. Started in 1908, this church has been called "the Parthenon of the Corrugated Iron Style."[33] Designed and built in the Batho African location by Father Edgar Rose, an Anglican priest, it was demolished in 1954 because of the Group Areas Act (Fig. 73). Basing his design on the great English Gothic cathedrals, Rose used a typical long nave, crossing, transepts, and choir. The section of the building was basilican with a nave and lower side aisles. Both the west end and the transepts were to be flanked by twin towers. The crossing was also surmounted by a tower capped by a form of mansarded roof. As the long nave and the western towers were not built, the church assumed the form of a Greek cross. Built completely of a wooden framework and covered with corrugated iron, it achieved for the humble mat-erial an unusual monumental status. Its demolition was a great loss to South African architecture.

Modernity, Community Centres, and African Inspiration: The Post-war Years
Until the Second World War historical styles served as the only models for churches; but after a lull in the post-war years, a new era of church architecture began when historically based styles were no longer considered most appropriate forms for places of worship, and some experimentation by architects took place, under the influence of the International Style or Modern Movement, which favoured concrete frames, flat roofs, and the use of modern materials like steel windows.[34] The new architecture, primarily concerned with functional buildings such as houses, showed little interest in the traditional or symbolic, and consequently a number of these newer buildings seem to lack a spiritual dimension.

Some architects did seek to blend old and new. The Holy Trinity Catholic church, Musgrave Road, in Durban, designed by the architects A. Woodrow and A. Collingwood and built in 1958, is an example of this attitude. A variation on the traditional basilican model,[35] it is, according to tradition, oriented east–west with a bell tower emphasizing its corner lot. Many traditional materials such as sandstone for the exterior, marble floors, and mosaics are used. The architects wished to achieve a traditional atmosphere in a contemporary manner, to emphasize verticality and the natural beauty of materials.

More radical in its break from tradition was the chapel of St. Peter at the Hammanskraal seminary near Pretoria, designed by the architect A. Konya and built in 1966 (Fig. 42).[36] Similar to a curved cone, its roof is covered in copper sheeting and is supported by a series of laminated wooden beams placed on concrete buttresses, rather than by walls. Between the buttresses are curtains of glass. Inside, the altar is a simple block of red granite. The main entrance to the church is a large wooden door ornamented with carvings in sapele, a local wood. Possibly influenced by overseas examples such as the Liverpool Cathedral (1967), a number of other circular churches with central altars were built in this period. They were also inspired by liturgical reforms, such as those of the Second Vatican Council (1962–67), in having the priest face the congregation from behind an altar table.

During the 1960s modernism also spread into the Dutch Reformed Church, influencing a series of buildings built chiefly in the new, predominantly Afrikaans suburbs around the major cities. Certain architects, like Johan de Ridder, favoured by a number of congregations, developed a personal style.[37] The Gereformeerde Kerk in Krugersdorp, built in 1962, can be considered typical of De Ridder's work. It is, quite traditionally, a large preaching box focused on the pulpit and communion table. However, new structural techniques and stronger materials allowed much wider spans and thus freed the plan from some of its earlier limitations. A wider variety of plan forms was one result, along with more adventurous roof shapes, often presented as folded planes reminiscent of prisms – possibly a local manifestation of the influence of the famous American architect Frank Lloyd Wright. Modern materials, such as the local facebrick, were used externally and internally, as were such elements as steel windows. Ornamentation and works of sacred art remained minimal.

In recent years the various denominations in South Africa, influenced by ecumenism and by concern for the poor, have often seen their buildings more as a focus for community life than as isolated "monumental" structures. To this end there are more rooms, with a diversity of function; and the place of worship itself, less dominant both in the plan and in the mass of the building, is now often the focus of a complex of spaces. An example is the Cathedral of the Holy Cross, Gaborone, in Botswana, a complex completed in 1979 and containing the cathedral itself, a chapel, a hall, general offices, and a library.[38] The architects, Munnik, Visser, Black & Fish, in association with P. Vintcent, designed the building to be modest but to portray its Christian message explicitly, in understandable visual terms. The complex is sited on a prominent corner of the town and the L-shaped building forms an outdoor space – the equivalent of the Sotho *khota* – for open-air services (Fig. 75). The principal material of the building is brick used both internally and externally. A tower in the re-entrant angle of the building is about the only element in the complex obviously derived from European traditions.

A great deal of Christian worship in South Africa, possibly most of it, has taken place outdoors, enabled by the generally mild climate. As late as the early 1950s it was observed in connection with Methodist missionary work in Zululand that "in at least one hundred places every sabbath day services are held in private kraals or under the shade of trees."[39] On Sunday afternoons in most South African cities one still sees small groups of people, often members of African Initiated Churches (AICs), holding services on public or waste land. Many Christians, among them Pentecostals, also worship in unconventional churches like homes, warehouses, and carparks, and also in buildings originally designed to serve one purpose, for example, a theatre or a garage (Fig. 74), but now used or adapted for use as a church.

Monumental church architecture in South Africa, the principal concern of this chapter, has, until recently, closely followed conventions set elsewhere, a reflection of the expatriate background of its patrons, ministers, and architects. Increasing use of local materials and increasing variety of styles has characterized the past few decades, along with a more self-conscious desire to situate South African church architecture in the cultures and political struggles of the country. Finally, in harmony with trends in global Christianity, there has been an accelerating evolution in conceptions of the function of church buildings: beyond the two basic forms of preaching box and the pulpit–altar combination towards new notions of the church as a community centre as well as a place of worship.

22

Millennial Christianity, British Imperialism, and African Nationalism

WALLACE G. MILLS

Religion, and specifically Christianity, is often portrayed as a tool of the dominant classes. Yet religion has helped shape the political ideas and the behaviour of most groups and classes in South Africa in ways that are more complex, contradictory, and changing than this portrayal suggests. Christian beliefs about the end of the world, or eschatology, have been particularly influential, though frequently overlooked by scholars who deem them too esoteric, quaint, or fantastic for serious study. Eschatological stances embody crucial perceptions about the world (cosmology) and about history and can thus profoundly influence political action. Protestantism, the predominant branch of Christianity in South Africa, harbours two significantly different eschatologies – postmillennialism and premillennialism, the latter also called "chiliasm" or "adventism."[1] Both views have long existed in Christianity, but during the eighteenth century, in Britain and North America especially, postmillennialism become dominant, peaking in the early nineteenth century.[2] After a long period of relative decline, premillennialism began a comeback over the nineteenth century and helped shape fundamentalism in the twentieth.[3] Both traditions have been influential among South African blacks and whites.

Postmillennialists believe that the Second Coming of Christ will occur after the millennium or thousand years of peace foretold in the twentieth chapter of Revelation. Postmillennialism is optimistic about the trend of human history, believing that God will use human instruments to perfect human nature and society. The Kingdom of God (the millennium) will be formed gradually through individual conversions and societal improvement.[4] While Christians' first priority is to evangelize their neighbours, they should also strive, through political action, to eliminate social evils such as slavery, drunkenness, and prostitution. Millennial society will be universal, and to achieve it, Christians must evangelize and improve societies throughout the entire world. De Jong attributes the remarkable surge in Anglo-American mission activity from the 1790s almost entirely to the postmillennial eschatological imperative: most missionaries were not striving simply to transform African societies into replicas of their home societies, which they regarded as far from perfect; they were also striving to achieve in Africa a better, less sinful, society than they had known at home. Kate Crehan, in her interesting Marxist analysis of the ideology underlying the great outburst of mission activity from the 1790s, notes that the onset of this outburst coincided with the French Revolution and the "fear and panic" experienced by the ruling classes. Most missionaries and their supporters, however, came from the lower middle and upper working classes, not from the "ruling classes." Her analysis also overlooks the enormous optimism and expectations of the mission enterprise. Nevertheless it may be said that eschatological curiosity mushrooms during times of significant change and upheaval as people attempt to discern "the signs of the times" in the unfolding of events.[5]

Premillennialism, too, can generate a powerful missionary impulse, but with the expectation that only a minority will accept the offer of salvation and be converted. As the famous American evangelist, D.L. Moody declared, "I look upon this world as a wrecked vessel. God has given me a lifeboat and said to me, 'Moody, save all you can.'"[6] Premillennialists start from the conviction that the world is evil and growing increasingly corrupt. The Kingdom of God will be inaugurated only after existing societies and political systems are destroyed in a series of cataclysmic events predicted in the book of Revelation, culminating in the great battle of Armageddon. Then Christ, along with his resurrected followers, will physically return and establish a theocratic state for a thousand years (the millenium). His return can take place at any moment ("like a thief in the night") and only those Christians in a state of grace at that precise moment will be saved from eternal damnation. Christians must accordingly maintain a constant state of readiness and high personal piety, while also warning their neighbours of the horrible fate awaiting the "unsaved." Premillennialists usually argue that though they "are in theworld, ... they are not of the world."[7] Striving to keep themselves uncontaminated from the world, they tend to regard political affairs as ephemeral, trivial, and dangerously distracting from the real duties of the Christian. The cataclysm and transformation of the world will come from the outside of history, in Christ's coming. Premillennialists usually admonish one another to "watch and pray" – and wait. While there are exceptions, for the vast majority of premillennialists, politics cannot be given high priority.

Postmillennialism and Christian Views of Imperialism

A new and dynamic postmillennialism came with missionaries to South Africa at the turn of the nineteenth century, roughly at the same time as the advent of British rule. The missionaries' first priority was the evangelization of African peoples, but the actions and policies of imperial officials often stood in their way. In spite of their frequently expressed reluctance, missionaries were drawn very early into political action, sometimes in opposition to officials of the empire. Although most missionaries were British and patriotic, they were not simply agents of the empire nor unalloyed enthusiasts for its expansion. The relationship between Christianity and imperialism was complex, ambiguous, and changing.

The first missionaries in South Africa did not necessarily assume that the empire was a force for good or that Christianity and empire were mutually supportive. In Britain, the supporters of Christian missions opposed imperial policy makers on the issue of slavery and the slave trade, which most mission enthusiasts wished to curtail and abolish, and on the policies of the East India Company, which tried to keep missionaries out of India. Many supporters of empire, while claiming to be Christians, saw the propagation of Christianity as inappropriate in imperial contexts. In South Africa missionaries had to confront another issue – white settlers and their harsh treatment of indigenous peoples. The efforts of some missionaries,

338

especially the Rev. John Philip of the London Missionary Society, to secure equality for Khoisan and whites before the law antagonized many white colonists and not a few imperial officials (see pp. 38–39).

While considering themselves good British subjects, many missionaries and their supporters asserted that Christians had a prophetic calling to denounce social evils such as slavery and political wickedness, to hold the empire to a high moral purpose, and to regard the governance of indigenous peoples as a God-given trust. On the desirability of extending the imperial frontiers their views frequently fluctuated. Few wanted the withdrawal of imperial control, which frequently seemed the least evil of the available options. Hence they often condemned imperial policies without rejecting the empire itself. During the early decades of the nineteenth century, many missionaries, including the missionary lobby in England known as "Exeter Hall," opposed further extensions of colonial control over African peoples, and their views prevailed in the 1837 report of the Aborigines Committee that recommended no annexations "without the previous sanction of an Act of Parliament."[8] In 1837, bowing to missionary pressure, Lord Glenelg at the colonial office forced the Cape government to withdraw from Queen Adelaide Province, a newly annexed region beyond the colony's eastern border between the Kei and Keiskamma rivers. Wesleyans, however, whose work embraced white as well as black communities, supported the annexation.[9]

In the early decades of the century, missionaries intended to convert entire African societies; under Christian African leaders these agrarian communities would conform to strict evangelical Christian piety and avoid the ills and vices of industrial Britain. Missionaries wanted to isolate Africans from white settlers, perhaps only nominally Christian, who might set a bad example and introduce Africans to new vices such as alcohol and prostitution. Missionaries wanted to convert African leaders and people en masse, and then, as advisors, to direct the transformation of their societies into independent Christian communities. To this end many missionaries opposed annexations that would subject African societies to settler-dominated colonial governments and throw them open to unruly white intruders. However, the extension of white settlement in the Great Trek of the 1830s, and rapidly escalating economic and political pressures from the Cape Colony, made the policy of isolation increasingly less viable.

Though they intermittently yielded to pressures from Christian abolitionists and "Exeter Hall," British statesmen did not regard "trusteeship" as an over-riding determinant of imperial policy. One cabinet minister remarked in 1828: "Britain could not conquer the world out of 'mere humanity' just because Britons believed that only under their rule were people happy."[10] Nevertheless, missionaries and the humanitarian lobby appealed to the imperial government to protect African peoples, not only from the Cape Colony, but from the two Voortrekker republics and from Natal, annexed by Britain in 1843. The most dramatic examples were the help given by French missionaries to Moshoeshoe in achieving a British protectorate for Basutoland (1868) and the long campaign of the LMS missionary John Mackenzie to have a British protectorate declared over the Tswana (accomplished in 1885) (see chap. 6, *passim*). In both cases missionaries intended to protect African peoples from incursions from the two Boer republics established after the

Great Trek. Later, when European powers began their "scramble for Africa" in the 1870s, British missionaries increasingly threw their support behind the British government, which seemed preferable both to foreign governments like Portugal or Germany and to private colonizers like Cecil Rhodes's British South Africa Company.

Missionaries' attitudes to imperialism were widely influenced by their convictions about the linkages between commerce and Christianity, an aspect of their theory of God's role in history. Postmillennial supporters of missions generally accepted the Newtonian Enlightenment view that the universe was like a Great Clock operating in accordance with fixed laws established by God, its designer and creator. These physical laws operated to achieve the transcendent moral purposes of God, the redemption and salvation of humanity. God employed "even the selfish and acquisitive motivations of men to promote the general good – which, to an evangelical, meant supremely the spread of the gospel." Thus, explains Brian Stanley, the "nineteenth-century evangelicals responded to the age of utilitarianism with a moral theology which enshrined 'usefulness' in the cause of the gospel as chief among the Christian virtues." Providence arranged things so that those nations who benefited others were, in return, rewarded; and foreign mission activity was the most important benefit Britain conferred on other nations. In this scheme commerce was "the means whereby providence welded together duty and interest, the channel through which the reflex benefit of Britain's missionary role in the world returned to her own advantage."[11]

Postmillennialists believed that Christianity opened "not only the prospect of eternal life but also the road to unlimited social and economic development,"[12] which they usually called "civilization." Development could best be promoted through market economies, private property, free trade, the use of ploughs and irrigation to maximize production, and increased levels of consumption.[13] The three Cs (Christianity, civilization and commerce) were closely interlinked and reinforced each other. When missionaries exhorted Africans to wear European clothes and use European goods and utensils, they fostered commerce. To generate the income not only to support this new consumption but also to make the missions viable, they advocated increased production and economic development. Increased trade and economic activity, in turn, would help the spread of the gospel. As David Livingstone, the most famous advocate of Christianity and commerce, put it:

> When a tribe begins to trade with another it feels a sense of mutual dependence; and this is a most important aid in diffusing the blessings of Christianity, because one tribe never goes to another without telling the news, and the Gospel comes in to be part of their news, and the knowledge of Christianity is thus spread by means of commerce.[14]

The trinity of Christianity, commerce, and civilization is often interpreted as evidence that missions were driven by the needs and interests of European capitalists. But while chambers of commerce strongly applauded Livingstone's speeches in 1858, it was the religious public not the captains of industry who subscribed most of the money for his scheme of evangelizing Africa. Missionaries themselves grew to question the mutual benefit of commerce and Christianization. By the late 1860s, "Christian confidence in the redemptive function of commerce was waning" and even began to be repudiated.[15] As John Smith Moffat (an LMS missionary turned colonial administrator) argued in 1903, "I do not believe in missionaries or societies putting themselves under obligation to the rich men in South Africa. The time is coming when there will be a life-and-death struggle on the native question. The capitalists are worse than the Boers, and we who stand by the native will have to fight to the death over the question."[16]

Certain nineteenth-century missionaries were attracted to imperialism, which they saw as a necessary means of reversing the disappointing results of their efforts to evangelize Africa. Even where they had been accepted and welcomed, missionaries had won fewer and less perfect conversions than they had expected. In most African societies, a reaction against Christianity had developed, and missionaries, rightly or wrongly, blamed this on the chiefs. Many missionaries concluded that before the gospel could take deep root, African political authorities must be destroyed, if necessary by colonial conquest and annexation. Thus, the Wesleyan missionary, J. C. Warner, writing in the wake of the Seventh and Eighth Frontier Wars in the 1850s, asserted:

> And above all, as they have so resolutely and so perseveringly refused to give to the Gospel even an attentive hearing; it seems to me that the way on which they themselves are so obstinately bent is the one which God will make use of to bring about this desirable object; and that the sword must first – not *exterminate* [sic] them, but – break them up as tribes, and destroy their political existence; after which, when thus set free from the shackles by which they are bound, civilisation and christianity will no doubt make rapid progress among them.[17]

Warner's stance was not necessarily or primarily a result of British patriotism, for German, American, and Norwegian missionaries held the same views about British imperialism and the Zulu monarchy.[18] However, there was an implicit racism in his belief that Africans would benefit more from imperial rule than from the rule of their own chiefs.[19]

After 1870, imperial sentiment in Britain and in British colonies became more fervent, taking on the colours of a civil religion.[20] J. R. Seeley, the influential historian and author of *The Expansion of England*,[21] argued that a national church should be closely associated with the State. "Religion is the great State building principle," he wrote. "As the Church without the State becomes a mere philosophical, or quasi-philosophical sect, so the state without the Church (i.e. without a living conscious nationality) is a mere administrative machine."[22] "The province of religion ... is much more national and political, much less personal, than is commonly supposed."[23] For Seeley and increasing numbers of imperialists, the history of the empire was evidence that God was using Britain in shaping world affairs. The haphazard but continuous expansion of the empire in spite of the reluctance of British governments was "an unmistakable indication of divine overruling."[24] The empire was, Lord Rosebery declared in 1900, "human and yet not wholly human, for the most heedless and the most cynical must see the finger of the divine."[25] Justifying the South African War in 1900, Bishop Westcott stated flatly, "We hold our Empire in the name of Christ."[26]

While most imperialists had a sense of mission and destiny, the motivating power of many was not Christian at its core. Rider Haggard, the imperialist novelist who wrote widely about South Africa, referred more frequently to fate than to God, and Cecil Rhodes, the quintessential Victorian imperialist and son of an Anglican priest, abandoned Christianity altogether. For many late-Victorians, imperialism was a religious substitute for a Christianity in which they no longer believed. Imperialism gained strength from its capacity to mean different things to different people. Thus, the imperialists' contention that the empire was a providential agency to bring "law, justice and order" to large areas of the globe, could be given a Christian meaning or not. Moreover, since imperial authorities usually protected missionaries, Christians could see the empire as reinforcing the Christian mission. The flourishing of missions in the late-Victorian era could be cited as evidence of the empire's potential for good in the world. Thus, on one level, Christianity, especially in its missionary outreach, gave a patina of "moral purpose" to the ideology of empire. Accordingly, by the end of the century, Christians were much more inclined to see empire and Christianity as complementary entities than they had been at the beginning.

Another reason for more muted criticism of imperialism may have been the arrival in South Africa of increasing numbers of premillennialist missionaries in the last two decades of the century.[27] The Student Volunteer Movement, aggressive in its approach to evangelization, held "councils of war" and called for Christian "conquest" of the unevangelized parts of the world. Its leaders hailed the expansion of British and American imperialism as a providential development for "the evangelization of the world in this generation."[28] Disinclined to devote their energies to political and economic affairs, premillennialists were only rarely directly involved in imperial activities, but their noninvolvement was also noncritical and inadvertently served imperial purposes.

Ironically, just as missonaries had become most enthusiastic about imperialism at the end of the century, the power of imperialism was about to wane around the world. In South Africa, the union of the four colonies in 1910 would drastically weaken British power and bring to the fore a new political movement, African nationalism.

Millennialism and African Nationalism

The emergence of African political activity in South Africa, often labelled African nationalism, has long received attention from historians, who usually accord a crucial role to Christianity, though they put exclusive emphasis, perhaps wrongly, on separatist Ethiopian churches (see pp. 212–16). For a deeper understanding of the connections between Christianity and African nationalism one needs to examine Africans' own eschatological outlooks.

Among the Xhosa, two responses to white intrusion and conquest were personified in the prophets Nxele and Ntsikana (pp. 71–73) in the second decade of the nineteenth century.[29] Nxele, attempting to tap into the power of the whites, incorporated elements of Christianity, while remaining firmly rooted in African religion and cosmology. His attack on Grahamstown in 1819 came to symbolize the possibility of African military resistance. Ntsikana, on the other hand, adopted Christianity, though in a distinctively African idiom, and became the first "to be a

Christian while remaining an African." His emphatic rejection of military resistance came to symbolize the non-violent response. In the short run, the overwhelming majority of Xhosa adopted Nxele's option. Ntsikana's following remained very small, and, after his death in 1821, the two leaders of his following, Soga and his son Dukwana, abandoned Ntsikana's non-violent policy and struggled against colonial conquest; both died fighting in the last of the Frontier Wars in 1877–78.[30]

In the longer run Ntsikana's policy proved the more effective. The futility of the military option was borne in upon the Xhosa by successive defeats in 1819, 1835, 1846–48 and 1851–53. The cattle-killing of 1856–57, when the Xhosa sacrificed their cattle and grain to bring a resurrection of both cattle and people and a restoration of Xhosa independence, was a desperate extension of the military option. Attempting to tap into supernatural forces, the Xhosa turned to ideas, such as resurrection and the need for purification, that Nxele had introduced almost forty years earlier.[31] An ensuing famine compounded the effects of the military defeats and convinced some Xhosa that the material and spiritual resources of Xhosa society were inadequate to stave off conquest and its devastating effects. For decades after Nxele's death, many Xhosa, refusing to believe that he was dead, anticipated that he would return and lead them against the whites. As a result, "'*Kukuza kukaNxele*' (the return of Nxele) was the byword for a vain hope."[32]

Although force was invoked by the Xhosa one last time in 1877–78, the onset of mass conversion to Christianity in the 1860s[33] may have shown that many Xhosa were shifting from Nxele's perspective to that of Ntsikana. They were converting to a postmillennial Christianity. Almost immediately, African Christians, under missionary influence, began a temperance movement; they replaced missionaries as leaders of the Independent Order of True Templars (I.O.T.T.) in the 1880s; by the 1890s they had complete control of the organization. Largely at the behest of African clergy and laity, total abstinence (including abstinence from African beer – *utywala*) was now for all practical purposes a requirement for African membership in the churches, though abstinence was rarely demanded of whites. By the 1870s, Africans in the Cape began a political campaign to reduce the number of canteen licences issued or to prohibit liquor sales to Africans; they sent petitions to parliament, addressed parliamentary committees, and appeared before hearings on canteen licences. In the temperance movement they learned how to manage voluntary organizations and how to conduct a political campaign under the Western parliamentary system. Temperance played an analogous role in the history of the women's suffrage movement in Britain, the white Dominions, and the United States.[34]

In the 1880s, the African Christian elite who were emerging from the mission schools, particularly Lovedale, moved into parliamentary politics of the Cape Colony, the only white-ruled colony in southern Africa where some Africans had the vote. Reflecting Ntsikana's admonition to remain united,[35] one of their earliest attempts at political organization was called *Imbumba Yama Afrika*. As S. N. Mvambo wrote in 1883, "we must be united on political matters. In fighting for national rights, we must fight together."[36] The African Christians sought to enrol Africans who could meet the property or income qualifications on the voters' rolls, and began to debate and discuss political issues, especially in the newspaper *Imvo Zabantsundu*. In spite of the inequality and injustice they faced, this generation of African leaders was optimistic that economic and political opportunities would open up for Africans in the Cape Colony. Their version of the millennium was a non-racist society, in which individual talents and qualifications, particularly Christianity and "civilization," would determine one's status, not skin colour.

The African elite believed, as did whigs in the British political tradition, that progress towards democracy and greater equality was inevitable. Founding their optimism on Britain's historic record on issues like Khoisan equality, the abolition of slavery, and the retrocession of Queen Adelaide Province, they arrived at an exaggerated reliance on British rhetoric about "trusteeship," confident that the British government was the chief bulwark against the inequitable impositions of the white settlers. In petitioning for the abrogation of the Registration Act of 1887, which restricted the African vote in the Cape Colony, a group of Christian Africans stated, "We therefore pray your Most Gracious Majesty that the brave and generous English Nation and the British Legislature will not abandon us to the tender mercy of those who are stronger than we are."[37] Imperialists such as Rhodes, hoping to reconcile colonial whites including Afrikaners to the empire and to enrol them as partners in the expansion of the empire north to Cairo, wanted to end meddling from London ("eliminate the imperial factor"), especially in the treatment of Africans by colonial whites. Faced with such naked intentions, African leaders accordingly favoured more British involvement in South Africa, rather than less. Despite an almost unbroken series of disappointments and "sell-outs" by Britain from the 1880s (including the Registration Act, but notably Britain's failure to impose a franchise for Africans in the Boer republics they conquered in 1902), Africans, in desperation, continued appeals to the British government as late as the 1913 Land Act.

Nevertheless, from the 1890s to 1914, opportunities for Africans withered, even in the "liberal" Cape. Not only were Africans disillusioned by British imperialism, but the political dominance of white settlers became almost absolute in the Union of South Africa created in 1910. As racial prejudice and inequality grew, the optimistic, progressive cosmology that was rooted in postmillennialism increasingly seemed to conflict with Africans' experience of reality. In the churches too, many Africans were disillusioned by racial discrimination. Some responded by seceding to form independent churches, although these did not all abandon postmillennialism. P.J. Mzimba, who seceded from the Free Church of Scotland and founded the Presbyterian Church of Africa (PCA) in 1898, retained the theological positions and the rules of order of the Free Church of Scotland. He continued his political activities, such as rallying African voters during elections, begun in the 1870s.[38] So too, some leaders of the African Methodist Episcopal Church participated in the founding of the African National Congress in 1912.[39]

Yet, in this period, premillennialism arrived in South Africa, brought in part by new missionaries sent by the older societies. Andrew Murray's preaching of revivalism among whites had little direct impact on Africans, but he helped found the South Africa General Mission in 1889 supported principally by British and American premillennialists. Most important, David Bryant, from the Christian

Catholic Church in Zion, Illinois, had begun baptizing Africans in Johannesburg no later than 1904,[40] reinforcing the flowering of a host of "Zionist" independent churches (see pp. 216–17, 229–30).

A new mixture of fundamentalism, Pentecostalism, and premillennialism offered alternative views of the world and of history. For many Africans, a more pessimistic premillennial outlook seemed to embody their experience in church and society, where justice did not prevail, indeed where injustices multiplied. Those who gave up on improving "this world" and its institutions, including the established missions and churches, tended to withdraw into independent churches. There were, of course, many direct and concrete reasons for withdrawal, such as racial discrimination by missionaries, disputes over money, career disappointments, and so on, but a deepening pessimism underlay many decisions to secede.

Premillennialism usually involves some degree of political quietism, and, with a few exceptions among the earlier Ethiopian leaders, the majority of independent church leaders displayed a disinclination, even aversion, to active political participation. Bengt Sundkler found that most separatist leaders agreed with sentiments such as: "I tell my people, don't take any interest in this colour bar. Forget about it, forget about politics." Sundkler rarely found "radicals or even the politically conscious" as members in the independent churches. "Broadly speaking, the politically awake and active, if subscribing still to 'Christianity' at all, are found in other Churches, and not among 'the Native Separatists.' The Separatists go out of their way to state that they take no part in politics."[41] In accordance with a premillennial view, most leaders of independent churches have focused on improving the spiritual and physical health of their followers, and on offering them hope in the life after death, rather than on attempting change in the political order.[42]

But what of the conflicts with political authorities frequently cited as evidence that religious separatism can be revolutionary? In some cases the conflicts in question might not have been initiated or intended by the separatists themselves. Governments often interpret acts of withdrawal, non-involvement, or non-conformity as politically motivated insubordination or even rebellion, as in several conflicts between chiefs and colonial officials in Bechuanaland early in the twentieth century.[43] A few separatists did take part in the Bambatha Rebellion in Natal (1906–08), as did a few Christians from the regular churches, but neither group instigated, and none was a major factor in, the disturbances. White assertions to the contrary must be seen as paranoid and hostile, in the absence of supporting evidence.[44]

Two premillennial movements are widely regarded as political: the events leading to the massacre of Enoch Mgijima's Israelite followers at Bulhoek, near Queenstown, in 1921, and Wellington Buthelezi's Garveyite movement in the Transkei in the 1920s. Claiming that Africans were descendants of the lost tribes of Israel, Mgijima, who had been disowned by both the Wesleyans and Moravians for his radical eschatological views and linked briefly with an African American sect in 1912, emphasized the Old Testament in his eclectic theology; he preached a violent second coming and an imminent millennium. To await this event, God, he said, had ordered the "Israelites" to occupy some municipal land at Bulhoek, and they did so. Ordered by the authorities to move, Mgijima and the Israelites did not budge. When a large contingent of armed police arrived to enforce the removal order, the Israelites attacked with home-made weapons; thereupon the police killed more than 160. Here the initiative for aggression had come primarily from the authorities, against the Israelites who sought simply to await their release from the travails of this world. The Israelites did not occupy land as part of a revolutionary assault on white political power, and their resistance, consistent with premillennialism, depended for triumph purely on the expectation of external supernatural intervention.[45]

Buthelezi's Garveyism in the 1920s was in the same mould. He believed that African–Americans would intervene in South Africa to free Africans from the white government. Although he urged his followers to refuse to pay a new poll tax, thus challenging the government, he also bitterly criticized the ANC and the Industrial and Commercial Workers Union (ICU), the leading union among Africans. He preached "a radical separatism" and non-involvement of any kind.[46] His movement, like Mgijima's, lies closer to the cattle-killing than to the main stream of African nationalism.

Other Africans, however, persisting in the Ntsikana tradition and postmillennial expectations, continued to believe in the possibility of progress. No longer assured that the non-racist society they visualized could be achieved easily, most continued to work for change in the regular churches and plunged more deeply into political activity. African political organizations and activities proliferated after the turn of the century,[47] most notably the African National Congress (ANC), founded (with a different name) in 1912 with the active participation of clergy and Christian laymen: the Rev. John Dube was elected its first president, the Rev. E. J. Mqoboli its first senior chaplain, and the Rev. Walter Rubusana an honorary president. Marxism and Africanism would later emerge as very significant ideologies in African nationalism, but the strongest and most consistent influence in the early twentieth century was the vision and hope that were rooted in postmillennial Christianity. It fostered the vision of gradually perfecting society and, at least until the state of emergency after the Sharpeville massacre in 1960, the rejection of violence. Moreover, as among Western Christians whose postmillennialism began to evolve into the Social Gospel (see chap. 23, *passim*) in the late nineteenth and early twentieth centuries, much of the impulse toward moderate socialism in African nationalist circles can be attributed to this stream of Christianity.

23

The Benevolent Empire and the Social Gospel: Missionaries and South African Christians in the Age of Segregation

RICHARD ELPHICK[1]

Mandhlakazi ka Ngini, a Zulu, was puzzled: was he wrong to continue "worshipping *amadhlozi* [spirits of the dead]"? He confided to James Stuart in 1916 that, though some Christian doctrines, such as the Incarnation and eternal life, were difficult to believe, he was inclined to become a Christian. But Stuart, a former Natal official, sought to dissuade him. Missionaries, he said, had imposed on Africans "a creed of another race widely different in civilization." They had tried to induce Africans "to accept their particular forms of Christianity as the Truth, whereas Christianity itself is losing its hold in a remarkable way in England and other countries."[2]

Stuart's attempt to discourage an African from accepting Christianity reflects two profoundly significant movements that were well under way by 1916 – the Christianization of much of Africa, and the dechristianization, and secularization, of much of western Europe. Between 1884 and 1911 the number of black Christian communicants in South Africa had grown fivefold – from 60,154 to 322,673 – and new converts continued to flood in, mostly responding to African evangelists, some of whom were preaching under missionary oversight, and others in independent African Initiated Churches (AICs). According to the 1911 census, 26 percent of Africans in the newly proclaimed Union of South Africa claimed to be Christians, and that figure would continue to rise, reaching, by one calculation, 76 per cent by the early 1990s. By then, the percentages were even higher in some locales: 92.4 per cent of the residents in Shoshanguve, an African township near Pretoria, claimed at that time to be affiliated with a Christian body, while 76 per cent said they attended church at least once a week.[3]

In Britain, by contrast, church attendance and membership had begun to decline significantly from the period of the First World War – just when Stuart had his conversation with Mandhlakazi. The fall-off, noticeable first among Protestants, later among Catholics, has continued, leaving, by the 1990s, a mere 10 per cent of the British population as Christian churchgoers. Over the same period, secularization – a related but distinct process[4] – intensified dramatically, as new elites in the arts, the universities, the media, the professions, and the state slowly pushed Christian thought and the Christian clergy to the margins of Britain's intellectual, social, and political life.[5]

The successful Christianization of mission fields in Africa, combined with the decline of Christianity in countries sending missionaries to Africa, formed the backdrop to a remarkable transformation of the Protestant missionary enterprise – the rise of a new social and political activism that South Africans sometimes called "Social Christianity." This term, and its more famous American equivalent "the Social Gospel," denoted a loosely articulated set of theological affirmations and practical strategies that churches in North America and Britain had adopted to counter the social ills created by industrialization, as well as to shore up their own declining public influence. By 1916, many Protestant missionaries in South Africa were seeking, in alliance with Africans and Christian white settlers, to craft a Christian response to the social and cultural crises inflicted on Africans by rural impoverishment, urbanization, and racially discriminatory policies enacted by the all-white parliament. These missionaries selectively adopted Social Gospel themes from Britain and America – themes that would powerfully affect the witness of black and white Protestants in pre-apartheid South Africa, shaping, among other things, a powerful strand of African nationalism that would remain vital into the apartheid era. The Roman Catholic Church, too, was deeply engaged during these years in the social application of Christianity, most notably in its schools, hospitals, and agricultural settlements (pp. 196–200). But as a minority church in a country still marked by considerable anti-Catholicism, it remained aloof, for the most part, from the movements discussed in this chapter.

Denouncing "The Sinful Kingdom": Social Christianity as a Solution to Converging Crises

By the early twentieth century many Protestant missionaries in South Africa accused their nineteenth-century predecessors of having been narrowly concerned "to save the individual [African] from impending and eternal judgment." These new critics wanted, in the words of the American missionary James Dexter Taylor, to go beyond personal salvation to embrace "the prophet's vision of the social, economic and even hygienic betterment of life that would result from a real filling of life with the spirit of God."[6] To be fair, many nineteenth-century missionaries had in fact been deeply concerned about social issues; the more radical among them – for example, some missionaries of the London Missionary Society and Bishop Colenso of Natal – had entered politics to promote justice for their African converts. And even the most resolutely apolitical missionaries had often been engaged, not only in planting a church, but also in educating youth, dispensing medicines, and striving to reshape the family life, sexual mores, domestic architecture, agricultural methods, and other facets of their African adherents' culture. As part of this project of social engineering they had built up impressive networks of institutions – churches, schools, dispensaries, hospitals, agricultural settlements – that contemporary Americans, in referring to their U.S. equivalents, called the "Benevolent Empire." Social Christians of the twentieth century inherited the South African Benevolent Empire, infused it with their new Social Gospel ideology, and used it as a base on which to build their political and social power.

By the time of the 1911 census, 1,589 Protestant missionaries (7.5 percent of all Protestant missionaries in the world) were working in South Africa and running 610 mission stations, most of them substantial African settlements, as well as 4,790 "outstations." (In Natal the missions held an additional 127,211 acres in trust from government as "Mission Reserves" for African occupation.)[7] Most mission stations, and many outstations, had schools as well as churches. Protestants administered 3,029 elementary schools, 16 "industrial and training" schools, 43 boarding and high schools, and 41 schools or classes for training clergy and teachers. At the same time, 313 Roman Catholic missionary priests and 1,667 missionary sisters laboured in South Africa, many of them in the 299 Catholic schools.[8] Roughly 4.8 per cent of the total African population (adults as well as children) were now studying in the mission schools,[9] virtually their only access to skills needed in the new colonial economy. At the apex of the missions' educational pyramid were the secondary schools (most prominently, Lovedale, run by Presbyterian Scots), which were educating 5,433 students, many of whom would join the black elite of the next generation. In 1916 the South African Native College would be founded at Fort Hare, the only institute of tertiary education for Africans in southern Africa. Though itself undenominational, Fort Hare provided denominational hostels for its students and was, by its constitution, to be staffed exclusively by "professing Christians . . . of missionary sympathies."[10]

Most Protestant mission stations were headed by a married male missionary, who was an ordained minister assisted by his wife and by a staff of African teachers and evangelists. The missionary saw his principal tasks as building Christian congregations and administering Christian schools. This programme contrasted sharply with Protestant mission practice in some other long-occupied mission fields, where missionaries, facing greater resistance to evangelism than in South Africa, had broadened their ministries to stress the social and medical needs of a non-Christian society. In China, for example, with fewer Christians than black South Africa, missionaries in 1911 ran 18 colleges and universities, and 438 boarding and high schools; they administered, in addition, 207 hospitals in China, compared to only five hospitals and nine dispensaries in South Africa. In South Africa only 0.4 per cent of Protestant missionaries were physicians, compared to 4.7 per cent worldwide. The entire Protestant missionary force in South Africa operated a mere four orphanages, two "rescue homes," and four "industrial homes."[11]

These statistics lent partial support to the Social Christians' claim that their predecessors in South Africa had been interested chiefly in saving souls. Protestant missions in South Africa, dominated by church-builders and educators, had practised their social ministry primarily in isolated rural communities. Only a few missionaries – gifted amateurs often acting alone – had exercised broad political influence. The Social Christians of early twentieth-century South Africa sought, by contrast, to unite and mobilize the fragmented Benevolent Empire through local and national interdenominational committees and through well-publicized congresses. By sponsoring research projects and developing specialized ministries they hoped to attend to South Africa's social ills and combat what they saw as its political malformations.

The missionaries would need the close collaboration of African Christians, who comprised most of the missions' evangelists and teachers, and many of their pastors. Of all the non-menial employees of Protestant missions, 85 per cent were black in 1911 (95 per cent in a well-established mission such as the American Board).[12] Protestant mission strategists in the nineteenth century had firmly believed that missionaries in a new field should rapidly educate and ordain young men as ministers, then leave them to manage their own "native church."[13] Yet in South Africa the missionaries were reluctant to ordain blacks, even the most successful evangelists. They believed that blacks were incapable, as yet, of the demanding tasks of a pastor – managing money, rebuking sin, and administering complex organizations. Under pressure from their home boards, missionaries did ordain Africans from the late nineteenth century, but by 1911, after more than a century of mission activity, only 401 ordained Africans (compared to 649 ordained missionaries) were ministering in mission-related churches in South Africa. Missionaries often refused to treat the African clergy as their professional equals and brothers in Christ. Consequently many Africans, embittered by their treatment as second-class ministers, quarrelled with the missionaries over money, status, and authority – few of these squabbles concerned Christian doctrine or disagreements over principles of church governance.

The frustrations of the black clergy erupted most dramatically in the Ethiopian secessions, which in the 1880s and 1890s engulfed most Protestant missions (see chap. 12, *passim*). The missionaries in turn felt betrayed by their African colleagues, whose grievances they only vaguely comprehended, and feared the loss of missionary control over the entire Benevolent Empire. Yet most black clergy declined to join the separatist Ethiopian movement and remained – many, no doubt, reluctantly and warily – in the missionary churches. Moreover, some Ethiopians later returned to their former missions, or joined other mission-related churches.[14]

Still, the more perceptive among the missionaries concluded that new arrangements must be devised to accommodate the aspirations of African moderates while maintaining, at least temporarily, a measure of missionary oversight. The American Board and the Scots Presbyterians created separate African churches under African leadership, but with close ties to the missions. The Anglicans integrated white and black within the same diocesan structure, and granted African clergy considerable voice in the Provincial Missionary Council, where resolutions on social issues were often considered. Missionaries slowly withdrew from parish or congregational management, where the likelihood of conflict with African clergy was most acute, and moved instead into specialized fields like education and medicine, into the growing ecclesiastical bureaucracies, and into social and political activism. The transition was slowest in the German Lutheran and some of the recently formed Anglo-Saxon missions, and fastest in the older Anglo-Saxon missions, such as the London Missionary Society, the Anglicans, the Scots, the American Board, and the Methodists. Between 1911 and 1938 the number of ordained Africans in Protestant mission-related churches (that is, excluding Roman Catholic and African Initiated Churches) exploded by 520 per cent: by 1938 black pastors outnumbered ordained missionaries by a ratio of 2.6 to 1. During the same period the Benevolent Empire continued to expand, and came to resemble more closely its counterparts in India and China. The Protestant educational establishment in South Africa almost doubled in size, while the number of Protestant hospitals jumped from 5 to 25, dispensaries from 9 to 76, and the number of missionary physicians from 7 to 29.[15]

Early in the twentieth century, the missionaries – increasingly able to motor around the countryside and travel by railway to national conferences – became aware of large-scale social threats to the missions throughout South Africa. Most of the older mission societies had begun their work in rural areas and had witnessed, in the late nineteenth century, the development of prosperous, largely Christian, peasant communities. By 1905, however, when the South African Native Affairs Commission asked for written comment on the past two decades of economic change among Africans, fewer than half the respondents reported overall improvement.[16] Four years later, James Henderson, the missionary principal of Lovedale, alerted the third General Missionary Conference that "native communities are becoming more and more impoverished"; he suggested that a "prime duty of missionaries" was to engage in a "great and sustained effort for securing and putting upon a stable basis the material prosperity of the Native people." This may have been the first time in a South Africa-wide missionary gathering that the Social Gospel was clearly proclaimed.[17]

Henderson, like most other missionaries, at first attributed rural poverty to defects in African culture and to missionaries' failure to train their converts in modern agricultural and business techniques. But as the rural crisis deepened in the 1920s, Henderson, after several studies of African families' income and expenditures, concluded that Africans were enmeshed in a relentless legal and economic system created in colonial conquest and tightened by discriminatory legislation, particularly by the Natives Land Act of 1913. African land ownership was now confined to a disproportionately meagre share of the South African land. As Africans' population increased, their lands deteriorated rapidly, and more and more young men were forced to find work in the white-dominated economic sector; here they received inadequate wages and were blocked from advancement by a legislated "colour-bar." Henderson concluded in 1928, far in advance of most white observers, that whites and blacks were part of a single economy, in which racism and injustice doomed Africans to increasing misery. Thus, missionaries should stop blaming Africans or themselves for African poverty, but should rather follow the example of the prophet Amos and "denounce evil in the name of the Lord . . . and give warning saying, 'Behold the eyes of the Lord are upon the sinful kingdom.'"[18]

Other missionaries responded to cries for help from African converts who had carried their faith into the burgeoning cities of South Africa. In 1894 the American Board dispatched Herbert Goodenough to Johannesburg to administer several Witwatersrand churches, including one founded by Africans in Pretoria; in 1899 it assigned Fredrick Bridgman to follow up evangelistic work begun by Africans in Durban. Goodenough and Bridgman ministered in the cities as they had in the country, but at an accelerated pace. They raced to secure land for their churches amidst feverish land speculation and booming construction, and laboured to organize congregations, open schools, settle disputes, and discipline immoral behaviour. In Durban, Bridgman's wife, Clara Bridgman, conducted prayer meetings for women and founded temperance societies. Missionaries and their African associates struggled to keep up with the demand for churches and schools, confident that Africans converted in the large cities would carry the gospel back to the rural areas of southern Africa. Yet their confidence was mingled with anxiety that the moral temptations of the city, especially for men unaccompanied by wives – the missionaries focused chiefly on drinking, gambling, prostitution, homosexuality, and pornography – would undermine the marital standards of the missions, promote crime, and spread malnutrition and disease. "What are we doing to stem this tide of evil?" asked Goodenough. "What *can* we do? If we tell them of salvation from sin, they don't want to be saved from sin. If we tell them of Heaven, Heaven is a long way off and the women and the beer are very near."[19] The missionaries moved on to identify the social conditions that caused the temptations of the city; they tried to persuade white-ruled municipalities to provide healthy "municipal locations" for Africans, and to supply rudimentary services. Bridgman's frenetic activities along these lines made him, said an admiring colleague in 1911, the "unofficial Protector of Natives" in Durban; over the past year Bridgman had significantly influenced the plans for the Durban location, induced the Town Council to erect a hostel "for the proper housing of native women temporarily in Durban," served on the Executive of the Native Affairs Reform Committee, and delivered "influential lectures" on controlling Africans' access to liquor. He had, moreover, tried in vain to save one African, "almost certainly wrongly convicted," from the gallows.[20]

When, shortly thereafter, Bridgman moved to Johannesburg to take over Goodenough's work, he was deeply distressed by the conditions of Africans on mine compounds and in town locations. "The utter darkness of night [in the unlighted locations is] a fitting picture of the black pall cast over the community by brazen sin, prevailing poverty, sickness, and troubled hearts." In thus equating problems that more secular observers might assign to separate spheres – "sin" to morality, "poverty" to economics, "sickness" to medicine, and "troubled hearts" to psychology – Bridgman struck a holistic stance characteristic of the Social Gospel. He could no longer limit himself to a spiritual gospel that would perpetuate the "mediaeval fallacy of saving souls while ignoring the body in which the soul lives." "Woe unto me," Bridgman exclaimed, "if I preach not the gospel of social as well as individual regeneration." In practical terms, he wanted to create two or three social centres to minister to the totality of human needs. "Attached to the central church there should be a hall for public gatherings, lectures, concerts, etc. There should also be provision for social, reading, and game rooms. Bowling alleys and a kitchen and lunch counter would be valuable adjuncts. And here should be located a medical dispensary . . ." By 1919 Bridgman had brought to South Africa the Rev. Ray Phillips, a youthful American proponent of the Social Gospel brimming with energy and optimism. Along with his equally energetic wife, Phillips organized athletics in the mine compounds, Pathfinders groups (like Boy Scouts) for boys, and "the first supervised playground . . . in Africa . . . for children of any color." Most significantly, he founded an "Educated Boys Club," where young men would gather weekly to put on plays and concerts, and debate with one another and "with prominent European officials and others interested in native affairs."[21]

The Social Gospel was new, not because – as its proponents often claimed – it addressed social or political issues for the first time, but because it did so on a larger scale and with more specialized personnel, and because it identified the whole of society, not just the church or mission station, as its principal target. The Social Christians in South Africa claimed that circumstances had forced the social dimension of Christianity upon them; they took up social issues solely to express God's love to Africans immune to theological appeals. They denied that they intended to engage directly in politics, but, in practice, they regularly sought aid from persons in power. "Nothing seems to attract much attention here in Johannesburg that does not have the patronage of some high Lord, His Worship the Mayor, or etc.," said Ray Phillips. He needed, he claimed, influential supporters to "do something to alleviate the spirit of distrust and unrest prevailing among the natives."[22]

Many Johannesburg Africans of Phillips's acquaintance had, by the early 1920s, become intensely politicized. The parliament of the new Union of South Africa had been seeking to perpetuate white dominance and to shape black–white relations through a series of discriminatory laws inspired by a loosely articulated ideology of "segregation." The most dramatic of these steps was the Natives Land Act of 1913, which, among other provisions, permitted the forceful eviction of black "squatters" from many white-owned farms in the Orange Free State. The suffering of evicted squatters, well documented by African activists, in particular by Sol Plaatje, hardened African opposition to white dominance. The principal missionary bodies, such as the Transvaal Missionary Association and the Anglican Provincial Board of Missions, denounced the act at the outset. But some missionaries, for example, Henderson at Lovedale, defended it, if cautiously, until mounting evidence of its dire consequences compelled him to reverse his stand.[23]

Blacks themselves led the mounting protest against discriminatory legislation. However, many missionaries (particularly the British and Americans) responded to the new political situation by extending their political activity from the local to the national level. They lobbied for or against legislation, publicized injustices, and offered themselves as mediators between blacks and whites. They sought, as a means to these ends, to streamline the massive but decentralized Benevolent Empire into an efficient organization, and to recruit allies among "moderate" Africans and white "friends of the native."

Selectively Appropriating the Social Gospel

In Britain and North America the principal Protestant churches had, for some time, been turning to the Social Gospel to combat the perceived evils of an industrial society. Its more radical advocates, like the American theologian Walter Rauschenbusch, said in 1907 that a "social crisis" was a consequence of the nineteenth century's failure to deliver its promised freedom and prosperity. Gross inequalities in landholding; "ugly, depressing, coarsening" factory work; periodic unemployment; declining purchasing power of workers' wages; undernourished and overworked women; disease-ridden children; a "wedge of inequality" that threatened to polarize society and undermine democracy; the corruption of morals through competition and greed – these formed the seamy side of the "age of progress" that the churches would ignore at their spiritual and institutional peril.[24] In the face of such distressing problems, many clergy, around the turn of the century, were shifting away from the traditional formula of revivalism – that individuals must be saved as a precondition to reforming society – toward a conviction that social reform was a precondition of individual redemption.[25] This shift of emphasis entailed, for some, a theological evolution from stressing the transcendence of God to stressing the "immanence" of God. By asserting that God was immanent (present) in the social and political processes of the day, the Social Gospellers intended, not just to claim individuals from individual sin, but by combating social injustices to usher in the Kingdom of God. Thus they continued the nineteenth-century postmillennial belief that the Kingdom could come through historical processes, before Christ's Second Coming (chap. 22, *passim*).

Since Social Christians conceived of salvation as a gradual process, to be accomplished by slowly altering the human environment, they believed the church should be like the leaven in a loaf – gradually Christianizing society through social reform and education. In more radical formulations this process would replace evangelism altogether.[26] A number of mission theorists, particularly in the United States, shared this perspective early in the twentieth century. Among them was James Dennis, whose *Christian Missions and Social Progress*, a massive three-volume study of the social impact of missions worldwide, accompanied by the first reliable statistics on global mission, inspired missionaries to greater social action, in South Africa and around the world.[27]

So influential was the Social Gospel in the U.S. that, in 1908, the newly created Federal Council of Churches, speaking for 17 million Protestants, adopted the "Social Creed of the Churches," which committed member churches to "the most equitable division of the product of industry that can ultimately be devised."[28] In England, where the churches faced a working-class flight from Christianity more threatening than any in America, the Social Gospel movement, though interdenominational, became particularly strong in the Church of England. Many Anglican leaders began to deride earlier Christian charity as mere "ambulance work." Mounting a theological critique of individualism and of private property, they advocated a number of mildly socialist measures, such as payment of a "living wage," worker participation in industrial management, and taxes on inherited wealth. In 1908 Lord William Cecil, in an address to the Pan-Anglican conference, pronounced himself "almost out of place in speaking as a person with no belief in socialism."[29] The Church of Scotland, for its part, decided in 1904 to replace its evangelistic programs with "social work in homes and 'labour colonies' for the elderly, disabled, inebriate, delinquent and unemployed." In 1908 the United Free Church of Scotland (whose missionaries ran Lovedale in South Africa) set up a Committee on Social Problems, and began a flurry of inquiries into "housing conditions, unemployment, child welfare, and allied matters."[30]

The Social Gospel also reached South Africa via a branch of the American "home missions" begun in the years after the Civil War. These missions concentrated on Christianizing and educating the emancipated black slaves in the defeated southern states; they devoted more funds to southern blacks' welfare than the federal government did.[31] A beacon of Christian commitment to southern regeneration was Hampton Normal and Agricultural Institute, founded by General Samuel Chapman Armstrong, a son of Presbyterian missionaries to Hawaii. Hampton made it possible for poor African–American students to work their way through school, learning – along with academic subjects – agriculture and trades. They were exposed to an "incessant varied activity of mind and body, with proper relaxation and amusement in an atmosphere of Christian influence and sympathy."[32] Hampton's most illustrious graduate, Booker T. Washington, modelled the school he established, Tuskegee Normal and Industrial Institute, on Hampton. He expanded on the themes of hard work, self-help, and moral formation in a Christian setting. Tuskegee was "strictly undenominational, but . . . thoroughly Christian," Washington claimed, as its "preaching service, prayer-meetings, Sunday-school, Christian Endeavour Society, Young Men's Christian Association, and various missionary associations testify." Washington was a strong advocate of practical Christianity – he said he wanted his students to "mix up with their religion zeal and habits of thrift, economy, carpentry . . ." – and an admirer of liberal white denominations, especially the Unitarians and Congregationalists. By 1901, when Washington published his autobiography, *Up From Slavery*, which, also in Zulu translation, came to have enormous impact in South Africa, Hampton, Tuskegee, and other schools modelled on them were strongly supported by a network of northern churches, Christian philanthropists, and, increasingly, by large corporations. Tuskegeeism could be extolled as a distinctly American application of the Social Gospel to the problems of race and rural poverty.[33] Washington's well-publicized view that "agitation of questions of social equality is the extremest folly,"[34] and his silence in the face of rising segregation in the United States, made his brand of the Social Gospel all the more appealing to missionaries, to white paternalists in South Africa, and to many blacks as well. Many South Africans of all races made their way to Tuskegee and were deeply impressed by their experience.

Both the industrial "socialist" and the rural Tuskegeean strand of the Social Gospel stressed Christian charity and reconciliation between contending social groups. Both proposed to empower the oppressed through education and moral formation. But the means differed: the "industrial" form of the Social Gospel, as enunciated in powerful and respected churches in Britain and America, often criticized the structure of society and challenged both capitalism and the dominant classes. The Tuskegeean approach, by contrast, reflected the predicament of an economically and socially deprived black minority whose political position was worsening; it eschewed formal politics, at least in the short run, and it sought to elevate blacks with the aid of white patrons. It was the Tuskegee model, and not the industrial, that was to have profound impact in South Africa.

Ups and Downs in the Benevolent Empire's Alliances

The extensive network of mission institutions in South Africa was, at the turn of the century, administered by fifty-two Protestant societies, and several Catholic orders, each with a somewhat distinct theological and social agenda. Most missionaries worked in semi-isolation even from their co-religionists. To foster some measure of common purpose, regular conferences of Protestant missionaries began in Natal in 1881, and were later established in the Transvaal (1907), Transkei (1909), Swaziland (1911), and Ciskei (1925). The first General Missionary Conference (GMC) for the whole of South Africa was held in 1904, its initial aims to eliminate competition and overlap among missions and to debate contentious issues, such as Ethiopianism, polygamy, and bridewealth. Meeting in different cities every three or four years (except during the First World War), each GMC attracted about a hundred delegates, who read and debated position papers, and adopted resolutions, with considerable attention from the press. The conference proceedings, and the actions of the GMC executive between conferences, were dominated by five bodies heavily influenced by the ideal of Social Christianity (the Anglicans, the Scots Presbyterians, the American Board, the Suisse Romande mission, and the Paris Evangelical mission) and by certain elements in the Dutch Reformed Church.[35]

The social and political plight of Africans rapidly came to dominate the GMC proceedings. In 1912 the conference, guided by reports of several commissions, passed a series of resolutions to be presented, variously, to the Minister of Native Affairs, the municipalities of the Union, or the Chamber of Mines. Some of the demands were compatible with the segregationist ideology that was crystallizing among white leaders – "native townships should be established . . . and a measure of local self-government shall be secured"; but others were integrationist – interracial marriage should be recognized and Africans should be given "fixity of tenure in towns." On civil rights, the missionaries were, alternately, conservative (advocating movie censorship and prohibition of alcohol sales in municipal townships), and liberal (seeking abolition of trials by white juries in interracial rape cases and proposing that African criminals be dealt with "through reformative and not purely punitive discipline.") Their liberal concern for personal and economic liberty was apparent in their denunciation of the Native Settlement and Squatters Bill, a 1911 precursor – never passed by parliament – of the Natives Land Act. They labelled the bill an effort to "force on the Natives a form of serfdom."[36]

The Social Christians' socio-political policies – conservative and liberal alike – derived from the paternalist assumption of nineteenth-century Protestant missions that Western Christians had a duty to raise up lost societies by controlling or at least by guiding them. Though, by 1912, they had extended their doctrine of the Kingdom to embrace the whole of society, the Social Christians still assumed that social salvation would spring in the first place from the salvation of individuals. In this they were distinctly more conservative than some Social Gospel thinkers overseas. They also hoped that the development of healthy Christian families and churches (as defined by the prevailing standards of Anglo-Saxon countries) would leaven the lump of society. They were, accordingly, indignant at any force or institution that might inhibit the regeneration, spiritual or economic, of individuals, families, and local communities. They could be equally critical of cultural influences, such as drink and risqué movies, and of discriminatory legislation, such as the Squatters Bill. Rarely did they appeal in the abstract to ideals like liberty or interracial equality – both difficult to envisage in South Africa for a long time to come. They did, however, believe that Africans, their societies transformed in Christ, had a right to progress to economic prosperity and citizenship. Whether such progress was best accomplished by separating or integrating the races was a matter, not of theological principle, but of pragmatic calculus.

So, too, with issues concerning women. Though the 1912 GMC conference was influenced by feminist concerns prominent in the international missionary movement and in American Social Gospel circles,[37] the missionaries were not demanding equal treatment for women, whose proper social role they regarded as distinct from that of men. Rather, they wished to foster conditions that would allow women to maintain their sexual "purity." They called, for example, for "carriages reserved for women, and including lavatory accommodation . . . on all long-journey trains." They also demanded social conditions that would provide women with wholesome employment, and enable them to perform their roles as Christian wives and mothers. They accordingly advocated government intervention in the "rescue and reformation" of prostitutes and the establishment of "Native settlements" at some distance from the mines, where "women can find employment, with houses providing conditions of health and decency."

Knowing that most South African whites were indifferent or hostile to their agenda, and anxious to recruit allies inspired by the vision of Social Christianity, the 1912 GMC sent a message of greeting to the newly established South African Native National Congress (SANNC, later renamed the African National Congress or ANC). The SANNC was dominated by members of the African middle class, virtually all educated in mission schools. Many of them had been convinced – through the influence of a respected missionary, or from association in Christian settings with white South Africans – that Christianity could not only raise up Africans to "civilization" but also ensure them justice in a multiracial South Africa. This optimism had been fed, in many cases, by travel and study in the United Kingdom, and, more frequently, in the United States, under the auspices of organizations like the African Methodist Episcopal Church (AME), the American Board Mission, or the Phelps-Stokes fund of New York. During visits to the United States such aspiring African politicians as John Dube, D.D.T. Jabavu, and Dr. Alfred Xuma were profoundly inspired by the Tuskegee philosophy of self-help and practical Christianity and by the prospects of working in alliance with sympathetic whites.

In the Cape, where Africans such as John Tengo Jabavu (D.D.T. Jabavu's father) had long combined a political career with active leadership in a Christian church, a strong body of prominent Christian Africans existed by the time of Union. The Cape Christians were joined by *kholwa* (middle-class Africans) from Natal and by Christian African doctors, lawyers, and ministers on the Witwatersrand. Together they formed a national elite that historians have variously labelled "African nationalists" (because the organization they founded would later combat white supremacy), or the "petty bourgeoisie" (because they were mostly small-business people or professionals), or "moderates" (because they advocated only constitutional forms of protest). They could, with equal justice, be called African Social Christians.

The founding executive of the SANNC was dominated by dedicated Christians, among them the Rev. John Dube (president), the Rev. Walter Rubusana and Sefago Mapogo Makgatho (vice-presidents), Pixley ka Isaka Seme (treasurer), and Solomon Plaatje (secretary).[38] Dube, who had founded Ohlange, a black-run school in Natal modelled closely on Tuskegee, believed, along with most Social Christians of his time, that Christianity must provide both for the "inward workings in the individual's eternal life" and for "those more material blessings of mental and social improvement with which the missionary has combined it." His "war cry," he told Congress, was "Onward! Upward! Into the higher places of civilization and Christianity." His strategy – to "gain the good will of the Government" – proved futile, as did his appeal to politicians in the United Kingdom to get the 1913 Land Act annulled. In 1917, with his prestige steadily eroding among more radical members of the Congress, he resigned.[39]

The SANNC's appeal to Britain harked back to the nineteenth-century missionaries' strategy of seeking British government intervention against colonial governments in southern Africa. After 1910, as British influence in the region waned, missionaries and Christian Africans began to search for allies among South African whites, particularly among politicians of the old "Cape liberal" tradition, such as Jacobus W. Sauer, the Minister of Native Affairs. But Sauer fostered the Natives Land Act, whose consequences were profoundly disillusioning. The 1924 electoral victory of J.B.M. Hertzog, an outspoken segregationist and Afrikaner nationalist, made matters worse. Though missionaries continued to enjoy access to ministers in the governments of Hertzog (1924–39) and J.C. Smuts (1939–48) – especially to J.H. Hofmeyr, a Social Christian who was twice a prominent cabinet member in the years between 1933 and 1948 – it was obvious almost from 1910 that parliamentary legislation would rarely transcend the prejudices and interests of the overwhelmingly white electorate. Missionaries and their African allies, in line with their elitist instincts and the logic of the Social Gospel, sought to cooperate with prominent white sympathizers outside of party politics. In particular, they turned to the more liberal members of the Native Affairs Department, many of whom, particularly in the Transkei, were offspring of missionary families and had close ties to Lovedale, Fort Hare, and the black Christian bourgeoisie.[40]

Equally important to the missionaries was the emergence of a small, highly influential group of white paternalist theorists, who sought to cooperate with the network of the Benevolent Empire, and with members of white and black elites, in pursuit of a juster society. Though the characteristic views of these paternalists can be traced back to the South African Native Affairs Commission of 1905, its most coherent formulations were offered in books by three white Natalians: *Black and White in South East Africa* by Maurice Evans (1909), *The Education of the South African Native* by Charles T. Loram (1917), and *The History of Native Policy in South Africa* by Edgar Brookes (1924). These writers argued that Africans, who were buffeted by massive social and cultural upheaval, especially in the cities, were losing their traditional moral and social "restraints" but not replacing them with the restraints of Western culture. Falling into immorality, criminality, and poverty, the mass of Africans posed a serious threat to the security of white South Africa. At the same time, black leaders, their views warped by an overly "bookish" education, were dangerously resentful and rebellious. The paternalists warned against what they regarded as two diametrically opposed errors – to keep blacks "repressed," as in the former Boer republics, or to "assimilate" them wholly to Western culture and society, as the Cape liberals wanted. The solution, the paternalists believed, was to encourage blacks to develop and advance, but in *partial* segregation from whites. They roundly criticized earlier missionaries, not only for preaching assimilationism, but also for expressing unreasonably negative views of African culture and for presenting the Christian gospel only as a matter of individual salvation. But they defended missionary education, provided it became less "bookish" and more adapted to Africans' needs, and vigorously supported missionaries as the best hope for "constructively" channelling black ambitions. Only missionaries could prevent potentially rebellious religions, such as Ethiopian

Christianity and perhaps Islam, from spreading among South African blacks. Only missionaries, helped by whites "of good will," could bring South Africa back from the brink of social disaster.[41]

Many missionaries were gratified by this line of analysis, which dovetailed nicely with their ambitions to be agents of social regeneration. They agreed wholeheartedly with the paternalists that Christianity was a more "social," less individualistic, religion than their predecessors had realized. Most of them, too, like many black leaders until the late 1920s, were sympathetic to variants of partial segregation that would give Africans space for development, even while they opposed segregationist measures they deemed unjust.

Missionaries, African Christians, and white paternalists formed a loose alliance in the early 1920s, meeting in such venues as the Bantu Men's Social Centre (BMSC), established in 1924 by Ray Phillips, a home for religious, athletic, musical, theatrical, and academic activities for the black Johannesburg elite.[42] The Johannesburg Joint Council, a forum of whites and blacks that had begun in 1921, moved its meetings to the BMSC; its members regularly discussed black–white relations, issued policy papers, and made representations to local and national governments. Similar Joint Councils were subsequently established in the principal cities and towns of the Union, reaching a total of thirty-seven in 1935. They drew their members largely from among socially conscious black and white Christians, who expressed their views largely in the language of the Social Gospel.[43]

The bridge-building of the Social Christians faced competition, in the early 1920s, from more radical political movements, particularly on the Witwatersrand, then a site of severe labour unrest. In the ANC (the former SANCC) and in the new black trade union movement, mission-oriented Africans (whose enemies called them the "good boys") were under pressure from Garveyite nationalists and Communists, both outspokenly hostile to missionaries, though not necessarily to Christianity itself. Clements Kadalie, the national secretary of the Industrial and Commercial Workers Union, speaking to the General Missionary Conference in 1928, denounced the churches for being "thoroughly reactionary and drifting from Christ's teaching" throughout history. The churches had, he said, sided "with the rich against the poor, opposing every effort toward social and economic freedom of the masses." Though Kadalie's inflammatory wording caused great offence, his call that the churches "devote more time and effort to the improvement of the material lives of men and women and less to the so-called spiritual side of things" was quite in line with the Social Gospel convictions of many in his missionary audience – as the Anglican Bishop of Johannesburg pointed out in reply. When, in 1946, Kadalie wrote his memoirs, he commented benignly on white and African–American missionaries, as did his contemporary, the Zulu trade unionist George Champion. Even the former communist leader, Edward Roux, remembered the missionaries of the 1930s as "in many ways the natural allies of the communists and the only other disinterested friends the Africans had in the country."[44]

Faced with more radical competitors, the missionaries redoubled their efforts on behalf of the Social Gospel. From 1912 every General Missionary Conference issued resolutions on social questions. The 1921 GMC cut back its discussion of traditional missionary concerns to a mere three papers and devoted, instead, seven papers to social and economic issues (and one to publishing, one to education, and one to music). It denounced the suffering caused by the Land Act and demanded increased facilities for training Africans as doctors and nurses, higher wages for Africans, and better African housing in towns. Although, in response to traditionalist missionaries, whose motto was "Back to the souls, back to the Gospel," the 1925 GMC was devoted to "The Evangelisation of Africa," it also passed resolutions on social reform. It demanded a commission, with African representation, to study ways to alleviate the harsh penalties imposed on Africans and replace them with "commonly accepted principles of modern criminology." It expressed its "gravest concern [about] the repressive tendency of much recent legislation affecting natives and urge[d] upon the Cabinet the pressing need for some reconsideration" of the Land Act, excessive taxes on Africans, and colour bars in industry. In 1928, the GMC declared that "the Native has the same right as the White man to combine for the purpose of collective bargaining," and that more blacks should be employed in the civil service. In 1932 it concentrated its fire on two issues: relief measures for African victims of the Depression and government provision of medicine and medical education for Africans.[45]

If the Social Christians were to go beyond issuing resolutions and were to influence government action, they needed support from the Dutch Reformed churches (DRC), whose membership embraced the overwhelming majority of Afrikaans-speaking whites. Several missionary-minded leaders of the Cape DRC – among them Johannes du Plessis, professor of missions at Stellenbosch and a frequent speaker on the international missionary circuit (pp. 137–38) – were broadly sympathetic to the Social Gospel, though not to racial integration. Mission-oriented Africans such as D.D.T. Jabavu, a professor at Fort Hare, and Sol Plaatje had denounced the DRC as an "anti-Native church," because of its support of the Land Act.[46] But with DRC missionaries flocking in large numbers to the GMC conventions, and with their leaders prominent on GMC committees and at the podium, English-speaking missionaries and their associates, particularly the education activist C.T. Loram, determined to co-opt the DRC into their plans. In 1923 the Federal Council of the four DRC churches convened a conference, in Johannesburg, of missionaries and African leaders; a number of Africans and DRC leaders read papers on the "Native Question" and agreed on a series of mildly segregationist resolutions proposed by Edgar Brookes. Loram later told a DRC synod that "from that Conference I date the future of your Church's dealings with Natives,"[47] and Jabavu declared it a "milestone" in interracial understanding. The Rev. Z.R. Mahabane of the ANC said it had "restored the confidence of the Bantu people in the ruling race, and removed the causes of suspicion and mistrust."[48] Such loose accords among blacks, paternalist English-speakers, and Afrikaners were possible before the Nationalists' election victory of 1924. Thereafter, the hitherto inchoate ideology of segregation was clarified into an unambiguous tool of white supremacy, forcing Brookes, Jabavu, and a number of other Social Christians to renounce it.[49]

DRC leaders who cooperated with the Social Christians had to fend off attacks from outraged members of their own churches. One angry correspondent wrote to *De Kerkbode*, the official paper of the four DRC churches, that "Our Church . . .

must realize that her calling in the first instance is to the whites and not to the natives." Another writer said that, although blacks' "eternal interests" must concern Afrikaners, "it is impossible to fraternize in society: we must be brothers in the spirit. [Blacks] stand too far below us in the area of morals. Friendly advances in practical life are impossible, and according to God's Word also sinful."[50] A second "European–Bantu" conference, convened by the Dutch Reformed Federal Council in 1927, was denied the use of the Dutch Church Hall in Cape Town. It was able, nonetheless, to reach a measure of consensus, including objections to certain features of Prime Minister Hertzog's "Native Bills," then under discussion in parliament; it kept silent on issues, such as the Cape franchise, that divided the DRC delegates from blacks and sometimes from liberal whites.[51]

But more serious opposition to the Social Christians was now forming in the DRC of the Orange Free State. In 1931, it drew up a "Mission Policy," which was adopted in 1935 by the Federal Council of the Dutch Reformed churches of all four provinces. The Dutch Reformed churches declared that they would make greater use of "medical, agricultural, industrial and literary activities," – an endorsement of the Social Gospel – but also made clear that they could not accept some of the social goals of the more liberal churches and missions. They stressed, in particular, their "antipathy to the idea of racial fusion" and to "social equality in the sense of ignoring differences of race and colour . . . in daily life." Yet the Dutch Reformed churches desired to assist "Native and Coloured . . . to develop into self-respecting Christian nations." This influential Mission Policy, which substantially foreshadowed the apartheid ideology of the next decade, was a line drawn in the sand. After 1935 English-speaking missionaries and their African allies continued to try to cooperate with the DRC in fostering African "development," but they did so in the certainty that they and the DRC were working toward different ultimate ends.[52]

By the 1930s radicalism had waned in African nationalist circles, and the Social Christians had again become ascendant. The ANC, under the presidency of Seme (1930–37) and Mahabane (1937–40), and with the Anglican priest James Calata as general secretary from 1936, was generally weak. It had meagre support from the black masses and was, in the words of one historian, "part think tank, part debating society."[53] It issued resolutions and drafted reports, rather like the missionary and philanthropic organizations with which its leaders cooperated. In 1935 D.D.T. Jabavu founded, with Seme, the All African Convention, seeking to keep Cape African voters on the common electoral roll, from which parliament removed them in 1936. Jabavu, like Dube before him, combined three careers – international Christian leader, educator, and African politician – all three rooted in the Social Gospel agenda. He called on the churches to address "Labour conditions, Pass Laws, Land [and] Segregation," and, at the same time, stressed "the evangelistic side of our work . . . to win more followers for [Jesus'] banner to the glory of His Heavenly Kingdom and to the Salvation of the Bantu Race." He saw this fusion of socio-political and spiritual power as rooted in the African world view and wholly contrary to secularizing tendencies that were driving religion to the margins of life in Western countries. "In the African mind there is a oneness about things, oneness about religion, together with daily life and wealth and work and discipline." More than those African leaders whose personal crusades brought them into conflict with cautious or autocratic missionaries, Jabavu was staunchly loyal to the missionary movement. He told an American audience in 1931: "Every [South African] black man who is a leader of any importance is a product of missionary work. Outside of missionary work there is no leadership."[54]

The conservative tack in black politics and the struggles over Hertzog's "Native Bills" kept the Social Gospel alliance alive for another decade. In 1929 eight eminent South Africans gathered in the home of the missionary Ray Phillips to found the South African Institute of Race Relations (SAIRR): along with Jabavu, Du Plessis, Loram, and Brookes – all activist Social Christians – they included a Quaker, Howard Pim, and a son of a Welsh clergyman, J.D. Rheinallt Jones, who would become the secretary of the SAIRR and its guiding hand in the 1930s and early 1940s. In his younger years Jones had taken a radical Social Gospel stance, stating in 1918, in a talk on "The Church and Labour," that "we must say good-bye to all our ideas about individual rights such as property." In 1927 he told the Natal Missionary Conference that Christianity's "greatest contribution has been to make mankind divinely rebellious against the forces of reaction and evil."[55] Under his direction, however, the SAIRR became cautious, avoided party politics, and accommodated itself to certain segregationist projects. It also steered the black–white dialogue in a more secular direction, taking over from the Dutch Reformed Church the task of organizing the "Bantu–European" conferences (and a "Coloured–European" conference in 1933). It also coordinated the Joint Councils and brought them together in national congresses. By now, as Rheinallt Jones pointed out in 1934, the Joint Councils were doing "the work which the Missionary Associations used to find it necessary to take up." It was, he added, "to the credit of the missions that . . . public interest has now been so much aroused that at the last [Joint Council] conference the majority of the European delegates were "non-missionary."[56] In fact, by the late 1930s the leading intellect among liberal white activists was R.F.A. Hoernlé, professor of philosophy at the University of the Witwatersrand, a son of missionaries but himself an agnostic.[57] Many advocates of the Social Gospel had long maintained that the churches should undertake certain roles only until succeeded by secular bodies; for them, the transfer of responsibility from missionaries to other Christian activists, or even to agnostics, was not a Christian retreat from society but society's embrace of Christian principles, a sign that the leaven of the Spirit was at work, that the Kingdom was approaching.

Simultaneously, under the influence of the international missionary movement, which was then evolving into a world-wide ecumenical movement, the Social Christians in South Africa sought to replace the GMC with a "Christian council" like the Federal Council of Churches in the United States. Christian councils founded in the mission fields of Japan, India, and China reflected progressive missionary leaders' conviction that missions should yield their leadership to the new non-Western churches. The members of a Christian council would be, not individuals as in the GMC, but organizations; these would include churches as well as missions. Whereas such a reorganization in South Africa would strengthen the voice of black clergy and laity – a consequence intended by mission theorists – it would, ironically, strengthen even more the voice of South African whites, who dominated the principal churches and often opposed the missionaries' activist pro-grammes. Yet missionaries, among them James Dexter Taylor, pressed strongly for such a Christian council, not only to undertake "research" and "practical service," but also to develop a "united Christian view-point upon the great problems of social and racial adjustment which challenge the Church in South Africa." Taylor's vision that the churches speaking with one voice would be a "vital force in the shaping of public opinion and the influencing of legislation"[58] was precisely what many white clergy and more conservative missionaries feared.

As plans crystallized for a Christian council, the mission activists constantly reassured the DRC and the German missions of the modesty of their intentions. In 1936, two years after John R. Mott of the International Missionary Conference tri-umphantly toured South Africa, the Christian Council of South Africa (CCSA) was founded – with a constitution that emphasized evangelism, study, and service, and said nothing about politics. Its first meetings were less free and vigorous than those of the past GMCs. Africans, as anticipated, were much better represented than in the old GMC, and some, the Rev. Z.R. Mahabane among them, urged the council to address political injustices such as the recent abolition of the Cape franchise. But the white CCSA leaders were eager to cement relationships with the Dutch Reformed churches, and accordingly concentrated on luring DRC clergy into prominent positions and encouraged the use of Afrikaans in council business; for the most part they tiptoed around divisive racial issues. These conciliatory efforts notwithstanding, the Afrikaner leaders noted that the gulf separating them from English-speakers on "most questions affecting the relationship between Europeans and Natives" was becoming "more and more clear." The Transvaal Dutch Reformed Church, briefly active in the council, withdrew in 1944 under the influ-ence of the Cape synod. No Lutheran organization, up to then, had joined the CCSA, except for the small Church of Sweden Mission.[59] The spectrum of Christian opinion on the early CCSA was thus distinctly narrower than the earlier consensus of the Benevolent Empire, which had embraced some Afrikaners, many Lutherans, and a number of influential blacks. Conservative whites now drifted away from the consensus; so did many blacks, who increasingly lost faith in mis-sionaries and in other white allies.

In the 1940s – under the pressure of the World War, urban unrest, and the 1948 electoral victory of the National Party with its allegiance to apartheid – African politics again entered a more radical phase. Alfred Xuma, a distinguished Johannesburg physician and a close ally of Calata, was ANC president from 1940 to 1949. Like Dube, Jabavu, and many other blacks, Xuma had been deeply inspired by the Tuskegee experiment. During a fourteen-year stay in the United States he had come to appreciate the value of cooperating with white Christian lib-erals, but, at the same time, he had derived from the African Methodist Episcopal Church (AME), a strong conviction that blacks must run their own organizations. On his return to South Africa he maintained close ties with the AME and the American Board Mission, and worked actively with Christian whites in the Joint Councils. He was less patient than many Africans with the paternalism of whites and their willingness to compromise with segregation. At different times he clashed with Fredrick Bridgman's widow Clara, and with Loram, Hoernlé, and Rheinallt

Jones. Yet to his death (1962) he would remain a liberal, an advocate of Christian morality, and an active booster of missions on the international circuit. As president of the ANC he was widely credited with revitalizing the organization and praised for carrying its campaign against white supremacy to the newly founded United Nations in New York. His tactics remained strictly constitutional; in 1949, under pressure from the yet more radical Youth League of the ANC, he was replaced by James Moroka, an advocate of more militant action.[60]

After 1948, the Nationalist government moved South Africa abruptly to the right, and many blacks countered by moving to the left. Still, the ethos of Social Christianity, and the interracialism it implied, did not disappear. Many blacks, Afrikaners, and English-speaking leaders retained interracial contacts made in an earlier era; they were still convinced that Christianity offered a powerful prescription for the ills of South African society, its racial polarization in particular. But the buoyancy among Social Christians of the early years had dissipated, as white South Africans' indifference to their message evolved into active hostility. In liberal circles, Social Christianity lost ground to secular organizations and secular modes of thought. In the early years of apartheid a number of politically prominent Social Christians worked increasingly in secular settings. Albert Lutuli, for example, who had served on the council of the American Board's Adams College and had represented the American Board in a 1948 tour of the United States, slowly drifted away from the missionaries. As ANC president from 1952, he displeased the missionaries by associating with left-wing members of the Congress alliance. And yet, Lutuli, who received the Nobel Peace Prize in 1961, was publicly identified with Christian principles throughout his career, his most famous speech in this regard "The Road to Freedom is via the Cross."[61]

For their part, many Christian whites, along with a few blacks, were attracted to the multi-racial Liberal Party, founded in 1953. Among them were the novelist Alan Paton, the party's national chairman from 1956 and later its president, and Edgar Brookes, who was national chairman in the 1960s.[62] The churches and the South African Council of Churches (the former CCSA), in turn, became deeply involved in the anti-apartheid struggle, but increasingly under the leadership of blacks, and inspired by more radical "prophetic" theologies of liberation (see pp. 374–82 and chap. 25 *passim*). By the 1970s the Social Christians' vision of reconciling the elites of the different races and of regenerating society through evangelism, education, and social work seemed impotent before the repressive and apparently stable structures of apartheid.

Secularization and Segregation: The Missionaries' Stamp on the Social Gospel

As Mandhlakazi's 1916 conversation with James Stuart reminds us, Christianity was declining in Britain and North America just as it began to grow rapidly in South Africa. British and North American church leaders were adopting the Social Gospel in part to avoid being sidelined in social debate; in doing so they embraced the secular world and, in turn, risked being secularized by it. In Canada, for example, where Social Gospel influences are widely credited with influencing Canadian political ideologies, social legislation, and perhaps even foreign policy, the "optimists" among scholars argue that the Social Gospel "gave birth to the emerging social sciences and movements of social and political reform, thus preserving and enshrining religious values in the nation's culture." The "pessimists," by contrast, argue that, "in a frantic search for social relevance, . . . the Protestant clergymen unwittingly capitulate[d] to secularism and, by too easily resolving theology into social science and reform, ensure[d] their own irrelevance." In any case, the political and social influence of Canada's Protestant churches declined during the twentieth century, as did levels of church membership and attendance. The question is whether the Social Gospel slowed or hastened that decline, and whether, in their decline, the churches imparted a distinctively Christian tone to the newly secularized Canada (in, for example, social welfare legislation and policies of foreign aid) or were, in fact, fatally subverted by it.[63]

In South Africa, as in Canada and other countries, Social Christianity was embraced by Christians eager to help the churches combat societal pathologies. As in Canada, the Social Gospellers appeared, on one level, to be launching a counter-offensive against secularization (especially in resisting the state's impingement on the hoped-for regeneration of African society). On another level it could be said that they were themselves secularizing the church (by focusing on social issues, adopting social-science language, and engaging in political advocacy). Yet the paradoxical relationship between Social Gospel and secularization worked differently in the two cases. In inter-war South Africa, the Benevolent Empire (schools, hospitals, and the like) were much more powerful and indispensable than in Canada (or in the United States or Britain). The South African state, too, was far weaker in its ability (and willingness) to administer and provide services to its poorer citizens. As a consequence, Social Christians retained an influential role in South African social and political discourse longer than their counterparts in countries that were secularizing more rapidly. Even in the 1970s and 1980s many North American visitors to South Africa were struck by the prominent role of the churches in civic life, and by the use of Christian language by all sides in the struggle over apartheid.

Yet no counterpart to the Canadian "optimists" could claim that the Social Gospel had shaped post-1948 South Africa. For the Nationalist government rejected, not only the Social Christians' specific demands for justice, but also their principal assumption: that blacks should be trained for eventual participation and leadership in South African political life. Under the Bantu Education Act of 1953 – arguably the most significant factor in the secularization of South Africa – the mission schools, once the cornerstone of the Benevolent Empire and power base of the Social Gospel, fell into the hands of a government dedicated, at least in theory, to preparing blacks for a destiny separate from whites. Though some missionaries anticipated advantages in the government take-over – it seemed consistent with benign patterns of secularization of education elsewhere[64] – none could claim, in the language of the Social Gospel, that the Spirit of Christ was leavening the loaf of society. Most could see clearly that the state had seized Christian assets and was determined to turn them to new ends.

Nationalization of the mission schools effectively ended a century and a half of missionary prominence in the social and political life of South Africa. The missionaries, most of them outsiders to both black and white South African society, had articulated a social vision in which Africans would be "raised" to the best in

Western culture as the missionaries defined it. When, in the Social Gospel era, they realized that they needed to work "with" (not just "for") Africans, their paternalism broadened into an interracial elitism, as they allied themselves with blacks who were, on the whole, as elitist as they. In addition, the missionaries' international network of globetrotting philanthropists and experts strengthened their instinctive paternalism and imparted to them, and to many South African liberals, the belief that the country's problems would yield to friendly discussion among "reasonable men" of influence drawn from the various races and ethnicities in South Africa. This conviction proved even less realistic in South Africa than in the countries where it had originated. As long as blacks had any hope of being admitted to the full benefits of South African citizenship, the paternalist missionary program of giving them the means to advance made some sense. But when the door to citizenship was slammed shut, as it was after 1948, it seemed that the elitist programme of the Social Christians had been a disastrous mistake. It could be argued that Social Christianity had distanced the African elites from the masses and had weakened their role in organizing popular resistance.

Deep into the twentieth century missionaries defined their task as bringing the gospel to a distinct body of "natives," who would dwell, ideally, on their own land under their own leaders. This perspective neatly meshed with the analysis of inter-war American experts on "race relations," who assumed that South Africa's principal problem was to accommodate the clashing interests of distinct races. But it also retarded the full realization that, by the 1920s, whites and blacks must be seen as increasingly enmeshed in a single, unequal economic system, and that blacks must be increasingly understood as workers and peasants, rather than as "natives." Missionaries, with their grassroots experience, were among the first to identify and articulate this profound social shift. However, their inherited assumptions inhibited them from seriously connecting with the socialist strands of the Social Gospel developed in industrialized countries. They accordingly gave only the wariest of support to Africans organizing around their economic interests.

For similar reasons, many missionaries did not oppose segregationist measures that promised special services to blacks (such as mother-tongue education in primary schools or "industrial education"), or that appeared to protect blacks from white encroachments. In retrospect, it is obvious that the chain of segregationist legislation from 1910 to 1948, by multiplying whites' advantages over blacks, laid a solid foundation for apartheid. But many contemporaries foresaw positive benefits for blacks in segregation. Although most missionary leaders were outspokenly hostile to the two most dramatic pieces of segregationist legislation in this period, the Natives Land Act of 1913 and the Native Representation Act of 1936, a number voiced guarded approval. The 1920 Native Affairs Act, which extended the segregationist structure of African councils and created a union-wide Native Conference of African leaders and an all-white Native Affairs Commission, now seems to have been the first step in the long march to separate Bantu authorities and the establishment of apartheid's "independent homelands." This Act was in part a response to missionaries' demands for regular channels through which Africans could express their views to government. Some missionaries supported the Act, as "a step in the right direction," as a "solid foundation" for future consideration of the "Native Question," and, in addition, as an opportunity for Africans to gain political skills. Dr. A.W. Roberts, a missionary at Lovedale, served for eleven years on the Native Affairs Commission created by the Act; C.T. Loram, a close ally of the missionaries, served fifteen years. Soon, however, Roberts and Loram learned that the commission provided them only slight, and dwindling, opportunities to influence government policy. Some African Christians, too, supported the act; John Dube, speaking for the Natal ANC, called it "the best attempt yet made to meet the requirements of the bulk of the native people." Others condemned it; Z.R. Mahabane charged, on behalf of the Cape ANC, that it perpetuated "the objectionable principle of political segregation."[65] The 1923 Natives (Urban Areas) Act, now seen as the foundation of urban segregation, was also, in part, a response to missionary demands that government oversee the dangerous and unhealthy African settlements in South African cities. The ANC welcomed the first drafts of the Urban Areas Bill but rejected its final form. It was praised by such Christian organs as the *Christian Express* and the Anglican *Church Chronicle*, which called it a "half-loaf" that would allow Africans to build their own homes in town locations. But more sceptical missionary voices worried that these Africans would only lease, not own, their houses, while other Africans would be denied access to town at all. What would happen, the critics asked, to "Natives evicted from farms [by the Natives Land Act], if they no longer have 'cities of refuge' to which to flee?"[66]

When they opposed segregation, missionaries were acting on the universalism at the root of their enterprise, their belief in the oneness of all people in Christ. A Scottish missionary, refuting arguments for ecclesiastical segregation in 1907, argued that for those "who have a living faith in [Christ's] power and in the indwelling of His Spirit union of Black and White in one Church is the only possibility."[67] When, on the other hand, the missionaries supported segregationist measures, they were animated by the traditional missionary concern to protect "child races" and "raise" them through moral uplift. A strategy for reconciling universalism and segregation was succinctly put by J.W. Williams, bishop of the Anglican missionary diocese of St. John's, who said in his diocesan charge of 1920, that Jesus, while bridging "the infinite gulf" between "the All-holy God and sinful man," had also "covered the insignificant differences of race and colour and language and training which separate man from man." Yet it was obvious to Williams that, at a more practical level, the differences between whites and blacks were "vast and unmistakable," whites having benefited from "training of 15 centuries" in the skills of "civilization." White Christians must therefore deny both the "inherent inferiority [of blacks], and their actual equality." They must, he contended, demand for them *"equality of opportunity."* Blacks "must be free in their development, free alike from the cupidity of wealth and the oppression of labour." They must have, as well, the "protection necessary for them, if they are to develop unhindered, undestroyed, by the dangerous habits of a civilisation with which they cannot cope." And, finally, as taxpayers, they had a "right to a voice in the making of laws."[68] This, then, was the crux of the missionaries' paternalist view: whites owed blacks opportunity, aid, protection, and slow advancement to political adulthood. Issues of full equality and total integration could be postponed to a distant future.

The Protestant missionary enterprise was rooted in the experience of conversion – the transformation of individuals in a personal confrontation with Jesus. Many early twentieth-century missionaries had experienced personal conversions – some, like James Henderson, at the Keswick conventions in England.[69] Such missionaries embraced the Social Gospel with the assurance that Jesus could transform societies as fundamentally as they themselves had been transformed. They embraced education, social work, and politics as extensions not as replacements of evangelism. African proponents of the Social Gospel such as Dube, Xuma, Jabavu, and Lutuli – second- or third-generation Christians who had acquired their faith through long exposure – eagerly took up the notion of social transformation, perhaps in part, as Jabavu claimed, because the secular–sacred dichotomy was foreign to their African cosmology.

The Social Christians of the inter-war years, unlike the anti-apartheid Christians of the 1970s and 1980s, rarely claimed to be "prophetic." Their goal was not to demolish a repressive structure, but to let God transfigure society through the slow gestation of Christ's Kingdom in its midst. An inescapable component of their plan was to convert whites and to persuade them to treat blacks as fellow citizens. To this end the Social Christians regularly exhorted whites from the pulpit and in the religious press. Occasionally, too, they mounted large crusades, such as the United Missionary Campaign of 1925, when Donald Fraser, a former Scottish missionary, preached in twenty-six South African cities. Fraser summoned all Christians, but primarily whites, "to be a witness by life and work and word to the Lord Jesus Christ," and to abandon their fears of a so-called "black menace." There is, proclaimed Fraser, "no menace when people are determined to do justice to one another."[70] The strategy of the political activists, such as Loram, Rheinallt Jones, and Brookes, was to conciliate whites by appealing to their Christian sentiments, not by threatening or condemning them. "We were anxious," said Brookes in recalling his service in South Africa's parliament as a senator representing African interests, "to appear as co-operative and reasonable South Africans, putting a good case reasonably to our fellow-citizens . . . I fear that, like many liberals in many countries, we were over-optimistic about the reasonableness of our fellow-men."[71] The hope that white South Africans would experience a "change of heart" (a modified notion of conversion) continued to animate South African liberals long after the heyday of Social Christianity. Its most powerful expression was, perhaps, Alan Paton's 1948 novel *Cry, the Beloved Country*.

Aspects of the missionaries' world view (their paternalism and elitism, their ambivalence about segregation, their "race-relations" emphasis, and their optimism about converting whites) appear, in hindsight, to have led the Social Christians seriously to misread the South African situation. The inter-war churches have accordingly been condemned by some recent writers as "Servants of Power."[72] Yet without missionaries there would likely have been little Social Christianity in South Africa at all. The missionaries' power base in South African education, medicine and social work – along with their international network of contacts with educational institutions, donors, and philanthropists – allowed generations of blacks to gain a Western education, many through overseas travel and study. Social Christians, white and black, evolved a South African political ideology of interracial cooperation that took deep root, most significantly, in the African National Congress. The missionaries' universalist message, and their optimism about the transformative power of the Christian gospel, emboldened several generations of whites and blacks to contend for universal values in a society pulled powerfully toward hierarchy, segregation, and racial oppression. The Social Gospel in South Africa led, neither to the Kingdom of God, as its advocates hoped, nor to the "secular city," as critics of the North American Social Gospel have charged. But it did inspire a dissenting tradition of faith in human equality and the possibility of ethnic and racial conciliation that, once purged of its paternalism, inspired powerful strands of resistance in the era of apartheid.

24

Creation and Apartheid: South African Theology since 1948

EUGENE M. KLAAREN

Theology in South Africa is serious and flourishing, a force even in politics, where leaders from all quarters call on God. Invoking God as "the Almighty," D.F. Malan, the Dutch Reformed minister who led the National Party to electoral victory in 1948, declared that "Afrikanerdom is not the work of man but a creation of God." Invoking God as "the Liberator," the disenfranchised black township authors of the *Kairos Document* of 1985 condemned the "State theology" of apartheid as "tyranny" and "idolatry."

Despite its political preoccupation, South African theology is serious about doctrine, relying heavily on the Bible and engaging all facets of traditional Christian theology: creation and salvation; God and humanity; Jesus Christ and the Holy Spirit; first things, last things, and the role of the church in the world. The relations between politics and doctrine work both ways: in the prolonged South African crisis, historic theological teachings, such as the doctrine of salvation, have become politically and culturally influential, even as political doctrines of liberation and reconciliation have taken on theological significance. South African theology accordingly has paid respectful attention to Karl Barth, the greatest European theologian of the mid-twentieth century, whose massive *Church Dogmatics* and Barmen protest (1934) against "German Christianity," were forged amidst spiritual and social crises similar to those of South Africa.[1]

South African theology has drawn much from abroad, is less secularized than European, and less individualized than American theology. In one respect it resembles the mixture of traditional, liberation, and evangelical theologies in Latin America. In both South Africa and Latin America the theological enterprise is invigorated by the presence of local spiritualities and by a constant struggle with social injustice. But South African theologies are distinctive in that they are predominantly Protestant, and have been marked in various ways by coming to terms with over forty years of apartheid.[2]

This survey is selective, especially in its focus on broad Christian understandings of creation evident in theologians' views of the world. Such views of the world have coloured the responses to apartheid along each of four prominent lines of South African theology: Afrikaner, English-speaking, Black, and African.[3] Doctrinal elaborations of creation stand out in South African theologies, more so than in Latin American liberation theology, which has generally taken creation for granted.[4] Unlike European and U.S. theologians, few South African theologians take the natural sciences and technology as raising the major questions for religious thought; nor, unlike many theologians of the industrialized world preoccupied with ecological degredation, do they equate creation with nature. In South African theology creation is conceived primarily in *social* terms, and the challenging questions for its theologies of creation are often found among hidden or marginalized people.

The Settings of Theological Thought

In the countryside, and later in the city, white Afrikaans-speakers came to understand themselves as a people under God. Their popular theological views have been shaped by the national myth of the Great Trek, when, re-enacting the Jews' exodus from Egypt, the Afrikaners withdrew from the Cape Colony and founded two republics in the South African interior. At memorial sites across South Africa, particularly at the Voortrekker monument in Pretoria that celebrated the Greak Trek, Afrikaner nationalists have commemorated God's covenant with their people.[5]

Formal Afrikaner theology is written at seminaries in Stellenbosch, Pretoria, and Potchefstroom, and at the University of South Africa. Most Afrikaans theology departments are organized along traditional divisions of biblical, historical, systematic, and practical theology, with the addition of missiology since the 1950s. The seminaries, financially supported by both government and church, have trained most Afrikaner theologians, although many have also pursued advanced study in Germany and the Netherlands, a number at the Free University of Amsterdam. After the Cottesloe Consultation of 1960, however (see pp. 148–49), Afrikaner theology, save in some important respects, drifted into isolation from other theological currents inside and outside South Africa.

The white English-speaking community, which urbanized earlier, has created a theology with a more complex intellectual and also imperial heritage; conservative and liberal political ideals have coexisted in it, in a shifting amalgam of Anglo-Catholicism, evangelicalism, and social gospel. Beginning in the late 1960s a number of Congregational, Methodist, and Presbyterian theologians assumed the ecumenical role of interpreting South African theology to the international community, a role Afrikaner theologians had largely abandoned.[6] Their theology evolved in traditionally English universities in South Africa such as the University of Cape Town, Rhodes, and the University of Natal at Pietermaritzburg, and was shaped by European- and American-trained scholars who had been influenced by Barth's theology, Reinhold Niebuhr's social ethics, and Dietrich Bonhoeffer's Christian witness against Nazism.[7]

Black theology has had a higher profile than others in South Africa, partly because of its dramatic birth when, in the 1970s, black students broke away from white-dominated liberal organizations. Black theology has retold the story of the Exodus as the liberation and formation of a new people, rather than stressing the covenant and chosen people themes characteristic of Afrikaner theology. It has contributed to new rituals, such as mass political funerals, and a sacred calendar commemorating Sharpeville, Soweto, and other sites of massacre in South Africa.

The activist settings in which Black theology is written – from the townships to the former "homelands," from the streets to universities in white urban centres – contrast with the more traditional, established settings in seminaries and universities where the white theologies are principally developed. Pastors of the new black consciousness boldly practised their anti-apartheid ministry anticipating the birth of a new nation, with their political leaders still in prison. The "Black Consciousness" and "Black Theology" movement developed powerfully during the 1970s at the Federal Theological Seminary, an ecumenical centre sited at Alice in the eastern Cape, and later at Imbali, Pietermaritzburg. There it became an occasional sanctuary for refugees from political conflicts in Natal. The University of the Western Cape at Bellville also became a radical centre of black thought in defiance of the designs of the apartheid theorists who had founded it. Some Black theologians went overseas to study at non-denominational seminaries and universities in New York City, Berkeley, Cambridge, Chicago, and Groningen in the Netherlands. Partly inspired by the late 1960s Black theology by James Cone of Union Seminary,[8] South African Black theology has gone its own way, without discarding all links with Black theology in the U.S.

African theology, unlike Black theology, has emerged in rural and traditional settings, in the ministry of informally educated African preachers. It is largely oral, sometimes prophetic, and expressed in the worship of a vast range of churches, especially the African Initiated Churches (AICs). Over the last forty years the AICs have grown enormously, making a place for themselves not only in rural areas but in urban townships as well. Written African theology, while common throughout Africa, is rare in South Africa.

Creation Under Law: Afrikaner Theology

Twentieth-century Afrikaner theology was shaped, in part, by the neo-Calvinist tradition epitomized by the Dutch statesman and theologian, Abraham Kuyper (1837–1920) and developed in South Africa by Hendrik G. Stoker and others at the University for Christian Higher Education at Potchefstroom, modeled on Kuyper's Free University of Amsterdam. It was also shaped by an evangelical tradition of revivals and missions rooted in Scottish evangelicalism, brought to the Dutch Reformed Church of the Cape Colony (the NGK) in the first half of the nineteenth century, and nurtured well into the twentieth century by the leading theologian and spiritual writer, Andrew Murray, Jr. But, after 1948, neo-Calvinism and evangelicalism took on distinctly South African forms as they consorted with the ruling powers in the country. A third tradition, drawn from the neo-orthodoxy of Karl Barth in Europe, impinged on Afrikaner theology after the 1960s.[9]

Different theological webs have been woven by Afrikaners from these three traditions. Particularly systematic and explicit is the neo-Calvinist theology of the small Gereformeerde Kerk (GK). For two decades before 1948, H. G. Stoker, South Africa's leading neo-Calvinist philosopher and a member of the GK, developed a theologically informed philosophy of creation, its focal point the Idea of Creation (*Skeppingsidee*).[10] His theory, which spread well beyond the GK, affirmed that all reality, including the diversity of creation, is bound by God's law. In this "comprehensive world and life view," knowledge conforms to the order(s) of creation, as does morality by virtue of the conscience with which each person is created.[11]

In 1957, at a decisive point in the history of higher education in South Africa, Stoker advocated separate universities for Africans, whites, and Coloureds. Liberal notions of freedom that stood in the way of this policy were, he argued, ultimately mistaken in stressing individual autonomy and racial integration at the expense of "group relations." At this "crossroads" of policy and theory, Stoker strongly urged the extension of apartheid education, which he took to be firmly supported in the comprehensive philosophy of lawful creation.[12]

In the Stoker tradition all creation exists under law. His theory is even more closely knit and thorough than that of the contemporary Dutch neo-Calvinist philosopher, Herman Dooyeweerd,[13] whose philosophy of the Cosmonomic Idea some South Africans regarded as too liberal. At Potchefstroom in the 1960s and 1970s, strict Afrikaner neo-Calvinism continued under Stoker's successor, J.A.L. Taljaard, whose law-and-order model of creation was elaborated in *Polished Lenses: A Philosophy That Proclaims the Sovereignty of God Over Creation and Also Over Every Aspect of Human Activity*. For Taljaard, the Creator is the Lawgiver, and the relation between Creator and creation is one of law and order. The Creator taught humanity to be obedient to the "mandates" of creation and divinely authorized rule. Sin is chiefly "disobedience," and salvation, the "eternal correction of such rebellion," is the restoration of the order of creation. The Bible is construed as the source of norms and principles, history as "the unfolding differentiation of lawful spheres provided by the Lawgiver," in opposition to secular doctrines of progressive evolution in society and culture. Orders of creation, and creaturely diversity, were emphasized in Taljaard's thoroughgoing promotion of apartheid.[14]

The neo-Calvinist line of thought also affirmed distinctly sovereign social spheres (such as family, school, church, state, and so on), each under the absolute sovereignty of the Creator. This was a teaching frequently used to support apartheid. But in the 1970s and 1980s, a few academics at Potchefstroom appealed to sphere sovereignty in criticizing the economic and political injustices of Christian nationalism and state apartheid.[15] However, the paradigm of divinely lawful creation has remained dominant at Potchefstroom, evident in its programme to develop international Christian educational institutions, for example, in southern African states like Zimbabwe.

In the white Nederduitse Gereformeerde Kerk (NGK), the church of the vast majority of Afrikaners, there has generally been less uniformity of doctrine than in the GK. After the stunning National Party triumph in 1948, South Africa's social and ideological edifice of grand apartheid was erected. Afrikaners dominated politics and the military, and made inroads into industry, with the support of NGK pastors, educators, and missionary and ecclesiastical officials who provided a general theology of culture rooted in neo-Calvinism and evangelicalism. At its most ambitious this theology embraced and legitimated Afrikaner nationalism and aimed to resolve South Africa's "racial problem," while protecting "Western civilization" from liberalism and communism.

If the building of apartheid was supported by the law and order structure of neo-Calvinism, it was also rendered more comfortable for whites by the spiritual solace of the evangelical tradition. To be sure, a number of leading evangelicals who stimulated a massive missionary effort among Afrikaners (see pp. 146–68), preached spiritual equality, under God, of white and black Christians. Yet the egalitarian promise of missions was undercut by doctrines of white trusteeship that led to the establishment of subordinate insititutions for blacks. Practical folk, the evangelicals had no doctrinal system or comprehensive paradigm of creation with which to confront the model of law-and-order. A broad theology of culture, stitched together from neo-Calvinist rigour and evangelical piety, ensured the dominance of Afrikanerdom and apartheid.

Despite the overwhelming pro-apartheid bent of Afrikaner theology – and its growing isolation from currents in world theology – some vigorous theological dissidents, such as Nico Smith and Beyers Naudé, drew from the wells of evangelical piety in their protests. Smith left the white NGK to lead an African Dutch Reformed (NGKA) congregation in Mamelodi township. Naudé, the most prominent dissenter, was a force in the early anti-apartheid Christian Institute and the South African Council of Churches; he drew on Barth's critical theology, on ecumenism, and on liberation theology, which Afrikaner theologians rarely used. For both of these two dissenters, there was an unmistakable (and recognizably Afrikaner) devotion to principle, and a willingness to endure ostracism from the Afrikaner community for the sake of that principle. A more moderate critic from the inside, David Bosch, taught a missionary theology stressing that salvation is for all creation – souls and bodies, individuals and social structures, blacks and whites, Third and First World societies. Enlarging the range of Afrikaner theology, he merged the evangelical and social sides of missions, an achievement both sides often found difficult to accept.[16]

In contrast to Naudé, Smith, and Bosch is the work of Johan Heyns, who taught in several seminaries, including Stellenbosch. A systematic theologian, Heyns seems to some a critical reformer like Barth; to others his leading category of the Kingdom of God seems a legacy of Dooyeweerd's Cosmonomic idea and Stoker's Skeppingsidee. Only a full examination of his multi-volume dogmatics and social ethics,[17] and perhaps more importantly, his work as an NGK moderator in the years of P. W. Botha's so-called "reform of apartheid," can test which of these two views is more correct.

In any case, Heyns's view of the church shared the traditional Afrikaner emphasis on creation, and with Barth, focused on an ever-active divine Word, but unlike Barth's highly emphasized doctrine of the Word as three-fold (incarnate, written, and preached), Heyns stressed three prior modes – Creation, Providence, and Salvation – of the Word. In effect, he underscored an older theology of the sovereign Kingdom of God, which he spelled out in "five basic elements" – "God is King"; "The King reigns"; "The King rules over his subjects"; "The King's subjects obey him"; "The King's subjects are blessed" – in which the neo-Calvinist paradigm of creation under law was maintained.[18]

Yet Heyns also held that the church, like the state and other social spheres, has a responsibility of its own for the Kingdom. Echoing Barth, he highlights the "dynamism" of the Kingdom against static rule. No nation, people, or race is an ordinance of creation.[19] His view of the church as a "sign" or "witness" suggested that it should not simply preach and administer but call itself and society to account.[20] If he was not shaking the foundations of Afrikaner law-and-order theology, he was rattling the cage.

By the decade of the 1980s, systematic theology in the NGK had to face a growing crisis of apartheid and the South African state. The new constitution of 1983, the black insurrection, the imposition of states of emergency, and the theological challenge of *The Kairos Document* produced by black township pastors and some academics[21] stimulated more rethinking of theology and apartheid. In the 1970s, an evangelical and *verligte* ("enlightened" or moderate) Reformed theologian, Adrio König, initiated a revisionary theology keyed to eschatology (or the ending of all things). Convinced that systematic theology must re-immerse itself in the Bible,[22] König argued, in his *Eclipse of Christ in Eschatology: Toward a Christ-Centered Approach*, that not only the crucifixion, resurrection, and ascension of Jesus, but the content of his entire life, had eschatological significance. In *Here Am I* he cites the Old Testament as support for a personal God, unlike other gods, who identified himself to Abraham and set out to surprise man by actively intervening in history.[23] König's subsequent volume on creation charts a revisionary path; it asserts that creation by the Word, like other biblical concepts of the "process" of creation, has been greatly exaggerated in dogmatic theology. Far from stressing beginnings, or the nature of the Creator, his theology draws attention to, as its English title puts it, *New and Greater Things*. God "... can do *again* what he did at creation – and even *more* than that." König clearly aims to escape the notion, long dominant in NGK thought, that soteriology (the doctrine of salvation) is a backward-looking effort to restore the original order of creation.[24] His volume gives virtually no attention to law and order in creation.[25]

The *Option for Inclusive Democracy: A Theological–Ethical Study of Appropriate Social Values for South Africa*, written by theological and legal leaders in Stellenbosch in 1987, is a more directly revisionist Afrikaner theology.[26] In the wake of many official and some unofficial church documents, such as *The Kairos Document*, it suggests another model for creation, namely, service. Critical of Afrikaner efforts to balance a spiritual unity of humanity with mundane diversity (as in apartheid philosophy), the *Option* argues that reciprocal service among people is key:

> ... unity is created when very different people become involved with each other – to the advantage of all. The key to this statement is a proper understanding of the meaning and fundamental significance of the Biblical concept of *diakonia*, i.e., service. This word expresses the nature of God's relationship with the world. Through creation and re-creation, God *serves* us with life, grace and love.

Most pointedly, the Stellenbosch *Option* proposes a bill of basic and specific "personal" rights, decidedly novel in the Afrikaner theological tradition, heretofore limited chiefly to "group" rights.

Afrikaner theology generally argues that biblical revelation will prove consistent with revelation in creation. Unlike Barth, it does not make the doctrine of Christ (Christology) the alpha and omega of revelation. Its "principial" method, (that is, the forging of norms and principles to guide *volk* and nation, church and society) stresses law and order in divine and in human rule.[27]

Creation Under Gospel: South African English Theology

White English-speaking theology in South Africa, in the decades after 1948, developed its dual heritage of evangelical spirituality and concern for basic civil rights.[28] Although not wedded to a *volk*, its influence has been strengthened by the wealth and prestige of the English churches and also of the English universities, where theologians have been prominent in departments of religious studies. It has used historical criticism, a traditional staple in English biblical scholarship in South Africa, to develop an anti-apartheid theology.[29]

In shaping a theology of creation the English have drawn much from Barth, including his stress on the God who creates and also his de-emphasis of the nature of original creation. Theirs is a critical theology of created realities and events, born in an ongoing social crisis unlike the more intense crises of world war that provoked Barth's dialectics. If there is a paradigm in this English-speaking theology, it is not law but history and the related social meaning of the Gospel.

One English-speaking scholar, in an important (and unanswered) critique of the NGK's 1975 Synodical Report in defence of apartheid, *Human Relations and the South African Scene in the Light of Scripture*, challenged not only apartheid, but the theology used to undergird it. Douglas Bax, a Presbyterian pastor and Calvin scholar, argued that the Report's claim, based on the story of the tower of Babel, that apartheid was anchored in a diversity created at creation, was not only historically uncritical, but incompatible with the New Testament, and against the grain of Calvin's theology. Bax further held that the Report introduced a natural theology demeaning to the sufficiency of Jesus Christ and that it relativized the Gospel. Against neo-Calvinism's independent theology of creation, Bax subordinated creation to redemption and, like Barth, criticized claims of continuities between acts of God and the institutions of human creation.[30]

In the 1970s and 1980s, Charles Villa-Vicencio, among the English South African theologians, drew on Barth and Dietrich Bonhoeffer (executed by the Nazis in 1945), and on Latin American liberation theologians, like Gustav Gutiérrez and Juan Luis Segundo,[31] to assail the "uncivil civil religion" of Afrikanerdom. Condemning "the structural violence of apartheid," and the "neo-Constantinian" co-optation of the church by the state, Villa-Vicencio urged the formation of an alternative church. His more recent work explores issues of reconstruction and nation-building in terms of civil and socio-economic rights. Similarly, James Cochrane has drawn critical attention to the church's neglect of labour issues.[32]

In contrast with the "principial" approach of Afrikaner theology and hermeneutics, the historical or "contextual" English-speaking theology uses classic Christian beliefs, such as the doctrine of original sin, to symbolize South African racism, nationalism, and class oppression. It calls for solidarity with the oppressed, and loyalty to God's own "preferential option for the poor."

For two decades John de Gruchy, Professor of Christian Studies at the University of Cape Town and an international Bonhoeffer scholar, has sought to forge an ecumenical theology in South Africa, partly by drawing on European and African spirituality (as in *Cry Justice*), and on a Bonhoeffer-based teaching of Providence as God's passionate activity in Christ's suffering. De Gruchy's "Kingdom of God perspective" emphasizes an historical understanding of social creation, particularly the cost, to the rich and powerful, of racial and economic reconciliation. In his 1991 work, *Liberating Reformed Theology*, the most contextualized systematic theology published recently in South Africa, he places Calvin and certain South Africans, such as Ntoane, Naudé, and Boesak in dialogue with major Latin American liberation and European dialectical theologians. He resists identifications of God with the Absolute and the Lawgiver, and emphasizes God's freedom in choosing to side with the poor. Evil, for De Gruchy, is less disobedience than "idolatry," especially "greed for land, ... privilege and power at the expense of others," which demeans the glory of God. Against such evils God in Christ has "set [us] free to love and obey." Confession of sins is not enough; social conversion, democracy, and a new covenantal accountability of government to the disadvantaged are required.[33]

The work of the popular Roman Catholic theologian, Albert Nolan, fosters "peoples' theologies" in workshops across South Africa sponsored by the Institute for Contextual Theology. Though it may have affected white students most, his work also shares in projects of Black theology. Nolan's provocative *God in South Africa* is a sharply contextualized and clear statement of liberation theology-in-practice.[34] Along with the more academic work of De Gruchy, Villa-Vicencio, and Cochrane, it is clear that an important critical and constructive current of white English-speaking theology has emerged. In 1948 such achievements would not have been predicted, given the dominance of Afrikaner theology.

A Liberating Creation: Black Theology

South African Black theology, which exploded in the era of apartheid, is a theology of struggle – in the township, church, and university. Yet those who develop and propagate it also have a profound commitment to teaching. Comparing two decades of his teaching in South Africa with teaching at New York's Union Seminary, a leading South African Black theologian contrasted the sharp political consciousness of his South African students with what he described as the confused consciousness of his American students.[35]

Black theology, in its forceful opposition to Afrikaner law-and-order creationalism, responded with a liberating theology of creation. In a number of early and controversial articles drawn from his 1968 thesis, *Creation and the Church*, Manas Buthelezi, a Lutheran pastor, provided a systematic critique of South African ecclesiology. He addressed the existential cry of a black pastor, "Why am I created black?" with a creation-oriented anthropology, keyed to the spontaneity and agency of the black church, and rooted in the conviction, long popular in South Africa, that all people are made in the image of God.[36]

So, too, Alan Boesak's controversial 1976 theology of black power and black history, *Farewell to Innocence*, promoted a creational view that empowers human beings, especially subjugated persons, like Africans, Coloureds and Indians in South Africa. Urging a piety of courage and deed, Boesak, a Calvinist, constructed a theological and political identity of blackness, which he later applied in public resistance to the 1983 Constitution that was designed to exclude blacks and to co-opt Coloureds and Indians in the continuance of apartheid.[37] The 1982 Belhar Confession of the NGSK, the Dutch Reformed Church for Coloureds, sharply distinguished its own faith from that of the NGK by declaring an unusual *status confessionis* (see pp. 153–54) in the church at large, inspired, in part, by Boesak's lead in the NGSK and the World Alliance of Reformed Churches, of which he was president. The Belhar Confession recalled Barth's Barmen Declaration in its focus on the Lordship of Jesus Christ, but its further stress on divine justice, in condemning apartheid as a heresy, is more creational than its European precursor and shows Black theology's shift to more radical views of social creation.[38]

The systematic theology of Simon Maimela, a professor at the University of South Africa, stresses divine "creativity," God's love "in process," and human "co-creation," and advocates the socio-political task of liberation to "complete" what God began at creation.[39] Maimela argues that God's command is, at heart, creative and works together with human creativity. Also critical of liberalism, he provocatively affirms human creatures as "little gods." Like liberation, the empowerment of created black subjects is elemental to a new South African theological discourse of "the subject," and crucial to overcoming subordination.[40] Maimela's *God's Creative Activity Through the Law*, while crediting Barth's favouring of gospel over law, shows that the subjugation of law to christology does not itself provide criteria for developing just laws in a still colonial society like South Africa. Law is invented and is not pre-existing. A theology of justice and power, he argues, is "overdue." Maimela is the most systematic Black theologian to date.

The black pastor and writer Tshenuwani Simon Farisani's polemical theology of creation presents a dialogue in which "the Creator" criticizes European/Afrikaner "Ministers of Law and Order," renamed "little creators" of the "native, kaffir, Bantu," to highlight the emergence of black and African subjects, especially those who have been forcibly removed from their land.[41]

Partly because of its seriousness about creation – embracing religion and politics, community and land, culture and society, African and European history, and African–American and Latin American liberation movements – Black theology is more far-reaching and pluralistic than some have realized.[42] It has explored subjects as diverse as Maimela's immersion of Black theology in processes of world history (including nuclear weapons issues), Takatso Mofokeng's focus on the world-overturning work of Jesus Christ, and Buti Thlagale's and Itumeling Mosala's class-based analyses of external and internal colonialism.[43] Its practical impact has included Buthelezi's, Boesak's, and Mosala's various contributions to the upsurge of black consciousness among students, the NGSK's Belhar Confession and the "Apartheid is a heresy" protest, the mediating but radical leadership of Archbishop Desmond Tutu and Boesak in the United Democratic Front, and *The Kairos Document*'s urging of liberation without excluding reconciliation.

Black theology's Christ- and people-centred struggle for liberation, like its realistic yet hope-filled view of humanity, is a *gospel* of liberation. Tutu's calls for liberation and reconciliation are rooted in an incarnational, as well as an African, spirituality. Boesak heralds Christ the liberating Lord who confronts injustice. Mofokeng's work, *The Crucified Among the Crossbearers*, has a radical and crucified Jesus Christ at its centre, though his christology is more Spirit-driven, and communal, than Barth's. Similarly Maimela, though less christological than Barth, asserts the indispensability of justification by faith.[44]

Liberation is more than a theme in Black theology; it articulates its vision. Its biblical paradigms are the Exodus of the people of Israel from Egypt and the ministry of Jesus.[45] The liberating "finger of God" is discerned in events. Jesus' prophetic statement, "I have seen Satan fall," is expounded by Boesak as a new

Exodus of the oppressed from the power of a satanic state. Liberation theology calls for resistance among oppressed people, freeing them from the fears which have led them to deny the reality of evil.[46] And it is eminently practical, demanding, for example, the redistribution of land stolen from Africans by colonists.[47]

Mofokeng has written, "It is not certain any more that the [old] language, which used to kindle the light of hope and the fire of active faith in the oppressed, will continue to be the most effective witness to God as He continues to bring down opposition to his sovereignty and to the liberation of His oppressed creation." The tension between the old and the new theological language has occasioned a remarkable degree of self-criticism within South African Black theology, unusual in movements so young.[48] Debate arose early about Boesak's political preaching of the Word of liberation, primarily to middle-class Coloureds involved to some degree in the anti-apartheid movement. Some Black theologians objected to Boesak's giving precedence to the (biblical) Word of God over God's revelation in the people's struggle. Later, Mofokeng mediated the issue by stressing, on the one hand, the centrality of the oppressed, and, on the other, using biblical language to invoke the free Spirit of God dwelling in an obediently struggling community, both biblical and contemporary.[49]

Mofokeng, among others, further sharpened the "epistemological break" with dominant Western theology by "deepening the subject," or enlarging the understanding of who is active in history. Without letting go of the historic agency of the whole black community, he also emphasized workers, and solidarity with student resisters in a non-youth culture. He welcomed black contributions to the issue of gender, particularly black feminist and womanist theology from the U.S.[50]

In 1989, Mosala, an Old Testament scholar and Marxist social analyst, published *Biblical Hermeneutics and Black Theology in South Africa*, which advocates historical tools of socio-economic interpretation, in contrast to a personalizing and existential appropriation of the Word of God, which he claims masks the Bible's own ambiguity on exploitation, and may reproduce it. Equally critical of idealism in liberal scholarship, Mosala asks which biblical texts are truly liberating in the ongoing struggle.[51] His book stands out in Black theology for its capacity to relate virtually all topics to the social interpretation of sacred texts. At the same time it addresses the relations of social production and cultural reproduction, the roles of ideology in society and theology, the efficacy of oral and written theological claims, and the criteria for an adequate theology of southern African society. Yet neither Mosala nor any other South African theologian has yet produced a comprehensive and critical theology of society; Mosala, however, has raised the stakes.

Over its brief and tumultuous course, Black theology has been the leading voice of liberation theology in South Africa. In opposing theological justifications of apartheid, it has offered its own constructive theology of a liberating creation. Like Afrikaner theology, but with an opposite method and aim, it has openly addressed the issues of power in its own time.

The Potential of Creation in African Theology

While African theology flourished in much of Africa since the mid-1950s, it has been a minor force in South Africa, some have said because it is too apolitical and too rural in its imagery to find an audience in the urban struggles.[52] Yet some of the most rural AICs have built up powerful alternative sacred spaces; other AIC leaders have formed a pan-African nationalism virtually equivalent to African theology.[53] There may, in fact, be more African theology than one finds in books. And, if, as some historians have claimed, the torch of evangelical spirituality has been passed from missionaries to Pentecostals and to revivalists in the AICs, then there may well prove to be immense potential in the conjunction of African spirituality and biblical, charismatic religion.[54]

The most visible proponent of African theology in South Africa, Gabriel M. Setiloane, now retired from a professorship at the University of Cape Town, combines ecumenical and evangelical, African and European, conservative and radical emphases. Beginning in the 1950s, Setiloane travelled throughout Africa during "the exciting times" of Kwacha/Uhuru and military coups, and studied African missiology and culture at ecumenical centres in England, and theology in the United States. His evangelical concerns are reflected in his writing on church growth, but his best-known work, *The Image of God Among the Sotho-Tswana*, 1976, synthesizes history, anthropology, and theology.[55]

Compared to the prophetic Black theologians, Setiloane appears as a sage who relates memorable African stories and rituals. He has made deep historical soundings and advanced the claims of African cosmologies over European ones. Yet there is a holism to his African theology, one that refuses to exclude European achievements just because they have often proven culturally destructive for Africans.

A certain edge in Setiloane's method is evident in his well-known poem "I am an African," of 1973,[56] a dialogue with a (European) catechist.

> They call me an African
> African indeed am I:
> Rugged son of the soil of Africa,
> Black as my father, and his before him;
> As my mother and sisters and brothers, living
> and gone from this world.
>
> They ask me what I believe ... my faith.
> Some even think I have none
> But live like the beasts of the field.
> "What of God, the Creator
> Revealed to mankind through the Jews of old,
> the YAHWEH: I AM
> Who has been and ever shall be?
> Do you acknowledge him?"
> My fathers and theirs, many generations before, knew Him.
> They bowed the knee to Him
> By many names they knew Him,
> And yet 'tis He the One and only God
> They called Him
> UVELINGQAKI:

The first One
Who came ere ever anything appeared:
UNKULUNKULU:
The BIG BIG ONE,
So big indeed that no space could ever contain Him.
MODIMO:
Because His abode is far up in the sky.
They also knew Him as MODIRI:
For He has made all:
and LESA:
The spirit without which the breath of man cannot be.

Setiloane's poem affirms the Jesus who comes late to Africa, whose healing words, and bloody "sheep or goat" sacrifice cleanses "... all MANKIND: Black and White and Brown and Red ..." In his 1986 *African Theology: An Introduction*, he cherishes an African myth of genesis in a sharp polemic against Europeans, who, he says, have forgotten their own myths and can only tell stories of God, Adam, and Eve playing hide-and-seek in a garden.

In Setiloane's myth we all come from a hole in the ground; men, women, children, and animals are ushered into this world by divine and mysterious forces. His book was addressed to the youth of the anti-apartheid struggle, to counteract European images of the African that often have generated self-hate and socio-cultural destruction, and to remind them of African intellectual and spiritual resources.

Central to this version of African theology is a powerful reorientation toward God and creation, and an angry polemic against the merely personal Father of European missionaries, translators, and theologians.[57] For Setiloane, MODIMO (whom one should shudder to name, unlike other spirits) is the numinous, resourceful, and pervasive divine power in all powers, including human community, the ancestors (living dead), personal energies, and the whole community of creation at large – including land, which is more than a gift to us because we, in turn, are given to it.

Criticisms that Setiloane stresses transcendence at the price of presence, spirituality at the expense of relevance, or that he is merely a "Tswana theologian," are off target. Though he cautions African youth against the "bandwagon" of liberation, asserting that the "soul of Africa" is at stake in opposing apartheid, Setiloane gives an old sage's advice that sometimes one must seize the sword to destroy a civil authority that is destroying others and itself.[58]

Setiloane has achieved the first formal African theology in South Africa. Another witness to the potential of African theology in South Africa has surfaced in a remarkable 1985 AIC Report, *Speaking for Ourselves*. One of its authors, Archbishop N.H. Ngada of the United Independent Believers in Christ Church of Kwa Thema township, who was present at the beginnings of Black theology, organized grass roots theological workshops to equip the profound spirituality of AIC churches. He has written that

... there is one enormous omission throughout the whole history that has been written by outsiders. The work of the Holy Spirit throughout our history has simply been left out ... We believe that our Churches were founded by the Spirit ... "The Spirit blows where he wills" (John 3: 8). That is why you cannot trace one single line of human influence in our history. Our Churches often sprang up here and there, spontaneously ... We have always been aware of the world of spirits. It is part of our African heritage, our African instinct. We know that there are evil spirits or demons and that they can take possession of a person ... But we believe that the Spirit of God is more powerful than any other spirit ... As we try to systematize our theology we shall have to find a way of expressing the oneness of the powerful activity of the Spirit as we experience it. There are different rites like healing, exorcism, *isiwasho* (purification), baptism and activities like consulting the prophets about our problems and speaking in tongues or prophesying; but there is only one Spirit who does all these things ... Our theology will have to find a way of expressing the unity in diversity here.[59]

How much the vision of this AIC theology, and Setiloane's for that matter, will be worked out in the educational institutions of South Africa remains to be seen. But, with the ending of apartheid, African theology in some form is likely to benefit from a new interest in Africa among South African Christians.

South African theology is remarkably vital, not only in universities and churches, but in social and political life as well. Public theology may be an endangered species in Europe and the U.S. but it has been creative and influential in South Africa for over forty years.[60] It has addressed many more doctrines and issues than are presented in this chapter, salvation and reconciliation for example, but issues of creation have stood at the nub of debates of four main lines of theology in the country. Contending views of divine (and human) creation – shaped by discourses of law, history, liberation, and community – have permeated all South African theologies, despite their differing stances on apartheid.

25

Christianity and the Anti-Apartheid Struggle: The Prophetic Voice within Divided Churches

PETER WALSHE

The struggle against apartheid in South Africa was theological, as well as political. When prophetic Christianity confronted segregation and the apartheid state, challenging the passivity of the diverse denominations and their *de facto* acceptance of the *status quo*, the Christian church itself became a site of political struggle. As Gregory Baum reminds us: "Religion is ambiguous; it is the bearer of diverse and sometimes contradictory trends; it is both the creator of ideologies and the bearer of utopias."[1]

"Christ as Common Lord and King": Early Signs of Prophetic Christianity

Signs of prophetic Christianity emerged in the early twentieth century as South Africa's black political culture began to articulate a vision of a just, non-racial society. Among African political leaders there was a strongly reactive response to racist measures such as the colour-bar clause of the South Africa Act (1909), and the territorial segregation of the Natives Land Act (1913). The African National Congress (ANC), founded in 1912, offered an alternative to this racially based system of oppression. In 1936, the All African Convention, a united-front organization, which included the ANC, protested against the Representation of Natives Act and its destruction of the Cape common voters roll. Then, in the Defiance Campaign of the 1950s, after the 1948 election to power of the Afrikaner National Party, the ANC and its allies offered passive resistance to apartheid's racist legislative programme. Black political organizations also strove against the economic interests that undergirded white racism, rejecting migratory labour and the colour bar on the mines and in industry, and calling for recognition of black trade unions, adequate housing, improved educational, medical, and welfare services, workman's compensation, and pensions.

Several ideological influences converged to support this evolving political culture.[2] Traditions among the Bantu-speaking peoples emphasized communal values and equality, particularly a commitment to an equitable distribution of rights of land usage. As the Rev. Malusi Mpumlwana wrote: "A human being is a human being because others are."[3] The non-racial elements in the political tradition of the Cape Colony also influenced black leaders, although to a diminishing extent after Africans were disenfranchised under the constitution of 1910 and the Representation of Natives Act. So, too, the civil rights struggle in the U.S. fostered non-racial ideals among black South Africans, who came to revere African–American leaders such as Frederick Douglass, Booker T. Washington, and W.E.B. Du Bois. Approximately a dozen young Africans attended Negro colleges in the U.S. and some of them assumed key roles in launching the ANC. In recent decades, Marxism has added to the liberation movement's political ideology an emphasis on class analysis, helping to inoculate Africans from the virus of a counter, black racism.

Generations of political leaders, particularity within the ANC, also drew on Christian values for the building of a broader political community. There was, they believed, an ethical imperative to move beyond narrow identities of family, clan, ethnicity, and race. The Rev. Zaccheus Mahabane, a Methodist minister, president of the Cape Congress and president of the ANC in the mid-1920s and late 1930s, maintained in 1925 that, "the universal acknowledgment of Christ as common Lord and King [would] break down the social, spiritual and intellectual barriers between the races."[4] Dr. A. B. Xuma, ANC president from 1940 to 1949, a physician trained in the U.S., Hungary, and Scotland, pointed out in 1944, that "the liberation movement is not anti-white in seeking full scope for African progress"; rather it was "working for the good of all South Africans, working to promote the ideals of Christianity, human decency and democracy."[5] At the unveiling of a tombstone for the Xhosa poet S.E.K. Mqhayi, Xuma described "our African Shakespeare" as a great Christian committed to a future in which "there must be neither white or non-white, but a common citizenship, a united South African nation."[6]

The failure of the white churches to confront racism in any effective way had, however, by the 1920s produced an under-current of disillusionment and even cynicism among some black activists. The racist constitution and the injustices of the Natives Land Act contradicted the vision of human equality embodied in Christianity. In 1927, Clements Kadalie, founder of the Industrial and Commercial Workers Union (ICU), engaged in a public correspondence with Bishop Carey of Bloemfontein. In response to Carey's request that Kadalie control the ICU's provocative speakers, Kadalie retorted that throughout history and in every denomination the church had strayed from Christ's teaching, siding with the rich against the poor, and opposing every effort towards social and economic freedom for the masses.[7] An unidentified speaker at an African political meeting in Johannesburg, probably in the same year, asserted:

> If I had two bags of mealies (corn) and my neighbour had none I shared my mealies, as a matter of course. When the missionary came to our villages, he told us that we were doing right in this matter. He put his stamp of approval on that way of doing. He said, "That's the Christian way, too. Keep on in that fashion." But when we left the mission station and came to the big city, what did we find? Why, we found that the missionary didn't know what he was talking about. We learned that it is the custom for civilized men to grab all they can for themselves and hang on to it. The most successful man is he who grabs the most; cuts the throats of his competitors, and advances himself to the top... The missionary did not know all this when he taught us, or he deliberately lied to us, for he did not equip us for success. We must give up this impractical Christianity if we wish to be successful in this white man's civilization.[8]

After the apartheid government had begun implementing its policies without resolute opposition from the churches, Albert Lutuli, a devout Congregationalist and president of the ANC during the 1950s, writing after the Sharpeville massacre and the banning of the ANC and other anti-apartheid organizations in 1960, issued a warning:

> The Churches have simply submitted to the secular state for far too long; some have even supported apartheid. While it is not too late for white Christians to look at the Gospels and redefine their allegiance, I warn those who care for Christianity, who care to go to all the world and preach the Gospel, that in South Africa the opportunity is three hundred years old. It will not last forever. The time is running out.[9]

In the wake of the slaughter of black schoolchildren in 1976 and the banning of the Black Consciousness Movement in 1977, the Roman Catholic Bishop Mandlenkhosi Zwane repeated Lutuli's warning. Some black Christians, whom he termed "rejectionists of concern," were turning their backs on institutional Christianity, and an increasing number, particularly among the younger generation, were rejecting Christianity altogether – he called them "rejectionists of anger." "The large number of black Christians whom you might call good cultic Christians," consoled themselves with escapist liturgies accepting an unchangeable *status quo*. The "rejectionists of concern" could not follow Christianity "as projected by whites and their church institutions ... yet they are deeply committed Christians." Cultic practices alone no longer impressed them; they could no longer "be won over by pious and sanctimonious platitudes." But Zwane's greatest fear was for the "rejectionists of anger," especially those young blacks from high schools, seminaries, colleges, and universities who "totally rejected God as revealed by what they saw as the white man's Christianity. For them the church in South Africa has been and continues to be part of the oppressive system. Christianity was used as a means to colonise, suppress and alienate the blacks ... They view every white man's institution as an instrument of oppression – his industry, his education and his Christianity." Writing in 1979, shortly before his death, Bishop Zwane predicted that apartheid would "eventually conscientize *all* the blacks in South Africa to a violent rejection of the entire system and those who benefit from it." At the same time he was pessimistic about reversing the drift of blacks from organized Christianity, "given the kind of church we have in Southern Africa." Politically conscious Africans were not taking parish life seriously; in turn they were often labelled, even by fellow Christians, as communists, anarchists or agitators. Zwane argued that for the church to undertake the struggle for justice as an integral part of its mission, a miracle would have to occur, but, as "God is present even in such a situation, miracles could still happen."[10]

Before the 1980s: No Miracle as Yet

The Dutch Reformed churches supported segregation. The English-speaking churches, on the other hand, failed to offer a prophetic, alternative voice: they condemned apartheid at annual conferences and in pastoral letters, but, in practice these churches were part of the racially oppressive system. Long-established custom, reinforced by the Urban Areas Act of 1923 and the Group Areas Act of 1950, led to segregated parishes, church schools, and hospitals. In 1957 the Roman

Catholic bishops told their flock that it was "a blasphemy to attribute to God the sins against charity and justice which are the necessary accompaniment of apartheid." It was a ringing declaration, but not until 1979 were Catholic seminaries integrated, and then only after the bishops (overwhelmingly white) were confronted by black seminarians and priests, who were a small minority within the clergy of a church whose membership was overwhelmingly (80 per cent) black.[11]

Outstanding individuals challenged the pervasive passivity. Father Trevor Huddleston of the Anglican Community of the Resurrection joined the Defiance Campaign, and stood in the forefront of resistance to the destruction of the African township of Sophiatown under the Group Areas Act. He went on to play a principal role in the Congress of the People, which, in 1955, produced the Freedom Charter. In consequence, he was recalled to England the next year by his order.[12] A second Anglican priest, Michael Scott, was imprisoned in 1946 for joining Indian passive resisters in Durban in their protest against the Smuts government's Asiatic Land Tenure and Indian Representation Acts; and, soon thereafter, he was declared a prohibited immigrant. Scott continued to fight in exile against apartheid and South Africa's occupation of South West Africa.[13] The Rev. Arthur Blaxall, the Anglican General Secretary of the Christian Council, developed a support network for political detainees during the Treason Trial of the late 1950s.[14] The Anglican Bishop of Johannesburg, Ambrose Reeves, visited the wounded after the Sharpeville massacre in 1960, took affidavits from witnesses, and published his exposé, *Shooting at Sharpeville*.[15] Both Blaxall and Reeves were deported. Although more cautious than these personalities and focused on ecclesiastical concerns, the Anglican Archbishop of Cape Town, Geoffrey Clayton, and the Roman Catholic Archbishop of Durban, Denis Hurley, in 1957 led ecumenical opposition to a bill designed to enable the Minister of the Interior to bar Africans from attending churches in white areas.[16]

The white-led denominations themselves, in contrast to such courageous individuals, were out of touch with anti-apartheid movements. Members of the ecclesiastical hierarchy were conspicuously absent from the non-violent Defiance Campaign of the 1950s. In the words of Helen Joseph, the "Church turned its back on the ANC, the ANC never turned its back on the Church." She described going into homes during the Defiance Campaign, where "we'd find fifteen or twenty people bunched up in the house waiting for us. And we started with a prayer."[17] The political scientist Tom Lodge described the "mood of religious fervour [that] infused the resistance."

> When the (Defiance) Campaign opened it was accompanied by days of prayer, and volunteers pledged themselves at prayer meetings to a code of love, discipline and cleanliness. *Manyanos* [members of church-based, township women's welfare groups] wore their uniforms and accompanied Congress speeches with solemn hymn singing, and even at the tense climax of the Campaign in Port Elizabeth people were enjoined on the first day of the strike "to conduct a prayer and a fast in which each member of the family will have to be at home;" thereafter they attended nightly church services.[18]

Although this historical context was foundational, the origins of a formal or explicit South African liberation theology lay in the 1960 Cottesloe Conference of the World Council of Churches convened in the aftermath of the 1960 Sharpeville shootings. During and after this conference the Rev. Beyers Naudé of the *Nederduitse Gereformeerde Kerk* (NGK) confronted, first, his own white denomination, then others, and finally the state itself.[19] In 1960, he launched an ecumenical publication, *Pro Veritate*, and, in 1963, organized the non-racial, ecumenical Christian Institute of Southern Africa. In June 1968, the Institute, in co-operation with the South African Council of Churches (SACC), issued "A Message to the People of South Africa," essentially a white initiative, rooted in a rejection of apartheid on the basis of the "good news that in Christ, God had broken down the walls of division between God and man, and therefore also between man and man."[20]

The growing Black Consciousness Movement (BCM) and its associated Black theology soon influenced this new theological initiative. Steve Biko, Barney Pityana, Abraham Tiro, Malusi Mpumlwana, and others, initiated the South African Students Organization, which led the BCM. Young theologians, among them Manas Buthelezi, Bonganjalo Goba, Sabelo Ntwassa, and Allan Boesak, laid the theological foundations. Then Biko was murdered in prison, Tiro assassinated, and Pityana and Mpumlwana tortured. After their release from prison, Pityana and Mpumlwana became Anglican priests: Mpumlwana was a leader within the Order of Ethiopia; Pityana directed the World Council of Churches' Programme to Combat Racism. Manas Buthelezi became a Lutheran bishop, joining the theological efforts of bishops Mandlenkhosi Zwane and Desmond Tutu. Zwane, in 1976 named Bishop of Swaziland, became the most effective spokesman for black Catholics in Southern Africa. Tutu, consecrated Bishop of Lesotho in 1976, was appointed General Secretary of the SACC, and, in 1984, received the Nobel Peace Prize for his leadership in the non-violent struggle against apartheid. He was elected bishop of Johannesburg, and, in 1986, Archbishop of Cape Town.

In dialogue with black theology, and influenced by European political theology as well as liberation theology emanating from Latin America, Naudé and his colleagues in the Christian Institute moved from the older, liberal approach of *noblesse oblige* – of a benevolent working *for* the poor – to a participatory working *with* the poor for the empowerment of the oppressed. By 1977, when the government banned the Christian Institute, as well as the South African Students Organization and other BCM groups and their leaders, Naudé and his colleagues were confronting the state and the churches with a series of radical commitments. They supported BCM community projects, encouraged seminars on black theology, and reached out to marginalized Christians in the African Initiated Churches (AICs). They criticized the function of capitalism in South Africa, supported economic sanctions against the regime and conscientious objection to the military draft, and called for the unbanning of the ANC, to be followed by negotiations for a new South African constitution.

By the 1980s a resurgent protest movement focused on the township councils that had been established to control and tax urban blacks, and on the tricameral constitution of 1983 with its separate white, Coloured, and Indian assemblies. The colour-bar had by then been dismantled in certain public places and, in 1979, African trade unions had been recognized in law. Yet the principal foundations of apartheid remained firmly in place: the Population Registration Act, the Natives Land Act, and the Group Areas Act maintained the essentials of social segregation. The new constitution entrenched ethnic or group politics, with African political representation confined to the tribal "Homeland" governments, and to the deeply resented and co-opted township councils.

The new constitution was designed to broaden the regime's political base when the pressures were increasing from the liberation and trade union movements, and overseas enemies of apartheid. It failed in this goal, triggering instead mass protests that even the most brutal means could not suppress. By 1985 the country was under a state of emergency, the black townships were occupied by the army, and vigilantes were preying on anti-apartheid groups. Recurrent school boycotts had coalesced into a virtual insurrection. Widespread torture of political detainees, many in their early teens, occurred. Death squads, associated with either the police or the army, had begun targeting anti-apartheid activists: between 1985 and 1989, at least 50,000 individuals were detained without trial, and more than 5,000 protesters were slain in the drive to destroy the liberation movement. Within such a context, prophetic Christianity became more articulate and more broadly based in its support of the liberation struggle. In this regard, the 1985 *Kairos Document* (see pp. 168–69) was seminal, heralding a sharp escalation in the confrontation between activist Christians and the apartheid state.[21]

Although the Christian Institute itself had failed in its attempt to dislodge the white NGK from its defence of apartheid, Naudé sought to build trust and to nurture dialogue with the black Reformed churches: the NGSK for Coloureds, the NGKA for Africans, and the small Reformed Church in Africa for Indians (see pp. 151–54).[22] Gradually each of these developed its own critical responses, the most intense confrontation occurring between the NGK and the NGSK led by the Rev. Allan Boesak. In 1978 the NGK had rejected a call to dismantle segregated structures in order to form a united denomination. A prophetic pressure group, the Alliance of Black Reformed Christians in Southern Africa (ABRECSA), and the NGSK branded the NGK's defence of apartheid as heretical: "We unequivocally declare that apartheid is a sin, and that the moral and theological justification of it is a travesty of the Gospel, a betrayal of the Reformed tradition, and a heresy."[23] In the face of the NGK's continued refusal to condemn apartheid, the World Alliance of Reformed Churches, at its Ottawa gathering in 1982, confirmed that charge of heresy and also elected Boesak as its president.

The NGSK now declared a *status confessionis* – a moment of truth in which the Gospel itself was understood to be at stake. In the hope of establishing a non-racial church, the NGSK adopted the Belhar Confession, inspired by the Barmen Declaration of the confessing church in Nazi Germany (see p. 153). Under these pressures, the NGK dropped its biblical defence of apartheid but nonetheless, on pragmatic grounds, continued to support the existing ethnic churches, the regime's reforms, and the new racially based constitution. For example, in 1983 the regional synod of the NGK in the Western Cape overwhelmingly rejected a proposal that it should "categorically condemn apartheid as a sin."[24]

Comparable struggles were underway within a number of South African denominations. The South African Council of Churches, now under black leadership, functioned as an ecumenical vanguard for prophetic Christianity, but its mainline member churches were polarized, largely along racial lines.[25] The Roman Catholic Church, too, remained divided, though its bishops condemned apartheid and the new constitution in a series of pastoral letters.[26] A small number of black Catholic clergy spoke out in their support, among them Bishop Zwane, the Rev. Buti Tlhagale of Regina Mundi parish in Soweto, and the Rev. Smangaliso Mkhatshwa, general secretary of the Southern African Catholic Bishops' Conference (see pp. 205–7). But, although Justice and Peace Commissions were set up in an effort to motivate the parishes, with few exceptions, most of the clergy and white congregations refused to support a prophetic stand, while most black laity remained cautious and essentially passive. Although the Catholic Bishops' Conference launched a pastoral plan to remedy this malaise, the Vatican was not particularly supportive.[27] In 1988 the Papal Nuncio alarmed and irritated the South African bishops by warning against political involvement.[28] Pope John Paul II, in his 1989 visit to Southern Africa, adopted a pacifist approach that reflected little understanding of the depth of black desperation.[29]

Evangelicals and Pentecostals were likewise divided. Although prophetic dissidents emerged from within each cluster of churches, neither offered a critique of the established political order, and both condemned liberation theology. Only a minority of Evangelicals and Pentecostals criticized their faiths' other-worldly theologies, whose effect was to abet the *status quo* (see pp. 238–41). Africa Enterprise, an evangelical organization whose South African director, Michael Cassidy, had trained in the U.S. with Billy Graham, had little sympathy for liberation theology. Unwilling to encourage overt confrontation with the state, the group preferred reconciliation conferences designed to build bridges, particularly with the white Dutch Reformed churches and the corporate world.[30]

Although the many hundreds of AICs, whose membership embraced almost one-third of all South Africa's Christians, tended to adopt an apolitical stance, some did coalesce into an African Independent Churches Association and joined the SACC.[31] Others supported the apartheid regime. Bishop Isaac Mokoena, for example, came out against the repeal of the Mixed Marriages Act, which outlawed inter-racial unions. He organized a still-born United Christian Reconciliation Party, and travelled abroad on several occasions to oppose economic sanctions, whereupon, in 1987, President P.W. Botha awarded him a "Decoration for Meritorious Services."

More complicated was the stance of the Zion Christian Church, by far the largest of the independent churches, with a membership approaching two million. A haven from white political domination and economic exploitation, it was essentially separatist, avoiding confrontation with the state, and posing no direct threat to apartheid structures.[32] During the 1980s the church's vast annual gatherings at Moria (its new Jerusalem in the northern Transvaal) were addressed by South African cabinet ministers, and in 1985 by President Botha, who congratulated the church for keeping religion and politics separate, and for dutiful obedience to the state.[33] Below the surface, however, a growing number of Zionists had been politicized against apartheid by the turmoil of the townships, and by their membership in trade unions.[34]

The state's manipulation of religion was more extensive than these links with particular African independent churches suggest. When the Christian League of South Africa was launched in 1977 to discredit the SACC and any strain of liberation theology, at least 340,000 rands from a government slush fund fuelled the effort.[35] Three years later, the Catholic Defence League was established to support the South African Defence Force in its "heroic struggle" against communism.[36] The League, made up of white lay Catholics, was designed to counter the Bishops' Conference's strongly worded pastoral letters supporting conscientious objectors and the non-violent liberation struggle against apartheid. The bishops, in turn, challenged Catholics to root out racist structures and practices within their Church.[37] Right-wing Christianity was regularly used to bolster the apartheid regime, as when the sermons of American evangelist Jimmy Swaggart, on a 1986 visit to South Africa at the height of repression in the townships, were broadcast by state radio and television as part of a propagandistic holy war against communism, against the liberation movement, and particularly against the ANC, which was constantly presented as a front for Moscow.[38]

"Not Only in Words and Sermons and Statements": Ecumenical Campaigns Against Apartheid

A small but growing number of Christians, some holding high church offices and nearly all working in ecumenical structures, had, by the 1980s, begun to criticize what Boesak called "the theology we have inherited from western Christianity: the theology of accommodation and of acquiescence; an individualistic other-worldly spirituality which has no interest in the realities of the world, except to proclaim the existing order God-ordained."[39] The gathering strength of this movement can be seen most clearly in the South African Council of Churches, the Southern African Catholic Bishops' Conference, the Institute for Contextual Theology, and Diakonia.

After the 1977 banning of the Christian Institute and the Black Consciousness Movement, the SACC sharpened its critique of apartheid. Under the leadership of three remarkable South Africans, it became more activist. Bishop Tutu, general secretary of the SACC from 1978 to 1985, who had come to the position from Lesotho, with close personal ties to the Black Consciousness Movement, contributed enthusiastically to the development of Black theology, at first moving cautiously toward a pro-sanctions stand but by the mid-1980s becoming more assertive.[40] When Tutu was elected bishop of Johannesburg, and later archbishop of Cape Town, Naudé was invited to replace him in 1985 as general secretary. Only recently unbanned after seven years and now a minister in the *Kerk in Afrika*, Naudé helped during the next three years of severe repression to strengthen the SACC's international contacts.[41] The third of these general secretaries was the Rev. Frank Chikane, who took over the SACC in 1988. Chikane had been detained on four occasions and severely tortured; he also had been rejected by his pentecostal Apostolic Church for his prophetic, activist stand. Before taking up his responsibilities at the SACC, Chikane had joined the staff of the Institute for Contextual Theology, where he read widely among liberation theologians and entered into a fruitful partnership with Albert Nolan, a South African Dominican.[42]

By the 1980s the SACC was administering a range of ambitious outreach pro-grammes, for which 95 per cent of the funding came from overseas. An extensive network supplied legal and material aid for thousands of detainees, and support for hard-pressed trade unionists. When the state of emergency was declared and black townships were occupied by the army in 1985 and 1986, the SACC set up crisis centres to offer first aid, instructions on how to cope with tear gas, legal assistance, and temporary shelter from vigilantes. With the first trickle of conscientious objec-tors in the late 1970s, and the End Conscription Campaign gathering strength after 1983, the Council lent its support. It also backed the rent boycotts, designed to impoverish the co-opted township councils, and the boycotts of elections for these councils and for the three ethnic chambers set up under the new constitution.[43]

Tutu, Naudé, and Chikane strengthened the SACC's contacts with exiled orga-nizations, in particular the ANC, building trust at the Harare (1985) and Lusaka (1987) conferences held in cooperation with the World Council of Churches. At these gatherings, representatives of church organizations and exiled movements explored contextual theology, more particularly the Kairos Document, and con-demned the apartheid regime as illegitimate.[44]

During these years the Southern African Catholic Bishops' Conference came to work more closely with the SACC, though usually speaking out in a lower key. Archbishop Hurley, president of the Conference for most of the decade, a board member of the Christian Institute until its banning, and a close friend of Naudé, played a key role in facilitating this growing ecumenical co-operation, thus con-firming his role as spokesman for a strain of liberation theology gaining acceptance within the Bishops' Conference and among a minority of clergy and laity – black and white.

During the 1980s the work of the Bishops' Conference was promoted by the forceful Fr. Smangaliso Mkhatshwa, a political activist, who was detained, tor-tured, and banned for six years during his tenure as General Secretary of the Bishops' Conference. Yet he was able to assume a crucial role in prodding the still predominantly white Conference towards an understanding of the brutality of repression and the harsh realities of black politics.[45] While most Roman Catholic parishes dragged their feet, the prophetic voice of the bishops was heard in pastoral letters, reports, and press releases. They identified themselves in 1977 with the struggle for black empowerment and confessed the persistence of racism within the church itself;[46] they decisively condemned the 1983 constitution, endorsed election boycotts, and issued detailed reports on police and army violence in the townships and on Defence Force atrocities in Namibia. In addition, white Catholic schools were integrated. This occurred in a hesitant manner in the late 1970s, but then with determination and a spirit of defiance as the tumultuous decade of the 1980s unfolded.[47]

In working with the SACC, the Bishops' Conference co-sponsored an exposé of the government's continuing policy of relocations; it supported the restructuring of schools and syllabuses, and encouraged the use of protest liturgies – including anti-apartheid national days of prayer.[48] The conference firmly supported the End Conscription Campaign, as in 1989 when 800 white South Africans coordinated public resistance to the draft. A pastoral plan organized in 1989, "Community

Serving Humanity," attempted to recover the insights of Vatican II (see pp. 206, 209) in developing more consultative processes in church affairs, encouraging small Christian communities, and stimulating action for justice in all parishes.[49] In the early 1980s the bishops formed a Church and Work Commission dedicated to support of trade unions.[50] They defended black and white activists in the Young Christian Students and Young Christian Workers;[51] they sponsored a Natal agricultural pilot project to distribute church land to black families and to nurture a cooperative movement. In 1986 they sent a high-level delegation to the ANC's headquarters in Lusaka, where a joint communiqué was issued.[52]

Of all the initiatives taken by the bishops, perhaps the most threatening to the state was their backing of *The New Nation* in 1984, a newspaper committed to becoming a voice for blacks. Its first editor, Zwelakhe Sisulu, youngest son of the veteran ANC leader Walter Sisulu and leading feminist and Christian activist Albertina Sisulu, was soon detained; but the paper survived despite hounding by censors and an interruption of three months' publication on account of its persistent reporting on the liberation movement and the brutalities of state repression.

The Institute for Contextual Theology (ICT), founded in 1981 in Johannesburg, became the cutting edge of liberation theology, or what the Institute preferred to call "contextual theology" – in part, to distinguish South African initiatives from those in Latin America. The South African movement, it was argued, needed to take account not only of race and class exploitation as in Latin America, but of the more complex range of Christian denominations, Islam, and the rich heritage of African religion in South Africa.

The Institute acted as a catalyst for the Kairos Document of 1985, signed by 150 clergy, laity, and academic theologians. Christians were called to unmask and confront the structures of evil and injustice or to betray their faith. The document condemned the theology of the state and declared as idolatrous the use of religion to bolster tyrannical, racist structures. The God invoked in the preamble to the new South African constitution, was "as mischievous, sinister and evil as any of the idols that the prophets of Israel had to contend with." The prevailing theology of the church was criticized as a naive search for premature reconciliation, the product of a dualistic, other-worldly spirituality based on an inappropriate model of personal conflict resolution. With the entrenched evils of apartheid, there could be no grounds for reconciliation or compromise; only after repentance and a commitment to dismantling injustice could reconciliation come. A reformed apartheid achieved through appeals to the white state was an abomination.

By contrast, said the Kairos Document, prophetic theology supported and empowered God's poor and oppressed. Rooted in the Jewish and Christian scriptures and informed by an understanding of South African history, it judged the apartheid state as divisive and tyrannical, as an enemy of God. Christians, called to love their enemies, were also called to confront evil:

> The most loving thing we can do for *both* the oppressed *and* for our enemies
> who are oppressors is to eliminate the oppression, remove the tyrants from
> power and establish a just government for the common good of *all the people*.

The church would have to take sides; it would "have to be involved at times in civil disobedience," preaching the message of hope "not only in words and sermons and statements but also through its actions, programmes, campaigns and divine services."[53]

Diakonia was a Durban-based pastoral centre supported by Roman Catholic Archbishop Hurley and six mainline Protestant churches. Begun in 1976, just after the crushing of the Black Consciousness Movement, Diakonia was open to liberation theology from Latin America. At first it found it difficult to move beyond a low-keyed commitment to charity, education, and the polite raising of consciousness in the parishes, but, as its black and white staff worked in the townships and the level of state violence increased, and after the publication of the Kairos Document in 1985, its discussions, publications, parish and seminary workshops took on a sharper analytical edge. Diakonia was also drawn into activism by co-operation with the End Conscription Campaign, support of the families of detainees, work with communities threatened by relocation orders, and by an outreach programme for black unions. Protest liturgies and marches were organized – for example, to prisons where detainees were held without trial.

The South African Council of Churches, the Catholic Bishops' Conference, the Institute for Contextual Theology, and Diakonia were not particularly effective in reaching out pastorally to migrant workers and to the working classes. Nevertheless in delegitimizing the apartheid regime, and in encouraging South Africans of all denominations to support the liberation movement, they brought down upon themselves the wrath of the state. After the 1985 military occupation of the townships, hundreds of clergy and church workers were detained, many of them tortured; others were banned and severely restricted. Foreign missionaries and lay volunteers were deported, particularly seminary teachers with an interest in liberation theology, and individuals with trade-union contacts. Death squads assassinated a number of Christian activists, such as Diliza Matshoba, an educator in the SACC's Division of Justice and Reconciliation, and Dr. Fabian Ribeiro, beloved physician of Mamelodi township. Bombs and arson destroyed church buildings, student and trade union offices. In Johannesburg in 1988 a massive bomb devastated the headquarters of the South African Council of Churches, Khotso House, and shortly thereafter arson gutted the Catholic Bishops' Conference building in Pretoria.[54]

Leading Christian activists, including Tom Manthata (a field worker for the Council of Churches), Patrick Lekhota (publicity secretary for the United Democratic Front or UDF, and a Roman Catholic), Moses Chikane (ex-Transvaal Secretary of the UDF and a worker for the Catholic Bishops' Conference) and their associates were charged with treason in the "Delmas" trial, which began in 1985 and dragged on for the remainder of the decade. They were accused of planning to overthrow the state through the use of non-violent, mass protests. Later the group of twenty-two was reduced to four, who were convicted of treason; but their conviction was eventually overturned by the South African Supreme Court.

"A Christian Presence in the Struggle": Prophetic Christianity and the Crisis of the Regime

In early 1988 Christian activists moved to the forefront of the struggle. When the United Democratic Front (UDF) was formed in 1983 to oppose the new constitution, the SACC, SACBC, ICT and Diakonia had all given their support. The Rev. Allan Boesak issued the first public call to establish the UDF, and along with Rev. Frank Chikane, Beyers Naudé, and Archbishop Desmond Tutu, was among the UDF's patrons; Albertina Sisulu was one of its vice-presidents. Inspiring and confrontational, these Christian leaders were eloquent spokespeople for the Front's non-racial ideals.[56] They were not committed to a "third way" – that is, to the creation of separate, specifically Christian organizations espousing particular "Christian" solutions to society's ills – but to the popular liberation movement's struggle for justice. As Boesak explained in his 1979 address to the SACC: "It is not a Christian struggle I am pleading for, it is for a Christian presence in the struggle that I plead."[57] With the state of emergency reimposed in 1986, a countrywide Day of Prayer for the Removal of Unjust Government was called to coincide with the tenth commemoration of the schoolchildren massacred on 16 June 1976.[58]

As the death tolls mounted and outdoor meetings were banned, church buildings and congregations became centres for protest. Funerals, usually of the young, became the liturgical focus of entire communities. At the 1985 funeral of a murdered trade unionist, Andries Raditsela, attended by thousands of grieving people, Bishop Simeon Nkoane, the Anglican Suffragan Bishop of Johannesburg, spoke of "God's broken heart."[59] There were many comparable events, as when the people of Cradock in the eastern Cape mourned four heroes – Matthew Goniwe, Sparrow Mkhonto, Sicelo Mhlawuli, and Fort Calata – murdered by a death squad in June of that year.[60] When two young activists, Robert Waterwitch and Caroline Williams, died in a Cape Town bomb explosion in 1989, Roman Catholic Bishop Lawrence Henry and seven priests celebrated Mass, and Archbishop Tutu and the Rev. Boesak were in the congregation.[61]

By the mid-1980s, the ANC had established a department of religion. Articles on liberation theology were appearing in its monthly publication *Sechaba*. At the World Council of Churches conferences in Harare and Lusaka, ANC leaders affirmed their respect for and in some cases their personal commitment to liberation theology. Church leaders, in turn, pledged themselves to non-violent action while recognizing that many individuals, in good conscience, had reluctantly turned to the use of force.[62]

By the time Pretoria "cracked down" yet again in February 1988, banning eighteen persons and the political activities of the Congress of South African Trade Unions (COSATU) and the UDF – the core of the Mass Democratic Movement – the meshing of prophetic Christianity and the liberation struggle was far advanced. The government imposed new sweeping restrictions on funerals. It forbade hymns, songs, and sermons, and limited attendance at funerals to those who held tickets issued by the police. Leaders of prophetic Christianity now helped launch the Defiance Campaign of 1988. The first step was an ecumenical service of witness in Cape Town at St. George's Cathedral that challenged the legitimacy of the apartheid regime, protested the bannings, and refused to accept restrictions on funeral services. Archbishop Tutu, Catholic Archbishop Naidoo, the Rev. Allan Boesak (moderator of the NGSK), the Rev. Khoza Mgojo (president of the Methodist Church of South Africa), and the Rev. Frank Chikane (the general secretary of the SACC) together led a procession to Parliament to deliver a petition in defiance of the emergency restrictions prohibiting public demonstrations. All were arrested and water cannons fired to disperse their followers.[63] A tough, public exchange of letters ensued between Tutu and President Botha, and later one between Chikane and Botha. Botha's correspondence was threatening, bitter, and personal: the churchmen, he said, were stooges manipulated by communists, traitors to their Christian calling. He called upon them not to pursue "secular and revolutionary objectives," but to be "messengers of the true Christian religion, and not of Marxism and atheism."[64]

Chikane now called for widespread civil disobedience. An emergency convocation of church leaders in Johannesburg pledged support and, after some hesitation and tense debate over tactics, launched a "Standing for the Truth Campaign." Along with the Mass Democratic Movement, they rejected Botha's attempts to reform apartheid as deceitful. Apartheid, they declared, had to be abolished. The 1988 elections for township councils were successfully boycotted; so were the following year's elections for the Coloured and Indian chambers of the tricameral Parliament.[65]

Perturbed by the regulation of funerals, more and more clergy began to reject state interference.[66] The Council of Churches and the Catholic Bishops' Conference informed the government that, should its Foreign Funding Bill become law, they would defy monitoring and restricting of their overseas support.[67] When students, held in detention without trial, some for more than a year, went on a hunger strike in 1989 to demand release or trial, Tutu and Chikane acted as their negotiators. Eventually an agreement for their release was reached with the Minister of Justice, not a moment too soon since several young men were close to death. When a leading activist, the young intellectual Sandile Thusi, broke his fast after 37 days, he did so by taking the Eucharist.[68]

By the end of 1989, disciplined protest marches were surging through the urban areas: 10,000 strong in Port Elizabeth and East London, 20,000 in Cape Town and Durban, 80,000 in Johannesburg.[69] Individuals and organizations simply unbanned themselves, forcing the state into both reluctant concessions and spasmodic repression. The Mass Democratic Movement, boosted by the now vigorous participation of leading ecclestical personalities and some of their denominational and ecumenical organizations, had regenerated its shattered structures.

After Botha's successor, F. W. de Klerk, was installed as President in February 1989, a "Conference for a Democratic Future" was called by the liberation movement. It gathered in December 1989, with 15 per cent of the delegates from churches and ecumenical organizations.[70] De Klerk now intensified negotiations with veteran leaders of the African National Congress; he released Govan Mbeki, Walter Sisulu, and several of their colleagues from prison; he unbanned the ANC, the South African Communist Party, the Congress of South African Students, the Pan Africanist Congress, and other organizations. In February 1990 Nelson Mandela was released unconditionally after 27 years of imprisonment.

"A Broken and a Contrite Spirit": Christians Confront Their Past and Future

De Klerk's government now faced a difficult task – to bolster its waning but considerable power by groping for some moral legitimacy. De Klerk declared the apartheid era to have been a costly and regrettable mistake, though he did not label apartheid itself a moral obscenity or a religious heresy. He also asserted the regime's responsibility for law and order during the transitional period to majority rule. The Broederbond, a secret society that had long coordinated the Afrikaner power structure – through its military, police, civil service, corporate, media, parliamentary, and clergy members – was shaken by the splintering of the Afrikaner National Party and the formation of the Conservative Party in 1983. Yet it had recovered sufficiently to coordinate the regime's survival strategies, with backing from the white Dutch Reformed Church (NGK). Resisting calls for repentance and compensation for past injustices, the NGK also rejected appeals for full church unity with the NGSK, the NGKA, and the (Indian) Reformed Church in Africa.

While De Klerk's image as a "man of peace" gave him a two-thirds majority in the March 1992 referendum of white voters on continued negotiations with the liberation movements, the Conservative Party and groups even further to the right refused to come to the negotiating table, finding allies instead in Buthelezi's Inkatha and the two "homeland" governments in the Ciskei and Bophuthatswana. Mandela, the ANC, and its allies had to manoeuvre in this hazardous terrain, organizing and disciplining their massive but volatile support. Supporters of Inkatha and the ANC repeatedly clashed, in Natal and on the Witwatersrand, with white extremists in the military and police encouraging the violence. The PAC's military wing, the Azanian People's Liberation Army, temporarily revived its anti-white campaign of terror. The thousands of returning exiles encountered unemployment, and members of the ANC's guerrilla wing, uMkhonto weSizwe (Spear of the Nation), were angered as negotiations faltered with no immediate prospect of integration into a reconstructed military or police force.

Prophetic Christian leaders struggled, in this context of social transition, to chart a dual ministry: intervention and mediation in the short run, reconstruction in the long run. They wanted to check the spread of violence through monitoring and mediation, while nurturing the process of negotiations. Their goals, however, were those of the liberation movement: formation of a multi-party transitional executive, election of a constituent assembly, and passage and implementation of a non-racial constitution bolstered by a comprehensive bill of rights. The prophetic church also backed a set of social and economic commitments – from land redistribution to support of the women's movement – designed to produce a more egalitarian yet pluralistic society and to challenge inequities in the international economic system.

The release of Mandela and the unbanning of organizations sparked an intense debate within the SACC on mediation versus prophetic ministry. Its general secretary, Frank Chikane, responded by distinguishing three approaches: mediation from a position of power, mediation from a position of powerlessness and neutrality, and mediation with the commitment to justice. The way forward, he argued, was the latter. Restitution in the pursuit of justice would have to be an integral part of the reconciliation process. Under Chikane's leadership the SACC established four task forces: on economic justice, on political justice, on violence, and on education for democracy.[71] It remained to be seen whether the Council's member churches would translate these commitments into effective practice.

Recognizing the importance of Christian initiatives within the new flux of South African polities, and hoping to limit the influence of the prophetic church, President de Klerk proposed a National Conference of Church Leaders to draw together as wide a spectrum of opinion as possible. The SACC rebuffed this intervention of the state into church affairs, but it did authorize General Secretary Chikane to cooperate with other church organizations in sponsoring a broadly based conference. The resulting Rustenburg Conference included 230 representatives of ninety-seven denominations, forty church associations and ecumenical agencies, for example, Diakonia and ICT. It also attracted leaders from denominations that had long harboured suspicions of liberation theology and had even supported the 1980s efforts to reform apartheid, among them the NGK, the Baptist Union, the Apostolic Faith Mission Church, the Evangelical Presbyterian Church in South Africa, the white-dominated Lutheran churches, evangelicals like the Rhema churches, and several African AICs that were not members of the SACC. Nevertheless, the agenda was set by the proponents of contextual theology, those within the churches who had confronted the apartheid state during the 1980s.[72]

All the delegates at Rustenburg, though differing on some issues, agreed on "the unequivocal rejection of apartheid as a sin." The final Declaration advised that "repentance and practical restitution" were necessary for God's forgiveness and for justice as a step toward reconciliation. Apartheid was condemned "in its intention" – a point with which the NGK had special difficulty – in its implementation, and in "its consequences as an evil policy." The victims of apartheid were remembered "with sorrow" and tribute was paid to those who resisted it. Church leaders who had supported or refused to confront apartheid confessed their misusing of the Bible, "ignoring of apartheid's evil," and "spiritualizing of the Gospel by preaching the sufficiency of individual salvation without social transformation." Some had been "bold in condemning apartheid but timid in resisting it." Those who benefited from apartheid had been "guilty of colonial arrogance towards black culture," allowing state institutions "to do our sinning for us." The victims of apartheid acknowledged their "own contribution to the failure of the church"; many had responded with "timidity and fear, failing to challenge our oppression." Some had become "willing instruments of the repressive state machinery," achieving privilege within apartheid structures. With a "broken and contrite spirit," the Conference asked for "the forgiveness of God and of our fellow South Africans." South Africa's predominantly white elite would have to accept "affirmative acts of restitution in health care, psychological healing, education, housing, employment, economic infrastructure and especially land ownership." Those gathered at Rustenburg called for a popularly elected constituent assembly and a new constitution that would enshrine the "value of human life created in the image of God," with a bill of rights "subject to the judiciary alone," a common voters' roll, and a multi-party democracy within a unitary state.

A year later Emilio Castro, general secretary of the WCC arrived at Cape Town and convened "Cottesloe II," a consultation of the WCC with the SACC's member churches. As with the churches' reaction to the Rustenburg declaration, the response to this gathering was to be a major disappointment. Denominational attendance at the Cape Town consultation was patchy, and the turnout at follow-up ecumenical services around the country was well below that of the earlier vibrant, populist responses at funerals of anti-apartheid activists. The clear, anti-racist goal had given way to a confusing political transition. Reflecting on Rustenburg and Cottesloe II, Beyers Naudé expressed alarm: impressive ecumenical statements were not inspiring a growing mass of church-goers to move from the confines of their parish liturgies into the various organizations of the liberation movement to check political violence and contribute to the formation of public policies that might empower the poor. As with the Kairos Document, the real tragedy, Naudé argued, was not that some Christians simply rejected it while others criticized it, "but that the churches which were sympathetic did not take up the challenge and act upon it." Like Kairos, these recent declarations did "not seem to have made any practical difference to the daily life and witness for social justice in the churches."[73]

If, in the changed political context, the denominations were disappointingly inert, key political figures in the liberation movement were looking to the church with mounting expectations. In December 1992, Nelson Mandela addressed the Free Ethiopian Church of Southern Africa at its centennial celebration in Potchefstroom, declaring that in the struggle against the heresy of apartheid, the contribution of the "broad ecumenical movement in South Africa and internationally" had been unparalleled. With apartheid collapsing, the church could "not afford to retreat to the cosiness of the sanctuary"; rather it had to act "as a midwife to the birth of our democracy." The church ought to warn against superficial changes that would simply add "a sprinkling of affluent blacks" to the white power structure. It should be involved in "national reconciliation underpinned by confession and restitution." On the other hand, while the church was to "take an active part in the building of a new nation in South Africa," it "was not to be subordinated, in any way, to the government of the day or any other societal institution."[74]

Looking back now at the emergence of a prophetic Christian voice in South Africa, we can discern its early articulation in African politics, particularly after the formation of the ANC in 1912. Later it was heard within the churches, among Anglicans in particular – as when Trevor Huddleston and a small number of clergy identified with the liberation movement during the Defiance Campaign of the 1950s. The consciousness of the need for justice gathered strength after the Cottesloe Conference of 1960, the formation of the Christian Institute in 1963, and the decisive influence of the Black Consciousness Movement and its Black theology during the 1970s. By the 1980s, prophetic Christian leaders worked for ecumenical cooperation, joined the liberation movement, and struggled to end apartheid. When the state responded with intensifying repression, church institutional structures became a source of support for the hard-pressed but gathering Mass Democratic Movement.

But what of the future? The SACC, which relied essentially on the international churches for its financial support, has seen its budget slashed in recent years, necessitating major cutbacks in staff and programmes; ecumenical organizations like Diakonia and ICT are facing comparable financial stress.[75] The Pastoral Plan of the Roman Catholic church, a parish educational program, has been in operation for five years without startling results in terms of activism. Other denominations face comparable inertia in their parishes. The white NGK, despite its repentance for the effects of apartheid, continues to resist the challenge to disengage from the Broederbond and to merge into a unified non-ethnic church with the NGSK, the NGKA, and the Reformed Church in Africa.[76]

In this context, two issues may be of vital importance for South Africa's future. The first is whether prophetic witness will renew its strength and contribute to sustaining the country's predominantly black political culture of racial tolerance and non-racial ideals – in a time when whites experience a loss of power and the redress of black communities' grievances about inequality and economic exploitation are slow in coming. The second and related issue is whether the prophetic church, having experienced the compromises of a relatively peaceful political transition, will be able to articulate a theology critical of the continuing structural injustices (social sin) of South African society. Whites will be inclined to cling to their economic privilege, while assertive, increasingly powerful black elites will tend to defend their class interests in the new political system, in the corporate world, the civil service, military, police, the professions, and trade unions. Who will further the vision of a more just society? Who will work to empower the poor? In the words of Jean-Marc Ela, who drew upon his experiences among the poverty-stricken Kirdis of north Cameroon: "How to speak about God in the living conditions of the poor in African societies torn apart by many forms of neo-colonial violence, is the question which should mobilize African churches."[77]

NOTES

ELPHICK / INTRODUCTION: CHRISTIANITY IN SOUTH AFRICAN HISTORY / PAGES 1–15

1. *Census of the Union of South Africa, 1911: Report and Annexes* (Pretoria: Government Printing and Stationery Office, 1913), 924–5; Patrick Johnstone, *Operation World: The Day-to-Day Guide for Praying for the World* (Grand Rapids: Zondervan, 1993), 493–8.

2. J.W. Hofmeyr and K.E. Cross, *History of the Church in Southern Africa: A Select Bibliography of Published Material to 1980* (Pretoria: University of South Africa, 1986) and *History of the Church in Southern Africa: A Select Bibliography of Published Material 1981 to 1985* (Pretoria: University of South Africa, 1988).

3. For recent analyses of this predicament, see N. Southey, "History, Church History, and Historical Theology in South Africa," *Journal of Theology for Southern Africa*, 68 (September 1989): 5–16; and Richard Elphick, "Writing Religion into History: The Case of South African Christianity," *Missions and Christianity in South African History*, ed. Henry Bredekamp and Robert Ross (Johannesburg: Witwatersrand University Press, 1995).

4. For an important synthesis that embraces other religions besides Christianity see David Chidester, *Religions of South Africa* (London and New York: Routledge, 1992).

5. For a review of leading ideas in the theory of micro- and macro-narratives see Kerwin Klein, "In Search of Narrative Mastery: Postmodernism and the Peoples without History," *History and Theory*, 34, 4 (1995).

6. James T. Campbell's important *Songs of Zion: The African Methodist Episcopal Church in the United States and South Africa* (New York and Oxford: Oxford University Press, 1995) was published too late to influence many of the chapters in this book.

7. The centrality of Evangelical Protestantism to nineteenth-century religious life in the United States is an organizing theme of such general histories of American religion as Sydney E. Ahlstrom, *A Religious History of the American People* (New Haven and London: Yale University Press, 1972) and Mark A. Noll, *A History of Christianity in the United States and Canada* (Grand Rapids: Eerdmans, 1992).

8. Some of the evidence is reviewed in Richard Gray, *Black Christians and White Missionaries* (New Haven and London: Yale University Press, 1990).

9. Richard Elphick, "Mission Christianity and Interwar Liberalism,"in *Democratic Liberalism in South Africa: Its History and Prospect*, ed. Jeffrey Butler, Richard Elphick and David Welsh (Middletown: Wesleyan University Press; and Cape Town: David Philip, 1987), 68.

10. Owen Chadwick, *The Secularization of the European Mind in the Nineteenth Century* (Cambridge: Cambridge University Press, 1975), 93–103.

11. See, for example, Deborah M. Valenze, *Prophetic Sons and Daughters: Female Preaching and Popular Religion in Industrial England* (Princeton: Princeton University Press, 1985) on British Primitive Methodism; Edith L. Blumhofer, *Aimee Semple McPherson: Everybody's Sister* (Grand Rapids: Eerdmans, 1993) on American Pentecostalism; and David Martin, *Tongues of Fire: The Explosion of Protestantism in Latin America* (Oxford: Blackwell, 1990) on Latin American Pentecostalism.

12. Maureen Swan, *Gandhi: The South African Experience* (Johannesburg: Ravan, 1985), 236.

13. Lamin Sanneh, *Translating the Message: The Missionary Impact on Culture* (Maryknoll, NY: Orbis, 1990); Galatians 3:29, NIV.

1 / GERSTNER / THE REFORMED CHURCH UNDER DUTCH RULE / PAGES 16–30

1. A minority argued for an active decree of damnation. The passive view is clearly taught in both the Belgic Confession (Article 16), and the Canons of Dort (First Head of Doctrine, Article 6). Later Lutheranism strongly rejected any doctrine of predestination to damnation, although Luther had accepted such.

2. "The Heidelberg Catechism," in *The Creeds of Christendom*, ed. Philip Schaff, 3 vols. (New York: Harper and Brothers, 1877), 316.

3. On Dort's opinions on slavery and their impact in colonial South Africa see Robert C.–H. Shell, *Children of Bondage: A Social History of the Slave Society at the Cape of Good Hope, 1652–1838* (Middletown: Wesleyan University Press, 1994). See also his English translation in "De Ethnicorum Pueris Baptizandis: Reformed Opinions on Baptism of Heathens, The Synod of Dort (1618–19)," South African Library, Cape Town.

4. Johannes Cocceius, *God-gelertheit, in de Byzondere Grondstukken der Christelijke Religie* (Amsterdam:

Johannes van Someren, 1676), 91, 95. Although Cocceius does speak of an overarching covenant of grace in the above passage, elsewhere in this same work at pp. 38–43 he outlines his extreme understanding of the inferiority of the state of a believer under the old covenant. For a more detailed discussion of the Voetian–Cocceian discussion see Jonathan N. Gerstner, *The Thousand Generation Covenant: Dutch Reformed Covenant Theology and Group Identity in Colonial South Africa 1652–1814* (Leiden: E.J. Brill, 1990), 68–74.

5. Joel R. Beeke, *Assurance of Faith: Calvin, English Puritanism, and the Dutch Second Reformation* (New York: P. Lang, 1991); F. Ernest Stoeffler, following the classic studies of Ritschl and Heppe, "Evangelical Pietism," in *The Rise of Evangelical Pietism* (Leiden: E.J. Brill, 1965) on use of the term "Second Reformation."

6. *Psalmen, Lofzangen ende Geestelyke Liedekens* (Amsterdam: Weduwe van Gerband Schragen, 1713), 23.

7. See Gerstner, *Thousand Generation Covenant*, 5–29, for further discussion of this point.

8. The form was consistently altered over the years in an "internal holiness" direction. *Ibid.*, 48–58.

9. Simon van der Stel, "Instructie ... aan Wilhelm Adriaan van der Stel," *Collectanea*, ed. C. Graham Botha (Cape Town: Van Riebeeck Society, 1924), 24.

10. "The Combined Church Assembly to the Classis of Amsterdam," 13 February 1759, in C. Spoelstra, *Bouwstoffen voor de Geschiedenis der Nederduitsch Gereformeerde Kerk in Zuid-Africa*, 2 vols. (Amsterdam: Hollandsch-Afrikaansche Uitgevers, 1907), vol. 1, 277. The Moravian missionary Georg Schmidt identified Roman Catholicism as "false Christianity" (see his *Tagebuch*, 78).

11. Jan Hoge, *Die Geskiedenis van die Lutherse Kerk aan die Kaap*, Archives Yearbook for South African History, 1938/II (Cape Town: Cape Times Ltd., 1938) 62–69; and Gerstner, *Thousand Generation Covenant*, 32–42.

12. See J.P. Claasen, *Die Sieketroosters in Suid-Afrika 1652–1866* (Pretoria: N.G. Kerkboekhandel, 1977), 22–9.

13. See also *Ecclesiastical Records of the State of New York*, ed. Edwin Tanjore Corwin (Albany: J.B. Lyon, 1901–16), vol. 1, 236.

14. For references to sick comforters as "dominee," see Spoelstra, *Bouwstoffen*, vol. 2, 427 [Paul Roux of Drakenstein, 2 June 1715], 429 [Bosman and Van Hoorn, 4 January 1715]; and *Dagboek van Adam Tas, 1705–1706*, ed. Leo Fouché (Cape Town: Van Riebeeck Society, 1970), 50 [Johannes Simonius].

15. For rare examples of scandals, see Spoelstra, *Bouwstoffen*, vol. 1, 220–1, 223–8; vol. 2, 91–2, and Gerstner, *Thousand Generation Covenant*, 81–2 [Rev. Rudolph Cloppenburg's matrimonial case]; and S.P. Engelbrecht, *Die Kaapse Predikant van die Siewentiende en Agtiende Eeuw* (Cape Town and Pretoria: HAUM and J.H. de Bussy, 1952), 30 [suicide of Rev. Hercules van Loon].

16. See Gerstner, *Thousand Generation Covenant*, 99–102 [cases of Rev. Pierre Simond, E. F. Le Boucq, Salomon van Echten, Petrus van der Spuy and J. H. von Manger].

17. As cited in H.D.A. du Toit, "Predikers en hul Prediking in die Nederduitse Gereformeerde Kerk van Suid-Afrika" (D.D. dissertation, University of Pretoria, 1947), 337.

18. Gerstner, *Thousand Generation Covenant*, 103–4.

19. The Rev. H. Kroonenburg (on behalf of the Combined Church Assembly) to the Classis of Amsterdam, 27 February 1756, in Spoelstra, *Bouwstoffen*, vol. 1, 267.

20. Willem J. van Zijl, *Van Skeepskis na Wakis tot Boekrak* (Cape Town: Lux Verbi, 1992), 81–111.

21. Michiel Christiaan Vos, *Merkwaardig Verhaal* (Amsterdam: H. Hoveker, 1850), 116.

22. W. E. B. Paravicini di Capelli, *Reize in de Binnen-Landen van Zuid-Afrika*, ed. W.J. De Kock (Cape Town: Van Riebeeck Society, 1965), 231; Gerstner, *Thousand Generation Covenant*, 113.

23. For the use of music in Dutch Reformed services, see Robert Percival, *An Account of the Cape of Good Hope* (London: C. Andr. Baldwin, 1804; repr., New York: Negro Universities Press, 1969), 206 ["It is a practice for them to be continually chanting hymns and psalms and before meals they uniformly use a long prayer or grace"]; and Adam Tas, *Dagboek*, 59 [Tas's psalm-singing at home].

24. Schmidt, *Tagebuch* (13 December, 1742), 448.

25. James Campbell, *Travels in Africa* (London: Black, Parry Co. and T. Hamilton, 1815; repr., Cape Town: C. Struik, 1974), 59.

26. Lichtenstein, "De Reize van H. de Graaf's Gezelschap naar Boetsjoeanaland in 1805," *Reize in Zuid-Afrika*, E.C. Gode Molsbergen, vol. 2: *Tochten naar het Noorden* (The Hague: M. Nijhoff, 1916), 266–7. George Thompson records an almost identical service of family worship except that this farmer, Schalk Burger, himself preached. *Travels in South Africa* (London: Henry Colburn, 1827; repr., Cape Town: Africana Connoisseurs Press, 1962), 329.

27. John Barrow, *An Account of Travels into the Interior of Southern Africa in the Years 1797 and 1798* (London: A. Strahan, 1801 and 1804), vol. 1, 82.

28. Minutes of the Church Council of Drakenstein, 18 March 1717, in Spoelstra, *Bouwstoffen*, vol. 2, 434; *Gedenkboek van die Gereformeerde Kerk in Suid Afrika: 1859–1959* (Potchefstroom: Die Kerkblad, 1959), 330, 324 [diverse views of these writers over the hymn-singing controversy].

29. This practice was noted with dismay by several visitors to the Cape, including Peter Kolb. *Naauwkeerige en Uitvoerige Beschrijving van de Kaap de Goede Hoop*, 2 vols. (Amsterdam: Balhazar Lakeman, 1727), 309.

NOTES

30. Jan van Riebeeck, *Van Riebeeck's Journal*, 3 vols. (Cape Town: A.A. Balkema, 1952), vol. 2, 43, 405–6.

31. "Journal of Zacharias Wagenaer" in H.C.V. Leibbrandt, *Précis of the Archives of the Cape of Good Hope: Journal 1662–1670* (Cape Town: W.A. Richards and Sons, 1901), 67–8; Gerstner, *Thousand Generation Covenant*, 179–83.

32. Lichtenstein, *Travels in South Africa in the Years 1803, 1804, 1805 and 1806*, trans. Anne Plumptre, 2 vols. (London: Henry Colborn, 1812, 1815; repr., Cape Town: Van Riebeeck Society, 1928, 1930), vol. 1, 116.

33. This book, originally presented by the Dutch Reformed Church in Swellendam, can be found at the University of Cape Town Library, Rare Book Collection.

34. See Gerstner, *Thousand Generation Covenant*, passim.

35. Some synodical decisions of the Dutch Reformed Church included a fourth group, gypsies.

36. Baptismal Records of the Cape Town Congregation in the Dutch Reformed Church Archives Cape Town.

37. Willem Barentsz Wylant to the Classis of Amsterdam, 20 April 1655, in Spoelstra, *Bouwstoffen*, vol. 1, 5.

38. Two committed suicide, two died as prisoners on Robben Island.

39. C. A. L. van Troostenburg de Bruijn, *Biographisch Woordeboek van Oost Indische Predikante*, s.v. "Daniel van Arckel" (Nijmegen: P. J. Milburn, 1893), 15. Sadly the Khoikhoi infant died the same month she was baptized. "Minutes of the Church Council of Cape Town, March 3, 1669," Dutch Reformed Church Archive, File G1 1/1 1/2. These events are also recorded in Peter de Neyn, *Lust-hof der Huwelyken* (Amsterdam: Johannes Rotterdam, 1730), 229.

40. Rev. Phillipus Baldaeus, a visiting minister in transit to Indonesia had to be ordered by the Council of Policy to baptize slave children with no European parentage (Spoelstra, *Bouwstoffen*, vol. 1, 29–30); Rev. Jacobus Overney (1679) wrote to the classis about the procedure and was told not to baptize such children in light of the rulings of the Synod of Dort (Spoelstra, *Bouwstoffen*, vol. 1, 28, vol. 2, 10). This direction of classis apparently was implemented, but then reversed by Van Reede tot Drakenstein in 1685, who noted, "Even white children, indisputably descended from Christian fathers, remained unbaptized." "Journaal van zijn Verblijf aan de Kaap," *Bijdragen en Mededeelingen van het Historisch Genootschap* (*Gevestigd te Utrecht*), 62 (Utrecht: Kemink en Zoon, 1941):184.

41. See Shell, *Children of Bondage*, 345, 375–6.

42. Cape Town baptism register, Cape Town Dutch Reformed Church Archive, File F G1 8/1–8/2.

43. Spoelstra, *Bouwstoffen*, vol. 1, 64–65.

44. "Journal of Zacharias Wagenaer," 13 September 1665, in *Précis of the Archives of the Cape of Good Hope: Journal 1662–1670*, 155.

45. François Valentyn, *Description of the Cape of Good Hope with the Matters Concerning It*, 2 vols. (Amsterdam, 1726; Cape Town: Van Riebeeck Society, 1971 and 1973), vol. 2, 259.

46. The form for the administration of the Lord's Supper is in many ways a counter-balance to the baptismal form's positive view of the spiritual state of all baptized. The Lord's Supper was denied to the "spiritually unfit."

47. Adam Tas, *Diary*, 23 December 1705, atp. 130.

48. Eric Anderson Walker, *The Great Trek* (London: Adam and Charles Black, 1934), 53; John M. Carter, *The Dutch Reformed Church in South Africa* (Edinburgh: W. and C. Inglis, 1869), 130–2.

49. Kolb, *Naauwkeurige en Uitvoerige Beschrijving*, vol. 2, 309; Charles Peter Thunberg, *Travels in Europe, Africa and Asia, Performed Between the Years 1770 and 1779*, 3 vols. (London: W. Richardson and J. Edgerton, n.d.), vol. 2, 159, 255; Lichtenstein, *Travels*, vol. 1, 175.

50. Chris Loff, "The History of a Heresy" in *Apartheid is a Heresy*, ed. John W. de Gruchy and Charles Villa-Vicenzio (Cape Town, David Philip; Grand Rapids: Eerdmans, 1983), 10–23.

51. Gerstner, *Thousand Generation Covenant*, 250–2.

52. Willem Barentsz Wylant to the Classis of Amsterdam, 20 April 1655, in Spoelstra, *Bouwstoffen*, vol. 1, 4.

53. *Das Tagebuch und die Briefe von Georg Schmidt, dem Ersten Missionar in Südafrika (1737–1744)*, ed. H. C. Bredekamp and J. L Hattingh (Bellville: University of the Western Cape Press, 1981), 44, 46.

54. The Cape Town Church Council to the Classis of Amsterdam, 9 April 1703, in Spoelstra, *Bouwstoffen*, vol. 1, 35.

55. Church Council of Drakenstein to the Classis of Amsterdam, 4 April 1703, in Spoelstra, *Bouwstoffen*, vol. 1: 35.

56. "Journal of Isbrand Goske," 29 July 1674, in *Précis of the Archives of the Cape of Good Hope: Journal 1671–74 and 1676*, 209.

57. *Tagebuch*, ed. Bredekamp and Hattingh, 344 (author's emphasis).

58. For an overview of the development of the Moravian mission see Bernhard Krüger, *The Pear Tree Blossoms: A History of the Moravian Mission Stations in South Africa, 1737–1869* (Genadendal: Genadendal Printing Works, 1966).

59. H. A. van Reede tot Drakenstein, "Journaal van zijn Verblijf aan die Kaap," *Bijdragen en Mededeelingen van het Historisch Genootschap* (*Gevestigd te Utrecht*), vol. 62, 184.

60. Petrus van der Spuy, *Dank-altaar Gode ter eer opgericht, of eene Plegtige Redenvoering ter Gelegenheid van's Ed. Comps Hondert Jaarige Possessie des Gouvernement van Cabo de Goede Hoop: In een Verklaring en*

Toepassing van Ps. CXLVII vers 12, 13 en 14, 8 April 1751 (Utrecht: Gysbert Tieme van Paddenberg en Abraham van Paddenberg, 1753), 28.

61. William J. Burchell, *Travels in the Interior of Southern Africa*, 2 vols. (London: Longman, Hurst, Rees, Orme, Brown, and Green, 1824; repr., London: Batchworth Press, 1953), vol. 2, 111.

2 / ELBOURNE & ROSS / THE CHURCHES OF EUROPEAN IMMIGRANTS / PAGES 31–50

1. On this whole process, see W. R. Ward, *The Protestant Evangelical Awakening* (Cambridge: Cambridge University Press, 1992).

2. Gillian L. Gollin, *Moravians in Two Worlds: A Study of Changing Communities* (New York: Columbia University Press, 1962), 25–50, 148–85; W. R. Ward, "The Renewed Unity of the Brethren: Ancient Church, New Sect or Interconfessional Movement?," *Bulletin of the John Rylands University Library of Manchester*, 70 (1988): 77–92, and *Protestant Evangelical Awakening*, chap. 4.

3. Elizabeth Elbourne, "'To Colonize the Mind': Evangelical Missionaries in Britain and the Eastern Cape, 1790–1837" (D.Phil. thesis: University of Oxford, 1992), 59–62; Ward, *Protestant Evangelical Awakening*, chs. 7, 8.

4. Scotland had a tradition of such revivals going back to the covenanting time of the 1640s. For an introduction to the literature on Methodism and the evangelical revival, see John Walsh, "Origins of the Evangelical Revival," in *Essays in Modern Church History*, ed. G.V. Bennett and J.D. Walsh (London: Adam and Charles Black, 1966); and D. Hempton, *Methodism and Politics in British Society: 1750–1850* (London: Hutchinson, 1984).

5. Roger H. Martin, *Evangelicals United: Evangelical Stirrings in Pre-Victorian England, 1795–1830* (Metuchen, NJ: Scarecrow Press, 1983).

6. See Deborah Valenze, *Prophetic Sons and Daughters: Female Preaching and Popular Religion in Industrial England* (Princeton: Princeton University Press, 1985), esp. 19–22.

7. See Michael Crawford, "Origins of the Eighteenth Century Evangelical Revival: England and New England Compared," *Journal of British Studies*, 26 (1987), on Ferguson's tenets.

8. Jan Boneschansker, *Het Nederlandsch Zendeling Genootschap in zijn Eerste Periode: Een Studie over Opwekking in de Bataafse en Franse Tijd* (Leeuwarden: Dijkstra, 1987), esp. 72–4.

9. Jean-François Zorn, *Le Grand Siécle d'une Mission Protestante: la Mission de Paris de 1822–1914* (Paris: Karthala et Les Bergers et Les Mages, 1993), 357–61, 554–65.

10. See Robert Hoffmann, "Die Neupietische Missionsbewegung vor dem Hintergrund des soziale Wandels um 1800," *Archiv für Kulturgeschichte*, 59 (1977): 445–70; W.O. Henderson, *The Life of Friedrich Engels*, 2 vols. (London: Cass, 1976), vol. 1, 4–5; Eduard Kriele, *Geschichte der Rheinischen Mission*, vol. 1: *Die Rheinische Mission in der Heimat* (Barmen: Verlag des Missionshauses, 1928), 39.

11. Hoffmann, "Neupietsche Missionsbewegung." See also Friedrich Engels, "Briefe aus dem Wuppertal," *Marx–Engels Gesamtausgabe* (Berlin: Dietz Verlag, 1985), vol. 1, III: 32–52 [an attack on 'hypocrisy' of Pietist mill-owners, among them his own grandfather].

12. See *Jahresbericht der Rheinische Missionsgesellschaft*, 17 (1847): 128–9.

13. *Das Tagebuch und die Briefe van Georg Schmidt, dem Ersten Missionar in Südafrika (1737–1744)*, ed. Bredekamp and Hattingh (Bellville: University of the Western Cape Press, 1981), 26, passim; Bernhard Krüger, *The Pear Tree Blossoms: A History of the Moravian Mission Stations in South Africa, 1737–1869* (Genadendal: Genadendal Printing Works, 1966), 11–46.

14. *The Genadendal Diaries: Diaries of the Herrnhut Missionaries H. Marsveld, D. Schwinn and J.C. Kühnel, Volume 1 (1792–1794)*, ed. H.C. Bredekamp and H.E.F. Plüddemann (Bellville: University of the Western Cape Institute for Historical Research, 1992), 68.

15. Russel Viljoen, "Khoisan Labour Relations in the Overberg Districts during the Latter Half of the 18th century, c. 1755–1795" (M.A. thesis: University of the Western Cape, 1993), esp. 205–16.

16. Richard Elphick and V.C. Malherbe, "The Khoisan to 1828," in *The Shaping of South African Society, 1652–1840*, ed. Elphick and Giliomee (2nd ed., Cape Town: Maskew Miller Longman, 1989), 22–8; Susan Newton-King, "The Enemy Within: The Struggle for Ascendancy on the Cape Eastern Frontier, 1760–1799" (Ph.D. thesis: University of London, 1992), 226-90; V.C. Malherbe and Susan Newton-King, *The Khoikhoi Rebellion in the Eastern Cape, 1799–1802* (Cape Town: UCT Centre for African Studies, 1981), passim.

17. Theophilus Hahn, *Tsuni-//Goam: The Supreme Being of the Khoi-khoi* (London: Trübner, 1881), 122–45; Alan Barnard, *Hunters and Herders of Southern Africa: A Comparative Study of the Khoisan Peoples* (Cambridge: Cambridge University Press, 1992), 251–63; Winifred Hoernlé, *The Social Organization of the Nama and Other Essays*, ed. Peter Carstens (Johannesburg: Witwatersrand University Press, 1985); Sigrid Schmidt, *Katalog zur Khoisan-Volksverzählungen des südlichen Afrikas*, 2 vols. (Hamburg: Helmut Buske Verlag Quellen zur Khoisan Forschung 6.1 & 6.2, 1989).

18. *Periodical Accounts Relating to the Missions of the Church of the United Brethren, Established among the Heathen*, 4 (1808): 422–3.

19. Russel Viljoen, "Revelation of a Revolution: The Prophecies of Jan Parel, alias 'Onse Liewe Heer'," *Kronos*, 21 (1994): 1–21; V.C. Malherbe, "Hermanus and His Sons: Khoi Bandits and Conspirators in the Post-

NOTES

Rebellion Period (1803–1818)," *African Studies,* 41 (1982): 192–3.

20. Robert Ross, *Cape of Torments: Slavery and Resistance in South Africa* (London: Routledge and Kegan Paul, 1982), esp. 13, 20–21; Nigel Worden, *Slavery in Dutch South Africa* (Cambridge: Cambridge University Press, 1985), esp. 41–51, 97–8.

21. Father Guy Tachard, *Voyage de Siam, des Pères Jésuites envoyés par le Roy aux Indes et à la Chine* (Paris: Arnoud Seneuz and Daniel Horthemels, 1686), cited in R. Raven-Hart, *Cape of Good Hope: The First Fifty Years of Dutch Colonisation as Seen by Callers,* 2 vols. (Cape Town: A.A. Balkema, 1970), vol. 2, 279; see also Marius F. Valkhoff, *New Light on Afrikaans and "Malayo-Portuguese"* (Louvain: Éditions Peeters, 1972), 88.

22. Repealed in 1812. See *Records of the Cape Colony,* ed. G. McC. Theal, 36 vols. (London: Swann Sonnenschein, 1895–1906), vol. 8, 500.

23. Robert Shell, "Religion, Civic Status and Slavery from Dordt to the Trek," *Kronos,* 19 (1992): 43; J.S. Marais, *The Cape Coloured People, 1652–1937* (London: Longmans, Green, 1939; repr. Johannesburg: Witwatersrand University Press, 1968), 168.

24. Viljoen, "Khoisan Labour Relations," 205–16.

25. Bredekamp and Plüddemann, *Genadendal Diaries,* passim; Krüger, *The Pear Tree Blossoms,* 47–120; Russel Viljoen, "Moravian Missionaries, Khoisan Labour and the Overberg Colonists at the End of the VOC Era, 1792–95," 49–64; Robert Ross, "The Social and Political Theology of the Western Cape Missions," both in *Missions and Christianity in South African History,* ed. Henry Bredekamp and Robert Ross (Johannesburg: Witwatersrand University Press, 1995), 101–4.

26. On Van der Kemp, see Ido H. Enklaar, *Life and Work of J. Th. van der Kemp, 1747–1811: Missionary Pioneer and Protagonist of Racial Equality in South Africa* (Cape Town: A.A. Balkema, 1988); W.M. Freund, "The Career of Johannes van der Kemp and His Role in the History of South Africa," *Tijdschrift voor Geschiedenis,* 86 (1973); A.D. Martin, *Dr. Van der Kemp* (London: Livingstone Press, n.d.); Elizabeth Elbourne, "Concerning Missionaries: The Case of Dr. Van der Kemp," *Journal of Southern African Studies,* 17 (1991).

27. Nigel Garth Penn, "The Northern Cape Frontier Zone, 1700–1815" (Ph.D. thesis: University of Cape Town, 1995), 411–12.

28. LMS-SA 1/3/C: Van der Kemp, "Journal of the Caffre Mission," 2 July–28 Sept. 1800; LMS-SA 1/3/D: Van der Kemp to LMS, 28 Dec. 1800.

29. Penn, "Northern Cape Frontier Zone," 430.

30. Martin Legassick, "The Northern Frontier to c.1840: The Rise and Decline of the Griqua People," in *The Shaping of South African Society,* ed. Elphick and Giliomee; Robert Ross, *Adam Kok's Griquas: A Study in the Development of Stratification in South Africa* (Cambridge: Cambridge University Press, 1976); John Campbell, *Travels in Southern Africa Undertaken at the Request of the Missionary Society* (London: Black, Parry, and T. Hamilton, 1815), 252–3.

31. V.C. Malherbe, "The Life and Times of Cupido Kakkerlak," *Journal of African History,* 20 (1979): 365–79; Jane Sales, *Mission Stations and Coloured Communities of the Eastern Cape, 1800–1852* (Cape Town: A.A. Balkema, 1975), 75–7; Bredekamp and Plüddemann, *Genadendal Diaries,* passim.

32. Report of the Select Committee on Aborigines, British Parliamentary Paper 535 of 1836, evidence of James Read Junior, 594.

33. John Barrow, *Travels in the Interior of Southern Africa, in the Years 1797 and 1798* (London: T. Cadell and W. Davies, 1801), 148; Bredekamp and Plüddemann, *Genadendal Diaries,* 91, 193, 239; E. Elbourne, "Early Khoisan Uses of Mission Christianity," in *Missions and Christianity in South African History,* ed. Bredekamp and Ross.

34. LMS-SA 14/2/B: George Barker to LMS, 6 Oct. 1834.

35. For evidence of Khoikhoi resentment over theft of land in the Third Frontier War and after, see V.C. Malherbe and Susan Newton-King, *The Khoikhoi Rebellion;* Barrow, *Travels,* vol. 2, 110 (citing Klaas Stuurman); for Andries Stoffels's recollections, CA A50, "Minutes of a Philipton Meeting," and miscellaneous Cape papers on Kat River settlers at Rhodes House, Oxford.

36. LMS-SA 2/2/D, Van der Kemp to LMS Directors, 1802 Annual Report; see also Enklaar, *Van der Kemp,* 110–24; Sales, *Mission Stations,* 17–20.

37. LMS-SA 2/2: Van der Kemp to LMS, Annual Report, 1801.

38. LMS-SA 2/A/2: Read to LMS, Botha's Place, 18 March 1802. The "Report of the Commission of Circuit for the Districts of Graaff-Reinet, Uitenhage and George," cited in Theal (ed.), *Records of the Cape Colony,* vol. 9, 75, still complained about extreme Khoikhoi lawlessness in 1812.

39. On pre-millenarianism and the belief in God's judgements on nations, see chapter 22, and Boyd Hilton, *The Age of Atonement: The Influence of Evangelicalism on Social and Economic Thought, 1795–1865* (Oxford: Clarendon Press, 1988).

40. Van der Kemp to Van Ryneveld, 19 July 1802, cited in Bannister, *Humane Policy,* clix-clxv.

41. LMS-SA 3/1/A: Janssens to Van der Kemp, 28 Feb. 1805 (LMS translation).

42. The document in question is printed *in extenso* in P.J. Idenburg, *The Cape of Good Hope at the Turn of the Eighteenth Century* (Leiden: Universitaire Pers, 1963), 84

404

43. "Minutes of the First Conference Held by the African Missionaries at Graaff-Reinet (1814)," ed. F.A. Steytler, *Hertzog-Annale van die Suid-Afrikaanse Akademie vir Wetenskap en Kuns*, 3 (1956): 110.

44. Elbourne, "'To Colonise the Mind'," chaps. 5 and 6; Susan Newton-King, "The Labour Market of the Cape Colony, 1807–1828," in *Economy and Society in Pre-Industrial South Africa*, ed. Shula Marks and Antony Atmore (London: Longman, 1980), 171–207; Elphick and Malherbe, "The Khoisan to 1828"; D. van Arkel, G.C. Quispel and R. Ross, "Going Beyond the Pale: On the Origins of White Supremacy in South Africa," in *Beyond the Pale: Essays on the History of Colonial South Africa*, ed. R. Ross (Hanover: University Press of New England, 1993), 90–102.

45. LMS–SA, 14/2/B: George Barker to LMS, 6 Oct. 1834.

46. Doug Stuart, "'O That We Had Wings': Race, Sexual Politics and the Missionaries" (paper presented to the Institute of Historical Research, London, 29 Oct. 1990); "The 'Wicked Christians' and the 'Children of the Mist': Missionary and Khoi Interactions at the Cape in the Early Nineteenth Century," *Collected Seminar Papers of the Institute of Commonwealth Studies, London: The Societies of Southern Africa in the Nineteenth and Twentieth Centuries*, vol. 18, 1–13.

47. On Philip, see Andrew Ross, *John Philip (1775–1851): Missions, Race and Politics in South Africa* (Aberdeen: Aberdeen University Press, 1985) and W.M. Macmillan, *The Cape Colour Question: A Historical Survey* (London: Faber and Gwyer, 1927).

48. Stanley Trapido, "From Paternalism to Liberalism: The Cape Colony, 1820–1824," *International Review of History*, 12 (1990): 73–104; J.B. Peires "The British and the Cape, 1814–1834," in *Shaping of South African Society*, ed. Elphick and Giliomee, 490–9; On the wider picture, C.A. Bayly, *Imperial Meridian: The British Empire and the World, 1780–1830* (London and New York: Longman, 1989).

49. John Philip, *Researches in South Africa*, 2 vols. (London: James Duncan, 1828); *The Kitchingman Papers: Missionary Letters and Journals 1817 to 1848 from the Brenthurst Collection, Johannesburg*, ed. Basil A. le Cordeur and Christopher C. Saunders (Johannesburg: Brenthurst Press, 1976), 68, on Philip's instructions to individual stations.

50. Elphick and Malherbe, " The Khoisan to 1828," 47–50; Peires, "The British and the Cape," 497–8; see also the Bourke papers, Rhodes House, Oxford.

51. LMS–SA 14/2/B: George Barker to LMS, 6 Oct. 1834.

52. Cited in Macmillan, *Cape Colour Question*, 216.

53. Leslie C. Duly, "A Revisit with the Cape's Hottentot Ordinance of 1828," in *Studies in Economics and Economic History*, ed. M. Kooy (London: Macmillan, 1972), 26–56.

54. Edna Bradlow, "The Khoi and the Proposed Vagrancy Legislation of 1834," *Quarterly Bulletin of the South African Library*, 39, 3 (1985): 99–103; much raw material is contained in *Report of the Select Committee on Aborigines*, British Parliamentary Papers 535 of 1836, 723–63, and 435 of 1837, 151–74.

55. *South African Commercial Advertiser*, 25 June 1834, letter from "A Hottentot."

56. MS–SA14/2/B: George Barker to LMS, 6 Oct. 1834.

57. Barnabas Shaw, *Memorials of South Africa*, 2nd ed. (London: Adams & Co., 1840), 317–20; Tillman Dedering, "Southern Namibia c.1780–c.1840: Khoikhoi Missionaries and the Advancing Frontier" (Ph.D. thesis: University of Cape Town, 1989), esp. 131–235 and "The Murder of William Threlfall: The Missionaries in Southern Namibia and the Cape Government in the 1820s," *South African Historical Journal*, 24 (1991): 90–111.

58. Cited in Brigitte Lau, *Southern and Central Namibia in Jonker Afrikaner's time* (Windhoek: Archeia, 1987), 82.

59. Elfriede Strassberger, *The Rhenish Mission Society in South Africa, 1830–1950* (Cape Town: Struik, 1969), 63–78; W. Peter Carstens, *The Social Structure of a Cape Coloured Reserve: A Study of Racial Integration and Segregation in South Africa* (Cape Town: Oxford University Press, 1966), notably 23 and chs. 8 and 9; "Opting Out of Colonial Rule: The Brown Voortrekkers of South Africa and their Constitutions," 2 parts, *African Studies*, 42 and 43 (1983–4): esp. 42: 144–50; Shaw, *Memorials*, esp. chaps. 9–13.

60. "Bastaard," their common appellation, was offensive, and "Griqua" promoted a sense of dignified self-awareness.

61. Martin Chatsfield Legassick, "The Griqua, the Sotho–Tswana and the Missionaries, 1780–1840: The Politics of a Frontier Zone" (Ph.D. thesis: UCLA, 1969); Ross, *Adam Kok's Griquas*; H.A. Parsons, "The Coinage of Griquatown," *Numismatic Calendar*, 35 (1927); *The Missionary Letters of Gottlob Schreiner, 1837–1846*, ed. Karel Schoeman (Cape Town: Human and Rousseau, 1991), chaps. 2, 3.

62. Prosper Lemue to Société des Missions Évangéliques, 23 March 1831, published in *Journal des Missions Évangéliques (JME)*, 6 (1831): 318–320.

63. Schoeman, *Schreiner*, 93.

64. Hendrick Hendricks as reported in Philip to Shaw, LMS Philip papers, 3/1/C, cited in Legassick, "The Griqua," 428.

65. Legassick, "The Griqua," chaps. 10 and 11; Ross, *Adam Kok's Griquas*, 28; Timothy Keegan, "Dispossession and Accumulation in the South African Interior: The Boers and the Tlhaping of Bethulie,

NOTES

1833–1861," *Journal of African History*, 28, 2 (1987): 191–209; Werner van der Merwe, "Die Berlynse Sendelinge van Bethanie (Oranje-Vrystaat) en die Kora, 1837–1856," *South African Historical Journal*, 17 (1985): 40–63.

66. Bisseux to Directors, PEMS, 22 Nov. 1830, *JME*, 6 (1831): 70.

67. Freund, "Van der Kemp," 380; P.S. de Jongh, "Sendingwerk in die Landdrosdistrikte Stellenbosch en Tulbagh (sinds 1822 Worcester), 1799–1830" (M.A. thesis: University of Stellenbosch, 1968), 19–24.

68. Bredekamp and Plüddemann, *Genadendal Diaries*, 264.

69. Elizabeth Elbourne, "Early Khoisan Uses of Mission Christianity," *Kronos*, 19 (1992): 12–13.

70. See letter, presumably from Ds. Arie Vos of the LMS, Tulbagh, 26 June 1824 in *Nederduitsche Zuid-Afrikaansche Tijdschrift*, 1 (1824): 234.

71. *Godsdienstverslag*, Graaff-Reinet, 8 Oct. 1838, CA NGKA R3/2.

72. P.J.J.S. Els, "Kerkplanting by die Suid-Afrikaanse Sendinggenootskap: 'n Sendingswetenskaplike Ondersoek na Gemeentevorming in die Suid-Afrikaanse Gestig" (Ph.D. thesis: University of Stellenbosch, 1971). See Robert Shell, *Children of Bondage: A Social History of the Slave Society at the Cape of Good Hope, 1652–1838* (Johannesburg: Witwatersrand University Press, 1994), 358. In 1937 the Society came under the NGK Synod.

73. A.H. Huussen Jr. and S.B.I. Veltkamp-Visser, *Dagboek en Brieven van Mewes Jan Bakker (1764–1824): Een Friese Zendeling aan de Zuidpunt van Afrika* (Amsterdam: Suid-Afrikaanse Instituut, 1991), 70.

74. *Ibid.*, 78. Dominees also owned slaves, e.g. both Borcherds and Van Lier; cf. S.B.I. Veltkamp, "Meent Borcherds: Predikant in Overgangstijd (Jengum 1762 – Stellenbosch 1832)" (Ph.D. thesis: Unisa, 1977), 258; T.N. Hanekom, *Helperus Ritzema van Lier: Die Lewensbeeld van 'n Kaapse Predikant uit die 18de Eeu* (Cape Town and Pretoria: N.G. Kerk Uitgewers, 1959), 298.

75. Ross, "Social and Political Theology."

76. Daumas to Directors, n.d., in *JME*, 11 (1836): 155.

77. For the celebration of Ordinance 50 by the Bethelsdorp Khoikhoi on the visit to Dr. Philip in 1830, see the journal of Samuel Rolland, 17 Feb. 1830, *JME*, 5 (1830): 240–50 and *South African Commercial Advertiser*, 20 Mar. 1830, and subsequent issues.

78. The Khoi claimed that the Xhosa had only recently moved into the region. LMS–SA 11/3/D: Read to Orme, 30 July 1829; CA A50, "Minutes of a meeting held at Philipton."

79. LMS–SA 23/3/A: James Read senior and junior to LMS, Kat River, 12 Nov. 1847.

80. Donovan Williams, *When Races Meet: The Life and Times of William Ritchie Thomson, Glasgow Society Missionary, Government Agent and Dutch Reformed Minister, 1794–1891* (Johannesburg: A.P.B. Publishers, 1967), 118–19.

81. See also Robert Ross, "James Cropper, John Philip and the *Researches in South Africa*,"in *Africa and Empire: W.M. Macmillan, Historian and Social Critic*, ed. Hugh Macmillan and Shula Marks (London: Temple Smith for the Institute of Commonwealth Studies, 1989), 140–52.

82. Thomas Fowell Buxton papers, Rhodes House, Oxford, vol. 13, 125–45: Priscilla Buxton to John Philip, 20 Sept. to 17 Dec. 1833; *Edinburgh Review*, 58 (Jan. 1834): 363.

83. Thomas Pringle, *Narrative of a Residence in South Africa*, 2nd ed. (London: Moxon, 1835), 279–80.

84. Sales, *Mission Stations*, 125, 132; James Read Snr., "Account of the Labour of Native Teachers Supported by Private Individuals and Churches in England in Connection with Philipton Congregation, Kat River," 1 April 1844, LMS SA 20/1/C; Christopher C. Saunders, "Madolo, a Bushman Life," *African Studies*, 36 (1977): 145–52.

85. Noël Mostert, *Frontiers: The Epic of South Africa's Creation and the Tragedy of the Xhosa People* (London: Jonathan Cape, 1992), 834–5; *Rev F.G. Kayser: Journal and Letters*, ed. Chris Hummel (Cape Town: Maskew Miller Longman for Rhodes University, Grahamstown, 1990), 164–81; Le Cordeur and Saunders, *Kitchingman Papers*, 249–50.

86. The Wesleyan agent Jacob Links, for example, was never described as anything other than an "assistant" when he was murdered with the white missionary "martyr" Threlfall in Namaqualand, even though Links was a seasoned agent and Threlfall completely inexperienced. See note 57.

87. Jan Christiaan Visagie, "Die Katriviernedersetting, 1829–1839" (Ph.D. thesis: Unisa, 1978), 55–316; Tony Kirk, "Progress and Decline in the Kat River Settlement, 1829–1854," *Journal of African History*, 14 (1973): 411–28.

88. LMS–SA 26/1/C: Read to LMS, 13 April 1851.

89. Stanley Trapido, "The Emergence of Liberalism and the Making of 'Hottentot Nationalism' 1815–1834," *The Societies of Southern Africa in the 19th and 20th Centuries*, Collected Seminar Papers of the Institute of Commonwealth Studies, vol. 17, 34–59.

90. See Uithaalder to Kok, 11 June 1851, Orange Free State Archives, HC 1/1/3, also printed in *Further Correspondence Relative to the State of the Kaffir Tribes*, British Parliamentary Paper 1428 of 1852, 152; Uithaalder and others to Cathcart, 17 Jan. 1855, in *Translation of a Communication Received by the Governor from Certain Rebel Hottentots Now Without the Colony, Addressed Jointly to the Governor and to the*

Parliament, Cape Parliamentary Paper, C6, 1855; Mostert, *Frontiers*, 1151–2.

91. Mostert, *Frontiers*, 1152, 1158.

92. *The Trial of Andries Botha* (Cape Town: Saul Solomon, 1852).

93. Mostert, *Frontiers*, 1146.

94. Both phrases come from a sermon given in Wellington on the eve of emancipation by the Rev. Isaac Bisseux; see Bisseux to Directors, 23 Dec. 1834 in *JME*, 10 (1835): 113–14.

95. John Nicholas Carel Marincowitz, "Rural Production and Labour in the Western Cape, 1838 to 1888, with Special Reference to the Wheat Growing Districts," (Ph.D. thesis: University of London, 1985); Krüger, *The Pear Tree Blossoms*, 196; Hallbeck to Bell, 8 April 1839, in CA CO 485.

96. Pamela F. Scully, "Liberating the Family? Gender, Labor and Sexuality in the Rural Western Cape, South Africa, 1823–1853" (Ph.D. thesis: University of Michigan, 1993), esp. 71–4, 191, 222–34, 351–8, shows that at Genadendal very few mothers of small children worked, whereas at Synthal (Tulbagh) 53 of 59 women did mainly day work. According to the Cape of Good Hope, Legislative Council, *Master and Servant: Addenda to the Documents on the Working of the Order in Council of the 21st July 1846* (Cape Town: Saul Solomon, 1849), nearly all children over 12 worked without apparently being tied by apprenticeship.

97. V.C. Malherbe, "Indentured and Unfree Labour in South Africa: Towards an Understanding," *South African Historical Journal*, 24 (1991): 90–111; D. van Arkel, G.C. Quispel and R.J. Ross, "Going Beyond the Pale," 94–102.

98. For descriptions of slave vulnerability to masters' sexual demands, see e.g. Patricia van der Spuy, "Slave Women and Family Formation in Nineteenth Century Cape Town" (unpublished paper, University of Cape Town, 1993), 129–32.

99. Elizabeth Helen Ludlow, "Missions and Emancipation in the South Western Cape: A Case Study of Groenkloof (Mamre), 1838–1852" (M.A. thesis: University of Cape Town, 1992), 182–5.

100. This calculation is made from figures from *Master and Servant: Addenda* and the *Cape of Good Hope Statistical Blue Book for 1849* (Cape Town: Saul Solomon, 1849); for this purpose the rural Western Cape has been reckoned to be the western division of the colony (east to and including George), minus Cape Town and the districts of Clanwilliam and Beaufort West, since figures for the Namaqualand stations were not available.

101. Robert Ross, "Emancipation and the Economy of the Cape Colony," *Slavery and Emancipation*, 14, 1 (1993): 131–48; Ludlow, "Missions and Emancipation," 206; Marincowitz, "Rural Production and Labour," 178–9.

102. G.C. Cuthbertson, "The Impact of the Emancipation of Slaves on St Andrew's Scottish Church, Cape Town, 1838–1878," *Studies in the History of Cape Town*, 3 (1980): 49–63.

103. Elizabeth Helen Ludlow. "The Work of the London Missionary Society in Cape Town, 1812–1841" (B.A. Hons. thesis: University of Cape Town, 1981), 44f.

104. *Godsdienstverslagen*, CA NGK archives R1/2.

105. *Jahresbericht der Rheinische Missionsgesellschaft*, 12 (1840–1): 12–14.

106. Krüger, *The Pear Tree Blossoms*, 185.

107. Letter from Schwester Henriette Külpmann, 19 June 1844, *Das Missionsblatt, herausgegeben von der Missions-Gesellschaft zu Barmen*, 19, 23 (1844).

108. Ross, "Emancipations and the Economy", 145; Vivian Bickford-Smith, "Meanings of Freedom: Social Position and Identity among Ex-slaves and Their Descendants in Cape Town, 1875–1910," in *Breaking the Chains*, ed Worden and Crais, 289–312.

109. Edna Bradlow, "The 'Great Fear' at the Cape of Good Hope, 1851–2," *International Journal of African Historical Studies*, 22, 3 (1989), 401–21; John Marincowitz, "From 'Colour Question' to 'Agrarian Problem' at the Cape: Reflections on the Interim," in *Africa and Empire*, ed. Macmillan and Marks, 157–60; see E. Helen Ludlow, "Groenkloof after the Emancipation of Slaves (1838–1852): Leavers, Soldiers and Rebels," in *Missions and Christianity*, ed. Bredekamp and Ross.

110. William Ellis, *Three Visits to Madagascar during the Years 1853, 1854, 1856 ...* (London: John Murray, 1858), 244.

111. Stanley Trapido, "White Conflict and Non-White Participation in the Politics of the Cape of Good Hope, 1853–1910" (Ph.D. thesis: University of London, 1970), 384–5; Krüger, *The Pear Tree Blossoms*, 256–7.

112. Vivian Bickford-Smith, "Keeping Your Own Council': The Struggle between Householders and Merchants for Control of the Cape Town Municipal Council in the Last Two Decades of the Nineteenth Century," *Studies in the History of Cape Town*, 5 (1984), 200–1.

113. Trapido, "White Conflict and Non-White Participation," chap. 10; Bill Nasson, *Abraham Esau's War: A Black South African War in the Cape 1899–1902* (Cambridge: Cambridge University Press; Cape Town: David Philip, 1991), especially chaps. 4 and 7.

114. Cuthbertson, "Impact"; I.J. van der Walt, "Eiesoortige Kerkvorming as Missiologiese Probleem met Besondere Verwysing na Suid-Afrika" (thesis for the Doctorate of Theology: Potchefstroom University of Christian Higher Education, 1960), 477; Els, "Kerkplanting," 163ff.

115. Strassberger, "Rhenish Mission Society," 28–9; *Jahresberichte der Rheinische Missionsgesellschaft*, 18

(1847): 82.

116. Ludlow, "The LMS in Cape Town," 60ff; on Grahamstown, there is a mass of correspondence in the LMS archives, notably the whole of file LMS–SA 19/3/A.

117. But see James Read Sr., "Account of the Labour of Native Teachers Supported by Private Individuals and Churches in England in Connection with Philipton Congregation, Kat River," 1 April 1844, LMS SA 20/1/C [reference to a 'native' teacher at Kat River accused of 'brain fever' for rejecting orthodox doctrines].

118. Richard Lovett, *The History of the London Missionary Society, 1795–1895*, 2 vols. (London: H. Frowde, 1899), vol. 1., 575–9; the quotations are from a letter by Robert Moffat and David Livingstone cited on page 574; Ellis, *Three Visits to Madagascar*, 241–3; A. Appel, "Bethelsdorp: Van Politieke Simbool tot Alledaagse Werklikheid," *South African Historical Journal*, 18 (1986): 166–8; Marincowitz, "Rural Production and Labor," 180–7; Ross, *Adam Kok's Griquas*, 78.

119. Bechler v. Van Riet, cited in *Cases decided in the Supreme Court of the Cape of Good Hope*, ed. M.W. Searle, vol. 5 (Cape Town: Juta, 1902), 203–8.

120. Bernhard Krüger and P.W. Schaberg, *The Pear Tree Bears Fruit: The History of the Moravian Church in South Africa–West (II) 1869–1960, with an Epilogue 1960–1980* (Genadendal: Moravian Book Depot, 1984), 18–19; Kerry Ward, "The Road to Mamre: Migration and Community in Countryside and City in the Early Twentieth Century," *South African Historical Journal*, 27 (1992): 198–224.

121. William Eric Brown, *The Catholic Church in South Africa: From Its Origins to the Present Day* (London: Burns and Oates, 1960); *The Cape Diary of Bishop Patrick Raymond Griffith for the Years 1837 to 1839*, ed. J.B. Brain (Mariannhill: for the Southern African Catholic Bishops' Conference, 1988). On the Methodists, see letter by William Shaw to Bell, 2 April 1839, CA CO 485.

122. Chris Loff, "The History of a Heresy," in *Apartheid is a heresy*, ed. John W. de Gruchy and Charles Villa-Vicencio (Cape Town: David Philip; Grand Rapids: Eerdmans, 1983), 10–23.

123. See Ross, "Social and Political Theology" [Hallbeck's 1836 letter on the occasion of the centenary of Genadendal]; Terence Ranger, "The Local and the Global in Southern African Religious History," in *Conversion to Christianity: Historical and Anthropological Perspectives on a Great Transformation*, ed. Robert W. Hefner (Berkeley: University of California Press, 1993) 65–98.

124. A. Ross, *John Philip*, esp. 52–116.

125. See J.S. Marais, *The Cape Coloured People*, 33–5.

126. On squares and straight lines, Peter Anderson, "No-Man's Land: Landscaping Neutrality on the Cape Frontier" (unpublished paper presented at African Research seminar, Oxford University, 11 June 1991).

127. LMS–SA 8/1/B: Read to Mrs Hamilton, 6 April 1819, enclosed in Mrs. Hamilton to LMS, 20 April 1819.

128. LMS–SA 18/4/B: C. Sass to LMS, Theopolis, 15 Sept. 1842. On clientage at Kat River: see Kirk, "Kat River Settlement," 416–19.

129. See for example the arguments (in different polemical contexts) of William Foster of Bethelsdorp in 1828 and of George Barker of Paarl in 1842: LMS–SA 18/2/B: Barker to LMS, Paarl, 8 Feb. 1842; LMS–SA 10/C/1: William Foster to George Burder, Bethelsdorp, 17 June 1826.

130. Hahn, *Tsuni-//Goam*, 118.

131. LMS–SA 18/1/C, W. Elliot to LMS, 3 June 1841. For the debate about respectability in relation to social control and the meaning of evangelical religious movements in a developing capitalist society, see E.P. Thompson, *The Making of the English Working Classes* (London: Victor Gollancz, 1963); F.M.L. Thompson, *The Rise of Respectable Society* (London: Fontana, 1988); T. Laqueur, *Religion and Respectability: Sunday Schools and Working Class Culture, 1780–1850* (New Haven and London: Yale University Press, 1976); Bernard Semmel, *The Methodist Revolution* (London: Heinemann, 1974).

132. Barnard, *Hunters and Herders*, 192, Winifred Hoernlé, *The Social Organisation of the Nama and Other Essays*, ed. Peter Carstens (Johannesburg: Witwatersrand University Press, 1985), 57–89; John Edwin Mason, "Hendrik Albertus and his Ex-slave Mey: A Drama in Three Acts," *Journal of African History*, 31 (1990): 423–45.

133. E.g. Frans Mager's speech reported in "Adjourned Public Meeting at Philipton, Kat River, Resumed August 12th," *South African Commercial Advertiser*, 6 September 1834.

134. Scully, "Liberating the Family?", chap. 8. In their defence, missionaries stated that they would not have expelled a woman who showed proper remorse.

135. William Philip to John Philip, 25 May 1843, CA VC 1415; Gary Baines, "The Origins of Urban Segregation: Local Government and the Residence of Africans in Port Elizabeth, c.1835–1865," *South African Historical Journal*, 22 (1990): 74–6.

136. LMS–SA 18/4/A, W. Elliot to LMS, 12 August 1842.

137. *South African Commercial Advertiser*, 21 Nov. 1838.

138. Missionaries were much firmer on the use of those narcotics which did not form part of their own culture, notably dagga (*Cannabis sativa*). See e.g. *Bericht der Rheinischen Missionsgesellschaft*, 2 (1831): 29.

139. Brian Harrison, *Drink and the Victorians: The Temperance Question in England, 1815–1872* (London: Faber and Faber, 1972), 64–127.

140. See note 34.

141. *South African Commercial Advertiser*, 6 Sept. 1834. See also Andries Stoffels's outspoken comments at the second anniversary meeting of the Kat River Temperance Society, in the *Graham's Town Journal*, 10 April 1834.

142. LMS–SA 18/5/C: Read Snr. to LMS, Annual Report of the Kat River Mission.

143. Pamela Scully, "Liquor and Labor in the Western Cape, 1870–1900," in *Liquor and Labor in Southern Africa*, ed. Jonathan Crush and Charles Ambler (Athens and Pietermaritzburg: Ohio and Natal University Presses, 1992), 56–77.

144. LMS–SA 18/1/C; James Read Snr. to LMS, Philipton, 26 May 1841.

145. Scully, "Liberating the Family?," chap. 6, esp. 299.

146. See James Read Sr., "Account of the Labour of Native Teachers Supported by Private Individuals and Churches in England in Connection with Philipton Congregation, Kat River," 1 April 1844, LMS SA 20/1/C.

3 / DAVENPORT / THE CHURCHES OF EUROPEAN IMMIGRANTS / PAGES 51–67

1. See Rodney Davenport "The Consolidation of a New Society: The Cape Colony," in *Oxford History of South Africa*, vol. 1 (Oxford: Clarendon, 1969), 275.

2. Andries Dreyer, *Bouwstoffe vir die Geskiedenis van die Nederduits-Gereformeerde Kerke in Suid-Afrika*, vol. 3 (Amsterdam: Dusseau, 1936), 8–23.

3. Considerations of cost and convenience led to the stabilization of synods on a quinquennial basis from 1829, and this necessitated the grant of enlarged provisional powers to the Ring assemblies. See Adriaan Moorrees, *Die Nederduitse Gereformeerde Kerk in Suid-Afrika, 1652–1873* (Cape Town: SA Bybelvereniging, 1937), 553, 577–9.

4. Moorrees, *Die Nederduitse Gereformeerde Kerk*, 622–5.

5. Tobias N. Hanekom, *Die Liberale Rigting in Suid-Afrika: 'n Kerkhistoriese Studie* (Cape Town: HAUM, 1951), 309.

6. William E. Brown, *The Catholic Church in South Africa* (London: Burns and Oates, 1960), 6–9; Barnabas Shaw, *Memorials of South Africa* (Cape Town: Struik, 1970 facsimile of 1820 original), 51, 91–2, 145–6.

7. Margaret Donaldson in *A History of Christianity in South Africa*, ed. Johannes W. Hofmeyr and Gerald J. Pillay (Cape Town: HAUM, 1994), 81–8.

8. See *The Unity of Christendom: A Correspondence Relating to Proposals for Union between the English and Dutch Reformed Churches in South Africa* (Cape Town, 1871), and Johannes du Plessis, *The Life of Andrew Murray of South Africa* (London, Edinburgh and New York: Marshall Bros., 1919), 254–9. For the expansion of Anglican dioceses, see the chronological list given in Osmond Victor, *The Salient of South Africa* (London: SPG, 1931), 114, and Peter Hinchliff, *The Anglican Church in South Africa* (London: Darton, Longman and Todd, 1963), passim.

9. For the activities of the LMS, see chapters 2 and 4 of this volume.

10. Andrew Ross, *John Philip (1775–1851)* (Aberdeen: Aberdeen University Press, 1986), chap. 4.

11. D. Roy Briggs and Joseph Wing, *The Harvest and the Hope: The Story of Congregationalism in Southern Africa* (Johannesburg: United Congregational Church of Southern Africa, 1970), 102–5; Norman Etherington, *Preachers, Peasants and Politics in South-East Africa, 1835–1880* (London: Royal Historical Society, 1976), 24–5.

12. Briggs and Wing, *The Harvest and the Hope*, 110–21.

13. Frank Quinn and Gregory Cuthbertson, *Presbyterianism in Cape Town: A History of St. Andrew's Church, 1829–1979* (Cape Town, privately printed, 1979), 3–5, 15–20; *Dictionary of South African Biography* (Cape Town: Nasionale Boekhandel, 1968–), vol. 1, 5–7 [Adamson]; vol. 3, 632 [Morgan] and 754–5 [Stegmann].

14. Edwin Pons, *The Southern and Central Streams of Presbyterianism in Africa* (Kitwe, privately printed, 1982).

15. William Shaw, *The Story of My Mission in South-Eastern Africa* (London: Hamilton and Adams, 1860); David Hammond-Tooke, *The Journal of William Shaw* (Cape Town: Maskew Miller Longman, 1988); Celia Sadler, *Never a Young Man: Extracts from the Letters and Journals of the Rev. William Shaw* (Cape Town: HAUM, 1967); *Dictionary of South African Biography*, vol. 1 (1968): 711–14 [Shaw].

16. Sidney Hudson-Reed, *By Taking Heed: The History of Baptists in Southern Africa, 1820–1977* (Roodepoort: Baptist Publishing House, 1983). The trend towards ethnic separation, initially noticeable with the German Baptists, also became characteristic of other Continental Lutheran colonial churches.

17. According to S.P. Engelbrecht, *Geskiedenis van die Nederduitsch Hervormde Kerk van Afrika*, 3rd ed. (Cape Town: HAUM, 1953), 7, this name implies "that the religion (*religie*) of the Church is reformed (*gereformeer*), and that its form of service (*godsdiens*) is restored (*hervorm*) and purged of false Roman doctrines."

18. Engelbrecht, *Nederduitsch Hervormde Kerk*, 15.

19. Du Plessis, *Andrew Murray*, 57–67.

20. Engelbrecht, *Nederduitsch Hervormde Kerk*, 12–13, 16. For the dispute over non-biblical psalms in the Cape church, see Spoelstra, *Die "Doppers" in Suid-Afrika, 1760–1899* (Johannesburg: Nasionale Boekhandel,

NOTES

1963), 46, 50, 63–6.

21. An idealized picture is given by Spoelstra at pp. 16–32. His depiction of their religious roots is qualified by Johan Gerstner, *The Thousand Generation Covenant: Dutch Reformed Covenant Theology and Group Identity in Colonial South Africa, 1652–1814* (Leiden and New York: E.J. Brill, 1991), chap. 6, esp. 111–14, 159–71.

22. *Dictionary of South African Biography*, vol. 3 (1977): 488–90 [Kuyper, A.]; Abraham Kuyper, *Calvinism* (1898, repr., Grand Rapids: Eerdmans, 1931); Johannes A.S. Oberholster, *Die Gereformeerde Kerke onder die Kruis in Suid-Afrika: Hul Ontstaan en Ontwikkeling* (Cape Town: HAUM, 1956).

23. Notably the repeal of the Test and Corporation Acts in 1828, and the Catholic Emancipation Act of 1829, the foundation of London University without a religious test in 1837, and the admission of dissenters to Oxford and Cambridge degrees in 1851 and to fellowships in 1871. The Methodist Church became an independent denomination in 1795, and the Catholics were granted the right to set up their own dioceses in 1851.

24. Stephen H. Toulmin and June Goodfield, *The Discovery of Time* (London: Pelican, 1965), chaps. 7–9.

25. The example of Kuenen is chosen because he seems to have been closely read by leaders of the new liberalism in both the Dutch and English communities at the Cape, notably by Thomas François Burgers and John William Colenso. See S.P. Engelbrecht, *Thomas François Burgers* (Pretoria: J.H. de Bussy, 1946), 12–13, 28; Jeff Guy, *The Heretic* (Johannesburg: Ravan Press; and Pietermaritzburg: University of Natal Press, 1983), 108, 119, 150, 175. Kuenen's Hibbert Lectures in 1882, entitled *Natural Religions and Universal Religions*, was an early exercise in comparative religion which attempted to distinguish "particular" religions from "universal."

26. Hanekom, *Liberale Rigting*, 293–6, 433–40; Du Plessis, *Andrew Murray*, 174–5.

27. Engelbrecht, *Geskiedenis* (Pretoria: HAUM, 1946), 6–14.

28. In 1859–1900 the Stellenbosch Seminary trained 240 theological students, as against the 25 who went overseas for training (Hanekom, *Liberale Rigting*, 280). Andrew Murray was a strong supporter of the changes (Du Plessis, *Andrew Murray*, 174–55).

29. Engelbrecht, *Burgers*, 35–6.

30. Peter Hinchliff, *Anglican Church*, 82–3.

31. Guy, *The Heretic*, chap. 9; Owen Chadwick, *The Victorian Church*, 3rd ed. (London: A. and C. Black, 1971), vol. 2, 90–7.

32. Kathleen Boner, "Dr F.C. Kolbe: Priest, Patriot and Educationist" (D.Litt. et Phil. thesis: Unisa, 1980), 50–6, 80–4.

33. Emlyn C.S. Wade and George G. Phillips, *Constitutional Law*, 5th ed. (London: Longmans Green, 1955), 480–1.

34. On Gorham's case see Chadwick, *Victorian Church*, vol. 1, 259–61.

35. *Ibid.*, vol. 2, 309–24.

36. The Eton College case, 1852. See Hinchliff, *Anglican Church*, 88, 98, 124–5.

37. *Dictionary of South African Biography*, vol. 3 (1977): 373–4, [Kotze J.J.].

38. William E.G. Solomon, *Saul Solomon: The Member for Cape Town* (Cape Town: Oxford University Press, 1948) chaps. 4 and 15; Leslie McCracken, *New Light at the Cape of Good Hope: William Porter, the Father of Cape Liberalism* (Belfast: Ulster Historical Foundation, 1993), 126–7.

39. For a discussion of the difficulties experienced by the London Missionary Society in adhering to the voluntary principle, see Margaret Donaldson, "The Voluntary Principle in the Colonial Situation: Theory and Practice," in *Voluntary Religion*, ed. W.J. Shiels and Diana Wood (Oxford: Blackwell, for the Ecclesiastical Historical Society, 1986), 381–90; and Briggs and Wing, *The Harvest and the Hope*, 110–21.

40. See Walter Mears, "Government Contributions to the Salaries of Clergymen at the Cape, 1806–1875" (unpublished pamphlet in personal possession, n.d.), 18–19. Figures based on the *Cape of Good Hope Blue Book, Ecclesiastical Return* (1874), 1–63.

41. Hanekom, *Liberale Rigting*, 316–41; Jan Hofmeyr, *Life of J.H. Hofmeyr (Onze Jan)* (Cape Town: Van de Sandt de Villiers, 1913), 66.

42. Hinchliff, *Anglican Church*, 106–17.

43. The first Lambeth Conference had helped in the process by agreeing in 1867 that Anglican communities throughout the world, constituted as separate provinces adhering to the faith and doctrine of the Church of England, could govern themselves as independent units – but with no central authority owing to the exceptional status of the Church of England as an established church under the Crown.

44. A resurgence of the jurisdictional dispute took place during the early twentieth century, and led to the formal establishment – or re-establishment, according to the point of view – of the Church of England in South Africa. See Hinchliff, *Anglican Church*, 221–5; Anthony Ive, *The Church of England in South Africa: A Study of Its History, Principles and Status* (Cape Town: Church of England Information Office, 1966).

45. This followed from the Eton College case. See Hinchliff, *Anglican Church*, 124–5. For the later split between the Church of the Province and the Church of England in South Africa in the twentieth century, see Ive, *Church of England in South Africa*, and Hinchliff, *Anglican Church*, 221–5.

46. Du Plessis, *Andrew Murray*, 233–5.

47. For the Trek and trekker churches, see chap. 7 of this volume and Engelbrecht, *Nederduitsch Hervormde*

Kerk, passim.

48. Hanekom, *Liberale Rigting*, 411–12.

49. See André du Toit, "'The Cape Afrikaners' Failed Liberal Experiment," in *Democratic Liberalism in South Africa: Its History and Prospect*, ed. Jeffrey Butler, Richard Elphick and David Welsh (Middletown, Connecticut: Wesleyan University Press; Cape Town: David Philip, 1987), 51–7; Hanekom, *Liberale Rigting*, 341–74.

50. See Rodney Davenport, *The Afrikaner Bond: The History of a Cape Political Party, 1880–1911* (Cape Town: Oxford University Press, 1966).

51. Davenport, *Afrikaner Bond*, 51–3, 173; J.D. du Toit ("Totius"), *S.J. du Toit in Weg en Werk* (Paarl: Drukkerij, 1917), 369–73; Oberholster, *Gereformeerde Kerke onder die Kruis* 225–46.

52. See Dunbar Moodie, *The Rise of Afrikanerdom: Power, Apartheid, and the Afrikaner Civil Religion* (Berkeley: University of California Press, 1975), 68–72.

53. The Genootskap van Regte Afrikaners in Paarl pressed for Afrikaans, while J.H. Hofmeyr in Cape Town argued in favour of simplified Hollands. See Davenport, *Afrikaner Bond*, 29–34, 75–80.

54. Eduard C. Pienaar, *Die Triomf van Afrikaans* (Cape Town: Nasionale Pers, 1946), 244–67; Jan Hofmeyr, "Is 't Ons Ernst?" and Gustav Preller, "Laat 't Toch Ons Ernst Wezen," in *Hertzog-Annale*, 1, 2 (Oct. 1952): 14–50. Preller reputedly took short-hand notes while listening to the language of sermons.

55. Ernest Malherbe, *History of Education in South Africa* (Cape Town: Juta, 1925), vol. 1, 50–1, 60–1.

56. Rodney Davenport in the *Oxford History of South Africa*, vol. 1 (1969): 284, citing the Report on the State and Progress of the Government Schools of 1824.

57. Malherbe, *Education*, 109–19.

58. Davenport, *Afrikaner Bond*, 29–32; Ian Hexham, "Religious Conviction or Political Tool? The Problem of Christian National Education," *Journal of Theology for Southern Africa*, 26 (1979): 13–23.

59. Davenport, Afrikaner Bond, 31–4, 266–9. See also chap. 8 in this volume.

60. Augustus Wirgman, *History of the English Church and People in South Africa* (London: Longman Green, 1895), 111.

61. Shaw, quoted in Seton, "Wesleyan Missionaries and the Sixth Frontier War, 1834–5" (Ph.D. thesis, University of Cape Town, 1962), 396.

62. Patrick Harries, *Work, Culture and Identity: Migrant Labourers in Mozambique and South Africa, c.1860–1910* (London: Heinemann, 1993), 61–2, 76–9, 213–20; Hinchliff, *Anglican Church*, 157–8; see also chap. 18 in this volume..

63. Ross, *Philip*, 81; Anthony Dachs, "Missionary Imperialism: The Case of Bechuanaland," *Journal of African History*, 13 (1972): 647–58; Jean and John Comaroff, *Of Revelation and Revolution: Christianity, Colonialism and Consciousness in Southern Africa* (Chicago: Chicago University Press, 1991), vol. 1, 252–308.

64. Philip Mason, *The Birth of a Dilemma* (London: Oxford University Press, 1958) 120–2; Arthur Keppel Jones, *Rhodes and Southern Rhodesia* (Pietermaritzburg: University of Natal Press, 1983), 41–5.

65. Margaret Blunden, "The Anglican Church during the War," in *The South African War*, ed. Peter Warwick (Harlow: Longman, 1980), 279–91.

66. Blunden, "Anglican Church," 284–6; Arthur Davey, *The British Pro-Boers 1877–1902* (Cape Town: Tafelberg, 1978), 146–9.

67. Greg Cuthbertson, "Missionary Imperialism and Colonial Warfare: LMS Attitudes to the South African War, 1899–1902," *South African Historical Journal*, 19 (1987): 93–114.

68. Davey, *British Pro-Boers*, 151–2.

69. Ibid., 149–51; Greg Cuthbertson, "The Rev. H.J. Batts and the South African Baptist Movement" (Centenary address to the SA Baptist Historical Society, unpublished, 1977), 14.

70. Davey, *British Pro-Boers*, 153–6; Hope H. Hewison, *Hedge of Wild Almonds* (London: Currey, 1989).

71. *Lawrence Richardson: Selected Correspondence, 1902–1903*, ed. Arthur Davey (Cape Town: Van Riebeeck Society, 1977).

72. *Report of the Native Laws Commission* G.4–1883 (Cape Colony), Analysis and Index at pp. 535–59 for handling of specific themes in the minutes of evidence. Note especially references to polygamy and "bride-price" (*lobola*).

73. J.R. Cochrane, *Servants of Power: The Role of the English-speaking Churches, 1903–1930: Towards a Critical Theology via an Historical Analysis of the Anglican and Methodist Churches* (Johannesburg: Ravan, 1987), 73–92; M. Nuttall, *The Making of a Tradition, 1870–1970* (Johannesburg: CPSA/SPCK, 1970), 3–4.

74. Olive Schreiner, "Closer Union" (a letter to the *Transvaal Leader*, 22 December 1908), discussed in Rodney Davenport, "Olive Schreiner and South African Politics," in *Olive Schreiner and After: Essays on Southern African Literature in Honour of Guy Butler*, ed. M. van W. Smith and D. Maclennan (Cape Town: David Philip, 1983), 105–7.

75. *The Shaping of South African Society, 1652–1840*, Richard Elphick and Hermann Giliomee (eds.), 2nd ed. (Cape Town: Maskew Miller Longman, 1989), 109–83.

76. The evidence of John Philip and his associates before the Select Committee on Aborigines, which reported in London in 1837, was noteworthy.

NOTES

77. Seton, *Wesleyan Missionaries*, 209–10 [Shrewsbury], 393–6 [Shaw], 223–5, 387–92 [Boyce].

78. William Shaw, *Defence of the Wesleyan Missionaries in Southern Africa* (London: privately published, 1839).

79. Wirgman, *English Church*, 81; *The Cape Journals of Archdeacon N.J. Merriman, 1849–1855*, ed. Douglas Varley and H.M. Matthew (Cape Town: Van Riebeeck Society, 1957), 32, 49–50, 155. Merriman acquired a new sensitivity, undermined nevertheless by doubt, as experience of the frontier worked its way into his outlook.

80. *The Journal of John Ayliff 1821–1830*, ed. Peter Hinchliff (Cape Town: A.A. Balkema, 1971), 76; Barnabas Shaw, *Memorials*, 149, 166–7.

81. Bengt Sundkler, *Bantu Prophets in South Africa,* 2nd ed. (London: Oxford University Press, 1961) 38–42; Christopher Saunders, "Nehemiah Tile and the Thembu Church," *Journal of African History,* 11 (1970): 553–70; personal communication from Professor Calvin Cook on origins of the Bantu (later Reformed) Presbyterian Church. See also Janet Hodgson's discussion in chap. 4, pp. 26–35.

82. Sundkler, *Bantu Prophets,* 41; Hinchliff, *Anglican Church,* 200–5.

83. Hudson-Reed, *By Taking Heed,* 213–16. The position in other Baptist churches, however, is not clear.

84. For example Hinrich Lichtenstein, *Travels in Southern Africa in the Years 1803–1806,* ed. Ernest E Mossop (Cape Town: Van Riebeeck Society, 1928–30), vol. 2, 87–8, 443–7; George Thompson, *Travels and Adventures in Southern Africa*, ed. Vernon Forbes, 2 vols. (Cape Town: Van Riebeeck Society, 1967–8) vol. 2, 98. For doubts cast concerning homestead worship see Elphick and Giliomee, *Shaping of South African Society*, 185–91, and Gerstner, *Thousand Generation Covenant*, 169, 212–14.

85. Chris Loff, "The History of a Heresy" in *Apartheid Is a Heresy*, ed. John de Gruchy and Charles Villa-Vicencio (Cape Town: David Philip, 1983), 10–23; Susan R. Ritner, 'The Dutch Reformed Church and Apartheid," *Journal of Contemporary History*, 2 (1967): 17–37.

86. Gerstner, *Thousand Generation Covenant*, 3.

87. Quinn and Cuthbertson, *Presbyterianism in Cape Town*, 15–20.

88. Pons, *The Southern and Central Streams*, 5–6.

89. David Burchell, "The Origins of the Bantu Presbyterian Church of South Africa" (unpublished paper), and private information supplied by Professor Calvin Cook.

4 / HODGSON / CHRISTIAN BEGINNINGS AMONG THE XHOSA / PAGES 68–88

1. Jean and John Comaroff, *Of Revelation and Revolution: Christianity, Colonialism and Consciousness in South Africa*, vol. 1 (Chicago: University of Chicago Press, 1991), 250.

2. Richard Elphick, "Africans and the Christian Campaign in Southern Africa," *The Frontier in History: North America and Southern Africa Compared*, ed. H. Lamar and L. Thompson (New Haven and London: Yale University Press, 1981).

3. Janet Hodgson, *The God of the Xhosa* (Cape Town: Oxford University Press, 1982), 6–7.

4. J.B. Peires, *The House of Phalo* (Johannesburg: Ravan, 1981), chaps. 2–4.

5. Hodgson, *God of the Xhosa*, chap. 5.

6. Clifton Crais, *White Supremacy and Black Resistance in Pre-industrial South Africa* (Cambridge: Cambridge University Press, 1992), chap. 2; Peires, *House of Phalo*, 53–8.

7. Ngqika regularly visited Van der Kemp and was even taught the alphabet; J.T. van der Kemp, *Transactions of the Missionary Society*, vol. 1 (London: Bye and Law, 1795–1802), 416; Janet Hodgson, "Do We Hear You Nyengana? Dr J.T. Vanderkemp and the First Mission to the Xhosa," *Religion in Southern Africa*, 5, 1 (Jan. 1984): 3–5; Ido Enklaar, *Life and Work of Dr. J.T. van der Kemp 1747–1811* (Cape Town: A.A. Balkema, 1988), 85.

8. Van der Kemp, *Transactions,* vol. 1, 421–2.

9. *Ibid.,* 428.

10. His "Specimen of the Caffra Language" comprised about 800 words: see "Woordenlijst," in *Ibid.,* 442–58.

11. *Ibid.,* 397–8, 416, 432–4, 439–41.

12. H. Callaway, *The Religious System of the Amazulu* (London: Springvale Mission Press, 1870), 67–8.

13. Over the years the Xhosa patronized rainmakers from all the different groups with which they came into contact: Khoikhoi, San and Mfengu.

14. Van der Kemp, *Transactions,* vol. 1, 410–11, 416, 426–9; H.A. Reyburn, "The Missionary as Rainmaker," *The Critic,* 1, 8 (1933): 146–53.

15. Janet Hodgson, "A Study of the Xhosa Prophet Nxele," parts 1 and 2, *Religion in Southern Africa*, 6, 2 (1985): 11–36, and 7, 1 (1986): 2–23; Peires, *House of Phalo*, 69–71; Ezra Tisani, "Nxele and Ntsikana: A Critical Study of the Religious Outlooks of Two 19th century Xhosa Prophets and Their Consequences for Xhosa Christian Practice in the Easten Cape" (M.A. thesis: University of Cape Town, 1987).

16. Report of James Reid, 31 May 1816, *Transactions*, vol. 4 (London: Bye and Law, 1813–18), 278–93. Peires notes that Nxele's messianic claims should be understood in the classificatory rather than the literal sense of extended family relationships (Peires, *House of Phalo*, 57).

17. Isaac Wauchope, *The Natives and Their Missionaries* (Lovedale: Lovedale Press, 1908), 34.

18. According to the Cape Nguni myth of origin, in the beginning human beings were thought to have emerged with their stock from a cave, hole in the ground, or reed bed. Hodgson, *God of the Xhosa*, 18–23.

19. A. Kropf, *A Kaffir–English Dictionary*, ed. R. Godfrey, 2nd ed. (Lovedale: Lovedale Press, 1915), 499; Wauchope, *Natives*, 34.

20. W.K. Kaye as quoted in J.B. Peires, "The Central Beliefs of the Xhosa Cattle-Killing," *Journal of African History*, 28 (1987): 58.

21. Hodgson, "Xhosa Prophet Nxele," parts 1 and 2; Peires, *House of Phalo*, 134–6.

22. T. Pringle, *Narrative of a Residence in South Africa* (London: Moxon, 1835), 281.

23. Peires, *House of Phalo*, 58–63, 73–4; Noël Mostert, *Frontiers* (London: Jonathan Cape, 1992), chaps. 11–14.

24. Janet Hodgson, "The Genius of Ntsikana: Traditional Images and the Process of Change in Early Xhosa Literature," in *Literature and Society in Southern Africa*, ed. T. Couzens and L. White (Cape Town: Maskew Miller Longman, 1985), 24–40; and "The Symbolic Entry Point: Removing the Veil of Structure from the Study of Religious Movements," in *Religion Alive*, ed. G.C. Oosthuizen (Johannesburg: Hodder and Stoughton, 1986), 48–51.

25. Janet Hodgson, *Ntsikana's Great Hymn: A Xhosa Expression of Christianity in the 19th Century Eastern Cape* (University of Cape Town: Centre for African Studies, 1980), 27–67.

26. David Dargie, *Xhosa Music* (Cape Town: David Philip, 1988), 4–5, 105–6.

27. Makapela Noyi Balfour, the eldest son of Noyi, a disciple of Ntsikana's, was born about 1810: John Knox Bokwe, *Ntsikana: The Story of an African Convert*, trans. H. Jimba, 2nd ed. (Lovedale: Lovedale Press, 1914), 59.

28. *Ibid.*, 26.

29. *Ibid.*, 23–4; Janet Hodgson, "Ntsikana: History and Symbol. Studies in a Process of Religious Change among Xhosa-speaking People" (Ph.D. thesis: University of Cape Town, 1985), 163–94.

30. See Hodgson, "Ntsikana: History and Symbol," 195–203; Basil Holt, *Joseph Williams and the Pioneer Mission to the South-Eastern Bantu* (Lovedale: Lovedale Press, 1954).

31. Donovan Williams, *Umfundisi: A Biography of Tiyo Soga 1829–1871* (Lovedale: Lovedale Press, 1978), 63.

32. Tshatshu was to assist the pioneering of the Wesleyan Methodist and Glasgow Missionary Society missions too. P.J. Jonas, "Jan Tshatshu and the Eastern Cape Mission: A Contextual Analysis," *Missionalia*, 18, 2 (August 1990): 277–91.

33. Hildegarde Fast, "African Perceptions of the Missionaries and Their Message: Wesleyans at Mount Coke and Butterworth, 1825–35" (Ph.D. thesis: University of Cape Town, 1991), 7–16.

34. Joseph Williams, 14 April 1818, as quoted in Holt, *Joseph Williams*, 80.

35. Mrs. Williams, quoted by John Philip, *Researches in South Africa*, vol. 2 (London: James Duncan, 1828), 165.

36. Life of Charles Henry Matshaya, dictated to the Rev. J. Laing in Xhosa, first published in *Glasgow Missionary Record (GMR)*, 1842.

37. James Cochrane, *Servants of Power: The Role of English-speaking Churches 1903–1930* (Johannesburg: Ravan Press, 1987), 23; Crais, *White Supremacy*, chap. 5.

38. Theal quoted in E.G. Malherbe, *Education in South Africa, 1652–1922*, (vol. 1 Cape Town: Juta, 1925), 59.

39. "Christian fortresses would enable peaceable incursions to be made into the surrounding heathenism," J. Whiteside, *History of the Wesleyan Methodist Church of South Africa* (London: Juta, 1906), 171. See also Fast, "African Perceptions," chap. 2.

40. Mount Coke (Xhosa, 1824), Butterworth (Xhosa, 1827), Morley (Mpondo, 1829), Clarkebury (Thembu, 1830), Buntingville (Mpondo, 1830). J. du Plessis, *A History of Christian Missions in South Africa* (Cape Town: Longmans Green, 1965), 173–5; Whiteside, *History*, 169–97.

41. Robert Shepherd, *Lovedale, South Africa: The Story of a Century 1841–1941* (Lovedale: Lovedale Press, 1940), chaps. 1 and 2.

42. The Moravian mission was Enon, and the Berlin missions, Bethel, Itemba and Emmaus. Du Plessis, *Christian Missions*, 243, 215–18.

43. Elphick, "Christian Campaign," 280–1.

44. *GMS Quarterly Paper, 4* (1828): 3; *Scottish Missionary and Philanthropic Register (SMPR)*, 9 (1828): 356–8, 475–6.

45. Donovan Williams, "Social and Economic Aspects of Christian Missions in Caffraria, 1816–1854," part 1, *Historia*, 31, 2 (1985): 33–48; Colin Bundy, *The Rise and Fall of the South African Peasantry* (London: Heinemann, 1979; Cape Town: David Philip, 1988), 42–3; Peires, *House of Phalo*, 76–7.

46. Ethnic composition included Xhosa, Mfengu, Gonaqua or Gona and Gqunukhwebe (Xhosa–Khoikhoi), and Coloured people (white–Xhosa–Khoikhoi). Williams, "Social and Economic Aspects," part 2, *Historia*, 31, 1 (1986): 25–56.

NOTES

47. Crais, *White Supremacy*, 82, 103; Williams, *Historia* (1985): 33–40. The building of a watercourse at Burnshill was held up when Ngqika's great wife declared the whole hill where he was buried to be sacred.

48. Numerous references in *SMPR* (1825–41); Whiteside, *History*, 179, 186, 220, 307.

49. *GMS* Report for 1827, 16.

50. The Wesleyans used the Sunday School system. M.J. Ashley, "Universes in Collision: Xhosa, Missionaries and Education in 19th Century South Africa," *Journal of Theology for Southern Africa*, 32 (Sept. 1980): 34–6; *GMS*, Report for 1825, 15.

51. The New Testament was published in 1846 and the Old Testament in 1857: R.H.W. Shepherd, *Bantu Life and Literature* (Lovedale: Lovedale Press, 1955), 26–33.

52. Whiteside, *History*, 195, 261.

53. *SMPR* (1833): 303; *Glasgow Missionary Society Quarterly*, 16 (Feb. 1837): 8; *Caffrarian Messenger* 16 (Feb. 1845): 242.

54. See Lamin Sanneh, *Translating the Message: The Missionary Impact on Culture* (Maryknoll: Orbis, 1991).

55. Williams, *Umfundisi*, chaps. 7, 8.

56. Hodgson, *Ntsikana's Great Hymn*, 11–21.

57. Mostert, *Frontiers*, chaps. 18–20; Peires, *House of Phalo*, chaps. 6–9.

58. In 1830 there were 60 African traders with a government licence costing £3: Shepherd, *Bantu Literature*, 25.

59. J. Lewis, "An Economic History of the Ciskei *c*. 1848–1900" (Ph.D. thesis: University of Cape Town, 1984), 62–7.

60. Janet Hodgson, "Soga and Dukwana: The Christian Struggle for Liberation in Mid 19th Century South Africa," *Journal of Religion in Africa*, 16, 3 (1986): 187–208. See also Williams, "Social and Economic Aspects," part 1, *Historia*, 31, 20 (1985): 40–8.

61. Fast, "African Perceptions," 151–8; R.A. Moyer, "A History of the Mfengu of the Eastern Cape, 1815–65" (Ph.D. thesis: University of London, 1976). For the current debate on the origins of the Mfengu, see Alan Webster, "Unmaking the Fingo: The War of 1835 Revisited," in *The Mfecane Aftermath*, ed. Carolyn Hamilton (Johannesburg and Pietermaritzburg: Witwatersrand and Natal University Presses, 1995), 241–76; and Jeffrey Peires, "Paradigm Deleted: The Materialist Interpretation of the Mfecane," *Journal of Southern African Studies*, 19 (1993): 295–313.

62. F.A van Jaarsveld, "The Afrikaner's Idea of His Calling and Mission in South African History," *Journal of Theology for Southern Africa*, 19 (June 1977): 17.

63. "Robert Godlonton, Editor of the *Graham's Town Journal*," in F. Fleming, *Kaffraria and Its Inhabitants* (London: 1853), Appendix III, p. 139.

64. J.M. Bowker, *Speeches, Letters and Selections* (Grahamstown: Godlonton and Richards, 1864; repr. Cape Town: Struik, 1962), 116–25, 131–2.

65. *SMPR*, 13 (1832: 340–1; David Chidester, *Religions of South Africa* (London and New York: Routledge, 1992), 39–43.

66. *GMS* Reports for 1827, 134, and 1841, 41.

67. *SMPR* (1845): 112.

68. H. Calderwood, *Caffres and Caffre Missions* (London: Nisbet, 1858), 210–11.

69. Whiteside, *History*, 210; G. Thom, "Kama," in *Trailblazers of the Gospel*, ed. D. Crafford (Pretoria: Institute for Missiological Research, 1991), 28–33.

70. Several "intelligent" Xhosa responded, saying "let us have access to knowledge in English, for it is a river, and unlike our rivers – it is ever flowing and ever full." *GMS* Report of 1841, vol. 13, 1–2; Leon de Kock, "'Drinking at the English Fountains': Missionary Discourse and the Case of Lovedale," *Missionalia*, 20, 2 (August 1992): 116–38.

71. R.H.W. Shepherd, *Lovedale South Africa 1824–1955* (Lovedale: Lovedale Press, 1971), 14–15.

72. *GMS* Report for 1828, vol. 4, 6.

73. See for example the Female Education Society: Margaret Donaldson, "The Invisible Factor: 19th Century Feminist Evangelical Concerns for Human Rights," in *Women Hold Up Half the Sky*, ed. Denise Ackerman and others (Pietermaritzburg: Cluster Publications, 1991), 207–19; Shepherd, *Lovedale South Africa*, 34–6.

74. Whiteside, *History*, 196–7.

75. W.C. Holden, *The Past and Future of the Kaffir Races* (London: privately printed, n.d.; repr. Cape Town: Struik, 1963), 487; A.E. du Toit, *The Earliest South African Documents on the Education and Civilization of the Bantu* (Pretoria: Communications of the University of South Africa, 1963).

76. Quoted in N. Majeke, *The Role of the Missionaries in Conquest* (Johannesburg: Society of Young Africa, 1952), 70.

77. *SMPR*, 13 (1832): 378–9; *GMS* Report for 1841, vol. 13,16.

78. Peires, *The Dead Will Arise* (Johannesburg: Ravan Press, 1989), 1–30.

79. Janet Hodgson, "Mission and Empire: A Case Study of Convergent Ideologies in 19th Century Southern Africa," *Journal of Theology for Southern Africa*, 38 (March 1983): 33–58.

414

80. For an analytical discussion of the cattle-killing see Peires, *Dead Will Arise*, chaps. 2–4.

81. Richard Gray, *Black Christians and White Missionaries* (New Haven and London: Yale University Press, 1990), 67–8. See also William Gqoba's "Great Discussion" between Present-world (non-Christian) and World-to-come (Christian) quoted in A.C. Jordan, *Towards an African Literature* (Berkeley and London: University of California Press, 1973), 64–5.

82. Peires, *Dead Will Arise*, 79, 90, 136–8; Hodgson, *Ntsikana's Great Hymn*, 41–3, 46.

83. See Great-heart in John Bunyan's *Pilgrim's Progress*.

84. Charles Brownlee was given the Xhosa nickname "Napakade" during the cattle-killing because he repeatedly denied the rising of the ancestors. Charles Brownlee, *Reminiscences of Kafir Life and History* (1896; 2nd. ed., Lovedale: Lovedale Press, 1916; repr. Pietermaritzburg: University of Natal Press, 1977), 127.

85. Kropf, *Dictionary*, 245, 319; J.W. Appleyard, *The Kafir Language* (King William's Town: Wesleyan Missionary Society, 1850), 135, 262, 264; J.L. Döhne, *A Zulu–Kafir Dictionary* (Cape Town: Gregg Press, 1857), 221.

86. Peires, *Dead Will Arise*, 30–6.

87. The expected parting of the sea to engulf the English reflects missionary teaching on Exodus and the identification of oppressed people with the Israelites' deliverance from bondage. Peires, *Dead Will Arise*, 98. Cattle-killing theology posited a move from an individualistic other-worldly salvation to a corporate salvation available to all believers. Whereas evangelical doctrine preached a Christ who ascended and transcended the earthly reality, the Xhosa exegesis of the Second Coming envisioned everlasting life breaking into this world, accompanied by Christ and the ancestors, in order to resolve the pressing this-worldly needs of the Xhosa.

88. Bishop Gray to Williamson, 31 July 1857, Muniment Room Archives, St. George's Cathedral, Cape Town.

89. For the effects of the cattle-killing see Peires, *Dead Will Arise*, chaps. 7–9.

90. M.J. Ashley, "Features of Modernity: Missionaries and Education in South Africa," *Journal of Theology for Southern Africa*, 38 (March 1982): 49–58.

91. Shepherd, *Lovedale South Africa*, 27–38.

92. Shula Marks quoted in De Kock, "Drinking at the English Fountains," 131.

93. For Tiyo Soga's literary achievements, including the translation of *Pilgrim's Progress* (*Uhambo Lomhambi*), see Williams, *Umfundisi*, chap. 8, and for his hymns, *The Journal and Selected Writings of the Reverend Tiyo Soga*, ed. Donovan Williams (Cape Town: A.A. Balkema, 1983), 195–8.

94. Williams, *Umfundisi*; *Selected Writings*; and "The Emergence of Black Consciousness in Caffraria," *Historia*, 32, 2 (Sept. 1987): 56–67.

95. Hodgson, "Soga and Dukwana," 201–3.

96. Janet Hodgson, "A Study in the Dynamics of the Oral and Written Transmission Process," in *Oral Studies in Southern Africa*, ed. H.C. Groenewald (Pretoria: Human Sciences Research Council, 1990), 54–67; "Fluid Assets and Fixed Investments: 160 Years of the Ntsikana Tradition," in *Oral Tradition and Literacy*, ed. R. Whitaker and E. Sienaert (Durban: Natal University Oral Documentation and Research Centre, 1986), 189–202.

97. André Odendaal, "African Political Mobilisation in the Eastern Cape" (Ph.D. thesis: Cambridge University, 1983), 25–32; Williams, *Umfundisi*, chaps. 7, 9.

98. Wallace G. Mills, "The Taylor Revival of 1866 and the Roots of African Nationalism in the Cape Colony," *Journal of Religion in Africa*, 8, 2 (1976): 114.

99. Ibid., 105–22; Whiteside, *History*, 267–77; Daryl M. Balia, *Black Methodists and White Supremacy in South Africa* (Durban: Madiba Publications, 1991), chap. 2.

100. David Coplan, *In Township Tonight* (Johannesburg: Ravan Press, 1985), 26–40, 76.

101. Hodgson, "A Study in the Dynamics," 54–67.

102. André Odendaal, *Vukani Bantu! The Beginnings of Black Protest in South Africa to 1912* (Cape Town: David Philip, 1984), 1–16.

103. Les Switzer, "Reflections on the Mission Press in South Africa in the 19th and Early 20th Centuries," *Journal of Theology for Southern Africa*, 43 (June 1983): 5–14.

104. André Odendaal, "South Africa's Black Victorians: Sport and Society in South Africa in the 19th Century" (paper presented at the University of the Witwatersrand History Workshop, 1987).

105. They had been educated at Zonnebloem College and St. Augustine's College, Canterbury.

106. Bundy, *South African Peasantry*, 32–64.

107. Janet Hodgson, *Princess Emma* (Johannesburg: Ad Donker, 1987), 136, 153–6.

108. R. Hunt Davis, "School vs. Blanket and Settler: Elijah Makiwane and the Leadership of the Cape School Community," *African Affairs*, 78, 310 (1979): 12–31; Mandy Goedhals, "Ungumpriste: A Study of the Life of Peter Masiza, the First Black Priest in the Church of the Province of Southern Africa," *Journal of Theology for Southern Africa*, 68 (Sept. 1989): 17–28; Edward Roux, "Jabavu and the Cape Liberals," *Time Longer Than Rope* (Wisconsin: University of Wisconsin Press, 1964), 53–77; Shepherd, *Bantu Life*, 70–78 [Makiwane and Bokwe], 90–3 [Jabavu]; Dominique Perrot and Francis Wilson, *Outlook on a Century* (Lovedale: Lovedale Press, 1972), 177–80 [Mzimba], 182–5 [Jabavu], and 185–8 [Khama]; C.C. Saunders, "The New Elite in the Eastern Cape and Some Late 19th Century Origins of African Nationalism" (University of London collected seminar

NOTES

papers, 1969–70), 44–55; Odendaal, *Vukani Bantu*, chap. 1.

109. The following year she passed the nursing examination of the Cape Colony: Shepherd, *Bantu Life*, 132–3.

110. Hodgson, *Princess Emma*.

111. Whiteside, *History*, 324.

112. *Occasional News from St Cuthbert's* (CPSA Archives, University of the Witwatersrand), 5 (1903): 9 and 6 (1903): 5.

113. Tiyo Soga, 1 January 1867, as quoted in Williams, *Selected Writings*, 119.

114. A Special Correspondent, "Dukwana's Rebellion," *Christian Express* (July 1878): 7–8.

115. Hodgson, "Soga and Dukwana," 204–5.

116. *Cape Times*, 9 July 1878.

117. Lecture given by the Rev. Robert Johnston to the Presbyterian Young Men's Mutual Improvement Association, Port Elizabeth, 1878, and "Personal Reminiscences of Sandilli and Dukwana," *The Kaffrarian Watchman*, 16 September 1878.

118. Whiteside, *History*, 32; Shepherd, *Lovedale South Africa*, 44–5.

119. Stewart defended a Lovedale education as "economically of more value to the country … and less danger than if left in a state of utter ignorance and barbarism." Shepherd, *Lovedale South Africa*, 53. See Stewart's register of 2,000 students in *Lovedale: Past and Present* (Lovedale: Lovedale Press, 1887).

120. Hunt Davis, "Makiwane," 13–14; S. Trapido, "African Divisional Politics in the Cape Colony, 1844–1910," *Journal of African History*, 9, 1 (1968): 79–98.

121. Jordan, *Towards an African Literature*, 77–102.

122. Odendaal, "African Political Mobilisation," 54–9. Three years later, the Imbumba yama Nyama (South African Native Association) attempted to establish wider African unity, symbolic legitimation coming for Ntsikana's last words. But it remained regionally bound. They saw themselves as Africans rooted in their African past and present and seeking an African future. *Ibid.*, 59–68.

123. "Intlanganiso ye nqubelo pambali yama Ngqika." *Ibid.*, 86–8.

124. Also called Peddie Native Association or "Manyano Lwabantsundu." *Ibid.*, 90.

125. J.T. Jabavu's predominantly Mfengu following supported the Afrikaner Bond-dominated South African Party and *Imvo Zabantsundu* newspaper, while the Xhosa–Thembu alliance led by the Rev. W.B. Rubusana and A.K. Soga adhered to the South African Native Congress and *Izwi Labantu* newspaper and supported the Progressive Party. Odendaal, *Vukani Bantu*, 11–16.

126. The Fingo celebration was held at Emqwasheni on 14 May. The Xhosa commemoration was first known as Manyano lo Buzalwana Bohlanga Lwama-Xosa (The Union of the Brotherhood of the amaXosa Nation). See M. Pelem, *Umongameli we Sikumbuzo so Mprofiti u-Ntsikana Gaba* (King William's Town, c.1918), and *Umongameli WoManyano Luka-Ntu* (Umtata, 1920). See also numerous entries in the correspondence column of *Imvo*, May, June, and July 1909, and 1910.

127. Canon James Calata, Anglican priest at Cradock, was president of the NMA from 1936 to the 1960s, and secretary-general of the ANC from 1936 to 1949. The Rev. Walter Stanley Gawe, another Anglican priest, was for a long time chaplain of the NMA and president of the Cape ANC in the late 1950s. When the Congress Youth League was formed in 1944, Nxele became a symbol of militant black resistance.

128. Stewart editorial quoted in Wilson, *Outlook*, 155; Greg Cuthbertson, "'Cave of Adullam': Missionary Reaction to Ethiopianism at Lovedale, 1898–1902," *Missionalia*, 19, 1 (April 1991): 57–64.

129. Balia, *Black Methodism*, 52–67; C.C. Saunders, "Tile and the Thembu Church: Politics and Independency on the Cape Easten Frontier in the Late 19th Century," *Journal of African History*, vol. 11, 4 (1970): 553–70.

130. L. Mzimba, "The African Church," in *Christianity and the Natives of South Africa*, ed. J.D. Taylor (Lovedale: Lovedale Press, 1928), 86–95; Cuthbertson, "'Cave of Adullam'," 57–8.

131. Balia, *Black Methodism*, 68–85; Sigqibo Dwane, *Issues in the South African Theological Debate* (Johannesburg: Skotaville, 1989), 83–101.

132. Hodgson, "Symbolic Entry Point," 58–60; B.W. Ntsikana, *Ityalike ye Sikumbuzo Sika Ntsikana* (Port Elizabeth, 1945).

133. David Chidester, "Religion Alive, Religious Studies Unborn: A Theoretical Review of Recent Research on African Indigenous Churches," *Journal for the Study of Religion*, 1, 2 (September 1988).

5 / ETHERINGTON / CHRISTIAN BEGINNINGS AMONG ZULU AND SWAZI / PAGES 89–106

1. This and subsequent paragraphs on Gardiner are drawn from his own *Narrative of a Journey to the Zoolu Country in South Africa* (London: W. Crofts, 1836), 14, 32–3, 37, 39, 42–3, 52–3, 57, 67–8, 71, 77, 122, 127, 131–4, 151, 161–3, 169–71, 177–80, 213.

2. *Ibid.* 395.

3. McKinney to the Secretary for Home Correspondence, 7 Feb. 1846, series 6, vol. 19, Archives of the American Board of Commissioners for Foreign Missions (henceforth, ABC), Houghton Library, Harvard University.

4. Wilder to the Secretary of the American Board, 3 Feb. 1848, ABC 6, vol. 24.

5. Anderson to the American Zulu Mission, 25 Mar. 1857, ABC 2.1.1, vol. 23.

6. Quoted in Clifton J. Phillips, "Protestant America and the Pagan World" (Ph.D. thesis: Harvard University, 1954), 243–4.

7. Anderson to the South African Mission, 12 July 1843, ABC 2.1.1, vol. 6.

8. Lindley to Anderson, 1 Dec. 1837.

9. N. Adams to Anderson, 30 May 1843, ABC 15.4, vol. 2.

10. A. Grout to Anderson, 20 Feb. 1850, ABC 15.4, vol. 4.

11. H. F. Fynn, Report on Zulu Affairs, 2 Jan. 1857, folio 1/3/6, Secretary for Native Affairs Papers, Natal Archives (henceforth, SNA).

12. The complex background to the split is comprehensively treated in Jarle Simensen, with V. Gynnild, "Norwegian Missionaries in the Nineteenth Century," in *Norwegian Missions in African History, vol. 1: South Africa 1845–1906*, ed. J. Simensen (Oslo: Norwegian University Press, 1986), 23–32. Simensen argues that there was an undeniable issue of social class involved in this schism. Unlike Schreuder, most of the clergy who worked under him lacked higher education and emerged from rural backgrounds.

13. The position taken by Schreuder is outlined at length in Per Hernœs "The Zulu Kingdom, Norwegian Missionaries and British Imperialism 1845–1879," in *Norwegian Missions in African History*, ed. Simensen, vol. 1, 1:114–71; and O. G. Myklebust, *H. P. S. Schreuder, Kirke og Misjon* (Oslo: Glyldendal Norsk Forlag A/S, 1980), esp. 274–9.

14. Halfdan E. Sommerfelt, *Den Norske Zulumission* (Christiania: Wm. Gram, 1865), 286.

15. W. Wendebourg, *Louis Harms als Missionsmann* (Hermannsburg: Druck und Verlag der Missionshandlung, 1910), 44.

16. Georg Haccius, *Hannoversche Missionsgeschichte* (Hermannsburg: Druck und Verlag der Missionshandlung, 1909–14), vol. 2, 222–3.

17. *Ibid.*, 243–50; F. Speckman, *Die Hermannsburger Mission in Afrika* (Hermannsburg: 1876), 3.

18. Thornley Smith, *The Earnest Missionary: A Memoir of the Reverend Horatio Pearse* (London: Wesleyan Mission House, 1868), 242; Wendebourg, *Louis Harms*, 249.

19. Mpande had objected to communities of Hermannsburg men settling like "soldiers" in his kingdom. See August Hardeland to T. Shepstone, 14 Aug. 1860, SNA 1/1/10.

20. The standard work on De Mazenod is Jean Leflon's *Eugène de Mazenod*, 3 vols. (Paris: Plon, 1957–65).

21. *Règles et constitutions à l'usage des frères convers de la Congrégation de la Très-Sainte et Immaculée Vierge Marie* (Marseilles: OMI, 1859).

22. *Histoire universelle des missions catholiques*, ed. Simon Delacroix (Paris: Grund, 1967), vol. 1, 324; Leflon, *Eugène de Mazenod*, vol. 3, 690; W. E. Brown, *The Catholic Church in South Africa from Its Origins to the Present Day* (London: Burns and Oates, 1960), 38, 41.

23. J.F. Allard, Journal, 19 Feb. and 22 July 1860, Oblate Archives, Rome. For a brief account of its troubles, see Norman Etherington, *Preachers, Peasants and Politics in Southeast Africa, 1835–1880* (London: Royal Historical Society, and Boyle and Brewer, 1978), 38–40. At the end of the nineteenth century, Catholics reoccupied the mission. See Joy Brain, *Catholics in Natal*, vol. 2, *1886–1925* (Durban: Archdiocese of Durban, 1982), 105–11.

24. Joseph Jackson, Jr. to William Arthur, 9 Sept. 1860, Natal District Papers, Archives of the Wesleyan Methodist Missionary Society, University of London (hereafter, WMMS).

25. William Arthur, *Tongues of Fire* (London: 1956), 104–5.

26. Etherington, *Preachers, Peasants and Politics*, 29.

27. Albert C. Outler, *John Wesley* (New York: Oxford University Press, 1964), 16.

28. J. Whiteside, *History of the Wesleyan Methodist Church of South Africa* (London: Elliot Stock, 1906), 357; William Shaw, *The Story of My Mission* (London: Hamilton, 1860), passim.

29. Charles Roberts to the Secretaries, 28 Oct. 1866, WMMS. For the revivalist's own account, see William Taylor, *Christian Adventures in South Africa* (London: Jackson, Walford and Hodder, 1867).

30. A. T. Bryant, *Olden Times in Zululand and Natal* (London: Longmans, 1929), 326–7.

31. Allison, Report of Indaleni Circuit for 1847, Synod Minutes, 1848, WMMS.

32. See Owen Watkins, "Swazi Mission, 1883," 20 July 1883, Methodist Papers 6/2, Natal Archives.

33. J. W. Colenso, *An Ordination and Three Missionary Sermons* (Cambridge, 1855), 35–6.

34. J. W. Colenso: *The Good Tidings of Great Joy, Which Shall Be to All People* (London, 1854), 17; *Ten Weeks in Natal: A Journal of a First Tour of Visitation among the Colonists and Zulu Kafirs of Natal* (Cambridge: Macmillan, 1855), 79.

35. Colenso, unaddressed letter, 9 Nov. 1855, folio D8, Archives of the United Society for the Propagation of the Gospel, Rhodes House, Oxford University (henceforth, SPG).

36. Colenso, unaddressed, 8 Aug. 1857, D8, SPG.

37. Colenso to Hawkins, 5 Feb. 1856, D8, SPG.

38. Alice Mackenzie, diary for 1859, typescript in Colenso Papers, Killie Campbell Africana Library of the University of Natal, Durban.

NOTES

39. Jeff Guy, *The Heretic: A Study of the Life of John William Colenso, 1814–1883* (Pietermaritzburg: University of Natal Press, 1983), 53.

40. A. T. Wirgman, *Life of James Green* (London: Longmans, Green, vol. 1, 1909), 24–5. For a discussion of Callaway's role as a medical missionary, see Norman Etherington, "Missionary Doctors and African Healers in Mid-Victorian South Africa," *South African Historical Journal*, 19 (1987): 77–92; and Rodney Davenport, "Christian Mission in the South African Melting-pot in the Nineteenth Century," *Studia Historicae Ecclesiasticae*, 18 (1992): 54–7.

41. The idea that the missionaries had been using an inappropriate Xhosa word, *Utixo*, was first suggested to Colenso by the Methodist missionary, James Allison; see Colenso, *Ten Weeks in Natal*, 56–7.

42. Maurice's influence on Colenso is treated in Guy, *The Heretic*, 24–30.

43. Colenso, *Remarks on the Proper Treatment of Cases of Polygamy, as Found Already Existing in Converts from Heathenism* (Pietermaritzburg: May and Davis, 1855). See also his *Ten Weeks in Natal*, 252–3; Lewis Grout, *The Autobiography of the Reverend Lewis Grout* (Brattleboro, VT: Clapp and Jones, 1905); Smith, *The Earnest Missionary*, 223; Wendebourg, *Louis Harms*, 300; Haccius, *Hannoversche Missionsgeschichte*, vol. 2, 362. Others involved in the controversy were T.D. Woolsey, President of Yale University, and August Hardeland of Hermannsburg, who backed Colenso but was dismissed by Harms.

44. *Annales de la propagation de la foi*, 39 (1867): 46.

45. *St. Paul's Epistle to the Romans: Newly Translated, and Explained from a Missionary Point of View* (Ekukanyeni, 1861); *The Pentateuch and the Book of Joshua Critically Examined*, 4 vols. (London: Longman, Roberts, and Green, 1862–3).

46. See Colenso to Domville, 19 Dec. 1865, 29 June 1867, and 20 Aug. 1870, folio B, Colenso Papers, Campbell Library, University of Natal.

47. Colenso to Shepstone, 11 Nov. 1869 and 2 April 1873, folio N., Colenso Papers, Campbell Library. See note by Harriette Colenso, covering her father's complicity, on the latter.

48. O. Stavem, *The Norwegian Missionary Society: A Short Review of its Work among the Zulus* (Stavanger: Norwegian Missionary Society, 1918), 23, 36; R. Robertson, Journal, Dec. 1864 to Jan. 1865, E17, SPG.

49. Speckmann, *Die Hermannsburger Mission*, 378–509.

50. Etherington, *Preachers, Peasants and Politics*, 84.

51. That Grout's mistake remained a rankling memory at the Zulu court is confirmed by Per Hernœs, "The Zulu Kingdom, Norwegian Missionaries and British Imperialism 1845–1879," in *Norwegian Missions*, ed. Simensen, vol. 1:105.

52. Robertson to Bullock, 1 Sept. 1869, E24, SPG; *The Net Cast in Many Waters*, 4 (1869): 26–7.

53. Speckmann, *Die Hermansburger Mission in Afrika*, 425.

54. The Zulu form is *kafula*. Colenso ascribed the use of the word in Zululand to the misconception that the settler term derived from the Zulu verb *kafula*, "to spit out, as chewed food"; fragment of a letter, n.d. folio Z, Colenso Papers, Campbell Library.

55. James Cameron to Secretaries, 1 Aug. 1866, WMMS.

56. Milward to Boyce, 10 Sept. 1873, WMMS.

57. Special reasons for these exceptions are outlined in Etherington, *Preachers, Peasants and Politics*, 68–9.

58. Callaway to Hawkins, 6 Feb. 1863, D25, SPG.

59. N. Etherington, "Mission Station Melting Pots as a Factor in the Rise of South African Black Nationalism," *International Journal of African Historical Studies*, 9 (1976): 592–605.

60. The enormous land purchases made possible under Abbot Pfanner by contributions from Central Europe are set out in Brain, *Catholics in Natal*, vol. 2, 148–57.

61. Rood to Clark, 8 July 1876, ABC 15.4, vol. 8.

62. A. Grout, Report of Umvoti Station for the Year Ending 18 May 1864, ABC 15.4, vol. 6.

63. Illing, Quarterly reports, Sept. 1872, Mar. 1876 and Mar. 1877, E27, E31 and E32, SPG.

64. J. Allsopp, testimony of 1881, in *Evidence Taken Before the Natal Native Commission, 1881* (Pietermaritzburg: Government Printer, 1882), 22.

65. General letter from the Zulu Mission to R. Anderson, 12 Sept. 1849, ABC 15.4, vol. 4.

66. H. M. Cameron to Mason, 29 March 1879, WMMS.

67. Bridgman to Shepstone, 20 Oct. 1864, Secretary for Native Affairs, 1/1/14, Natal Archives (hereafter, NA). H. M. Cameron to Mason, 29 March 1879, WMMS.

68. Illing, 3 March 1869, Quarterly report for 30 June 1879, D37 and E34, SPG.

69. Illing, Quarterly reports, 30 June 1876 and 31 March 1877. E31 amd E32. SPG.

70. *Natal Bluebook*, 1880. The government issued statistics sporadically, for long periods (as in 1865–75) not at all, relied on missionaries to supply returns, and often failed to receive them from schools not aided by government grants.

71. On the self-supporting ideal, see Andrew Walls, "British Missions," in *Missionary Ideologies in the Imperialist Era*, ed. T. Christensen and W.R. Hutchison (Copenhagen: Aros, 1982), 162. This "three self policy" was associated in Britain with Henry Venn, and in the American Board with its secretary, Rufus Anderson.

72. Annual Report of Amanzimtoti Seminary, 22 May 1877, ABC 15.4, vol. 8.

73. The American Zulu mission had launched a Native Home Missionary Society in 1860. Though converts responded enthusiastically to the challenge, the venture was a creature of the white missionaries, not an African initiative.

74. J. Calvert to Perks, 28 Aug. 1876, WMMS.

75. O. Watkins, "Swazi Mission, 1883," 20 July 1883, Methodist Papers, 6/2, Natal Archives.

76. Personal communication to the author by H.S. Msimang in an interview at Edendale, 10 Feb. 1970. Sheila Meintjes in her unpublished dissertation on Edendale (Ph. D. thesis: University of London: 1990) felicitously translates *nontlevu* as "babblers."

77. Pinkerton to Clark, 17 July 1875, ABC 15.4, vol. 8.

78. Jackson, Jr. to the Secretaries, 7 Feb. 1860, WMMS. For another interesting account, see *Missions-Berichte* (1872): 382–91.

79. For accounts of these and other movements see Bengt Sudkler, *Bantu Prophets in South Africa*, 2nd ed. (London: Oxford University Press, 1961), 39–41, 314–15; E. Roux, *Time Longer Than Rope* (Madison: University of Wisconsin Press, 1966), 79–84, 99; N. Etherington, "African Economic Experiments in Colonial Natal, 1845–80," *African Economic History*, 5 (1978): 1–15.

80. Etherington, *Preachers, Peasants and Politics*, 146–50.

81. Toleration for these customs varied from denomination to denomination. The Americans condemned them all, although a minority of the mission defended *lobola* as a pillar of marriage. Except for Bishop Colenso and August Hardeland of the Hermannsburg Mission, polygamy was universally denounced. And even those two churchmen would only admit polygamists who had married *before* joining the church. Lutheran, Anglican and Catholic missions condemned beer drinking only when carried to excess.

82. Rood to Clark, 7 June 1869, ABC 15.4, vol. 7.

83. Report of the Native Institute for 1871, American Zulu Mission papers, 22, iv/1/1, Natal Archives. Rood to Clark, 7 June 1869, ABC 15.4, vol. 7.

84. For more examples equating women's position in Nguni society with slavery, see Allard to Mère Véronique, 18 Aug. 1852 and 2 Feb. 1855, Archives of the Oblates of Mary Immaculate, Rome; Bridgman to Clark, 27 Feb. 1868, ABC 15.4, vol. 6; Journal of Henry Callaway, 1 July to 30 Sept. 1860, SPG.

85. Kirkby to Secretaries of the Society, 28 February 1866, WMMS.

86. Wisner to Newton Adams, 21 August 1834, ABC 1.01, vol. 12.

87. See, for example, C. Posselt writing in *Missions-Berichte* (1848): 20.

88. Mrs. Laura Bridgman to Clark, 9 November 1869, ABC 15.4, vol. 6. One of the children did grow up to be a member of the American Zulu Mission.

89. Bridgman to Clark, 24 July 1873, ABC 15.4, vol. 8.

90. K. Lloyd to Treat, October 1863, ABC 15.4, vol. 7.

91. K. Lloyd to Mrs. Parker, forwarded to American Board, January 1868, ABC 15.4, vol. 6. The references to Paul strongly suggest the influence of Bishop Colenso. Daniel Lindley, who became Katherine Lloyd's father-in-law in 1870, was according to Colenso "exceedingly friendly" to him and "made some progress in the study of my books," one of which was *St. Paul's Epistle to the Romans: Newly Translated, and Explained from a Missionary Point of View*.

92. K. Lloyd to Clark, 3 June 1870, ABC 15.4, vol. 7.

93. Edwards to Clark, 14 June 1869. She later requested that this letter be burnt, lest it be used against her by her enemies in the mission.

94. Morris to Clark, 17 July 1879, ABC 15.4, vol. 8.

95. For a particularly complex and interesting case see Resident Magistrate Mesham to Shepstone, 8 September 1854, 1/3/3 SNA.

96. See L. Grout to Anderson, 23 November 1848 and 21 March 1849, as well as extracts from his journals for 1848, ABC 15.4, vol. 5. Missionaries would always protect them, and sometimes their property as well, from passing by levirate marriage to their deceased husbands' brothers. See Resident Magistrate Blaine to Shepstone, 1 March 1859, and J. Allsopp to Shepstone, 23 Jan. 1875, SNA, Natal Archives. The whole subject is covered at length in Etherington, *Preachers, Peasants and Politics*, 95–9.

97. Etherington, *Preachers, Peasants and Politics*, 137–40.

98. Brain, *Catholics in Natal*, vol.2, 135–46.

99. Markham, Quarterly report, 5 Feb. 1878, E33, SPG.

100. *Proceedings and Report of the Commission Appointed to Inquire into the Past and Present State of the Kafirs in the District of Natal, 1853* (Pietermaritzburg, 1854), 14.

101. It was reported that on the day the coastal column of the invading army engaged the enemy Robertson could be seen sniping at Zulu soldiers from the cover of a supply wagon: Case of the Mission Station of the Church of England at Kwamagwaza, Government House papers, 2284, Natal Archives.

102. The affair is treated in detail in N. Etherington, "Why Langalibalele Ran Away," *Journal of Natal and Zulu History*, 1 (1978) :1–24.

NOTES

103. Colenso's campaigns on behalf of Langalibalele and Cetshwayo are magisterially narrated by Guy in *The Heretic*, 193–348.

104. See N. Etherington, "Christianity and African Society," in *Natal and Zululand from Earliest Times to 1910: A New History*, ed. A. Duminy and B. Guest (Pietermaritzburg: University of Natal Press, 1989), 294–5; and *Preachers, Peasants and Politics, 23*. For an insight into the technicalities of land granting to missionaries see Pilcher to the Secretaries of the Wesleyan Methodist Missionary Society, 6 Sept. 1862, WMMS.

105. Natal Blue Book, 1865. David Welsh, *The Roots of Segregation* (Cape Town: Oxford University Press, 1971), 206 notes that much of the annual grant was commonly not spent.

106. Colenso to Allnutt, 12 Nov. 1855, folio E, Campbell Library, and unaddressed letter, 9 Nov. 1855, D8, SPG; Pearse to Jenkins, 8 May 1857, 3/1/2, Methodist Missionary Papers, Natal Archives; Fynn to the Colonial Sec., 31 Aug. 1857, NA 1/3/6.

107. Mann to Shepstone, 25 July 1864, First Annual Report on Industrial Training, 1/1/14 NA. Subsequent reports were sporadic. A report by Governor Bulwer to the Legislative Council in 1879 found reports extant for 1864–65, 1868 and 1877; LC no. 15, 2nd Session, 1879–80.

108. For only a handful of many examples, see W. Campbell to Shepstone, 28 March 1860, NA 1/1/10; W. Mellen to Shepstone, 25 Oct. 1859, NA 1/1/9; A. Tønnesen to Secretaries, 31 March 1862, E9, SPG.

109. Brain, *Catholics in Natal*, vol. 2, 135–6.

110. *Ibid.*, 142.

111. *Witness*, 12 June 1889, quoted in *ibid.*, 144.

112. The story of this contest has been told by several scholars drawn to the key issues of reserve lands and Ethiopian churches. Shula Marks, *Reluctant Rebellion*, (Oxford: Oxford University Press, 1970); B. M. Norman, "Responsible Government in Natal and the American Zulu Mission: 1893–1907" (B.A. Hons. thesis: University of Natal, 1982); Carmel McKeough, "Reluctant Defender: The Transformation of a Conservative Mission into a Liberal Political Opposition in the Colony of Natal, 1893–1910" (B.A. Hons. thesis: University of Adelaide, 1982).

113. Shantha Bloemen "The Impact of the American Zulu Mission in Natal from 1890 to 1910" (B.A. Hons. thesis: University of Western Australia, 1992), 39–49.

6 / BECK / MONARCHS AND MISSIONARIES AMONG TSWANA AND SOTHO / PAGES 107–120

1. See Gabriel M. Setiloane, *The Image of God Among the Sotho–Tswana* (Rotterdam: A.A. Balkema, 1976), 9–19. Setiloane uses the combined term "Sotho-Tswana" throughout his book in all references to these people.

2. J.T. du Bruyn, *Die Aanvangsjare van die Christelike Sending onder die Tlhaping, 1800–1825* (Pretoria: Government Printer, 1989), 24–44.

3. John Campbell, *Travels in South Africa*, 3rd ed. (London: T. Hamilton, 1815), vi.

4. *Ibid.*, 208–9.

5. Those sent were John Evans, Robert Hamilton, Joseph Williams, and George Barker.

6. Robert Moffat, *Missionary Labours and Scenes in Southern Africa* (London: Snow, 1842), 229.

7. Contemporary accounts of the battle of Dithakong by Robert Moffat and John Melvill are to be found, respectively, in Moffat's *Apprenticeship at Kuruman*, ed. I. Schapera (London: Chatto and Windus, 1951), 77–103, and George Thompson, *Travels and Adventures in Southern Africa*, vol. 1 (Cape Town: Van Riebeeck Society, 1967) chaps. 15 and 16. For a recent debate see Julian Cobbing, "The Mfecane as Alibi: Thoughts on Dithakong and Mbolompo," *Journal of African History*, 29 (1988): 487–519, and contributions by Elizabeth Eldredge and Guy Hartley in *The Mfecane Aftermath*, ed. Carolyn Hamilton (Wits and Natal University Presses, 1995).

8. Schapera, *Apprenticeship*, xxvii; Jean and John Comaroff, *Of Revelation and Revolution: Christianity, Colonialism, and Consciousness in South Africa* (Chicago: Chicago University Press, 1991), 252–308.

9. See, for example, Moffat, *Apprenticeship*, 51, 56–7, 63, 71.

10. *Ibid.*, xxvi.

11. Moffat, *Missionary Labours*, 249.

12. *Ibid.*, 244; Anthony Sillery, *The Bechuanaland Protectorate* (London: Oxford University Press, 1952), 14–15.

13. *David Livingstone.: Family Letters 1841–1856*, ed. I. Schapera (London: Chatto and Windus, 1959), 1:13.

14. J.J. Freeman, *A Tour of South Africa* (London: John Snow, 1851), 258–94.

15. Following the excellent study by the French historian, Claude H. Perrot, *Les Sotho et les missionaires éuropéens au XIXe siècle* (Abidjan: Annales de l'Université d'Abidjan, 1970), 10.

16. V. Ellenberger, *A Century of Mission Work in Basutoland (1833–1933)*, trans. Edmond M. Ellenberger (Morija: Sesuto Book Depot, 1938), 9.

17. *Ibid.*, 20.

18. Moshoeshoe to Directors, 18 Sept. 1855, *Journal des missions évangéliques* (1856): 54, cited in Leonard Thompson, *Survival in Two Worlds: Moshoeshoe of Lesotho, 1786–1870* (Oxford: Clarendon Press, 1975), 77.

19. See Thompson, *Survival in Two Worlds*, 202–3.

20. *Ibid.*, 91–5.

21. For a discussion of Moshoeshoe's conversion, see Thompson, *Survival in Two Worlds*, 320–4.

22. *Ibid.*, 99.

23. The "Bechuana Mission" of the Wesleyan Missionary Society along the Caledon River Valley began in 1833, and included stations at Thaba Nchu (Rolong), Umpukane (Kora), Platberg and Lishuani (Griqua), and Imperani (Tlokwa). See *The Wesleyan Mission in the Orange Free State, 1833–1854*, ed. Karel Schoeman (Cape Town: Human and Rousseau, 1991).

24. See Thompson, Survival in Two Worlds, 120–32; and Jean-François Zorn, *Le Grand Siècle d'une mission protestante: La mission de Paris de 1822–1914* (Paris: Les Bergers et Les Mages, 1993). 384–5.

25. Perrot, *Les Sotho*, 46.

26. *Ibid.*, 53, 56–7, 125; Zorn, *Le Grand Siècle*, 391–2. Ellenberger argues that the missionaries had two motives: Christian and political. He believes they feared English retaliation against Moshoeshoe and his people for murder and theft, and concludes that they were wrong to become involved in Sotho civil matters. Ellenberger, *Century of Mission Work*, 78–80.

27. Perrot, *Les Sotho* 60–70.

28. Zorn, *Le Grand Siècle*, 378–82, 386–92.

29. Thompson, *Survival in Two Worlds*, 255–6; Perrot, *Les Sotho*, 166–7.

30. Thomas Tlou and Alec Campbell, *History of Botswana* (Gaborone: Macmillan, 1984), 133.

31. Mackenzie took over the work begun by the Hermannsburg missionary, Christoph Heinrich Schulenburg.

32. Perrot, *Les Sotho*, 142–3.

33. Thompson, *Survival in Two Worlds*, 318; Perrot, *Les Sotho*, 149–52.

34. Perrot, *Les Sotho*, 145–8.

35. *Ibid.*, 145.

36. *Ibid.*, 132–3.

37. John Widdicombe, *Fourteen Years in Basutoland* (London: The Church Printing Company, 1891) 72.

38. Perrot, *Les Sotho*, 117–19, 150–2, 160.

39. *Ibid.*, 118.

40. *Ibid.*, 119, 164–5. The Dieterlen quotation, cited by Perrot, comes from Hermann Dieterlen and Frederic Kohler, *Livre d'or de la mission du Lessouto* (Paris: Societé des Missions Évangéliques, 1912), 489 (my translation).

41. J. Mutero Chirenje, *Chief Kgama and His Times, c. 1835–1923: The Story of a Southern African Ruler* (London: Rex Collings, 1978), 71–81.

42. For discussion of Kgama and the establishment of the British protectorate, see Sillery, *The Bechuanaland Protectorate*, 115–28.

43. See Lamin Sanneh, *Translating the Message: The Missionary Impact on Culture* (Maryknoll, New York: Orbis Books, 1989). Perrot argues that by making Sotho a written language the missionaries "contributed to national unification." See Perrot, *Les Sotho*, 27. Compare *The Creation of Tribalism in Southern Africa*, ed. LeRoy Vail (London: James Currey; and Cape Town: David Philip, 1989), 1–19, and Jean and John Comaroff, *Of Revelation and Revolution*, 213–30 for suggestions of countervailing influences.

44. Sanneh, *Translating the Message*, particularly 181–90. See also Steven Kaplan, "The Africanization of Missionary Christianity: History and Typology," in *Indigenous Responses to Western Christianity*, ed. Steven Kaplan (New York: New York University Press, 1995), 9–28, and other essays in this volume for a global comparative perspective on this issue.

45. For a discussion of the "politics of language" in the context of Christian missionaries and the Tswana see Jean and John Comaroff, *Of Revelation and Revolution*, 213–30, and Paul Landau, *The Realm of the Word: Language, Gender and Christianity in a Southern African Kingdom* (Portsmouth, N.H.: Heinemann, 1995).

46. Jean and John Comaroff, *Of Revelation and Revolution*, 231–6, 240 [discussion of "sacred" schooling and use of hymns]; Setiloane, *Image of God*, 144–9, 156–7 [missionary attempts to make people literate and sing hymns in the indigenous language as the "most universally employed method of evangelisation"].

47. Ellenberger, *Century of Mission Work*, 35, 38, 66–8, 119–29, 159–60, 163.

48. *Ibid.*, 193.

49. *Ibid.*, 193–5.

50. *Journal des missions évangéliques* (1892): 111, and Dieterlen, *Livre d'or*, 489, cited in Perrot, *Les Sotho*, 119.

7 / HEXHAM & POEWE / CHRISTIANITY IN TRANSORANGIA / PAGES 121–134

1. Cf. Leonard Thompson "The Difaqane and Its Aftermath, 1822–1836," in *The Oxford History of South Africa*, ed. Monica Wilson and Leonard Thompson (London: Oxford University Press, 1969), vol. 1, 391–405; J. Cobbing "The Mfecane as Alibi: Thoughts on Dithakong and Mbolompo," *Journal of African History*, 29, 2 (1988): 487–519; *The Mfecane Aftermath*, ed. Carolyn Hamilton (Johannesburg and Pietermaritzburg: Wits and Natal University Presses, 1995) [papers of a conference devoted to the Mfecane debate, especially those by Neil

NOTES

Parsons, Andrew Manson and Margaret Kinsman].

2. Cf. *The Bantu-Speaking Peoples of Southern Africa*, ed. W.D. Hammond-Tooke (London: Routledge and Kegan Paul, 1974), 56–102, 177–93, 201–9.

3. See his *Missionary Labours and Scenes in Southern Africa* (London: John Snow, 1842), and *Apprenticeship in Kuruman*, ed. I. Schapera (London: Chatto and Windus, 1951).

4. Denys W.T. Shropshire, *The Church and Primitive Peoples* (London: SPCK, 1938), 107–51, 400–23; W.C. Willoughby, *The Soul of the Bantu* (London: SCM, 1928), 198–265; cf. G.C. Oosthuizen, Irving Hexham and others, *Afro-Christian Religion and Healing in Southern Africa* (Lewiston: Edwin Mellen, 1989); R. Grove, "Scottish Missionaries, Evangelical Discourses and the Origins of Conservation Thinking in Southern Africa, 1820–1900," *Journal of Southern African Studies*, 15 (1989): 163–87.

5. Moffat, *Missionary Labours*, 260–8.

6. Gabriel M. Setiloane, *The Image of God Among the Sotho–Tswana* (Rotterdam: A.A. Balkema, 1976), 13–19, 77–86, 89–106, and "Modimo: God among the Sotho–Tswana," *Journal of Theology for Southern Africa*, 4 (September 1973): 6–17; P. Bolink, "Modimo Macroanthropos" (unpublished paper delivered at the 13th Congress of the International Association for the History of Religions, University of Lancaster, 15–22 August 1975).

7. Cf. Ninian Smart, *The Religious Experience of Mankind* (New York: Charles Scribner's Sons, 1969). And see Rudolf Otto, *The Idea of the Holy*, trans. John W. Harvey (London: Oxford University Press, 1923).

8. J.A. van Rooy, "Language and Culture in the Communication of the Christian Message as Illustrated by the Venda Bible" (Th.D. thesis: Potchefstroom University, 1971); Shropshire, *The Church and Primitive Peoples*, 279–304; and B.A. Pauw, *Religions in a Tswana Chiefdom* (Oxford: Oxford University Press, 1960, repr. 1964), 12–40.

9. Setiloane, "Modimo," 11.

10. See Irving Hexham, "Lord of the Sky-King of the Earth: Zulu Traditional Religion and Belief in the Sky God," *Studies in Religion* (Waterloo), 10, 3, (1981): 273–85; and *Texts on Zulu Religion*, ed. Irving Hexham (Lewiston: Edwin Mellen Press, 1987). Contrast the view of N. Etherington with respect to the Zulu high god at p. 100, of this book.

11. Despite a dearth of published primary material on African religions in Transorangia during the nineteenth century, leads are provided in Henri A. Junod, *The Life of a South African Tribe* (2nd rev. ed., London: Macmillan, 1927), and W.C. Willoughby, *The Soul of the Bantu* (London: SCM, 1926), and *Nature-Worship and Taboo: Further Studies in "The Soul of the Bantu"* (Hartford: Hartford Seminary Press, 1932).

12. See Christoph J.H. Muller, *Die Oorsprong van die Groot Trek* (Cape Town: Tafelberg, 1974); Leonard Thompson, "The Great Trek, 1836–54," in *The Oxford History of South Africa*, ed. Monica Wilson and Leonard Thompson (London: Oxford University Press, 1969), vol. 1, 405–25; Eric Walker, *The Great Trek* (London: Adam and Charles Black, 1938).

13. *Totius: Versamelde Werk*, ed. V.E. d'Assonville (Cape Town: Tafelberg, 1977), vol. 10, 48 [translation]. See Irving Hexham, *The Irony of Apartheid: The Struggle for National Independence of Afrikaner Calvinism Against British Imperialism* (New York: Edwin Mellen Press, 1981), 36–7.

14. The most recent books to expound the basic themes of this interpretation of South African history, are Willem A. de Klerk, *The Puritans in Africa* (London: Rex Collings, 1975); *Ideology on a Frontier: The Theological Foundation of Afrikaner Nationalism, 1652–1910* (Westport: Greenwood Press, 1984); and Jonathan Neil Gerstner's stimulating *The Thousand Generation Covenant: Dutch Reformed Covenant Theology and Group Identity in Colonial South Africa, 1652–1814* (Leiden: E.J. Brill, 1991), and his chapter in this volume. All of these authors accept as a fact the innate piety of Boer society in the Calvinism of the earliest settlers.

15. See André du Toit, "No Chosen People: The Myth of the Calvinist Origins of Afrikaner Nationalism and Racial Ideology," *American Historical Review*, 88, 1 (1983): 920–52; "Puritans in Africa? Afrikaner 'Calvinism' and Kuyperian Neo-Calvinism in Late Nineteenth-Century South Africa," *Comparative Studies in Society and History*, 27, 2 (1985): 209–40; and "Captive to the Nationalist Paradigm: Prof. F.A. van Jaarsveld and the Historical Evidence for the Afrikaner's Ideas on his Calling and Mission", with Van Jaarsveld's reply, *South African Historical Journal*, 16 (1984): 48–81. See also Hexham, *Irony*; and "Modernity or Reaction in South Africa: The Case of Afrikaner Religion", in *Religion and Modernity*, ed. William Nichols (Waterloo: Wilfrid Laurier University Press, 1988) 62–88; and "Dutch Calvinism and the Origins of Afrikaner Nationalism," *African Affairs* (London, Spring 1980): 195–208.

16. Walker, *Great Trek*, 182; S.P. Engelbrecht, *Geskiedenis van die Nederduitsch Hervormde Kerk van Afrika* (Cape Town and Pretoria: H.A.U.M., De Bussy, 1953), 30–46, 100–24.

17. See *The Diary of Erasmus Smit*, ed. H.F. Schoon (Cape Town: Struik, 1972).

18. See Edwin W. Smith, *The Life and Times of Daniel Lindley, 1801–1880* (London: Epworth Press, 1949).

19. See, for example, *Young Mrs. Murray Goes to Bloemfontein*, ed. Joyce Murray (Cape Town: A.A. Balkema, 1954), 127.

20. Recognition of the clan structure of traditional Boer society was confirmed in discussions with Professor Bouker Spoelstra and the late Professor David Bosch.

21. Local church minute books show that between 1902 and 1920 individuals belonging to the Gereformeerde Kerk faced church discipline for courting members of other religious communities.

22. Professor Johan Snyman and several prominent Transvaal Afrikaners told us they knew that during the nineteenth century members of their families had been polygamous.

23. Cited in Smith, *Daniel Lindley*, 160. These comments refer to Natal Boers, most of whom moved to Transorangia in 1843.

24. Cited in R.C. Germond, *Chronicles of Basutoland* (Morija, Lesotho: Morija Sesuto Book Depot, 1967), 65.

25. James Chapman, *Travels in the Interior of South Africa, 1849–1863*, ed. Edward C. Tabler (Cape Town: A.A. Balkema, 1971), 18.

26. *Ibid.*, 20; dated 1849. Boer dislike of missionaries is also commented on at pages 40, 84.

27. See *Letters of the American Missionaries, 1835–1838*, ed. D.J. Kotze (Cape Town: Van Riebeeck Society, 1950), 215, 230, 262; Germond, *Chronicles*, 223; J. Spiecker, *Er führet mich auf rechter Strasse* (Gütersloh: C. Bertelsmann, 1903), 15, 65.

28. *The Memoirs of Paul Kruger: Four Times President of the South African Republic. Told by Himself*, trans. A. Teixeira de Mattos (London: T. Fisher Unwin, 1902), 37.

29. Henri A. Junod, *The Life of a South African Tribe*, vol. 2: *Mental Life* (1927, repr. New York: University Books, 1966), 452–79, and A.T. Bryant, *Zulu Medicine and Medicine-men* (Cape Town: C. Struik, 1966). Bryant appears to have originally written his book in the 1920s. Therefore, it probably reflects African beliefs and practices prior to 1910. Junod's own researches took place in the 1890s.

30. Irving Hexham was given a very detailed account of these cures by an Afrikaner medical doctor whom he interviewed in 1981.

31. *Doctor to Basuto, Boer and Briton, 1877–1906: Memoirs of Dr. Henry Taylor*, ed. Peter Hadley (Cape Town: David Philip, 1972), 130. This comment is not dated but, in context, clearly comes from around 1885 from the Ficksburg area of the Orange Free State. Further insights into Boer folk medicine and superstitions are to be found in Isidore Frack, *A South African Doctor Looks Backward and Forward* (Pretoria: Central News Agency, 1943). There are also numerous entries in the archives of the Gereformeerde Kerk prior to 1910 which involve Afrikaners who were censured by the local church council for consulting "Malay doctors," "Slamaaiers," etc.

32. Irving Hexham gathered information on this topic in 1972–74 and later in 1981. Because many elderly folk told what their parents had taught them on these matters he is confident that the picture he is describing is accurate for before 1910.

33. See Hexham, *Irony*, 80–1.

34. Exact details cannot be provided because of confidentiality.

35. Provincial Synod of the GK, Orange Free State, 1910, article 39; 1911, article 15. After 1911 problems such as witchcraft disappear from GK records at both local and provincial levels.

36. Confidentiality prevents identification. Today the best known example of a man born with the caul is Nicholaas van Rensburg, the "prophet" of Lichtenburg. See Sybrand Botha, *Profeet en Krygsman: Die Lewensverhaal van Siener van Rensburg* (Johannesburg: Nasionale Pers, n.d.). The book was probably published in the late 1930s or early 1940s. A collection of his prophecies can be seen in the Ossewa Brandwag Archives at the University of Potchefstroom.

37. A group of elderly predikants provided information on this topic. The stories dated from around 1918 but drew upon ideas which went back well into the nineteenth century.

38. Interview in 1981 with a 93-year-old Afrikaner woman who held many of these beliefs although she acknowledged that she would never mention them to her predikant.

39. Du Plessis, *The Life of Andrew Murray of South Africa* (London: Marshall Brothers, 1919), 85; P. B. van der Watt, *Die Nederduitse Gereformeerde Kerk, 1824–1905* (Pretoria: N.G. Kerkboekhandel, 1980), 51–7; *Ons Nederduitse Gereformeerde Kerk*, ed. D.T. Hanekom (Cape Town: N.G. Kerk-Uitgewers, n.d.), 132–200.

40. The term "indigenous" is used in this connection because Van der Hoff's church, unlike the NGK, was created in Southern Africa.

41. See S.P. Engelbrecht, *Geskiedenis van die Nederduitsch Hervormde Kerk van Afrika* (Pretoria: J.H. de Bussy, 1953); Hinchliff, *The Church*, 61; J. du Plessis, *Andrew Murray*, 139–41; Walker, *History*, 266; T.R.H. Davenport, *South Africa: A Modern History*, (3rd ed.; London: Macmillan; and Toronto: University of Toronto Press, 1987), 86–9.

42. Protestant theologians who rejected Christian orthodoxy were initially called "rationalists" or "liberals" because of their commitment to "modern thought." During the 1860s, in the Netherlands and South Africa the term "moderns," later the term "modernist," came into use. See Du Plessis, *Andrew Murray*, 190, 212, 235; Andrew Murray, *A Lecture on the Modern Theology* (Cape Town: Pike and Byles, 1868). The Dutch title of this work was *Het Moderne Ongeloof*, i.e. modern unbelief. Theodore Christlieb, *Modern Doubt and Christian Belief*, trans. H.U. Weitbrecht (New York: Scribner, Armstrong and Co., 1874); and Abraham Kuijper (Kuyper), *Lectures on Calvinism* (New York: Fleming H. Revell, 1898, repr. Grand Rapids: Wm. B. Eerdmans, 1931),

NOTES

19–40.

43. His "liberalism" and theological views were strongly attacked by Frans Lion Cachet. See Davenport, *South Africa*, 90.

44. Hinchliff, *The Church*, 62.

45. Du Plessis, *Andrew Murray*, 144; Hinchliff, *The Church*, 62–3.

46. This strange paradox of a church which produced the most radical theology but political reaction is commented on briefly by John de Gruchy, in *The Church Struggle in South Africa* (Grand Rapids: Eerdmans; Cape Town: David Philip, 1979), 20–1, 76.

47. See J.P. Jooste, *Die Geskiedenis van die Gereformeerde Kerk in Suid Afrika, 1859–1959* (Potchefstroom: The Potchefstroom Herald, 1959); Hinchliff, *The Church*, 63–4.

48. B. Spoelstra, *Die "Doppers" in Suid-Afrika 1760–1899* (Cape Town: Nasionale Boekhandel, 1963), 150–5.

49. Some Doppers argue that their nickname "Dopper" came from a conservative lifestyle that extinguished the new light of the Enlightenment, from the Dutch "domper," a device used to quench the flame of a candle. See Spoelstra, *Die "Doppers,"* 16–32; and, W. Postma, *Doppers* (Bloemfontein: Het Westen, 1918), 11–16.

50. G.C.P. van der Vyver, *Professor Dirk Postma, 1818–1890* (Potchefstroom: Pro-Rege, 1958), 177–87, 223–6.

51. Church historians differ in their interpretation of these events. See Van der Vyver, *Postma*, 177–267 (esp. 202–44); Engelbrecht, *Geskiedenis*, 141–66; Hinchliff, *The Church*, 63–4; Spoelstra, *Die "Doppers,"* 157–68; *Gereformeerde Kerk Almanak* (Burgersdorp: Gereformeerde Kerk) for 1868 and 1899.

52. See Hexham, *Irony*, passim.

53. After 1915 members of the Gereformeerde Kerk continued to play an important role in the Nationalist movement. But in general the church, as a church, withdrew from direct political activity.

54. See P.B. van der Watt, *John Murray, 1826–1882: Die Eerste Stellenbosse Professor* (Pretoria: N.G. Kerkboekhandel, 1979).

55. J.D. du Toit singled out holiness meetings for criticism in a series of articles and booklets because, in his view, they encouraged the Anglicization of Afrikaners. See J.D. du Toit, *De Streversvereeniging Bevordeeld van Gereformeerd Standpunt* (Potchefstroom: Potchefstroom Herald, 1905); and *De Christelijk Strevers Vereeniging: Antwoord* (Pretoria: Van Schaik, 1906).

56. See F.B. Meyer, *A Winter in South Africa* (London: National Council of Evangelical Free Churches, 1908), 92, 101–3; and H.S. Bosman, *Een Terugblik op Kerkelijke en Godsdienstige Toestanden in de Transvaal* (Cape Town: Van de Sandt de Villiers, 1923).

57. See Davenport, *South Africa*, 90; Engelbrecht, *Geskiedenis*, 216–48; T.N. Hanekom, *Die Liberale Rigting in Suid-Afrika: 'n Kerkhistoriese Studie* (Stellenbosch: CVS Boekhandel, 1952), 186–9.

58. The liberal strategy was to obtain a court ruling that a Cape Ordinance of 1843 limited membership of the NGK to persons living within the boundaries of the Cape Colony, because many evangelical members of the Synod were missionary preachers active beyond those boundaries. By excluding them from the Synod the liberals hoped to weaken the evangelical group in the Cape and gain control of the Church's key institutions. See Du Plessis, *Andrew Murray*, 208–36.

59. *Ibid.*, 311–29, 353–72, 394–413.

60. Peter Hinchliff, *The Anglican Church in South Africa* (London: Darton, Longman and Todd, 1963), 75–81, 153–66, 179–205. Regarding the growth of the Anglican church in Transorangia, Hinchliff notes that in the year 1895, "no figures at all are given for the three northern dioceses, Bloemfontein, Pretoria and Mashonaland"(178). The role played by the Anglican, Methodist and some other English-speaking churches is severely criticized in James Cochrane, *Servants of Power* (Johannesburg: Ravan Press, 1987); and Charles Villa-Vicencio, *Trapped in Apartheid* (Maryknoll, New York: Orbis; Cape Town: David Philip, 1988).

61. W.E. Brown, *The Catholic Church in South Africa: From its Origins to the Present Day* (New York: P.J. Kennedy and Sons, 1960), 170–93.

62. See Roy Coad, *A History of the Brethren Movement* (Exeter: Paternoster Press, 1976), 28–9, 203; and H. Pickering, *Chief Men Among the Brethren* (London: Pickering and Inglis, 1931), 185–6.

63. Information of this topic comes from Steven Hayes of the Department of Missions at the University of South Africa.

64. Walter J. Hollenweger, *The Pentecostals* (Peabody, Mass: Hendrickson, 1988), 120–2. Hollenweger gives far greater details in his twelve-volume German edition.

65. For a partial discussion of this theme see Irving Hexham, "Possible Theosophical Influences on the Rise of African Independent Churches in the Early Part of the Twentieth Century," in *Afro-Christian Religion at the Grassroots in Southern Africa*, ed. G.C. Oosthuizen and Irving Hexham (Lewiston: Edwin Mellen, 1991), 364–92. Information on the Swedenborgians comes from members of the group, and Dr. Hennie Pretorius. Kurt Widmar provided information on the Mormons. The activities of Jehovah's Witnesses are discussed in Erhard Kamphausen, *Anfänge der kirchlichen Unabhängigkeitsbewegung in Südafrika* (Frankfurt am Main: Peter Lang, 1976), 464–9.

PAGES 121–134

66. Meyer, *Winter,* 233–4 is highly critical of English-speaking churches.

67. Du Plessis, *Andrew Murray,* 187–207, 311–29. See Meyer, *Winter,* 54–5, 209–20.

68. Du Toit, *De Streversvereeniging* and *Strevers Vereeniging: Antwoord*; see D'Assonville, *Totius,* vol. 6, 202–14.

69. See S.B. Spies, *Methods of Barbarism?* (Cape Town: Human and Rousseau, 1978), 118, 215, 262, 363, 381.

70. Hexham, *Irony,* 69–71; see Marthina Elaine Botha, "Partikuliere Volksorg in die Afrikaanse Volkskultuur met Verwysing na die ATKV (SAS en H), 1930–1964," (Ph.D. thesis: Potchefstroom Universiteit vir CHO, 1970), 97–117; J.H. Coetzee, *Die Barmhartigheidsdiens van die Gereformeerde Kerk in Suid-Afrika, 1859–1949* (Potchefstroom: Pro-Rege, 1953). For an historical study of social work within the NGK see J.P. Claasen, *Die Sieketroosters in Suid-Afrika, 1652–1866* (Pretoria: N.G. Kerkboekhandel, 1977). More recent NGK social work is dealt with in *Kerk en Huisgesin,* ed. G. Cronjé (Cape Town: N.G. Kerk-uitgewers, 1958).

71. See Donald Denoon, *A Grand Illusion* (London: Longman, 1973).

72. Albert Grundlingh, "Collaborators in Boer Society," in *The South African War,* ed. Peter Warwick (London: Longman, 1980), 276–7, has noted deep division within Afrikanerdom brought about by the war, even to the extent of deserters having to set up their own "Scoutskerk"; but many Afrikaners interviewed in the 1970s repeatedly told how the "Church" had literally saved people's lives by providing them with food, clothing and shelter.

73. The growth of church attendance among English-speaking whites appears similar to that of the Boers until 1900. After that there is a marked increase in the involvement of the Boers in Christian activities.

74. See R.G. Wagner, "Coenraad de Buys in Transorangia," *The Societies of Southern Africa in the 19th and 20th Centuries,* ed. Shula Marks, 4 (1973): 1–8; Robert Ross, "Griqua Power and Wealth: An Analysis of the Paradoxes and their Interrelationship," The Society of Southern Africa in the 19th and 20th Centuries, 4 (1973): 9–18; Martin Legassick, "The Frontier Tradition in South African Historiography," *The Societies of Southern Africa in the 19th and 20th Centuries,* ed. Shula Marks, 2 (1971): 1–33.

75. J. du Plessis *A History of Christian Missions in South Africa* (London: Longmans, Green, 1911), 101–7 remains a basic source. The other essential source is C.P. Groves *The Planting of Christianity in Africa,* 4 vols. (London: Lutterworth, 1948–1958, repr. 1964). This chapter uses these works to provide its essential structure. Other books like D.R. Briggs and Joseph Wing, *The Harvest and the Hope: The Story of Congregationalism in South Africa* (Johannesburg: United Congregational Church, 1970) were also consulted.

76. The son of the Methodist missionary Samuel Broadbent (1794–1867). He was born near present-day Wolmaransstad on 1 July 1823 and eventually became a missionary to India.

77. W.J. Gordon Mears, *Methodism in the Transvaal* (privately published, 1972), 2–3.

78. *Ibid.,* 13. Similar figures for the Orange Free State were not available to the authors. In general, statistics on various missions are hard to obtain. The best are to be found in the *Condensed Report of the Statistical Committee of the United Missionary Conference* (Lovedale: Mission Press, 1889), which gives information about the situation in 1883. Unfortunately many other statistical summaries, such as those found in Du Plessis, *Missions,* 464, and various census reports are for the whole of South Africa and not Transorangia.

79. *Condensed Report,* 30–5.

80. James Stewart, *Dawn in the Dark Continent* (1903, repr. Edinburgh: Oliphant Anderson and Ferrier, 1906), 140.

81. Gustav Warneck, *History of Protestant Missions* (Edinburgh: Oliphant Anderson and Ferrier, 1901), 219.

82. *De Maandbode,* 15 September 1897; Abraham Kuyper, *The South African Crisis,* trans. A.E. Fletcher (London: Stop the War Committee, 1900), 20–7; Gereformeerde Kerk, *Algemene Vergadering Notule, Transvaal 1910,* art. 49.

83. See Kuyper, *South African Crisis,* 72–5.

84. See J.D. du Toit, *Die Methodisme,* first published 1903; *Totius: Versamelde Werke,* ed. V.E. d'Assonville (Cape Town: Tafelberg, 1977), vol 6, 129–240.

85. See *Condensed Report,* 18; Hinchliff, *Anglican Church,* 144–7, 155–62, 188–92; Edwin Farmer, *The Transvaal as a Mission Field* (London: Wells, Gardner, Darton and Co., 1900), 59–76.

86. See W.E. Brown, *Catholic Church,* 170–93. Unfortunately no statistics appear to be available for this period.

87. The Plymouth Brethren came into existence in 1827–8 and sent their first missionary overseas in 1828 and to Transorangia in the 1850s. See Coad, *History,* 28–9, 203; and Dan Crawford, *Thinking Black* (London: Morgan and Scott, 1912).

88. See Edwin W. Smith, *Aggrey of Africa: A Study in Black and White* (London: SCM, 1929), 164–84. See also David B. Coplan, *In Township Tonight!* (Johannesburg: Ravan Press, 1985), 37–46.

89. See J.M. Cronjé, *Born to Witness* (Pretoria: N.G. Boekhandel, 1982), 39–45, 53–5, 63–5; Du Plessis, *Christian Missions,* 284–7; and Du Plessis, *Andrew Murray,* 373–93. For their evangelical ethos, see Spoelstra, *Die "Doppers,"* 57–61; G.C.P. van der Vyver, *Postma,* 396–400; and W.L. Maree, *Lig in Soutpansberg* (Pretoria: N.G. Kerkboekhandel, 1962).

425

90. The Hermannsburg missionaries were the worst paid, receiving, on those occasions when their pay actually materialized, the equivalent of $150 per year, in 1899; other German missionaries received around $250, while British missionaries were in the $400 range. By contrast ministers of the Afrikaans churches received around $600 per year.

91. The Rev. Markus Nietzke gave some invaluable insights and very kindly obtained a number of rare texts used in this section.

92. See Elfriede Strassberger, *The Rhenish Mission Society in South Africa, 1830–1950* (Cape Town: C. Struik, 1969).

93. D.W. van der Merwe, *Die Geskiedenis van die Berlynse Sending-genootskap in Transvaal, 1860–1900* (Pretoria: Die Staatsdrukker, 1984), and *Die Berlynse Sending-genootskap en Kerkstigting in Transvaal, 1904–1962* (Pretoria: Die Staatsdrukker, 1987).

94. Cf. Georg Haccius, *Hannoversche Missionsgeschichte* (Hermannsburg: Druck und Verlag der Missionhaus, 1920).

95. Cf. Fritz Hasselhorn, *Bauermission in Südafrika: Die Hermannsburger Mission im Spannungsfeld der Kolonialpolitik, 1880–1939* (Erlangen: Verlag der Ev.-Luth. Mission, 1986), 99, 214–15.

96. Cf. Hasselhorn, *Hermannsburger*, 53, 65; D. Julius Richter, *Geschichte der Berliner Missionsgesellschaft, 1824–1924* (Berlin: Verlag der Buchhandlung der Berliner Ev. Missionsgesellschaft, 1924), 230, 232, 373.

97. Richter, *Geschichte*, 221, 230, 232; Peter Delius, *The Conversion* (Johannesburg: Ravan Press, 1984), 53, says "Sekhukhune ... suspected (with some cause) that the missionaries were agents of the Z.A.R." That Delius's ambiguous statement creates an entirely false impression about the role of the Berlin missionaries through the over-simplification of a highly complex situation is confirmed by the ongoing work of Ulrich van der Heyden.

98. Cf. Hasselhorn, *Hermannsburger*, 53 ; J. Spiecker, *Er führet mich*, 15.

99. Cf. *Report of the Centenary Conference of the Protestant Missions of the World held in Exeter Hall (June 9th–19th) London 1888*, ed. J. Murray Mitchell (London: James Nisbet and Co., 1889), 306–8; Spiecker, *Er führet mich*, 26–7; Richter, *Geschichte*, 233–6.

100. Cf. Richter, *Geschichte*, 233–42.

101. *Ibid.*, 233–4.

102. Cf. Glenda Kruss, "A Critical Review of the Study of Independent Churches in South Africa"; and J.J. Kritzinger, "What the Statistics Tell Us about the African Indigenous Churches in South Africa"; both in *Religion Alive: Studies in the New Religious Movements and Indigenous Churches in Southern Africa*, ed. G.C. Oosthuizen (Johannesburg: Hodder and Stoughton, 1986), 21–32, 253–61.

103. See Peter Delius in *The Land Belongs to Us* (London: Heinemann, 1984), 153, 158–78. For a different assessment see Ulrich van der Heyden, *Alexander Merensky: Erinnerungen aus dem Missionsleben in Transvaal, Südafrika, 1859–1882* (Berlin: Cognoscere, forthcoming).

104. Ivan der Heyden, 241; cf. Delius, *The Land Belongs to Us*, 159–78.

105. Cf. Hasselhorn, *Hermannsburger*, 100 ; Richter, *Geschichte*, 371.

106. According to R. Wagner, ample evidence exists in the Transvaal Archives to show that these charges were correct (private communication).

107. Richter, *Geschichte*, 367, 703–7. This incident is depicted in the Australian film "Breaker Morant." Cf. *Breaker Morant and the Bushveldt Carbineers*, ed. Arthur Davey (Cape Town: Van Riebeeck Society, 1987), and R.L. Wallace, *The Australians at the Boer War* (Canberra: Australian Government Publishing Service, 1976), 367, 372–9.

108. Cf. Hasselhorn, *Hermannsburger*, 65–8; and Richter, *Geschichte*, 367.

109. Delius, *Land Belongs to Us*, comments on the spread of Christianity through migrant labour, while Peter Warwick, *Black People and the South African War, 1899–1902* (Cambridge: Cambridge University Press, 1983), documents the impact of the concentration camp system and the war in general on blacks.

110. Hexham, *Texts on Zulu Religion*, 411–29.

111. See Alexander Merensky, *Erinnerungen aus dem Missionsleben in Transvaal 1859–1882* (Berlin: No. 43, Buchhandlung der Berliner Evangel. Missionsgesellschaft, 1899 (1888); and Gustav Warneck, *Abriss einer Geschichte der Protestantischen Missionen von der Reformation bis auf die Gegenwart* (Berlin: Verlage von Martin Warneck, 1901). Karla Poewe is currently working on this issue.

112. Hinchliff, *The Church*, 72.

113. See Rodney Stark and William Sims Bainbridge, *The Future of Religion* (Berkeley: University of California Press, 1985).

114. Roger Finke and Rodney Stark, *The Churching of America 1772–1990: Winners and Losers in our Religious Economy* (New Brunswick, NJ: Rutgers University Press, 1992) Oosthuizen and Hexham, *Afro-Christian Religion*.

115. Cf. Public Record Office, London, *South Africa*, CO 537, 1904, "Ethiopianism Report;" cf. John Buchan, *Prester John* (London: Thomas Nelson, 1910).

116. Edgar Brookes, *The History of Native Policy in South Africa from 1830 to the Present Day* (Cape Town: Nasionale Pers, 1924), 442–3.

117. Bengt Sundkler, *Bantu Prophets in South Africa* (London: Lutterworth Press, 1948).

118. As late as 1989 we were told by a respected black South African scholar that the prophet Isaiah Shembe died after he jumped off a cliff in the mistaken belief that he could fly. This story is quite untrue, but it does illustrate the continuation of prejudice against AICs.

119. The Thembu Church of the Rev. Nehemiah Tile was founded in 1884; German mission records indicate that similar movements in Transorangia predate Tile's movement. Cf. Kamphausen, *Anfänge*, 76–89.

120. See A. Lee, *The Native Separatist Church Movement in South Africa* (Cape Town: n.p., 1926), 29–31.

121. See *The Scriptures of the Amanazaretha of Ekuphakameni*, ed. Irving Hexham (Calgary: Calgary University Press, 1994), xxvi–xxix, 7–11; and Absolom Vilakazi, "Isonto Lamanazaretha: The Church of the Nazarites" (M.A. thesis: Hartford Seminary, 1954), 31–7.

122. See E.K. Lukhaimane, "The Zion Christian Church of Ignatius (Engenas) Lekganyane, 1924–1948: An African Experiment with Christianity" (M.A. thesis: University of the North, 1980), 9–23.

123. See *Empirical Studies of African Independent / Indigenous Churches*, ed. G.C. Oosthuizen and Irving Hexham (Lewiston: Edwin Mellen Press, 1992), 1–3.

124. On the issue of Christian identity see F.B. Welbourn, *East African Christian* (London: Oxford University Press, 1965), 191–202.

125. One example of success is the Hermannsburg mission which experienced a consistent growth rate of over 15 per cent until 1899, after which the growth rate declined to around 5 per cent. Cf. Hasselhorn, *Hermannsburger*, 128. Rodney Stark and Lynne Roberts, "The Arithmetic of Social Movements: Theoretical Implications," *Sociological Analysis*, 43, 1 (1982): 53–67, analyses the significance of growth rates.

126. Cf. Charles Henry Robinson, *The Conversion of Europe* (London: Longman, Green, 1917), 348–436.

127. For an extensive discussion of church growth and growth rates in the context of American society, which challenges many of the "certainties" of American church history on the basis of statistical analysis, see Finke and Stark, *Churching*.

128. To date relatively little has been published about or even by the wives of nineteenth-century missionaries.

129. It is important to recognize that the criticism of nineteenth-century missions and missionary methods is not restricted to the secular press. Many evangelical writers, like Charles Kraft and members of the Fuller School of Church Growth, are among the severest critics of missions. An earlier example of such criticism is to be found in James Stewart, *Dawn*, 292–7, 307–28. In accepting such a negative assessment of the missionary enterprise many missionaries and mission leaders, as well as later commentators, commit the fallacy of treating growth in terms of static numbers, not growth rates calculated as a percentage of the total membership at any one time.

130. While this is commonly recognized among Blacks, it is equally true for Boer society, as oral interviews in the early 1970s and 1981 showed.

8 / KINGHORN / THE AFRIKANER CHURCHES / PAGES 135–154

1. The GK did not develop this concept. It took it over from the "anti-revolutionary" theology of Abraham Kuyper.

2. Ferdinand Deist, *Wetenskapsteorie en Vakmetodologie in Bybelwetenskaplike Navorsing in Suid-Afrika* (Pretoria: HSRC, 1990), vol. 2, 63ff.

3. Irving Hexham, *The Irony of Apartheid* (Lewiston: Edwin Mellen, 1981), 147–68.

4. For a general, insider history, see G.D. Scholtz, *Die Geskiedenis van die Nederduitse Hervormde of Gereformeerde Kerk van Suid-Afrika* (Elsiesrivier: Nasionale Handelsdrukkery, 1956).

5. Johannes du Plessis, *The Life of Andrew Murray of South Africa* (London: Marshall Bros, 1919). Du Plessis concludes this biography with the question: "Is it too much to prophesy that Andrew Murray's works will take their place upon our bookshelves next to Augustine and à Kempis … ?"

6. In 1910, as the editor of the *Kerkbode* (The Church Herald, the official paper of the NGK), Du Plessis had spoken out strongly against one W.A. Joubert for having chosen to do postgraduate studies in (anti-humanist) Kuyperian theology at the Free University of Amsterdam, rather than standard theology at Utrecht. Du Plessis argued that the theology of Amsterdam was not NGK theology, but "the new inhibiting, strictly confessional tendency of Kuyper …" This was an early indication of things to come, for Du Plessis's most hostile opponents later came from the growing circle of Kuyperian anti-modernists.

7. The entire court proceedings were published afterwards in *Die Kerksaak tussen Prof. J. du Plessis en die Ned. Geref. Kerk in Suid-Afrika* (Cape Town: Nasionale Pers, 1932).

8. F.S. Malan, *Ons Kerk en Prof. Du Plessis* (Cape Town: Nasionale Pers, 1933), 281.

9. The report was published in five volumes dealing with the economic, psychological, educational, medical and sociological deprivation of "poor whites", under the title *Die Armblankevraagstuk in Suid-Afrika / The Poor White Problem in South Africa* (Stellenbosch: Pro Ecclesia, 1932).

10. *Kerk en Stad* (Stellenbosch: Pro Ecclesia, 1947), 42ff, 289ff (my translation).

11. For detail see T. Dunbar Moodie, *The Rise of Afrikanerdom* (Los Angeles: UCLA Press, 1975), 197ff; Heribert Adam and Hermann Giliomee, *The Rise and Crisis of Afrikaner Power* (Cape Town: David Philip, 1979), 145ff.

NOTES

12. See *Kerk en Stad*; P.F. Greyling, *Die Nederduits Gereformeerde Kerk en Armesorg* (Cape Town: Nasionale Pers, 1939); Louis L.N. Botha, *Die Maatskaplike Sorg van die NG Kerk in SA* (Paarl: Paarl Drukpers, 1956).

13. *South African Outlook*, 7 (1 Feb. 1933).

14. *Handelinge van die Federale Raad van Kerke* (1935): 94–9 (my translation).

15. *Die Gereformeerde Vaandel*, 7 (April 1939): 104–9 (my translation).

16. *Die Sendingraad van die NG Kerke in SA: Sy Ontstaan, Doel en Strewe* (1944): 73ff (my translation).

17. *Rassebakens: Offisiële orgaan van "Die Afrikanerbond vir Rassestudie"* (1939): 58 (my translation).

18. F.J.M. Potgieter and H.G. Stoker, *Koers in die Krisis* (Stellenbosch: Pro Ecclesia), vol. 1, vii (my translation).

19. Nico J. Diederichs, *Nasionalisme as Lewensbeskouing en sy Verhouding tot Internasionalisme* (Bloemfontein: Nasionale Pers, 1936), 62ff (my translation).

20. Deist, *Wetenskapsteorie*, 120 (my translation).

21. *Ibid.*, 121.

22. Jacobus D. Vorster, "Die Rassevraagstuk volgens die Skrifte," *Die Gereformeerde Vaandel*, 15 (Aug. 1947): 4–6 (my translation).

23. *Agenda van die 22ste Sinode van die Ned. Geref. Kerk van Suid-Afrika* (1951): 184, 187 (my translation).

24. P.J. Viljoen, *Handelinge van die 21ste Vergadering van die Raad van Kerke* (11 May 1949), 222ff (my translation).

25. *Die Naturellevraagstuk: Referate Gelewer op die Kerklike Kongres van die Gefedereerde Ned. Geref. Kerke in SA, Byeengeroep deur die Federale Sendingraad* (Bloemfontein, 4–6 April 1950).

26. See John Lazar, "Verwoerd versus the 'Visionaries': The South African Bureau of Racial Affairs (Sabra) and Apartheid, 1945–1961," in *Apartheid's Genesis, 1935–1962*, ed. Philip Bonner, Peter Delius and Deborah Posel (Johannesburg: Ravan Press and Witwatersrand University Press, 1993), 362–92.

27. The average salary of a white, educated person at the time was approximately 4,500 rands per year.

28. For more on the above trends and figures, see Dionne Crafford, *Aan God die Dank* (Pretoria: NGKB, 1982), vol. 1, 175ff.

29. Johann Kinghorn, *Die NG Kerk en Apartheid* (Johannesburg: Macmillan, 1986), 111ff.

30. Carefully documented by Abraham Lückhoff, *Cottesloe* (Cape Town: Tafelberg, 1978).

31. *Ibid.*, 60 (my emphasis).

32. *Kerk en Samelewing* (1990): 39f (my translation and emphasis).

33. *Agenda van die 22ste Sinode*, 189ff (my emphasis)

34. *Ras, Volk en Nasie en Volksverhoudinge in die Lig van die Skrif* (Cape Town: NGKU, 1974), 72 (my translation).

35. *Agenda van die 4de Vergadering van die Algemene Sinode van die NG Kerk in Afrika* (1975): 112, 121ff (my translation).

36. Daan Cloete and Dirk Smit, *A Moment of Truth* (Cape Town: Tafelberg, 1984), 7–10, 39ff.

9 / DE GRUCHY / THE ENGLISH-SPEAKING CHURCHES / PAGES 155–172

1. The Church of England, which was the church of the British colonial establishment, became a separate province of the Anglican communion in 1870. Named the Church of the Province of South (now Southern) Africa (CPSA), it is in communion with Canterbury. Like the CPSA, the Church of England in South Africa (CESA) also traces its origins to the colonial church, but is not part of the Anglican communion. The CPSA, which is Anglo-Catholic by tradition, is much larger than the CESA, which is strongly evangelical. CESA has not been involved in the ecumenical movement in South Africa. See Peter B. Hinchliff, *The Anglican Church in South Africa: An Account of the History and Development of the Church of th Province* (London: Darton, Longman and Todd, 1963); Anthony Ive, *A Candle Burns in Africa: The Story of the Church of England in South Africa*, 2nd ed. (Hillcrest: Church of England, 1992).

2. The Salvation Army and the Society of Friends (Quakers) do not normally identify themselves as churches.

3. Peter B. Hinchliff, *The South African Rite and the 1928 Prayer Book* (London: Mowbray, 1960).

4. See for example Bishop Walter Carey, of Bloemfontein's tract, *Dutch and British in South Africa: An Appeal to the British Section* (n.p., n.d.).

5. See Leo Kuper, "African Nationalism in South Africa, 1910–1964," *The Oxford History of South Africa*, ed. Monica Wilson and Leonard Thompson, vol. 2 (Oxford: Clarendon Press, 1971), 434.

6. Peter Walshe, *The Rise of African Nationalism in South Africa* (Berkeley: University of California Press, 1971), 38, 158f.

7. This is the major theme of Charles Villa-Vicencio, *Trapped in Apartheid* (New York: Orbis; Cape Town: David Philip, 1988); see, for example, 65ff.

8. See, for example, the address on "The Exclusion of the Bantu" by the Rev. Z.R. Mahabane, President of the Cape National Congress, 1921 in *From Protest to Challenge : A Documentary History of African Politics in South Africa 1882–1964*, vol. 1: *Protest and Hope*, ed. Thomas Karis, Gwendolen M. Carter and Gail Gerhart (Stanford: Hoover Institute Press, 1972), 290ff.

428

9. *The Christian Express* (1 Nov. 1912): 163.

10. See Article 12 of the 1919 Constitution of the SANNC.

11. James Cochrane, *Servants of Power: The Role of the English-speaking Churches, 1903–1930* (Johannesburg: Ravan Press, 1987), 133.

12. "The Attempted Revolution on the Rand," *Church Times* (London), (22 April 1922); editorials in *Christian Express* (March 1922, April 1922) published in *Outlook on a Century: South Africa 1870–90*, ed. Francis Wilson and Dominique Perrot (Lovedale : Lovedale Press and Sprocas, 1973), 339f, 342.

13. C. Howard Hopkins, *John R. Mott: 1865–1955* (Grand Rapids: Eerdmans, 1979), 294f.

14. Ruth Rouse and Stephen Charles Neill, *A History of the Ecumenical Movement 1517–1948*, 2nd ed. (London: SPCK, 1967).

15. *Proceedings of the Twenty-eighth General Assembly*, East London (September 1927), 159.

16. *Ibid.*, 48.

17. Leslie A. Hewson, *An Introduction to South African Methodists* (Cape Town: Methodist Publishing House, 1950), 89.

18. Hopkins, *John R. Mott*, 675f; Elfriede Strassberger, *Ecumenism in South Africa: 1936–1960* (Johannesburg: SACC, 1974), 134ff.

19. Strassberger, *Ecumenism*, i.

20. On the founding of FEDSEM and the saga of black theological education in South Africa from the 1950s, see Aelred Stubbs (ed.), *The Planting of the Federal Theological Seminary of Southern Africa* (Alice: Lovedale Press, 1973); Simon Gqubule, "An Examination of the Theological Education of Africans in the Presbyterian, Methodist, Congregational, and Anglican Churches in South Africa from 1860–1960" (Ph.D. thesis: Rhodes University, Grahamstown, 1978); and Roger D.T. Cameron, "Some Political, Ecumenical and Theological Aspects of the History of the Federal Theological Seminary, 1963–1975" (M.A. thesis: University of Cape Town, 1984).

21. Presbyterian Church of South Africa, *Proceedings and Decisions of General Assembly* (1984): 317–18, 351.

22. For documentation and commentary see *Journal of Theology for Southern Africa*, 23 (June 1978), and 40 (1982).

23. See John W. de Gruchy, *The Church Struggle in South Africa*, revised ed. (Grand Rapids: Eerdmans; Cape Town: David Philip, 1986), 55.

24. See Johann Kinghorn (ed.), *Die NG Kerk en Apartheid* (Johannesburg: Macmillan, 1986), 90ff.

25. Michael E. Worsnip, *Between Two Fires: The Anglican Church and Apartheid* (Pietermaritzburg: University of Natal Press, 1991); Freda Troup, *In Face of Fear: Michael Scott's Challenge to South Africa* (London: Faber and Faber, 1950); R.G. Clarke, "For God or Caesar: An Historical Study of Christian Resistance to Apartheid by the Church of the Province of South Africa, 1946–1957" (Ph.D. thesis: University of Natal, 1983).

26. Alan Paton, *Apartheid and the Archbishop: The Life and Times of Geoffrey Clayton* (Cape Town: David Philip, 1973), 151ff.

27. Trevor Huddleston, *Naught for Your Comfort* (London: Fontana, 1956); Clarke, "For God or Caesar," 94ff.

28. Garth Abraham, *The Catholic Church and Apartheid: The Response of the Catholic Church in South Africa to the First Decade of National Party Rule 1948–1957* (Johannesburg: Ravan, 1989), 62ff.

29. See Thomas Karis, "The Congress Movement," in *From Protest to Challenge*, ed. Thomas Karis, Gwendolen M. Carter and Gail Gerhart, vol. 3 (Stanford: Hoover Institute Press, 1977), 30; Nelson Mandela, *Long Walk to Freedom* (Randburg: Macdonald Purnell, 1994), 156–7.

30. See Villa-Vicencio, *Trapped in Apartheid*, 95–107.

31. T.R.H. Davenport, "The Triumph of Colonel Stallard: The Transformation of the Natives (Urban Areas) Act between 1923 and 1937," *South African Historical Journal*, 2 (1970): 94ff, on the 1937 Act.

32. De Gruchy, *The Church Struggle*, 60f; Alan Paton, *Apartheid and the Archbishop*, 275–82.

33. Abraham, *The Catholic Church and Apartheid*, 111.

34. A.H. Lückhoff, *Cottesloe* (Cape Town: Tafelberg, 1978); De Gruchy, *The Church Struggle*, 62f.

35. *Cottesloe Consultation: The Report of the Consultation among South African Member Churches of the World Council of Churches, 7–14 December 1960* (Johannesburg, 1961), 74f.

36. John W. de Gruchy and Charles Villa-Vicencio (eds.), *Apartheid is a Heresy* (Grand Rapids: Eerdmans; and Cape Town: David Philip, 1983), 148f.

37. "Cottesloe Statement," 16(a), in *Cottesloe Consultation*, 75.

38. Peter Walshe, *Church Versus State in South Africa: The Case of the Christian Institute* (New York: Orbis, 1983).

39. *World Conference on Church and Society, Official Report* (Geneva: WCC, 1967).

40. Pauline Webb and Barney Pityana (eds.), *A Long Struggle: World Council of Churches Involvement in South Africa* (Geneva: WCC, 1994).

NOTES

41. De Gruchy, *The Church Struggle*, 115ff.

42. Sydney Hudson-Reed, *By Taking Heed ... The History of Baptists in Southern Africa 1820–1977* (Roodepoort, Transvaal: Baptist Publishing House, 1983), 231.

43. See Robert Fatton, Jr., *Black Consciousness in South Africa: The Dialectics of Black Resistance to White Supremacy* (Albany: State University of New York Press, 1986); N. Barney Pityana, Mamphela Ramphele, Malusi Mpumlwana and Lindy Wilson (eds.), *The Bounds of Possibility: The Legacy of Steve Biko and Black Consciousness* (Cape Town: David Philip, 1991).

44. On the connection between UCM and SASO see Basil Moore, "Black Theology: In the Beginning," *Journal for the Study of Religion*, 4, 2 (September 1991): 23.

45. See Itumuleng Mosala and Buti Tlhagale (eds.) *The Unquestionable Right to be Free* (Maryknoll, NY: Orbis, 1986).

46. De Gruchy, *The Church Struggle*, 138f.

47. *Ibid.*, 169ff.

48. Kinghorn, *Die NG Kerk en Apartheid*, 117ff. Kinghorn notes a breakaway to the NGK in Afrika by white clergy disillusioned by NGK policy, e.g. Nico Smith.

49. Alan Brews, "Vulnerable to the Right: The English-speaking Churches"; Michael Worsnip, "Low Intensity Conflict and the South African Church"; Roger A. Arendse, "The Gospel Defence League: A Critical Analysis of a Right Wing Christian Group in South Africa"; all in *Journal of Theology for Southern Africa*, 69 (December 1989).

50. Hudson-Reed, *By Taking Heed*, 401f.

51. Richard Quebedeaux, *The New Charismatics* (New York: Doubleday, 1976).

52. *An Anglican Prayer Book, 1989: Church of the Province of Southern Africa* (London: Collins, 1989).

53. *Ecunews*, 4 (27 February 1980), 11.

54. John W. de Gruchy, "Towards a Confessing Church," in De Gruchy and Villa-Vicencio, *Apartheid is a Heresy*, 75ff.

55. De Gruchy and Villa-Vicencio, *Apartheid is a Heresy*; G.D. Cloete and D.J. Smit, *A Moment of Truth: The Confession of the Dutch Reformed Mission Church* (Grand Rapids: Eerdmans, 1984).

56. John W. de Gruchy, "The Church and the Struggle for South Africa," Buti Tlhagale and Itumuleng Mosala (eds.) in *Hammering Swords into Ploughshares* (Johannesburg: Skotaville, 1986).

57. See Charles Villa-Vicencio (ed.), *Theology and Violence: The South African Debate* (Johannesburg: Skotaville, 1987).

58. See Allan Boesak and Charles Villa-Vicencio (eds.), *When Prayer Makes News* (Philadelphia: Westminster, 1986).

59. *The Kairos Document: Challenge to the Church*, 2nd ed. (Johannesburg: Skotaville, 1986).

60. *The Kairos Document*, 9.

61. See the discussion in Klaus Nürnberger and John Tooke (eds.), *The Cost of Reconciliation in South Africa* (Cape Town: Methodist Publishing House, 1988); Anthony Balcomb, *Third Way Theology: Reconciliation, Revolution and Reform in the South African Church during the 1980s* (Pietermaritzburg: Cluster Publications, 1993).

62. *Evangelical Witness in South Africa* (Dobsonville, South Africa: Concerned Evangelicals, 1986).

63. "The Church Overseas," 10 November 1924, Bishop Wilfred Parker's Scrapbook, CPSA Archives.

64. Phoebe Swart-Russell, "The Ordination of Women to the Priesthood: A Critical Examination of the Debate within the Anglican Communion, 1961–1986" (Ph.D. thesis: University of Cape Town, 1988); see also *Journal of Theology for Southern Africa*, 66 (1989).

65. Leslie A. Hewson, *An Introduction to South African Methodists*, 100.

66. Cherryl Walker, *Women and Resistance in South Africa* (London: Onyx Press, 1982; 2nd. ed. New York: Monthly Review Press; Cape Town: David Philip, 1991), 32f.

67. Walker, *Women and Resistance*, 189f.

68. Denise Mary Ackermann, "Liberating Praxis and the Black Sash: A Feminist Theological Perspective" (D.Th. thesis: University of South Africa, 1990), 137ff.

69. *Ibid.*, 231.

70. Louw Alberts and Frank Chikane (eds.), *The Road to Rustenburg: The Church Looking Forward to a New South Africa* (Cape Town: Struik Christian Books, 1991); Denise Ackermann, Jonathan A. Draper and Emma Mashinini (eds.), *Women Hold Up the Half the Sky in Southern Africa* (Pietermaritzburg: Cluster Publications, 1991).

71. Sheena Duncan, "Some Reflections on Rustenburg," in Ackermann et al., *Women Hold Up Half the Sky*, 386; see also John W. de Gruchy, "From Cottesloe to Rustenburg and Beyond: The Rustenburg Conference in Historical Perspective," *Journal of Theology for Southern Africa*, 74 (March 1991).

72. "The Cape Town Statement," *Journal of Theology for Southern Africa*, 77 (December 1991).

73. Speech delivered by Nelson R. Mandela, President of the ANC to the Free Ethiopian Church of Southern Africa, Potchefstroom, 14 December 1992.

PAGES 173–194

10 / SCRIBA WITH LISLERUD / LUTHERAN MISSIONS AND CHURCHES / PAGES 173–194
We wish to thank Richard Pierard for helpful comments on an earlier draft.

1. Lutherische Monatshefte, 34, 4 (April 1995): 46; 2.22. Lutheran World Information, 1 Jan. 1994), 9.

2. Georg Scriba, "Die Zeichen der Zeit: Lutherische Kirche im Spannungsfeld Süd-afrikas," in *Lutherische Mission in Südafrika*, ed. Heinrich Bammann (Hermannsburg: Evangelische Lutherisches Missionswerk in Niedersachsen [ELM], 1990) 198.

3. *Condensed Report of the Statistical Committee of the United Missionary Conference* (Lovedale: Lovedale Mission Press, 1889). These figures referred to 1884.

4. Johannes Christian Hoekendijk, *Kirche und Volk in der deutschen Missionswissenschaft*, ed. E. Pollmann, Th.B. vol. 35: *Mission und Ökumene* (Munich: Chr. Kaiser-Verlag, 1967), 71–5. Peter Beyerhaus, *Die Selbständigkeit der jungen Kirchen als missionärisches Problem* (Wuppertal-Barmen: Verlag der Rheinischen Missions-gesellschaft, 2nd. edn., 1959), 78–96 especially mentions Gustav Warneck and Bruno Gutmann in this connection.

5. Augsburg Confession, art. VII. See Georg Scriba, "Kirche als Ziel der Mission: Volkskirche oder Weltkirche? Dargestellt am Beispiel der Hermannsburger Mission in Südafrika" (Masters thesis: Erlangen, 1974), 98, 125.

6. John Hoge, *Die Geschichte der ältesten evangelisch–lutherischen Gemeinde in Kapstadt: Ein Beitrag zur Geschichte des Deutschtums in Südafrika* (München: Reinhardt, 1939), 52. The original Afrikaans version is in *Archives Year Book for South African History* (1938, vol. 2).

7. Reino Ottermann, *The Centenary of the Synod 1895–1995* (Cape Town: Evangelical Lutheran Church in Southern Africa, 1995), 11–16, 90–124; Reino Ottermann, "Aus der Geschichte der Lutherischen Kirche am Kap" (Windhoek: Afrikanischer Heimatkalender, 1968), 64–7.

8. At the suggestion of the Dutch Governor Janssens, Baviaanskloof was renamed Genadendal in 1804. J. du Plessis, *A History of Christian Missions in South Africa* (London, 1911; reprint, Cape Town: C. Struik, 1965), 84.

9. Georg Schmidt, *Das Tagebuch und die Briefe von Georg Schmidt, dem ersten Missionär in Südafrika (1737–1744). Dagboek en Briewe van George Schmidt, eerste sendeling in Suid-Afrika (1737–1744)*, ed. H.C. Bredekamp and J.L. Hattingh (Cape Town: Instituut vir Historiese Navorsing, 1981).

10. Bernhard Krüger, *The Pear Tree Blossoms: A History of the Moravian Mission Stations in South Africa, 1737–1869* (Genadendal: Moravian Book Depot, 1966); Bernhard Krüger and P.W. Schaberg, *The Pear Tree Bears Fruit: The History of the Moravian Church in South Africa: Western Cape Province, 1869–1960* (Genadendal: Moravian Book Depot, 1984).

11. Gustav Menzel, *Die Rheinische Mission: Aus 150 Jahren Missionsgeschichte* (Wuppertal: Verlag der Veneinigten Evangelischen Mission, 1978); G.B.A. Gerdener, *Recent Developments in the South African Mission Field* (Cape Town and Pretoria: N.G. Kerk-Uitgewers, 1958), 83–6.

12. Siegfried Knak, "Berliner Missionsgesellschaft," in *Evangelisches Kirchenlexikon*, ed. H. Brunotte and O. Weber (Göttingen: Vandenhoek u. Ruprecht, 1956), vol. 1, 400.

13. Harald Winkler, "The Divided Roots of Lutheranism in South Africa: A Critical Overview of the Social History of the German-speaking Lutheran Missions and the Churches Originating from their Work in South Africa" (M.A. dissertation: University of Cape Town, 1989), 25–7, sees Botshabelo as the model mission station of the Berlin Mission Society.

14. Julius Richter, *Geschichte der Berliner Missionsgesellschaft 1824–1924* (Berlin: Buchhandlung der Berliner Missionsgesellschaft, 1924); Helmut Lehmann, *150 Jahre Berliner Mission* (Erlangen: Erlanger Taschenbücher, 1974); Helmut Lehmann, *Zur Zeit und zur Unzeit: Geschichte der Berliner Mission 1918–1972*, 3 vols. (Berlin: Berliner Missionswerk, 1989); Daniel Werner van der Merwe, "Die Geskiedenis van die Berlynse Sendinggenootskap in Transvaal, 1860–1900," *Argiefjaarboek vir Suid-Afrikaanse Geskiedenis*, 46 (Pretoria: Die Staatsdrukker, 1983); Daniel Werner van der Merwe, "Die Berlynse Sendinggenootskap en Kerkstigting in Transvaal, 1904–1962," *Argiefjaarboek vir Suid-Afrikaanse Geskiedenis*, 50 (Pretoria: Die Staatsdrukker, 1987); Linda Zöllner and J.A. Heese, *The Berlin Missionaries in South Africa and their Descendants* (Pretoria: Human Sciences Research Council, 1984); Gerdener, *Recent Developments*, 83.

15. Georg Haccius, *Hannoversche Missionsgeschichte*, 4 vols. (Hermannsburg: Verlag der Missionshandlung, 1909, 1910, 1914, 1920); Winfried Wickert, *Und die Vögel des Himmels wohnen unter seinen Zweigen: Hundert Jahre Bauernmission in Südafrika* (Hermannsburg: Missionshandlung, 1949); Hinrich Pape, *Hermannsburger Missionäre in Südafrika: Lebens-und Arbeitsberichte mit Bildern; Ein Beitrag zur südafrikanischen Missionsgeschichte* (Pretoria: Hinrich Pape, 1986, 1991); W. Wendebourg, *Louis Harms, als Missionsmann: Missionsgedanken und Missionsstaten des Begründers der Hermannsburger Mission* (Hermannsburg: Missionshandlung, 1910), 285–6.

16. Aunice Ernest Nsibande, "Historical Development of the Evangelical Lutheran Church: South Eastern Region" (M.Th. thesis: University of South Africa, 1981), 21.

17. Gerdener, *Recent Developments*, 86.

18. Joan Millard, "Grass-roots Pioneers of Transvaal Methodism," *Missionalia*, 17 (Nov. 1989): 193.

19. G. Scriba, *The History of the United Evangelical Lutheran Church in Southern Africa* (unpublished:

431

NOTES

Kroondal, 1989).

20. Wilhelm Bodenstein, *25 Jahre der Hermannsburger deutsch evangelisch–lutherischen Synode in Südafrika* (Hermannsburg: Verlag der Missionshandlung, 1937); Georg Scriba, "Auf dem Wege zur Synode: Die Entstehung der Hermannsburger deutsch evangelisch–lutherischen Synode, 1911" (unpublished paper: Kroondal, 1989).

21. Scriba, "Auf dem Wege zur Synode," 1–3.

22. *Lutherische Kirche treibt Lutherische Mission: Festschrift zum 75 jährigen Jubiläum der Bleckmarer Mission, 14.6.1892–1967*, ed. Friedrich Wilhelm Hopf (Hermannsburg: Bleckmarer Mission, 1967); Johannes Schnackenberg, *Geschichte der freien ev.–luth. Synode in Südafrika, 1892–1932* (Celle: Otto Romberger, 1933); Carl Eggers, *Geschichte und Entwicklung unserer Synode von 1890 ab aus Copien zusammengestellt* (unpublished collection, 1951); Georg Scriba, *Einheit lutherischer Missionen und Kirchen in Natal* (unpublished: Durban, 1976), 21–2.

23. Jarle Simensen (ed.), *Norwegian Missions in African History*, vol. 1: *South Africa 1845–1906* (Norwegian University Press: Oslo, 1986).

24. By 1926 there were seven missionaries, eight black pastors and forty-one evangelists at 4 main stations and 60 out-stations, with 6,796 baptized members. Gerdener, *Recent Developments*, 93.

25. By 1955 the number of church members had grown to 16,572, on 7 main stations and 155 out-stations. Three hospitals and three dispensaries with over 5,000 patients and 1,000 outpatients had been erected by 1955. *Ibid.*, 93.

26. Nsibande, "Historical Development," 23.

27. In 1955 the mission had nine stations in South Africa with 21,000 members, served by 11 missionaries and 16 black ordained pastors and 56 trained evangelists. The CSM erected 3 hospitals at Bethany in Dundee, Ceza in Zululand and Appelsbosch in Natal and 72 government-aided and private schools, with 7,200 pupils. Gerdener, *Recent Developments*, 96–7.

28. Gunnar Lislerud, "Christian Origins to c. 1910: A Call to Missions" (unpublished: Oslo, 1992). The Gustav Adolf changed to the Nordic church of Transvaal, St. Johannes Kelvin, in 1975 (Rev. D. Harms, personal communication).

29. Fritz Hasselhorn, *Bauernmission in Südafrika: Die Hermannsburger Mission im Spannungsfeld der Kolonialpolitik, 1880–1939* (Erlangen: Erlanger Monographien, 1988), 56. Hasselhorn (p. 101) concludes that black aspirations for independence were to be suppressed by administrative means and by emphasizing the leadership role of the missionary. A synod for the Tswana region was only reconstituted in 1957.

30. Ottermann, "Aus der Geschichte," 64–7; Ottermann, *Centenary of the Synod*, 17–24.

31. Georg Scriba, "Auf dem Wege," 3–5. The term *prases* (president) was used in Germany to denote a pastor of pastors without implying the hierarchical office of a "bishop" as in the Roman Catholic tradition.

32. Georg Scriba, "Historical Review of ELCSA(N-T): The Evangelical Lutheran Church in Southern Africa (Natal–Transvaal)" *Communicatio: The Annual Newsletter of the ELCSA(N-T)* (1993): 8.

33. Van der Merwe, *Berlynse Sendinggenootskap en Kerkstigting*, 14; Lehmann, *150 Jahre Berliner Mission*, 132–3.

34. H. Schlyter, *The History of the Co-operating Lutheran Missions in Natal, 1912–1951* (Moorleigh: Mission Press, 1953).

35. In 1972 this publication was taken over by the SACC, together with the ecumenical publication *Ministry*, and has since been published as the *Journal of Theology for Southern Africa*. Georg Scriba, "Einheit lutherischer Missionen und Kirchen in Natal," (unpublished), 17.

36. This sub-committee of the CLM was changed in 1969 to an "Indian Church Council," which was independent of the mission societies and subsequently joined the South Eastern Regional Church. Scriba, "Einheit," 17.

37. *Ibid.*, 25.

38. As early as 1889, during the visitation of the Hermannsburg mission director in South Africa, the idea of one Lutheran church in South Africa was seen as a goal. Georg Haccius, *Denkschrift über die von 1887–1889 abgehaltene General-Visitation der Hermannsburger Mission in Südafrika* (Hermannsburg: Missionshandlung, 1890), 20–1.

39. Minutes of Constituent Assembly, para 8 (Christianenburg: 1958).

40. Winkler, "Divided Roots," 44; Georg Scriba, "Kirche als Ziel der Mission," 69.

41. Constitutional Assembly: Evangelical Lutheran Church, 5th–10th July 1960, Kwa Mondi, Eshowe, Zululand: *Minutes*, para. VI.A.

42. "United Testimony" and "Church Practice and Discipline," ed. Gunnar Lislerud (Durban: Lutheran Publishing House, 1961), 60–2.

43. Theodor Homdrom, "The Problem of Lutheran Unity in South Africa" (M.Th. thesis: Luther Theological Seminary, 1959); Heinrich Schlag, "Lutherische Zusammenarbeit und Einigungsversuche im Südlichen Afrika" (Masters thesis: Hamburg, 1966); Wolfgang Albers, "Evangelisch–Lutherische Kirche im Südlichen Afrika: ELCSA(SER) – ELCSA (TswR)" (Masters thesis: Hamburg, 1970); Scriba, "Kirche als Ziel der Mission"; Hans

PAGES 173–194

Florin, *Lutherans in South Africa* (original reprint Benoni, 1965; revised, Durban: Lutheran Publishing House, 1967). The bishops' dates were confirmed by Bishop Zulu.

44. Scriba, "Kirche als Ziel der Mission," 69–72; G. Pakendorf, "Die gegenwertige und zukünftige Gestalt der Féderation der evangelisch–lutherischen Kirchen im Südlichen Afrika (FELKSA)," Kirchliches *Aussenamt, Brückenschlag: Berichte aus den Arbeitsgebieten des kirchlichen Aussenamtes der Evangelischen Kirche in Deutschland*, vol. 3: *Afrika* (Stuttgart: Quell Verlag, 1970), 228–9. The churches, with their dates of independence, were: the Rhenish Mission Church in SWA (1957), ELC in Southern Rhodesia (1959), ELCSA Tswana Regional Church (1959), ELCSA South East Region (1960), DELKSWA – German Evang.–Luth. Church in SWA (1960), ELCSA Ovambocavango (1960), Moravian Church Western Cape (1960), ELCSA (Transvaal Church) (1961), ELCSA (Cape Church) (1961), ELCSA Transvaal Region (1962), ELCSA Cape–Orange Region (1963); ELCSA (Hermannsburg) (1963), and the Moravian Church, Eastern Cape (1966). The two Lutheran free churches became independent later (LCiSA in 1967, FELSiSA in 1972).

45. Nsibande, "Historical Development," 45–6.

46. Their position was defined by an advisory Lutheran Mission Council and their placements discussed with Home Boards in a Joint Committee for South Africa: *ibid.*, 48–52.

47. Scriba, "Einheit lutherischer Missionen," 23ff.

48. DELKSWA – German Evang.–Luth. Church in SWA, ELCSA (Transvaal Church), ELCSA (Cape Church), and ELCSA (Hermannsburg). Within UELCSA the two churches, ELCSA (Hermannsburg) and ELCSA (Transvaal) merged in 1981 to form the ELCSA (Natal–Transvaal).

49. Scriba, "Kirche als Ziel der Mission," 73.

50. The participating churches in FELCSA were: ELC Rhodesia, ELCSWA (Ovambocavango), ELCSWA (Rhenish Mission Church), DELKSWA, ELCSA (Cape Church), ELCSA (Transvaal Church), ELCSA (Hermannsburg), ELCSA (South Eastern Region), ELCSA (Transvaal Region), ELCSA (Tswana Region), ELCSA (Cape–Orange Region), Moravian West Cape, Moravian East Cape, the individual congregations of St. Olav's (Durban), St. Kelvin (Johannesburg), and the Indian Congregational Council (ICC) under the auspices of the CLM in Natal. Scriba, "Einheit Lutherischer Missionen," 25–6.

51. The Indian Council decided to join ELCSA. The congregation of St. Olav split on this issue, the larger part remaining an independent congregation with no affiliation to a Lutheran church body.

52. Scriba, "Einheit lutherischer Missionen," 29–30.

53. *LUCSA: Lutheran Communion in Southern Africa*, ed. Friedrich Graz (Bonaero Park: LUCSA, 1995), 8, 14, 16. (Each church was asked to write a short history of one page.)

54. Georg Scriba, *A Historical Review of the United Evangelical Lutheran Church in Southern Africa: Church and Culture* (Report for the General Meeting in Cape Town, 8 Dec. 1989, 25th anniversary of UELCSA: unpublished, 1989), 9.

55. In 1995 member churches of LUCSA were (with approximate membership numbers): ELCM in Malawi (10,800), ELCZ in Zimbabwe (70,000), ELCB in Botswana (16,583), IELA in Angola (16,000), IELM in Mozambique (1,108), ELCIN in Namibia (470,000), ELCRN in Namibia (250,000), ELCIN(DELK) in Namibia (6,850); and in South Africa, the Moravian East (49,350), Moravian West (50,000), ELCSA (615,135), ELCSA(Natal–Transvaal) (11,100), and ELCSA (Cape Church) (6000). Friedrich Graz, *Report of the Executive Director*, in *Documentation for the Second General Conference of LUCSA*, Harare, 3–7 April 1995, Information Brochure.

56. A.P. Smit, *God Made It Grow: History of the Bible Society Movement in Southern Africa 1820–1970* (Cape Town: Bible Society of South Africa, 1970), 195–203, 212–17, 223–5.

57. Hoekendijk, *Kirche und Volk*, 71–5; Beyerhaus, *Selbständigkeit der jungen Kirchen*, 78–96.

58. Lislerud, "United Testimony" and "Church Practice and Discipline."

59. Axel-Ivar Berglund, *Report on the Missiological Institute, Umphumulo, on Concepts of Death and Funeral Rites* (Umphumulo: Lutheran Theological College, 1969).

60. Minutes of the Second General Conference of LUCSA in Harare, 3–7 April 1995.

61. Millard, "Grass-roots Pioneers of Transvaal Methodism," 195; Heinrich Bammann, *Tshimologo ya Efangele mo Bakweneng ba Mogopa ka David Mokgatle: le tswelelopele ya yona mo kerekeng ya luthere mo ELCS odi* (Rustenburg: Lutheran Book Depot, 1991); Hasselhorn, *Bauernmission*, 43, 48, 52; Du Plessis, *Christian Missions*, 376–7.

62. Heinrich Filter, *Paulina Dlamini, Servant of Two Kings* (Pietermaritzburg: Shooter and Shuter, 1986), 82–4.

63. *Ibid.*, 114.

64. Lehmann, *150 Jahre Berliner Mission*, 88–9; Van der Merwe, *Berlynse Sendinggenootskap en Kerkstigting*, 10–12; Julius Richter, *Geschichte der evangelischen Mission in Afrika* (Gütersloh: C. Bertelsmann, 1922), 376, 426. Personal information about writer's second marriage from the Rev. Ntshabeleng. lecturer at the LTC, Umphumulo.

65. Aunice Ernest Nsibande, "The Founding of Umphumulo Seminary," in *Dynamic African Theology: Umphumulo's Contribution*, ed. H. Nelson, P. Lwandle, and V. Keding (Durban: Pinetown Printers, 1992), 6–8; Nsibande, "Historical Development," 68.

NOTES

66. Gunnar Lislerud, "The History of the Lutheran Seminary Umphumulo" (unpublished manuscript, 1992). See the chapter "Church mergers and consciousness movements."

67. Schlyter, *The History of the Co-operating Lutheran Missions in Natal 1912–1951*, 24.

68. This was to be a joint ecumenical venture by the Anglican, Congregational, Methodist, and Presbyterian churches, supported by the Theological Education Fund (TEF) under the World Council of Churches (Lislerud, "Lutheran Seminary Umphumulo"). It later moved to Pietermaritzburg, where it was closed in 1993–4.

69. Günther Wittenberg, "History and Challenges of Lutheran Theological Education in Pietermaritzburg," in *Lutheran Theology in Southern Africa*, ed. Georg Scriba (Pietermaritzburg: Lutheran House of Studies, 1993).

70. Aunice Ernest Nsibande, "The Black Theologian and the Black Church," in *Dynamic African Theology*, ed. Nelson, Lwandle, and Keding, 28–30.

71. Florin, *Lutherans in South Africa*, 71.

72. *World Missionary Atlas*, ed. Harlan P. Beach and Charles H. Fahs (New York: Institute of Social and Religious Research, 1925), 134–5, 147–8, 160.

73. Florin, *Lutherans in South Africa*, 72.

74. Richard Elphick, personal communication.

75. D Siegfried Knak, *Zwischen Nil und Tafelbai: Eine Studie über Evangelium, Volkstum und Zivilisation, am Beispiel der Missionsprobleme unter den Bantu* (Berlin: Heimatsdienst-Verlag, 1931).

76. Florin, *Lutherans in South Africa*, 85–6.

77. Winkler, "Divided Roots," 64.

78. Wolfram Kistner, *Outside the Camp: A Collection of Writings by Wolfram Kistner*, ed. H. Brandt (Johannesburg: South African Council of Churches, 1988).

79. Winkler, "Divided Roots," 72.

80. Bernhard Lange, "One Root Two Stems: A Study on the Origin and Consequences of the Constitution of the First Missionary Congregation of the Hermannsburg Mission Society in South Africa" (Church History III project, University of Natal, Pietermaritzburg, 1988); Winkler, "Divided Roots."

81. Winkler, "Divided Roots," 73.

82. Florin, *Lutherans in South Africa*, 67.

83. *Ibid.*, 74–5.

84. G. Lislerud (ed.), *The Lutheran Teaching on the Two Kingdoms and its Implications and Possibilities for the Witness of the Church in the South African Society* (Umphumulo: Lutheran Theological College, Umphumulo, 1968); Albers, *Evangelisch–Lutherische Kirche*, 153–5; *Lutheran Churches: Salt or Mirror of Society? Case Studies on the Theory and Practice of the Two Kingdoms Doctrine* (Geneva: Lutheran World Federation, 1977).

85. Albers, *Evangelisch–Lutherische Kirche*, 156; Winkler, "Divided Roots," 59–61.

86. Karlheinz Schmale (ed.), *State and Church: Lectures of the Church Leaders Seminar of the FELCSA, April 1968*, (Rustenburg: Hermannsburg Mission Book Depot, 1969).

87. A.W. Habelgaarn and K. Schmale, *Appeal to Lutheran Christians in Southern Africa Concerning the Unity and Witness of Lutheran Churches and their Members* (signed on behalf of the Conference of FELCSA held on 11–13 February 1975 and sent to all FELCSA member churches, Braamfontein 1975).

88. Hans-Jürgen Becken (ed.), *Salvation Today for Africa* (Durban: Lutheran Publishing House, 1974), 1.

89. J.S. Matthews, *Dossier: ELCSA's Contribution to the Liberation Struggle in South Africa*, in Evangelical Lutheran Church of South Africa, Sixth General Assembly, 5–9 December 1989 [for 1988], (Johannesburg: ELCSA, 1989) 18.

90. Carl-J. Hellberg, *A Voice of the Voiceless: The Involvement of the Lutheran World Federation in Southern Africa 1947–1977* (Lund: Sceab Verbum, 1979); Lutheran World Federation, *Reports on the Assemblies*, (Geneva: various dates, especially Reports on the Sixth and Seventh Assemblies).

91. Klaus Kremkau (ed.), *EKD und Kirchen im Südlichen Afrika: Das Problem der kirchlichen Einheit im Rassen-Konflikt* (Bielefeld: EKD: Eckart-Verlag, 1974); Rudolf Hinz, "Die Evangelische Kirche in Deutschland und die Kirchen im Südlichen Afrika, 1973–1986," *Sonderdruck aus kirchliches Jahrbuch für die Evangelische Kirche in Deutschland, 1984*, vol. 2: *Kirchen im südlichen Afrika* (Gütersloh: Verlagshaus Gerd Mohn, n.d.).

92. Friedrich Graz (ed.) *Handreichung der Generalsynode der Vereinigten Evangelisch–Lutherischen Kirche im Südlichen Afrika* (Pietermaritzburg: unpublished, 1983), 13–31; Scriba, *A Historical Review of UELCSA*, 10.

93. "Constitution of the Evangelical Lutheran Church in Southern Africa," in *Handbook of the Evangelical Lutheran Church in Southern Africa*, ed. Mervin Assur (Johannesburg: ELCSA, 1984), 15–44.

94. Constitution of the Evangelical Lutheran Church in Southern Africa (Natal–Transvaal); Statutes of ELCSA (Natal–Transvaal), Constitution 1 Jan. 1991 (Kempton Park: ELCSA (Natal–Transvaal), 1991).

95. Scriba, "Die Zeichen der Zeit," 189ff.

11 / BRAIN / THE ROMAN CATHOLIC CHURCH / PAGES 195–210

1. See K.S.Latourette, *A History of the Expansion of Christianity*, vols. 4, 5, 6 (Grand Rapids: Zondervan Publishing House, 1973).

2. The terms "vicariate" and "vicar apostolic" were introduced by the pope to replace diocese and bishop when, in the 16th century, the powerful kings of Spain and Portugal claimed and enforced their right to appoint bishops to the dioceses within their territories, especially in South America.

3. Most of the Catholics living in Devereux's diocese were Irish soldiers or discharged soldiers who had had little formal education.

4. P. R. Griffith, *The Cape Diary of Bishop Patrick Raymond Griffith for the Years 1837 to 1839*, ed. J. B. Brain (Pretoria: Southern African Catholic Bishops' Conference (SACBC), 1988).

5. These are the Holy Childhood Society, Society for the Propagation of the Faith, and the Society of St. Peter Claver, all of which collect and distribute funds to overseas missions.

6. Francis L. Coleman, *A History of St Aidan's* (Grahamstown: ISER, Rhodes University, 1980); Judy Ann Ryan, "An Examination of the Achievements of the Jesuit Order in South Africa, 1879–1934" (M.A. thesis, Rhodes University, 1990).

7. W.E. Brown, *The Catholic Church in South Africa from its Origins to the Present Day* (London: Burns and Oates, 1960), 25–6, 86–7.

8. Brown, *Catholic Church in South Africa*, 182–3; *Catholic Magazine of South Africa*, 8:147. See also Kathleen Boner, "Dr F.C. Kolbe: Priest, Patriot and Educationist" (D.Litt. et Phil. thesis: Unisa, 1980).

9. Brown, *Catholic Church in South Africa*, 183.

10. Brain, *Catholics in Natal*, vol. 2 (Durban: Archdiocese of Durban, 1982), 44–6.

11. E. de Mazenod, *Letters to Ceylon and Africa 1847–1860*, vol. 4 (Rome: General Postulation, OMI, 1980), 206.

12. The first Zulu grammar and the first Zulu dictionary were published in London in 1855, for the use of Colenso's group, and were not yet available in Natal.

13. J.B. Brain, *Catholic Beginnings in Natal* (Durban: Griggs, 1975), 81–3.

14. It is the opinion of some anthropologists that the majority of Sotho men were monogamists, only the chiefs being rich enough to practise polygamy.

15. Brown, *Catholic Church in South Africa*, 140.

16. A complete account of the Trappists in the eastern Cape is to be found in A.A. Weiswurm, *The Dunbrody Episode: The Futile Attempt to Establish the Trappists in the Sunday's River Valley of the Cape Province, South Africa: A Documentation* (Mariannhill: Mariannhill Mission Press, 1975).

17. For details of this mission method see J. B. Brain, *Catholics in Natal*, vol. 2, chap. 3.

18. R. Kneipp and others, *Mariannhill and its Apostolate: Origin and Growth of the Congregation of the Mariannhill Missionaries* (Reimlingen: St. Joseph's Mission Press, 1964), 61.

19. The daughter houses of Mariannhill bought and established before 1909 were Reichenau (1886), Einsiedeln (1887), Mariathal (1887), Oetting (1887), Kevelaer (1888), Lourdes (1888), Centocow (1888), Rankweil (1888), Maria Ratschitz (1890), Maria-Zell (1893), Emaus (1894), Maria Telgte (1895), Maryhilf (1895), Clairvaux (1896), Citeaux (1896), Mariatrost (1896), St. Bernard's Mission (1896), Hardenberg (1896), Maria Linden (1897), Himmelberg (1901), St. John (1900), Maria Stella (1901), St. Joseph (1908), Keilands (1909). There were also two in Rhodesia – Monte Kassino and Triashill.

20. Brain, *Catholics in Natal*, vol. 2, 161–2.

21. *South African Catholic Magazine*, 5, 54 (June 1895): 329.

22. For details of the development of the various Mariannhill missions see J. Dahm, *Mariannhill: seine innere Entwicklung, sowie seine Bedeutung für die katholische Missions- und Kulturgeschichte Südafrikas* (Mariannhill: Missionsdruckerei, 1950), 138–47.

23. For details of these problems see J.B. Brain, *The Catholic Church in the Transvaal* (Johannesburg: Missionary Oblates of Mary Immaculate, 1991), chap. 5.

24. *Ibid*, 133 ff.

25. The original Natal vicariate was subdivided many times. In 1879 the Zambezi mission was confined to the Society of Jesus; in 1886 the Transvaal was separated and at the same time Basutoland, the Orange Free State, and the Diamond Fields were combined in the Vicariate of the Orange Free State under Bishop Anthony Gaughren, OMI. In 1894 a separate prefecture of Basutoland was formed, and made into a vicariate in 1909. Two further vicariates, Maseru and Leribe, were created later. The Transvaal was subdivided in 1910 when Belgian Benedictines took over the Pietersburg prefecture; this was in turn subdivided to create the prefecture of Louis Trichardt–Tzaneen staffed by the Irish Missionaries of the Sacred Heart. Both are now dioceses. The Kimberley diocese was subdivided several times between 1884 and 1940. The Orange Free State vicariate, based on Bloemfontein, was split to allow the Holy Ghost Fathers (Spiritans) to work in the Kroonstad prefecture and in 1948 there was a further subdivision, creating the diocese of Bethlehem. After 1921 many more vicariates or prefectures were created and allocated to various congregations. In 1921 Mariannhill, Swaziland and Eshowe were created vicariates apostolic. After the establishment of the hierarchy in 1951 the diocese of Natal became the archdiocese of Durban while northern Natal was separated to form part of the diocese of Volksrust (now Dundee diocese). Keetmanshoop vicariate was formed in 1949 and Bechuanaland prefecture in 1959. Klerksdorp was separated from the Transvaal as a prefecture in 1965 and became a diocese, under the Oblates of Mary

NOTES

Immaculate of the Belgian Province, in 1978. From the original Natal vicariate twenty of the present dioceses were created, making each more manageable and allowing many different Orders and congregations to engage in missionary work. For an account of their work in East and South Africa, see G. Sieber, *The Benedictines of Inkamana* (Ertabtei St. Ottilien, Eos Verlag, 1995).

26. D.H. St. George, "A Lay Apostle of the 19th Century: Saturnino do Valle," *Études Oblats,* 25, 2 (1966): 1–22.

27. Memoirs of Natal Missions: Father Saby, 1895–1923 (Archdiocesan Archives, Durban).

28. Memoirs of Father Leo Muldoon (typescript in Catholic History Bureau, Johannesburg).

29. The first black priests were sent from Mariannhill to Rome to be trained in the 1880s and 1890s (Brain, *Catholics in Natal,* vol. 2, 251–4).

30. H. Daniel-Rops, *A Fight for God* (London: Dent, 1966), 291–3.

31. L. Brouckaert, "Better Homes, Better Fields, Better Hearts: The Catholic African Union, 1927–1939" (B.A. Hons. essay: University of the Witwatersrand, 1985).

32. Archbishop Denis Hurley believes that this period, between the wars, was the time emphasizing the three Ds: Duty, Devotion and Doctrine.

33. The report of a committee, chaired by Paul Sauer, to formulate an "apartheid" policy before the election, quoted in G.Abrahams, *The Catholic Church and Apartheid: The Response of the Catholic Church in South Africa to the First Decade of National Party Rule 1948–1957* (Johannesburg: Ravan Press, 1989), 21.

34. The Catholic weekly founded in Cape Town in 1920 and financed by the Catholic Publishing Company, subsidized by the bishops. The editor at this time was Father Louis Stubbs.

35. Letters, dated 21 March 1939 and 2 Sept. 1948, Hennemann papers, Archdiocesan Archives, Cape Town, *The Things That Make for Peace: A Report to the Catholic Bishops and the Church in Southern Africa,* ed. B. Connor (Pretoria: SACBC, 1985), appendix 1–2, 217–19.

36. *Ibid.,* 24.

37. H. A. de Wet, "Die Roomse Kerk in Suid Afrika," *Kerkbode,* 70 (1953): 346.

38. Quoted in Abrahams, *The Catholic Church and Apartheid,* 26.

39. D.M. Bixby, "The Roman Catholic Church and Apartheid in Education" (Honours dissertation: University of Cape Town, 1977), 63; Abrahams, *Catholic Church and Apartheid.* Schools run by Seventh-Day Adventists also continued but were not receiving a government subsidy.

40. Quoted from the Chairman's Report, in Bixby, "The Roman Catholic Church and Apartheid in Education."

41. This view was held by several priests including the late Father D.H. St. George, who opposed the bishops' decision from the first. Hastings holds that Christian marriage and family should be the priority in propagating the Christian faith. Hastings, *Christian Marriage in Africa* (London: SPCK, 1973).

42. A "black spot" was defined as a place in the midst of a white area where a small number of blacks were living permanently or temporarily.

43. See the following examples from the League's newsletter *Candidus:* "Meddling into Matters of State Security" by A.H. da Fonseca, 17 July 1964; "Puerile Ranting and Raving" by K.T. Rawlings, 22 July 1964; "Hurley Taken to Task" by M. Andrews, 19 Sept. 1983.

44. A. Hastings, *A History of African Christianity 1950–75* (Cambridge: Cambridge University Press, 1979), 173–4.

45. B. Hinwood, "The Dutch Reformed Churches and the Catholic Church; Some Areas of Agreement and Disagreement," in *Towards Christian Unity,* ed. G. O'Reilly (Pretoria: SACBC, Pastoral Action series no. 30, 1983).

46. The commissions deal with Christian service; seminaries; priests, deacons and religious; Christian education and worship; ecumenism and inter-religious affairs; immigrants and refugees; laity; social communication; justice and reconciliation; finance; church and work; theology; marriage officers.

47. The Catholic bishops of South Africa, Mozambique, Angola, Zimbabwe and Lesotho also meet from time to time through the Inter-Racial Meeting of Bishops of Southern Africa (Imbisa), to learn of developments in one another's countries. A Symposium of Episcopal Conferences of Africa and Madagascar (Secam), consisting of the bishops' conferences of Africa and Madagascar, also meets regularly

48. I am indebted to Father Dominic Scholten OP for information on the secretariat, on Lumko and on a number of other points in the recent period.

49. The first published work of translation was undertaken by Father Joseph Gérard, who translated the Gospel of St. Luke into Sesuto (South Sotho); he also translated the catechism for the use of his neophytes. Mariannhill missionaries began to work on a Zulu translation of the Bible soon after their arrival, the first section, consisting of extracts, being published in 1887.

50. Dr. Newton Adams of the American Board Mission was the first to translate parts of the Bible into Zulu in 1846. The first complete Zulu edition appeared in 1883.

51. His best known works are *Olden Times in Zululand and Natal* (London: Longmans, 1929); *The Zulu People Before the White Man Came* (Pietermaritzburg: Shuter and Shooter, 1949); *Bantu Origins, the People and*

their Language (Cape Town: Struik, 1963). They have been much debated by modern scholars. See *The Mfecane Aftermath: Reconstructive Debates in Southern African History*, ed. Carolyn Hamilton (Johannesburg and Pietermaritzburg: Witwatersrand and Natal University Presses, 1995).

52. SACBC, Minutes of plenary session 1987, 102–3.

53. The late Chris Hani, Patrick Lekota, and many of the present black leaders are products of Catholic education.

54. Brain, *Catholic Church in the Transvaal*, 245.

55. The office bearers of the Commission of the Laity are present and give their reports at the plenary sessions of the SACBC.

56. One such occasion resulted in the publication of *The Laity in Dialogue with their Bishops: Consultation Between the Laity and the Bishops during the Plenary Session of the SACBC, February 1975* (Pretoria: SACBC, 1975).

57. See Brain, *Catholics in Natal*, vol. 2, 98–9 [case of Mother Tiefenbrock, superior of the King William's Town Dominican Sisters versus Bishop Charles Jolivet over the transfer of a teacher from Oakford], and Brain, *Catholic Beginnings in Natal*, 88–9 [a dispute in Lesotho]; and Brown, *Catholic Church in South Africa*, 306–7 [appeal by the Filles de Jésus to the Sacred Congregation of Religious against Bishop Delalle, who lost his case].

58. SACBC, Pastoral Action series no. 2, 14–15.

59. Quoted in *Southern Cross*, 28 Jan. 1970.

60. The signatories were Fathers P. Mangaliso Mkhatshwa, D. Moetatele, J.L. Louwfant, C. Mokoko, and A. Mabona.

61. These are Bloemfontein, Cape Town, Durban, Eshowe, Klerksdorp, Mariannhill, Umtata, Witbank, Johannesburg (auxiliary), Durban (auxiliary).

62. A discussion of these suggestions is to be found in Brain, *The Catholic Church in the Transvaal*, 252–7.

63. E. Norman, *Roman Catholicism in England from the Elizabethan Settlement to the Second Vatican Council* (Oxford: Oxford University Press, 1985), 111–12.

64. Brown, *Catholic Church in South Africa*, 339.

65. I am indebted to Archbishop D.E. Hurley for this phrase, which accurately describes the position of the Catholic Church in South Africa in earlier times.

12 / PRETORIUS & JAFTA / AFRICAN INITIATED CHURCHES / PAGES 211–226

1. J.J. Kritzinger, "The Numbers Game," *African Insight*, 23: 4 (1993), 248; Patrick Johnstone, *Operation World* (Carlisle, U.K.: OM Publishing, 1993), 494. Although reliable AIC statistics do not exist and are often exaggerated, the figures given here take some of the more realistic estimates into account. See also note 70.

2. Allan Anderson, *Tumelo: The Faith of African Pentecostals in South Africa* (Pretoria: Unisa, 1993), 138.

3. David Bosch, "Introduction," in Inus Daneel, *Quest for Belonging* (Gwero: Mambo Press, 1987), 9.

4. Janet Hodgson, "'Don't Fence Me In': Some Problems in the Classification of African Religious Movements," in *Exploring New Religious Movements*, ed. A.F. Walls and W.R. Shenk (Elkhart: Mission Focus, 1990), 89–90.

5. David Barrett, *Schism and Renewal in Africa* (London: Oxford University Press, 1968), 46–7. More than 40 terms are listed.

6. Paul Makhubu, *Who Are the Independent Churches?* (Johannesburg: Skotaville, 1988), 5.

7. L.N. Mzimba, "The African Church," in *Christianity and the Natives of South Africa*, ed. J.D. Taylor (Lovedale: General Missionary Conference of South Africa, 1928), 89.

8. Bengt Sundkler, *Bantu Prophets in South Africa*, 2nd ed. (London: Oxford University Press, 1961), 17.

9. Daneel, *Quest for Belonging*, 31.

10. The Social Welfare section of one government department has about 7,500 files on such churches dating from as early as the 1890s.

11. Richard Elphick, "Writing Religion into History: The Case of South African Christianity," in *Missions and Christianity in South African History*, ed. Henry Bredekamp and Robert Ross (Johannesburg: University of the Witwatersrand Press, 1995), 23. For a detailed analysis of approaches to some major studies on AICs, see Hennie Pretorius, *Historiography and Historical Sources Regarding African Indigenous Churches in South Africa* (Lewiston: Edwin Mellen, 1995), esp. 33-51.

12. See Sundkler, *Bantu Prophets*, 53–5, 302; Makhubu, *Independent Churches*, 5–15. For issues regarding classification and terminology see Hodgson, "Don't Fence Me In," 83–94. The Zion City–Zion-Apostolic distinction follows Glenda Kruss, "Religion, Class and Culture: Indigenous Churches in South Africa, with Special Reference to Zionist-Apostolics" (M.A. thesis: University of Cape Town, 1985), 74–5, 260–5. Among others, Kruss uses statistical analysis and the comparison of name lists to illustrate the emergence of the second sub-type (pp. 159–65). On the reasons for our typology see Hennie Pretorius, "Nikhonza phi na? Comments on Church Typology," in *Traditional Religion and Christian Faith*, ed. Gabriele Lademann-Priemer (Ammershoek bei Hamburg: Verlag an der Lottbeck, 1993), 135-47.

13. Hodgson, "Don't Fence Me In," 85–6. See also chap. 4 of the present volume.

NOTES

14. O.F. Raum, "Von Stammespropheten zu Sektenführern," in E. Benz, *Messianische Kirchen, Sekten und Bewegungen im heutigen Afrika* (Leiden: Brill, 1965), 62.

15. Cf. Erhard Kamphausen, *Anfänge der kirchlichen Unabhängigheitsbewegung in Südafrika* (Frankfurt: Lang, 1976), 84–108, 121–2; Sundkler, *Bantu Prophets*, 38–9.

16. Trevor Verryn, *A History of the Order of Ethiopia* (Cleveland, Transvaal: Central Mission Press, 1972), 17–30. For causes of the wider AIC movement see Barrett, *Schism*, 83–158; Makhubu, *Independent Churches*, 20–38; Sundkler, *Bantu Prophets*, 29–32, 295–7.

17. Kamphausen, *Anfänge*, 423–6.

18. Norman Etherington, "The Historical Sociology of Independent Churches in South East Africa," *Journal of Religion in Africa* 10, 2 (1979): 113–15, 120.

19. G. Shepperson, "Ethiopianism: Past and Present," in *Christianity in Tropical Africa*, ed. C.G. Baëta (London: Oxford University Press, 1968), 249–50.

20. Verryn, *Order*, 14–17; Kamphausen, *Anfänge*, 248–52.

21. J.M. Chirenje, *Ethiopianism and Afro-Americans in Southern Africa, 1883–1916* (Baton Rouge: Louisiana State University Press, 1987), 2.

22. Kruss, "Religion, Class and Culture," 74, 98, 261. She has stressed that after the discovery of gold the shift of the economic fulcrum of South Africa from the Cape to the Witwatersrand gave impetus to the Ethiopian movement.

23. For successive interpretations see D.D. Stormont, "The Ethiopian Movement Amongst the Native Churches of South Africa" (manuscript, Cory Library, Rhodes University, Grahamstown, 1902); A. Lea, *The Native Separatist Church Movement in South Africa* (Cape Town: Juta, 1926), 73–85; Sundkler, *Bantu Prophets*, 38–47; J.H. van Wyk, "Die Separatisme en Inheemse Kerklike Bewegings onder die Bantoe in die Sothogroep," 2 vols. (unpubl. report, HSRC, Pretoria, 1973); Kamphausen, *Anfänge*; Chirenje, *Ethiopianism*.

24. Kamphausen, *Anfänge*, 109, 120–4, 140, 145; Shepperson, *Ethiopianism*, 251.

25. Shula Marks, *Reluctant Rebellion: The 1906–8 Disturbances in Natal* (London: Oxford University Press, 1970), 76, 295, 310, 326–36; Sundkler, *Bantu Prophets*, 68–9.

26. Chirenje, *Ethiopianism*, 84, 111.

27. André Odendaal, *Vukani Bantu! The Beginning of Black Protest Politics in South Africa to 1912* (Cape Town: David Philip, 1984), 29, 84; cf. Kamphausen, *Anfänge*, 470–1, 473–4.

28. Odendaal, *Vukani*, 86.

29. Kamphausen, *Anfänge*, 473–80, 628; Chirenje, *Ethiopianism*, 159, 162; Alan Cobley, "The 'African National Church': Self-determination and Political Struggle among Black Christians in South Africa to 1948," *Church History*, 60, 3 (Sept. 1991): 356–7.

30. Shepperson, *Ethiopianism*, 256.

31. Cobley, "Self-determination," 361–3.

32. Lordvyck Xozwa, *Methodist Church in Africa: History of the Church*, Occasional Papers no. 2 (Grahamstown: Cory Library, 1989), 42. UMHOBE kaDONKI Thina singabantwana – be-Afrika emnyama, Siphuma kulo lonke – Elo mzantsi Afrika. SingamaWesil' amnyama – Sivela kwizizwe zonke. Size kuThixo wethu – Sizis' imithandazo.Thina singabantwana – be-Afrika emnyama.Size kuthandazela – Inkululeko yabaNtsundu.

33. *World Christian Encyclopaedia*, ed. David Barrett (Oxford: Oxford University Press, 1982), 623, 625–6.

34. Makhubu, *Independent Churches*, 5, 6, 10, 106.

35. Chirenje, *Ethiopianism*, 164–5.

36. Bengt Sundkler, *Zulu Zion and Some Swazi Zionists* (London: Oxford University Press, 1976), 16; Kamphausen, *Anfänge*, 462; Absolom Vilakazi (ed.), *Shembe: The Revitalization of African Society* (Braamfontein: Skotaville, 1986), 153–4; Makhubu, *Independent Churches*, 4.

37. Shepperson, *Ethiopianism*, 254.

38. Quoted by Kamphausen, *Anfänge*, 459.

39. Although no comprehensive work on the history of the origins of Zionism in South Africa – let alone the movement as a whole – has as yet been written, see Sundkler, *Zulu Zion*, 13–67; G.C. Oosthuizen, *The Birth of Christian Zionism in South Africa* (KwaDlangezwa: University of Zululand, 1987), 11ff.

40. Sundkler, *Zulu Zion*, 33.

41. *Ibid.*, 66.

42. Kruss, "Religion, Class and Culture," 125, 128, 132; Sundkler, *Zulu Zion*, 317.

43. Sundkler, *Zulu Zion*, passim.

44. Kruss, "Religion, Class and Culture," 135, 139.

45. H. Häselbarth, "The Zion Christian Church of Edward Lekganyane," in *Our Approach to the Independent Church Movement*, ed. H.J. Becken (Mapumulo, Natal: Missiological Institute, 1966), 64. For a history of this church and Moria itself see Katesa Schlosser, *Eingeborenenkirchen in Süd- und Südwest-Afrika* (Kiel: Mühlau, 1958), 184–93; Van Wyk, *Separatisme*, 850–61, 867–70; Anderson, *Pentecostalism*, 78–82.

46. Sundkler, *Zulu Zion*, 161. For a history of this church and its "Shembe village" at Ekuphakameni see

Schlosser, *Eingeborenenkirchen*, 227–40; R. Papani, *Rise Up and Dance and Praise God* (Durban: Local History Museum, 1992), p. 36 note 3: "*UbuNazaretha* is based on an ascetic Old Testament cult described in Numbers 6, and its adherents are thus rightly known as Nazirites (after the Ancient Hebrew *nazir*, a person consecrated to God). More often seen in the literature is the variant but incorrect spelling 'Nazarites'." A major project for the collection and interpretation of ubuNazaretha has well progressed. For a unique translation of the writings of the founder Isaiah Shembe, see Irving Hexham, *The Scriptures of the amaNazaretha of Ekuphakameni* (Calgary: University of Calgary Press, 1994).

47. Vilakazi, *Shembe*, 155–6.

48. Quoted by Robert Edgar, *Because They Chose the Plan of God: The Story of the Bulhoek Massacre* (Johannesburg: Ravan, 1988), 38–9.

49. Sundkler, *Bantu Prophets*, 72–3. This church's history and its holy place are described in Schlosser, *Eingeborenenkirchen*, 129–55; cf. Edgar, *Plan of God*.

50. Gary Baines, "An Alternative and Exclusive Community: 'Bishop' Limba and the Church of Christ in New Brighton, c.1929–1949" (paper read at Conference on People, Power and Culture: The History of Christianity in South Africa, 1792–1992, University of the Western Cape, 1992), 8–14.

51. Institute for Contextual Theology, *Speaking for Ourselves* (Braamfontein: The Institute, 1985), 30.

52. James Kiernan, *The Production and Management of Therapeutic Power in Zionist Churches Within a Zulu City* (Lewiston: Edwin Mellen, 1990), 37.

53. Kruss, "Religion, Class and Culture," 152–5.

54. Hans-Jürgen Becken, "Patterns of Organizational Structures in the African Independent Church Movement in S.A.," *Africana Marburgensia*, 1, 2 (1968).

55. Kruss, "Religion, Class and Culture," 193.

56. Mia Brandel-Syrier, *Black Woman in Search of God* (London: Lutterworth, 1962), 231.

57. Sundkler, *Zulu Zion*, 79.

58. Kiernan, *Power*, 44.

59. Van Wyk, *Separatisme*, 826–31, 836, 839–40, 847; cf. Institute for Contextual Theology, *Speaking*, 18–20; Anderson, *Pentecostalism*, 82–4.

60. Vilakazi, *Shembe*, 75.

61. B.E. Ngobese, "The Concept of the Trinity among the AmaNazaretha," in *Empirical Studies of African Independent / Indigenous Churches*, ed. G.C. Oosthuizen and I. Hexham (Lewiston: Edwin Mellen, 1992), 97.

62. *Constitution of the Christian Catholic Apostolic Church in Zion* (n.p., n.d.).

63. Ngobese, *Trinity*, 97.

64. J.B. Ngubane, "The Role of Amadlozi / Amathongo as Seen in the Writings of W.B. Vilakazi" (paper read at a Forum, Federal Theological Seminary, Pietermaritzburg, 1983), 3.

65. Stan Nussbaum, "Liturgical Associations in the Nazarite Association of Lesotho," in *Afro-Christian Religion at the Grassroots in Southern Africa*, ed. G.C. Oosthuizen and I. Hexham (Lewiston: Edwin Mellen, 1991), 223.

66. G.C. Oosthuizen, "Divine / Prophet Parallels in the African Independent Churches and Traditional Religion," in *Empirical Studies*, ed. Oosthuizen and Hexham, 175.

67. *Constitution*, 1.

68. E.K. Lukhaimane, "Crisis in the Zion City Church" (paper read at NERMIC Conference, Durban, University of Natal, 1990), 20.

69. Inus Daneel, "The Liberation of Creation: African Traditional Religious and Independent Church Perspectives," *Missionalia*, 19, 2 (August 1991).

70. "A Million Zionists Massed at Moria to Pray," *Weekly Mail* (Johannesburg) 24, 9 (April 1992).

71. Kritzinger, "Numbers Game," 2, 10: "There are simply not enough people to make all the claims possible."

72. Johan Claasen, "Independents Made Dependents: African Indigenous Churches and Government Recognition," *Journal of Theology for Southern Africa*, 91 (June 1995): 31.

73. *Ibid.*, 25, 32–3; Sundkler, *Zulu Zion*, 282–8.

74. Makhubu, *Independent Churches*, 101.

75. *Ibid.*, 67–9; Institute for Contextual Theology, *Speaking*, 30–1; Anderson, *Pentecostalism*, 127–30, 133; *Religion Alive*, ed. G.C. Oosthuizen (Johannesburg: Hodder and Stoughton, 1986), 234.

76. Anderson, *Pentecostalism*, 127–8.

77. H.N. Ngada, "The Brigadier and the Churches," *Challenge*, 13 (March 1993): 5.

78. Oosthuizen, *Religion*, 240; Wilbert Shenk, "The Contribution of the Study of New Religious Movements to Missiology," in *Exploring*, ed. Walls and Shenk, 196.

13 / ANDERSON & PILLAY / THE PENTECOSTALS / PAGES 230–241

1. Vinson Synan, *The Spirit Said "Grow"* (Monrovia: MARC, 1992).

2. The term "Pentecostal-type" refers here to those African Initiated Churches with historical, theological, and

NOTES

liturgical affinities with the Pentecostal movement. These churches, which embrace one third of the black population of South Africa, have an emphasis on the Holy Spirit, especially manifested in prophetic healing practices, and other Pentecostal beliefs like adult baptism by immersion and speaking in tongues.

3. A. H. Anderson, "African Pentecostalism in a South African Urban Environment: A Missiological Evaluation" (D.Th. thesis: University of South Africa, 1992), 23–4. Figures quoted there are taken from the official 1991 South African census report.

4. D. W. Dayton, *Theological Roots of Pentecostalism* (Metuchen, N.J.: Scarecrow Press, 1987), 35–54.

5. M.E. Dieter, "Wesleyan-Holiness Aspects of Pentecostal Origins: As Mediated through the Nineteenth-Century Holiness Revival," in *Aspects of Pentecostal–Charismatic Origins*, ed. Vinson Synan (Plainfield: Logos, 1975), 57–76.

6. D.W. Dayton, "From 'Christian Perfection' to the 'Baptism of the Holy Ghost'," in *Aspects*, ed. Synan, 48.

7. Dieter, "Wesleyan-Holiness Aspects," 68–9.

8. W.W. Menzies, "The Non-Wesleyan Origins of the Pentecostal Movement," in *Aspects*, ed. Synan, 86.

9. Dayton, *Theological Roots*, 136–7.

10. Edith L. Blumhofer, "The Christian Catholic Apostolic Church and the Apostolic Faith: A Study in the 1906 Pentecostal Revival," in *Charismatic Experiences in History*, ed. Cecil M. Robeck (Peabody: Hendrickson, 1985), 131.

11. I. MacRobert, *The Black Roots and White Racism of Early Pentecostalism in the USA* (Basingstoke: Macmillan, 1988), 56, 81.

12. R.M. Anderson, *Vision of the Disinherited: The Making of American Pentecostalism* (New York: Oxford, 1979), 122.

13. V. Synan, *The Holiness-Pentecostal Movement in the United States* (Grand Rapids: Eerdmans, 1971), 114.

14. *Ibid.*, 32. A photograph taken at Azusa Street in 1907 shows Lake and Hezmalhalch together with Seymour and other early Pentecostal leaders.

15. Menzies, "Non-Wesleyan Origins," 90–5.

16. B.G.M. Sundkler, *Zulu Zion and Some Swazi Zionists* (London: Oxford University Press, 1976), 18.

17. *Ibid.*, 30.

18. B.G.M. Sundkler, *Bantu Prophets in South Africa* (Oxford: Oxford University Press, 1961), 48.

19. Sundkler, *Zulu Zion*, 51.

20. Sundkler, *Bantu Prophets*, 48.

21. Sundkler, *Zulu Zion*, 52.

22. C.P. Watt, *From Africa's Soil: The Story of the Assemblies of God in Southern Africa* (Cape Town: Struik, 1992), 20–1.

23. Sundkler, *Zulu Zion*, 53.

24. Quoted in C.R. de Wet, "The Apostolic Faith Mission in Africa: 1908–1980. A Case Study in Church Growth in a Segregated Society" (Ph.D. thesis: University of Cape Town, 1989), 64

25. De Wet, "Apostolic Faith Mission," 39.

26. *Ibid.*, 161.

27. *Ibid.*, 311.

28. Quoted in De Wet, "Apostolic Faith Mission," 34.

29. *Ibid.*, 38.

30. I.S. v.d. M. Burger, *Geloofsgeskiedenis van die Apostoliese Geloofsending van Suid-Afrika 1908–1958* (Johannesburg: Evangelie Uitgewers, 1988), 167.

31. In De Wet, "Apostolic Faith Mission," 51–2.

32. Burger, *Geloofsgeskiedenis*, 175.

33. Sundkler, *Bantu Prophets*, 48.

34. At this time, a circular in Zulu and Sesotho was sent by the AFM executive to those in "kindred bodies" inviting them to unite with the AFM. The AFM held that "If all the struggling Native Bodies could be picked up and consolidated a National Service would be rendered." De Wet, "Apostolic Faith Mission," 63.

35. Sundkler, *Zulu Zion*, 55–6, note 54.

36. De Wet, "Apostolic Faith Mission," 63.

37. The ZCC puts its official beginning at 1910, which appears to be the year that Lekganyane received his divine call.

38. In W. Hollenweger, *The Pentecostals* (London: SCM, 1974), 171–2n.

39. *Ibid.*, 120.

40. Sundkler, *Zulu Zion*, 50–1.

41. C. Hanekom, *Krisis en Kultus* (Pretoria: Academica, 1975), 39.

42. E.K. Lukhaimane, "The Zion Church of Ignatius (Engenas) Lekganyane, 1924 to 1948: An African Experiment with Christianity" (M.A. thesis: University of the North, 1980), 14.

43. *Ibid.*, 15.

44. The official ZCC founding date of 1910 appears to refer to the call of Lekganyane to the ministry and not

to the actual commencement of the ZCC.

45. Hanekom, *Krisis en Kultus*, 41.

46. Sundkler, *Zulu Zion*, 79–82. Most of the information on St. John is drawn from this source.

47. Sundkler, *Zulu Zion*, 81.

48. Statistics from Martin West, *Bishops and Prophets in a Black City* (Cape Town: David Philip, 1975), 2; J.J. Kritzinger, *Die Onvoltooide Sendingtaak in die PWV Gebied* (Pretoria: University of Pretoria, 1975), 170; Central Statistical Services, "Summarised Results before Adjustment for Undercount," *Population Census* (Pretoria, 1992) 121–3; A.H. Anderson, *Bazalwane: African Pentecostals in South Africa* (Pretoria Government Printer: Unisa, 1992), 58–9.

49. We have made use of two unpublished manuscripts by Drs. Isak Burger and Christo de Wet in this section on the AFM.

50. The information obtained here on the recent history of the AFM results from interviews during July and August 1991 with Edgar Gschwend, first President of the AFM Composite Division, George Mahlobo, General Secretary, and Japie Lapoorta, Vice-President. We also had access to an unpublished secretarial report of the Committee for Unity of the AFM for the period 1985 to 1991.

51. The material on the FGC is largely drawn from an unpublished manuscript by Dr. I. G. Lemmer du Plessis.

52. This property is now the headquarters of the Irene Association of the FGC, as explained later.

53. This information results from telephone interviews conducted during July and August 1991 with Cornelius van Kerken, General Overseer of the United Assemblies Association, Henry van der Vent, Secretary General of the same Association, and Lawrence Rowlands and Marius Herholdt of the Irene Association.

54. In a telephone conversation with the General Secretary of the Irene Association, Lawrence Rowlands, we were told that his association felt strongly about the need to ensure "protective mechanisms" that would enable churches to worship God in their own culture and language. Henry van der Vent assured us that these types of preconditions were not acceptable to the United Assemblies Association, as they were seen as an attempt to perpetuate apartheid. Equally unacceptable is the attempt on the part of the white churches to secure greater local autonomy, which would result in the possibility of the white churches hiving off on their own and taking their money and property with them. The United Assemblies say that this is not their idea of an integrated church.

55. C.P. Watt, *From Africa's Soil* (Cape Town: Struik, 1992), 23. We have largely drawn from Watt for the information on the AOG.

56. The information here is also as a result of conversations during August 1991 with several AOG leaders, including the Chairman of the General Executive, John Bond; the General Secretary, Victor Nkomonde; an Executive member and Chairman of the predominantly Coloured and Indian "Association," Colin La Foy; and another Executive member, Dan Lephoko.

57. Watt, *From Africa's Soil*, 22.

58. *Ibid.*, 39.

59. Watt has in effect conveniently sidestepped the issue with his emphasis on what he terms the division between "indigenous" (including white) and "expatriate" (including black) streams. He calls this "a pragmatic response to the South African situation."

60. *Ibid.*, 57.

61. Quoted in De Wet, "Apostolic Faith Mission," 60.

62. *Ibid.*, 160.

63. *Ibid.*, 93, 95–6.

64. *Ibid.*, 165.

65. *Ibid.*, 135.

66. *Ibid.*, 163.

67. *Ibid.*, 179–80.

68. On one occasion he was reported to have been preaching on a farm where he was told to sleep in the fowl-house. In the middle of the night he was wakened by the white farmer and asked to pray for his sick wife. This he did, and the farmer thereupon apologized for having put him in the fowl-house. To this Letwaba replied: "It is all right, sir, to put me there, my Master slept in a stable, and I am only a black worm" (in *ibid.*, 70).

69. Translated from the original Afrikaans by the author, *ibid.*, 69–70.

70. *Ibid.*, 143.

71. Frank Chikane, *No Life of My Own* (Braamfontein: Skotaville, 1988), 49.

72. R. Sider "Interview with Rev. Frank Chikane," *Transformation*, 5, (1988): 9–12.

73. Chikane, *No Life*, 77, 182.

74. Watt, *From Africa's Soil*, 178.

75. *Ibid.*, 112.

76. *Ibid.*, 149.

77. A.A. Dubb, *Community of the Saved: An African Revivalist Church in the East Cape* (Johannesburg: Witwatersrand University Press, 1976), 119–20.

78. *Ibid.*, 27.

NOTES

79. J.N. Horn, "The Experience of the Spirit in Apartheid South Africa," *Azusa*, 1, 1 (1990): 31.

80. Translated from Afrikaans quoted in *ibid.*, 29.

81. *Ibid.*

14 / MALOKA / CHRISTIANITY IN THE GOLD MINE COMPOUNDS / PAGES 242–252

1. Francis Wilson, *Labour in the South African Gold Mines* (Cambridge: Cambridge University Press, 1972), 157–8, based on Chamber of Mines statistics.

2. Patrick Harries, *Work, Culture and Identity: Migrant Labourers in Mozambique and South Africa, c.1860–1910* (London: James Currey, 1994), 213; Deborah Gaitskell, "Devout Domesticity? A Century of African Women's Christianity in South Africa," *Women and Gender in South Africa*, ed. Cherryl Walker (Cape Town: David Philip, 1990), 253; Deborah Gaitskell, "Female Mission Initiatives: Black and White Women in Three Witwatersrand Churches, 1903–1939" (Ph.D.: University of London, 1981), 6.

3. Latimer Fuller, *The Romance of a South African Mission* (Leeds: Richard Jackson, 1907); Herbert Bennet, *Romance and Reality: The Story of a Missionary on the Rand: Being a Sequel to "The Romance of a South African Mission"* (Leeds: Richard Jackson, 1920), 21. For correspondence regarding missionaries, *Leselinyana la Lesotho* (15 July, 1 August and 1 October 1993; 14 January, 3 June 1911; 22 January 1917; 27 April 1928; and 19 May 1937). For the flexible relationship between compounds and locations before the Native Grievances Enquiry Report of 1913, see Philip Bonner in *Labour, Townships and Protest*, ed. Belinda Bozzoli (Johannesburg: Ravan Press, 1979), 273–97.

4. *Africa's Golden Harvests* (henceforth *AGH*), December 1913, 44.

5. *Leselinyana* (22 January 1915; 22 January 1917; 28 February 1928; 27 April 1928; 18 December 1935; 19 May 1937); *Bulletin de la mission suisse en Afrique du Sud* (1908): 150.

6. *AGH* (December 1913; March 1914; August 1914); Central Archives Depot (SAB), GNLB 383, 13/14.

7. GNLB 383, 13/14.

8. J. du Plessis, *A History of Christian Missions in South Africa* (London: Longman, Green, 1911), 303–99; J.D. Taylor, *Christianity and the Natives of South Africa: A Year-Book of South African Missions* (Alice: Lovedale Institution Press, 1928).

9. Albert W. Baker, *Grace Triumphant: The Life Story of a Carpenter, Lawyer and Missionary in South Africa from 1856 to 1939* (Glasgow: The Author, 1939), 101.

10. Baker, *Grace Triumphant*, 101–14; *Bulletin* (1896–97), 219–20; SAB, RAD 160, 4025–62 [E.H. Mabille's "Claim for Compensation"]; Daniel P. Kunene, *Thomas Mofolo and the Emergence of Written Sesotho Prose* (Johannesburg: Ravan Press, 1989), 33; Harries, *Work, Culture and Identity*, 213; Lesotho National Archives (LNA), S7/7/18.

11. *Bulletin* (1904): 38; (1905): 86; *Leselinyana* (1 November 1929); Harries, *Work, Culture and Identity*, 213.

12. Harries, *Work, Culture and Identity*, 213; Gaitskell, "Devout Domesticity," 253; Gaitskell, "Female Mission Initiatives," 6; V. Ellenberger, *A Century of Mission Work in Basutoland, 1833–1933* (Morija: Sesuto Book Depot, 1938), 352–7; B. Moreillon, "My First Three Weeks on the Rand," *Basutoland Witness* (*BW*), 4 (March–April 1950).

13. Fuller, *Romance of a South African Mission*, 10; South African Library, Archives of the Paris Evangelical Missionary Society (APEMS), Mf.818; Mf.847; Mf.849.

14. Bennet, *Romance and Reality*, 33.

15. Fuller, *Romance of a South African Mission*, 17; *AGH* (May 1914; August 1914; December 1913; June 1924; April 1921; July 1923; April 1917); Du Plessis, *History of Christian Missions*; Ray E. Phillips, *The Bantu are Coming: Phases of South Africa's Race Problem* (Stellenbosch: Students' Christian Association of South Africa, 1930), 142–52.

16. *Leselinyana* (1 November 1906); *Bulletin* (March 1943): 195.

17. *Leselinyana* (6 April 1938; 1 August 1934); *Journal des missions évangéliques* (*JME*) (1928): 84–90; (1942–5): 131–2; Ellenberger, *Century of Mission Work*, 182.

18. Bennet, *Romance and Reality*, 59.

19. *Ibid.*, 58, 60.

20. *AGH*, (August 1914): 113.

21. *Ibid.* (June 1911): 2.

22. SAB, GNLB 383, 13/14. The Anglicans also managed to convince the mine authorities that they taught their converts to obey the law and mine authorities; see Bennet, *Romance and Reality*, 59.

23. *AGH* (August 1914); *Bulletin* (1904): 272–4; Bennet, *Romance and Reality*, 68–9; Harries, *Work, Culture and Identity*, 217; J. Dexter Taylor, "The Rand as a Mission Field," *International Review of Missions*, 25 (October 1926): 653.

24. *Umteteli* (1 October 1921).

25. Bennet, *Romance and Reality*, 30.

26. SAB, GNLB 383, 13/14.

27. *AGH* (June/July 1918); Taylor, "The Rand as a Mission Field," 70; *Bulletin* (1905): 83–4; (1924–5): 113–14; (March 1943): 195; Bennet, *Romance and Reality*, 30.
28. *Bulletin* (1924–5): 113.
29. *Ibid.*
30. Taylor, "The Rand as a Mission Field," 653.
31. *Leselinyana* (25 September 1935; 24 May 1939); *JME* (1934): 355; (1942–5): 132; B.G.M. Sundkler, *Bantu Prophets in South Africa* (London: Oxford University Press, 1948), 80–7.
32. George Mabille, "Spiritual Gold Digging on the Rand," *BW*, 4 (March–April 1950): 22.
33. *Standard and Diggers News* (31 December 1896); T. Dunbar Moodie, "Ethnic Violence on South African Gold Mines," *Journal of Southern African Studies*, 18 (1992); *Rand Daily Mail*, (31 May 1910; 1 June 1910; 3 June 1910); Union of South Africa, *Report of the Native Grievances Inquiry, 1913–14*, U.G. 37, 14.
34. J.E. Selikane, "Church of Basutoland," *BW*, 4 (March–April 1950), 10.
35. The type of South African ghetto music and culture popular by the 1920s.
36. These types of dances and music were linked to the migrant labour system in Lesotho. Sexually provocative dances gave a great role to women, who jumped about to the sound of rattles and drums.
37. On marabi, famo, and focho, see David B. Coplan, *In Township Tonight: South Africa's Black City Music and Theatre* (London: Longman, 1985), 94–101; on Basotho women on the Rand, see Phil Bonner, "'Desirable or Undesirable Basotho Women?': Liquor, Prostitution and the Migration of Basotho Women to the Rand, 1920–1945," in *Women and Gender*, ed. Walker.
38. E.A. Makhele, "The Tragedy of Basuto Life on the Rand," *BW*, 7 (October–December 1953): 55.
39. J. M. Mohapeloa, *From Mission to Church: Fifty Years of the Work of the Paris Evangelical Missionary Society and the Lesotho Evangelical Church* (Morija: Sesuto Book Depot, 1985), 18; *JME* (1929): 227; T. Verdier, "L'alcoolisme au Lessouto," *JME*, 1 (1930); E. Mphatsoe, "The Blue Cross Association in Basutoland," *BW*, 8 (July–September 1954).
40. *JME* (1928), 88; *Leselinyana* (1 August 1893; 1 August 1934; 8 August 1934).
41. Malefane, "Work of the Lord," 5.
42. A Sotho dance performed for recreational purposes. Interview with Samuel Nonyana, born 1914.
43. Malefane, "Work of the Lord," 6.
44. *JME* (1942–45): 132. For the experience of the Anglicans, see Bennet, *Romance and Reality*, 33.
45. Baker, *Grace Triumphant*, 106.
46. *Leselinyana* (1, 8 August 1934).
47. Coplan, *In Township Tonight*, 37, 71–6; *JME* (1942–45): 131–2; *Leselinyana* (12 October 1938; 1 June 1938; 23 February 1917; 14 August 1935; 5 February 1936; 16 February 1938; 13 March 1935; 18 March 1921; 26 March 1926; 3 November 1937; 3 March 1937; 12 May 1937; 12 October 1932; 25 May 1938); *Mochochonono* (12 September 1934; 13 March 1937; 7 August 1937).
48. *JME* (1928): 89; *Leselinyana* (18 December 1925; 28 November 1930; 18 July 1934; 10 February 1928; 12 October 1932); Harries, *Work, Culture and Identity*, 216.
49. Phillips, *Bantu are Coming*, 138; *Bulletin* (March 1943): 196; Fuller, *Romance of a South African Mission*, 21; *AGM* (July 1923; June 1924).
50. *Leselinyana* (18 July 1934; 10 February 1928; 12 October 1932; 25 November 1930; 18 December 1925); *JME* (1928): 84–90.
51. *JME* (1928): 89.
52. *AGH* (June 1911): 1.
53. *Ibid.* (March 1915).
54. Harries, *Work, Culture and Identity*, 217; *AGM* (March 1914); *JME* (1927): 373.
55. *Umteteli* (7 December 1929).
56. *Leselinyana* (18 July 1934; 10 February 1928; 12 October 1932; 25 November 1930; 18 December 1925); *Mochochonono* (14 September 1946).
57. Harries, *Work, Culture and Identity*, 216–18; S. Moroney, "Mine Married Quarters: The Differential Stabilisation of the Witwatersrand Workforce, 1900–1920," in *Industrialisation and Social Change in South Africa: African Class Formation, Culture and Consciousness, 1870–1930*, ed. Shula Marks and Richard Rathbone (London: Longman, 1982), 264–7; Stimela J. Jingoes, *A Chief is a Chief by the People: The Autobiography of Stimela Jason Jingoes* (London: Oxford University Press, 1975), 63; interview with Samuel Nonyana Mokoaleli.
58. *JME* (1928): 145.
59. E. Labarthe, "Mission Work in Johannesburg," *BW*, 62 (July 1962): 4.

15 / GAITSKELL / WOMEN'S CHRISTIAN ORGANIZATIONS / PAGES 253–267
1. *Minutes of Annual Conference, Methodist Church of South Africa*, 1940, 246–7.
2. *New Dimensions. The Report of the Bishop of Willesden's Commission on the Objects and Policy of the Mothers' Union* (London, 1972), 198, 216.

NOTES

3. Mia Brandel-Syrier, *Black Woman in Search of God* (London: Lutterworth, 1962), 97.

4. See figures in Leonard Thompson, *A History of South Africa* (New Haven and London: Yale University Press, 1990), 243, Table 1.

5. Methodist Missionary Society Archives (MMS), School of Oriental and African Studies, London University, 1180, File of Rev. A.A. Kidwell, unsigned letter, 24 August 1919.

6. From "Annual Report of General Secretary. By Mrs Howse, 1919–1920," in *The Story of the Methodist Women's Auxiliary in South Africa* (Cape Town, 1961), 12.

7. See further Deborah Gaitskell, "Praying and Preaching: The Distinctive Spirituality of African Women's Church Organisations," in *Missions and Christianity in South African History*, ed. Henry Bredekamp and Robert Ross (Johannesburg: Witwatersrand University Press, 1995).

8. This is the heart of the argument in Deborah Gaitskell, "Devout Domesticity? A Century of African Women's Christianity in South Africa," *Women and Gender in Southern Africa to 1945*, ed. Cherryl Walker (Cape Town: David Philip; and London: James Currey, 1990).

9. Helen Joseph, *If This Be Treason* (London: Hutchinson, 1963), 165.

10. Thoko Mpumlwana, "My Perspective on Women and their Role in Church and Society," in *Women Hold Up Half the Sky: Women in the Church in Southern Africa*, ed. Denise Ackermann, Jonathan A. Draper, Emma Mashinini (Pietermaritzburg: Cluster Publications, 1991), 371.

11. Julia Wells, "Women's Resistance to Passes in Bloemfontein during the Inter-war Period," *Africa Perspective*, 15 (1980): 22–4. See also Julia C. Wells, We *Now Demand: The History of the Women's Resistance to Pass Laws in South Africa* (Johannesburg: Witwatersrand University Press, 1993), 40.

12. William Beinart, "*Amafelandawonye* (The Die-hards): Popular Protest and Women's Movements in Herschel District in the 1920s," in William Beinart and Colin Bundy, *Hidden Struggles in Rural South Africa: Politics and Popular Movements in the Transkei and Eastern Cape 1890–1930*, (London: James Currey, 1987), 262; Helen Bradford, "'We Are Now the Men': Women's Beer Protests in the Natal Countryside, 1929," in *Class, Community and Conflict: South African Perspectives*, ed. Belinda Bozzoli (Johannesburg: Ravan Press, 1987), 308–10.

13. Julia Wells, "'The Day the Town Stood Still': Women in Resistance in Potchefstroom, 1912–1930," in *Town and Countryside in the Transvaal: Capitalist Penetration and Popular Response*, ed. Belinda Bozzoli (Johannesburg: Ravan Press, 1983), 286.

14. See Beinart, "*Amafelandawonye.*"

15. "Manyano and Die-hard," *Umteteli wa Bantu* (6 July 1924): 5. I am much indebted to Jeff Opland for copies of his translations of some of Mgqwetho's poems (based on preliminary versions prepared by Phyllis Ntantala). See further J. Opland, "Nontsizi Mgqwetho: Stranger at the Gates," in *Power, Marginality and African Oral Literature*, ed. L. Gunner and G. Furniss (Cambridge: Cambridge University Press, 1995).

16. See note 43.

17. Gaitskell, "Devout Domesticity?", 271.

18. See Jacklyn Cock, "Domestic Service and Education for Domesticity: The Incorporation of Xhosa Women into Colonial Society," in *Women and Gender*, ed. Walker.

19. For further elaboration, see Deborah Gaitskell, "At Home with Hegemony? Coercion and Consent in the Education of African Girls for Domesticity in South Africa before 1910," in *Contesting Colonial Hegemony: State and Society in Africa and India*, ed. Dagmar Engels and Shula Marks (London: German Historical Institute and Academic Press, 1994). See also Sheila Meintjes, "Family and Gender in the Christian Community at Edendale, Natal, in Colonial Times" and Heather Hughes, "'A Lighthouse for African Womanhood': Inanda Seminary, 1869–1945," in *Women and Gender*, ed. Walker.

20. Methodist Church of South Africa, Transvaal and Swaziland District: African Women's Prayer and Service Union, *Manyano-Kopano Jubilee Celebrations* (1959).

21. *Foreign Field* (FF) (Feb. 1916): 133.

22. "African Women's Prayer Union (Manyano) Rules," typescript in the possession of Ruth Allcock, London.

23. *FF* (April 1913): 251.

24. *Transvaal Methodist* (November 1923).

25. Archives of the United Society for the Propagation of the Gospel (USPG), Women's Work (WW) Reports Africa, Dss Julia, 1908.

26. *Umlandu Wesililo Samabandla 1912–1962*, Rhodes House, Oxford, "A History of the Isililo of the Churches," anniversary pamphlet, comp. T.F. Mbili.

27. This issue is explored more fully in Deborah Gaitskell, "'Wailing for Purity': Prayer Unions, African Mothers and Adolescent Daughters, 1912–1940," in *Industrialisation and Social Change in South Africa*, ed. Shula Marks and Richard Rathbone (London: Longman, 1982).

28. *FF* (April 1913): 253.

29. Mothers' Union Overseas Records, London. No. 5, Africa: "Grahamstown Diocese. South Africa," May 1910 (ts.); and Sixth Annual Report of the Mothers' Union in the Diocese of Grahamstown, South Africa, 1911.

30. *The Watchman* (Feb. 1946): 6.

31. *SWM [Society of Women Missionaries] Journal* (April 1936): 8.

32. Marc Epprecht, "Domesticity and Piety in Colonial Lesotho: The Private Politics of Basotho Women's Pious Associations," *Journal of Southern African Studies*, 19, 2 (June 1993): 210.

33. See further, Gaitskell, "Devout Domesticity?" 261.

34. Mrs. D.W. John, "The Transvaal Women's Associations (now 'Women's Auxiliaries')," in *The Story of the Methodist Women's Auxiliary in South Africa*, 46.

35. Mrs. John, "The Transvaal Women's Associations," 47–53.

36. *Ibid.*, 30–41, 48–53.

37. Methodist Church of South Africa, *Women's Auxiliary: General Report of the Year 1930* (hereafter WA Report 1930), 6, 54.

38. *Umlandu*, 5–8.

39. *The Story of the Methodist Women's Auxiliary*, 29.

40. *Ibid.*, 15.

41. *Ibid.*, 53.

42. *WA Report 1930*, 33, 25, 53.

43. *Transvaal Methodist* (TM) (Nov. 1923): 30; *FF* (Sept. 1921): 232, (April 1913): 253, (Feb. 1916): 132.

44. *Annual Report, American Board of Commissioners for Foreign Missions 1904*, "Report of the Deputation Sent by the American Board to its Missions in South Africa in 1903," 22–3. See also MMS, Transvaal District Synod Minutes 1912–1925: an animated "Report of Service conducted by J.B. Mabona, Asst. African Minister, at Fordsburg Native Wesleyan Church, Jany. 18th, 1922."

45. Allcock Papers, Mrs. Allcock to her family, 15 Oct. 1924.

46. This suggestion was offered by Gervase Clarence-Smith.

47. USPG, E, "Work Amongst the Native Women in Johannesburg and the Reef," 1920.

48. *Cape to Zambezi* (May 1937): 27.

49. American Board Mission Archives, Houghton Library, Harvard University: 15.4 v.48, Amy Cowles to Miss Lamson, 22 April 1926.

50. Isabel Hofmeyr, "Jonah and the Swallowing Monster: Orality and Literacy on a Berlin Mission Station in the Transvaal," *Journal of Southern African Studies*, 17, 4 (December 1991): 642.

51. Ruth Finnegan, *Oral Literature in Africa* (Oxford: Clarendon Press, 1970), 184, 91; Harold Scheub, *The Xhosa Ntsomi* (Oxford: Clarendon Press, 1975); Elizabeth Gunner, "Songs of Innocence and Experience: Women as Composers and Performers of *Izibongo*, Zulu Praise Poetry," *Research in African Literatures*, 10, 2 (1979).

52. Aylward Shorter, *Prayer in the Religious Traditions of Africa* (Nairobi: Oxford University Press, 1975), 8.

53. Wallace G. Mills, "The Role of African Clergy in the Reorientation of Xhosa Society to the Plural Society in the Cape Colony, 1850–1915" (Ph.D. thesis: University of California, Los Angeles, 1975), 25–7, 298 note 6; A.F. Christofersen, *Adventuring with God: The Story of the American Board Mission in Africa* (Durban, 1967), 93–4.

54. Harriet Ngubane, *Body and Mind in Zulu Medicine* (London: Academic Press, 1977), 84, 93–4.

55. Finnegan, *Oral Literature*, 147–8.

56. Berthold A. Pauw, *Christianity and Xhosa Tradition* (Cape Town: Oxford University Press, 1975), 96.

57. *WA Report*, 1930, 13, 16, 25.

58. *Ibid.*, 28, 34.

59. *The Story of the Methodist Women's Auxiliary in South Africa*, 10.

60. I owe this valuable insight to David Anderson.

61. St. Cuthbert's Report, Tsolo (1916).

62. MMS, 1141, Aliwal North Quarterly Report, June 1917.

63. See Deborah Valenze, *Prophetic Sons and Daughters: Female Preaching and Popular Religion in Industrial England* (Princeton: Princeton University Press, 1985).

64. Primitive Methodist Missionary Society, *Annual Report* (1927): 57; MMS 845, Kidwell to Ayre, 4 December 1938.

65. Wesleyan MMS, *Annual Report (1931)*, 72.

66. Leslie Hewson, *An Introduction to South African Methodists* (Cape Town: Standard Press, 1950), 76–80; Christofersen, *Adventuring*, 92.

67. *Manyano–Kopano Jubilee Celebrations*.

68. USPG, E, from O. Victor, 1922; *SWM Journal* (April 1936): 8.

69. *Umlandu*, chap. 2.

70. Allcock Papers, Mrs. Allcock to her family, 15 October 1924.

71. MU Overseas Records, No. 5 Africa. St. John's Diocese [Transkei]. Mothers' Union Assistant Organiser's Report 1962 [by Mrs. Juliet Xaba].

72. *Umlandu*.

73. *TM* (Oct. 1938): 3–4.

NOTES

74. *FF* (Feb. 1916): 132–3.
75. MMS 1180, A.A. Kidwell, unsigned letter, 24 August 1919.
76. *WA Report,* 1930, 8.
77. MMS 842, Allcock to Burnet, 2 April 1924.
78. *The Story of the Methodist Women's Auxiliary,* 12.
79. *Ibid.,* 19.
80. *Ibid.,* 54–5.
81. See above, note 15.
82. Epprecht, "Domesticity and Piety," 223.

16 / SHELL / BETWEEN CHRIST AND MOHAMMED / PAGES 268–277

I would like to thank Mary Caroline Cravens, Achmat Davids, Sandy Rowoldt and Shāmil Jeppie for help on previous drafts. I would especially like to thank Anthony Whyte for much new data on nineteenth-century Cape Islam.

1. *The Shaping of South African Society, 1652–1840,* ed. Richard Elphick and Hermann Giliomee (2nd edition, Middletown: Wesleyan University Press, 1991), 557–8.

2. C. Spoelstra, *Bouwstoffen voor de Geschiedenis der Nederduitsch-Gereformeerde Kerken in Zuid-Afrika* (Amsterdam: Hollandsch-Afrikaansche Uitgevers-Maatschappij, 1906–36), vol. 1, 3, 33–4; vol. 2, 15. "'t Sal ons liev sijn, in het toekomende daervan wederom sulke aangename berigten te ontfangen; gelijk wij U. Eerw. hertelik geluk wenschen, ende ons verblijden over de bekeering, die wij hoopen dat oprecht sijn sal, van den Muhammedaan, die aldaar sijne belijdenisse gedaan heeft. Wij wenschen met U. Eerw., dat God den vloek eenmaal geheel van Chams geslachte afwende; de volheid der heydenen doe ingaan, en gantsch Israel saligmake!" (Classis Amsterdam to Drakenstein Church Council, 21 Dec. 1703, *ibid.,* vol. 2, 15).

3. Robert Shell, *Children of Bondage: A Social History of the Slave Society at the Cape of Good Hope, 1652–1838* (Middletown: Wesleyan University Press, 1994), 330–70.

4. George McCall Theal, *Records of the Cape Colony* (Cape Town Government Printer, 1904) (hereafter RCC), *Statutes of India,* vol. 9, 131–2; William Wright, *Slavery at the Cape of Good Hope* (New York: Negro Universities Press, 1969, originally published 1831), 4–5.

5. The following question and answer is from an interrogation in the Cape torture chamber: [Question:] "Of hij, gev. [Santrij] onder schijn van heijligheit alle die weggelopende slaven en bandieten niet tot sijn devotie gekreegen en tragten te brengen?" A[ntwoord:] "Dat hij [gev.] sulx gedaan hebben omdat hij Paap was en dat sulx een Javaanse maneer is." The Hague, Algemeen Rijksarchief (AR): VOC 4071, "Interrogatie" (20 December 1712), fol. 586.

6. The reference to "'t parlement den vagabonden" is in AR: VOC 4071, "Criminele Processstukken, Eisch en Conclusie" (20 January 1713), fol. 554; Santrij's full name and title was "Joudaan Tappa van Cheribon, Javaans Paap," and he was 40–50 years old: *ibid.,* fol. 541 and 558–9.

7. François Valentyn, *Oud en Nieuw Oost Indien* (Dordrecht and Amsterdam, 1724–1726, 5 vols.), vol. 3 (Section 4), 123; vol. 5, 47ff.

8. *Ibid.:* "zyn Sappa (of uitgekaaude pinang) die by wagwierp, als een heilighed eerbiedig opgeraapt, bewaard."

9. Suleman Essop Dangor, *Shaykh Yusuf* (Mobeni: Iqra' Research Committee, 1982).

10. CAD (Cape Archives Depot): CJ 3318 Bandietrollen, fols. 217–19; 237–8; 314–15; 355; 391–2; 410–11; 427–8; 449; 456; 484; 488; 511; 515; 526; 551; 579; 617 and passim.

11. Convict estimate from James C. Armstrong, June 1995, personal communication; School of Oriental and African Studies (SOAS), University of London, Council for World Mission Archives, L.M.S. Series, South African Correspondence, Box 11, Folder 3, Jacket A, Elliot to Miles (1 January 1829).

12. "Evidence of Two Mahometan Priests" (13 December 1824) in Imperial Blue Book, *Papers Relative to the Condition and Treatment of the Native Inhabitants of Southern Africa within the Colony of the Cape of Good Hope, or Beyond the Frontier of that Colony,*" part 1, 207. For other nineteenth-century examples of father–son relationships in the clergy, see Shamil Jeppie, "Leadership and Loyalties: The Imams of Nineteenth Century Colonial Cape Town" (seminar paper, Southern African Research Program, 28 October 1992), 11–12, reprinted in *Journal of Religion in Africa* (December 1995).

13. Johann Georg Bövingh, *Kurze Nachricht von den Hottentotten* (Hamburg: Bey Casper Jahkel, 1714), 3.

14. "Evidence of Two Mahometan Priests" (13 December 1824), 208.

15. *Ibid.*

16. The word "Malay" was used extensively, but erroneously, by nineteenth-century travellers to describe Cape Muslims. To this day confusion exists. Few ethnic "Malays" or Malay-speaking people were brought to the Cape. Cape Muslims more properly derived from African, Bouginese, Chinese, European, Khoikhoi, Malagasy and Indian origins. Islam at the Cape was mainly a result of conversion there, and not the result of transplanting of Muslims from the Indonesian archipelago. An innocent confusion possibly arose for linguistic reasons (Malay was also a spoken language among early Cape Muslims). But Christian sources nearly all used the word "Malay" even when talking of converts from other areas. This allowed for a strong negative reaction from audi-

ences, based on the two main co-ordinates of Victorian prejudice – race and religion (exemplified in the Cape slur *Slameier*, a Muslim Malay). The confusion persisted and later was fused with the ethnic agenda of the apartheid regime. In the post-apartheid era, Malay identity is again being pushed to the fore by some Muslims who wish to empower themselves locally and internationally by association with the Malaysian government. Cf. Shamil Jeppie, "Politics and Identities in South Africa: Reflections on the Tricentenary Celebration of Islam in South Africa" (conference paper, American Council for the Study of Islamic Societies, Villanova University, 20–22 April 1995), 11–13.

17. John Schofield Mayson, *The Malays of Cape Town* (Cape Town: Africana Connoisseurs Press, 1963, first published in 1855), 24.

18. "Facts that Concern Both White and Coloured Throughout South Africa" (Cape Town: South Africa News Co. Ltd., n.d.), South African Library, S.A.B.P., ii.

19. I am grateful to Shamil Jeppie and Gigi Edross for this information; personal communication, 7 October 1995.

20. SOAS: Council for World Mission Archives, L.M.S. Series, South African Correspondence, Box 12, Folder 4, Jacket B, Philip to the Directors, L.M.S., 14 January 1831.

21. SOAS: Council for World Mission Archives, L.M.S South African Correspondence, Box 11, Folder 3, Jacket C, Elliot to Arundel, 6 June 1829.

22. I am grateful to Achmat Davids for these references.

23. Karel Schoeman, "'Maart van Mozambiek': Andries Verhoogd, a Slave in the Service of the London Missionary Society," *Quarterly Bulletin of the South African Library*, 49, 3 (March 1995): 140–9.

24. *South African Commercial Advertiser* (10 December 1834), 2, col. 2.

25. *Cape of Good Hope Government*, G.6-'92: *Results of a Census of the Colony of the Cape of Good Hope as on the Night of Sunday the 5th of April, 1891* (Cape Town: Richardson, 1892), 118–19.

26. I. H. Enklaar, *Life and Work of Dr. J. T. van der Kemp, 1747–1811* (Cape Town: Balkema, 1988), 163.

27. Evidence of Two Mahometan Priests" (13 December 1824), 208; *ibid.* (10 January 1825), 210.

28. Lucy Duff-Gordon, *Letters from the Cape by Lady Duff Gordon* (London: Oxford University Press, 1927), 37.

29. Dutch Reformed Church Archives, Cape Town: S.A.S.G. [Zuid-Afrikaansch Zendeling Genootskap] (1816) v/1/6/12.

30. SOAS: Council for World Mission Archives, L.M.S. Series, South African Correspondence, Box 11, Folder 1, Jacket C, Elliot to the Directors, 24 July 1828, n.p.

31. SOAS: Council for World Mission Archives, L.M.S. Series, South African Correspondence, Box 12, Folder 4, Jacket B, Philip to Directors, 14 January 1831, n.p.

32. *RCC*, "Letter from the Earl of Caledon to Viscount Castlereagh" (4 February 1808), vol. 6, 271.

33. W. W. Bird, *The State of the Cape Colony in 1822* (Cape Town: Struik, 1964, reprint of 1823 edition), 349, note iii.

34. *The Report of the Wesleyan-Methodist Missionary Society, for the Year Ending December, 1828* (London: Mills, Jowet and Mills, [1828?]), 55–6.

35. E.C.W. Hengherr, "Emancipation and After: A Study of Cape Slavery and the Issues Arising from It, 1830–1843" (M.A. thesis: University of Cape Town, 1953), 14.

36. John Edwin Mason, Jr., "Fit for Freedom: The Slaves, Slavery, and Emancipation in the Cape Colony, South Africa, 1806 to 1842" (Ph.D. thesis: Yale University, 1992), 539–46 (my pagination is from a disk and the pages might be different from the copy deposited at Yale).

37. Robert Shell (ed.), "Katie Jacobs: An Oral History of a Cape Wet Nurse," *Quarterly Bulletin of the South African Library*, 46, 3 (March 1992): 94–9.

38. Petrus Borchardus Borcherds, *An Autobiographical Memoir* (Cape Town: Robertson, 1861), 202.

39. *The Cape Journals of N.J. Merriman, 1848–1855* (Cape Town: Van Riebeeck Society, 1957), 8–9.

40. Duff-Gordon, *Letters from the Cape*, 69.

41. G.6-'92: *Census 1891*, "Birthplaces of the People," 88–9.

42. Thomas Fothergill Lightfoot, "The Cape Malays," in *Sketches of Church Work and Life in the Diocese of Cape Town*, ed. Allan George Sumner Gibson (Cape Town: S.A. Electric Printing and Publishing Company, 1900), 30.

43. Gustav Bernhard August Gerdener, "Mohammedanism in South Africa," *South African Quarterly*, 11 (January 1915): 55.

17 / SHAIN / CHRISTIANITY AND THE JEWS / PAGES 278–285
I wish to thank the University of Cape Town for its financial assistance towards research for this study. I am also grateful to Margo Bastos for her research assistance.

1. At no time did Jews comprise more than 4.7 per cent of the total white population and one per cent of the total population.

2. Gustav Saron, "Boers, Uitlanders, Jews," in *The Jews in South Africa: A History*, ed. Gustav Saron and

NOTES

Louis Hotz (Cape Town: Oxford University Press, 1955), 185. For the republican constitutions, see George W. Eybers, *Select Constitutional Documents Illustrating South African History 1795–1950* (New York: Routledge, 1918), 285ff. (O.F.S.), 362–410 (Transvaal). For jury service, see Sheila M. Aronstam, "A Historical and Socio-Cultural Survey of the Bloemfontein Jewish Community with Special Reference to the Conception of Jewish Welfare Work" (D.SS. thesis: University of the Orange Free State, 1974), 68.

3. *De Volksstem*, 17 August 1892.

4. There was no evidence of religious discrimination in the Cape of Good Hope Constitution Ordinance of 1852. See Eybers, *Constitutional Documents*, 45ff.

5. *Cape Town Mail*, 28 October 1848.

6. *Cape of Good Hope Statutes*, Act 16, 1860.

7. *Cape of Good Hope Statutes*, Act 11, 1868.

8. The *Cape of Good Hope Literary Gazette* (16 June 1830) had expressed pleasure at Hebrew being taught at Cape Town's South African College. In fact the periodical quoted with approbation John Wesley's view that "Hebrew was of divine origin and therefore perfect."

9. Louis Herrmann, *The Cape Town Hebrew Congregation: A Centenary History 1841–1941* (Cape Town: Hebrew Congregation, n.d.), 19.

10. *Graaff-Reinet Advertiser*, 14 August 1861.

11. Abraham Addleson, "In the Eastern Province," in *The Jews in South Africa: A History*, ed. Saron and Hotz, 307.

12. "When the Community was Young," *Jewish Affairs* (August 1949): 36.

13. 6 February 1882.

14. *Cape Argus*, 3 October 1883.

15. *Oudtshoorn Courant*, 1 February 1888.

16. *The Press*, 25 November 1891. An eloquent sermon by Cape Town's Unitarian Reverend D.P. Faure on behalf of the Russian Jewish Relief Fund similarly attested to the goodwill between Jew and Christian. See *Cape Argus*, 25 February 1891.

17. For the evolution of the anti-Jewish stereotype see Milton Shain, *The Roots of Antisemitism in South Africa* (Charlottesville: The University Press of Virginia, 1994; and Johannesburg: Witwatersrand University Press, 1994), chaps. 1–3.

18. See Milton Shain, *Jewry and Cape Society: The Origins and Activities of the Jewish Board of Deputies for the Cape Colony* (Cape Town: Historical Publication Society, 1983), chaps. 1–3.

19. John Atkinson Hobson, *The War in South Africa: Its Causes and Effects* (London: Nisbet, 1900), 189.

20. *De Kerkbode*, 18 January 1897.

21. *Ibid.*, 24 March 1898.

22. *Land en Volk*, 7 December 1898.

23. See for example its concern about Kruger's association with "Hollanders and Jews," *Land en Volk*, 29 December 1892.

24. *Land en Volk*, 7 December 1898.

25. *Land en Volk*, 18 January 1899.

26. *The Press*, 12 December 1898.

27. *Cape Times*, 1 April 1899.

28. *Cape Times*, 3 April 1899.

29. Gideon Simonowitz, "The Background to Jewish Immigration to South Africa and the Development of the Jewish Community in the South African Republic, Between 1890 and 1902" (B.A. Hons. thesis: University of the Witwatersrand, 1960), 90. See also Manfred Nathan, *Paul Kruger, His Life and Times* (Durban: Knox, 1941), 36ff. and Richard Mendelsohn, *Sammy Marks: The Uncrowned King of the Transvaal* (Cape Town: David Philip, 1991).

30. See *The Star*, 15 August 1899.

31. See, for example, *De Kerkbode*, 21 June 1898; 28 March 1895; 12 December 1896; 28 August 1898.

32. See *The Press*, 24 February 1894.

33. See *Cape Times*, 11 November 1903.

34. See Moshe P. Grosman, *A Study in the Trends and Tendencies of Hebrew and Yiddish Writings in South Africa since the Beginning of the Early Nineties of the Last Century to 1930*, 3 vols. (Ph.D. thesis: University of the Witwatersrand, 1973), 182.

35. *The Owl*, 27 March 1903.

36. See, for example, the comments of M.C. Bruce in *The New Transvaal* (London: Alston Rivers Limited, 1908), 71–2.

37. See, for example, the comments of the one-time Cape Colony Prime Minister, J.G. Sprigg, *Legislative Assembly Debates*, 27 July 1894.

38. *Cape Times*, 16 July 1906.

39. See, for example, the comments of W.P. Schreiner (*Cape Times*, 16 July 1906) and Sir James Rose Innes

(*South African Jewish Chronicle*, 3 August 1906).

40. *South African Jewish Chronicle*, 23 January 1914.

41. See Shain, *The Roots of Antisemitism in South Africa*, chaps. 4–6.

42. For details see Michael Cohen, "Anti-Jewish Manifestations in the Union during the Nineteen-Thirties" (B.A. Hons. thesis: University of Cape Town, 1968), 67–9.

43. *Die Transvaler*, 1 October 1937.

44. See Patrick J. Furlong, *Between Crown and Swastika: The Impact of the Radical Right on the Afrikaner Nationalist Movement in the Fascist Era* (Johannesburg: Witwatersrand University Press; and Middletown, CT.: Wesleyan University Press, 1991). Edna Bradlow, "Immigration into the Union, 1910–48: Policies and Attitudes" (Ph.D. thesis: University of Cape Town, 1978).

45. Sandra Braude, "Combatting Anti-Jewish Propaganda: The South African Society of Jews and Christians 1937-1951," *Jewish Affairs* (October–November 1991): 32. This was not the only resolution emanating from the church. In 1938, for example, the Methodist Church Conference passed a resolution deploring the spread of antisemitic doctrines and propaganda. See *Cape Times*, 1 November 1938.

46. For a brief overview see Sandra Braude, "Combatting Anti-Jewish Propaganda."

47. See Braude, "Combatting Anti-Jewish Propaganda," 33–4.

48. William Henry Vatcher, *White Laager: The Rise and Fall of Afrikaner Nationalism* (London: Pall Mall Press, 1965), 68–75.

49. *South African Jewish Times*, 11 January 1943. In 1944 a motion expressing abhorrence at the suffering inflicted on the Jews of Europe was passed unanimously at an Anglican Synod: see *Zionist Record*, 11 August 1944. The provincial Synod also passed a motion noting with grave disquiet the increase of racial antagonism, including antisemitism in South Africa: see *Natal Mercury*, 1 November 1944.

50. Sharon L. Friedman, "Jews, Germans and Afrikaner-Nationalist Press Reactions to the Final Solution" (B.A. Hons. thesis: University of Cape Town, 1982), chap. 4.

51. The National Party was organized along federal lines with each province maintaining an autonomous structure.

52. *South African Jewish Times*, 6 November 1964.

53. *Brakpan Herald*, 9 May 1969.

54. *South African Observer*, March 1976.

55. See Gideon Shimoni, *Jews and Zionism: The South African Experience 1910–1967* (Cape Town: Oxford University Press, 1980), chap. 10.

56. See Gustav Saron, "A University's 'Private Affair' or State Policy?," *Jewish Affairs* (January 1962): 6.

57. See *Zionist Record*, 16 March 1973.

58. See *Sunday Times*, 27 October 1974, and *Zionist Record*, 22 July 1983.

59. *The Star*, 19 January 1977.

60. *Jewish Affairs*, September, 1978, 151.

61. *Ibid.*; and see Sergio DellaPergola and Allie A. Dubb, "South African Jewry: A Sociodemographic Profile," *American Jewish Year Book*, vol. 88 (New York, Philadelphia: American Jewish Committee and Jewish Publication Society, 1988), 86.

62. *The Star*, 4 April 1984.

63. Melville L. Edelstein, *What Do Young Africans Think?* (Johannesburg: SA Institute of Race Relations, 1972).

64. Melville L. Edelstein, "The Urban African Image of the Jew," *Jewish Affairs* (February 1972): 8.

65. Marcia Leveson, "The Jewish Stereotype in Some South African Fiction: A Preliminary Investigation," in *Waters Out of the Well: Essays in Jewish Studies*, ed. Reuben Musiker and Joseph Sherman (Johannesburg: University of Witwatersrand Library, 1988), 278–82.

66. "The Attitudes of Whites and Black Elites Towards Anti-Semitism," in *Opinion Surveys: Research for a New South Africa* (Pretoria: Human Sciences Research Council, 1990).

18 / PILLAY / CHRISTIANITY AMONG INDIAN SOUTH AFRICANS / PAGES 286–296

1. Resolution cited in C.T. Ferguson-Davie, *The Early History of Indians in Natal* (Durban: SA Institute of Race Relations, n.d.), 3.

2. M. Palmer, *The History of Indians in Natal* (Cape Town: Natal Regional Survey 10, 1957), 21f; *Report of the Indian Immigrants* [Wragge] *Commission* (1887), 99; *Natal Mercury*, 19 Jan. 1865.

3. Cited in Ferguson-Davie, *Indians in Natal*, 88.

4. The Wragge Commission (p. 70) estimated their number to be about 1,000. By 1891 this had increased to 6,000 – still less than 10 per cent of the total Indian population in Natal (*Colony of Natal Census Report*, 1891).

5. *Natal Mercury*, 20 June 1955; Ferguson-Davie, *Indians in Natal*, 10; *Coolie Commission Report* (1872), 7; *Wragge Commission Report*, 81.

6. Leonard Thompson, "Indian Immigration in Natal 1860–1872," *Archives Year Book for South African History* (1952/II): 57–58; Palmer, *History of Indians in Natal*, 49–50.

NOTES

7. *Report of the Coolie Commission* (1872), 49–50.

8. Ferguson-Davie, *Indians in Natal*, 22.

9. These included Law 3 of 1885; the proclamation of April 1899; Act 37 of 1919; the Transvaal Asiatics' Land and Trading Bill of 1939; the Trading and Occupation Land (Transvaal and Natal) Restriction Act [the 'Pegging Act'] of 1943; and the Asiatic Land Tenure ... Act of 1946, all aimed at restricting Indian business and residential areas.

10. The Group Areas Act of 1950, as frequently amended, resulted in the rigid demarcation of areas to which Indian South Africans were restricted for the ownership or occupation of property in all parts of South Africa.

11. J.B. Brain, *Christian Indians in Natal 1860–1911* (Cape Town: Oxford University Press, 1983) is the best available source for the statistics on the Christian immigrants to 1911.

12. Brain, *Christian Indians*, 195.

13. Letter of Sabon to Fabre, 28 March 1862 cited in *ibid.*, 197.

14. Information about the early Roman Catholic Indian Mission may be found in J.B. Brain's two other works, *Catholic Beginnings in Natal and Beyond* (Durban: Griggs, 1975) and "The History of the Roman Catholic Church in Natal 1886–1925" (D.Litt. et Phil. thesis: University of South Africa, 1987), published as *Catholics in Natal*, vol. 2 (Durban: Archdiocese of Durban, 1982). See also W.E. Brown, *The Catholic Church in South Africa, from its Origin to the Present Day* (London: Burns and Oates, 1960).

15. R.S. Stott to Hoole, Dec. 1871 cited in Brain, *Christian Indians*, 204.

16. R.S. Stott to Boyce, 14 Oct. 1873, in *ibid.*, 204.

17. Brain, *Christian Indians*, 201f; S.H. Stott, *A Nonagenarian's Experiences and Observations in Many Lands* (London: Epworth Press 1927); Wesleyan Methodist Church of South Africa, Natal District Division, *Is It Nothing to You? Work Among the Indians of Natal* (Port Elizabeth: J.W. Ware, 1922); *Faith Marches On: 150 Years of Methodism in Southern Africa* (Cape Town: Methodist Missionary Department, 1956); A.J. Choonoo, *Methodist Church of South Africa: A Brochure in Commemoration of the 90th Anniversary of the Durban and Coastal Methodist Indian Mission 1862–1952* (Durban, 1952); G. Mears, *Methodist Missions to the Indians of Natal* (Cape Town: Methodist Missionary Dept, 1957); *Natal Methodist Indian Mission, Centenary Brochure 1862–1962* (Durban, 1962); Methodist Church of South Africa, Pietermaritzburg Indian Circuit, *Seventy-fifth Anniversary Brochure of Thomas Street Church 1897–1972* (Pietermaritzburg, 1972).

18. Brain, *Christian Indians*, 212f; *Historical Records of the Church of the Province of South Africa*, ed. C. Lewis and G.E. Edwards (London: SPCK, 1934); B.B. Burnett, *Anglicans in Natal: A History of the Diocese of Natal* (Durban: St. Paul's Parish, 1955); P.E. Goldie, *The Centenary of St. Cyprian's Church, Durban 1870–1970* (Durban: Knoxprint, 1970).

19. Brain, *Christian Indians*, 20–221.

20. Telegu Baptist Mission, *First and Second Annual Reports* (1903, 1905); A. Jacob and J.P. Cornelius, *Indian Baptist Mission Golden Jubilee Brochure 1903–53* (Durban: Coastal, 1953); D.N. Nathaniel, "The Origin and Development of the Indian Baptist Church in South Africa 1900–1978" (M.Div. thesis: University of Durban–Westville, 1979); T.D. Pass, "Light and Shade: A Survey of Indian Baptist Progress in South Africa" (Dip.Th. thesis: Baptist Theological College of Southern Africa); M. Rungiah, Natal Indian Baptist Association, *Golden Jubilee Souvenir Brochure 1914–1964* (Clairwood: Mercantile, 1964); *The Diamond Jubilee of Indian Baptist Work in South Africa 1903–78*, ed. N. Timothy (Durban: Colortel, 1978).

21. "Education: A Story of Success," in *Centenary of Indians 1860–1960*, ed. S.R. Pather (Durban: n.p., 1960), 185–9.

22. Brain, *Christian Indians*, 218–19.

23. Hilda Kuper, *Indian People in Natal* (Pietermaritzburg: Natal University Press, 1960).

24. G.C. Oosthuizen, *Pentecostal Penetration into the Indian Community* (Durban: Human Sciences Research Council, 1975), 49–62.

25. P. Hey, *The Rise of the Natal Indian Elite* (Pietermaritzburg: University of Natal Press, 1961); E. Brookes and C. Webb, *A History of Natal* (Durban: University of Natal Press, 1965), 260.

26. *Moving to the Waters* (Durban: Bethesda, 1975). This history of the first 50 years of Bethesda was written by G.C. Oosthuizen at the invitation of J.F. Rowlands to mark the Golden Jubilee celebrations. It contains important biographical information. See also G.J. Pillay, *Religion at the Limits?* (Pretoria: University of South Africa, 1994), especially chap. 2 for reference to the key primary sources, in particular the sources of oral information.

27. The following editions of *Moving Waters*, the monthly magazine edited by J.F. Rowlands, are useful sources for the historical detail presented here: Feb. 1940; May 1941; March, December 1942; Feb., March 1943; Feb. 1947; Nov. 1949; Aug., Dec. 1952; Aug., Sept., Oct., Nov. 1953; Feb. 1954; March, June 1955; Nov. 1956; March 1958; May, Aug., Oct., Dec. 1973; Dec. 1975.

28. Refer to *Moving Waters*, Aug. 1952; Aug., Sept., Oct. 1953; Oct., Nov. 1954, for details about these campaigns.

29. *Moving Waters* (Feb. 1954): 14.

30. *The Golden Jubilee Brochure* (AFM Indian Mission), and D. Reddy, *The Gospel on Bicycle Wheels* (1979) (on the history of the Mount Edgecombe Assembly) are two brochures that have valuable information on the

Indian mission.

31. See Pillay, *Religion at the Limits?*, chap. 2 for more information on the AFM.

32. Interviews with F. Langeland-Hansen and David Nadesen; Pastor Hansen's sermons, which include frequent references to the church's history; Pillay, *Religion at the Limits?*, chapter 2; also W.F. Millan, "Early History: Assemblies of God," part 2, *Fellowship*, 5 (1978): 7.

33. Interview with Stephen Govender; Oosthuizen, *Pentecostal Penetration*, 87f; Pillay, *Religion at the Limits?*, chap. 2.

34. Pillay, *Religion at the Limits?*, 147–8.

35. Detailed information on these independent Pentecostal churches may be found in *ibid.*, 4.

36. *The Leader,* 4 (1955); *Daily News,* 16 June 1973.

37. *The Graphic,* 12 Nov. 1955.

38. *The Hindu Heritage in South Africa*, ed. R.S. Nowbath and others (Durban: Hindu Maha Sabha, 1961), 92.

39. The early Indian pastors of Bethesda, V.R. Enoch, F. Victor, C. Geoffrey and J. Vallen, all absolved Rowlands from a charge of disrespect for Hindus. On the contrary, Rowlands held that other believers must be respected but that Christians should be free to share their faith with others.

40. *The Leader,* 21 Oct. 1955.

41. S. Neill, *Christian Faith and Other Faiths* (London: Oxford University Press, 1961), 70–98; M.M. Thomas, *The Acknowledged Christ of the Indian Renaissance* (London: SCM, 1969).

19 / OPLAND / CHRISTIANITY AND LITERATURE / PAGES 297–315

The author is grateful to The British Academy for the award of a grant that facilitated the research for this chapter, and to the research committee of Vassar College for further financial aid.

1. M. van Wyk Smith, *Grounds of Contest: A Survey of South African English Literature* (Kenwyn: Juta, 1990), i and 22–4.

2. A.M. Lewin Robinson, *None Daring to Make Us Afraid: A Study of English Periodical Literature in the Cape Colony from its Beginnings in 1824 to 1835* (Cape Town: Maskew Miller, 1962).

3. Smith, *Grounds of Contest*, 22; see also Stephen Gray, *Southern African Literature: An Introduction* (Cape Town: David Philip, 1979).

4. Ralph Trewhela, *Song Safari: A Journey Through Light Music in South Africa* (Johannesburg: Limelight Press, 1980), 18.

5. Smith, *Grounds of Contest*, 70.

6. Pauline Smith, *The Little Karoo* (London: Jonathan Cape, 1925) 143–9 passim.

7. Michael Chapman, *South African English Poetry: A Modern Perspective* (Johannesburg: Donker, 1984), 10–11.

8. *Die Afrikaanse Patriot 1876: 'n Faksimilee-weergawe van die Eerste Jaargang* (Cape Town: Tafelberg, 1974), 14.

9. See G. Dekker, *Afrikaanse Literatuurgeskiedenis*, 12th ed. (Cape Town: Nasou, 1972) and J.C. Kannemeyer, *Die Afrikaanse Literatuur 1652–1987* (Pretoria and Cape Town: Academica, 1988).

10. *Journals of Andrew Geddes Bain*, ed. Margaret Hermina Lister (Cape Town: Van Riebeeck Society, 1949), 198 and 202.

11. Kannemeyer, *Afrikaanse Literatuur*, 24.

12. *Die Afrikaanse Patriot*, 3.

13. *Ibid.*, 7–9.

14. *Ibid.*, 60.

15. Kannemeyer, *Afrikaanse Literatuur*, 46.

16. *Ibid.*, 47.

17. André Brink, *Mapmakers: Writing in a State of Siege* (London: Faber, 1983), 26 and 112.

18. See P.J. Schutte, *Sendingdrukperse in Suid-Afrika 1800–1875* (Potchefstroom: Potchefstroomse Universiteit vir Christelike Hoër Onderwys, 1971) and Albert S. Gérard, *African Language Literatures: An Introduction to the Literary History of Sub-Saharan Africa* (Harlow: Longman, 1981).

19. R.H.W. Shepherd, *Lovedale South Africa 1824–1955* (Lovedale: Lovedale Press, 1971), 4.

20. See Frank R. Bradlow, *Printing for Africa: The Story of Robert Moffat and the Kuruman Press* (Kuruman: Kuruman Moffat Mission Trust, 1987).

21. Text in *Izwi Labantu*, ed. Jeff Opland and Peter Tshobisa Mtuze (Cape Town: Oxford University Press, 1994), 62.

22. Shepherd, *Lovedale*, 104.

23. Jeff Opland, "The transition from oral to written literature in Xhosa, 1823–1909," *Oral Tradition and Literacy: Changing Visions of the World*, ed. R.A. Whitaker and E.R. Sienaert (Durban: Natal University Oral Documentation and Research Centre, 1986), 141–2.

24. See Janet Hodgson, "Soga and Dukwana: The Christian struggle for liberation in mid-19th century South

NOTES

Africa," *Journal of Religion in Africa* 16 (1986): 187–208.

25. The Xhosa texts of most of the works mentioned in the preceding two paragraphs may be found in Opland and Mtuze, *Izwi Labantu*. On the early history of Xhosa literature, see Albert S. Gérard, *Four African Literatures: Xhosa, Sotho, Zulu, Amharic* (Berkeley: University of California Press, 1971) and A.C. Jordan, *Towards an African Literature: The Emergence of Literary Form in Xhosa* (Berkeley: University of California Press, 1973).

26. *Isigidimi*, 3 March 1871.

27. As translated in D.P. Kunene, *Heroic Poetry of the Basotho* (Oxford: Clarendon Press, 1971), xii.

28. C.F. Swanepoel, "Southern Sotho poetry, 1833–1931," *South African Journal of African Languages* 10 (1990): 266 and 267.

29. On Sotho literature, see also G.H. Franz, "The literature of Lesotho," *Bantu Studies* 4 (1930): 145–80, and Gérard, *Four African Literatures* and *African Language Literatures*.

30. See Peter Burke, *Popular Culture in Early Modern Europe* (Aldershot: Wildwood House, 1978, repr. 1988), ch. 1.

31. D.D. Stormont, "Literature for native Christians," *Report of the Proceedings of the Second General Missionary Conference for South Africa held at Johannesburg July 5–11, 1906*: 70.

32. For contrasting views of Shepherd as Director of the Lovedale Press, see Jeffrey B. Peires, "Lovedale Press: Literature for the Bantu revisited," *English in Africa* 7 (1980): 71–85; and Jeff Opland, "The publication of A.C. Jordan's Xhosa novel *Ingqumbo Yeminyanya* (1940)," *Research in African Literatures* 21 (1990): 135–47.

33. Jeff Opland, "The isolation of the Xhosa oral poet," *Literature and Society in South Africa*, ed. Tim Couzens and Landeg White (Cape Town: Maskew Miller Longman, 1984), 104; information from Cory Library for Historical Research, Rhodes University, MS 16,321c.

34. *Christian Literature for the Bantu of Southern Africa*, ed. C.B. Brink (Johannesburg: Continuation Committee of South African Churches, 1957).

35. On Gqoba, see Jordan, *Towards an African Literature*.

36. See Jeremy Cronin, "'Even under the rine of terror': Insurgent South African poetry," *Research in African Literatures* 19 (1988): 12–23; and Tony Emmett, "Oral, political, and communal aspects of township poetry in the mid-seventies," *English in Africa* 6 (1979): 72–81.

37. *Zemk'inkomo Magwalandini*, ed. W.B. Rubusana, 2nd ed. (Frome and London: W.B. Rubusana, 1906, repr. 1911), 232 and 233.

38. *Words that Circle Words: A Choice of South African Oral Poetry*, ed. Jeff Opland (Johannesburg: Donker, 1992), 112.

39. *Ibid.*, 112–13.

40. R.M. Sobukwe, "A collection of Xhosa riddles," *African Studies* 30 (1971): 149.

41. All Manisi's oral poems cited here are in my collection. Translations have been prepared with the poet's assistance.

42. But see Opland, "The isolation of the Xhosa oral poet."

43. David J. Darlow, *The Mendi: A Poem* (Lovedale: Lovedale Press, 1940), 7.

44. W.G. Bennie, "Two Xosa poems in English renderings," *The Critic* 4 (1936): 103–4.

45. James J. R. Jolobe, *Poems of an African* (Lovedale: Lovedale Press, 1946), 20–1.

46. See Ngqika's praises in Opland, *Words that Circle Words*, 217–18.

47. Jolobe, *Poems*, 25.

48. See Elizabeth Gunner, "New wine in old bottles: Imagery in the izibongo of the Zulu Zionist prophet, Isaiah Shembe," *Journal of the Anthropological Society of Oxford* 13 (1982): 99–108.

49. *Musho! Zulu Popular Praises*, ed. and trans. Liz Gunner and Mafika Gwala (East Lansing: Michigan State University Press, 1991), 67–71.

50. Opland, *Words that Circle Words*, 278.

51. Jeff Opland, "Nontsizi Mgqwetho: Stranger in town," *Power, Marginality and African Oral Literature*, ed. Graham Furniss and Liz Gunner (Cambridge: Cambridge University Press, 1995) 162–84.

52. Translations of Mgqwetho's poetry are based on preliminary versions prepared by Phyllis Ntantala.

20 / SMITH & DARGIE / SOUTH AFRICAN CHRISTIAN MUSIC / PAGES 316–326
A. Christian Music in the Western Tradition: Barry Smith (pages 316–319)

1. "Hymns and Other Sacred Songs," *Standard Encyclopedia of Southern Africa* (Cape Town: Nasou, 1972), 6:11–17.

2. *Ibid.*

3. R.R. Langham-Carter, *Old St. George's: The Story of Cape Town's First Cathedral* (Cape Town: Balkema, 1977).

4. "Hymns and Other Sacred Songs," 11–17.

B. *African Christian Music*: David Dargie (pages 319–326)

5. A. Kropf, *A Kafir-English Dictionary*, 2nd ed. (Lovedale: Lovedale Press, 1915), 67.

6. *Caffrarian Messenger* 8 (April 1843): 194.

7. *Incwadi yamaculo yesiKolo zika Krestu* (Lovedale: Lovedale Press, 1864); *The Journal and Writings of the Reverend Tiyo Soga*, ed. Donovan Williams (Cape Town: Balkema, 1983), 195. Williams wrongly alleges it may be "the first hymn book ever to be published in Xhosa."

8. A bibliography of Xhosa hymn books may be found in Janet Hodgson, *Ntsikana's Great Hymn: A Xhosa Expression of Christianity in the Early 19th Century Cape* (Cape Town: University of Cape Town, 1980), Bibliography V.

9. The diatonic ("white note") system is exemplified in the (European) key of C major, without the use of chromatic (black) notes. On the Xhosa bow-harmony system, see D. Dargie, *Xhosa Music* (Cape Town: David Philip, 1988), chap. 6. Some peoples of southern Africa use systems similar to the Xhosa in some degree, while others have very different systems – for example, with different scale intervals. Nonetheless all over southern Africa church songs use the African diatonic system – the diatonic system adapted to the ear of the people. This adaptation can mean that the same song sounds different in, say, Kavango, Namibia, from its Xhosa version. But, especially in large townships, an overall similarity of style has emerged among most church musicians.

10. See also D. Dargie, *Xhosa Zionist Church Music* (Johannesburg: Hodder and Stoughton, 1987) for further discussion and analysis.

11. Xhosa traditional rites and ceremonies, and their related music, are discussed in Dargie, *Xhosa Music*, chap. 2.

12. This process is encouraged in O. Hirmer and D. Dargie, *The Training of Hymn Leaders* (Germiston: Lumko, 1977).

13. See D.D. Hansen, *The Life and Work of B.K. Tyamzashe: A Contemporary Xhosa Composer* (Grahamstown: I.S.E.R., Rhodes University, 1968). Tyamzashe acknowledged Ntsikana as his inspiration. Ntsikana's influence is clear in the *Gloria* of 1965, but the song is also linked melodically and rhythmically to another traditional Xhosa song: cf. Dargie, *Xhosa Music*, 131.

14. Weman's experience of working with Zulu church music is reflected in H. Weman, *African Music and the Church in Africa* (Uppsala: Svenska Institutet foer Missionsforskning, 1960).

15. In 1985 Lumko Institute moved from "old" Lumko to Germiston. For a list of Lumko music publications, recordings and books, see *Lumko Music Publications Catalogue* (Germiston: Lumko Institute, 1991).

16. "*Nkosi sikelel' iAfrika*" was composed by Enoch Sontonga in 1892, and published in "*Umteteli waBantu*," 11 June 1927. It was later republished in many hymn-books, and also in a series of fine sol-fa compositions by African composers published by Lovedale.

17. Thus the song was described in the programme notes written by Hugh Tracey, accompanying a recording of the Four Hymns of Ntsikana by a choir led by S.T. Bokwe, the son of J.K. Bokwe, in 1957; cf. Disc TR 26, of the I.L.A.M., Rhodes University, Grahamstown, and the *Tracey by the Roadside* series of disc recordings. Ntsikana's conversion is described in Janet Hodgson, *Ntsikana's Great Hymn*, and in her *Ntsikana: History and Symbol: Studies in a Process of Religious Change Among Xhosa-speaking People* (Ph.D thesis: University of Cape Town, 1985).

18. The *uhadi* is a large gourd-resonated percussion bow; cf. Dargie, *Xhosa Music*, chapter 3; and, for bow versions of Ntsikana's song, pages 202–6, with recordings on the accompanying cassette tape.

19. The four hymns as transcribed by Bokwe may be found in J.K. Bokwe, *Ntsikana: The Story of an African Convert*, 2nd ed. (Lovedale: Lovedale Press, 1914); and transcribed into staff notation in Dargie, *Xhosa Music*, 198; Dargie compares the significant differences found in the version by Bokwe's son (cf. footnote 14).

20. The *Journal of Tiyo Soga* presents Tiyo Soga's black consciousness, and his devotion to Ntsikana's song. The story of "old" Soga is told in Hodgson, *Ntsikana: History and Symbol*.

21. Dargie, *Xhosa Zionist Church Music*.

22. Dargie, *Xhosa Zionist Church Music*, 2.

23. Dargie, *Xhosa Zionist Church Music*, 4ff; audio (tape no. 115); and video recordings of this service are included in the Lumko publications.

24. The Xhosa, like many other African peoples, did not make drums traditionally. Today both diviners' and Zionists' drums are made in the pattern of the British military bass drum: Dargie, *Xhosa Music*, 43–4; and P.R. Kirby, *The Musical Instruments of the Native Races of South Africa*, 2nd ed. (Johannesburg: Witwatersrand University Press, 1968), 44–5.

25. Photographs of Zionist services, illustrating "i-merry-go-round" and the musical instruments used, are in Dargie, *Xhosa Zionist Church Music*.

26. On Methodist songs see M. Stephenson, *African Music in the Methodist Church of Southern Africa: A Case Study in the Western Cape* (M.A. thesis, University of Cape Town, 1985). On song classification see Dargie, *Xhosa Zionist Church Music*, 15. In regard to *iingoma zamaWesile* some Xhosa people, in English, sometimes refer to the "Whistle Church" – i.e. the Wesleyans.

27. These comments are based on research material, as yet unpublished, gleaned by this writer, and also on

453

personal experience at funerals of police victims and protest gatherings in the 1980s.

28. This lenient attitude was reflected in a paper presented by the Zulu Catholic priest and theologian, Rev. Jabulani Nxumalo, O.M.I., at an anthropology conference at old Lumko, 1981.

29. J. Hodgson, "The Faith Healer of Cancele: Some Problems in Analyzing Religious Experience among Black People," *Religion in Southern Africa* 4:1 (January 1983): 13–29.

30. D. Dargie, "The Influence of 'Indigenous' Church Music on the Roman Catholic Church," *Religion Alive*, ed. G.C. Oosthuizen (Johannesburg: Hodder & Stoughton, 1986).

31. Dargie, *Xhosa Zionist Church Music*, 14–15, passim.

32. Such a performance may be seen on Lumko Video, MV03, "Xhosa Church Music", in a mass celebrated in the Catholic Church, Fingo Village, Grahamstown, in 1989: a performance of the stately hymn "Immortal, invisible, God only wise," in Xhosa accompanied by bells, clapping and dancing – a Western hymn transformed into something exuberantly African.

21 / RADFORD / CHRISTIAN ARCHITECTURE / PAGES 327–336

1. Hans Fransen and Mary Alexander Cook, *Old Buildings at the Cape* (Cape Town: A. A. Balkema, 1987), 420.

2. Jakob Rosenberg and others, *Dutch Art and Architecture 1600–1800* (Harmondsworth: Penguin, 1966), 243.

3. Fransen and Cook, *Old Buildings*, 43.

4. *Ibid.*, 135.

5. *Ibid.*, 43.

6. *Ibid.*, 33.

7. William Burchell, *Travels in the Interior of South Africa* (Cape Town: Struik, 1967), 106.

8. *Ibid.*, 43.

9. Hans Fransen, *Classicism, Baroque, Rococo and Neo-Classicism at the Cape* (Pietermaritzburg: University of Natal, 1987).

10. Fransen and Cook, *Old Buildings*, 285.

11. Ronald Bentley Lewcock, *Early Nineteenth Century Architecture in South Africa* (Cape Town: A.A, Balkema 1963), 261.

12. Lewcock, *Early Nineteenth Century Architecture*, 266.

13. *Ibid.*, 269.

14. *Ibid.*, 273.

15. Quoted in *Ibid.*, 275.

16. Derek Japha and others, *Mission Settlements in South Africa* (Cape Town: University of Cape Town, 1993), 16.

17. *Ibid.*, 15.

18. Roger Dixon and Stefan Muthesius, *Victorian Architecture* (London: Thames & Hudson, 1978), 182ff.

19. Lewcock, *Early Nineteenth Century Architecture*, chap. 12.

20. Brian Kearney, *Architecture in Natal 1824–1893* (Cape Town: A.A. Balkema 1973), 109.

21. Fransen and Cook, *Old Buildings*, 84.

22. Doreen Greig, *A Guide to Architecture in South Africa* (Cape Town: Timmins, 1971), 123–4.

23. Fransen and Cook, *Old Buildings*, 82.

24. T.B. Floyd, *Town Planning in South Africa* (Pietermaritzburg: Shuter & Shooter, 1960), 36.

25. Gilbert Herbert, *Pioneers of Prefabrication* (Baltimore: Johns Hopkins University Press, 1978), 97.

26. Desirée Picton-Seymour, *Victorian Buildings in South Africa* (Cape Town, A.A. Balkema, 1977), 383.

27. Fransen and Cook, *Old Buildings*, 387.

28. *Ibid.*, 439.

29. Doreen Greig, *Herbert Baker in South Africa* (Cape Town: Purnell, 1970), 78.

30. *Ibid.*, 150ff.

31. Information supplied by National Monuments Council, Transvaal Branch.

32. Greig, *Guide to Architecture*, 44.

33. Barrie Biermann, *Boukuns in Suid-Afrika* (Cape Town: A.A. Balkema, 1955), 92.

34. Gilbert Herbert, *Martienssen and the International Style* (Cape Town: A.A. Balkema, 1975), 232ff.

35. *South African Architectural Record*, June 1959.

36. *South African Architectural Record*, July 1966.

37. Greig, *Guide to Architecture*, 167.

38. *Architecture S A*, September 1979.

39. Methodist Missionary Department, *Methodist Missions, Missionaries and Ministers*, pamphlet No. 5, (Rondebosch, Cape, n.d.), 40.

22 / MILLS / CHRISTIANITY, IMPERIALISM, AND AFRICAN NATIONALISM / PAGES 337–346

1. These are, of course, the more extreme and sharply defined positions. Many have tended to regard Biblical eschatological passages as too obscure and speculative to be understood and have preferred to leave the future to the wisdom of God.

2. See J. A. de Jong, *As the Waters Cover the Sea: Millennial Expectations in the Rise of Anglo-American Missions 1640–1810* (Kampen: J.H. Kok, 1970); also William G. McLoughlin, Jr., *Modern Revivalism* (New York: Ronald Press, 1959), 100–7.

3. See Ernest R. Sandeen, *The Roots of Fundamentalism: British and American Millenarianism 1800–1930* (Chicago and London: University of Chicago Press, 1970).

4. Samuel Hopkins, the president of Yale University, estimated that it would probably take 150–200 years: *A Treatise on the Millennium* (New York: Arno, 1972; reprint of 1793 edition), 83–98.

5. Kate Crehan, "Missionaries and ideology in early nineteenth century South Africa," papers of the Conference on "Whites in Africa, Past, Present and Future," Oxford, 1978.

6. McLoughlin, *Modern Revivalism*, 257.

7. John 17: 11, 16, but there are many similar references.

8. British Parliamentary Papers, 7 (1837): 78–9.

9. Brian Stanley, "Nineteenth century liberation theology: Nonconformist missionaries and imperialism," *The Baptist Quarterly* 32 (1987): 9–12.

10. G.C. Bolton, *Britain's Legacy Overseas* (Oxford: University Press, 1973), 18–19.

11. Brian Stanley, "'Commerce and Christianity': Providence theory, the missionary movement, and the imperialism of free trade, 1842–1860," *The Historical Journal* 26 (1983): 72–5; also, Brian Stanley, *The Bible and the Flag* (Leicester, Eng.: Apollos, 1990), 70–4.

12. Stanley, "Commerce and Christianity," 71. For an example of the postmillennial vision see Hopkins, *A Treatise*.

13. Crehan, "Missionaries and ideology," has an extensive analysis of such ideas, in a Marxist framework.

14. Cited in Stanley, "Commerce and Christianity," 75.

15. Stanley, "Commerce and Christianity," 83–94.

16. Robert U. Moffat, *John Smith Moffat, Missionary: A Memoir* (New York: Dutton, 1921), 46.

17. John Maclean, *A Compendium of Kafir Laws and Customs* (1858; repr. London: Cass, 1968), 112.

18. Norman Etherington, "South African missionary ideologies 1880–1920: Retrospect and prospect," ed. Torbin Christensen and William R. Hutchinson, *Missionary Ideologies in the Imperialist Era: 1880–1920.* (Arhus, Denmark: Aros Publishers, 1982), 194–5. All except Bishop Colenso did an about-face on the question of annexation.

19. Greg Cuthbertson, "War, imperialism and the British nonconformist conscience," *Theologia Evangelica*, 17 (June 1984): 71.

20. See Wallace G. Mills, "Victorian imperialism as religion, civil or otherwise," *The Man on the Spot: Essays on British Empire History*, ed. Roger D. Long (Westport, Conn.: Greenwood Press, 1995), 21–43. On the concept of a "civil religion" see Robert N. Bellah, "Civil Religion in America," *Daedalus*, 96 (Winter 1967): 1–21; also, *American Civil Religion*, ed. Russell E. Richey and Donald G. Jones (New York: Harper and Row, 1974); Robert N. Bellah and Phillip E. Hammond, *Varieties of Civil Religion* (Harper and Row, 1980); and Dunbar Moodie, *The Rise of Afrikanerdom* (California: University of California Press, 1975) for his notion of the Afrikaner civil religion.

21. See R. T. Shannon, "John Robert Seeley and the idea of a national church," *Ideas and Institutions of Victorian Britain*, ed. Robert Robson (London: G. Bell & Sons, 1967).

22. C.A. Bodelsen, *Studies in Mid-Victorian Imperialism* (New York: Howard Fertig, 1968), 162–3, note 2.

23. Bodelsen, 153, note 1 (italicized in original).

24. Stanley, "Commerce and Christianity," 73.

25. Cited in Wendy R. Katz, *Rider Haggard and the Fiction of Empire* (Cambridge and New York: Cambridge University Press, 1987), 27.

26. Shannon, "John Robert Seeley," 240.

27. Some premillennialists argued that Christ would not return until all peoples in the world had heard the gospel. Thus, carrying the gospel to all the world would speed up the Second Coming. While some of the premillennialists went to the mission fields under the auspices of long-established societies, many new societies emerged. There were non-denominational missions, which included the South African General Mission and the Student Volunteer Movement. As new fundamentalist denominations were formed (especially in North America), they too began to send missionaries.

28. Clifton J. Phillips, "Changing attitudes in the student volunteer movement of Great Britain and North America, 1886–1928," *Missionary Ideologies*, ed. Christensen and Hutchinson, 131–45.

29. Jeffrey Peires, *The House of Phalo* (Berkeley: University of California Press, 1982), 67–74; also, "Nxele, Ntsikana and the origins of Xhosa religious reaction," *Journal of African History*, 20 (1979): 51–61.

30. Janet Hodgson, "Soga and Dukwana: The Christian struggle for liberation in mid-19th century South

NOTES

Africa," *Journal of Religion in Africa* 16 (1986): 187–208.

31. See J. B. Peires, *The Dead Will Arise* (Johannesburg: Ravan Press, 1989). Although some elements were borrowed or influenced from Christianity, it was a Xhosa movement.

32. *House of Phalo*, 74.

33. See Wallace G. Mills, "The Taylor Revival of 1866 and the roots of African nationalism in the Cape Colony," *Journal of Religion in Africa*, 8 (1976): 105–22.

34. Wallace G. Mills, "The roots of African nationalism in the Cape Colony: Temperance, 1866–1898," *International Journal of African Historical Studies*, 13 (1980): 197–213. See also Stanley Trapido, "'The friends of the natives': Merchants, peasants and the political and ideological structure of liberalism in the Cape, 1854–1910," *Economy and Society in Pre-Industrial South Africa*, ed. Shula Marks and Anthony Atmore (Oxford: University Press, 1980), 266.

35. Hodgson, "Soga and Dukwana," 189. In his last instructions to his followers as he lay dying, Ntsikana "ordered them to remain strongly united, *njenge mbumba yamanyama*, referring to the ball of scrapings from a tanned hide which forms an inseparable mass when dry."

36. Leo Kuper, *An African Bourgeoisie* (New Haven and London: Yale University Press, 1965), 193.

37. *From Protest to Challenge*, ed. Thomas Karis and Gwendolen M. Carter, 4 vols. (Stanford: Hoover Institution Press, 1972–77), vol. 1: 15.

38. Christopher C. Saunders, "The New African Elite in the Eastern Cape and Some Late Nineteenth Century Origins of African Nationalism," *The Societies of Southern Africa in the 19th and 20th Centuries*, 1 (London, 1969–1970): 55; Stanley Trapido, "African divisional politics in the Cape Colony, 1884 to 1910," *Journal of African History*, 9 (1968): 88–91.

39. J. Mutero Chirenje, *Ethiopianism and Afro-Americans in Southern Africa, 1883–1916* (Baton Rouge and London: Louisiana State University Press, 1987), p. 162. Out of over 230 Africans, about 6 to 10 AME and other independent church adherents are identified in biographies in Karis and Carter, *From Protest to Challenge*, vol. 4.

40. See Walter J. Hollenweger, *The Pentecostals*, trans. R. A. Wilson (London: SCM Press, 1972), 111–16. Although his immediate impact was in the Nederduitse Gereformeerde Kerk, Andrew Murray's (1828–1917) influence through his books extended to British and North American fundamentalists. On Bryant, see *ibid.*, p. 120.

41. *Bantu Prophets in South Africa*, 2nd ed. (London: Oxford University Press, 1961), 304–5.

42. See Wallace G. Mills, "The Fork in the Road: Religious Separatism Versus African Nationalism in the Cape Colony, 1890–1910," *Journal of Religion in Africa*, 9 (1978): 51–61. I was perhaps too categorical and Christopher Saunders raised some objections in "African Nationalism and Religious Independency in Cape Colony: A Comment," *Journal of Religion in Africa*, 9 (1978): 205–10. See also my "Rejoinder," *ibid.*, pp. 189–92. There were certainly exceptions, but the general thrust of my argument stands.

43. Chirenje, *Ethiopianism*, 94–7, 144–6; also, Chirenje, *A History of Northern Botswana 1850–1910*, (London: Associated University Presses, 1977), 201–28.

44. Shula Marks, *Reluctant Rebellion* (London: Oxford University Press, 1970), 326–36.

45. Robert Edgar, "The Prophet Motive: Enoch Mgijima, the Israelites, and the Background to the Bulhoek Massacre," *International Journal of African Historical Studies*, XV, 3 (1982) 401–22; also, Robert Edgar, *Because They Chose the Plan of God: The Story of the Bulhoek Massacre* (Johannesburg: Ravan Press, 1988).

46. William Beinart, "Amafelandawonye (the die-hards): Popular Protest and Women's Movements in Herschel District in the 1920s," in William Beinart and Colin Bundy, eds., *Hidden Struggles in Rural South Africa* (London: James Currey and Berkeley: University of California Press, 1987), 250–5. Other groups in the Transkei during the same period were urging that animals introduced by whites, especially pigs, should be slaughtered as a form of purification in preparing for the coming of the African–Americans.

47. See Karis and Carter, *From Protest to Challenge*; Peter Walshe, *The Rise of African Nationalism in South Africa* (London: C. Hurst, 1970); André Odendaal, *Black Protest Politics in South Africa to 1912* (Totowa, New Jersey: Barnes & Noble, 1984); André Odendaal, *Vukani Bantu! The Beginnings of Black Protest Politics in South Africa* (Cape Town: David Philip, and Totowa, New Jersey: Barnes and Noble, 1984).

23 / ELPHICK / CHRISTIANS IN THE AGE OF SEGREGATION / PAGES 347–369

1. I am grateful to Jeffrey Butler, Eugene Klaaren and Richard Vann for helpful comments on an earlier draft.

2. *The James Stuart Archive of Recorded Oral Evidence Relating to the History of the Zulu and Neighbouring Peoples*, ed. C. de B. Webb and J.B. Wright (Pietermaritzburg: University of Natal Press; and Durban: Killie Campbell Africana Library, 1979), vol. 2, 184–5.

3. "Tabular View of Mission Work in South Africa 1884," *Condensed Report of the Statistical Committee of the United Missionary Conference* (Lovedale: Lovedale Mission Press, 1889); *Census of the Union of South Africa, 1911: Report and Annexures* (Pretoria: Government Printing and Stationery Office, 1913), 924–5; Patrick Johnstone, *Operation World: The Day-by-Day Guide for Praying for the World*, 5th ed. (Grand Rapids: Zondervan, 1993), 493–8. Johnstone's figures incorporate statistics from the former "homelands" now reunit-

ed with South Africa. On Shoshanguve see Allan Anderson, *Bazalwane: African Pentecostals in South Africa* (Pretoria: University of South Africa, 1992), 129–30.

4. Peter Berger, *The Sacred Canopy: Elements of a Sociological Theory of Religion* (New York: Anchor, 1969), 107. Though dechristianization and secularization often reinforce one another, we must carefully distinguish the two terms. The United States, for example, has been radically secularized in the twentieth century without experiencing substantial dechristianization. South Africa, for its part, has experienced (comparatively belated) secularization accompanied by dramatic Christianization. By dechristianization I mean simply a decline in rates of church attendance, church membership, and assent to Christian doctrines. By secularization I mean, in Peter Berger's formulation, "the process by which sectors of society and culture are removed from the domination of religious institutions and symbols." Secularization, says Berger, can include such varied processes as "separation of church and state, ... expropriation of church lands, ... emancipation of education from church authority, ... decline of religious contents in the arts, in philosophy, in literature, and, most important of all, ... the rise of science as an autonomous, thoroughly secular perspective on the world."

5. Paul Badham, "Religious Pluralism in Modern Britain," in *A History of Religion in Britain*, ed. S. Gilley and W.J. Sheils (Oxford: Blackwell, 1994), 488–9; Alan D. Gilbert, *The Making of Post-Christian Britain: A History of the Secularization of Modern Society* (London: Longman, 1980), 76–8.

6. J. Dexter Taylor, "The Social Motive in Evangelism," *South African Outlook* (1 December 1933): 238–9.

7. *South African Native Affairs Commission, 1903–5* (Cape Town: Cape Times, 1905), vol. 1, 19.

8. *World Atlas of Christian Missions*, ed. James S. Dennis, Harlon P. Beach and Charles H. Fahs (New York: Student Volunteer Movement for Foreign Missions, 1911), 109, 128. The figures on Catholic education apparently exclude white pupils and their teachers.

9. Using as a population base the 1911 census figure for Africans of 4,019,006.

10. Alexander Kerr, *Fort Hare, 1915–48: The Evolution of an African College* (Pietermaritzburg: Shuter and Shooter; and London: C. Hurst, 1968), 11; *The Christian Handbook of South Africa: Die Suid-Afrikaanse Kristen-Handboek* (Lovedale: Lovedale Press, 1938), 94.

11. *World Atlas of Christian Missions*, 84, 118–19, 123. The Roman Catholic figures are not available in this source.

12. *Ibid.*, 94–5.

13. William R. Hutchison, *Errand to the World: American Protestant Thought and Foreign Missions* (Chicago: University of Chicago Press, 1987), 81.

14. Most famously, the Ethiopian followers of James Dwane who severed their ties with the (African-American) African Methodist Episcopal Church and joined the Anglican Church.

15. Catholic mission schools were much smaller, but their 27 hospitals had almost as many beds as all the Protestants combined: Catholics had 954 beds, Protestants 1,065. Joseph I. Parker, *Interpretative Statistical Survey of the World Mission of the Christian Church* (New York and London: International Missionary Council, 1938), 33–5, 70–1, 182–3, 226.

16. Ninety-eight residents of the Cape, Transvaal, Natal, and the Orange River Colony gave written responses to the question "What is your opinion of (a) the status and condition of the native men and women compared to that of 20 years ago: (b) Their present resources; (c) Their earning power; (d) Their cost of living?" Of these, 26% said that Africans' position had deteriorated, 42% that it had improved; 16% gave a mixed assessment, and 15% discerned no change. *South African Native Affairs Commission, 1903–5*, vol. 5, 1–431. The questionnaires were tabulated for me by Thomas Policelli and statistically analyzed by Anthony Whyte.

17. James Henderson, "The Problems of the Older Mission Fields," *Report of the Proceedings of the Third General Missionary Conference* (Cape Town: Townshend, Taylor and Snashall, 1909), 104–5.

18. J. Henderson, "The Native Economic Crisis and Some Ways Out," *The Realignment of Native Life on a Christian Basis: Being a Report of the Proceedings of the Seventh General Missionary Conference of South Africa* (Lovedale: Lovedale Institution Press, 1928), 97–111 (quotation on p. 109); James Henderson, "The Problem of Native Poverty," in *Christianity and the Natives of South Africa: A Year-Book of South African Missions*, ed. J. Dexter Taylor (Lovedale: Lovedale Institution Press, 1927 or 1928), 24–32.

19. Harvard University, Archives of the American Board (hereafter cited as ABC), 15.4(23), item 61, D.D. Goodenough, The Johannesburg Field, 24 July 1909, 9.

20. ABC 15.4(29), item 60, Annual Report [J.D. Taylor], 1911, 5–6.

21. ABC 15.4(29), item 168, Annual Report – Transvaal [F.B. Bridgman], June 1917, 7–9; ABC 15.4(29), item 202, Ray Phillips to Foreign Department, 11 May 1919, 2–3.

22. *Ibid.*, 2, 3.

23. Harvey M. Feinberg, "The 1913 Natives Land Act in South Africa: Politics, Race, and Segregation in the Early 20th Century," *International Journal of African Historical Studies*, 26, 1 (1993): 65–109; "Mr. Sauer's Land Bill," *Christian Express* (hereafter CE), 1 May 1913, 70–1; "Mr. Sauer's Land Bill, II," CE, 2 June 1913, 84–5; Brian Willan, *Sol Plaatje: South African Nationalist, 1876–1932* (Berkeley: University of California Press, 1984), 165; "The Native Land Act," CE, 1 Oct. 1914, 148–9.

24. Walter Rauschenbusch, *Christianity and the Social Crisis* (New York: Macmillan, 1907; repr. New York:

NOTES

Harper and Row, 1964), 211–86.

25. Ramsay Cook, *The Regenerators: Social Criticism in Late Victorian English Canada* (Toronto: University of Toronto Press, 1985), 176.

26 Hutchison, *Errand to the World*, 104.

27. James S. Dennis, *Christian Missions and Social Progress*, 3 vols. (New York: Fleming H. Revell, 1897–1906); *World Atlas of Christian Missions*.

28. *Ibid.*, 172-76; Susan Curtis, *A Consuming Faith: The Social Gospel and Modern American Culture* (Baltimore: Johns Hopkins University Press, 1991), 16–19.

29. E.R. Norman, *Church and Society in England, 1770–1970: A Historical Study* (Oxford: Clarendon Press, 1976), 222, 221, 301.

30. Callum G. Brown, *The Social History of Religion in Scotland since 1730* (London: Methuen, 1987), 193; A.C. Cheyne, *The Transforming of the Kirk: Victorian Scotland's Religious Revolution* (Edinburgh: Saint Andrew's Press, 1983), 150.

31. Ralph E. Luker, *The Social Gospel in Black and White: American Racial Reform, 1885–1912* (Chapel Hill: University of North Carolina Press, 1991), 13.

32. Louis R. Harlan, *Booker T. Washington: The Making of a Black Leader, 1856-1901* (London: Oxford University Press, 1972), 58–70; the quotation is on p. 62.

33. Robert Michael Franklin, *Liberating Visions: Human Fulfillment and Social Justice in African–American Thought* (Minneapolis: Fortress Press, 1990), 24-30; Luker, *Social Gospel*, 125–36; Harlan, *Black Leader*, 196–7; Booker T. Washington, *Up From Slavery* (repr. Oxford and New York: Oxford University Press, 1995), 116.

34. Harlan, *Black Leader*, 219.

35. The more pietistic Lutherans and members of the small evangelical missions attended the conferences in large numbers but said little. Only one Roman Catholic, and four delegates of the large African Methodist Episcopal church, attended the eight GMC meetings. The only conference speaker from either church was Charlotte Maxeke, the influential AME educator, evangelist, and social worker, who acted as a link between the white-dominated missions and the AME. On Maxeke, see James T. Campbell, *Songs of Zion: The African Methodist Episcopal Church in the United States and South Africa* (New York: Oxford University Press, 1995), 282–94.

36. *Report of the Proceedings of the Fourth General Missionary Conference of South Africa* (Cape Town: Townshend, Taylor and Snashall, 1912), 28–34.

37. An enormous literature on these topics has recently emerged, especially in the historiography of temperance and missionary movements in the United States. See, for example, Barbara Leslie Epstein, *The Politics of Domesticity: Women, Evangelism, and Temperance in Nineteenth-Century America* (Middletown, CT.: Wesleyan University Press, 1981); Ian Tyrell, *Woman's World, Woman's Empire: The Woman's Christian Temperance Union in International Perspective, 1880–1930* (Chapel Hill: University of North Carolina Press, 1991); Patricia Hill, *The World Their Household: The American Woman's Foreign Mission Movement and Cultural Transformation, 1870–1920* (Ann Arbor: University of Michigan Press, 1985); Jane Hunter, *The Gospel of Gentility: American Women Missionaries in Turn-of-the-Century China* (New Haven: Yale University Press, 1984).

38. Peter Walshe, *The Rise of African Nationalism in South Africa: The African National Congress, 1912–1952* (Berkeley: University of California Press, 1971), 33–37; *From Protest to Challenge: A Documentary History of African Politics in South Africa, 1882–1964*, ed. Thomas Karis and Gwendolen M. Carter, vol. 4: *Political Profiles, 1882–1964*, by Gail M. Gerhart and Thomas Karis, 24–6, 68–9, 127, 134–5, 137–9.

39. Manning Marable, "African Nationalist: The Life of John Langalibalele Dube" (Ph.D. thesis: University of Maryland, 1976), 226, 228, 134.

40. Saul Dubow, *Racial Segregation and the Origins of Apartheid in South Africa, 1919–36* (Basingstoke: Macmillan, 1989), 80, 101.

41. Maurice S. Evans, *Black and White in South East Africa: A Study in Sociology* (London: Longmans, Green, 1911), 92–125; Charles T. Loram, *The Education of the South African Native* (London: Longmans, Green, 1917), 46–78; Edgar H. Brookes, *The History of Native Policy in South Africa from 1830 to the Present Day* (Cape Town: Nasionale Pers, 1924), 436–80.

42. Steven D. Gish, "Alfred B. Xuma, 1893-1962: African, American, South African" (Ph.D. thesis: Stanford University, 1994), 103. Tim Couzens, "'Moralizing Leisure Time': The Transatlantic Connection and Black Johannesburg," in *Industrialisation and Social Change in South Africa: African Class Consciousness, 1870–1930*, ed. Shula Marks and Richard Rathbone (London: Longman, 1982), 318–19.

43. Richard John Haines, "The Politics of Philanthropy and Race Relations: The South African Joint Councils c.1920–1955" (Ph.D thesis: University of London, 1991), 98-9, 105, 236, 294–300; Jeffrey Butler, "Interwar Liberalism and Local Activism," in *Democratic Liberalism in South Africa: Its History and Prospect*, ed. Jeffrey Butler, Richard Elphick, and David Welsh (Middletown: Wesleyan University Press; and Cape Town: David Philip, 1987), 86.

44. *Seventh General Missionary Conference*, 128–31; *South African Outlook* (hereafter *SAO*), 2 Jan. 1928, 2; Robert A. Hill and Gregory A. Pirio, "'Africa for the Africans': The Garvey Movement in South Africa, 1920–1940," in *The Politics of Race, Class and Nationalism in Twentieth-Century South Africa*, ed. Shula Marks and S. Trapido (London and New York: Longman, 1987), 223–26; Clements Kadalie, *My Life and the ICU: The Autobiography of a Black Trade Unionist in South Africa* (London: Frank Cass, 1970), 47–8, 50, 56, 85; A.W.G. Champion, *The Views of Mahlathi: Writings of A.W.G. Champion, a Black South African*, ed. M.W. Swanson (Pietermaritzburg: University of Natal Press; and Durban: Killie Campbell Africana Library, 1982), 187 (see also 58); Edward Roux, *Time Longer Than Rope: A History of the Black Man's Struggle for Freedom in South Africa* (Madison: University of Wisconsin Press, 1966), 277, 279.

45. *Report of the Proceedings of the Fifth General Missionary Conference of South Africa* (Durban: Commercial Printing Co., 1922), 17–29; *The Evangelisation of South Africa: Being the Report of the Sixth General Missionary Conference* (Cape Town: Nasionale Pers, 1925), 16-19; *Seventh General Missionary Conference*, 18–26; *Evangelism: The Message and the Methods: A Report of the Proceedings of the Eighth General Missionary Conference of South Africa* (Lovedale: Lovedale Press, 1932), 17–23.

46. D.D.T. Jabavu, "Native Unrest: Its Cause and Cure, I," *CE*, 1 Oct. 1920, 154; Plaatje, *Native Life*, 148.

47. *European and Bantu, Being Papers and Addresses Read at the Conference on Native Affairs . . . 27th to 29th September, 1923* (n.p.: Federal Council of the D.R. Churches, 1924), esp. 41–55; C.T. Loram, "The Dutch Reformed Church and the Native Problem," *SAO*, 2 Feb. 1925, 33–40; quotations on 34, 36.

48. "De Johannesburgse Konferentie: Indrukken van Verscheide Voormannen," *Kerkbode*, 10 Oct. 1923, 1373.

49. Paul B. Rich, *White Power and the Liberal Conscience: Racial Segregation and South African Liberalism, 1921–60* (Johannesburg: Ravan Press, 1984), 33–4; D.D.T. Jabavu, "The Segregation Fallacy," in *The Segregation Fallacy and Other Papers* (Lovedale: Lovedale Institution Press, 1928).

50. W.J. van Zyl, "Die Naturel en die Witm··· in Suid-Afrika," and "Sendingvriend," "Algemene Sendingkonferensie van Suid-Afrika," *Kerkbode*, 1º Aug. 1925, 1090, 1089.

51. *Programme of the European–Bantu Conference . . . January 31–February 2, 1927* (Cape Town, n.d.); Howard Pim, "The Native Bills," *SAO*, 2 Apr. 1928, 69; "De Konferentie over Naturellen-Zaken: Indrukken op de Konferentie van Verschillende Kanten," *Kerkbode*, 16 Feb. 1927, 234–5.

52. "The Mission Policy of the D.R. Church of the O.F.S. Province," *SAO*, 1 June 1931, 113–14; *Handelinge van die Viertiende Vergadering van die Raad van die Kerke Gehou op 16 Mei 1935 en die Volgende Dae* (n.p., n.d.), 94–9. I have quoted the English translation in G.B.A. Gerdener, *Recent Developments in the South African Mission Field* (Cape Town and Pretoria: N.G. Kerk-Uitgewers, 1958), 269–75. See also J.C. Adonis, "Die Afgebreekte Skeidsmuur Weer Opgebou" (Doctoral thesis: Free University of Amsterdam, 1982), 78–81.

53. Gish, "Xuma," 170.

54. Catherine Ann Higgs, "The Ghost of Equality: D.D.T. Jabavu and the Decline of South African Liberalism, 1885–1959" (Ph.D. thesis: Yale University, 1993), 87, 160, 189, 182.

55. Witwatersrand University Archives, Rheinallt Jones papers, "The Church and Labour," SA 3.2.2. (quotation on p. 13); "The Foundations of Missionary Policy," SA 3.2.4, unpaginated.

56. "Recent Inter-Racial Conferences," *SAO*, 2 Oct. 1933, 186–7; J.D. Rheinallt Jones, "Missionary Co-operation," *SAO*, 2 April 1934, 71.

57. Richard Elphick, "Mission Christianity and Interwar Liberalism," *Democratic Liberalism*, ed. Butler, Elphick, and Welsh, 69, 73, 79.

58. J. Dexter Taylor, "A National Christian Council for South Africa," *SAO*, 2 June 1930, 110–11.

59. The Anglican Church also briefly disaffiliated itself from the conference in the early 1940s. Elfriede Strassberger, *Ecumenism in South Africa 1936-1960 with Special Reference to the Mission of the Church* (Johannesburg: South African Council of Churches, 1974), 139–43; 157–63.

60. Gish, "Xuma," 49–55, 90–1, 112–13, 158-62, 298, 308.

61. Paul B. Rich, "Albert Luthuli and the American Board in South Africa," in *Missions and Christianity in South African History*, ed. Henry Bredekamp and Robert Ross (Johannesburg: Witwatersrand University Press, 1995), 196–205; A.J. Lutuli, "The Road to Freedom is via the Cross," in *From Protest to Challenge*, ed. Karis and Carter, vol. 2: *Hope and Challenge, 1935–1952*, ed. Thomas Karis (Stanford: Hoover Institution Press, 1973), 486–9; Albert Luthuli, *Let My People Go* (New York: Meridien, 1962), 136–9.

62. Douglas Irvine, "The Liberal Party, 1953–1968," in *Democratic Liberalism*, ed. Butler, Elphick, and Welsh, 119, 132.

63. The terms "optimist" and "pessimist" are Michael Gauvreau's; he spells out the two interpretations in *The Evangelical Century: College and Creed in English Canada from the Great Revival to the Great Depression* (Montreal and Kingston: McGill–Queen's University Press, 1991), 5. On missions and Canada's international outlook see Robert Wright, *A World Mission: Canadian Protestantism and the Quest for a New International Order, 1918–1939* (Montreal and Kingston: McGill–Queen's University Press, 1991), esp. 256–7.

64. For example, Ray Phillips: see Rich, "Albert Luthuli," 203.

65. "The Native Affairs Bill," *CE*, 1 July 1920, 100; "Native Affairs," *Church Chronicle*, 10 June 1920, 229;

NOTES

Walshe, *African Nationalism*, 101; "Testimony of Z.R. Mahabane," in *From Protest to Challenge*, ed. Karis and Carter, vol. 1, 115.

66. Walshe, *African Nationalism*, 102–6; Wilfred Parker, "Serfdom of the Native: The Land Question," *SAO*, 1 Jan. 1923, 10; 2 April 1923, 74–5; 1 June 1923, 122–3; Editorial, *Church Chronicle*, 14 June 1923, 179; "Half a Loaf" [Letter from Arthur Cardross Grant], 12 July 1923, 216; *Official Report of the Eighth Provincial Missionary Conference* (1923), 12; Walshe, *African Nationalism*, 103–5.

67. "The United Free Church Missions," *CE*, 1 June 1907, 91.

68. J.W. Williams, "Extracts from a Charge," *CE*, 1 May 1920, 73–4 (italics mine).

69. *Forerunners of Modern Malawi: The Early Missionary Adventures of Dr. James Henderson, 1895–1898*, ed. M.M.S Ballantyne and R.H.W. Shepherd (Lovedale: Lovedale Press, 1968), 6.

70. "The United Missionary Campaign," *SAO*, 2 Feb. 1925, 31–3; *ibid.*, 2 March 1925, 51.

71. Edgar H. Brookes, *A South African Pilgrimage* (Johannesburg: Ravan Press, 1977), 78.

72. James R. Cochrane, *Servants of Power: The Role of the English-speaking Churches, 1903–1930: Toward a Critical Theology via an Historical Analysis of the Anglican and Methodist Churches* (Johannesburg: Ravan Press, 1987). Cochrane is much more critical of the Social Christians than I have been in this chapter. Part of the discrepancy is due to his concentration on the churches, while I have focused mostly on the missions. For another radical critique see Charles Villa-Vicencio, *Trapped in Apartheid: A Socio-theological History of the English-speaking Churches* (Maryknoll: Orbis; and Cape Town: David Philip, 1988), 65–92.

24 / KLAAREN / THEOLOGY SINCE 1948 / PAGES 370–382

1. For selections from Barth's 12-volume *Church Dogmatics* (1932–67), and the text of the Barmen Declaration, see Clifford Green's *Karl Barth: Theologian of Freedom* (London: Collins, 1989).

2. As of this writing (1993) apartheid has officially ended, but how its legacy will be handled is unknown.

3. On the importance of the presupposition of creation in Western worldviews, see *Creation: The Impact of an Idea*, ed. Daniel O'Connor and Francis Oakley (New York: Scribners, 1969); Eugene M. Klaaren, *Religious Origins of Modern Science: Belief in Creation in Seventeenth-Century Thought* (Grand Rapids: Eerdmans, 1977; Lanham, MD: University Press of America, 1985); Nicholas Wolterstorff, *Until Justice and Peace Embrace* (Grand Rapids: Eerdmans, 1983); and David B. Burrell, *Freedom and Creation in Three Traditions* (Notre Dame: Notre Dame, 1993). For an excellent study of apartheid and NGK theology, see Johann Kinghorn, "The theology of separate equality: A critical outline of the DRC's position on apartheid," in *Christianity Amidst Apartheid*, ed. Martin Prozesky (London: Macmillan, 1990), 57–80, and *Die NG Kerk en Apartheid* ed. Johann Kinghorn (Johannesburg: 1986). See also note 26.

4. For an explanation, and exception, see Vitor Westhelle, "Creation motifs in the search for a vital space: A Latin American perspective," *Lift Every Voice: Constructing Christian Theologies from the Underside*, ed. Susan Brooks Thistlethwaite and Mary Potter Engel (New York: Harper and Row, 1990), 128–40.

5. See Albert Grundlingh and Hilary Sapire, "From feverish festival to repetitive ritual: The changing fortunes of Great Trek mythology in an industrializing South Africa, 1938–1988," *South African Historical Journal* 21 (1989) 19–38.

6. The *Journal of Theology for Southern Africa*, begun in 1972 and based at the University of Cape Town, has become the most internationally known theological journal from South Africa. For a survey by its editor, see John de Gruchy, "South African theology comes of age," *Religious Studies Review* 17, 3 (1991).

7. For Bonhoeffer's works, see John de Gruchy, *Dietrich Bonhoeffer: Witness to Jesus Christ* (London: Collins, 1988).

8. See James Cone's *Black Theology and Black Power* (New York: Seabury Press, 1969).

9. Jaap Durand, "Afrikaner piety and dissent," *Resistance and Hope: South African Essays in Honour of Beyers Naudé*, ed. Charles Villa-Vicencio and John de Gruchy (Cape Town: David Philip; Grand Rapids, Michigan: Eerdmans, 1985), 50. See also J. Durand, *Skepping, Mens, Voorsienigheid* (Pretoria: N.G. Kerkboekhandel, 1982), and the work of Johan Heyns, notes 17, 18, 20 below.

10. For a collection of Stoker's writings, see H.G. Stoker, *Oorsprong en Rigting* (2 vols.; Cape Town: Tafelberg-Uitgewers, 1967, 1970).

11. *Ibid.*, 1: 319–22, 2: 202ff.

12. H.G. Stoker, "At the crossroads: Apartheid and university freedom in South Africa," [originally published in *Race Relations Journal* XXIV (1957)], republished in H.G. Stoker, *Oorsprong en Rigting*, 1: 209–22.

13. Dooyeweerd's main work was published in the Netherlands as a philosophy of the law idea (*Wetsidee*), in 1935 and 1936. A second English edition and translation was published as the philosophy of the "Cosmonomic Idea" under a different title: Herman Dooyeweerd, *A New Critique of Theoretical Thought*, trans. David H. Freeman and William S. Young (4 vols.; Philadelphia: Presbyterian and Reformed Publishing Co., 1953–1958).

14. J.A.L. Taljaard, *Polished Lenses* (Potchefstroom: Pro Rege, 1976), passim. Taljaard's writings do not match the sophistication or accomplishments of his predecessor, but he was an influential teacher.

15. See, e.g., the works of M. Elaine Botha and B.J. van der Walt, and the *Koinonia Declaration* of 1977.

16. See also David J. Bosch, *Transforming Mission: Paradigm Shifts in Theology of Mission* (Maryknoll: Orbis

Books, 1991; and the *Festschrift* for Bosch: *Mission in Creative Tension: A Dialogue with David Bosch*, ed. J.N.J Kritzinger and W.A Saayman (Pretoria: S.A. Missiological Society, 1990). On Naudé, see *Resistance and Hope*, ed. Villa-Vicencio and De Gruchy.

17. J. Heyns, *Dogmatiek* (Pretoria: N.G. Kerkboekhandel, 1958), and *Teologiese Etiek* (3 vols.; Pretoria: N.G. Kerkboekhandel, 1982-89).

18. J. Heyns, *The Church* (Pretoria: N.G. Kerkboekhandel, 1980 (translation of *Die Kerk* [Pretoria: N.G. Kerkboekhandel, 1977]), chap. 1, et passim.

19. For several decades, beginning in the 1930s, if not before, use of the concept of creation ordinances (especially when tied to notions of the "diversity" of "groups") on the part of Afrikaner intellectuals (theological and otherwise) had the effect of directly tying apartheid, along with the *volk* and nation, to divine rule. Among other accounts, see T. Dunbar Moodie, *The Rise of Afrikanerdom: Power, Apartheid, and the Afrikaner Civil Religion* (Berkeley: University of California Press, 1975).

20. J. Heyns, *The Church*, 20-7, 203-25.

21. *The Kairos Document, Challenge to the Church: A Theological Comment on the Political Crisis in South Africa*, (2nd ed.; Johannesburg: Skotaville Publishers, 1986). See below for further discussion.

22. In 1972, König and a small group of Afrikaner theologians issued an open letter against apartheid. His systematic work has been shaped in relation to such European theologians as Barth, Gerrit C. Berkouwer, Hendrikus Berkof, Oscar Cullmann, and Gerhard von Rad. In European theology, after the ascendancy of Barth and in the context of a new Europe, Wolfhart Pannenberg and Jürgen Moltmann initiated new engagements with secular philosophies of science and history to reconstruct systematic theology in eschatological categories. See, e.g., W. Pannenberg, *Theology and the Philosophy of Science* (Philadelphia: Westminster Press, 1976), and J. Moltmann, *Hope and Planning* (New York, Harper, 1971).

23. A. König, *The Eclipse of Christ in Eschatology* (Grand Rapids: Eerdmans, 1989: adaptation and translation of *Jesus die Laaste. Gelowig Nagedink*, vol. 2 *Oor die Einde* [Pretoria: N.G. Kerkboekhandel, 1980]); A. König, *Here Am I!* (Grand Rapids: Eerdmans, 1982: translation of *Hier is Ek! Gelowig Nagedink*, vol. 1 *Oor God* [Pretoria: N.G. Kerkboekhandel, 1975]). König's eschatological turn was already announced in his 1970 dissertation on eschatological Christology.

24. A. König, *New and Greater Things: Re-evaluating the Biblical Message on Creation* (Pretoria: University of South Africa, 1988: translation of *Hy kan Weer en Meer. Gelowig Nagedink*, vol. 3, *Oor die Skepping* [Pretoria: N.G. Kerkboekhandel, 1982]), vii–viii.

25. In this respect, however, further volumes, in König's ongoing theological project, e.g., on anthropology, warrant examination. Kinghorn's general claim that NGK theology is a case of rationalizing apartheid ideology and economic development may be relevant here. See note 3.

26. Bernard Lategan, Johann Kinghorn, Lourens du Plessis, and Etienne de Villiers, *The Option for Inclusive Democracy* (Stellenbosch: Centre for Hermeneutics, 1987), 5, et passim.

27. However, in contrast to the ordering propensity of the principial approach, different modes of methodological criticism have also emerged. See the various inquiries into hermeneutics by Wentzel van Huysteen and Dirkie J. Smit, especially the latter's critique of the Yale method of narrative theology for resolving the social divisions of South Africa.

28. See Elphick's sketch of liberalism in South Africa and its relation to evangelical values of Christian missions. *Democratic Liberalism in South Africa: Its History and Prospect*, ed. Jeffrey Butler, Richard Elphick, and David Welsh (Middletown: Wesleyan University Press; Cape Town: David Philip, 1987); 3–17, 64–80.

29. See, for example, John de Gruchy, *The Church Struggle in South Africa* (2nd ed.; Grand Rapids: Eerdmans, 1986; London: William Collins; Cape Town: David Philip), James Cochrane's radical, *Servants of Power: The Role of English-speaking Churches 1903–1930* (Johannesburg: Ravan Press, 1987), and Charles Villa-Vicencio's bolder *Trapped in Apartheid* (Maryknoll: Orbis; Cape Town: David Philip, 1988).

30. Douglas Bax, *A Different Gospel: A Critique of the Theology Behind Apartheid* (Johannesburg: The Presbyterian Church of Southern Africa, 1979). See also the *Report, Human Relations ...* (Cape Town and Pretoria: Dutch Reformed Church Publishers, 1976 [official translation of *Ras, volk en nasie en volkereverhoudinge in die lig van die Skrif*, approved and accepted by the General Synod of the Dutch Reformed Church, October, 1974].

31. Gustavo Gutiérrez, *A Theology of Liberation* (Maryknoll: Orbis Books, 1973); Juan Luis Segundo, *Jesus of Nazareth Yesterday and Today*, (4 vols.; Maryknoll: Orbis Books, 1982–87).

32. Charles Villa-Vicencio, *Between Christ and Caesar* (Grand Rapids: Eerdmans; Cape Town: David Philip, 1986); *Theology and Violence: The South African Debate*, ed. C. Villa-Vicencio (Braamfontein: Skotaville Publishers, 1987; Grand Rapids: Eerdmans, 1988); C. Villa-Vicencio, *A Theology of Reconstruction: Nation-building and Human Rights* (Cambridge: University Press; Cape Town: David Philip, 1992); James Cochrane, *The Church and Labour in South Africa* (Braamfontein: Skotaville Publishers, 1987); *The Three-fold Cord: Theology, Work and Labour*, ed. J.R. Cochrane and G.O. West (Pietermaritzburg: Cluster Publications, 1991).

33. John de Gruchy, *Cry Justice!* (Maryknoll: Orbis Books, 1986), and "Providence and the shapers of history," in his *Bonhoeffer and South Africa: Theology in Dialogue* (London: Paternoster; Grand Rapids: Eerdmans,

NOTES

1984), chap. 2, and *Liberating Reformed Theology: A South African Contribution to an Ecumenical Debate* (Grand Rapids: Eerdmans; Cape Town: David Philip, 1991).

34. Albert Nolan, *God in South Africa: The Challenge of the Gospel* (Cape Town: David Philip; Grand Rapids: Eerdmans, 1988). See also his *Jesus Before Christianity* (Cape Town: David Philip, 1976; 3rd ed.; Maryknoll: Orbis Books; Cape Town: David Philip, 1992).

35. Prof. Takatso Mofokeng, personal communication.

36. Manas Buthelezi, "Creation and the Church: A study in ecclesiology with special reference to a younger church milieu" (Ph.D. thesis: Drew University, 1968). For articles published from this work, see the bibliography in Dwight Hopkins's *Black Theology USA and South Africa: Politics, Culture, and Liberation* (Maryknoll: Orbis Books, 1989), 232–3.

37. Allan Boesak, *Farewell to Innocence: A Socio-ethical Study on Black Theology and Power* (Kampen: Uitgeversmaatschappij J.H. Kok; Maryknoll: Orbis Books, 1976), and *Black and Reformed: Apartheid, Liberation and the Calvinist Tradition* (Maryknoll: Orbis Books, 1984).

38. The Belhar Confession, in *A Moment of Truth: The Confession of the Dutch Reformed Mission Church, 1982*, ed. G.D. Cloete and D.J. Smit (Grand Rapids: Eerdmans, 1984), translated from *'n Oomblik van waarheid* (Cape Town: Tafelberg-Uitgewers), 3. For the story of the *Belhar* see *ibid.*, and *Apartheid is a Heresy*, ed. J. de Gruchy and C. Villa-Vicencio (Cape Town: David Philip; Grand Rapids: Eerdmans, 1983).

39. Simon S. Maimela, *God's Creative Activity Through the Law* (Pretoria: University of South Africa, 1984), and *Proclaim Freedom to My People: Essays on Religion and Politics* (Johannesburg: Skotaville Publishers, 1987).

40. S. Maimela, *God's Creative Activity*, 192–209, 217.

41. Tshenuwani Simon Farisani, *In Transit: Between the Image of God and the Image of Man* (Trenton and Grand Rapids: Africa World Press and Eerdmans, 1990) 79–99.

42. See, e.g., the primary articles collected in the first and second anthologies of black theology: *The Challenge of Black Theology in South Africa*, ed. Basil Moore (Atlanta: John Knox Press, 1973); *The Unquestionable Right To Be Free: Essays in Black Theology*, ed. Itumeleng J. Mosala and Buti Tlhagale (Johannesburg: Skotaville Publishers, 1986). See also the following highly accomplished secondary studies: Dwight N. Hopkins, *Black Theology USA and South Africa* (Maryknoll: Orbis Books, 1989); Per Frostin, *Liberation Theology in Tanzania and South Africa* (Lund: University Press, 1988); Gerald O. West, *Biblical Hermeneutics of Liberation: Modes of Reading the Bible in the South African Context* (Pietermaritzburg: Cluster Publications, 1991); J.N.J. Kritzinger, "Black Theology – challenge to mission," (Ph.D. thesis: UNISA, 1988); Louise Kretschmar, *The Voice of Black Theology in South Africa* (Johannesburg: Ravan, 1986).

43. See, e.g., the surveys by Maimela and Mofokeng: Simon Maimela, "Current themes and emphases in black theology," *Unquestionable Right To Be Free*, ed. Mosala and Tlhagale, 101–112; Takatso Mofokeng, "Black theology in South Africa: Achievements, failures and the future," *Christianity Amidst Apartheid*, ed. Prozesky, 37–54.

44. Takatso Mofokeng, *The Crucified Among the Crossbearers: Towards a Black Christology* (Kampen: J.H. Kok, 1983); see also the collective theme of Christology in the inaugural issue of the *Journal of Black Theology in South Africa* 1, 1 (1987).

45. T. Mofokeng, "Black Theology in South Africa," 50.

46. Allan Boesak, *The Finger of God: Sermons on Faith and Responsibility* (Maryknoll: Orbis Books, 1982) (*Die Vinger van God* [Johannesburg: Ravan, 1979]), and *If This is Treason, I am Guilty* (Grand Rapids: Eerdmans, 1987) (*Als dit verraad is ben ik schuldig* [Baarn: Ten Have Publishers, 1986]), and *Comfort and Protest: The Apocalypse from a South African Perspective* (Philadelphia: Westminster Press, 1987).

47. See, e.g., the land theme of the *Journal of Black Theology in South Africa* 5, no. 2 (1991).

48. T. Mofokeng, "Black Theology in South Africa," 38. Black theology has not settled on one name for its method, but such terms as historical, critical, and praxis are frequent.

49. T. Mofokeng, "Black Theology in South Africa," 45.

50. See also the productive tension of claims about and of feminist theology by several leading editors and authors: Bernadette Mosala, "Black theology and the struggle of the black woman in southern Africa," and Bonita Bennett, "A critique of the role of women in the church," in *The Unquestionable Right To Be Free*, ed. Mosala and Tlhagale, viii, 129–33, 169–74; and Denise Ackermann, Jonathan Draper and Emma Mashinini, *Women Hold Up Half the Sky* (Pietermaritzburg: Cluster Publications, 1991).

51. Itumeleng J. Mosala, *Biblical Hermeneutics and Black Theology in South Africa* (Grand Rapids: Eerdmans, 1989). The forthrightness, nuance, and openness to African cultures of Mosala's Marxist analysis distinguish his work from vulgar Marxism as much as his public seriousness as a scholar, Methodist minister, and leading spokesman for AZAPO. On the difference of his "materialist" Biblical hermeneutics from Boesak's "Word of God" hermeneutics, see the important study by Gerald West, *Biblical Hermeneutics of Liberation: Modes of Reading the Bible in the South African Context*, which is keyed to the similarities as well as differences between Boesak and Mosala, p. 75, et passim. Everything is ideological, but ideology is not everything. Note especially the handling of black nationalism.

52. Matthew Schoffeleers, "Black and African Theology in southern Africa: A controversy re-examined," *Journal of Religion in Africa* 17 (1988).

53. David Chidester, *Religions of South Africa* (London and New York: Routledge, 1992), 223, et passim.

54. Richard Elphick, "Conversion and its effects in nineteenth-century South Africa" (unpublished paper, 1991).

55. G. Setiloane, *The Image of God among the Sotho–Tswana* (Rotterdam: A.A. Balkema, 1976); *Pangs of Growth: A Dialogue on Church Growth in Southern Africa*, ed. G. Setiloane and I. Peden (Johannesburg: Skotaville Publishers, 1988); G. Setiloane, "Civil authority – from the perspective of African theology," *Journal of Black Theology in South Africa* 2, 2 (1988) 10–23; G. Setiloane, "Land in the negotiations chamber: An Afrocentric approach," *Journal of Black Theology in South Africa* 5, 2 (1991), 29–39.

56. G. Setiloane, "I am an African," republished in John de Gruchy, *Cry Justice! Prayers, Meditations and Readings from South Africa* (Maryknoll: Orbis Books, 1986), 49–52.

57. G. Setiloane, *African Theology: An Introduction* (Johannesburg, Skotaville Publishers, 1986), 21–8.

58. G. Setiloane, *African Theology*, 43–5; G. Setiloane, "Civil Authority," 21–3. The readiness to seize the sword may be more radical than appeals to Revelation 13 to contest fence-sitting appeals to Romans 13.

59. *African Independent Churches: Speaking for Ourselves* (Braamfontein: Institute for Contextual Theology, 1985), 16, 27, 28.

60. Responses to South African theology from overseas have seldom been theological, even among theologians. Afrikaner theology has been largely ignored, even by Grand Rapids neo-Calvinists; see, e.g., Gordon J. Spykman, *Reformational Theology* (Grand Rapids: Eerdmans, 1992). But see also Nicholas Wolterstorff, *Until Justice and Peace Embrace* (Grand Rapids: Eerdmans, 1983). English theology has been read more as social commentary than as theology; see, e.g., Richard Neuhaus, *Dispensations: The Future of South Africa as South Africans See It* (Grand Rapids: Eerdmans, 1986). Black theology, however – and African theology to a lesser extent – has drawn analysis worthy of the subject; see, e.g., the five book-length secondary studies in note 42.

25/ WALSHE / CHRISTIANITY AND THE ANTI-APARTHEID STRUGGLE / PAGES 383–399
The author wishes to acknowledge the support of the John T. and Catherine T. MacArthur Foundation for this research. The themes of this chapter are developed at greater length in the author's *Prophetic Christianity and the Liberation Movement in South Africa* (Pietermaritzburg: Cluster Publications, 1995).

1. Gregory Baum, *Religion and Alienation* (New York and Toronto: Paulist Press, 1975), 107.

2. These influences, as outlined below, are explained in some detail in P. Walshe, *The Rise of African Nationalism in South Africa* (London, Berkeley, and Los Angeles: University of California Press, 1970). For the later phases, see also Walshe, *Prophetic Christianity and the Liberation Movement* and his preliminary study in the *Journal of Modern African Studies* 29 (1991), 27–60. For the later phases, see also P. Walshe, "South African Prophetic Christianity and the Liberation Movement," *Journal of Modern African Studies* 29 (1991), 27–60, and *Prophetic Christianity and the Liberation Movement in South Africa* (Pietermaritzburg: Cluster Publications, 1995), from which sections in this chapter dealing with the 1980s are taken.

3. Malusi Mpumlwana, "The Contextualization of Rights in South Africa: Is there a Unique Local Character to Rights?" in *Monitor* (Port Elizabeth), Special Edition, "Human Rights in South Africa, 1988," 1989: 91.

4. Walshe, *African Nationalism*, 88.

5. Johannesburg Joint Council, *Minutes of Ordinary Meeting, 11 September 1944*, Mimeo, "Address by President General, ANC," University of the Witwatersrand Library.

6. A.B. Xuma Papers 510326, Witwatersrand University Library, Johannesburg, "Address at Unveiling of S.E.K. Mqhayi Tombstone, 26 March, 1951."

7. *South African Outlook*, January 1928.

8. R.E. Phillips, *The Bantu Are Coming* (London: Student Christian Movement Press, 1930), 35–6.

9. A. Luthuli, *Let My People Go* (London: Collins, 1962), 119.

10. *A Man for All People: The Message of Bishop Mandlenkhosi Zwane* (London: Catholic Institute for International Relations, 1983) 32–6.

11. Peter Walshe, *Church Versus State in South Africa: The Case of the Christian Institute* (London: Hurst; and Maryknoll, New York: Orbis, 1983), 76–8 and 210–11.

12. Trevor Huddleston, *Naught for Your Comfort* (London: Collins, 1956).

13. Michael Scott, *A Time to Speak* (London: Collins, 1957).

14. Ernie Regehr, *Perceptions of Apartheid: The Churches and Political Change in South Africa* (Scottdale, PA.: Herald Press, 1979), 267–8.

15. John S. Pearl Binns, *Ambrose Reeves* (London: Gollancz, 1973), 121–5.

16. Alan Paton, *Apartheid and the Archbishop: The Life and Times of Geoffrey Clayton, Archbishop of Cape Town* (Cape Town: David Philip; New York: Scribners, 1973), 282–8.

17. M.E. Worsnip, *Between Two Fires* (Pietermaritzburg: University of Natal Press, 1991), 88.

18. T. Lodge, *Black Politics in South Africa Since 1945* (London: Longman, 1983), 43–4.

19. Walshe, *Church Versus State in South Africa*, chapters 3–7, esp. pp. 22–35, 61.

NOTES

20. G. Moss and I. Obery, *South African Review* 5 (Johannesburg, 1989), 18–23; South African Institute of Race Relations, *Survey* 1988/89, 552–3

21. *The Kairos Document: Challenge to the Church, A Theological Comment on the Political Crisis in South Africa* (Johannesburg: The Kairos Theologians; 1985).

22. Walshe, *Church Versus State in South Africa*, 188–91.

23. "ABRECSA Charter," included as an appendix in *Apartheid Is a Heresy*, ed. John de Gruchy and Charles Villa-Vicencio (Cape Town: David Philip; Grand Rapids: Eerdmans, 1983), 161.

24. "Dutch Reformed Church Synod," in *Ecunews* (Johannesburg: South African Council of Churches, November 1983), 17–18. See also, D.J. Smit, "A Status Confessionis in South Africa?" *Journal of Theology for Southern Africa*, 47 (June 1984): 21–46.

25. Charles Villa-Vicencio, "Church Unity and Political Diversity," *ibid*. 43 (June 1983): 33–45. These persisting tensions are recorded in *Ecunews* (Johannesburg). See the October 1983 issue, for example, on divisions within the churches over the new South African constitution.

26. Southern African Catholic Bishops' Conference, *Pastoral Letter of the Catholic Bishops on the Proposed New Constitution* (Pretoria, 1983).

27. Author's interviews in South Africa, 1990, *inter alia* with Rev. Buti Tlhagale, Director, Educational Opportunities Council, Johannesburg; Rev. Smangaliso Mkhatshwa, General Secretary, South African Catholic Bishops' Conference; Marilyn Aitken, Secretary, Justice and Peace Commission, Bishops' Conference; and Archbishop Denis Hurley, O.M.I., Durban. Southern African Catholic Bishops' Conference, *Community Serving Humanity* (Pretoria, 1989).

28. *Catholic Herald* (London), 30 January 1987, and *National Catholic Reporter* (Kansas City), 28 April 1989.

29. *Religious News Service* (New York), 12, 16, and 20 September 1988.

30. See South African Christian Leadership Assembly, *SACLA* (Johannesburg, 1979) for an account of its origins, aims, programmes, and organization. Also, John W. de Gruchy, "The Church and the Struggle for South Africa," *Hammering Swords into Ploughshares: Essays in Honor of Desmond Tutu*, ed. Buti Tlhagale and I. Mosala (Johannesburg: Ravan, 1988), 198–200. Michael Cassidy, *The Passing Summer* (London: Hodder and Stoughton, 1989), is the autobiography of the founder of the Africa Enterprise.

31. *ICT News* (Institute for Contextual Theology, Johannesburg), December 1984; "Speaking for Ourselves," (Johannesburg: African Independent Churches Association, 1985); and Martin West, *Bishops and Prophets in a Black City: African Independent Churches in Soweto, Johannesburg* (Cape Town: David Philip; and London: Rex Collings, 1975), 142–70.

32. Jean Comaroff, *Body of Power, Spirit of Resistance* (Chicago: University of Chicago Press, 1985), a detailed study of the Zion Christian Church and its social content.

33. *Ecunews*, November 1982, 14, and April 1985, p. 20. Also, *New York Times*, 8 April 1985.

34. Author's interviews in South Africa, 1990: Moss Chikane, Southern African Catholic Bishops' Conference, and Sisa Njikelana, General Secretary, National Education, Health and Allied Workers Union.

35. *Ecunews*, 17 November 1978, 15.

36. Archdiocese of Pretoria Commission for Justice and Peace, *The Catholic Defence League* (Pretoria, c. 1980), 1–8.

37. Catholic Secretariat, *Catholic Commitment on Social Justice: The Three Statements Made by the Catholic Bishops' Conference* (Pretoria, 1978).

38. *Evangelical Witness in South Africa* (Johannesburg, 1986), 31–2.

39. Allan Boesak, "Address to the South African Council of Churches," *South African Outlook* (July 1979), 102.

40. *Hope and Suffering: Sermons and Speeches of the Rt. Rev. Desmond Mpilo Tutu*, ed. Mothobi Mutloatse and John Webster (London and Grand Rapids: Eerdmans, 1984). Also, Shirley du Boulay, *Tutu: Voice of the Voiceless* (London and Grand Rapids: Eerdmans, 1988).

41. *Not Without Honour: Tribute to Beyers Naudé*, ed. Peter Randall (Johannesburg: Ravan Press, 1983); *Resistance and Hope: South African Essays in Honour of Beyers Naudé*, ed. Charles Villa-Vicencio and John W. De Gruchy (Cape Town: David Philip; and Grand Rapids: Eerdmans, 1985); "The Most Trusted White Man in South Africa: An Interview with Beyers Naudé," in *Sojourners* (Washington, DC), February 1988: 14–21; *Diakonia News* (Durban), March 1985: 6; *Ecunews*, April 1987: 10; and author's interview in South Africa 1990, with Naudé.

42. Frank Chikane, *No Life of My Own* (London: Catholic Institute for International Relations, 1988), and author's interview with Chikane in South Africa, 1990.

43. South African Council of Churches, *National Conference Reports* (Johannesburg) for the years 1980–88.

44. World Council of Churches, "Harare Declaration, December 1985," and "The Implications of Harare," *ICT News* (Johannesburg), March 1986: 3–6; *The Churches' Search for Justice and Peace in Southern Africa. Meeting in Lusaka, Zambia, 4–8 May 1987* (Geneva: Programme to Combat Racism, World Council of Churches, 1987); and South African Council of Churches, "Report on Lusaka," *Refugees and Exiles. National*

Conference Report, 1987 (Johannesburg, 1987), 64–9.

45. *Info* (Catholic Bishops' Conference, Pretoria), 20 July and 7 September 1987; "Onward Christian Soldiers," *New Nation* (Johannesburg), 18–24 June 1987, 7, interview with Fr. Smangaliso Mkhatshwa, Secretary General of the Catholic Bishops' Conference, after his release from detention; and author's interview with Mkhatshwa in South Africa, 1990.

46. General Secretariat of the Southern African Catholic Bishops' Conference, "Statement on the Current Situation," "Declaration of Commitment by the Church," and "Statement on Conscientious Objection," press releases (Pretoria), February 1977.

47. Southern African Catholic Bishops' Conference, *Pastoral Letter on the Proposed New Constitution of South Africa* (Pretoria, July 1983); *Pastoral Letter of the SACBC: The Municipal Elections of October 26, 1988* (Pretoria, 1988); *Report on Police Conduct During Township Protests, August–November 1984* (Pretoria and London, 1984); and *Report on Namibia* (Pretoria, 1982). For their resistance to apartheid in education, see P. Christie, *Open Schools: Racially Mixed Catholic Schools in South Africa, 1976–86* (Johannesburg: Ravan Press, 1990).

48. South African Council of Churches and Southern African Catholic Bishops' Conference, *Churches' Report on Relocations* (Johannesburg, 1984), and "Minutes of the Meeting of the SACC Division of Justice and Reconciliation Held on the 11th and 12th February 1986," 4. For examples of protest liturgies, see Southern African Catholic Bishops' Conference, *Inter Nos* (Pretoria), February and November 1987; *Ecunews*, 2 April 1987, pp. 6, 13, and 28–9; *ICT News*, June 1988, 5; and Southern African Catholic Bishops' Conference, "Letter to Parish Priests, 9 May 1988."

49. Southern African Catholic Bishops' Conference, *Community Serving Humanity* (Pretoria, 1989).

50. The Commission published a workers' newsletter, *Church and Industry* (Pretoria) from 1981.

51. Young Christian Students, "Annual Report, 1986," Johannesburg, and *YCS News* (Johannesburg), 5, 1, 1988.

52. "ANC/SACBC Communiqué and Press Conference," *Inter Nos*, May 1986, 11–14.

53. *The Kairos Document: Challenge to the Church*. References in the text are to pp. 6–7, 8–14, 20.

54. *Diakonia News* (Durban), June 1986, 4; *National Catholic Reporter* (Kansas City), 21 October and 4 November 1988; and *New Nation* (Johannesburg), October 1988, 13, 19.

55. *Ecunews*, June 1985, 15; South African Council of Churches, *Annual Report, 1987*, 102; *New York Times*, 16 and 19 November, and 15 December 1988.

56. United Democratic Front, "National Launch," Cape Town, 20 August 1983.

57. Allan Boesak, "The Black Church and the Future," *South African Outlook* (July 1979), 102, address to the South African Council of Churches.

58. South African Council of Churches, *June 16, 1986, Day of Prayer to End Unjust Rule of Apartheid: Call to Christians of the World Church* (Johannesburg: n.d.) and Southern African Catholic Bishops' Conference and South African Council of Churches, "Call to June 16 Day of Prayer," *Ecunews*, May 1986, 2–5.

59. *Ecunews*, May 1985, 14.

60. "The deaths of Matthew Goniwe, Sparrow Mkonto, Sicelo Mhlauli and Fort Calata," supplement in *Monitor* (Port Elizabeth Journal of the Human Rights Trust), March 1988, being the final address to the court by Arthur Chaskalson, who represented the Goniwe family. Later revelations confirmed that the decision to eliminate Goniwe was taken in the State Security Council. *Weekly Mail* (Johannesburg), 13, 20, 27 August 1992.

61. *Catholic News Service* (Boston), 9 August 1989, 3–4.

62. Cedric Mayson, "Converting Christian Subversion," *Sechaba* (London), September 1989, 27–30; Programme to Combat Racism, *The Churches' Search for Justice and Peace, Lusaka, 1987* (Geneva: World Council of Churches, 1987); South African Council of Churches, *Annual Report, 1987*, 64ff; and "ANC/SACBC Communique," *Inter Nos* (May 1986), 11–14.

63. South African Council of Churches, *Senzenina? The Day 300 Church Leaders, Clergy and Laity Marched on the South African Parliament* (Johannesburg, 1988), 1–2.

64. Letter from P.W. Botha to the Rev. F. Chikane, 24 March 1988, reprinted in *Preparation Material for Emergency Convocation of Churches in South Africa, 30–1 May 1988* (Johannesburg: South African Council of Churches), 51–2. See also, *Ecunews*, March 1988, 3–5; April 1988, 8–14.

65. *New Nation*, 9–15 November 1988, 6–7, 12; *New York Times*, 5 September 1989; and *Observer* (London), 10 September 1989.

66. *New Nation*, 10–16 March 1988, and Frank Chikane, *The Church and the South African Crisis* (London: Catholic Institute for International Relations, 1988), 7–10.

67. South African Council of Churches, *Annual Conference, 1989* (Johannesburg, 1989), "Annexure B: The General Administrative Secretary's Report," 6.

68. *New Nation*, 16 February 1989, and *National Catholic Reporter*, 3 and 17 March 1989.

69. *New York Times*, 15 and 30 October 1989; *In These Times* (Chicago), 27 September–3 October 1989, 9; and *Guardian* (New York), October 1989.

70. *Southscan* (London), 10 November 1989; *Guardian* (London), 17 August 1989; *New York Times*, 10 and

NOTES

11 December 1989; and author's interviews with Marilyn Aitken, Southern African Catholic Bishops' Conference, and Frank Chikane, South African Council of Churches in South Africa, 1990.

71. Frank Chikane, "The Church's Role During a Period of Transition," 1–11, an address given at a breakfast briefing, 12 August 1992, organized by Diakonia's Sociopolitical Development Programme (a Diakonia pamphlet, Durban).

72. National Initiative for Reconciliation, *Rustenburg Declaration: National Conference of Churches in South Africa*, Pretoria, November 1990, sections 1.1 to 2.6.

73. "Oom Bey Today: A Great Afrikaner Prophet Continues to Speak Out," *Challenge* (Johannesburg: Institute for Contextual Theology), December 1991, 2–5.

74. "Mandela's Challenge to the Church," Speech at the Centenary Celebrations of the Free Ethiopian Church of Southern Africa, 14 December, 1992, *Challenge*, 20–1.

75. *Ecunews*, December 1991, 7–8.

76. *Weekly Mail*, 25 February 1993; *Southern African Church News* (London), March 1993. For an example of continuing racial divisions in the denominations, see "Black and White Lutheran Youth Meet for First Time," *Southern African Church News*, April 1992.

77. Jean-Marc Éla, *My Faith as an African* (New York: Orbis, 1988), xvii.

INDEX

INDEX

INDEX

470

41 130; segregation of
66–7; *see also* Bantu
Presbyterian Church
Pringle, T. 297
Programme to Combat
Racism 163 164 165–6
169
prophecy 14 125 231
prophets 220 33-4 5, *see
also* cattle-killing, Nku,
C., Ntsikana, Nxele
Protestant missionaries 31
348–50
Protestant Reformation 2
16–17
Purcell, H. 317

Quakers 64
Quota Act, *see* Immigration
Quota Act

Raasel, W. 22
racism 142 144–5 167 213
344 345: in Pentecostal
movement 230 234–40;
white churches and
384–5; *see also* apartheid,
segregation
Railway Mission 200
rainmakers 70–1 79
Ramaphosa, C. 239
Rand Native Mission 244
Rand rebellion 1922 281
Read, J. Sr. 36–7 38 42 45
47 73 108
Read family 43 44 50
Reeves, Bp. A. 161 386
Reformed Church in Africa
(Indian) 388 396 399
Reformed Lutheran Church
in SA 186
Reformed tradition 17–18
religious pluralism 29
Renewed Unity of the
Brethren, *see* Moravians
Retief, Piet 62
Reveil 56
Reveley, H. 329
Rheinallt Jones, J.D. 362
363 368
Rhema Bible Church 237
Rhenish Missionary Society
32 39–41 45–6 55 130
131 175
Ribeiro, Dr. F. 393
Ricards, Bp. J.D. 196 197
198–9
Richardson, Lawrence 64
Richtersveld, missions in 40
right-wing Christianity
165–6 390

Robben Island 72 175 269
Roberts, O. 237
Roberts, Dr. A.W. 367
Robertson, R. 96 104
Robson, Rev. A. 48
Roebert, E. 237
Rolland, S. 110 118
Roman Catholic Church 3
6 7 9 127 171 195–210:
and apartheid 162–3 165
385–6 389 391; and edu-
cation 161 195 196–7
204–5 207; and Indians
287; and Social Gospel
196 348; and state 52
197; and women 10 208;
missionaries 115-16 197-
203 210, *see also* Oblates
of Mary Immaculate;
music 321–2; relations
with Dutch Reformed
Church 21 24 204 206;
segregation in 208–9
Romero, Bp. 153
Rood, D. 98 101
Rose, Fr. E. 334–5
Ross, J. 75
Roux, E. 359
Rowlands, A. 291
Rowlands, J.A. 291
Rowlands, J.F. 235 291–2
293 295–6
Royal School of Church
Music 319
Rubusana, Rev. W.B. 308
346 357
Ruffel, Fr. P. 205
Rungiah, Rev. J. 289
Rustenburg Conference 397
398
Rustenburg Declaration
171

Sabon, Fr. J.B. 198 287 289
Saint Ntsikana Memorial
Association (SNMA) 86
Sak River 34 35
Salem 65
Salvation Army 55 245
San 33 44 69, *see also*
Khoisan
Sandile 84–5
Sarhili 308
Sarndal, Pastor O. 187
Sauer, J.W. 358
Sauter, Fr. J.-B. 203
Scandinavian Evangelical
Lutheran Congregation
178
Schmidt, G. 19 21 22 23 27
28–9 33 34 174–5

Schreiner, Olive 64 281
Schreuder, H.P.S. 92–3 104
177–8 186
Schulenburg, C.H. 421n.31
Schutte, H. 327 329
Schwin, D. 34
Scott, Sir G. 331
Scott, J.O. 331
Scott, M. 161 386
Scottish evangelicalism 372
Scottish Free Church 53
Secor Dabar 56
secularization 8–9 11–12
347 364–5
Segoete, E.L. 307 308
segregation 5 64–7 87 103
360 366–7: and English-
speaking churches 156–7
160–1; in Anglican
Church 5 66; in Dutch
Reformed Church 5 47 66
140–1; in Pentecostal
churches 230–1 233–7
238–40 293–4 294; in
RCC 208–9
Segundo, J.L. 376
Sekese, A. 307
Sekgoma 114 117
Selby-Taylor, Bp. R. 159
Sello, T. 188
Seme, P. ka I. 357 361
Sending Gesticht (South
African Missionary
Society), Cape Town 40–1
46 274 328
separate development, *see*
apartheid
Sestigers 303
Setiloane, G.M. 122 380–1
382
settlers, relations with mis-
sionaries 34, 37, 42, 103,
105, see also Boers;
Voortrekkers
Seventh Day Adventist
Church 290
sewing 255 258
Sewushane, M. 188
sexuality 101 259–60
Seymour, W. 228–9 240
Sharpeville massacre 148
162 299 346 386
Shaw, B. 54 65
Shaw, Rev. W. 54 62 65 75
129 330
Shembe, I. 133 218 219
221 222 224 312
427n.118
Shepherd, Rev. R.H.W. 304
308
Shepstone, T. 92 95 96 104

INDEX

Tas, A. 26
Taylor, J.D. 348
Taylor, J.T. 363
Taylor, W. 83 94–5
Teenstra, M.D. 301
temperance movement 48–9
  83 156 259 343 351
Thaba Bosiu 110–11 115
Thaba Nchu 116
Theal, G.M. 307
Thembu, missions to 43
Thembu church 65 87 213
  427n.119
theological disputes 56-8
  136-8, *see also* Colenso,
  J.W.
theological training:
  Catholic 201–2; Lutheran
  176 187 189–90; PEMS
  246; Pentecostal 234 235;
  Reformed 57 136 137 371
theology: African 372
  379–82; African Initiated
  Churches 221–3;
  Afrikaner 371 372–5;
  English-speaking 371
  375–7; feminist 170 379;
  Lutheran 173–4; South
  African, influence of
  370–1; *see also* Black the-
  ology, liberation theology
Theophilus, E. 291
Theopolis 35 42 44–5
Thlagale, B. 378
Thlotse 115
Tholuck, F.A.G. 130
Thom, G. 38 53
Thomas, J. 288
Thompson, W.R. 42 62
Thomson, W. 75
thousand-generation
  covenant 24–6
Threlfall, W. 39
Thunberg, C.P. 27
Tikkuie, V. 33 34
Tile, N. 65 87 213
  427n.119
Tiro, A. 387
Tlhagale, Rev. B. 389
Tlhaping, relations with
  missionaries 107–8
tongues, speaking in 217
  228 230 231 233
Torres, C. 153
tot system 49
translation 12–13
Transorangia, missionaries
  in 35–6 39 121 129–33
Transvaal Missionary
  Association 353
Trappists 98 103 104–5

198–200
Tshatshu, D. (Jan Tzatzoe)
  74 79 301
Tswana 40, 118, and mis-
  sionaries 4 35 107 109
  113–14 116–17
Tswana, religion 109 121–2
Tulbagh church 329
Turner, Bp. H. 214
Turney, A. 229
Turney, H. 229
Tuskegee Normal and
  Industrial Institute 355
  363
Tutu, Abp. D. 155 165 168
  171 378 387 390 391
  394–5
Tyamzashe, B.K. 321
Tyhume mission 75 76–7
  78 85

Uithaalder, W. 44
Umphumulo 177 180 187
  189
Umphumulo Memorandum
  191–2
Umvoti mission 98 100 102
uniforms 223 257–8
Union Chapel of the
  Congregationalists 41
Unitarians of South Africa
  54
United Brethren, *see*
  Moravians
United Congregational
  Church of Southern Africa
  (UCCSA) 159 169
United Democratic Front
  393–4
United Evangelical
  Lutheran Church in
  Southern Africa (UELC-
  SA) 173 181 184 186 189
  193–4
United Free Church of
  Scotland 354
United Missionary
  Campaign (1925) 368
United Nations 146
United Pentecostal Mission
  of Natal 291
United Presbyterian Church
  of Scotland 83
Uniting Reformed Church
  of Southern Africa
  (URCSA) 136 154
unity 6 206: church:
  Anglican 66; Dutch
  Reformed 396 399;
  English-speaking churches
  157–60; Lutherans 180–5

191–2 194; Pentecostal
  234–5
Universities' Mission to
  Central Africa 95
University Christian
  Movement 164
University of the Western
  Cape Theology Faculty
  151 372
Untunjambili 181 189
Unzondelelo 99
Upton, R.S. 331
Uys, J. 62

Valentyn, E. 38 47
van Arckel, Rev. J. 22 25
van den Heever, C.M. 303
van der Hoff, D. 125 126
van der Kemp, J.T. 34–8 40
  44 53 69–71 72 273 304
van der Lingen, Rev.
  G.W.A. 61
van der Spuy, Rev. P. 29
van der Stel, S. 20–1 25
van der Stel, W.A. 20
van Dijk, L. 22 28
van Lier, Rev. H.R. 22 29
  40
van Prinsterer, G. 56
van Reede tot Drakenstein,
  H.A. 25 29
van Reenen, J. 27
van Riebeeck, J. 24
van Riebeeck, M. 24 28
van Wyk Louw, N.P., *see*
  Louw, N.P. van Wyk
Vatican Council, Second 9
  163 206 208 209–10 335
  392
Venter, F.A. 303
Venter, J.J. 126
vernacular literature, development of 307
Verwoerd, H.F. 145 148–9
  162 282
Vilakazi, B. 207
Villa-Vicencio, C. 376 377
Vintcent, P. 336
VOC, *see* Dutch East India
  Company
Voetius, G. 18–19 22 24 25
von Manger, Rev. J.H. 22
von Zinzendorf, Count
  N.L. 28 31 174 187
Voortrekkers, religion of
  122–8
Vorster, B.J. 284
Vorster, J.D. 138 143 283
Vos, Rev. M.C. 22 23 24 29
  274

Wagenaer, Z. 24 25 26
Wagener, Pastor 180
Walters, M.M. 303
Wangemann, Dr. H.T.
188–9
War of Hintsa 78
War of Mlanjeni 322
War of the Axe 78 94
War of the Guns 113 114
115
Warden, H.D. 112
Warneck, G. 129
Warner, J.C. 341
Washington, B.T. 354–5
383
Watkins, O. 100
Wauchope, I. 84
Weichardt, L. 281
Weir, Mrs. James 80
Wesley, J. 227
Wesleyan Methodist Prayer
Union 256
Wesleyan missionaries, see
Methodist missionaries
Wessels, G.R. 233–4
Widdicombe, Rev. J. 115
Wilder, H. 91
Williams, Dean F.H. 60
Williams, J. 5 71 72 73–4
Winkler, H. 191
Winter, J. 188–9 213
Wirgman, Canon A.T. 62
65
witchdoctors 124
Witt, O. 178
Wittenberg, Dr. G. 184
Wolpert, Fr. G. 207
women 10 84–5 190 198
220–1 356–7: as preachers
263–7; ordination of 160

169 208
Women's Help Society
256–7
women's organizations 170
253–60, see also
manyanos: American
Board Mission 256 257;
Anglican 256–7;
Methodist 253–5 256
258–61
Woodrow, A. 335
World Alliance of Reformed
Churches(WARC) 153
159 377 388
World Conference on
Religion and Peace 285
World Council of Churches
(WCC) 146 148 159 162
163 164 171 185 391
394, see also Programme
to Combat Racism
World Methodist
Conference 159
World Student's Christian
Federation 164
Wuppertal mission 175
Wylant, W.B. 24 27

Xaba, J.G. 214
Xhosa: and Christianity 4 5
68; and land 42 43 71;
converts 50 319; language
76; relations with missionaries 35 76–7; religion of
69–71
Xuma, Dr. A.B. 215 357
363–4 368 384

Yali-Manisi, D.L.P. 309–10
Yusuf, Shaykh 269 272

Zimbabwe, Dutch
Reformed Church in 146
147
Zion Apostolic Church 231
Zion Apostolic Faith
Mission (ZAFM) 231 232
Zion Christian Church of
the Transvaal 133
Zion Christian Church
(ZCC) 218 223–4 231
232 389
Zion City churches 217–19
Zionism 6 8 216–21: and
Pentecostalism 229
Zionist church 129
Zionist churches 10 100
345
Zionist–Apostolic churches
219-21, women in 220–1
Zondi, J. 215
Zonnebloem College, Cape
Town 83 85
Zulu, Bp. A. 163
Zulu, J. 178
Zulu, S.P. 183
Zulu: and Christianity 4 89;
converts 97–8 99 132;
relations with missionaries
97–8 99; religion of 90 96
122
Zulu Congregational
Church 214
Zulu Mbiana Congre-
gational Church 100
Zulu Mission 102
Zwane, Bp. M. 385 387
389

ACKNOWLEDGEMENTS AND SOURCES FOR ILLUSTRATIONS

Grateful acknowledgements are made to the following sources for the use of illustrations indicated:

Page vi: Photo Gary Isaac, courtesy the Rev. H. Pretorius.

Figs. 1, 3, 9, 42, 61–73, 75, page 30: Prof. Dennis Radford.

Figs. 4–5: P. Crafford, *Aan God Sy die Dank* (N.G. Kerkboekhandel, 1981).

Figs. 6–7, 11: Cape Archives (Elliott collection).

Figs. 8, 23, 27, 31 (sketch R. Batty), 33 (watercolour C.D. Bell), pages 88, 154: Africana Museum (Kennedy), Johannesburg.

Fig. 9: C.I. Latrobe, *Journal of a Visit to South Africa in 1815 and 1816* (1818, reprinted Struik, 1969), sketch R. Cocking.

Fig. 10: A.D. Martin, *Dr. Van der Kemp* (Livingstone Press, 1931).

Fig. 12: Moorcroft collection, Cory Library, Rhodes University, Grahamstown.

Fig. 13 (sketch by Capt. Miller), 14, 15, 17, 40, 55: South African Library, Cape Town.

Fig. 16: Stewart Papers, Lovedale.

Figs. 18–19: J. Chalmers, *Journal and Selected Writings of the Reverend Tiyo Soga* (Balkema, 1983).

Fig. 20: D.D.T. Jabavu, *The Life of J.T. Jabavu* (Lovedale Press, 1922).

Fig. 21: E. Casalis, *Mes Souvenirs* (Societé des Missions Evangeliques, Paris, 1922).

Fig. 22: P. Sanders, *Moshoeshoe, Chief of the Sotho* (Heinemann, London, and David Philip, Cape Town, 1975).

Fig. 24: R. Gordon, *Macrorie, Gentle Bishop of Maritzburg* (Simon van der Stel Foundation, 1973).

Figs. 25–6: T. Gutsche, *The Bishop's Lady* (Timmins, 1970).

Figs. 28–9: M. Dickson, *Beloved Partner: Mary Moffat of Kuruman* (Kuruman Moffat Mission Trust, 2nd ed. 1989).

Fig. 30: N.G.K. Archives, Cape Town.

Fig. 32: Painting by Thomas Annan, Scottish National Portrait Gallery, Edinburgh.

Fig. 33: A. Sillery, *The Story of an African Chief* (George Ronald, Oxford, 1954).

Fig. 34: W.D. MacKenzie, *John MacKenzie, South African Missionary and Statesman* (Hodder and Stoughton, 1902).

Fig. 35: D. Wylie, *A Little God* (Witwatersrand University Press, 1990) and McGregor Museum, Kimberley (Duggan-Cronin collection).

Figs. 36–7: P. Delius, *The Land Belongs to Us* (Ravan, 1983).

Fig. 38: Graham's Town Series, Rhodes University, courtesy Dr. K. Hunt.

Fig. 39: K. Boner, *Dr. F.C. Kolbe* (D. Litt. et Phil. thesis, UNISA).

Fig. 41: M. Dischl., *Transkei for Christ* (Queenstown Printing and Publishing Co., 1982).

Figs. 43, 45, 46: J.B. Brain, *Christian Indians in Natal, 1860–1911* (Oxford, 1983).

Fig. 44: G.C. Oosthuizen, *Pentecostal Penetration into the Indian Community* (H.S.R.C., Durban, 1975).

Fig. 47: C. Kuppusanie, *Religious Practices and Customs of South African Indians* (Sunray, 1983).

Fig. 48: R. Edgar, *Because They Chose the Plan of God* (Ravan, 1988).

Fig. 49 (photo Lynn Acutt), 50, 52 (photo *Drum*), page 241 (photo Lynn Acutt): B.G.M. Sundkler, *Bantu Prophets in South Africa* (Oxford, 1981).

Figs. 51, 60 (photo Rex Reynolds), page 88: *Illustrated History of South Africa* (Readers Digest, 1992).

Fig. 53: C. Hanekom, *Krisis en Kultus* (Academia, 1975), photo *The World*.

Fig. 54: J. du Plessis, *The Life of Andrew Murray of South Africa* (Marshall Brothers, 1919).

Fig. 56: G.C.P. van der Vyver, *Professor Dirk Postma, 1818–90* (Pro Rege Pers, 1958).

Fig. 57: N.H.K. Archives, Pretoria.

Fig. 58: T.R.H. Davenport, *The Afrikaner Bond, 1880–1911* (Oxford, 1966).

Fig. 59: T.F. Burgers, *Schetsen uit de Transvaal* (J.H.de Bussy, 1934).

Fig. 74: Photo the Rev. Makhuba, courtesy Mrs. Susan Sturman.

Fig. 76: S.E.K. Mqhayi, *Ityala Lamawele* (Lovedale Press, 1937).

Fig. 77: J.A. Loubser, *The Apartheid Bible* (Maskew Miller Longman, 1987).

Fig. 78: C. Saunders, *Beyond the Cape Frontier* (Longman, 1974), photo J. Opland.

Fig. 79: D. Owen, *Directory of Eastern Cape Black Leaders* (Albany Museum, 1996).

Fig. 80: A. Paton, *Journey Continued* (David Philip, 1988), photo Capricorn, courtesy *Living Magazine*.

Fig. 81: *Theologica Evangelica* 1986, XIX. I.

Fig. 82: McMillan collection, African Studies Library, U.C.T.

Fig. 83: Photo *The Star*.

Fig. 85: A.H. Luckhoff, *Cottesloe* (Tafelberg, 1978).

Figs. 86–8: A. Paton, *Apartheid and the Archbishop* (David Philip, Cape Town, and Rex Collings, London, 1973).

Figs. 89–90: R. Suttner and J. Cronin, *Thirty Years of the Freedom Charter* (Ravan, 1985).

Fig. 91: "Naming the Beast – the Changing Face of Apartheid" (pamphlet, Student Christian Movement of Britain and Ireland, 1980).

Fig. 92: F. Chikane, *No Life of My Own* (Skotaville, 1988).

Page 120: W.F. Lye (ed.), *Andrew Smith's Journal* (Balkema, 1975).

Cover illustration: Photo Sean Brown, courtesy Dr. Deborah Gaitskell.

The editors and publishers have done their best to acknowledge the illustrations to their correct sources; if any errors or omissions have been made, they will be corrected in subsequent impressions of the book.